AF837379

Law Made Simple

Now in its fifteenth edition, *Law Made Simple* is the perfect introduction to the English Legal System and combines an overview of both the legislation and case law relating to all the foundation subjects, including Contract, Torts, Land, Trusts, Criminal, Public and EU. Fully updated, this book acts as a clear and concise guide for students studying law at any level and takes into account developments across the curriculum. With that in mind, this edition includes additional questions and examples of the law in practice. It is suitable for students studying law at A-Level or as an excellent background for students thinking of embarking on the study of law or a related course at degree level.

David L. A. Barker is Solicitor of the Supreme Court of NSW and High Court of Australia; Emeritus Professor and Formerly Dean, Faculty of Law, University of Technology Sydney; and Former Dean, Faculty of Law, University of Westminster (formerly Polytechnic of Central London).

Law Made Simple

Fifteenth Edition

David L. A. Barker

BarkerAM, FAAL, LLB, MPhil, LLM, PhD, FCIS, FGIA, FCMI, FIML, FAICD

Solicitor of the Supreme Court of NSW and High Court of Australia; Emeritus Professor and Formerly Dean, Faculty of Law, University of Technology Sydney; Sometime Dean, Faculty of Law, University of Westminster (formerly Polytechnic of Central London)

Routledge
Taylor & Francis Group
LONDON AND NEW YORK

Designed cover image: Zolnierek / Getty Images ®

Fifteenth edition published 2026
by Routledge
4 Park Square, Milton Park, Abingdon, Oxon, OX14 4RN

and by Routledge
605 Third Avenue, New York, NY 10158

Routledge is an imprint of the Taylor & Francis Group, an informa business

First edition published by W. H. Allen & Co. Ltd, 1970
Fourteenth edition published by Routledge 2020

British Library Cataloguing-in-Publication Data
A catalogue record for this book is available from the British Library

Library of Congress Cataloging-in-Publication Data
Names: Barker, David, 1934– author.
Title: Law made simple / David L. A. Barker, Barker, AM, FAAL, LLB, MPhil, LLM, PhD, FCIS, FGIA, FCMI, FIML, FAICD, Solicitor of the Supreme Court of NSW and High Court of Australia; Emeritus Professor and Formerly
Dean, Faculty of Law, University of Technology, Sydney; Sometime Dean, Faculty of Law, University of Westminster (formerly Polytechnic of Central London)
Description: Fifteenth edition. | Abingdon, Oxon [UK] ; New York, NY : Routledge, 2026. | Includes bibliographical references and index.
Identifiers: LCCN 2025030610 | ISBN 9781032728285 (hardback) | ISBN 9781032728247 (paperback) | ISBN 9781003422808 (ebook)
Subjects: LCSH: Law—England.
Classification: LCC KD660 ‡b .B37 2026 | DDC 349.42 ‡2 23/eng/20250708—dcundefined
LC record available at https://lccn.loc.gov/2025030610

ISBN: 978-1-032-72828-5 (hbk)
ISBN: 978-1-032-72824-7 (pbk)
ISBN: 978-1-003-42280-8 (ebk)

DOI: 10.4324/9781003422808

Typeset in Joanna and DIN
by Apex CoVantage, LLC

Contents

Preface

As always, the compilation of this new edition has necessitated the rewriting of major parts of the text that reflect both the vast amount of legislation and the increase in case law which has taken place since the last edition was published in 2020.

The political changes which occurred in the United Kingdom Government in 2024 have already been reflected in the amendments to the English legal system, particularly with regard to legislation enacted since the election of a new Government in July 2024. There have also been some significant case decisions during that period as well.

Also, the European Withdrawal Act has now begun to take effect, although despite this, the European Union maintains a continued influence, especially by the European Convention on Human Rights. This has meant the ongoing retention of 'European Union Law' in Chapter 13. The demands of producing a text which covers the whole spectrum of English law continue to present a major challenge that increases with each new edition. As always, I am grateful to my wife, Catherine Barker, for her encouragement in the preparation of this edition, together with Jones Olatunji of AustLII for his provision of technical support and Chloe Herbert and Emily Kindleysides of Routledge for their professional advice and editorial assistance. I would also like to make a special thanks to Chris Mathews and Michelle Sanson for their contributions.

David L. A. Barker
2025

Note: The change constituted in the amended Civil Procedure legislation of substituting *claimant* for *plaintiff* has been reflected in the main body of the text. In this edition, the use of *plaintiff* has been retained in the case notes as it was the terminology used at the time of the relevant law report.

Table of cases

B

C

D

H

N

O

P

Q

R

S

T

U

Table of legislation

D

E

F

M

U

V

W

Y

Table of statutory instruments

Table of European law

Table of abbreviations

ABS	Alternative Business Structure
ACAS	Advisory, Conciliation and Arbitration Service
AP	Appeal Case
BAILII	British and Irish Legal Information Institute
CCT	common customs tariff
CDS	Criminal Defence Service
CFI	Court of First Instance
CIC	community interest company
CJEU	Court of Justice of the European Union
CLS	Community Legal Service
CLSA	Courts and Legal Services Act
CPR	Civil Procedure Rules
CPS	Crown Prosecution Service
CSI	Consultancy Service Index
DG	Directorates-General
ECB	European Central Bank
ECHR	European Convention on Human Rights and Fundamental Freedoms
ECJ	European Court of Justice
ECSC	European Coal and Steel Community
EEC	European Economic Community
EMU	Economic and Monetary Union
HRA	Human Rights Act
ILEX	Institute of Legal Executives
LCJ	Lord Chief Justice
LDP	legal disciplinary practices
MCC	magistrates' courts committee
MR	Master of the Rolls
OFT	Office of Fair Trading
PACE	Police and Criminal Act
PCC	police and crime commissioners
SOCA	Serious Organised Crime Agency
SRA	Solicitors Regulation Authority
TEU	Treaty on European Union

Chapter 1

Introduction

Key points

- the nature of law
- custom, morality and the law
- classification of law
- characteristics of English law

1.1 The nature of law

The term 'law' is used in many senses: we may speak of the laws of physics, mathematics, science or the laws of football. When we speak of the law of a State, we use the term 'law' in a special and strict sense, and in that sense, law may be defined as *a rule of human conduct, imposed upon and enforced among the members of a given State.*

People are by nature social animals, desiring the companionship of others, and in primitive times they tended to form tribes, groups or societies, either for self-preservation or by reason of social instinct. If a group or society is to continue, some form of social order is necessary. Rules or laws are, therefore, drawn up to ensure that members of the society may live and work together in an orderly and peaceable manner. The larger the community (or group or State), the more complex and numerous will be the rules.

If the rules or laws are broken, compulsion is used to enforce obedience. We may say, then, that two ideas underline the concept of law: (a) *order*, in the sense of method or system; and (b) *compulsion*—i.e. the enforcement of obedience to the rules or laws laid down.

1.2 Custom, morality and the law

On examination of the definition of law given previously, certain important points should be noted.

a Law is a body of rules

When referring to 'the law' we usually imply the whole of the law however it may have been formed. As we shall see later, much of English law was formed out of the customs of the people.

DOI: 10.4324/9781003422808-1

But a great part of the law has been created by legislation, i.e. the passing of laws. Common law and statutory law together comprise what is referred to as the 'Law of England'.

b Law is for the guidance of human conduct

People resort to various kinds of rules to guide their lives. Therefore, moral rules and ethics remind us that it is immoral or wrong to covet, to tell lies or to engage in drunkenness in private. Society may well disapprove of the transgression of these moral or ethical precepts. The law, however, is not concerned with such matters and leaves them to the individual's conscience or moral choice and the pressure of public opinion: no legal action results (unless a person tells lies under oath in a court, when he or she may be prosecuted for perjury). Thus, there is a degree of overlap between moral and legal rules, as depicted by the diagram 'Moral and legal rules'.

Sometimes Parliament does intervene, as illustrated by the **Criminal Justice and Immigration Act 2008** which abolished the common law offences of blasphemy and blasphemous libel (s. 79).

c Law is imposed

We sometimes think of laws as being laid down by some authority such as a monarch, dictator or group of people in whom special power is vested. In Britain we can point to legislation for examples of law laid down by a sovereign body, namely Parliament. The legal author John Austin (1790–1859) asserted that law was a command of a sovereign and that citizens were under a duty to obey that command. Other writers say that men and women in primitive societies formed rules themselves, i.e. that the rules or laws sprang from within the group itself. Only later were such rules laid down by a sovereign authority and imposed on the group or people subject to them.

d Enforcement

Clearly unless a law is enforced, it loses its effectiveness as a law and those persons subject to it will regard it as redundant. The chief characteristic of law is that it is enforced, such enforcement being today carried out by the State. Therefore, if *A* steals a mobile phone from B, *A* may be prosecuted before the court and may be punished. The court may then order the restitution of the mobile phone to its rightful owner, B. The 'force' used is known as a *sanction* and it is this sanction that the State administers to secure obedience to its rules.

e The State

A State is a territorial division in which a community or people lives subject to a uniform system of law administered by a sovereign authority, e.g. a parliament.

The United Kingdom, which comprises a parliamentary union of England, Wales, Scotland and Northern Ireland, is for our purposes the State. Parliament at Westminster legislates for England, Scotland and Wales (although, in accordance with recent devolution legislation, Scotland and Wales now have separate parliamentary assemblies which are empowered to legislate regarding specified internal affairs such as education), and also in respect of some matters (such as defence and coinage) for Northern Ireland. Scotland has its own legal system, different in many ways from that of England and Wales, and has been influenced by Roman and Continental law to a far greater extent.

f Content of law

The law is a living thing, and it changes through the course of history. Changes are brought about by various factors such as invasion, migration, contact with other races, material prosperity,

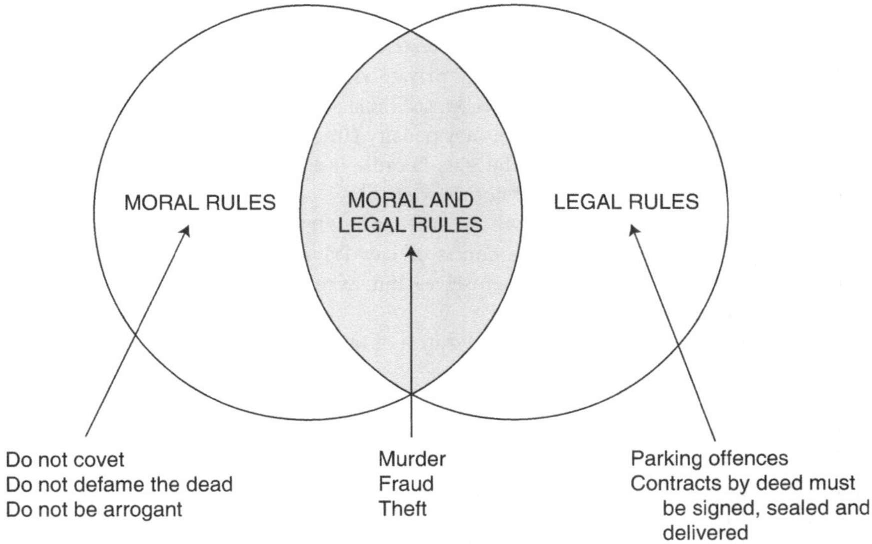

FIGURE 1.1 Moral and legal rules

education, the advent of new machines, new ideas or new religions. Law responds to public opinion and changes accordingly. Formerly, the judges themselves moulded and developed the law. Today an Act of Parliament may be passed to change it.

g Justice and law

People desire justice in their personal, social and economic dealings. There is no universal agreement on the meaning of justice, and ideal or perfect justice is difficult to attain in this life. People strive for relative justice, not perfect justice; and good laws assist to that end. It is the business of citizens in a democracy to ensure that wise laws are passed and that they are fairly administered in the courts of law. The importance of this concept has been emphasised in the recent decision of *Bates & Others v Post Office Ltd* (2019), involving the Post Office wrongfully prosecuting several of its postmasters. In addition, the **Post Office (Horizon System) Offences Act 2024** also provided for the quashing of convictions in England and Wales and Northern Ireland for certain offences alleged to have been committed while the Horizon system was in use by the Post Office.

1.3 Classification of law

Law may be classified in various ways. The four main divisions are as follows:

a criminal law and civil law
b public law and private law
c substantive law and procedural law
d municipal law and public international law

a Criminal law

Criminal law is that part of the law that characterizes certain kinds of wrongdoings as offences *against* the State, not necessarily violating any private right, and punishable *by* the State. Crime is defined as *an act of disobedience of the law forbidden under pain of punishment*. The punishment for crime ranges from death or imprisonment to a money penalty (fine) or absolute discharge. For example, to commit murder is an offence against the State because it disturbs the public peace and security, so the action is brought by the State and not the victim.

The police are the public servants whose duty is the prevention and detection of crime and the prosecution of offenders before the courts of law. Private citizens may legally enforce the criminal law by beginning proceedings themselves, but, except in minor cases of common assault, rarely do so in practice.

Civil law is concerned with the rights and duties of individuals towards each other. It includes the following:

i *Law of contract*, dealing with that branch of the law that determines whether a promise is legally enforceable and what its legal consequences are.

ii *Law of tort*. A tort is defined as a civil wrong for which the remedy is a common law action for unliquidated (i.e. unspecified or unascertained) damages, and which is not exclusively the breach of a contract, breach of trust or other merely equitable obligation. (Salmond: *Law of Torts*.) Examples of torts are nuisance, negligence, defamation and trespass.

iii *Law of property* is that part of the law that determines the nature and extent of the rights that people may enjoy over land and other property—for example, rights of 'ownership' of land or rights under a lease.

iv *Law of succession* is that part of the law that determines the devolution of property on the death of the former owner.

v *Family law* is that body of law regulating family relationships, including marriage and divorce, the treatment of children and related economic matters.

The preceding list contains the major branches of civil law. Its main distinction from criminal law is that in civil law the legal action is begun by the private citizen to establish rights (in which the State is not primarily concerned) against another citizen or group of citizens, whereas criminal law is enforced on behalf of or in the name of the State. Civil law is sometimes referred to as *private law* as distinct from *public law*.

b Public law

Public law comprises (i) constitutional law, (ii) administrative law and (iii) criminal law.

i *Constitutional law* has been defined as *the rules that regulate the structure of the principal organs of government and their relationship to each other and determine their principal functions*. This subject includes: choice of monarch, his or her powers and prerogative; the constitution of the legislature; powers and privileges of Members of Parliament; the relationship between the separate chambers of Parliament; the status of Ministers; the civil service; the armed forces; the police; the relations between the central government and local authorities; the making of treaties; admission and rights of aliens; the courts of justice; liberties of speech, of meeting, of association; and voting rights.

ii *Administrative law* is defined as *that body of legal principles that concerns the rights and duties arising from the impact upon the individual of the actual functioning of the executive instruments of government* (C.K. Allen: *Law and Orders*.) For example, administrative law determines the legal rights of a private citizen whose house a local authority intends to acquire compulsorily.

iii *Criminal law* has already been described, with its distinction from civil law.

c Substantive law

Substantive law is the body of rules of law in the preceding branches that regulate the rights, duties and liabilities among citizens and governments.

Procedural law lays down the rules governing the way a right is enforced under civil law, or a crime prosecuted under criminal law. Thus, a legal action is started by issuing a claim form in civil cases, by a summons or an arrest in criminal cases, and ends by the trial and judgment in the court itself, followed by the execution of the judgment. Procedural law governs the steps in the progress of the civil legal action or criminal prosecution.

The distinction between substantive law and procedural law is not always clear. It is an important rule of law that the prosecution may not (except in special circumstances) refer to the accused's bad character during the course of the trial, for this could clearly prejudice their case. (English law presumes that an accused person is innocent until proven guilty.) This rule may be regarded as either substantive or procedural, depending on the view taken of its nature.

d Municipal or national law

This is the law operative within a State. One branch of that law is the law relating to conflict of laws, otherwise known as *private international law*, which determines which national law governs a case in which there is a foreign element.

Thus Jenkins, a British subject, makes a contract in Rome with Boussac, a Frenchman, for the supply of footballs to a team in Madrid. If Jenkins now takes action against Boussac in an English court of law for alleged breach of contract, the court will have to determine by the rules of private international law which law is to be applied: English, Italian, French or Spanish.

However, the **International Criminal Court Act 2001** recognized the establishment of the International Criminal Court and the provision for offences under the Law of England, Wales and Northern Ireland corresponding to offences within the jurisdiction of the Court.

The Government has also enacted the **Private International Law (Implementation of Agreements) Act 2020** to implement the Hague Conventions of 1996, 2005 and 2007 whilst providing for the implementation of other international agreements on private international law. The purpose of the Act was to provide for the implementation of domestic law of international agreements on private international law. The Act contains two main sections—Section 1 referring to the three Hague Conventions which related to: protection of children, choice of court agreements, and child support, and Section 2 on implementation of other agreements on private international law.

e Public international law

This is the body of rules of law that govern the relationships between States, particularly the rules of war. Certain writers hold that since there is no world authority with power to enforce the rules or laws and that, as public international law is incompatible with national sovereignty, the essential characteristics of law are absent.

1.4 Characteristics of English law

The United Kingdom is a unitary State, not a federation of States. Nevertheless, it does not have a single system of law within that State. There are separate systems operating in (i) England and Wales, (ii) Northern Ireland and (iii) Scotland. Due to the closeness of the association since the twelfth century between England and Wales on the one hand and Northern Ireland on the other, these countries have similar legal systems. There are, however, differences between the law of Scotland, influenced by Roman law, and that of the remainder of the United Kingdom, although since the **Union with Scotland Act 1707**, these differences are now less marked on broad issues.

Two important links uniting the system are: (i) Parliament at Westminster is the supreme authority throughout the United Kingdom; (ii) The Supreme Court which, in 2009, replaced the House of Lords as the final court of appeal. English law is one of the great legal systems of the world, and a substantial proportion of it is ruled today by laws that came originally from this small island. What, then, are the characteristics of English law, which give it this pre-eminence? The most important are these:

a Continuous growth

English law is traceable to Anglo-Saxon times. The common law, i.e. judge-made law, which forms the basis of English law, has endured for 900 years and has continuously adapted itself to changing social and economic needs.

Old rules of law remain law despite their age, unless expressly repealed. Thus, in the case of *Ashford v Thornton* (1818), an appeal against alleged murder, the appealer claimed and was granted the ancient Norman right of trial by battle. In fact the appealer's opponent refused to fight, and the right was abolished by statute in 1819.

The **Treason Act 1351** is still good law and may be invoked today despite its age.

Whereas Continental countries have been subject to continual invasions, revolutions, declarations of independence and the like, the geographical separation of England from the Continent, coupled with the English person's traditional respect for law, has tended to preserve the independent and uninterrupted growth of English law.

The **Constitutional Reform and Governance Act 2010** is another example of this ongoing growth of the law. It deals with various matters, including provisions in respect of s. 3 of the **Act of Settlement 1701**, ratification of treaties and provision for a referendum on the voting system for parliamentary elections and general arrangements for the holding of referendums.

Regarding the role of the Crown, the **Succession to the Crown Act 2013** provided that, in future, succession to the Crown would not depend on gender, neither would a person be disqualified from succeeding to the Crown as a result of marrying a person of the Roman Catholic faith.

The **House of Lords Reform Act 2014** provided for the first time for the resignation or retirement of Peers from the House of Lords or their removal on conviction of a serious offence. Its provisions were amended by the **House of Lords (Expulsion and Suspension) Act 2015,** which authorised the House of Lords to expel or suspend a member for a definite period. They are then disqualified from being a member again.

b Absence of codification

A legal code is a systematic collection of laws so arranged as to avoid inconsistency and overlapping. Codification was a feature of Roman law and was adopted by nearly all Continental countries, notably France, Germany, Austria and Switzerland. The English common law was formed from the customs of the people. Under the Norman kings, these unwritten laws achieved a fairly uniform legal system. Certain parts of English law have only today been codified, e.g. the **Bills of Exchange Act 1882** and the **Sale of Goods Act 1979**, though the Law Commission is working towards a codification of criminal law and contract (**Law Commissions Act 1965**, see p. 35).

c Judicial character of the law

The early Norman judges were important figures appointed by the Crown whose justice they administered. The common law was largely 'judge-made' from the existing customary laws. It is from the records and reports of cases tried by the judges that we derive our knowledge of early case law. Judges formed or moulded the common law, and its growth and character can often be traced to outstanding men such as Bracton, Coke and Littleton. Although judges today may develop the common law within narrow limits, they are mainly concerned with interpreting and applying statute law, which is now the main source of legal development.

d Independence of judiciary

Justice requires that a judge be impartial and independent of either party to a particular legal dispute. The **Act of Settlement 1701** provided that judges of superior courts 'hold office during good behaviour, that their salaries be ascertained and established, and that they be removed only on the address of both Houses of Parliament'.

e Independence of lawyers

The two branches of the legal profession comprise barristers and solicitors. Each branch is controlled by an independent body that maintains high professional standards of education, training and conduct. Lawyers are not appointed by the State and are not civil servants. They are not subject to direct political control and, like the judges, are traditionally independent. Their relations with clients are based on confidence and protected by privilege; they cannot be compelled to disclose what passes between them during their professional dealings.

f Influence of procedure

Procedure has influenced substantive law. We shall see later that at one time the existence of a legal right depended on whether there was a suitable writ with which to begin the action. The writ system governed early law. Such procedural rules affected the law itself, and they have left their imprint.

g No reception of Roman law

English common law was of native growth and little influenced by Roman law, unlike the law of Continental countries and Scotland, which was shaped by it.

h The doctrine of precedent

To achieve some consistency in decisions, the courts developed the practice that the lower courts are bound to follow decisions in higher courts.

i Practical nature of the law

It was emphasized by the House of Lords in *Ainsbury v Millington* (1987) that it has always been a fundamental feature of the English judicial system that the courts decide disputes between the parties before them. They will not pronounce on abstract questions of law where there is no dispute to be resolved.

1.5 Useful webpages

British and Irish Legal Information Institute (BAILII) (www.bailii.org)

The official website of the Ministry of Justice. (www.justice.gov.uk)

1.6 Exercises

1. Distinguish between (i) a legal rule and (ii) a principle of morality.
2. Distinguish between criminal law and civil law and between public law and private law.
3. What are the main characteristics of English law?

Chapter 2

Sources of English law

Key points

- origins of the common law and the history of equity
- the role of legislation
- judicial precedent and its mode of operation within the English judicial system
- forms of legislation
- interpretation of statutes

2.1 Historical sources

English law has developed from several sources: custom, the rules worked out by the common-law courts and the courts of equity, canon law, the law merchant, legislation, etc. Moreover, the growth of substantive civil law has at common law been bound up with procedure, since a right existed only if it could be enforced.

The following is an outline of the sources of English law and of the courts and other institutions involved.

2.2 The common law

In Anglo-Saxon times there existed three distinct legal systems: *The Dane Law*, which had been adopted after the invasions and settlement of Danish and Scandinavian warriors in the coastal areas of northern and north-eastern England; *Mercian Law*, which bore traces of Germanic origin, following the Saxon invasions, and extended around the Midlands; *Wessex Law*, which applied in south and west England.

In each of the three systems the law was based on customs, and the customs varied from place to place and shire to shire. There was little distinction between criminal wrongs and civil wrongs at this time; the laws were generally primitive, but nevertheless served to produce such good order as could be expected. But there were courts of law where cases were heard. The Anglo-Saxon courts before 1066 were:

i The *Shire Court* (or *Moot*), presided over by the Sheriff, the Bishop and the Ealdorman, and attended by the lords and freemen of the county, with the priest. This court sat twice a year.

DOI: 10.4324/9781003422808-2

ii The *Hundred Court* ('hundred' means a division of a shire), presided over by the Hundredman, assisted by 12 senior thanes.

iii The *Franchise Courts*, granted to certain persons by the monarch. The grantees were entitled to the profits, for the suitors or litigants who brought their cases to court for trial were required to pay fees. In Norman times the franchise courts were sometimes taken over by the lords of the manor who, in deciding disputes between tenants of land, continued the practice of charging fees.

Of these three courts the shire court was the most important, but all enforced the local laws and all had jurisdiction to deal with obvious criminal offences, such as murder, theft, violence to person and property, and also the civil claims concerning ownership or possession of land or cattle—both very important sources of wealth.

The Anglo-Saxon system of keeping the peace was based on *frank-pledge*, a police organization that required every male over the age of 12 to belong to a 'tithing', a group of ten or more persons under a headman. All in the tithing were mutually responsible for the offences of the others and were bound to produce the offender in court if called upon. Those who did not submit to justice in the courts were declared outlaws and could be killed with impunity.

In most parts of England, the succession to land on the death of an owner was determined by the rule of *primogeniture*, i.e. the first-born son inherited his father's land. But in some places, it was different; e.g. in Kent, the system of landholding was known as *gavelkind* and, under it, all sons inherited equally. In Bristol and Nottingham, a system of *borough-English* applied which provided that the youngest son inherited.

The procedure and the proof of guilt in Anglo-Saxon courts were primitive. Trial might be by *ordeal*, which was in effect an appeal to God or the supernatural. It might consist of ducking someone in a pool, and he was guilty if the water 'rejected' him and innocent if he sank; or in an ordeal by fire a red-hot iron would be carried a distance of nine feet, whereby if the hands had not festered within a certain period after carrying the iron the offender had established his innocence.

Another form of proof in civil cases was *compurgation*. This consisted of the litigant repeating an oath word-perfect without stumbling. Sometimes the claimant was assisted by kinsmen who were oath helpers (or compurgators) and similarly swore. If they, too, repeated the oath successfully, the claimant had 'waged his law' and won, his claim. Juries (see p. 66) later superseded ordeal and compurgation.

Before the Norman Conquest there was no strong central government. The King with his council (or witan) had little control over his kingdom. Royal justice was difficult to obtain.

2.2.1 The Norman conquest

English legal development stems from 1066 when William of Normandy gained the Crown of England by right of battle. William and his Norman successors distinguished themselves in many ways. They possessed orderly minds and were efficient administrators. They crushed the rebellious English into submission and established a strong central government.

William owned all England: all other persons possessed land either as tenants (not owners) or subtenants of the King himself. Feudalism, based on land tenure, was introduced into England. No immediate change was attempted in regard to the customary laws of the English, for this would have been an insuperable task. Primitive people do not take kindly to radical alterations in their way of living.

The changes made by William I include the following:

a The King's Council (*Magnum Concilium*) was set up. Here foregathered the barons, lords, bishops and other important figures of the kingdom, on whose advice and wisdom the monarch relied. Here was the strong central government.

b A new feudalism was introduced. The King owned (in theory) all the land, and the barons, lords, bishops and freemen held of him as tenants or subtenants. All tenants, whether barons or freemen, were compelled to swear an oath of allegiance to the King himself. Freemen owed allegiance as subtenants not only to a lord of the manor but also to the King, an important fact making for closer royal control.

c Separation of lay courts and church (or clerical) courts, each with a definite jurisdiction. Bishops and clergy were henceforward to be tried in their own courts and Church (or canon) law was to be applied therein.

William and his successors achieved the uniformity of the law, making it the common law, by introducing the *general eyre*. This was a form of central control whereby representatives of the King were sent out from Westminster to all parts of the country to check the local administration in the shires. These representatives made records of the land and wealth of the country, they collected taxes and they adjudicated in disputes brought before them. In the course of time the general eyre became judicial rather than administrative. In the reign of Richard II, the eyre was abolished, but the important practice of sending members of the Royal Council continued. These representatives of the King were the original *royal judges* and derived their authority from the King's command by Royal Commissions, namely:

a the *Commission of Gaol Delivery*, empowering the judges to clear the gaols of untried prisoners

b the *Commission of Oyer and Terminer*, empowering the judges to hear (*oyer*) and determine (*terminer*) cases of serious crimes such as treason or felonies brought before them

c the *Commission of Assize*, which granted the judges jurisdiction over civil matters normally triable in the royal courts at Westminster

To appreciate the significance of the Commission of Assize, we should remember that whenever a plaintiff wished to bring an action in a civil matter against another person, he had to obtain a writ from the Lord Chancellor's writ office and serve it on his opponent. The writ commanded the defendant and the plaintiff to attend the royal courts at Westminster on a certain date, unless before that date (nisi prius) the King's justices could hear the case locally, i.e. where the action arose. Attendance at Westminster was itself no easy matter in those days; journeys were long, delays in London were likely and witnesses could not always be found to attend. So, a local hearing by the royal judges was a useful and attractive expedient readily grasped by those who could not obtain justice in the manorial court or other local courts—which were frequently corrupt, partial and unfair.

Here, then, were the royal judges, known as *itinerant justices*, granting better justice which naturally proved popular with the people. Henry II (1154–89) reorganized the system by dividing the country into *circuits* and putting the excursions from Westminster on a regular basis.

We have seen that the judges were originally men appointed from the King's Council; they might be bishops, barons or knights. Behind them stood the royal power as evidenced by the King's Commissions.

The original justices were, for the most part, untrained in law. When they visited a county court (the shires became counties after the Normans), they had to ascertain the customs applicable to the local court. The royal judges then applied the law thus discovered from the inhabitants. The twelfth and thirteenth centuries saw the introduction of *juries*. Juries were made up of local people who knew the facts of the local cases and the local customs relevant thereto, so that the justices could then enforce these customs in the name of the King.

On completing their circuits, the justices returned to the royal courts at Westminster. There they discussed together the customs ascertained in various parts of the country and their findings. By a process of sifting these customs, rejecting those that were unreasonable and accepting those that were not, and by the use of good sense and right reason, they formed a uniform pattern of customary law throughout England.

At the same time another important practice grew up: the judges began to apply the principle of *stare decisis* ('let the decision stand'). Whenever a new problem of law came to be decided, a rule was formed, and this rule was followed subsequently by all other judges. By this means, the law became more certain and predictable, and acquired the character of a legal system. So, out of the varied and different customs, there was formed what is now known as the common law of England, so called because it is the law common to all parts of England and Wales.

It is estimated that the formation of the common law was complete by about 1250 when Bracton wrote his famous *Treatise on the Laws and Customs of England*, which was the first exposition of a part of the law that was destined to reach all parts of the world.

2.2.2 The common-law courts

The King's Council, sometimes called the *Curia Regis*, was the central government of the kingdom, performing legislative, executive and judicial functions without distinction. From the King's Council, special courts were instituted to deal with particular kinds of cases in which royal justice was sought. The various courts staffed by royal judges developed in the following order:

a The Court of Exchequer

This was formed during the reign of Henry I and was primarily a government department concerned with national revenue. It was named the 'Exchequer' because the method of accounting involved the use of counters that were moved about on a chequered board. The department split into two branches: one administrative, collecting taxes and dues; the other judicial, dealing with disputes over taxation. The court extended its jurisdiction to hear common-law actions only remotely connected with the royal revenue. The judges of the court were known as Barons of the Exchequer.

b The Court of Common Pleas

The itinerant or circuit judges were sent out by royal authority to dispense justice in the counties. These judges sat in the communal and feudal courts (e.g. manorial courts) and they claimed jurisdiction over disputes between persons, e.g. in relation to land. Their justice became popular, and a special court called the *Court of Common Pleas* (so called because it dealt with pleas of the commoners as distinct from royal pleas, i.e. criminal cases) was set up to decide disputes of a civil nature between subject and subject. In 1273 the first Chief Justice was appointed. This court administered the common law and survived until the **Judicature Acts 1873–5**.

c The Court of King's Bench

This was the youngest and the most durable of the courts to emerge from the *Curia Regis*. It owes its name to the close connexion with the monarch, for the King himself used to sit at a bench with the judges to decide disputes. This close connexion with the *Curia Regis* and the King also gave it a unique importance. Its jurisdiction included criminal cases (in addition to those tried by the itinerant justices in the local courts), and also civil cases, concurrent with the jurisdiction of the Court of Common Pleas. But the King's Bench had a supervisory jurisdiction over the activities of all inferior courts, which it enforced by means of prerogative writs.

This court survives today as the Court of King's Bench with its civil, criminal and supervisory jurisdiction, and is under the control of the President of the King's Bench Division, who is assisted (as were former courts) by puisne judges.

Some mention should be made here of legal procedure. In medieval times criminals were arrested and placed in the gaols until they could be tried, either by the local manorial courts or by the royal judges when they came to the district. In civil cases, however, procedure was more technical. The proceedings in the common-law courts started with the issue of an 'original' writ (so named because it originated the proceedings), which was purchased from the main royal office, the Chancery.

The writ was a formal document addressed to the sheriff of the county where the defendant resided, commanding him to secure the presence of the defendant at the trial and setting out the cause of action or ground of claim of the claimant. For every civil wrong or cause of action, there was a separate writ. Important examples were the writ of trespass, the writ of debt and the writ of detinue (detinue alleged that the defendant detained an article or chattel from the claimant and would not return it). The claimant had to select the particular writ that he considered fitted the facts of his case.

The claimant attended the Writ Office of the Chancery, where a register of the various writs was kept, and applied for the writ most suitable to his claim. If there was no writ suitable to the civil claim made or the relief required by the law, the claimant was at a severe disadvantage. We may say, therefore, that the writ system dominated the civil law: for only where there was a remedy was there a right (which is expressed in the Latin phrase *ubi remedium ibi jus*). Moreover, if the wrong kind of writ were selected by the claimant, the common-law judges would reject the case and refrain from inquiring into its merits. Under the rigid procedure of the writ system, the remedy available to litigants became more important than the justice of the claim.

Some attempt to alleviate this system was made by the clerks in the Chancery. Where a writ was thrown out by the court, or where none existed to found the claim, the clerks endeavoured to accommodate litigants by issuing new writs, thus effectively expanding the rights available. At first the common-law judges tolerated this procedure and accepted some new writs; but later their attitude stiffened, and they refused to accept the new writs, since these amounted to new law.

The Provisions of Oxford, 1258, forbade the practice of creating new writs. As a result, certain wrongs went unremedied merely because they did not fall within the limits of an existing writ. However, some alleviation was attempted by the Statute of Westminster II, 1285, which empowered the clerks in the Chancery to issue writs *in consimili casu* ('in like case to'); i.e. existing writs could be adapted to fit new circumstances. However, full use was not made of this provision, and litigants' claims still went unsatisfied by the ineffectual writ system: the common law did not expand to meet the urgent and growing needs of the community. Complaints to the King and his Council regarding the inelasticity of the common law led to the emergence of the Court of Chancery and its special field known as *equity*.

2.3 Equity

In a general sense, equity means fairness. In English law, equity means that body of rules originally enforced only by the Court of Chancery. Equity has been described as 'a gloss [meaning a supplement] on the common law', filling in the gaps and making the English legal system more complete.

Petitions from persons unable to obtain justice in the common-law courts were sent to the King as 'fountain of justice'. These petitions were sometimes examined by the King and Council and the relief was granted or refused. Later, owing to pressure of business in the Council, the petitions were sent to the Lord Chancellor, who, as Chief Secretary of State and 'Keeper of the King's Conscience', dealt with them alone.

The petitions were usually in the form of allegations that:

a the common law was defective, e.g. the law of contract was undeveloped and inadequate to serve the growing needs of suitors
b the remedy of the common-law courts, namely damages, was not always a satisfactory relief

c the defendant was too powerful; people of wealth and power in a county could overawe a court and intimidate jurors
d the court lacked jurisdiction to decide certain cases, e.g. where foreign merchants were suitors

By the end of the fifteenth century the Chancellor had set up a separate court that dealt with petitions for relief. The Chancellor was not bound by the writ system or the technical and formal rules of the common law and considered petitions based on conscience and right.

At first the Chancellor used to consult the Council and sometimes the common-law judges, but eventually it became customary to summon the parties to the dispute to appear before the Chancellor alone to answer 'interrogatories' (specific questions relevant to the issue) and to unburden their consciences so that the truth could be ascertained and justice done.

The Court of Chancery proved popular with litigants, and this caused friction with the common-law courts. Jurisdiction was lost to the Chancery Court. Sometimes the courts of common law and the Chancery Court issued contradictory verdicts, and relations between the courts became difficult. The dispute came to a head under James I (1603–25) in the *Earl of Oxford's* case (1616). The common-law courts, headed by Chief Justice Coke, gave a judgment that was alleged to have been obtained by fraud. The Chancellor, Lord Ellesmere, issued an injunction preventing the successful party from proceeding to enforce the judgment, whereupon the dispute was referred to the King for decision. The King sought the views of Sir Francis Bacon (Attorney-General), who advised that *where common law and equity conflicted, equity should prevail*. Although competition between the courts of common law and equity continued, the right of the Chancellor to grant injunctions thereafter was not seriously challenged. Matters were finally resolved by the passing of the **Judicature Acts 1873–5** (see p. 15).

Despite its early popularity, equity as administered in the Chancery was subject to criticism. Its initial flexibility led to uncertainty in the seventeenth century, and the jurist John Selden observed that 'Equity varies with the length of the Chancellor's foot'. Whatever the demerits of the common law, it was possible to estimate a probable verdict by considering similar cases already decided and the statutes enforced. Equity, which was dispensed as a matter of conscience, was unpredictable and the relief granted by one Chancellor might be refused by his successor. Between flexibility and certainty there is much tension. Flexibility was advantageous because it gave relief from the rigidity of law, but could be disadvantageous if it led to uncertainty and hardship.

Eventually equity emerged from vagueness and conscience and became formalized. Lord Nottingham (Lord Chancellor in 1673–82) held that equity should be administered where possible in accordance with known principles and not by arbitrary discretion. Only where there was no precedent or where there was conflict in the rules or principles should conscience determine the matter.

Nottingham's work was carried on by others, in particular Lord Hardwicke (Lord Chancellor in 1736–56), who held that a judge exercising equity jurisdiction should follow existing principles. With the adoption of the system of precedent, equity became predictable and intelligible.

Lord Eldon (Lord Chancellor in 1801–6 and 1807–27) further developed equity, establishing a system of case law, so that by the beginning of the nineteenth century, equity became nearly as rigid as the common law.

2.3.1 Later history

The history of equity in the nineteenth century was notable for the delays that occurred in settling disputes and the confusion over jurisdiction. Lord Eldon's rule as Lord Chancellor has been described as 'ponderous' (one case is reported to have lasted ten years). The delays may have been caused by the numerous duties that the Lord Chancellor was called upon to perform. Today the Lord Chancellor is similarly burdened, although with different responsibilities, but now has a large staff to assist. In the nineteenth century complaint was also made of the cost of proceedings, and we should remember that the clerks and assistants in the Chancery Court received emoluments from the litigants themselves, a system that evoked much criticism.

The latter half of the nineteenth century was also a period of judicial reform that culminated in the **Judicature Acts 1873–5**. These Acts set up a new structure of courts known as the Supreme Court of Judicature (see p. 18). In addition, the Acts laid down four important principles:

a equity and common law should in future be administered side by side in all courts
b where there is a conflict between a rule of equity and a rule of common law with reference to the same matter, the rule of equity should prevail
c evidence could be given in court orally
d rules of the Supreme Court of Judicature were to be formulated regarding procedural matters

The result of the Acts was the fusion of the administration of both common law and equity. Certain matters, e.g. trusts, originally dealt with by the Court of Chancery, were assigned with other matters to the Chancery Division of the High Court. All courts could henceforward award common-law remedies, e.g. damages, and grant the special equitable remedies of which the following are the most important:

a *injunction*, an order of the court in the form of a decree compelling the defendant in a case to cease from doing certain acts;
b *specific performance* of contracts where the common law remedy of damages is inadequate to compensate the claimant.
c *rescission of contracts* (see p. 175);
d *rectification* (see p. 170);
e *relief against penalties* (see p. 200), *fraud and undue influence* (see p. 179).

These remedies are at the discretion of the court, unlike the common-law remedy of damages, which is 'of right'. The discretion is exercised on equitable principles, e.g. 'He who comes to equity must come with clean hands.'

2.4 Legislation, part I

It has already been emphasized that the basis of English law is the common law, whose principles are to be found today in the case law built up by the judges ever since the Norman Conquest.

The original role of the King and his Council was merely to maintain order and peace within the realm and to defend the State against external aggression. To keep order and peace, the King amended or altered existing law by issuing ordinances, provisions, assizes and charters, always with the advice of his Council. These ordinances, some temporary and some permanent, were in effect statutes, but their number was comparatively small.

The Rise of Parliament. Frequently the King was required to raise military forces and the money wherewith to carry out his duties and maintain his position within the State. This meant the taxation of those feudal tenants and freeholders under the King's protection and from whom he exacted allegiance. Accordingly, the Norman kings sometimes summoned the great vassals (barons, bishops and lords) to attend a 'parliament' (*parler*; to speak), a name first used in the thirteenth century.

In 1265 Simon de Montford summoned his famous parliament, which for the first time contained representatives from the cities and boroughs as well as the shires. The practice of summoning representatives of the important groups in the land continued, and by 1300 the three estates of the realm, namely (i) the Lords Spiritual (the archbishops and bishops), (ii) the Lords Temporal (barons and lords) and (iii) the Commons (knights and freemen from the cities, boroughs and the shires), met at Westminster. Sometimes the Lords and Commons met together, but more often in private and separate assemblies, to discuss what answers should be given 'in Parliament' to the King's demands for military supplies and money.

The grant of money to the King placed the Commons in a strong bargaining position, and eventually they began to present petitions or 'Bills' to the King requesting a change in the law in return for the grant of money. These petitions were originally requests; some were granted, and some were refused. Refusal meant a conflict between the Commons (expressing the will of the people) and the King with his advisers. But kings do not lightly relinquish their vast powers; many were despotic and claimed to rule by Divine Right.

In the time of the Tudors, Parliament was subjected to the wills of strong monarchs, including Henry VIII and Elizabeth I, who, while not overruling Parliament, ruled as they pleased *through* Parliament.

This uneasy balance of powers came to a head in the seventeenth century in the English Civil War (1642–51), fought between the Parliamentarians and the Royalists, which resulted in the trial and execution of King Charles I in 1649. His rule was replaced with a republican Commonwealth and then a Protectorate under Oliver Cromwell. The monarchy was restored to power with Charles II in 1660. James II (1685–8) also reverted to unwise and arbitrary methods of government, and again civil war broke out between the Royalists, supporting the King, and the Parliamentarians, supporting the Commons. James II fled to France, and, after the so-called 'Glorious Revolution' of 1688, William and Mary were invited to come to the throne of England. The Bill of Rights, 1689, meant that the King could not in future override Acts of Parliament or exercise the great powers of government without check from the representatives of Parliament. Because the Commons would grant money to the King for one year only, it became necessary for the King to call Parliament together at least once a year.

During the remainder of the seventeenth century, and in the eighteenth and nineteenth centuries, great constitutional developments took place. First, the growth of political parties; second, the rise of Cabinet government led by a Prime Minister; and, following the **Reform Act 1832**, the grant of universal franchise. Today Britain has what is described as a *constitutional monarchy*, the chief characteristic of which is that the monarch is nominally head of the State, but has lost practically all actual power. By convention the monarch acts in accordance with the will of the Government of the day (headed by a Prime Minister and a Cabinet), which is itself responsible to Parliament, composed of representatives of the people elected by popular vote.

Successive governments have interfered more and more positively with the social, economic and industrial aspects of national affairs. The Welfare State was brought about by legislation, and many areas of the common law (civil and criminal) have been revoked or reformed. It follows, therefore, that the main source of law today is legislation. A recent example of the use of legislation by government to achieve instant support to the community was the **Business and Planning Act 2020** which was legislation enacted to introduce various temporary and permanent measures aimed at supporting business during the COVID-19 pandemic. It included provisions for promoting economic recovery and growth, allowing certain sectors to operate more flexibly.

Legislation may take the form of:

a *statutes* or Acts of Parliament (see p. 24); and
b delegated legislation, mainly in the form of what are called *statutory instruments* (see p. 27).

2.4.1 European Union law

Some of the legislation enacted by the European Union institutions was directly applicable and immediately binding on the English courts. Other legislation was not so, but the Parliament of the United Kingdom was required to legislate on the matter. Obviously since the referendum in favour of the United Kingdom withdrawing from the European Union ('Brexit'), there has been a dramatic change in these arrangements (see Chapter 13).

2.5 Local custom, part I

We have described the common law as the unwritten part of English law or the common or universal custom of the realm. We have also mentioned that the principles of law formulated by the judges, which in fact make up the body of the common law, have been enforced by the courts of law for some 900 years.

It is well known that in some parts of England, certain local customs are observed that, while different in character from the general custom of the realm, are nevertheless regarded as conferring rights or imposing duties. Moreover, many such customs have existed from time immemorial. English law takes account of these local customary rights, and even though they are apparent exceptions to the general law, they may nevertheless be enforced.

2.6 The nineteenth century

The law and the procedure by which justice is administered are always open to public criticism. In the nineteenth century there were ample grounds for general dissatisfaction. It has already been noted that the principles of common law and those of equity were separate and were administered in different courts. Where a litigant in a common-law case (e.g. trespass) wished to obtain an equitable remedy or relief (e.g. an injunction), they had to commence a separate action in the Chancery Court, thus adding to expense and often causing great delay. The rules of common law sometimes conflicted with the principles of equity, so that confusion resulted. There was, moreover, a variety of courts, and some (e.g. the ecclesiastical courts and the Admiralty courts) had developed special rules and practices of their own. The system of appeals from the common law courts (civil and criminal) and the equity courts was irrational and confusing. The legal procedure for enforcing rights and obtaining remedies was inefficient, technical, antiquated and slow.

The deficiencies in the law itself and in its administration were obvious to ordinary citizens (as well as litigants). They were noted by Charles Dickens and other writers and were critically examined by outstanding political thinkers such as Jeremy Bentham (1748–1832).

Changes were, however, slow and piecemeal. As already mentioned (p. 15), the **Court of Probate Act 1857** took away the probate jurisdiction of the ecclesiastical courts and set up a new Probate Court. By the **Matrimonial Causes Act 1857**, a new Divorce Court was set up which took over the matrimonial jurisdiction of the old ecclesiastical courts.

The **Common Law Procedure Act 1854** empowered common-law courts to grant injunctions and to take account of certain equitable defences. The **Chancery Procedure Act 1852** enabled the Chancery Court to decide points of common law arising in equity proceedings, e.g. actions for breach of trust. The **Chancery Amendment Act 1858** enabled the Chancery Court to award damages (a common law remedy) in place of or in addition to its own equitable remedies, notably injunction and specific performance of contracts.

But the main reform was affected by the **Judicature Acts 1873–5**, from the recommendations of the Judicature Commission of 1867.

Immediately before this important Act came into effect, the following courts existed: King's Bench; Common Pleas; Exchequer; Chancery; Court of Probate; Court of Divorce; Court of Admiralty. Appeal courts were the Court of Appeal in Chancery and the Court of Exchequer. Appeals in criminal cases were heard by the Court of Crown Cases Reserved, established in 1848. This court was not affected by the reorganization of 1875.

2.6.1 Reorganization of the courts

The **Judicature Acts, 1873–5**, set up a Supreme Court of Judicature comprising (a) the Court of Appeal and (b) the High Court of Justice. The latter included:

i the Queen's Bench Division
ii the Chancery Division
iii the Common Pleas Division
iv the Exchequer Division
v the Probate, Divorce and Admiralty Division

By an Order in Council of 1881, made under the **Judicature Acts, 1873–5**, the Common Pleas Division and the Exchequer Division were merged with the Queen's Bench Division, thus forming three divisions that existed till 1970:

i the Queen's Bench Division
ii the Chancery Division
iii the Probate, Divorce and Admiralty Division

2.6.2 The House of Lords

The jurisdiction of the House of Lords as a final court of appeal was abolished by the **Judicature Act 1873**, mainly on the grounds that there were insufficient legally qualified peers (lay members of the House, by convention, had not attended judicial meetings). By the **Appellate Jurisdiction Act 1876**, the appellate jurisdiction was restored, and provision was made for the appointment of two Lords of Appeal in Ordinary. However, the long-term effect of the **Constitutional Reform Act 2005** eventually resulted in the House of Lords as a judicial court of appeal being replaced by a Supreme Court (see p. 39).

2.6.3 Reforming the rules

The **Judicature Acts** not only reformed the structure of the courts, but they also made fundamental changes in the administration of law and equity. All branches of the Supreme Court were empowered to administer law and equity and to grant legal remedies and equitable remedies. Moreover, all divisions of the High Court were competent to try *any* action. For administrative purposes and convenience, certain matters were reserved or allocated to each division, roughly corresponding to the jurisdiction of the courts that had been replaced.

The Acts further provided that, where a rule of equity and a rule of common law were at variance with reference to the same matter, the rule of equity should prevail. The Acts did not fuse law and equity into a single set of rules. The rules of common law and the principles of equity stem from different sources and are still distinct.* What the Acts did was to ensure that

* The modern opinion (Lord Denning and Viscount Simonds) is that law and equity are now fused.

for the future the two systems should be *administered* in the same courts. The rules of procedure, particularly in respect of the issue of writs, were simplified.

The relevant statute was the **Supreme Court Act 1981** which, to avoid confusion, was renamed the **Senior Courts Act 1981** and which has replaced the earlier legislation.

2.6.4 Legal sources

In English law substantive rules of law derive their authority from the following: judicial precedents, legislation, certain ancient textbooks and, to a very limited extent, local custom. These are called the legal sources.

2.7 Judicial precedent

The essentials of good law are, on the one hand, certainty; and on the other, uniformity and consistency. Common law was judge-made, i.e. the judges moulded or created out of the original customary rules the common law of England, whose principles are today found in case law.

Once a regular system of law reporting had developed and reports published, judges began to be guided by decisions in previous cases; eventually, it became the established practice that judges were bound to follow the decisions of higher courts in similar cases. The general rule established in the nineteenth century and consistently followed since was of binding precedent.

The hierarchy of courts in this matter is as follows:

Court of Justice of the European Communities. Its decisions on interpretation of the Treaties, validity of acts of Community institutions and interpretation of the statutes of Council bodies were until Brexit 2019 binding on all English courts, though apparently not binding on itself (see Chapter 13).

Supreme Court. This replaced the House of Lords. Its decisions bind all other courts, but not necessarily the Supreme Court itself.

Court of Appeal (Civil Division). Its decisions bind the High Court, county courts and Divisional Courts, and itself. However, in *Derby & Co. Ltd v Weldon and Others* (No. 3) (1989), a High Court judge held that in exercising a discretion to strike out a claim, the court in a first instance can disregard a recent Court of Appeal decision where there is a possibility that it may be reversed by the Supreme Court.

Court of Appeal (Criminal Division). Its decisions bind the Crown Court and the magistrates' courts. They probably bind the King's Bench Divisional Court. The Court normally follows its own decisions, but on occasion does not do so.

King's Bench Divisional Court. Its decisions bind the magistrates' courts but not the Crown Court (*Colyer*, 1974) and normally the Court follows its own decisions.

High Court. Decisions of its judges do not bind other High Court judges, but they do bind county court judges. If, however, the court is faced with two conflicting decisions on virtually the same point, then subsequent judges are bound to follow the second decision (*Colchester Estates v Carlton Industries* 1984).

It has not been determined whether decisions of the Crown Court are binding on magistrates' courts, but in effect they are not since they are not reported in the series of law reports and because appeals on points of law are by case stated to the Divisional Court of the Queen's Bench.

The two divisions of the Court of Appeal are of equal status and are not strictly bound by each other's decisions, but in practice, each does pay attention to the rulings of the other and each has a strong persuasive influence on the other to ensure certainty and uniformity of the law.

2.7.1 The Supreme Court and precedent

In 1966 the Lord Chancellor, on behalf of the Lords of Appeal in Ordinary, made the following pronouncement in the House of Lords:

> Their Lordships regard the use of precedent as an indispensable foundation upon which to decide what is the law and its application to individual cases. It provides at least some degree of certainty upon which individuals can rely in the conduct of their affairs, as well as a basis for orderly development of legal rules.
>
> Their Lordships nevertheless recognize that too rigid adherence to precedent may lead to injustice in a particular case and also unduly restrict the proper development of the law. They propose, therefore, to modify their present practice and, while treating former decisions of this House as normally binding, to depart from a previous decision when it appears right to do so.
>
> In this connexion they will bear in mind the danger of disturbing retrospectively the basis on which contracts, settlements of property and fiscal arrangements have been entered into and also the especial need for certainty as to the criminal law.
>
> This announcement is not intended to affect the use of precedent elsewhere than in this House.

2.7.2 Case law: advantages and disadvantages

Prof. William Geldart has enumerated the advantages of case law as:

a certainty
b possibility of growth
c the great wealth of detailed rules
d the practical character of these rules

The disadvantages, according to the same writer, are:

a rigidity: 'the binding force of precedent is a fetter on the discretion of the judge';
b the danger of illogical distinctions: 'a judge will often avoid following a rule which works hardship in a present case by laying hold of minute distinctions. Moreover, rules which are logically inconsistent with each other are sometimes developed along distinct lines of cases which ultimately meet and come into conflict';
c bulk and complexity: there are over 1,000 volumes of law reports containing some 400,000 cases. These may be regarded as cumbersome and the legal rules difficult to learn and apply. Although balanced against this is the fact that physical books of law reports have been replaced by online databases such as BAILII, CommonLII or WorldLII.

The points made by Prof. Geldart emphasize the need to achieve certainty and the need to ensure flexibility. While the former tends to make the law rigid, the latter tends to render the law uncertain and vague, but does allow for development to meet the new needs of society.

Judges of the senior courts, formerly known as the superior courts, may, on appeal, *overrule* a decision, *reverse* a decision or *disapprove* of a previous decision. Sometimes alterations can only be made by a statute that revokes previous law and reshapes the law to meet the changing conditions of people and society.

Overruling occurs where a higher court (e.g. the Supreme Court) decides a similar case on the basis of a different legal principle. The previous rule laid down (e.g. by the Court of Appeal) is then said to be overruled.

Reversal occurs where an appeal court reverses a decision given in a lower court from which the appeal emanated. Thus, in the case of *A v B*, a High Court may give judgment for *A*, while on appeal, the higher court gives judgment for B.

Disapproval occurs where a senior court, during its judgment, expresses doubt as to the validity of some previous rule but does not expressly overrule it.

- The doctrine of *stare decisis* ('to stand by past decisions') is the technical name given to the rule that judges must follow the precedents and principles of law declared by superior courts.
- *Ratio decidendi* is a technical phrase meaning the principle or reason for the decision. This portion of a judgment of a court is binding in similar cases that may subsequently be tried by lower courts. It is a vital part of a judgment and must be distinguished from *obiter dicta* ('things said by the way'), meaning those words delivered by a judge that are not essential to his or her decision. Thus, a judge in the course of a judgment might discuss a hypothetical situation: 'If, however, *A* had done this, and B had done that . . . I should have been obliged to find that *A* and B would be jointly responsible.' These words are said *obiter*, by the way, and are not binding. They might, however, be 'persuasive'; if the situation envisaged by the judge arose in fact at some later time, these words could have an influence on the judge trying that case.
- Judges of the High Court, county court judges and magistrates are absolutely bound by the decisions of the Supreme Court and Court of Appeal where those decisions are clearly in point. Such precedents which a judge *must* follow are called *binding precedents*. All other precedents are called *persuasive precedents*: these include decisions or principles laid down by the Judicial Committee of the Privy Council, decisions of Commonwealth courts or of the United States Supreme Court. A judge of one division of the High Court is not bound by the decision of another High Court judge, though each pays attention to the other's decisions to ensure certainty and uniformity of the law.
- Frequently, there will be no relevant decided case for a judge to turn to. Notwithstanding the many volumes of law reports and the thousands of cases reported, representing a 'wealth of detailed rules', there may be no certainty of the rule to be applied. The judge must declare what the rule should be by arguing from analogous cases. Since the common law is 'complete' and capable of providing a remedy for every wrong, where there is no apparent rule, the judge is expected to act creatively in declaring from his or her study of the common law, equity or jurisprudence what that rule should be.
- Obviously no two cases coming before the courts of law are identical. This fact enables a judge to point to some material difference that is justification for refusing to apply a rule of law previously laid down. The judge is *distinguishing* the present case from the earlier one, so avoiding hardship or injustice which was not envisaged when the earlier judgment was announced.

After hearing the evidence from both sides in a case and the address of counsel, the stage is reached when the judgment is delivered. The form the judgment takes is generally as follows:

a a statement of the relevant facts
b review of relevant precedents
c reasoning of the judge from one or more of the cases cited
d judgment, decree or order made

The judicial precedents that we have been considering are found in law reports.

2.7.3 Law reports

The records of Anglo-Saxon laws (or dooms) and of actual cases are few. Similarly, we have scant records of cases in the Norman period, and we have to remind ourselves that the common law was not completely formed until around AD 1250.

The first treatise on the English common law was written by Henricus de Bracton, who lived in the first part of the thirteenth century in the reign of Henry III. His work, in part a collection of cases, became the forerunner of the later law reports and was entitled *De legibus et consuetudinibus Angliae*. *Year Books*. These contained fragmentary reports of cases in the period between 1289 and 1535. They were written in Anglo-Norman, were technical and procedural in content (covering points of practice) and dealt with civil law rather than criminal law.

Abridgments. These were shortened versions of the Year Books that appeared in the sixteenth and seventeenth centuries and contained reports of cases, some of which were written by judges and counsel. *Private Publications*. Some notable sixteenth-century lawyers and judges prepared private publications of reports on contemporary and earlier cases. Some were copied from imperfect manuscripts and contained much trivial detail. However, by the sixteenth century, pleadings in civil cases were written down, so that it was possible thereafter to cite a case in support of a particular argument. The notable reports during this period are Plowden's Reports (1550–80), Coke's Reports (1572–1616), Bridgman's Reports (1614–21) and Lord Raymond's Reports (1694–1732).

The first *regular* reports were known as Term Reports and were published by Durnford and East (1785–1800). Once reporting of cases became systematic and regular, the reports became authorized, i.e. accepted by the courts as accurately representing the judgment made. Nevertheless the system of reporting was expensive, the standard of reporting deteriorated and there were often lengthy delays between a judgment and the appearance of its report.

Council of Law Reporting. Because of the multiplicity of law reports in the nineteenth century, the Council of Law Reporting was set up in 1865 and barrister reporters were appointed. A series of authorized reports was established under the control of the legal profession.

The Council of Law Reporting is a quasi-official body consisting of representatives of the Inns of Court and the Law Society. The Council employs an editor and a staff of reporters (who are barristers) and produces a uniform series of reports of cases in all the superior courts. Not all cases are reported; a selection is made by the editor. Where it is decided to report a case, a copy of the report made by the reporter is passed to the judge, who has an opportunity of revising the wording of his judgment. The reports so produced are known as the *Law Reports*. They include counsel's argument.

In 1953 the Council of Law Reporting began a weekly series known as the *Weekly Law Reports*.

The Council has no monopoly in the field of law reporting. Certain commercial companies produce reports, and the *All-England Reports*, which began in 1936, is an important example in this field. Moreover, *The Times* publishes summary reports of important cases the day after judgment, and weekly journals such as *The Solicitors' Journal* (established 1857) and the *Justice of the Peace* (established 1837) contain summary reports of cases. Section 115 of the **Courts and Legal Services Act** 1990 provides that a report by a solicitor or a person who has a Supreme Court qualification will have the same authority as if it had been by a barrister.

Where various reports of the same case reveal differences in wording, the *Law Reports* are taken to be the most authoritative since they are semi-official.

British and Irish legal materials, including most law reports, are also available electronically through the British and Irish Legal Information Institute (BAILII)—www.bailii.org. BAILII is based at the Institute of Advanced Legal Studies in London and in Ireland at University College, Cork. Its databases were formerly held in Australia on the servers of, and using technology developed by, the Australasian Legal Information Institute (AustLII—www.austlii.edu.au), which is a world leader in this field.

Since 11 January 2001, it has become even easier to refer to cases on the internet because of the introduction of what has been described as neutral citation. This new process does not refer to any particular published law report but instead indicates the year in which the judgment is given and the court which gave the judgment, so that [2018] UKSC means the tenth judgment of the Supreme Court for that year. For the Court of Appeal [Civil Division], it would be [2018] EWCA Civ1, and for the Court of Appeal [Criminal Division], it would be [2018] EWCA Crim1. Another transformation which has come about because of the internet is that all judgments have their paragraphs numbered successively throughout the judgment. This was another change to law reports which was introduced at the same time as neutral citation.

The law of the European Union is reported in the *European Case Reports* and the *Common Market Law Reports*. Reference should also be made to the *European Law Review* and the *Common Market Law Review*. *Reference to reports*. The claimant, previously designated as the plaintiff, is cited first and the defendant second; thus, '*Brown v Smith* [1968] 1 Q.B. 334' indicates that the report will be found in the first volume of Queen's Bench Division Reports of 1968 at p. 334. 'Ch' indicates Chancery Division Reports, while 'P' indicates those of the (former) Probate, Divorce and Admiralty Division. 'F' denotes the Family Division.

Reports of decisions of the Court of Appeal appear with the reports of the Division (although the Division has disappeared, the reports survive) from which the appeal is made. 'AC' indicates an appeal case heard in the Supreme Court or the Privy Council.

2.7.4 Citation of cases

Where cases are determined by a court at first instance (i.e. heard for the first time), the proceedings are cited thus:

Civil case

a *Brown v Jones* (1969)

Brown is the claimant; Jones is the defendant.

Criminal case

b *Regina* (or *R*) *v Smith* (1969)

Regina (the King) is the prosecutor; Smith is the defendant. Pronounced 'The King against Smith'.

Appeal

If Jones and Smith decide to appeal against the decisions at (a) and (b), the appeal cases will appear as previously shown, but in the past, the names were reversed as shown here:

a *Jones v Brown* (1969)
b *Smith v Regina* (1969)

Jones and Smith are known as appellants; Brown and Regina are known as respondents.

Admiralty cases

Where claims are made involving one ship only, the proceedings are named after the ship: e.g. *The Moorcock* (1889); *The Tubantia* (1924). Where two ships are involved, the owners of one claiming against the owners of the other, both ships are named.

2.7.5 Declaratory theory of the common law

The declaratory theory encouraged the development of precedent and enabled a large body of rules to develop from a few customary rules. The judge applying those rules to new cases merely *declared* or enunciated a pre-existing rule or principle of common law. In no sense was he or she creating new law. The declaratory theory of law applied only to the common law. It did not apply to equity, which is traceable to conscience, and whose principles were decided in many cases by individual judges. Moreover, many areas of jurisdiction, e.g. trusts, were not part of the common law at all. The development of equitable principles into a systematic form is attributable to the creativity of judges, such rules being improved and refined over the course of time.

2.8 Legislation, part II

The Sovereignty of Parliament means that Parliament is legislatively supreme and can make and unmake (i.e. repeal) laws to any extent. Moreover, there is no body that can declare its legal enactments to be of no effect; the only limit on the legislative power of Parliament is that it cannot bind its successors in power.

Any Act passed by Parliament that is of general application is absolutely binding on all persons within the sphere of Parliament's jurisdiction. However controversial a particular statute may be, a judge is *bound* to enforce its provisions, although there may be some scope for judges to interpret a new statute in a particular way.

2.8.1 Statutes

A statute may be defined as *an express and formal laying-down of a rule or rules of conduct to be observed in the future by persons to whom the statute is expressly, or by implication, made applicable.* A statute and a judgment may be contrasted thus:

Statute	Judgment
a Creates a new law	Usually disclaims any attempt to create new law
b Lays down general rules for the guidance of future conduct	Usually applies an existing law to a particular set of circumstances
c Is imperative	Gives reasons

The making of a statute. Parliament comprises the King, the House of Lords and the House of Commons. Although legislation may be introduced by both Houses, the effective chamber from which most legislation springs is the House of Commons. This lower House contains some 635 members representing geographical areas of the country called constituencies. Such Members of Parliament are elected at General Elections, held usually every five years, by the vote of all subjects over 18 years of age, unless disqualified.

The Government is formed by the party gaining a majority of seats in the House of Commons. A Prime Minister is appointed to lead the Government. He or she then forms their Cabinet from the important members of their party and appoints junior officials to various posts in the Government. When, however, no one party has a sufficient majority, or when a national emergency occurs, a coalition government may be formed by two or more parties temporarily uniting.

The Cabinet forms its policies of government and turns to legislation as the means of carrying the policies into effect, e.g. the **Local Government Act 1972** (as amended).

2.8.2 Stages in legislation

The first step in legislation is the *drafting* of the Bill. This is a skilful and sometimes long process requiring the services of Parliamentary Counsel, who are lawyers attached to the Treasury.

Once drafted, the Bill passes through the following stages to enable Parliament to consider and reconsider its provisions as thoroughly as possible:

a *First reading*. This is a formality. The Bill may be read a first time as a result of the House agreeing to a motion for leave to introduce it. The Bill is then printed and published.
b *Second reading*. Here the Minister or Member in charge of the Bill explains its purpose and the main issues of policy involved. The debate is limited to the purpose of the Bill and the means proposed for giving it effect. The House votes on the Bill. If the Bill survives the vote it passes to the next stage.
c *Committee stage*. At this stage the Bill is dealt with by (i) a committee of the whole House, (ii) a Select Committee or (iii) a Standing Committee. A Select Committee is a committee constituted on a party basis, while a Standing Committee is composed of 20–50 Members appointed to examine Public Bills, which, after a second reading, are not passed to a committee of the whole House or to Select Committees. The purpose of the Committee Stage is to consider the *details* of the Bill clause by clause.
d *Report stage*. Having passed the Committee Stage the Bill is formally reported to the House by the chairman of the committee. At the Report Stage the amendments made in the committee are considered by the House, which may make any additional amendments.
e *Third reading*. At this stage the Bill is reviewed in its final form. The debate is confined to verbal amendments only, not the principles of the Bill.

The House of Lords is the second tier in the legislative process, which allows for reflection on the merits or faults of the Bill and for criticism from different points of view.

After its third reading in the Commons, the Bill is sent to the Lords, where it goes through a procedure similar to that in the Commons. If the Bill is amended in the Lords, it is returned to the Commons for consideration of the amendments. These may be accepted or rejected, though an attempt is made to reconcile the two points of view. If agreement is impossible, the Commons can invoke its powers under the **Parliament Acts 1911** and **1949**, whereby it may present the Bill for Royal Assent after one year without the agreement of the Lords. A Money Bill must originate in the Commons and may be delayed by the Lords for one month only.

Royal Assent. Having passed the House of Lords, the Bill is ready for the Royal Assent, which may be given by the King personally or by three Lords Commissioners. The **Royal Assent Act 1967** now provides that an Act is duly enacted if the Royal Assent is notified to each House of Parliament, sitting separately, by either the Speaker of that House or the acting Speaker. The Royal Assent is now simply a formality. Once the Royal Assent is given, the Bill becomes an Act of Parliament and takes effect immediately (unless some future date is specified in the Act).

Private Members' Bills. At the beginning of a Parliamentary Session (a session lasts one year), the Cabinet lays down its legislative programme. It is still possible for a Private Member of the House (i.e. an MP who is not a member of the Government) to introduce a Bill on some matter of importance to him or her. If the Private Member's Bill is of general importance and receives the support of the House it may be adopted by the Government and so form part of its legislative programme. Otherwise the Member may have difficulty in securing the passage of the Bill through Parliament. The **Matrimonial Causes Act 1937** and the **Murder (Abolition of Death Penalty) Act 1965** were the Private Members' Bills of Sir Alan Herbert and Mr Sidney Silverman, respectively. A more recent example is the **Local Government (Religious etc. Observances) Act**

2015, introduced by Jake Berry MP, to affirm the rights of all councils and authorities to hold prayers before their meetings.

Private Bills. These are of two kinds: (i) local and (ii) personal.

Local Bills deal with purely local matters. Where a local authority or other public body wishes to acquire additional powers not available under the general law, it may obtain them by the promotion of a private Bill. After receiving Parliament's approval, the Bill becomes an Act of Parliament. Local Bills usually deal with the construction or alteration of bridges, canals, docks, ports, roads, railways, tramways, waterworks, etc., or with extending the powers of local authorities, gas, electricity or other public-utility undertakings.

Personal Bills relate to private estates, names, naturalization, divorce, peerage and other matters. Such Bills are rare and must be started in the House of Lords.

Conflict with common law. Because Parliament is omnipotent in the field of law, it follows that a statute may abolish any rule of common law or any criminal offence at common law.

2.8.3 Obsolescence

It is obvious that the social conditions of today are vastly different from those obtaining in medieval and Tudor times. Some case law laid down in earlier times and applicable to wholly different social situations may therefore have to be disregarded on account of obsolescence.

Statute law, on the other hand, does not become obsolete on account of age. We may instance the well-known case of *Ashford v Thornton* (1818), where the plaintiff asserted that a right of trial by wager of battle was available to him under a statute of Henry II. This long-forgotten statute was repealed the year after its existence was revealed by the plaintiff's application. The **Treason Act 1351** is still law despite its age, and was invoked in 1946 to prosecute a British subject for broadcasting enemy propaganda during the Second World War (*Joyce v Director of Public Prosecutions*, 1946).

Though statute law does not become obsolete by reason of age, nevertheless there are some Acts that are so inappropriate to the changed conditions of today that *in practice* they are not enforced. The **Sunday Observance Act 1677** forbids meetings or assemblies of people out of their own parishes on the Lord's Day for any sports and pastimes whatsoever. Every offender is to forfeit 3*s*. 4*d*. The **Profane Oaths Act 1745** made it an offence for any person to curse or swear (penalty 1*s*. for a day labourer, common soldier, sailor or seaman; 2*s*. for any person under the degree of gentleman; 5*s*. over the degree of gentleman). The Act was not enforced for many years and was finally abolished by the **Criminal Law Act 1967**.

2.8.4 Consolidation and codification

By *consolidation* we mean the combination of all the statutes relating to a given matter, such statutes being incorporated into one consolidating Act. The statute law in relation to the given matter is, therefore, readily accessible in one Act. For example, the road-traffic problem is a pressing one, and numbers of statutes and statutory instruments have been passed over the years regulating the different kinds of vehicles, their construction and their use on public roads. Amendments of road-traffic law appear yearly, and in time, there are so many alterations, revocations or improvements that it is difficult to ascertain the law. Hence there is a need for systematizing the law, and a consolidating statute is passed accordingly: in this case, the **Road Traffic Act 1972**.

The **Consolidation of Enactments (Procedure) Act 1949** was passed to enable consolidating statutes to receive Parliamentary approval speedily. The **Juries Act 1974**, the **Magistrates' Courts Act** 1952, the **Solicitors Act 1974** and the **Factories Act 1961** are examples of consolidating statutes made under this new provision.

Whereas consolidation means the combination of statute law only, *codification* is a term that means the enactment of a statute incorporating all previous statute law *and* case law on a particular subject. The **Sale of Goods Act 1893** and the **Partnership Act 1890** are examples of codification in English law.

Codification can mean, of course, a complete statement of *all* the law of a given State, and not, as in England, certain parts only. The French Civil Code is one example, though we may note that Germany and Switzerland have similar codes. The Law Commission (see p. 35) is charged with the duty of the codification of English law, a task that will take some years to fulfil.

2.8.5 Delegated legislation

Because Parliament is legislatively omnipotent, it can grant to some other person or body the power to make orders, regulations or rules that have the force of law. In strict legal theory, Parliament ought to retain in its own hands the power and duty to enact all the laws and the rules affecting the State. In practice, Parliament cannot discharge this duty mainly because it has so much to do and so little time in which to do it. It overcomes this difficulty by resorting to **delegated legislation**, sometimes called subordinate legislation.

Acts of Parliament nowadays tend to lay down general principles or policy and to leave the working out of the administrative details to subordinate authorities who are responsible for carrying the Acts into effect. For example, the **Road Traffic Act 1983** empowers the Minister of Transport to make regulations in respect of road-traffic matters by means of statutory instruments. So, too, the Home Secretary may make orders and regulations under the **Police Acts 1996, 1997, Police Reform Act 2002** and the **Police (Complaints and Conduct) Act 2012**, in relation to the government, administration and conditions of service of police, and the Secretary of State for Education and Science, may make orders under the **Education Act 2002**.

2.8.6 Forms of delegated legislation

Delegated legislation comprises:

a *Orders in Council*, i.e. Orders made by the King in Council, have been described as the most dignified form of subordinate legislation. In practice, the Minister of a Government department usually drafts and makes the Order in the name of the King, whose approval 'in Council' is a formality.

b *Statutory instruments, rules* and *orders* are normally made by Ministers in charge of Government departments, but such rules must be submitted to Parliament for approval.

c *By-laws* are made by local authorities, railways, water boards and other such bodies, and, like statutory instruments, draw their authority from Acts of Parliament. By-laws require the approval of the appropriate Minister before they have legislative force.

Government of a country of some 50 million people is a highly complex matter. The most that Parliament can manage in the legislative field is between 60 and 70 Acts of Parliament per session (one year). On the other hand, there are today more than 2,000 statutory instruments issued each year.

All the forms of subordinate legislation noted previously are enforced equally with statutes, provided the order or by-law is not *ultra vires* the Minister or local authority.

2.8.7 Growth of delegated legislation

The following reasons are advanced for the growth of delegated legislation:

a *Lack of Parliamentary time*. The legislature has insufficient time to deal with and debate all necessary measures for efficient government.

b *Urgency*. Parliament is not always in session, and its legislative procedures are slow. Emergencies and urgent problems arise, and delegated legislation is the best means of meeting the situation.

c *Flexibility*. A statute requires elaborate and cumbersome procedures for its enactment. It can be revoked or amended only by another statute. A ministerial order or statutory instrument can be made speedily; if it proves unworkable or impracticable, it can be quickly revoked.

d *Technicality of subject matter*. Modern legislation tends to be technical and detailed, e.g. road-traffic matters that may deal with 'special type' vehicles; building regulations; dangerous drugs regulations. Such legislation is best dealt with by Ministers (who are advised by experts familiar with the technical or scientific problem) rather than MPs who may be inexpert and unfamiliar with the technicalities involved.

e *Future needs*. Parliament cannot foresee the difficulties that may arise, particularly when new major schemes such as the National Health Service or National Insurance are launched. Future difficulties are better dealt with by delegated legislation rather than statutes.

2.8.8 Criticism of delegated legislation

The processes of government and, in particular, the making of statutes is continuously subject to critical examination and analysis. Among the criticisms frequently levelled against delegated or subordinate legislation are:

a *Matters of principle*. Because these are the primary concern of the legislature, Ministers ought not to be entitled to legislate by means of orders in respect of matters of principle.

b *Delegation of taxing power*. Parliament fought for years for the sole and exclusive right to tax. History shows that the right can be abused and should not be yielded to subordinate authorities or Ministers. The **Import Duties Act 1932** gave the Treasury the power to legislate on taxation by fixing import duties and altering the 'free list', thus usurping the right of Parliament alone.

c *Sub-delegation*. The **Emergency Powers (Defence) Act 1939** provides a clear example of five-tier legislation as it embraced: (i) the parent statute; (ii) regulations made under the statute; (iii) orders made under the regulations; (iv) directions made under the orders and (v) licences issued under the directions.

In its Report of 1946, the Select Committee on Statutory Instruments condemned the practice of delegation at four removes from Parliament of the power to make subordinate legislation.

d *Exclusion of the jurisdiction of courts*. The power of the courts to declare the regulations void on the ground of *ultra vires* ought not to be excluded either in the parent Act or the delegated legislation.

e *Authority to modify an Act of Parliament*. This power, known as 'the Henry VIII clause', enables a Minister to modify the Act itself and thus usurp the essential function and duty of Parliament.

f *Inadequate publicity*. The Press usually reports the effect of new statutes, but there is frequently inadequate publicity given to the numerous statutory instruments (over 2,000 annually) made by Ministers. A person charged with an offence against a statutory instrument of whose existence he or she was unaware has only a limited defence since ignorance of the law is normally no excuse (see s. 3(2) of the **Statutory Instruments Act 1946**).

2.8.9 Control of delegated legislation

The main forms of control over the power of a Minister to make delegated legislation are:

a consultation of interests
b control by the courts
c control by Parliament

a Consultation

In practice Ministers consult experts, both within their own departments and outside, and take the advice of various interests and bodies likely to be affected by proposed legislation. Thus road-traffic legislation would involve consultation with local authorities, surveyors, the police, the AA, the RAC, motor manufacturers and others likely to be intimately affected. Sometimes a Minister must, by statute, consult an advisory body or submit a draft of the statutory instrument to it for approval. For example, under the **Social Security Act 1980**, regulations proposed by the Secretary of State for Social Services must be submitted in draft to the Social Security Advisory Committee. Where Ministers propose to make rules of procedure for tribunals set up within their department, they must consult the Council on Tribunals (**Tribunals and Inquiries Act 1992**—see p. 61).

b Control by the courts

Rules and regulations made by Ministers and other administrative bodies under statutory authority are liable to be subject to challenge in the courts on two grounds: (i) *ultra vires* and (ii) unreasonableness. While a court cannot invalidate an Act of Parliament, it may declare that statutory instruments, rules or by-laws are void on the ground that they are *ultra vires*, i.e. beyond the powers conferred by the Act under which they were made. In practice, ministerial rules and orders are only rarely challenged on this ground because great care is usually taken by the legal advisers of the Minister on such matters.

By-laws may be challenged on the grounds of *unreasonableness*, by which is meant that they are partial and unequal in their operation as between different classes. If rules are manifestly unjust, if they disclose bad faith or if they involve 'such oppressive or gratuitous interference with the rights of those subject to them as can find no justification in the minds of reasonable men, the court might well say Parliament never intended to give authority to make such rules; they are unreasonable and *ultra vires*' (Lord Russell in *Kruse v Johnson*, 1898).

c Control by Parliament

(i) Parliament may revoke or vary the delegated power.

(ii) Certain Acts require that regulations made under them shall be laid before Parliament. This enables Members of Parliament to know what has been done by the Minister, or what is proposed.

(iii) A Select Committee on Statutory Instruments (SIs) was set up in 1944 to consider every SI, rule or Order laid before the Commons. A Special Orders Committee exists in the Lords to do similar work in that House.

In 1974, to avoid duplication in the two Houses, a Statutory Instruments (Joint Committee) was created comprising members of a Select Committee from the Commons and members of the Special Orders Committee of the Lords. The Joint Committee (which replaces the two former committees in the consideration of SIs) reports to each House on any order or regulation deserving special attention on the following grounds:

i that it imposes a charge on the public revenue, or imposes or prescribes charges for any licence or consent or for any services from a public authority

ii that it is made under an Act that precludes challenge in the courts

iii that it appears to make some unusual or unexpected use of the powers conferred by the statute under which it is made or there appears to be doubt as to whether it is *intra vires*

iv that there appears to have been unjustifiable delay in publication or laying before Parliament

v that for any special reason its form or purport calls for elucidation

vi that it purports to have retrospective effect

vii that the drafting is defective

The Joint Committee may require a department to submit a memorandum or explanatory note on any instrument and may request a representative of the department to appear and explain a document personally. Before the committee reports that the special attention of the House should be drawn to an instrument, it gives the department concerned the opportunity to provide an explanation.

2.8.10 Publication

HM Stationery Office publishes lists showing dates of issue of statutory instruments, and the **Statutory Instruments Act 1946** provides that:

> [I]t shall be a defence to prove that the instrument had not been issued by HMSO at the date of the alleged contravention, unless it is proved that at that date reasonable steps had been taken for the purpose of bringing the purport of the instrument to the notice of the public or of persons likely to be affected by it, or of the person charged.

2.8.11 Interpretation of statutes

It is important to realize that the rules of statutory interpretation originally arose from both statute and from the cases of common law. Prior to the influence of the English Parliament, the only form of statute was a decree from the monarch. Nevertheless, it was not until the establishment of the Model Parliament in 1295 that there was the development of a rudimentary system of the passing of bills in Parliament followed by royal assent approval. It was during the fourteenth century that there was a gradual evolution of the concept of the superiority of the binding nature of statutes over the common law, which led to the realization that there should be guidelines for their interpretation. It was this that gave rise to the common-law rules of statutory interpretation as set out in (b) later on. Today statutes are drafted by Parliamentary draftsmen, who are lawyers skilled in this highly important work. Despite the great care taken to ensure that all statutes are clear and exact, it is certain that in due time legal actions will arise on points of doubt and the courts will be called upon to interpret the meaning and to adjudicate.

The rules adopted by the judges to discover the meaning of an Act may be classified as (a) statutory definitions and (b) common-law rules.

a Statutory definitions

The Interpretation Act 1978 is a general statute that consolidates enactments regarding the construction of statutes and provides definitions and rules of construction. Thus, unless the contrary appears:

i words importing the masculine gender include females
ii words in the singular include the plural and words in the plural include the singular
iii the expression 'person' includes a body corporate, e.g. a limited company
iv expressions referring to writing are construed as including references to printing, lithography, photography and other modes of representing or reproducing words in a visible form

Modern statutes and statutory instruments frequently include a section expressly incorporating the **Interpretation Act 1978**.

A statute usually contains an *interpretation section* that explains the meaning of words in that statute. Thus, section 34 of the **Theft Act 1968** contains a definition of the words 'goods' as follows: 'For the purpose of this Act "goods", except in so far as the context otherwise requires, includes money and every other description of property except land, and includes things severed from the land by stealing.'

The *preamble* is an introductory statement appearing immediately below the official title of a statute, and sets out the purposes of the Act. Judges may refer to the preamble as an aid to interpretation.

All bills passed since the beginning of 1999 are the subject of explanatory notes, which are made public. These detail the background to the legislation and explain what the intended effects of particular provisions are expected to have. In *Cusack v London Borough of Harrow* (2013), it was emphasized that these were meant to be 'guidelines rather than railway lines.'

b Common-law rules

Where a statute is not clarified by reference to the preceding statutory guides, a judge may look to the following common-law rules:

i '*The Literal Rule*' lays down that words must be given their literal, grammatical meaning. Words in old statutes are given the meaning they had when the statute was passed, e.g. The Statute of Treason, 1351. Words appearing more than once must usually be given the same meaning throughout the Act. The duty of the court is to interpret the words that the legislature has used. If a statute so interpreted is clear and produces hardship, the remedy is to create a new statute; it is not the duty of a judge to fill in the gaps.

ii '*The Mischief Rule*', also known as the Rule in *Heydon's* case (1584), lays down that the court must look at the Act to see what 'mischief' or defect in the common law the Act was passed to prevent.

Four questions should be considered:

1. What was the common law before the Act was passed?
2. What was the mischief and defect for which the common law did not provide?
3. What remedies had Parliament resolved to provide?
4. What was the true reason for the remedy?

Judges were enjoined to make such construction 'as shall suppress the mischief and advance the remedy'.

iii '*The Golden Rule*' lays down that a judge should construe the statute in its grammatical and ordinary sense:

> It is a very useful rule in the construction of a statute to adhere to the ordinary meaning of the words used, and to the grammatical construction, unless that is at variance with the intention of the legislature to be collected from the statute itself, or leads to any manifest absurdity or repugnance, in which case the language may be varied or modified so as to avoid such inconvenience, but no further.
>
> (Parke, B., in *Becke v Smith*, 1836)

For example, section 57 of the **Offences Against the Person Act 1861** defines the offence of bigamy and provides: 'Whosoever being married shall *marry* any other person during the life of the former husband or wife . . . shall be guilty of bigamy'. Under English law a married person cannot 'marry', and to avoid absurdity or repugnance, the word 'marry' in this section means 'to go through the form of marriage' (*R v Allen*, 1872).

iv '*The Ejusdem Generis Rule*'. Where general words follow specific words, the general words must be construed as applying to the persons or things of the same class (*ejusdem generis*) as those already mentioned. Thus 'other person', 'other cattle', 'other animals' are vague and a reference in an Act to 'dogs, cats, and other animals' was held not to include lions and tigers, for 'other animals' meant those *ejusdem generis* with dogs and cats, i.e. domestic animals (*Evans v Cross*, 1938).

v *Expressio unius est exclusio alterius* (the express mention of one thing implies the exclusion of another). This means that where specific words are used in a statute and are not followed by general words, the statute applies only to those things mentioned.

vi *Noscitur a sociis* (the meaning of a word can be comprehended from its context). Ambiguous or doubtful words may be determined by reference to those words appearing in association with them.

vii *'The Exclusionary Rule'* excludes reference to parliamentary materials in interpreting an Act. However, if the Act is ambiguous or obscure, or its literal meaning leads to an absurdity, the court may have regard to the *Official Report of Debates* (usually referred to as *Hansard*) for assistance in interpreting the Act (*Pepper v Hart*, 1993).

2.8.12 Presumptions

Certain presumptions or rules of evidence must also be borne in mind. These presumptions apply to the construction of a statute, unless there are express words to the contrary. The following examples are some of the more important presumptions in law:

a The presumption against criminal liability, unless *mens rea* (guilty mind) is shown to exist. Proof of criminal intent is generally necessary to secure a conviction. Thus, a motorist involved in a road accident of which he or she was unaware could not rightly be convicted of 'failing to report the accident to the police within 24 hours', since the motorist was unaware of involvement, and the law does not compel the impossible (*Harding v Price*, 1948).

b The presumption against the ouster of jurisdiction of the courts. Thus, where a particular statute provides that tribunals be set up to determine questions arising in administration (as under the **National Service Act 1948**, to consider appeals for postponement of military service) and excludes the jurisdiction of the courts of law *expressly*, then the terms of the statute will be applied. Where no such express terms exist, the jurisdiction of the courts is not ousted.

c The presumption that the Crown is not bound by statute, unless expressly stated therein.

d The presumption that a statute does not alter the general principles of the common law, unless expressly so stated.

e The presumption against the infringement of international law.

f The presumption against the deprivation of property. Statutes empowering the acquisition of private property will be strictly construed. Where private property is taken away from an owner, the law infers that compensation will be paid unless there are clear words in the statute to the contrary.

g The presumption against arbitrary conduct and abuse of a power given by statute.

h The presumption that the legal meaning of an Act is that which corresponds to its literal meaning.

2.8.13 Reference to statutes

There are three forms of referring to an Act of Parliament: by its short title, by its official reference or by its full title.

a *Short title*. When we refer to an Act such as the **Theft Act 1968** or the **Data Protection Act 1998**, we are using its short title.

b *Official reference*. This shows the calendar year in which the Act was passed and the number of the Chapter (or Act) passed in that year. For example:

1968 CHAPTER 60

is the official reference to the **Theft Act 1968**, and

1998 CHAPTER 29

is the official reference to the **Data Protection Act 1998**.

c *Full title*. This gives the official reference and a short description of the object of the statute. For example, the full title of the **Theft Act 1968** is

ELIZABETH II
1968 CHAPTER 60

An Act to revise the law of England and Wales as to theft and similar associated offences, and in connexion therewith to make provision as to criminal proceedings by one party to a marriage against the other, and to make certain amendments extending beyond England and Wales in the **Post Office Act 1953** and other enactments; and for other purposes connected therewith.
The full title of the **Data Protection Act 1998** is

ELIZABETH II
1998 CHAPTER 29

An Act to make new provision for the regulation of the processing of information relating to individuals, including the obtaining, holding, use or disclosure of such information.

2.8.14 Reference to statutory instruments

The most common form of delegated legislation is the statutory instrument. Each statutory instrument is allocated a number, and reference to the instrument is to the year of issue followed by the number so allocated. For example,

S.I. 1968 No. 1911

relates to the Town and Country Planning (Planning Inquiry Commissions) Regulations, 1968.

The printing of Bills, Acts of Parliament and statutory instruments is done by Her Majesty's Stationery Office. The **Statutory Instruments (Production and Sale) Act 1996** enables the King's Printer as well as HMSO to print statutes and provides for the reception in evidence of lists of statutory instruments that do not bear the imprint of the King's Printer. Such documents are on sale to members of the public at His Majesty's Stationery Office in London.

2.8.15 European Community law (of the European Union)

Since 1 January 1973, the date of Britain's entry into the European Economic Community (**European Communities Act 1972**), a new source of law is added to what came before, namely the law of the European treaties (e.g. the Treaty of Rome, 1958) and of the secondary legislation made by the community institutions (e.g. the EU Council, the Commission and the Parliament). This law constitutes a new legal order standing alongside both the statute and common law and, in the event of conflict, takes *precedence* over them (*Torfaen Borough Council v B . . . Q* (1990)). This will be subject to the outcome of Brexit as and when it arises (see Chapter 13).

2.8.16 Human Rights Act 1998

The **Human Rights Act 1998** formally incorporates into English law the individual rights guaranteed by the European Convention on Human Rights.

The European Convention deals with many fundamental freedoms such as the prohibition of torture, inhuman and degrading punishment, prohibition of slavery and protection against retrospective criminal law. This new Act gives the United Kingdom a comprehensive code of rights that can be enforced by the courts.

Under the Act, Parliament still has the right to pass any law that it wishes, even if those laws are 'unreasonable and unjust'. However, Judges of the High Court will have the power to look carefully at these cases and compare them with the rights given by the European Convention. If they decide that our laws are not in keeping with the letter and spirit of these rights, they may make a declaration of incompatibility—declare them to be incompatible with the laws set out in the European Convention. The **Human Rights Act** provides a means by which these 'incompatible laws' may then be swiftly changed to bring them into line with the rights given by the European Convention.

The Act also recognizes the authority of the European Court of Human Rights to adjudicate on complaints from individual United Kingdom citizens who are appealing against a decision of the English Courts.

2.8.17 Law revision and reform

The law is open to the criticism that, in general, it is conservative. Many statutes are ancient, appertaining to a bygone age and feudal system; some common-law offences are inappropriate today. For example, the offences of challenging to fight, eavesdropping, being a common barrator, a common scold or common night walker were abolished only in 1967 by the **Criminal Law Act** of that year. Furthermore, it is argued that legal procedures are unduly formal and slow, and that the system of courts needs overhauling and remodelling.

Some of these criticisms may seem fair and reasonable, but it is clear that reform of the law and the machinery of the courts are matters that require careful planning. Nevertheless, law is a living thing and reform is continual. The agencies through which revision or reform is affected include the following:

a Law Reform Committee
b Criminal Law Revision Committee
c Law Commission
d Royal Commissions
e Committees appointed by Ministers or by Parliament
f Private Members' Bills
g Civil Justice Council

a The Law Reform Committee

The Law Reform Committee began in 1952 and took over the work of the Law Revision Committee set up in 1934. It was made up of judges and practising and academic lawyers, and dealt with civil law matters referred to it by the Lord Chancellor. Members of the committee and the general public could also raise matters and suggest subjects for consideration. The following statutes reformed parts of the civil law and were passed as a result of the recommendations of the committee:

The **Limitation Act 1939** (replaced by the 1980 Act)
The **Law Reform (Contributory Negligence) Act 1945**
The **Occupiers' Liability Act 1957**
The **Law Reform (Husband and Wife) Act 1962**

The Committee is now regarded as being defunct.

b The Criminal Law Revision Committee

While the Lord Chancellor is concerned with the Law Reform Committee and the reform of the civil law, the Home Secretary is primarily concerned with the administration of the criminal law. The Criminal Law Revision Committee (a standing committee) was set up in 1959 to examine aspects of the criminal law, to consider whether the law requires revision, and to make recommendations.

The committee has issued several reports; the seventh (Felonies and Misdemeanours) and eighth (Theft and Related Offences) have resulted in the **Criminal Law Act 1967** and the **Theft Act 1968**, respectively. It has now been superseded by the Law Commission.

c The Law Commission

The **Law Commissions Act 1965** set up a full-time commission whose duty is to keep under review the English law as a whole with a view to its systematic development and reform, including, in particular, its codification, the elimination of anomalies, the repeal of obsolete and unnecessary enactments, the reduction of the number of separate enactments and, generally, the simplification and modernization of the law. Pursuant to programmes approved by the Lord Chancellor, the commission undertakes the examination of particular branches of the law and the formulation, by means of draft Bills, of proposals for reform.

The five commissioners and a legal staff are appointed by the Lord Chancellor. In accordance with the **Law Commissions Act 2009**, s.1, there is a duty imposed upon the Lord Chancellor to lay an annual report before Parliament in which the outcome of Law Commission proposals for the relevant reporting year is stated and accounted for.

S.2 of the Act empowers the Lord Chancellor and the Law Commission to agree a protocol relating to the working relationship between the Commission and government departments.

On 7 February 2019 the Ministry of Justice (MoJ) published its tailored review of the Law Commission, highlighting the Government's continued support for the role and functions that the Commission carries out.

d Royal Commissions

Royal Commissions are appointed by the Crown on the advice of a Minister who names a chairman. The membership of each Royal Commission varies, but it usually reflects expert, professional and lay opinions. The duty of a Royal Commission is to investigate some matter of public importance, to take evidence and to make recommendations. On receipt of its report, the Government may give legislative effect to the recommendations. For example, the main recommendations of the **Royal Commission on Tribunals and Inquiries Act**, appointed in 1955, found expression in the **Tribunals and Inquiries Act 1958**, now consolidated in the **Tribunals and Inquiries Act 1992**.

e Committees appointed by Ministers or Parliament

Committees of experts may be appointed to consider particular aspects of the law for the purpose of revising it, e.g. those appointed by the Lord Chancellor to consider civil procedure and legal aid, and by the Secretary of State for Trade and Industry to consider revision of the law of copyright.

f Private Members' Bills

Private Members' Bills (see p. 25) may reform existing law in important respects. Examples include the **Inheritance (Family Provision) Act 1938**, the **Matrimonial Causes Act 1937,** the **Defamation Acts 1952** and the **Local Government (Religious etc. Observances) Act 2015** (see p. 23). Parliamentary time is, however, limited, and Government Bills must come first. Hence the Private Member's Bill is not the most important medium of reform.

2.9 Textbooks

The first important work on the English common law was Glanvil's *Tractatus de Legibus et Consuetudinibus Angliae*, produced in the twelfth century. This work was followed by Bracton's *De Legibus et Consuetudinibus Angliae*, written in the thirteenth century, and described by Maitland as 'the crown and flower of English medieval jurisprudence'. It contained references to decided cases.

Later works included Littleton's *New Tenures* (1481), Sir Matthew Hale's *History of the Common Law and Pleas of the Crown*, which appeared in 1730, Sir Edward Coke's *Institutes* (1628–41), Sir William Blackstone's *Commentaries* (1765) and Sir Michael Foster's *Crown Law* (eighteenth century).

The preceding works and a few other early works, written when law reporting had barely begun, are accepted as books of authority and therefore as an original source of common law.

The modern textbook is not a source of law and not a book of authority. However, such works may have persuasive authority; counsel may adopt the view of a distinguished academic writer and the court may accept that view of the law. In this way, the writer is influencing the law. Works by Cheshire, Dicey, Winfield, Salmond, Williams, and Smith and Hogan have often been referred to in this way, particularly on points that are not covered by authority or where there is some doubt about the authority. As Mr R. J. Walker has commented, 'On the whole the persuasive authority of a standard textbook is of considerable weight.'

Similarly, articles in legal journals such as the *Criminal Law Review*, the *Law Quarterly Review* and the *Cambridge Law Journal* have been referred to in the courts.

2.10 Local custom, part II

A *local custom* is a usage or rule that has gathered the force of law and is binding within a defined area upon the persons affected thereby. Common examples are local rights of way or rights of common. A useful case that exemplifies the operation of law is the following:

❖ CASE EXAMPLE

***Mercer v Denne* (1905)**

Defendant owned part of a beach and proposed to erect houses thereon. Local fisherman sought to stop him by claiming that they had a local customary right to dry their nets on the land. Witnesses proved that the custom dated back for some 70 years and reputedly earlier. This raised the presumption of antiquity. *Held*: that the defendant must not build the houses on the land; the local customary right was upheld.

The onus of proof of a local custom rests on the person claiming that such a custom exists. Judicial recognition will be given, and the custom will be enforced if it is:

a reasonable
b certain as to the subject matter of the right, the persons benefited by it and the locality;
c local, in the sense that the custom must be applicable to a district known to law, e.g. a parish, manor or shire
d of immemorial existence, i.e. must have existed from 'the commencement of legal memory': arbitrarily fixed at 1189, the first year of the reign of Richard I. Because of the difficulty of

proving this, courts presume that the custom existed then unless there is clear evidence of the contrary

e peaceably used. The custom must have been exercised peaceably, openly and as of right (*nec per vim, nec clam, nec precario*). If a right is exercised by permission, then it cannot be claimed to be exercised 'of right' for the right can only be exercised in accordance with the permission

f continuously observed. This does not mean that the right must have been continuously *exercised*, but that it could have been, the right to do so being observed without interruption

g compulsory. Once established the custom must be local common law and legally effective because it is right and enforceable

h not contrary to any statute

i consistent, in the sense of being consistent with other customs and not contradictory to them

Local customs must be distinguished from *conventional usages*, which are found and observed in particular occupations, trades, business or among professional groups. Following the analogy of the local custom, the courts have laid down certain principles. Every usage must be certain and reasonable and must have acquired notoriety (in the sense that the usage is well known and observed) in the trade or business to which it relates. In contracts, for example, there will usually be express terms, but in addition to these, the court may, in construing the contract, imply a term or terms where the parties are deemed to have contracted on that basis. Thus, if a usage is shown to exist in a class of workers entitling members to, say, three months' notice terminating their engagements, this usage or trade custom will apply unless expressly negatived by the contract itself.

❖ CASE EXAMPLES

Dashwood v Magniac (1891)

A had devised an estate to B with 'a power to cut timber for the repair of the estate'. Evidence was admitted showing what trees were included in the term 'timber' in the locality. *Held*: that 'timber' included beech in addition to the usual meaning of oak, ash and elm.

Grant v Maddox (1846)

Evidence was admitted in this case of a theatrical usage to show that the word 'year' in a theatrical contract means those parts of the year during which the theatre is open.

Smith v Wilson (1832)

A usage was proved and admitted that in a lease of a rabbit warren, the words 'thousand rabbits' meant in that particular locality 1,200.

A more recent example is *Egerton v Harding* (1974), where the duty to fence was held to be based on custom.

2.11 Useful webpages

Law Commission website (www.lawcom.gov.uk)

Government legislation website (www.legislation.gov.uk)

ILEX Legal sources website (www.cilex.org.uk)

Decisions of the Supreme Court (www.supremecourt.uk/decided.cases/)

Important Judgments published by the Court Service (www.justice.gov.uk/about/hmcts)

2.12 Exercises

1 What is meant by 'common law'?

2 Name the early common-law courts and give the jurisdiction of each.

3 What does 'equity' mean? Describe the growth of equity jurisdiction.

4 Of what importance was the *Earl of Oxford*'s case (1616)?

5 What is meant by 'mercantile law'? Whence did it derive, and who was mainly responsible for its incorporation into the common law?

6 What is canon law? With what matters did the canon law deal?

7 What courts existed before the Judicature Acts? What changes did the Acts make?

8 Describe the principal and the subsidiary sources of English law.

9 Distinguish between (i) *ratio decidendi* and (ii) *obiter dicta*. What is meant by *stare decisis*?

10 What are the advantages and disadvantages of case law?

11 What courts are bound by their own decisions?

12 What is the hierarchy of courts as regards judicial precedent?

13 What must be proved to enforce a local custom?

14 How far do judges make law?

15 What is meant by the phrase 'Sovereignty of Parliament'?

16 Define a statute, and distinguish between (i) a statute and (ii) a judgment of a court of law.

17 What forms of control over delegated legislation are exercised (i) by the courts and (ii) by Parliament?

18 What are the main rules applied by a court of law in the interpretation of a statute?

Chapter 3

The courts today

Key points

- the role of the Supreme Court
- differences between civil and criminal jurisdiction
- advantages and disadvantages of administrative tribunals
- arbitration and forms of alternative dispute resolution
- laypersons in the courts

3.1 Civil courts

3.1.1 The House of Lords and the Supreme Court

The **Constitutional Reform Act 2005**, which came into effect on 3 April 2006, changed the future role of the Lord Chancellor, the operation of a final United Kingdom court of appeal and the appointment of the judiciary.

In accordance with Part 3 of the Act, in October 2009, the United Kingdom Supreme Court replaced the former system of the Appellate Committee of the House of Lords. The court is housed in the former Middlesex Guildhall in Parliament Square, Westminster. Part 3 of the Act also provides for the appointment of Judges and Justices of the Supreme Court. The first members of the Supreme Court were the 12 persons who, immediately before s. 23 of the Act came into effect, were the current Law Lords, with the Lord Chief Justice taking on the additional title of the President of the Supreme Court.

The Supreme Court stands at the apex of the judicial system and is the final court of appeal in civil and criminal matters, unless a matter of European Union Law, which can be appealed to the European Court of Justice.

As the official website of the Supreme Court States:

> Courts are the final arbiter between the citizen and the State and are therefore a fundamental pillar of the constitution. The Supreme Court was established to achieve a complete separation between the United Kingdom's senior Judges and the Upper House of Parliament, emphasising the independence of the law Lords and increasing the transparency between Parliament and the courts.

DOI: 10.4324/9781003422808-3

Jurisdiction. In civil matters the court hears appeals from the Court of Session in Scotland, the Court of Appeal in Northern Ireland and the Court of Appeal (Civil Division) in England. There is no general right of appeal: leave of the Court of Appeal or the Supreme Court must first be obtained.

The **Administration of Justice Act 1969** provides a new form of appeal in *civil* actions from the High Court (or Divisional Court) direct to the Supreme Court, 'leapfrogging' the Court of Appeal. An appeal will lie only subject to the following conditions: (i) that, on application of any of the parties, the trial judge grants a certificate of appeal; (ii) that the certificate will only be granted if the judge's decision involves a point of law of *general public importance*; (iii) that this point of law either relates to the construction of an enactment or statutory instrument, *or* is one in respect of which the judge is bound by the Court of Appeal or the Supreme Court.

3.1.2 Judicial Committee of the Privy Council

The Privy Council originated as the *Curia Regis* of the Norman kings, to which reference has been made earlier (see p. 12). The Council retains certain advisory and formal functions, but it also exercises judicial authority through a committee known as the Judicial Committee of the Privy Council.

Composition. The 'court' is made up of all Privy Councillors who hold, or have held, high judicial office in the United Kingdom (including Justices of the Supreme Court), the Lord Chancellor, former Lord Chancellors and Commonwealth judges who are Privy Councillors. The quorum of the Committee is three, but in important cases, five members are usually present.

Jurisdiction. The Committee hears appeals from those Commonwealth countries that have retained the right of appeal (some such countries, on acquiring independence, abolished the right) and from colonial territories. It also hears appeals from:

i prize courts: jurisdiction extends over claims to captured ships during time of war
ii ecclesiastical courts
iii courts of the Isle of Man, the Channel Islands
iv tribunals of the medical, dental and opticians' professions

Procedure. The Committee sits as an advisory board and its procedure is informal. Judges, for example, are not robed. No judgment is given as in a court of law. The committee tenders advice to the monarch upon which an Order in Council is made to dispose of the issue in question. Dissentient opinions are not usually given (but see *Abbott*, 1977).

The decisions of the Judicial Committee are not binding on itself or on other courts of law of the United Kingdom, but a decision on appeal from a colony is binding on the colonial courts of that territory. In practice the judicial strength of the Committee is such that its decisions are treated with great respect by other courts (see, for example, the *Wagon Mound* case, p. 205). *Attorney General for Jersey v Holley* (2005) and *R v James and Karimi* (2006) are similar examples where the Court of Appeal (Criminal Division) has preferred to apply the Privy Council's judgment rather than that of the former House of Lords.

3.1.3 Court of Appeal (Civil Division)

This court is composed of the Master of the Rolls, the President of the Family Division and the Vice Chancellor of the Chancery Division, who are all *ex officio* judges, and 35 Lords Justice of Appeal. Normally, in civil cases, the Master of the Rolls and the Lords Justice of Appeal sit. However, any High Court judge may be requested by the Lord Chancellor to sit. Justices of the Supreme Court may also sit. The quorum of the court is three, and the court may sit in five divisions at the same time.

The court may uphold, amend or reverse the decision of a lower court, or order a new trial.

Jurisdiction. The court hears civil appeals from the High Court, county courts, the Restrictive Practices Court, the Employment Appeal Tribunal and other tribunals. It also hears appeals on interlocutory orders made by judges in chambers and, exceptionally, masters and registrars (e.g. directions on procedure, evidence and other preliminary matters before actual trial).

3.1.4 The High Court of Justice

The High Court consists of:

a the King's Bench Division
b the Chancery Division
c the Family Division

The three divisions are of equal competence, so each is empowered to try any action, but for administrative purposes and convenience, specific matters are allocated to each division as described in what follows.

The heads of the respective divisions are (a) King's Bench Division: The Lord Chief Justice, (b) Chancery Division: The Lord Chancellor (in practice the *Vice-Chancellor* presides) and (c) Family Division: The President. These are assisted by approximately 85 puisne judges who are allocated to each division. The Lord Chancellor may require any judge to sit in any division.

a The King's Bench Division

This court is composed of the Lord Chief Justice and approximately 60 puisne judges (High Court). It exercises three kinds of jurisdiction: (i) original (i.e. at first instance), (ii) appellate and (iii) supervisory.

i *Original jurisdiction.* This is of three kinds. As a result of the **Administration of Justice Act 1970**, the jurisdiction of the Admiralty Court (formerly a part of the Probate, Divorce and Admiralty Division) has now been added to the King's Bench Division. Further, a new Commercial Court has been added to deal with commercial cases involving traders and merchants, e.g. insurance claims. The main feature of this court is that procedure is more flexible than in other courts to enable disputes to be dealt with more quickly.

The effect of this reorganization is that the Division jurisdiction comprises: (i) all civil cases not specifically assigned to other Divisions of the High Court—these cases include tort cases, breaches of contracts and actions for the recovery of land, (ii) Commercial Court cases as described previously and (iii) Admiralty cases, i.e. claims and actions involving ships, e.g. collisions at sea, salvage, towage of ships to harbour and prize jurisdiction (during time of war).

When hearing cases, the judges sit alone, but in certain cases (e.g. defamation) a jury may be empanelled to assist the court. Jury verdicts may now be majority verdicts.

There is no limit to the amount that may be claimed in damages in the King's Bench. Some cases involve millions of pounds, e.g. the negligent sinking of a ship.

ii *Appellate jurisdiction* is exercised by two or three judges sitting as a 'Divisional Court' to hear appeals from a Solicitors' Disciplinary Tribunal and appeals under the **Rent Acts** and in some other cases. Appeal lies to a judge in chambers against an interlocutory order of a King's Bench Division master, and to a judge in the case of some appeals from tribunals.

iii *Supervisory jurisdiction* is exercised over inferior courts, tribunals and administrative authorities 'acting judicially', by means of the writ of habeas corpus and the prerogative orders of certiorari, prohibition and mandamus (see p. 60).

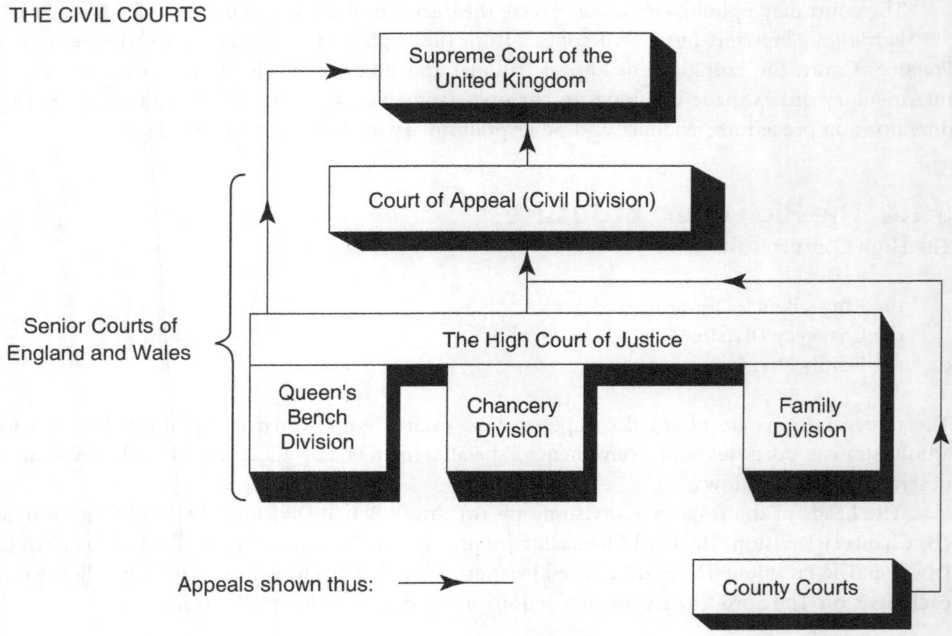

FIGURE 3.1 The civil courts

b The Chancery Division

The Chancery Division deals generally with matters that, before 1873, fell within the jurisdiction of the old Court of Chancery. Certain other matters have, however, been added by statute, e.g. bankruptcy claims and company matters.

Composition. The court is composed of the Lord Chancellor who never sits, the Vice-Chancellor, and at least four other puisne judges. In 1971 a Vice-Chancellor was appointed to take charge under the official president, the Lord Chancellor.

Jurisdiction of the division includes (i) the administration of estates of deceased persons; (ii) the dissolution of partnerships and taking of partnership accounts; (iii) mortgages and charges on land; (iv) trusts, both private and public (or charitable); (v) the sale of property subject to a lien or charge; (vi) company matters, e.g. dissolution and winding up; (vii) revenue matters, e.g. taxation; (viii) partition and sale of real estates; (ix) rectification and setting aside or cancellation of deeds or other written instruments; (x) bankruptcy matters; (xi) specific performance of contracts and (xii) probate (contentious matters only).

In addition, the Chancery Division hears appeals from certain lower courts, e.g. county courts, on such matters as bankruptcy or orders relating to trusts.

c Family Division

This Division was created by the **Administration of Justice Act 1970** and deals mainly with the following matters: divorce, granting decrees of judicial separation; decrees of nullity of marriage; orders as to the financial arrangements (maintenance) consequent upon decrees, e.g. for the wife, children or dependants; the marriage and wardship of minors; adoption; legitimacy; guardianship of minors; and non-contentious probate matters.

Probate jurisdiction (formerly exercised in the PDA Division) has been divided thus: contentious probate matters (e.g. where a dispute arises between *A* and B, and *A* claims a will to be valid which B disputes) is allocated to the Chancery Division; non-contentious probate matters are dealt with in the Family Division.

The Family Division comprises a President and 16 puisne judges. Judges sit alone, except when adjudicating at a Divisional Court of the Family Division to hear appeals, e.g. from magistrates' and county courts.

d The Business and Property Courts of England and Wales

The formation of the Business and Property Courts of England and Wales was announced in March 2017 and launched in June 2017. These courts would in future administer the following specialist courts and lists of the High Court:

i the Commercial Court (including the Admiralty Court and Mercantile Court);
ii the Technology and Construction Court (TCC); and
iii the Courts of the Chancery Division (including those dealing with financial services, intellectual property, competition and insolvency).

Note: As an outcome of the Briggs Review 2015/2016, there has been an ongoing reform of the court structure regarding the provision of electronic procedures in relation to the civil and family courts and tribunal proceedings. These reforms have already been incorporated into the **Civil Liability Act 2018** and **Courts and Tribunals (Judiciary and Functions of Staff) Act 2018**.

3.1.5 County Court

These courts were first established by the **County Courts Act 1846** to provide cheap, speedy and local justice—so obviating the need for bringing actions at Westminster or before the courts at nisi prius. The county courts proved efficient, and their jurisdiction has been enlarged from time to time. The **County Courts Act 1984**, which consolidated the **County Courts Act 1959** with certain later enactments, now governs the composition and the jurisdiction of these useful courts. In accordance with the **Crime and Courts Act 2013**, the **County Courts Act 1984** was amended to provide for the establishment of a single County Court.

Composition. One judge sits alone. Circuit judges are appointed by the Lord Chancellor. They must be barristers or solicitors of at least ten years' standing. In rare cases, a jury of eight persons may assist the court.

A *District Judge* (previously known as a registrar) of the court keeps the records of the court and performs the administrative work attached to it. They must be a solicitor of at least seven years' standing and are appointed by the Lord Chancellor. A registrar may hear and deal with certain small claims in place of the judge.

Jurisdiction. As a rule, the claimant must bring his or her claim or action in the court of the district where the defendant (or one of several defendants) dwells or carries on business. Actions relating to land must be brought in the court of the district where the land is situated.

Matters falling within the jurisdiction of the county courts include: (i) actions founded on contract or tort (except defamation) up to £50,000; (ii) equity matters (trusts, mortgages, etc.) up to £30,000; (iii) actions for the recovery of land, and questions of title to land, where the net annual rateable value does not exceed £1,000; (iv) bankruptcies;* (v) probate proceedings

* These financial limits are subject to regular review.

where the value of the deceased's estate is less than £30,000; (vi) winding up of companies with a paid-up capital of less than £120,000;* (vii) supervision of the adoption of infants; (viii) Admiralty matters (in some courts only) and (ix) actions in relation to rent restriction, hire purchase, landlord and tenant and similar matters as laid down by statute.

To relieve the burden of work falling on the Family Division of the High Court regarding divorce petitions, and with a view to reducing legal costs, the **Matrimonial Causes Act 1967** was passed, giving county courts a limited divorce jurisdiction. Under this Act the Lord Chancellor may designate any county court as a 'divorce county court' with power to hear and determine any *undefended* matrimonial cause.

Appeal from a county court lies to the Court of Appeal.

Since 1974 *small claims*, e.g. for debts, whether for goods sold, work done, money lent or for damages for personal injury negligence, where the amount in dispute does not exceed £1,000, may be dealt with informally before an arbitrator, who is usually the District Judge. The object is to enable persons to sue (and defend) actions without a solicitor, and without running up costs and long delays. A booklet is available at all county court offices showing the steps to be taken in simple actions of the kind described.

3.2 Criminal courts

The courts that hear criminal cases are:

a Supreme Court
b Court of Appeal (Criminal Division)
c Administrative Division of the High Court (formerly known as the Divisional Court of the King 's Bench Division)
d Crown Court
e magistrates' courts

3.2.1 Supreme Court

This court hears appeals from the Court of Appeal (Criminal Division) and from the Divisional Court of King's Bench Division. Either prosecutor or defendant may appeal, provided that the Court of Appeal or the Divisional Court (i) certify that a point of law of general public importance is involved in its decision and (ii) either the Court of Appeal (or the Divisional Court) or the Supreme Court gives leave to appeal on the ground that the point is one that ought to be considered by the House (**Administration of Justice Act 1960**). This is to prevent frivolous or minor cases from going to this final court.

Composition. This court is composed of the Lords of Appeal in Ordinary and other peers who have held high judicial office. The quorum is three, and each judge delivers a separate speech, the verdict being by a majority.

3.2.2 Court of Appeal (Criminal Division)

The **Criminal Appeal Act 1968** provides that the Court of Appeal shall consist of two divisions: one exercising civil jurisdiction and one criminal. The Act abolished the former Court of Criminal Appeal (created in 1907); its jurisdiction is now exercised by the Court of Appeal (Criminal Division).

Composition. The judges who sit in this court are the Lord Chief Justice, the Lords Justice of Appeal and judges of the King's Bench Division. A quorum of three is necessary.

The court may dismiss the appeal or allow it and may order that any conviction recorded in a lower court shall be quashed. The court may order a new trial (**Administration of Justice Act 1964**). An appeal as to the length of a person's sentence may be made by the person sentenced, where the sentence is considered too harsh or by the Attorney General, where the sentence is considered unduly lenient. In an appeal by the Attorney General, the Court of Appeal may increase or decrease the sentence, but in an appeal by an individual, the sentence may only be decreased. In *R v McIlKenny and Others* (1992), the court stated that it would allow an appeal only if the condition is unsafe or unsatisfactory, if there had been a wrong decision on a question of law or if there had been a material irregularity.

To hear these appeals, two courts sit full-time, while a third sits as and when required by the number of appeals listed.

In accordance with the **Criminal Appeal Act 1995**, the Court of Appeal can commission an investigation by a Criminal Cases Review Commission (appointed under the Act) and, where appropriate, report to the court's cases of wrongful conviction or sentence. The Criminal Cases Review Commission (Information) Act 2016 extended the Criminal Cases Review Commission's Powers to obtain documents and other material so that they could obtain them from a person who is not employed by or serving in a public body.

3.2.3 The Crown Court

Before 1971 the more serious indictable offences were tried by a High Court judge at assizes, and the less serious by a recorder or a bench of magistrates at quarter sessions.

The Royal Commission on Assizes and Quarter Sessions recommended replacing the old circuit system and sweeping reorganization. It resulted in the **Courts Act 1971**, which gave effect to most of the proposals. Only the main points can be noted here. The Act:

a abolished Assize Courts and Quarter Sessions Courts; and
b established the Crown Court.

Broadly, the Crown Court takes over all 'first instance' business above the magistrates' court level, and all appeal business of the Quarter Sessions mentioned previously.

Jurisdiction. The Crown Court has jurisdiction over indictable offences and offences triable either way for which a defendant has been committed by the magistrates for trial by the Crown Court. The Court also sentences offenders committed for sentence by magistrates' courts, e.g. where the magistrates' court finds the accused guilty but has insufficient powers to adequately deal with the defendant. The Crown Court acts as an appeal court to hear appeals from magistrates' courts. It has the power to revoke a community service order imposed by justices and substitute a sentence of its own. This cannot be exercised so as to impose a sentence longer than the justices had power to impose (*R v Ogden* (1996)). Finally, the Crown Court has an inherent jurisdiction to regulate its own practices, which has been exercised in a case not covered by existing regulation and precedent, in *R v Leicester Crown Court, ex. parte* Phipps (1997).

The judge in the Crown Court will be one of the following:

a A *High Court Judge*, a puisne judge of the King's Bench Division. His or her position is similar to that of his or her predecessor, sitting as an Assize Court Judge. The judge is appointed to one of six circuits.
b A *Circuit Judge* appointed by the Crown to serve in (1) the Crown Court and (2) a county court (see p. 43). He or she must be a barrister of ten years' standing or a recorder who has held the office for three years. They retire at 72 but may be allowed to extend their period of office till 75 years.

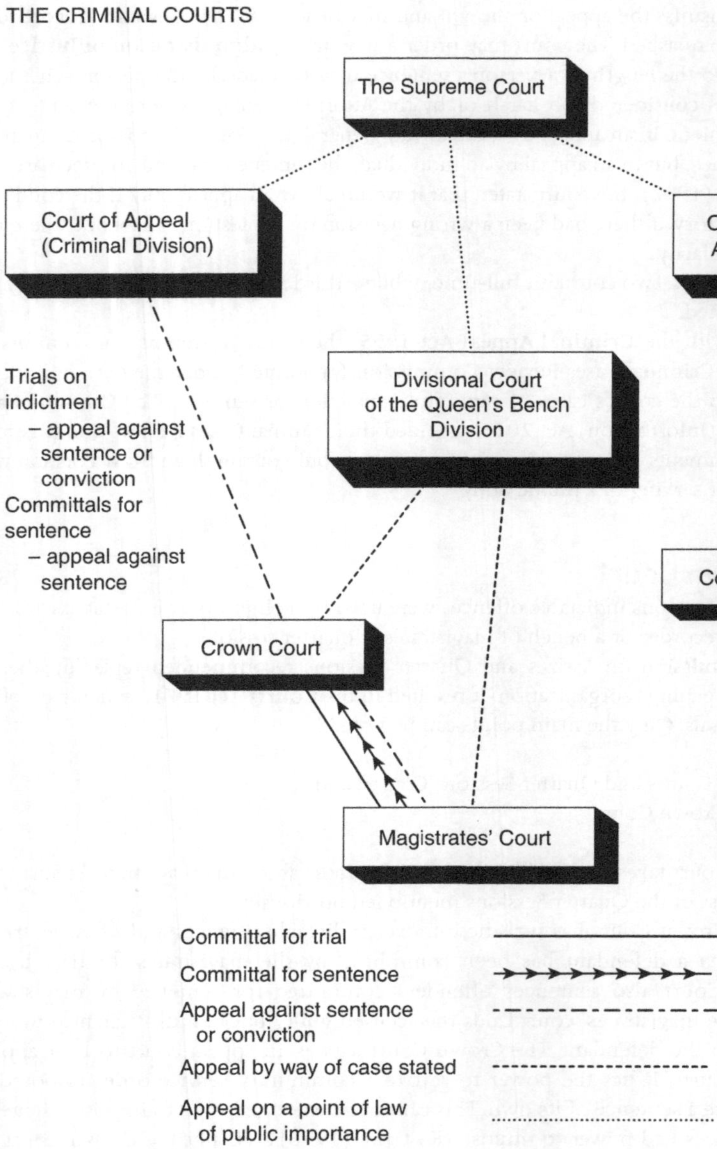

FIGURE 3.2 The criminal courts

c A *Recorder*, who is a part-time judge of the Crown Court. Appointments are made from barristers and solicitors of ten years' standing who are prepared to commit themselves to not less than one month's work on the bench each year.

At the Lord Chancellor's request, a Court of Appeal judge can sit in the Crown Court. All trials in the Crown Court take place before a jury.

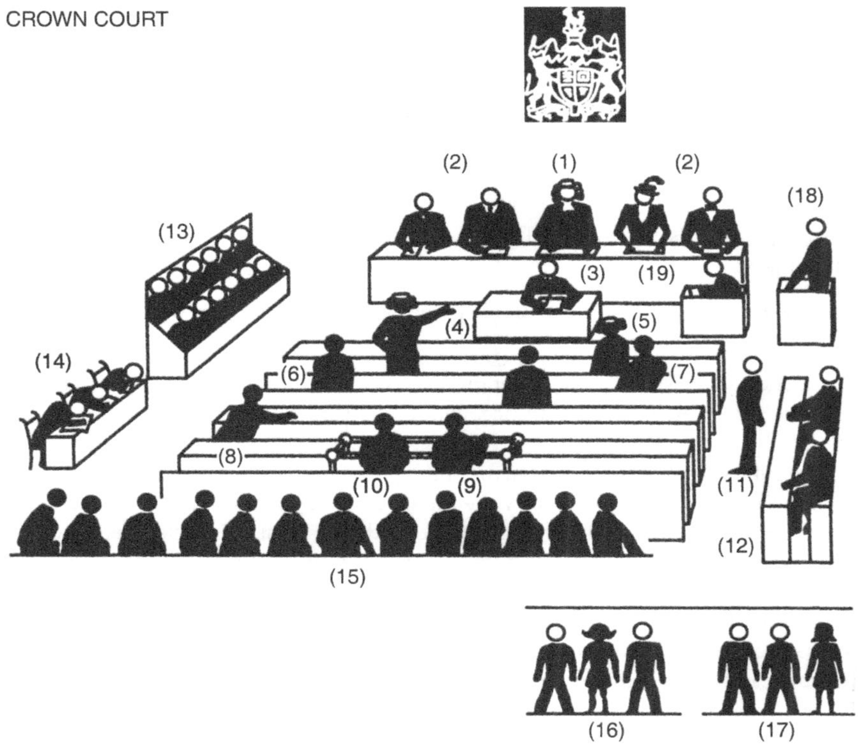

1. High Court Judge, Circuit judge or recorder
2. Justices of the Peace (not more than 4)
3. Clerk of the Crown Court
4. Defending Barrister (standing)
5. Prosecuting Barrister (seated)
6. Solicitor or solicitor's clerk in attendance (Defence)
7. Solicitor or solicitor's clerk in attendance (Prosecution)
8. Probation Officer
9. Accused
10. Warder from prison
11. Court Usher
12. Witnesses who have given evidence
13. Jury
14. Press reporters
15. Public
16. Witnesses for Prosecution outside court waiting to give evidence
17. Witnesses for Defence outside court waiting to give evidence
18. Witness
19. Shorthand writer

FIGURE 3.3 The Crown Court

The Crown Court has about 90 centres, chosen as far as practicable to be within travelling distance of the whole population. There are six circuits:

1 South-eastern (with London as its administrative centre)
2 Midland and Oxford (Birmingham)
3 North-eastern (Leeds)
4 Wales and Chester (Cardiff)

5 Western (Bristol)
6 Northern (Manchester)

On each of these circuits, the towns where the judges sit are classified in three types:

> *First-tier centres*, where High Court judges and Circuit judges deal with criminal cases, and High Court judges also take civil business.
>
> *Second-tier centres*, dealing only with criminal business, but served by both High Court and Circuit judges.
>
> *Third-tier centres*, served only by Circuit judges and Recorders who deal only with criminal cases.
>
> *How business is distributed*. The distribution of business in the Crown Court is determined by directions from the Lord Chief Justice, with the agreement of the Lord Chancellor.

The general rule is that the higher the status of the judge, the more serious will be the cases tried.

A High Court judge will always try the offences of murder and treason. Offences normally tried by a High Court judge include manslaughter and rape. Most indictable offences can be tried by any judge of the Crown Court. Offences triable either way will normally be tried by a Circuit judge or Recorder.

Lay magistrates have a role to play in the Crown Court. Not less than two and not more than four must sit for appeals and committals for sentence from magistrates' courts; and not more than four in other cases on indictment. They sit with the judge.

In the City of London, where the Crown Court is known as the Central Criminal Court, or more commonly the Old Bailey, the Lord Mayor and aldermen can sit with any judge in any type of case.

Crown Court and Solicitors. Solicitors of ten years' standing are eligible for appointment as Recorders. Moreover, if a solicitor holds the appointment of Recorder for five years, they may then be appointed a Circuit Judge. Solicitors have a limited right of audience in the Crown Court.

3.2.4 Appeal by way of case stated

This form of appeal may be used in magistrates' courts and in the Crown Court. The court to which an appeal is made is the Divisional Court of King's Bench, which is constituted by not less than two judges of that Division (the usual number sitting is three).

Where either party (prosecutor or defendant) is dissatisfied on a point of law with the decision of the Crown Court, that party may require the Crown Court to 'state a case' for the opinion of the Divisional Court of King's Bench. The Crown Court then states the case in writing, giving the facts and the reasons for the decision. The Divisional Court then adjudicates on the written evidence submitted and gives its ruling.

There are two points to be noted: (i) the appeal must be on a point of law, not fact; (ii) both prosecutor and defendant may appeal. This is contrary to the general rule that where the defendant is acquitted, the prosecution has no general right of appeal to a higher court.

The first justices were appointed in 1327 as 'conservators of the peace'. For more than 600 years, their successors, now known as justices of the peace or magistrates, have performed the duties of enforcing the common law and statute law and of preserving locally the public peace and good order.

In recent years Parliament has burdened the 900 magistrates' courts with enforcing increasing quantities of legislation, much of it highly complex. Magistrates' courts (or courts of petty sessions) today deal with more cases than any other court in the English legal system. For example, over 98 per cent of all criminal prosecutions in England and Wales are dealt with by magistrates. Magistrates also deal with some civil cases and perform certain administrative duties, particularly in licensing matters.

The responsibility for the finance, organization and management of these courts was transferred from the Home Office to the Lord Chancellor on 1 April 1992.

Further reorganization of the magistrates' courts system took place because of Part V of the **Access to Justice Act 1999**. This legislation established a new organizational unit, the magistrates' courts committee area (MCC), each administered by a magistrates' courts committee responsible for the administration of the magistrates' service within the commission area. Each MCC is comprised of 12 members, mostly lay magistrates, who are responsible for the appointment of a justices' chief executive who is not required to be legally qualified to manage the courts within an MCC area.

There are currently 26 MCCs in England and Wales, with 22 of these being in the Greater London Area under the auspices of a Greater London Magistrates' Courts Authority.

There are two kinds of magistrates:

a Justices of the Peace (lay magistrates); and
b District Judges (magistrates' courts) (formerly known as stipendiary magistrates).

MAGISTRATES' COURT

1. Chairman of Justices
2. Justices of the Peace
3. Legal Adviser
4. Prosecuting Lawyer (seated)
5. Defending Lawyer (standing)
6. Probation Officers
7. Defendant
8. Usher
9. Witness
10. Other witnesses
11. Press
12. Public

FIGURE 3.4 The magistrates' court

a Justices of the peace

These are laypersons appointed by the Lord Chancellor:

i in respect of counties on the recommendation of the Lord Lieutenant of the county, assisted by an advisory committee
ii in respect of large urban areas (e.g. Stoke on Trent) on the recommendation of its own advisory committee

The important features of the county and urban magistrates are that they are local people, with some knowledge of the areas for which they are appointed, who are prepared to give up a certain amount of their time (say, at least one day every two weeks) to the discharge of their judicial duties. They are unpaid (though they may receive out-of-pocket expenses when adjudicating).

The aim is to have on the bench a good cross-section of people of good character, of all social classes, male or female, who fairly represent the community. There are nearly 30,000 in England and Wales.

b District Judges (magistrates' courts)

District Judges (magistrates' courts) (formerly stipendiary magistrates) are full-time paid magistrates appointed by the Lord Chancellor and must be barristers or solicitors of at least seven years' standing. They have all the powers of two or more lay justices and are able to exercise jurisdiction in every commission area of England and Wales. Currently there are 98 such judges with 171 Deputy District Judges.

The *Legal Adviser (formerly Clerk to the Justices)* is the official of each magistrates' court who advises the justices on points of law and procedure, makes a record of evidence and prepares depositions (i.e. statements sworn on oath in the presence of an accused person) made by witnesses in cases sent forward for trial at the Crown Court (**Courts Act 1971**). They also perform the administrative work of the court, such as preparing information, summonses and warrants granted by magistrates and collecting fines.

The **Justices of the Peace Act 1949** provides that a clerk must be a barrister or solicitor of at least five years' standing. The Act also provides for the setting up in the counties and in those boroughs having a separate commission of the peace, of committees to supervise the administrative work of the magistrates' courts. The **Justices of the Peace Act 1997** consolidates the **Justices of the Peace Act 1979** and certain provisions of the **Police and Magistrates' Courts Act 1994** and came into force on 19 June 1997.

A (legal adviser) to the justices must not retire with the justices to consider their verdict, such matters being solely for the magistrates, but the justices may send for the legal adviser if advice is needed.

3.2.5 Jurisdiction of magistrates' courts

The jurisdiction of these courts falls under three main headings: (a) as a court of trial, (b) as a court of preliminary investigation and (c) miscellaneous.

a Court of trial

The jurisdiction is exercised by from two to seven justices, and the maximum punishment that may be imposed for any one offence is six months' imprisonment or a fine of £5,000. A single lay justice may try certain cases, such as simple drunkenness.

Criminal offences can be divided into three classes:

i Offences triable only on indictment. Offences will be such if there is no express statutory provision otherwise. They are triable by judge and jury in the Crown Court. An indictment is the document used in jury trials that states the offences and gives particulars.
ii Offences triable only summarily, i.e. in a magistrates' court. Offences that can only be tried summarily including riding a pedal cycle at night without lights, begging in a public place and being found drunk and incapable on the highway. A statute must expressly provide for such trial or prescribe a procedure for determining the matter (see s. 23 of the **Criminal Law Act 1977**).
iii Offences triable either way. Schedule 3 of the **Criminal Law Act 1977** lists over 60 offences triable either way, i.e. summarily or on indictment. The Act also provides that offences made so triable by earlier statutes will now be in this class. The magistrates must offer the defendant the choice of trial either in the Crown Court or by the magistrates. If the latter is chosen, the magistrates will try the case there and then, i.e. summarily. If the defendant chooses to be tried at the Crown Court, the magistrates will sit as a court of preliminary investigation.

The agenda of a typical magistrates' court reveals a wide variety of offences: petty theft, criminal damage, common assault, drunkenness, driving a motorcar without a driving licence, driving without insurance, failing to obey traffic signs, parking offences, driving without due care and attention and similar road traffic offences. Some offenders will be dealt with then and there (even though they qualify for trial by the Crown Court), while defendants who elect for trial by jury will be committed for trial if the prosecution makes out a prima facie case in respect of each. (A prima facie case is one which appears 'at first sight' or 'from the first impression' to be an offence.)

b Court of preliminary investigation

In this capacity the magistrates' court is called upon to determine whether an accused person, who is brought before it by means of a summons or by arrest, shall be committed to stand trial at the Crown Court.

- The prosecution calls its witnesses and produces exhibits (e.g. a gun or knife). The evidence of the prosecution witnesses is taken down in writing in the presence of the accused, and the document (called a deposition) is signed by the witness (called a deponent) and by the justices present at the hearing.
- The accused may give evidence and call witnesses in support, or he or she may reserve their defence until the actual trial. Usually, an accused reserves his or her defence.
- After hearing the evidence, the magistrates decide whether the prosecution has made out a prima facie case. If it has, the accused and the witnesses are bound over to attend the trial at the Crown Court. These proceedings are known as *committal proceedings*, and although they may be taken before one justice, in practice two or more lay magistrates usually preside over this important step in the judicial process. A stipendiary magistrate acts alone.
- If the prosecution has not made out a prima facie case against the accused, the magistrates must order a release.
- An accused committed for trial may be either remanded in custody (i.e. to a prison to await trial) or remanded on bail (i.e. released on condition that an appearance is made at the trial court at a later date when the case will be heard).

The **Criminal Justice Act 1967** provides that, in certain circumstances, an accused person may be committed for trial on written statements alone.

The Act also restricts the publication of reports of committal proceedings to purely formal matters, i.e. the identity of the court and magistrates, the names of the parties and the nature of the charges. The object is to avoid prejudicing the accused by pre-trial publicity. But the reporting restrictions can be lifted on application by the accused or one of the accused.

c Miscellaneous jurisdiction

In addition to the foregoing duties, the magistrates have a limited jurisdiction in regard to civil debts (e.g. unpaid income tax where the amount due is less than £30).

Other important duties include: (i) making matrimonial orders for separation and maintenance of spouses; (ii) affiliation orders; (iii) consent to marriage; (iv) guardianship of minors; (v) adoption of children; (vi) orders under the **Mental Health Acts 1959, 1983** and **2007** and (vii) orders in regard to children and young persons in need of care, protection or control.

3.2.6 Juvenile courts

Certain magistrates attached to a petty-sessional division form a special panel to deal with offences committed by children (i.e. persons under 14) and young persons (i.e. over 14 and under 17). The juvenile court is formed by three lay justices, under 65 years of age, one of whom must be a woman.

The juvenile court sits *separately* from the adult court: if it cannot sit in a different room, it must sit on a different day. Proceedings in juvenile courts are shielded from publicity. The press must not disclose the identity of the child or young person unless the court, in exceptional cases, permits.

Where a child or young person is charged jointly with an adult, the case is dealt with in an adult court, i.e. the usual magistrates' court.

In accordance with the **Youth Justice and Criminal Evidence Act 1999**, juvenile courts are, in certain circumstances, required to refer young offenders who have been convicted of certain offences to youth offender panels.

3.2.7 Appeals from magistrates' courts

Appeals from magistrates' courts are organized as follows:

a Where the defendant wishes to appeal against (i) conviction and/or (ii) sentence, appeal lies to the Crown Court.

b Where the defendant or prosecutor wishes to appeal on a point of law, appeal lies to the Divisional Court of King's Bench by way of 'case stated'.

c Appeals concerning separation and maintenance orders, affiliation, adoption and consent to marry lie to a Divisional Court of the Family Division.

d Further appeal may be made from the Divisional Court to the Supreme Court.

3.2.8 HM Courts and Tribunals Service

HM Courts and Tribunals Service was created on 1 April 2011. It integrated the HM Courts Service and Tribunals Service into one agency, providing support for the administration of justice in courts and tribunals. It operates as a partnership between the Lord Chancellor, the Lord Chief Justice and the Senior President of Tribunals.

The agency is responsible for the administration of the criminal, civil and family courts and tribunals in England and Wales and non-devolved tribunals in Scotland and Northern Ireland. It is intended to provide for a fair, efficient and effective justice system delivered by an independent judiciary.

The aim of the service is 'To run an efficient and effective courts and tribunals system, which enables the rule of law to be upheld and provides access to justice for all'. The stated objectives are: 'provide the supporting administration for a fair, efficient and accessible courts and tribunal system; support an independent judiciary in the administration of justice; drive continuous improvement of performance and efficiency across all aspects of the administration of the courts and tribunals; collaborate effectively with other justice organisations and agencies, including the legal professions, to improve access to justice; work with government departments and agencies, as appropriate, to improve the quality and timeliness of their decision making in order to reduce the number of cases coming before tribunals and courts.'

3.2.9 Leveson Review of Criminal Courts

On 12 December 2024 the Lord Chancellor and the Justice Secretary, the Rt Hon Shabana Mahmood, published information relating to a Courts review to be led by Sir Brian Leveson, which it claimed would see quicker justice for victims and keep streets safe. The review would consider the case for new 'intermediate courts' where cases too serious for magistrates' courts but not serious enough for the Crown Court could be heard by a judge, flanked by magistrates.

Sir Brian would also be asked to consider whether Magistrates should be empowered to look at more cases, freeing up capacity in the Crown Court to consider the more complex, serious crimes. By reclassifying some offences and extending magistrates' sentencing powers, certain trials could move to magistrates' courts. This would build on the decision to allow magistrates to hand out custodial sentences for up to 12 months, which had been announced earlier in 2024.

The review would also look at where technology could be used to drive efficiencies and improve how the Crown Court functions.

The review would build on previous reviews, such as the 2001 Review of the Criminal Courts in England and Wales by Lord Justice Auld and the 2015 report into Efficiency in Criminal Proceedings by Brian Leveson.

The Independent Review of Criminal Courts Part 1 was published in July 2025 (https://www.gov.uk/government/publications/independent-review-of-the-criminal-courts-part-1https://assets.publishing.service.gov.uk/media/686be85d81dd8f70f5de3c1f/35.49_MOJ_Ind_Review_Criminal_Courts_v8b_FINAL_WEB.pdf) and contains 45 recommendations, including increasing use of out-of-court resolutions by the police, and restrictions on the use of jury trials.

3.3 Other courts

3.3.1 Coroner's courts

The office of coroner and the coroner's inquest (or inquiry) are of ancient origin. The first coroners were appointed in the reign of Richard I in 1194. Originally, they had wide powers concerning local administration and the criminal law, but these have now been shed and the coroner of today carries out those duties laid down in the **Coroners Act 1988**, the **Administration of Justice Act 1982** and rules made thereunder. The **Coroners and Justice Act 2009** introduced some major reforms regarding the law in relation to coroners and the certification and registration of deaths. The legislation provided for a Chief Coroner to lead the service and re-designated several positions in the former coronial system so that there are now senior coroners, area coroners and assistant coroners. The legislation also introduced medical coroners to supplement the work of the coroners under the guidance of a National Medical Examiner.

The legislation also separated the functions of the coroners relating to deaths and coroners investigating treasure trove. The latter are designated as a coroner for treasure and assistant coroners for treasure. The **Judicial Review and Courts Act 2022** made two further major reforms to the operation of Coroner's Courts. These were: Allows virtual hearings in coroner's courts ('Virtual hearings'): and, Allows a coroner to discontinue an investigation where the cause of death becomes clear (i.e. by natural causes), without a post-mortem examination ('Discontinuing investigations where cause of death becomes clear').

- The main duties of the coroner are to investigate the death of any person that has been
  - i sudden
  - ii violent
  - iii unnatural (i.e. against the course of nature)
  - iv deaths of prisoners
  - v deaths of persons in mental institutions where there is no satisfactory medical evidence
  - vi deaths involving the police. The coroner may, however, hold an inquest into *any* case of death.
- A coroner *must* summon a jury when there is reason to suspect that death is due to murder, manslaughter, infanticide, a road accident, poisoning or notifiable disease. An inquest may be held in any place (e.g. a court or a private house). Proceedings are carried out in a formal manner. The public are admitted to the court except when this would be prejudicial to national security.
- The purpose of the inquest is to enable the coroner, with the aid of a jury when so required, to ascertain the identity of the deceased person and the place and cause of death. If some person has already been arrested and charged with the murder, manslaughter or infanticide of the subject of the inquest, the coroner must adjourn the inquiry until the criminal proceedings are ended.
- Money, coins, gold, silver, plate or bullion found hidden in the earth or a private place, the owner of which is unknown, is called *treasure trove* and belongs to the Crown. When such articles are uncovered, the coroner holds an inquest to establish whether they are, in fact, treasure trove. If so, the finder and the owner of the land on which they were found are customarily recompensed by the Treasury.
- A coroner must be a barrister, solicitor or a Fellow of the Chartered Institute of Legal Executives of at least five years' standing. They are appointed by the relevant local authority having a separate commission of the peace. The Lord Chancellor may remove a coroner for misbehaviour.

3.4 Court of Justice of the European Communities

Subject to the effect of the European Union (Withdrawal) Act 2018, European Union (Withdrawal) Act 2019 and the Retained EU (Revocation and Reform) Act 2023 (see Chapter 13).

The European Court of Justice has jurisdiction to give preliminary rulings on the interpretation of the Treaties, the validity and interpretation of acts of the Community institutions and the interpretation of the statutes of bodies established by an act of the Council. Any national court or tribunal may request the European Court to give a ruling on these matters and courts or tribunals from which there is no appeal must make such a referral.

The court consists of 15 judges assisted by nine Advocates-General. There is also a Court of First Instance with twelve members, established in 1988.

3.5 Administrative tribunals

In his book *Freedom Under the Law*, Lord Denning refers to administrative tribunals as:

> a separate set of courts dealing with a set of rights and duties. Just as in the old days there were ecclesiastical courts dealing with matrimonial cases and the administration of estates,

> and, just as there was the Chancellor dealing with the enforcement and administration of trusts, so in our day there are the new tribunals dealing with the rights and duties between man and the State.

In the last 50 years, successive governments have been concerned with regulating the social life of the community. Legislation for improving the general well-being has included the **National Health Service Act, National Insurance Act, Education Act, Housing Acts, Town and Country Planning Acts** and **Rent Restriction Acts**. Although the collective good and welfare are admirable aims, the effect of much legislation is that, while promoting the public interest, it also circumscribes the rights of the private individual. There are now over 2,000 such tribunals that hear over 200,000 cases a year.

For example, Adams owns a field that the local Education Authority proposes to purchase compulsorily as a site for a technical college. Adams may wish to retain this field and contest the right of the Education Authority to acquire it. If the field is compulsorily acquired, Adams may further dispute the amount payable to compensate him for his loss. Tribunals may decide (a) whether the field will be acquired and (b) the amount of compensation.

Similarly, Black is injured at work, which disables him from continuing his employment. He can claim a pension under Social Security legislation, but his claim may be repudiated by the Adjudication Officer on the grounds that it is not within the Act.

Many such disputes occur between a private individual seeking to protect their own private rights and a Minister, Government department, local authority or other person to whom authority has been given by law to administer a particular Act.

It may be argued that disputes of this kind ought to be decided in the traditionally impartial and fair atmosphere of a court of law that follows a known procedure and applies a known system of law—common law or statute. But we find that such disputes are frequently decided by special tribunals, not based on law but on grounds of policy and discretion and that, as far as possible, the tribunals endeavour to reconcile the rights of the individual with those of the public in whose general interest the particular legislation may have been passed.

The position occupied by administrative tribunals and the type of law applied therein, known as *administrative law*, is a matter of great importance. At this stage, therefore, we shall examine some of the reasons advanced for their creation, and the advantages and disadvantages that administrative tribunals display.

The *reasons* usually given for the establishment of administrative tribunals are:

a Ordinary courts are already overburdened with work, and additional jurisdiction would cause a breakdown.
b The costs of judicial proceedings in ordinary courts would be heavy.
c The courts of law are slow and the procedure elaborate.
d Matters involving a public service are best administered by specialists in that service, e.g. doctors at a medical appeal.
e Policy decisions are best settled by an administrative authority.

The *advantages* of administrative tribunals are said to be:

i Decisions are *quick*, and delays are avoided.
ii The procedure is *cheap*; usually no fees are payable.
iii The *informal* atmosphere and straightforward procedure suit the litigant.
iv They have wide *discretionary* power. This avoids the rigidity that the doctrine of precedent imposes on the courts of law.

v Tribunals are often staffed by *experts*, e.g. doctors on Pensions Tribunals determine disability or extent of injury.
vi Tribunals ensure *efficient administration* of social or economic policies found in statutes; while courts of law sift facts and decide on the basis of established rules of law different in character from social policy.

The *disadvantages* are said to be:

i Administrative tribunals are sometimes held in *private* and lack publicity. Suspicion may be aroused as to 'administrative justice'.
ii The parties are sometimes prohibited from being represented by lawyers. The inarticulate person is therefore at a disadvantage in explaining his or her case. Legal aid is not generally available (see p. 68).
iii Reasons for decisions are not always published.
iv Technical experts and administrators are not always capable of acting impartially or of sifting the facts.
v Tribunals sometimes include a civil servant of the Ministry that is directly involved in the dispute. He or she is, therefore, not sufficiently independent or impartial to give a just decision.
vi Rights of appeal are limited in some cases.
vii Discretion of a tribunal is sometimes so wide as to make decisions inconsistent and unpredictable.

The **Tribunals, Courts and Enforcement Act 2007** introduced major changes to the operation of the administration of tribunals. It created a new simplified legislative framework for tribunals, incorporating the merger of existing tribunals into a new generic First-tier Tribunal and Upper Tribunal. The Upper Tribunal primarily, but not exclusively, reviews and decides appeals arising from the First-tier Tribunal. It also provided for the future creation of new jurisdictions within the Act's framework.

In addition, the Act also placed the independence of the tribunal judiciary on a statutory footing and provided for the appointment of a Senior President of Tribunals.

3.5.1 Examples of tribunals

Social Security. Claims for benefits under the **Social Security Contributions and Benefits Act 1992** are dealt with locally by a Social Security officer. If disagreement arises, the applicant for benefit has a right of appeal to a local tribunal made up of a chairman, who is a lawyer, and two lay members, one representing employers' organizations and one representing employees' organizations. From the tribunal's decision appeal lies to the Social Security Commissioner, a barrister appointed by the Crown.

There is no right of appeal either on a point of law or fact from the Commissioner's finding. Some technical questions are reserved for decision by the Minister, who may refer the matter to a judge of the High Court. From the Minister's decision on such questions, there is a right of appeal to the High Court (whose decision is final).

Industrial injuries. There is a similar system of adjudication in respect of industrial injuries claims under the **Social Security Contributions and Benefits Act 1992**. The insured person must establish that the injury arose during the course of their employment. If the insurance officer disallows the claim, the applicant may appeal to the tribunal applicable to Social Security (see earlier mentions).

If the applicant establishes that the injury did arise in the course of employment, the next question to consider is the extent of the disablement. This claim is decided first by a medical board of two doctors. Further appeal lies to a medical appeal tribunal made up of two doctors with a lawyer as chairman. From the medical appeal tribunal appeal lies with the Social Security Commissioner.

Decisions of the Commissioner in Social Security and industrial injuries cases are published officially, and such decisions bind insurance officers and local tribunals.

Employment tribunals (formerly industrial tribunals). The **Industrial Training Act 1964** (replaced by the **Industrial Training Act 1982**) provided for the establishment of these tribunals. Later legislation has considerably increased their jurisdiction, particularly the **Trade Union and Labour Relations (Consolidation) Act 1992** and the **Employment Protection (Consolidation) Act 1978**. Most of the cases brought to the tribunals concern unfair dismissal or redundancy. The **Industrial Tribunals Act 1996** consolidated various enactments relating to industrial tribunals and the Employment Appeal Tribunal. In addition to these areas, the tribunals have jurisdiction over many aspects of industrial law. Thousands of cases are referred to the tribunals, which sit throughout the country.

In accordance with the **Employment Rights (Dispute Resolutions) Act 1998**, Industrial Tribunals were renamed Employment Tribunals with the title 'President of the Employment Tribunals (England and Wales)' replacing 'President of the Industrial Tribunals (England and Wales)'.

The principal aim of the 1998 Act was to improve access to justice in employment rights disputes by streamlining procedures before employment tribunals and by encouraging greater use of alternative methods of dispute resolution. The Advisory, Conciliation and Arbitration Service (ACAS) is empowered, subject to the Secretary of State's approval, to prepare, fund and promote an arbitrator's scheme for the resolution of unfair dismissal disputes.

The tribunal consists of a legally qualified chairman and two lay members (where the parties agree, the Chairman may sit with only one lay member).

The applicant may be legally represented or may be represented by a trade union official; he or she may send written representations setting out the facts and arguments; they may require the production of documents and may request the tribunal to order the attendance of any person to give evidence and to produce documents.

The decision of the tribunal, which is by majority, is given in writing with reasons therefore. The decision is subject to a right of appeal to the Employment Appeal Tribunal on a point of law.

Rent tribunals. Under the **Rent Acts**, the tenant of furnished accommodation may apply to a rent tribunal for the rent to be reduced. Similarly, the tenant of unfurnished accommodation below a certain rateable value may apply to a rent officer to fix a fair rent. Appeal from that decision lies with a rent assessment committee, which normally consists of a legally qualified chairman, a valuer or surveyor and a layperson.

Legal representation is allowed, hearings are open to the public and the press, and evidence is never taken on oath. If requested, reasons for the decisions of the rent assessment committee may be given in writing or orally. Appeal, on a point of law only, lies to the High Court.

Domestic tribunals. Domestic tribunals exist to determine questions, decide disputes and maintain discipline among members of a particular trade or profession. Thus, a trade union or a professional body may lay down its set of rules governing membership. If the rules are infringed, a tribunal may be set up to deal with the incident and it may punish or expel the offender.

Three important examples of domestic tribunals are:

a *Trade unions*. The disciplinary tribunals of trade unions are created by members themselves. A governing committee frames the rules of membership, rules constituting a tribunal, rules of procedure and the forms of punishment. Members who violate the rules may be expelled or fined by the disciplinary tribunal. The **Trade Union and Labour Relations (Consolidation) Act 1992** altered the law regarding trade unions. Trade unions maintain certain disciplinary powers regarding members, but where a wrong is alleged to have been done to a member, they have a right of appeal to an industrial tribunal, e.g. where he or she has been wrongfully expelled or refused the right to take part in the activities of a trade union.

Employees are protected from dismissal for belonging to a union or taking part in its activities. This protection extends to members of all independent unions.

b *Solicitors.* The **Solicitors Act 1974**, as amended by the **Administration of Justice Act 1982**, provides for the setting up of a committee to exercise disciplinary powers over solicitors. The disciplinary committee sits as a board with a minimum of three members, and follows the usual legal procedure of a court of law. The board may strike a solicitor off the roll, suspend him or her from practice, impose a fine of up to £3,000 or order the payment of costs. Appeal from the committee lies to the High Court.

c *Doctors and other medical practitioners.* The professional conduct committee of the General Medical Council has power under the **Medical Act 1983** to strike a doctor off the Medical Register for infamous conduct in his or her profession, and he or she can be barred from further practice. The **Medical (Professional Performance) Act 1995** sets out the rules governing the suspension or elimination of a person's name from the register. Appeal against the decision of the General Medical Council lies with the Judicial Committee of the Privy Council.

The General Dental Council has similar powers under the **Dentists Act 1984**, concerning dentists, and the Central Midwives Board has similar authority over midwives.

The **National Health Service Reform and Health Care Professions Act 2002** established a Council for the Regulation of Health Care Professionals. The intention of the legislation is to create a more uniform system for each of the professional health care bodies.

Another function is to provide an oversight of the self-regulatory functions conferred on each professional regulatory body, such as doctors, dentists, opticians, osteopaths and chiro- practitioners.

There are many more such tribunals, but a lack of space precludes their description.

3.6 Judicial control of administrative tribunals

A tribunal is another name for a court, but to avoid confusion, the term is applied to those bodies possessing judicial powers that operate outside the traditional courts of law. The essential purpose of a tribunal is to adjudicate in a dispute, to follow proper procedures, to act fairly and impartially and finally to reach a decision. We have seen that many of the tribunals have very wide powers; indeed, therefore, their judgments must be subject to the supervisory control of the courts of law. Such control is exercised mainly by the King's Bench Division, which continues the ancient jurisdiction of the original royal court of King's Bench.

As a rule, Parliament leaves the professional organizations to form their own rules and procedures to maintain control of their membership. Only in exceptional cases will the courts of law interfere with these. But where the administration of a statute, the exercise of powers under it and the setting up of tribunals to decide disputes are entrusted to a Minister, Parliament generally requires that certain rules be framed to ensure fairness in the administration of the statute and of tribunals set up thereunder. Nevertheless injustices do occur, and the purpose of this section is to examine the grounds on which the courts of law exercise their supervisory jurisdiction and the procedures that are followed.

Where a tribunal acts judicially it must follow certain unwritten rules of common law known as 'natural justice'. Natural justice embraces two sub-rules:

a the rule against bias ('no man may be a judge in his own cause'); and
b *audi alteram partem* ('hear the other side').

3.6.1 The rule against bias

A true judicial decision can be reached only if the judge is impartial. This is an obvious requirement in a court of law or a tribunal and is equally applicable to any other public body with power to affect an individual's rights. In *R v Rand* (1866) it was held that a judge is disqualified where (i) he or she has a direct pecuniary interest, however small, in the subject matter in dispute or (ii) there is real likelihood that the judge would have a bias in favour of one of the parties.

For example, if a judge is related to, or is a friend of, one of the parties to a dispute, there would be real likelihood of bias. It is immaterial whether a judicial decision was in *fact* biased, for as was said by Lord Chief Justice Hewart in *R v Sussex Justices, ex parte* McCarthy (1924): 'Justice should not only be done, but should manifestly and undoubtedly be seen to be done.'

As an example of pecuniary bias, we may quote:

❖ CASE EXAMPLE

***Dimes v Grand Junction Canal* (1852)**

Lord Chancellor Cottenham made decrees in a Chancery suit in favour of a canal company. Lord Cottenham held several shares in the company. *Held* (by the House of Lords): that the decrees be set aside on the ground of pecuniary interest. No bias was proved in fact, nor could it be shown that Lord Cottenham was in any way influenced by his shareholding.

As an example of likelihood of bias, we may quote:

❖ CASE EXAMPLE

***R v Sussex Justices, ex parte McCarthy* (1924)**

A was summoned before magistrates for a motoring offence. The acting clerk to the justices was a member of a firm of solicitors representing *A* in civil proceedings arising out of the same accident. The acting clerk did not advise the magistrates, but he retired with them to consider their decision. *Held*: that as the acting clerk was connected with the case in the civil action, he ought not to advise the magistrates in the criminal prosecution. Conviction accordingly quashed, even though the acting clerk took no part in the decision to convict and had not been asked by the justices to give his opinion or advice.

The second rule of natural justice is that a person has the right to be heard in their own defence. 'It is contrary to the spirit of our laws that anyone should be convicted without having an opportunity of being heard in their own defence' (*R v Benn and Church*, 1795).

The rule embraces the propositions that the party sued or prosecuted should have the opportunity to:

i know the case against them; and
ii state their case (orally or in writing).

A further rule is no doubt that parties have a right to be informed of the reason for the decision. The courts of law follow strict procedural rules that have been hammered out over the centuries to ensure fairness and are also guided by the provisions of the European Convention on Human Rights. Administrative tribunals, however, are not bound to follow these rules meticulously but must apply the general principles of justice as shown previously.

3.6.2 Supervision by the King's Bench Division

We have mentioned earlier that the monarch is 'the fountain of justice' and that one part of the jurisdiction of the King's Bench Division is supervisory. Thus, the King's Bench Division, acting for the Crown, supervises the administration of justice by inferior courts, administrative tribunals and other tribunals throughout the kingdom. Moreover, the King's Bench Division exercises supervisory control over Ministers of the Crown, civil servants, local authorities or other authorities purporting to exercise statutory powers. If such authorities act *ultra vires* (i.e. beyond the powers conferred on them by statute), the King's Bench Division may declare such excess of power to be void.

❖ CASE EXAMPLE

***Ridge v Baldwin* (1964)**

The Chief Constable of Brighton was dismissed from the force by the watch committee. The Chief Constable was not present at the meeting of the Committee, nor was he given an opportunity of stating his case. The Court of Appeal held in favour of the defendants. Ridge appealed to the House of Lords, which overruled the Court of Appeal. *Held*: that, first, there were disciplinary regulations (Police Regs) that laid down the procedure to be followed in dismissals; and, further, natural justice required that a hearing should have been given before the watch committee exercised its power. The failure to give a hearing as required by natural justice invalidated the dismissal.

The control exercised by the King's Bench Division is by means of prerogative orders of (a) mandamus, (b) prohibition and (c) certiorari. Before the **Administration of Justice (Miscellaneous Provisions) Act 1938**, these were known as prerogative writs.

a *Mandamus* is an order issuing out of the King's Bench Division commanding (mandamus; we command) a person or body to perform a duty imposed by common law or statute. The order is available to enforce administrative duties, e.g. to compel a local authority to produce its accounts for inspection by a ratepayer; or judicial duties, e.g. to compel a housing tribunal to hear and determine an appeal, or magistrates to decide a case in petty sessions.

b *Prohibition* is an order issuing out of the King's Bench Division to prohibit an inferior court or tribunal from continuing to exceed, or threatening to exceed, its jurisdiction. Thus, the order may be directed to recorders, magistrates, coroners and all statutory tribunals.

c *Certiorari* is an order removing the decision of an inferior judicial body to the King's Bench Division to have its legality inquired into. The word certiorari means 'to be informed'. The order may be used (i) to secure an impartial trial; (ii) to review an excess of jurisdiction; (iii) to challenge an *ultra vires* act; (iv) to quash a judicial decision made contrary to natural justice and (v) to correct errors of law on the face of the record.

An order of certiorari will lie 'wherever anybody of person having legal authority to determine questions affecting the rights of subjects, and having the duty to act judicially, act in excess of their legal authority' (Lord Atkin in *R v Electricity Commissioners* (1924)). Thus, it can be issued to magistrates' courts, administrative tribunals, disciplinary tribunals of the police and fire service and to arbitrators.

Applications for review were made under one of these prerogative writs, and the problem was that if the applicant claimed under the wrong writ, the whole application could fail.

In 1977 major changes were made to RSC Order 53, to provide a new form of procedure known as 'application for judicial review' that enables an applicant to seek any one or more of the remedies: certiorari, prohibition, mandamus, injunction, declaration or damages. This means that more than one remedy can be sought, and remedies can be claimed in the alternative.

3.6.3 Tribunals and Inquiries Act 1992

We have already mentioned some of the disadvantages of administrative tribunals (see p. 55–56). The wide powers granted to, and the procedures followed by, tribunals in disputes involving private rights of individuals caused considerable disquiet in the period following the Second World War. This came to a head in the *Crichel Down* case in 1954 (concerning the acquisition by a government department of land owned by a private individual), which revealed inefficient administrative procedures and apparent injustices. As a result, a committee was set up in 1955 by the Government under Sir Oliver Franks (later Lord Franks). Its terms of reference were to examine and make recommendations on (i) the constitution and working of tribunals set up by statute and (ii) the working of administrative procedures, e.g. the holding of an official inquiry or the hearing of appeals by a Minister as the result of objections, particularly in relation to the compulsory purchase of land.

This important committee reported in 1957, and some of its main recommendations passed into law in the **Tribunals and Inquiries Act 1958**. The **Tribunals and Inquiries Act 1992** (a consolidating Act) operates today.

The provisions of the Act include:

a. A *Council on Tribunals* shall be formed of 10–15 members appointed by the Lord Chancellor and Secretary of State for Scotland. (A Scottish committee is appointed to deal with Scottish matters.)
b. *Duties* of the Council are to keep under review the constitution and working of the tribunals listed in Schedule 1 of the 1971 Act and other tribunals and inquiries. The Council acts in an advisory capacity and does not itself hear appeals.
c. *Reports* of the Council are to be made annually and laid before Parliament.
d. *Chairmen* of the various tribunals to which the Act applies are selected by the appropriate Ministers from a panel of names suggested by the Lord Chancellor. This ensures that nominees have the qualifications, legal or otherwise, for the appointment.
e. *Membership* of tribunals can be terminated only with the Lord Chancellor's consent. The Parliamentary Commissioner is an *ex officio* member of the Council and the Scottish Committee.
f. *Reasons for decisions* made by tribunals must be given, if requested before or when the decision is given.
g. *Appeal* on a point of law to the High Court is given in the case of several tribunals (e.g. rent, schools and employment tribunals) where the right had not existed before the Act.
h. *Prerogative Orders*; judicial control by resort to certiorari, mandamus and prohibition is safeguarded.

3.6.4 The Inquiries Act 2005

The **Inquiries Act 2005** makes provision for any government minister to instigate an independent inquiry where it appears that particular events have given, or might give, cause for public concern.

3.7 Arbitration

Arbitration is the reference of a matter in dispute to one or more persons called arbitrators. In *Sodzawiczny v Ruhan* (2018) it was *held* that 'matter' included a defence, even if the claim to which it related did not fall within the arbitration agreement. We commonly find arbitrators, usually three, appointed to consider wage disputes between employers' and employees' organizations if both sides so agree. But arbitration may be used as an alternative proceeding to litigation. So instead of bringing an action in a court of law the parties may agree to submit a dispute to arbitration, and while it is not a court process, the decision of the arbitrator will be binding on the parties to the dispute.

The general principles upon which arbitration is based are set out in the **Arbitration Act 1996**, as follows:

a the parties are to obtain a fair resolution of disputes by an impartial tribunal without unnecessary delay
b the parties are to be given freedom to agree how to resolve their disputes
c the court is to intervene only in prescribed circumstances

Contracts often include a clause for arbitration in the event of disagreement between the parties, and an arbitration agreement is often incorporated in partnership agreements should disputes occur among partners. A clause may provide for the appointment of (a) a sole arbitrator or (b) two arbitrators (one may be appointed by each party to a dispute). Where the appointment of two arbitrators is expressly provided for, it is implied that they should appoint an umpire to take up the reference in the event of failure of the arbitrators to agree. High Court judges may now be appointed as arbitrators in certain cases. Members of the Bar are often appointed.

The *advantages* of arbitration are said to be:

a *Privacy*: the dispute, which may involve private and personal matters or confidential commercial matters, is not debated in open court.
b *Convenience*: the arbitration is held at a place and time convenient to the parties and the arbitrator(s).
c *Speedy settlement*: delays often met in litigation are overcome. Time is money in the business world today.
d *Informality*: technical procedural rules of a court of law are not rigidly applied.
e *Expert knowledge*: the arbitrator may be appointed because he or she is an expert in the matter under dispute. Frequently the matter is purely a factual one, not involving law at all.
f Where contracts involve a foreign element (see conflict of laws, p. 5), foreign courts may be more likely to enforce the arbitration award (as opposed to a court order) when the parties have clearly so agreed to arbitration.
g Expenses are generally less than litigation fees.

The *disadvantages* are said to be:

a The dispute may hinge on difficult points of law. An arbitrator may not have the requisite expertise.
b The doctrine of precedent does not apply. Each case is decided on its merits; and is therefore no guide to future similar cases.

Arbitration procedure is governed by the **Arbitration Acts** of **1950, 1975, 1979, 1996** and **2025**, together with Part V of the **Courts and Legal Services Act 1990** and the statutes that provide for statutory references. The court has unfettered discretion under the **Arbitration Act 2025** in deciding whether or not to appoint an arbitrator to a dispute. Unless the parties have agreed otherwise, the case must be decided according to the normal rules of English law and procedure. The parties often agree to dispense with strict rules of evidence. The arbitrator has the power to order discovery and inspection of documents and to examine witnesses, etc.

After hearing the evidence, it is usual for the arbitrator to notify each party when he or she has come to a decision, and they may require payment of their fees before publishing the award. The losing party may be required to pay the costs of the arbitration proceedings, including the arbitrator's fees.

If a losing party refuses to carry out the terms of an award, an order may be obtained from the High Court to compel its enforcement in the same way as a judgment of that court.

The High Court has jurisdiction on application with the consent of the arbitrator or the other parties to determine a question of law arising in the case.

In *Fleetwood Wanderers Ltd (T/A Fleetwood Town Football Club) v AFC Flyde Ltd* (2018), the claimant was successful in having an award set aside on the ground of serious irregularity by the arbitrator.

There is now a right of appeal to the High Court on a question of law arising out of the award with the consent of the parties or by leave of the court, unless validly excluded by agreement.

In this respect even where the words used are *final, binding* and *conclusive* in the arbitration clause they cannot be construed as an agreement that excluded the parties' rights of appeal in relation to a question of law under s.69 of the **Arbitration Act 1996** (*Shell Egypt West Manzala GmbH v Dana Gas Egypt Ltd* (Formerly Centurion Petroleum Corp), 2009).

The High Court is now more likely to adopt a pro-arbitration approach as illustrated by its decision in *Aquavita International SA v Indagro SA* (2022), where the High Court granted an anti-suit injunction restraining foreign proceedings that were commenced in breach of the arbitration agreement. The party which had commenced the foreign proceedings claimed that these were merely an interim measure to obtain security over a ship. However, in rejecting this argument, the Court took the view that although such interim measures were commonly allowed in support of arbitration to maintain the proceedings, the foreign proceedings in this particular case would have involved the granting of final relief which would follow from the enforcement of the parties substantive rights. If the foreign proceedings had been permitted, there would have been no relief to pursue in the arbitration, therefore preventing the parties' agreement to arbitrate.

There is a limited right of appeal with leave from the High Court to the Court of Appeal. In *Pioneer Shipping Ltd v BTP Tioxide Ltd* (1980) the Court of Appeal *held* that decisions of arbitrators in arbitrations begun after 1 August 1979 to which the 1979 Act applied, were only to be questioned on points of law if the judge gave leave, usually with no appeal from him or her to the Court of Appeal; and leave should not be given where the sole question is the proper interpretation of a commercial contract in a commercial sense, as an arbitrator is better placed to do that than a judge.

The court may remove an arbitrator for misconduct and set aside the award, and also the parties may agree upon circumstances in which an arbitrator's authority may be revoked.

The **Arbitration Act 2025** aims to modernize the arbitration process and prioritize the United Kingdom's position as a leading destination for dispute resolution by making some key reforms, including amendments to the **Arbitration Act 1996.** The Act focuses on streamlining procedures and enhancing the efficiency of arbitration.

The principal amendments introduced by the Act are as set out here:

a *The governing law of arbitration agreements*—In the absence of express agreement, the arbitration agreement by default will be governed by the law of the 'seat' of the agreement. The seat is a legal concept which refers to the jurisdiction in which the arbitration is deemed to take place.

This could mean that the governing law of the arbitration agreement could be different to the governing law of the of the contract.

b *Arbitrator immunity strengthened*—The Act strengthens the immunity of arbitrators from liability for acts or omissions in the discharge of their functions.

c *Summary disposal*—Arbitrators are given the express power to issue awards on a summary basis where they believe a party has no real prospect of succeeding on a claim or issue or in the defence of a claim or issue. This provision aims to enhance the efficiency of arbitration by allowing for the expedited resolution of unmeritorious claims.

d *Duty to disclose arbitrator conflicts*—The Act introduces a statutory duty for arbitrators to disclose any circumstances which might reasonably give rise to justifiable doubts as to their impartiality as reasonably practicable.

e *Emergency arbitrators*—the Act strengthens the role of emergency arbitrators by granting them powers similar to those of regular arbitrators, including the enforcement of peremptory orders and the ability to seek court assistance.

f *Court's powers with respect to third parties clarified*—The court's powers to support arbitration proceedings have been clarified by confirming that orders under section 44 of the **Arbitration Act 1996** in support of arbitration can be made against third parties (with those third parties having the usual rights of appeal against such orders).

g *Limits on jurisdictional challenges*—The Act provides a new framework for jurisdiction challenges whereby if a tribunal has already ruled on its own substantive jurisdiction, the court should not rehear the evidence or hear new evidence (unless it is newly available) and should not hear new objections (unless they were not previously known to the applicant or reasonably discoverable) unless the court considers that doing so is in the interests of justice.

3.8 Useful webpages

Law Reports—British and Irish Legal Information Institute BAILII (www.bailii.org)

The Supreme Court (http://supremecourt.gov.uk)

Judiciary website (www.judiciary.gov.uk/about-the-judicary-indetail/judicial+roles)

LSE Library Case Law: locating law reports (www.lse.ac.uk/library/subjectguides/law/Lawcaserep.aspx)

British Library—Help for researchers—Legal cases, law reports and judgments (England and Wales) (www.bl.uk/rehelp/findhelpsubject/busmanlaw/legalstudies/legalcases/legalcases.html)

HM Courts & Tribunals Service 'Framework Document' July 2014 at (https://assets.publishing.service.gov.uk/media/5a7efae440f0b6230268cbeb/hmcts-framework-document-2014.pdf)

3.9 Exercises

1 Outline the jurisdiction of the civil courts.

2 Describe the system of appeal in criminal cases.

3 Describe the composition and jurisdiction of: (a) county courts and (b) magistrates' courts.

4 What are the main duties of a coroner? What qualifications must he or she possess, and by whom is he or she appointed? p. 41

5 What is the importance of the **Tribunals and Inquiries Act 1992**, and what are its main provisions?

6 What part does a jury play in a court of law? What are (i) the advantages and (ii) the disadvantages of a jury trial?

7 Explain why the Criminal Defence System was established.

8 A party to arbitration proceedings considers that the arbitrator has wrongly applied the law. Advise the party how an appeal may be made and to whom.

Chapter 4

Procedure

The following is an outline of the procedure applicable to civil and criminal cases.

Key points

- the distinction between civil and criminal procedure
- operation of case management in civil proceedings
- commencement of civil proceedings
- enforcements of civil proceedings
- process by summons or warrant in magistrates' court
- meaning and use of bail
- indictment and arraignment in criminal proceedings

4.1 Juries

a The criminal jury

The criminal jury consisting of 12 persons of either sex is found in the Crown Court (see p. 45). Juries are not used in magistrates' courts. The sworn duty of the jury is to 'faithfully try the defendant and give a true verdict according to the evidence' (Criminal Procedure Rules 2025 Rule 25.6).

The defendant has a right of challenge to the array of jurors or to individual jurors. The Crown has a right to a provisional challenge to 'stand by' jurors. Those jurors objected to will be asked to stand down, and others will be empanelled to take their places.

Formerly the verdict of a jury had to be unanimous, but since the **Criminal Justice Act 1967,** a majority verdict may be allowed. The court cannot, however, accept a majority verdict unless the jury has been deliberating for not less than two hours, when the verdict need not then be unanimous if: (i) in a case where there are not less than 11 jurors, ten of them agree or (ii) in a case where there are ten jurors, nine of them agree. It must be stated in open court as to the number of jurors who respectively agreed to and dissented from the verdict (*R v Reynolds*, 1981).

Where a juror dies or is ill, provided that both sides agree and the number of jurors is not reduced below ten, the case may continue, and a verdict may be given.

DOI: 10.4324/9781003422808-4

b The civil jury

The civil jury is now a rarity. The general rule following the **Administration of Justice (Miscellaneous Provisions) Act 1938** is that the civil court has discretion in its use of a jury. A jury may, however, be ordered on the application of either party in cases of defamation, malicious prosecution, false imprisonment and cases of fraud (called deceit—see p. 271), unless the court considers that the trial will involve prolonged examination of documents or accounts, or a scientific or local investigation.

In actions in the Chancery Division, juries are not used. In defended divorce cases or contested probate actions, a jury may be applied for.

In High Court cases the jury comprises 12 persons and a majority verdict may be accepted. In county court actions, the jury numbers eight. In coroners' courts, the jury comprises from seven to 11 persons; the coroner may accept a majority verdict, provided that the number of dissentients does not exceed two.

When a judge sits without a jury, he or she determines questions of law and fact.

Qualifications of jurymen. The **Criminal Justice Act 1972** abolished the former property qualification for jury service in England and Wales. Further qualifications were introduced by the **Juries Act 1974**.

- The basic qualification is that of citizenship as evidenced by inclusion in the Electoral Register. Anyone between the ages of 18 and 70 registered as an elector who has lived here for five years or more since the age of 13 becomes liable for jury service.
- Payments in respect of jury service for travelling, subsistence and financial loss are made to jurors.
- Anyone who has been imprisoned in the past ten years is disqualified from serving on a jury as is anyone who has been on probation during the previous five years.
    - As a result of recommendations made by Sir Robert Auld in his Review of the Criminal Courts (2001) the Government introduced the **Criminal Justice act 2003,** whereby s. 321 and Sched. 33 amended the **Juries Act 1974**. This Act now provides that potential jury members must be
        - aged 18 to 70;
        - on the electoral register;
        - resident in the UK, Channel Islands or the Isle of Man for at least five years since the age of 13;
        - not a mentally disordered person; and
        - not disqualified from jury service.

        It also abolished all the grounds for exclusion from jury service that had formerly existed. The effect of the 2003 Act was to increase substantially the pool from which jurors are chosen by making more people eligible, such as lawyers and medical practitioners from 2004, than had previously been the case.

The *advantages* of trial by jury may be said to be:

a a finding of fact is better left to several persons than to one person
b juries represent the verdict of ordinary people
c there is public confidence in jury trials

The *disadvantages* of trial by jury are:

a jurors of 18 may be too inexperienced for jury service
b jurors have no physical or educational test for their task

c jurors may be too easily impressed and swayed by advocacy of experienced counsel
d juries are prone to leniency to an accused in certain cases, e.g. manslaughter by motor car
e local prejudice may exist in certain trials, and this may be reflected in local jurors
f corrupt influences, threats and intimidation from outside parties
g some trials are long and may cause inconvenience to jurors, who may suffer financially; the cost to the State will also be high

In *R v Abdroikof* (2007), the House of Lords considered membership of the jury of people who ordinarily work within the criminal justice system. It *held* that people should not sit as a juror if there was a conflict of interest which could lead to the possibility of them being regarded as biased.

The Law Commission Report 2013 recommended the creation of a new criminal offence for jurors guilty of conducting their own personal research during a trial. This was implemented by s.71 of the **Criminal Justice and Courts Act 2015.**

4.2 Legal services

The **Legal Aid Act 1949** created a scheme for providing legal aid to people within certain means limits, the expense to be paid out of the Legal Aid Fund financed by the State. A later Act made provision also for legal advice. The scheme was then amended by the Acts of 1974, 1979 and 1982 and the regulations made under them.

In 1988 a new Act was passed, the **Legal Aid Act 1988**, which introduced a new Legal Aid Scheme that came into force on 1 April 1989. This was largely an enabling Act (giving the Government the power to make changes to the Scheme by regulation).

The provisions of this Act were reinforced by the **Legal Aid, Sentencing and Punishment of Offenders Act 2012**. This incorporated the appointment of a Director of Legal Aid Casework who is given wide-reaching powers relating to legal aid in respect of both civil and criminal proceedings. One outcome of this legislation was the abolition (by ss. 38 and 39 of the Act) of the Legal Services Commission.

Note: The Legal Services Commission had been established by the **Access to Justice Act 1999** to replace the former legal aid system.

4.2.1 Legal Services Commission

The **Access to Justice Act 1999** replaced the former legal aid system by creating a Legal Services Commission to develop and administer a new system of legal aid in England and Wales.

In accordance with the Act the Commission has responsibility for two further services, the Community Legal Service (CLS), which deals with civil and family law cases, and the Criminal Defence Service (CDS), which provides legal assistance and representation to persons involved in criminal proceedings.

4.2.2 Community Legal Service

The Community Legal Service, which replaced the former legal aid scheme for civil litigation, is funded by a Community Legal Service fund. This is used to secure provision of appropriate legal services for the conduct of civil and family litigation. The Act states that such provision must be made within the resources made available to the Community Legal Service in accordance with 'priorities' set after consultation with the Lord Chancellor and taking into account the need for services that will effectively meet the needs of litigants. Included under this description are a wide variety of services, such as the provision of general information about the law and legal services, including the application of the law in particular services and the provision of help in the prevention or settling of disputes and the enforcement of decisions because of these actions.

The Community Legal Service is excluded from providing services that are funded as part of the Criminal Defence Service. It is also excluded from providing any assistance for any actions relating to a wide variety of circumstances that could give rise to a legal claim. These are specified in the Act as including negligence claims involving damage to property or personal injury (with some exceptions): conveyancing, boundary disputes, making of wills, trusts, defamation or malicious falsehood and matters of company or partnership law.

4.2.3 Criminal Defence Service

The Criminal Defence Service was established to maintain and develop a service in the interests of justice, for the active assistance and representation of persons who have been accused of or involved in committing a crime. Not only does this include trial, sentence and appeal, but also binding over, extradition (in certain circumstances), criminal contempt and proceedings involving the variation and discharge of supervision orders under the Children and Young People's Legislation.

In accordance with s. 58 of the **Courts and Legal Services Act (CLSA) 1990**, the Lord Chancellor was permitted to introduce conditional fee arrangements regarding civil actions, with criminal cases, family cases or those involving children being excluded. This meant that lawyers could agree to represent a client on the basis that they would receive no fee at all, but if the case was successful, they would receive double the amount they would normally receive.

This is known as the contingency fees scheme, as the lawyer's fee is contingent (conditional) upon him or her winning the case on behalf of the client.

Law Centres. Law Centres are local centres, with solicitors employed on a full-time basis, who will handle free of charge a person's case from start to finish, including representation in court or at a tribunal, if necessary. There are 14 in London, distributed in the Boroughs, and there are three outside London in Birmingham, Cardiff and Manchester. Finance for the centres is provided by local authorities and through the Government's Urban Aid Programme for areas in special need. Some are staffed with community social workers to deal with special social problems best settled through social or community means rather than by legal action.

Legal Advice Centres. These centres are for giving advice. If the applicant needs further help, they will be advised where to go, e.g. to a solicitor operating under the Legal Aid Scheme who will be able to devote adequate time to the applicant's case. There are about 40 legal advice centres in London, and about 50 outside London. Some operate in conjunction with the Citizens' Advice Bureau.

4.3 Laypersons in the courts

As to administration of the law today, we may note particularly the part played by laypersons (a) as justices of the peace, (b) as jurors and (c) as lay assessors who assist a professional judge or lawyer acting judicially in the special courts and administrative tribunals already described.

4.3.1 Justices of the peace

A description of the composition of the magistrates' courts and Crown Courts has already been given. All we need to note here is that there are some 28,000 lay justices regularly adjudicating on a wide variety of matters and performing numerous administrative duties. These justices deal with more than 98 per cent of the criminal cases in Britain. The relevant legislation is the **Justices of the Peace Act 1997.**

Lay justices appointed after 1 January 1966 are required to undergo training in the basic duties of their office. This does not render them lawyers but assists them in understanding the meaning of 'acting judicially' so that they may more efficiently administer justice to the local people, from whose numbers they are drawn and whose public interests they serve.

4.3.2 Juries

A detailed description of the different kinds of juries is given on pp. 66–68. It should be borne in mind that juries are composed of laypersons on whose shoulders rests the final determination of verdicts in criminal cases.

4.3.3 Lay assessors in special courts

Examples of this form of participation are found in:

a *The Admiralty Court of the Queen's Bench Division*. This is presided over by a High Court judge with jurisdiction to decide shipping disputes, collisions at sea, etc. There is no jury, but in suitable cases (e.g. negligent navigation), the judge may call on the assistance of two nautical assessors (Elder Brethren of Trinity House) who are competent to advise on technical maritime matters.

b *The Restrictive Practices Court*. The jurisdiction of this court has been dealt with on p. 41. It is a superior Court of Record and is composed of professional judges and persons experienced in commerce and business. Each court sits with a High Court judge and two laypersons.

c *Administrative Tribunals*. These have an increasingly important part to play in the lives of all people, and mention may be made of Rent Tribunals, National Insurance Tribunals, National Insurance Industrial Injuries Tribunals, Pensions Tribunals, National Health Service Tribunals, Transport Tribunals and those of the Area Traffic Commissioners.

Although the constitution of each may vary in detail, the common factor is the presence of laypersons, usually drawn from bodies such as local authorities, employers' organizations and employees' organizations. Usually the chairperson is legally qualified (**Tribunals and Inquiries Act 1992**), but the presence of the laypersons ensures that tribunals have the benefit of industrial or other experience.

4.4 The new civil procedure

General. Persons considering themselves to have a civil claim against another will normally consult their solicitor. If unable to afford this, they may first visit a Citizens' Advice Bureau and take advantage of the facilities available under the **Access to Justice Act 1999** (see p. 68). There is no obligation to consult a solicitor, but legal procedure is technical and detailed, and it is a matter of common sense to take advice from those who are experienced and qualified to give it.

- The first step for the solicitor is to ascertain whether a cause of action is disclosed or whether the matter may be resolved by a straightforward letter to, for example, a debtor asking for payment. This may be all that is required.
- If legal action is needed, the next step is to see whether the action will be taken in the county court or the High Court (the jurisdiction of each is dealt with on p. 41 and 43). No court can entertain an action unless it is legally empowered to do so.

The **Civil Procedure Act 1997** amends the law as to civil procedure in England and Wales. The Act provides for the making of Civil Procedure Rules (CPR) governing the practice and procedure to be followed in the civil division of the Court of Appeal, the High Court and county courts.

The origins of the reforms can be traced back to 28 March 1994, when Lord Woolf was appointed by the Lord Chancellor, Lord Mackay of Clashfern, to review the rules and procedures of the civil courts in England and Wales. The aims of the review were stated as being:

- the improvement of access to justice and reducing the cost of litigation;
- reducing the complexity of the rules and modernization of terminology and
- the removal of unnecessary distinctions of practice and procedure.

As a result of Lord Woolf's Interim Report published in June 1995 and his Final Report in July 1996, new rules were proposed that, having been amended, were promulgated as the Civil Procedure Rules (CPR) 1998, which came into effect on 26 April 1999.

The overriding objective of the new CPR was stated in CPR r. 1.1 as enabling the court to deal with cases justly, which should mean that parties would be on an equal footing: the saving of expense and the dealing with a case in a way that should be proportionate to the consent of the many involved, the importance of the case, the complexity of the issues, and the financial position of each of the parties. It should also ensure that it was dealt with expeditiously and fairly, at the same time allotting an appropriate share of the court's resources.

The person making a claim in a civil action previously called 'the plaintiff' has now been re-designated 'the claimant' while for those claims that were previously commenced by the issue of a writ, a formal legal document issued under the court seal setting out the nature of the claim, this has now been replaced by a claim form. This will incorporate the nature of the claim and the remedy that the claimant is seeking.

The new CPR is the same for both the county court and the High Court (and also the Civil Division of the Court of Appeal).

The only exceptions to the application of the CPR are:

- insolvency proceedings
- probate proceedings
- prize court proceedings
- Court of Protection proceedings
- family proceedings and adoption proceedings

The two overall themes incorporated within this new civil process are the need for greater judicial control over proceedings and the introduction of procedures that will demand the early identification of the real issues of the case.

In accordance with the Recommendations of the Woolf Final Report great emphasis has been laid on the control of litigation moving from the litigant to the court (i.e. judicial case management).

4.4.1 Case management

There is now a positive duty placed on the court to manage cases. Rule 1.4(1) states that 'The court must further the overriding objective by actively managing cases. The rule goes on to explain what this management involves.

CPR r. 1.4(2) Active case management includes:

a encouraging the parties to co-operate with each other in the conduct of the proceedings
b identifying the issues at an early stage
c deciding promptly which issues need full investigation and trial and accordingly disposing summarily of the others
d deciding the order in which issues are to be resolved

e encouraging the parties to use an alternative dispute resolution procedure if the court considers that appropriate and facilitating the use of such procedure
f helping the parties to settle the whole or part of the case
g fixing timetables or otherwise controlling the progress of the case
h considering whether the likely benefits of taking a particular step justify the cost of taking it
i dealing with as many aspects of the case as it can on the same occasion
j dealing with the case without the parties needing to attend court
k making use of technology
l giving directions to ensure that the trial of a case proceeds quickly and efficiently

Case management decisions are generally dealt with by masters for cases proceeding in the Royal Courts of Justice and by district judges in High Court, district registry and county court cases. The governing rule (CPR r. 2.4) gives the court a great deal of flexibility, allowing performance by any judicial officer, whether a district judge, master or judge, subject to any specific contrary provision in any enactment, rule or practice direction.

The preliminary stage of case management is mainly concerned with the allocation of a defended claim to the appropriate track. There is no 'automatic' allocation; each case requires a judicial decision. However, the general rule is in r. 26.7. Note in particular that the court will not allocate a claim to a 'lower' track unless all the parties' consent (r. 26.7(3)).

Allocation to the track is the main but not the only function at this preliminary stage of case management. The court will also consider striking out a statement of case (r. 3.4), summary judgment (r. 24.4) and whether to give case management directions pursuant to Part 27, 28 or 29 as appropriate.

The CPR therefore requires that the parties are required, as soon as a defendant has been filed, to complete an allocation questionnaire that will provide the court with details relating to the progress that has been made with seeking a resolution of the dispute with the other party, the preparation of evidence for the trial, together with relevant information relating to the likely length of the trial and an estimate as to costs.

This will also assist the court in allocating a case to one of the three tracks for an appropriate court hearing.

The small claims track will normally be limited to claims of £5,000 or under, excluding personal injury claims or housing disrepair claims that exceed £1,000, tenancy harassment or unlawful eviction claims and claims involving allegations of dishonesty.

A fast track is the normal track for claims broadly falling between £5,000 and £15,000 and which it is estimated will be disposed of by a trial that would not normally exceed a day.

The multi-track is the normal track for any claim not allocated to the small claims track or the fast track. Claims on the small claims or fast track will be in the county court, while claims on the multi-track will be in either the county court or the High Court.

4.4.2 Pre-action protocols

These are statements of understanding between legal practitioners and others about pre-action practice and which are approved by a relevant practice direction.

In his final Access to Justice Report, Lord Woolf recommended the development of pre-action protocols to build on and increase the benefits of early but well-informed settlements that genuinely satisfy both parties to a dispute (Ch. 10, para. 1).

The protocols are intended to provide a simple system for setting out guidelines of best practice by the provision of timetables for the exchange of information before litigation and thereby assisting each party in knowing the case that may have to be met.

If court proceedings do subsequently arise, the intention is that litigation will proceed quickly and efficiently from the issue of the claim because of the parties' compliance with the normal pre-action protocol.

Currently there are two pre-action protocols in operation. These are for Personal Injury Claims and for the Resolution of Clinical Disputes, both of which came into effect with the Civil Procedure Rules 1998 (CPR).

4.4.3 Commencement of proceedings

Part 7 of the CPR at r. 7.2(1) states that proceedings are started when the court issues a claim form at the request of the claimant. The claim form is now the sole form of originating process for all claims in the High Court and County Court. The term 'claim form' has replaced the terms 'High Court Writ' and 'County Court Summons'. In the new CPR law cases, it is the claimant (formerly a plaintiff) who makes a claim. A defendant may now respond by filing a defence to which the claimant may respond by filing a reply. The previous term 'pleadings' has been replaced by 'statements of case' and 'statement of claim' has been replaced by 'particulars of claim'. In accordance with Part 18 of the CPR (18.1(1)) the term 'obtaining further information' has been replaced by 'further and better particulars'.

4.4.4 The claim form

The standard method of commencing a claim under the CPR is by the court issuing a claim form prepared for or by the claimant, at the request of the claimant (r. 7.2(l)). The claim form is required by the CPR to set out essential details of the claim, incorporating a concise statement of the nature of the cause of action and a statement of the remedy sought. The claimant is also required to provide rather fuller particulars of the claim that must include a concise statement of the facts upon which he or she relies. Where practicable, the particulars of the claim should be set out in the claim form, although they can be provided in a separate document accompanying the claim form or filed separately (now described as 'statements of case').

4.4.5 Statements of truth

R. 22.1(l)(a) requires that every statement of case, a response complying with an order under r. 18.1 to provide further information or any witness statement, it must be verified by a statement of truth. The justification for this requirement is that it provides some guarantee that the statement is made with an honest belief as to the accuracy of its contents. In addition, in deletion to statements of case it means that it is less likely to include assertions that are groundless or speculative and, in certain circumstances, that a statement of case may be relied on as evidence.

In accordance with r. 32.14, in certain circumstances, a false statement made in a document verified by a statement of truth may lead to a liability for contempt of court.

4.4.6 Part 8—alternative procedure for claims

The Part 8 procedure is intended as an alternative procedure for claims where the nature of the relief or remedy sought, or the lack of factual dispute, would make the standard procedure initiated under Part 7 procedure unnecessarily cumbersome. It is intended to provide for a speedy resolution of claims without the need for statements of case, disclosure or expert evidence, etc. PD8, para 1.4 gives examples of the types of claims where this Part 8 procedure may be used, including where:

a a claim by or against a child or patient has been settled before the commencement of proceedings and the sole purpose of the claim is to obtain the approval of the court to the settlement
b a claim for provisional damages has been settled before the commencement of proceedings and the sole purpose of the claim is to obtain a consent judgment
c there is a claim for a summary order for possession against named or unnamed defendants occupying land or premises without the licence or consent of the person claiming possession, and the claim is unlikely to involve a substantial dispute of fact

In the event of the defendant believing it should not be used because there is a substantial dispute of fact and the use of the Part 8 procedure is not required or permitted by a rule or practice directions, the defendant nevertheless files an acknowledgement of service while at the same time proceeding to make an application for an order that the court does not have jurisdiction. Where this contains matters of evidence, it should be verified by a statement of truth.

In the event of the court upholding such an objection it has the power to order the claim to continue as if it were an ordinary claim not governed by Part 8.

All Part 8 claims are allocated to the multi-track (CPR, r. 8.9 (c)), but Part 26 (Case Management) does not apply and there is no requirement for parties to complete allocation questionnaires.

Most Part 8 claims will be disposed of with a hearing, although the court has discretion to deal with claims without a hearing or without the parties needing to attend court.

4.4.7 The trial

The trial date having been fixed, the action proceeds on the date named and, in the court, named.

Many things may cause delays, e.g. the illness of the claimant, defendant or an important witness and similar matters, so that adjournments may have to be made.

If, after all the documents have been served, the defendant does not appear at the court on the day named, the trial may proceed in their absence and judgment may be entered for the claimant, usually with costs. If, however, the claimant does not appear at the court and gives no explanation for their absence the action will generally be struck out for want of prosecution. The action may be reinstated for sufficient cause on the claimant's application.

On the assumption that both parties are present with their witnesses and their respective solicitors or counsel, the steps to be followed during the trial will take the following form.

At the trial before the judge, the usual procedure is as follows:

a Claimant's lawyer makes an opening speech, describing the issue to be resolved and explaining how it is proposed to prove the points at issue.
b Claimant's lawyer calls the claimant's witnesses and examines them. They are then cross-examined by the defendant's lawyer, in order to test the truth of what each witness says on oath.
c Defendant's lawyer calls the defendant's witnesses, who testify about what they know of the matter. Defendant's lawyer examines the witnesses, and they are cross-examined by the claimant's lawyer.
d Defendant's lawyer makes a speech to the judge, comments on the points relevant to the issue and, if a point of law is concerned, the statute or cases are brought to the notice of the judge. He or she asks for judgment in their favour.
e Claimant's lawyer makes a speech in reply, giving the claimant's side of the story, commenting on the relevant factors, arguing points of law and asking for judgment in favour of the claimant.

f The judge thereupon makes a decision. If sitting alone, the judge will give judgment, which is then entered on the court records. If a jury is present, the judge will address the jury on the facts and the law and ask them to consider their verdict.

4.4.8 Steps in a default action

A claimant claiming a debt or a specified sum of money (formerly a liquidated demand) must proceed by default action, not by an ordinary action. Judgment may then be entered by the claimant in default without the case going to trial if the defendant fails to take the appropriate steps, i.e. an acknowledgement of service, file a defence, counterclaim or admission, or pay into the court the sum claimed with costs. Even where the claim is for a debt or specified sum of money, there are some exceptions to the stated rule and an ordinary action must be brought, e.g. against a person under disability or to recover a sum secured by a mortgage.

The same initial steps must be taken by the claimant's solicitor as those taken in ordinary actions described previously. However, after the defendant has been served with a request filed under r. 12.4(1) and the claim form, the defendant may take one of the several courses:

a If the defendant, after receiving the request, does nothing within 14 days (i.e. the defendant defaults) the claimant may enter judgment.
b If, after receiving the request, the defendant pays into court either the whole amount claimed or an amount that the claimant is prepared to accept in settlement, the action will, in most cases, be stayed.
c If the defendant admits the whole, or part, of the debt claimed at a specified rate (say £40 per month) and the claimant (i) accepts the amount admitted and (ii) agrees to accept the mode of payment, judgment will be entered for the claimant.
d If the defendant admits the whole of the claim but the claimant does not agree to accept the mode of payment (say £40 per month), a date will be set by the court for the decision of the question of the mode of payment. Much depends on the means of the defendant about which inquiries will be made.
e If the defendant admits only a part of the claim, and the claimant does not wish to accept the amount admitted by the defendant and the form of payment that the defendant proposes, the court will set aside or vary a default judgment.
f If the defendant does not admit the claim at all, the court will again set aside or vary a default judgment.

4.4.9 The enforcement of county court judgments

There are, of course, rights of appeal against the judgments given in a county court. Generally, however, once judgment is given in the county court that is the end of the matter. The sum adjudged to be paid to the claimant is sent to the court; or to the claimant by the defendant; or, if the dispute is over the possession of land, the possessor either stays on in occupation or removes in favour of the claimant.

Where the judgment is ignored, however, we have to consider how the judgment is enforced by the court. There are two general kinds of enforcement: (a) those where a judgment is given for a sum of money and (b) other judgments (e.g. for possession of land or a chattel).

a Enforcing judgments for a sum of money

The following methods of enforcement are available:

i *Warrant of execution*

The warrant is issued under the authority of the court directing the bailiffs to seize sufficient of the property of the debtor, including money, negotiable instruments and goods, and to sell the same if need be to satisfy the amount of the judgment plus costs. The clothing and bedding of the debtor and his or her family and the tools of trade to a prescribed value may not be seized.

ii *Attachment of earnings order*

Under the **Attachment of Earnings Act 1971**, a county court is empowered to issue this order, which directs the employer of the judgment debtor to make periodical payments from the debtor's earnings and to pay the amounts so deducted to the collecting officer of the court at certain specified intervals. The sums so paid over by the employer are allocated to the judgment creditor in satisfaction of his or her judgment.

iii *Bankruptcy proceedings*

Where the judgment is above a prescribed sum, the judgment creditor may serve a bankruptcy notice on the debtor. If the latter does not pay the sum claimed, this omission will constitute an 'act of bankruptcy' and proceedings will ensue in the normal way.

iv *Garnishee proceedings*

This form of enforcement is available where a third party owes a sum of money to the judgment debtor. Thus, where *A*, the judgment creditor, is owed £100 by B, the judgment debtor, and X (a third party) owes £100 to B, garnishee proceedings may be issued against X, the garnishee, to pay the sum of £100 to *A*, the judgment creditor, instead of to B. The debt is thereby extinguished, and the judgment is satisfied.

v *Appointment of a receiver*

Where a judgment debtor refuses to pay the judgment debt and the debtor has lands or houses that yield rents and profits, the court may, on the application of the judgment creditor, appoint a receiver, who is thereupon an officer of the court to collect the rents and profits. These are applied to reduce the debt due. When the whole of the judgment debt (plus costs) is paid, the appointment of the receiver ends.

vi *Charging order*

Where the judgment debtor owns land and certain other forms of property, the judgment creditor may apply to the court for a charging order in accordance with the **Charging Order Act 1979** (as amended), the effect of which is that the property owned by the debtor is charged with the payment of the sum due on the judgment (plus costs). The property subject to the charge may be sold in settlement of the judgment debt, any surplus being handed over to the judgment debtor.

vii *Judgment summons*

In a few cases, a court may order a debtor to attend a hearing to provide information about their finances or explain why they haven't paid.

viii *Administration order*

Providing for the administration of an insolvent judgment debtor's estate by the court.

b Enforcing other judgments

Sometimes a county court is called upon to decide ownership of land or goods that the defendant refuses to give up in favour of the rightful owner or possessor. The following authorize enforcement in such cases.

i *Warrants of delivery or possession*

A warrant may be issued by the court to authorize the bailiff to take by force, if need be, the goods to be delivered to the person adjudged to have rightful ownership. Similarly, where a judgment for the recovery of land has been obtained, and the defendant will not give up the land, a warrant may be issued by the court to the bailiff to enter on the land and place the rightful owner in possession. Any interference with the bailiff is a punishable offence.

ii *Warrant of attachment*
A warrant may be issued by the court to attach the defendant for contempt. The warrant authorizes the bailiff to arrest the defendant and convey him or her to the prison named. This form of enforcement is available where a defendant willfully fails to comply with an order of the court.

4.4.10 Costs

The general rule regarding the costs involved in taking and defending actions, which include barristers' fees and solicitors' charges, together with court fees and other disbursements, are in the discretion of the court. Usually, the court orders the costs to be paid by the party losing the action.

4.4.11 Enforcement of judgments in the High Court

Once a judgment is made by the judge, it follows that the judgment will have to be obeyed. If the party, against whom judgment is given, pays the damages and costs awarded against them, that is the end of the matter. Sometimes the judgment is not obeyed, and the party to whom the money is due or, if land is in dispute, the party entitled to possession, will have to take steps, at his or her own expense, to enforce the judgment. There are two classes: judgments for payment of money, and judgments for other matters such as possession of land or goods. Writs of execution are issued by the court, as follows:

a *Fieri facias*. This is a writ that is directed to the sheriff commanding that out of the goods and chattels of the debtor the sheriff 'do cause to be made the sum endorsed on the writ' with interest and costs. The sheriff who acts through bailiffs thereby becomes entitled to take possession of the goods of the debtor, except the wearing apparel, bedding and tools of trade to a prescribed value, and to sell the goods in satisfaction of the writ. The sheriff can enter the lands of the debtor to do this.
b *Garnishee order*. This is like that described on p. 76.
c *Charging order* (see p. 76).
d *Appointment of a receiver* (see p. 76).
e *Sequestration*. The writ of sequestration authorizes commissioners (up to four) to enter the debtor's lands, to take possession and collect the rent and profits from the debtor's real and personal estate and to hold the land and personal estate until the debtor has paid the amount due. This writ is available where the debtor is in contempt of court by refusing or neglecting to obey the order of the court to pay the specified amount.
f *Attachment of earnings*. This is available to the plaintiff only where the defendant neglects or refuses to obey a maintenance order made by the High Court.
g *Committal to prison*. A rare method, but available where the defendant neglects or refuses to obey an order of the court.
h For possession of land or delivery of goods.

4.5 Criminal procedure

This section deals briefly with the procedure followed in the prosecution of a case in (a) a magistrates' court and (b) the Crown Court.

All criminal prosecutions are, in theory, taken in the name of the Crown and are cited: *Rex* (or *Regina*) *v Smith* (defendant). That form is followed in Crown Court proceedings. In summary trials, the Crown Prosecution Service will institute proceedings as prosecutor against a defendant (see p. 87).

But a private citizen may institute criminal proceedings. The **Criminal Procedure and Investigations Act 1996** covers disclosure, the issues that may be dealt with in advance at a preparatory hearing and the preparation of a code of practice regarding the conduct of criminal investigations.

4.6 Proceedings in magistrates' courts

4.6.1 Process by summons

Refer to page 339 and note the distinction between summary offences and indictable offences. This section deals with the procedure followed in the prosecution of a summary offence. These are by far the most numerous and include road traffic offences of all sorts.

Let us assume a simple case. X exceeds the speed limit when driving a car on the highway. X is stopped by a police officer who informs X that he or she will be reported for summons.

What happens now?

- The police officer submits the report and, from this, an **information** is prepared, the first legal process. An information is merely a statement that may be oral, but is usually written, setting out the details of the alleged offence.
- From the information, the clerk to the justices prepares a summons, which is signed by a JP.
- The summons is then served on the defendant. Service may be effected simply by handing X a copy personally, or more usually by sending a copy by post. The summons informs X of the date, time and place of the alleged offence and the statute (or common law rule) infringed. The summons commands the attendance of X at a court on a date named in the summons.
- In most cases the defendant X must appear at court. Indeed, if X does not attend the court the magistrates may issue a warrant for his or her arrest. Note that they *may* do so.
- In minor offences, however, the **Magistrates' Courts Act 1980** provides a procedure by which a defendant may avoid attendance at court by sending a form through the post to the clerk of the court pleading guilty. He or she may make any written explanation, which will be considered by the court. This saves much time, and the case is quickly disposed of, usually by a fine.

  Note: The **Judicial Review And Courts Act 2022** introduces a new automatic online conviction and standard statutory penalty (AOCSSP) procedure for specified summary only non-imprisonable offences, which will give defendants who wish to plead guilty the option of having their entire case completed online without the involvement of the magistrates' court. It enables prosecutors to provide defendants who are prosecuted for summary-only offences that are also initiated by police charge (in person at a police station) with the option to indicate a plea in writing/online and proceed view the existing procedure (referred to as 'pleading guilty by post') that is available under section 12 of the **Magistrates Court Act 1980** ('the MCA 1980').
- In the earlier illustration, if pleading 'Not Guilty', X (the defendant) should attend the court on the day named. He or she may consult a solicitor to assist in defence. On the facts, however, there is not likely to be a defence. If X was speeding due to being in a hurry to visit a seriously ill parent, X may consider this a defence. It is not a defence, however, though it may be a mitigating circumstance that the court may take into consideration when fixing the sentence if it finds the defendant guilty.
- A defendant who strongly wishes to contest the case will attend the court on the day named. When the magistrates are ready to hear the case, X's name will be called out. X will be directed to a position in the court (see diagram on p. 47). The alleged offence is read out to the defendant, who is asked to plead. X pleads 'Not Guilty'.

- First, the solicitor will give a short outline of the facts and then ask the police officer to enter the witness box and, after being sworn, to give evidence. X (or the solicitor) will be invited to ask any questions about the evidence of the officer.
- The solicitor for the prosecution may re-examine the officer to clear up any doubts raised by X (or X's solicitor).
- Any other prosecution witnesses will then be called to give their evidence and may be cross-examined by X or the defence solicitor.
- The prosecution is then at an end.
- X will now be invited to do one of two things: (a) to go into the witness box and be sworn on oath to give evidence of what happened or (b) to make a statement from outside the witness box giving his or her side of the story.
- If X adopts course (a), they will be liable to be cross-examined by the prosecuting solicitor to test the truth of what X says. X may then be re-examined by his or her own solicitor, if they have one. Otherwise, after both sides, i.e. the police (the prosecution) and X (the defendant) have given their versions, the justices announce their verdict of Guilty or Not Guilty.
- As to course (b), it will be apparent that the statement of a defendant who decides not to go into the witness box will not be as convincing as that of one who is prepared to testify in the witness box. But note—this decision is the defence's alone, and he or she is not forced to take either course. The defendant may say nothing at all.
- In the example given, the magistrates will decide on a penalty. It may be a fine, but this is a matter for the court, and there may be circumstances in which the court may give an absolute discharge.
- To sum up, this is the simplest example of a case often before a magistrates' court. In many cases in these courts, there are more serious matters, such as driving a car to the danger of the public, when there may be several witnesses for the defence and several for the prosecution. The burden of proving the guilt of the accused beyond reasonable doubt rests on the prosecution throughout the trial. The accused person is presumed innocent until the contrary is proved.

4.6.2 Process by warrant

A warrant is another means of starting a prosecution. Let us assume that X has stolen £100 from Y and that X has absconded.

- Y reports the matter to the police and gives a description of the offence and the offender.
- Theft is an 'arrestable offence'.
- After the police investigation, the police may apply to the magistrates for a warrant. First, an information in writing and on oath must be laid by the police before a magistrate, who may then issue a warrant for the arrest of X.
- The warrant authorizes the police to whom it is directed to arrest X. The warrant may direct that X, on arrest, be granted bail. This is entirely in the discretion of the magistrate.
- If X is arrested in some other part of the UK, he or she will be handed over by the police of that area to the police of the area where the offence occurred.
- X will then be brought before the court whence the warrant was issued to answer the charge of theft. The powers of a police officer regarding stop and search; entry search and seizure; arrest; detention and questioning, are now contained in the **Police and Criminal Evidence Act 1984**.
- On being brought before the court, the magistrates will give X a choice of being tried either by (a) the magistrates' court or (b) the Crown Court, since theft is an offence triable either way. (Sections 21, 22 and 23 of the **Criminal Law Act 1977** provide that in the case of

offences triable either way, even if the magistrates consider that the offence is more suitable for summary trial, they must commit to the Crown Court unless the accused consents to summary trial; that if they consider the offence more suitable for trial on indictment they must commit to the Crown Court; and that certain offences, e.g. criminal damage, where the value involved does not exceed £200 must be tried summarily.) Let us assume that the defendant opts for (a).

- The charge will be read out, and he or she will be asked to plead Guilty or Not Guilty. If the defendant does not plead one or the other or says anything that casts doubt on the plea of Guilty, a plea of Not Guilty will be entered.
- X will be given facilities to consult a solicitor who will advise on what course of action to take and how the defence should be conducted, i.e. obtaining evidence and witnesses for the defence. If he or she is unable to afford a solicitor, they may be granted by the court the services of a solicitor (see legal aid and advice, p. 68).
- X may apply for bail or for an adjournment to enable arrangements for a defence to be made with the solicitor. These matters are decided by the court.

When the case is ready for trial, the case proceeds in the normal way: the prosecuting solicitor outlines the main facts of the case.

- Witnesses are then called who are examined and may then be cross-examined.
- In accordance with the **Youth Justice and Criminal Evidence Act 1999,** provision is made for the protection of certain categories of witnesses (other than the accused), such as a juvenile (under 17 years of age) or a person suffering from a mental or physical disorder, from cross-examination by an accused.
- These special measures may include the witness giving evidence from behind a screen, by means of a live link or a video.
- Prosecution solicitor addresses the court.
- The defence solicitor addresses the court, calls witnesses who give evidence. They are examined, cross-examined and may be re-examined to clear up any points raised by the prosecution.
- The prosecution solicitor addresses the court, followed by the defence solicitor.
- At the conclusion of the case, the magistrates may retire to consider their verdict.
- The magistrates will, if they find the defendant guilty, then hear the antecedents (i.e. the history) of the accused. The magistrates then decide the appropriate penalty. If the magistrates find the case not proved, they will return a verdict of Not Guilty, and the defendant will go free from the court.
- A warrant of arrest may not be issued against a person 17 or over unless the offence is (i) indictable, (ii) is punishable by imprisonment or (iii) the address of the defendant is not sufficiently established for a summons (to be served on him) **(Criminal Justice Act 1967,** s. 24(2)).

Note: Anonymity of witnesses—the **Criminal Evidence (Witness Anonymity) Act 2008** makes statutory provision for the courts to grant witness anonymity orders in criminal proceedings where this is consistent with the right of the defendant to a fair trial. The enactment of this legislation was necessary because of the outcome of the House of Lords Judgment in *R v Davis* (2008) which concerned the use of anonymous witness evidence at a trial governed by the common law. This restricted the court's ability at common law to allow evidence anonymously during criminal trials.

Effects of time spent on police bail. The **Police (Detention and Bail) Act 2011** reversed the decision in *R v Davis* (on the application of *Chief Constable of Greater Manchester v Salford Magistrates Court*) (2011), where it was held that time spent on police bail counted towards the 96 hours in detention under the **Police and Criminal Evidence Act 1984** (PACE). The Act was passed to reverse the effects of the judgment and to clarify that periods on bail do not count towards the total detention period.

4.7 Proceedings in the Crown Court

Cases committed to the Crown Court by the magistrates are triable by judge and jury.

4.7.1 Indictment

This is a written or printed accusation of the crime for which a person is to be tried by the Crown Court. More than one person may be charged in an indictment, as where two or more persons are charged jointly or where the crime necessarily involves more than one person, e.g. conspiracy. Moreover, several crimes may be charged in an indictment. Each offence will be described in a separate paragraph called a 'count'.

A 'bill of indictment' must be given to the clerk of the court. When the judge (or recorder) is satisfied that the requirements of the law are complied with the clerk may be directed to sign the Bill and, when this is done, the document becomes an 'Indictment'.

Any person may prefer a bill of indictment before the Crown Court and, if it is properly drawn up and signed, a trial may take place. Where the Court of Appeal orders a new trial it will direct a fresh indictment to be preferred; a bill may be preferred by a judge of the High Court; and where a person commits perjury **(Perjury Act 1911)** in the Crown Court a bill of indictment may then and there be drawn up and the person may be charged, tried and convicted. The usual channel, however, is by means of preliminary investigation at the magistrates' court, followed by a committal for trial to the Crown Court.

What follows is a general description of a trial when, for example, a defendant, X, is charged with theft under the **Theft Act 1968**. Complicated trials (some have lasted 100 days) involve complex rules. Only the broad general procedure can be noted here.

4.7.2 Arraignment

The defendant, X, is 'arraigned' when the clerk of the court calls the defendant by name to the bar (i.e. the bar of the dock, see p. 47) and asks: 'How say you, are you guilty or not guilty?'

The actual pleading to this question, i.e. guilty or not guilty, must be by the defendant, not by the counsel.

Guilty pleas. Where the defendant pleads guilty, the prosecuting counsel outlines the broad facts of the case to the court, and the antecedents of the defendant are read out to the court by the police officer in charge of the case. Defendant's counsel may then make a speech in mitigation, pointing out any circumstances, e.g. upbringing, mental depressions, personal accidents, etc., that should be borne in mind by the court in fixing the sentence to be passed on the defendant. The judge, who may retire to consider the sentence, delivers his or her decision of the penalty in open court.

Not guilty pleas. In these cases, the procedure is as follows:

- A jury is empanelled from those potential members of the jury called to attend the court. They take the oath and are sworn to 'well and truly try the case according to the evidence'.
- After this, prosecuting counsel outlines the facts of the case, shows how it is proposed to prove the case, the number of witnesses intended to be called and the exhibits at the prosecution's disposal.

- Prosecuting counsel then calls witnesses. Each is examined and then cross-examined by defence counsel. Each may be re-examined by prosecuting counsel to clear up doubtful points.
- Defence counsel then outlines the defence. Counsel may, however, state that no case has been disclosed and that the defendant should go free. If that submission is accepted, the court makes its finding and may then free the prisoner.
- Usually there is a prima facie case, and the defence counsel, if calling witnesses to fact other than the defendant, may make an opening speech to the jury, after which defence witnesses are called. Each witness is examined, cross-examined by prosecuting counsel and re-examined by defence counsel.
- The defendant, X, may elect to go into the witness box and give evidence on oath. If this occurs, and the defendant wishes to protest his or her innocence, not only will defence counsel examine (question) him or her, but prosecuting counsel will also cross-examine the defendant. This is usually a vital moment in every trial since both what the defendant says and how it is said will be under close scrutiny by the jury and all those present in court.
- If this stage is successfully negotiated, the defendant will be re-examined by defence counsel. If the defendant elects not to go into the witness box, he or she may make any statement at all from the bar or other appointed place. Naturally any statement not on oath will not be as convincing as that which is subject to cross-examination under oath.
- Prosecuting counsel now makes a closing speech asking that the accused be found guilty. The last speech, however, will be that of defence counsel who will make a final plea to the jury.
- The judge (or recorder) then directs the jury on the law, sums up and explains that the burden lying on the prosecution is to prove that the accused committed the offence beyond reasonable doubt. The judge will also direct them as regards majority verdicts.
- The jury then retires and deliberates in secret without any interference from anyone. The verdict is theirs and theirs alone.
- If the jury disagrees (e.g. where eight consider the defendant guilty, while four consider him or her not guilty), the judge will order a retrial when a different jury will be empanelled.
- If the defendant is found guilty by the jury, defence counsel will make a plea in mitigation, bringing out those facts that ought to be borne in mind by the court before the sentence of the court is awarded by the judge.
- If the defendant is sentenced to prison, a committal warrant is prepared and the defendant is taken to the prison where the sentence is to be served.

The **Sentencing Act 2020** has 14 Parts and 29 Schedules, with Parts 2 to 13 comprising a code, the 'Sentencing Code which comprises the main sentencing regimes for England and Wales.

In accordance with s. 143 of the **Powers of the Criminal Courts (Sentencing) Act 2000,** forfeiture may be ordered of any property that has been used for the purpose of committing or facilitating the commission of an offence (or that was intended to be used for that purpose) by the person convicted of the offence.

Part III of the **Criminal Justice and Court Services Act 2000** made a number of changes relating to community sentences. Probation orders were renamed 'community rehabilitation orders', community service orders were renamed 'community punishment orders' and combination orders were renamed 'community punishment and rehabilitation orders'. Two new community orders that were introduced are an 'exclusion order', which prohibits an offender from entering a place for a period of up to two years and a 'drug abstinence order' whereby a person could be ordered to abstain from misusing specified Class A drugs. The **Offender Rehabilitation Act 2014** provides further support by supervision of offenders who have served custodial sentences of up to two years.

The **Crime (Sentences) Act 1997** set out the circumstances in which the court is required to impose a mandatory life sentence or minimum custodial sentence. S. 61 of the **Criminal Justice and Court Services Act 2000** reduced the minimum age for imprisonment from 21 years of age to 18.

4.7.3 Proceedings against children and young persons

All offences committed by children and young persons must be dealt with summarily by juvenile courts. These are special courts (see p. 52) set up for each petty sessional area, and are presided over by especially experienced JPs.

The following offences committed by either a child or a young person may not be dealt with summarily:

i homicide
ii where the child or young person is charged jointly with a person over 17 years and the court considers it necessary in the interests of justice that the defendants be committed for trial

In these classes of cases, the court of trial will be the Crown Court.

4.7.4 Arrest and habeas corpus

The police have wide powers of arrest both at common law and under statute. Private citizens also have powers of arrest, but in practice, they are not frequently used.

If a person is detained in custody (e.g. in police cells or a prison or elsewhere) he or she, or someone acting on his or her behalf, may apply for a writ of habeas corpus against the person, e.g. a police superintendent or prison governor, who detains them. The detaining person will be required to appear in court on a day named to justify the detention of the prisoner.

An application for such a writ is made to the Divisional Court of the Queen's Bench Division. If the court is not sitting, then an application may be made to a single judge who will inquire into the matter.

Where the imprisonment is lawful, the prisoner will be returned to custody. Otherwise, the court will order release. Under the civil law where a person has been imprisoned wrongfully, damages may be claimed against the person responsible. However, we should note that where a police officer has reasonable suspicion that an arrestable offence has been committed, he or she may arrest that person even though it turns out that no offence has been committed. In *Mohammed-Holgate v Duke* (1983), where P had been arrested for questioning and then released without being charged, the House of Lords held that such an arrest was not unlawful.

4.8 Standard works

The standard books used by lawyers are:

a *County Court Practice* for County Court proceedings (commonly called the Green Book)
b Annual Practice containing the rules of the Supreme Court (RSC for short) for High Court proceedings (commonly called the White Book)
c *Stone's Justices' Manual* for the law and procedure of magistrates' courts
d *Archbold Criminal Pleading, Evidence and Practice*
e *Blackstone's Criminal Practice*

4.9 Useful webpages

4.9.1 Civil procedure

Civil procedure—Wikipedia (https://en.wikipedia.org/wiki/Civil-procedure)

An overview of civil proceedings in England and Wales—Out-Law.com—Legal news and guidance from Pinsent Masons (www.out-law.com/en/topics/dispute-resolution-and-litigation/court-procedure/an-overview-of-civil-proceedings-in-england-and-wales/).

4.9.2 Criminal procedure

Criminal procedure rules—The Crown Prosecution Service (CPS) (www.cps.gov.uk/legal/a-to-c/criminal-procedure-rules) Criminal procedure rules—Ministry of Justice (www.justice.gov.uk/courts/procedure-rules/criminal/rulesmenu).

4.10 Exercises

1 Outline the procedure in bringing an ordinary action in a County Court.

2 What are the three kinds of indorsement of a High Court writ? What is meant by the phrase 'entering an appearance'?

3 Explain the meaning of: (a) Interrogatories, (b) an Order of Discovery and (c) Statement of Defence.

4 Describe the methods available for the enforcement of judgments in the High Court.

5 Explain the terms: (a) indictment; (b) arraignment; (c) habeas corpus.

6 Describe in broad outline the procedure to be followed in a Crown Court where the defendant pleads Not Guilty.

Chapter 5

The judiciary, law officers and the legal profession

Key points

- the roles of the Attorney General, Solicitor General, Masters and the Director of Public Prosecutions
- distinction between barristers, solicitors and legal executives

5.1 The Lord Chancellor—change in role

The **Constitutional Reform Act 2005**, which came into effect on 3 April 2006, changed the future role of the Lord Chancellor, the operation of a final United Kingdom court of appeal and the appointment of the judiciary.

The principal changes were the modification of the role of the Lord Chancellor so that he or she was no longer required to be a member of the House of Lords. The judicial role of the Lord Chancellor has now ended, and any previous judicial responsibilities formally exercised by the Lord Chancellor have been transferred to the Lord Chief Justice.

The respective functions of these two offices were agreed by the former Lord Chief Justice Lord Woolf and the Lord Chancellor Lord Falconer in January 2004 in a document described as 'the Concordat' and subsequently incorporated into the **Constitutional Reform Act 2005**.

As to the appointment of the Lord Chancellor, s. 2 of the Act states that the Lord Chancellor must simply appear to the Prime Minister to be qualified by experience. Subsection (2) states that this experience could have been gained as a government minister, a member of either Houses of Parliament, a qualified lawyer, a teacher of law in a university or 'other experience that the Prime Minister considers relevant'. In theory the Lord Chancellor no longer needs to be a lawyer—as happened in 2012 when a non-lawyer, Chris Grayling, was appointed.

5.2 Judges

a *The Lord Chief Justice* (LCJ) is appointed by the King on the advice of the Prime Minister and is head of the Court of Appeal (Criminal Division) and of the King's Bench Division as well as being a member of the House of Lords.

DOI: 10.4324/9781003422808-5

b *The Master of the Rolls* (MR) is appointed by the King on the advice of the Prime Minister and is head of the Court of Appeal (Civil Division) and also supervises the admission of solicitors to the Rolls of the Supreme Court.

c *The President of the Family Division* is appointed by the King on the advice of the Prime Minister and is responsible for the work of this Division of the High Court.

d Judges of the Supreme Court are appointed by the King on the recommendation of the Prime Minister, who can only recommend a person notified to him or her by the Lord Chancellor on the advice of a selection committee set up by the Lord Chancellor. There are 12 judges of the Supreme Court known as Justices of the Supreme Court.

e *Lords Justice of Appeal* are appointed by the King on the advice of the Prime Minister from among existing judges or barristers of at least 15 years' standing. They are judges of the Court of Appeal. They are 23 in number.

f *Judges of the High Court* are known as puisne judges and are appointed by the King on the recommendation of the Lord Chancellor from among barristers or solicitors of at least ten years' standing or circuit judges of at least two years' standing. Twelve judges are assigned to the Chancery Division, 45 to the King's Bench Division and 16 to the Family Division of the High Court.

All the judges referred to in (a) to (e) hold office 'during good behaviour' and may be removed by the Crown on an address presented by both Houses of Parliament. Their salaries are fixed by statute and form a charge on the Consolidated Fund. The effect of these two important provisions is to ensure judicial independence: a vital feature in the administration of law and justice within the State.

Judges of the High Court retire at the age of 75 and are eligible for pensions granted by statute.

g *Circuit judges*. These are judges appointed by the King on the advice of the Lord Chancellor to serve in (i) the Crown Court (see p. 45) and (ii) county courts (see p. 43). A circuit judge must be a barrister or solicitor of ten years' standing or a person who holds the office of a recorder (see later on in the chapter). The retiring age is 72, with the possibility of extension to 75. All county court judges who existed in 1971 became circuit judges, as did the recorders of Liverpool and Manchester, a number of whole-time chairmen and deputy chairmen of Quarter Sessions and certain other holders of judicial offices under the provisions of the **Courts Act 1971**.

h *Recorders*. Under the **Courts Act 1971**, these are designated *part-time* judges of the Crown Court. Appointments are made by the King on the recommendation of the Lord Chancellor to men or women of standing who are prepared to commit themselves to not less than one month's work on the bench each year. Barristers and solicitors of ten years' standing are eligible for appointment to this office. If a solicitor holds the appointment for five years, he or she may then be appointed a circuit judge (as stated previously).

5.3 Attorney General and Solicitor General

Together, the Attorney General and Solicitor General are known as Law Officers. Both are appointed by the Prime Minister. They are political appointments, and the holders are precluded from private practice while holding office.

a *The Attorney General* is a member of the House of Commons (not cabinet rank). His or her duties comprise the following:

   i represents the Crown in the courts in civil matters where the public interest is concerned and may prosecute in important and difficult cases in the criminal courts ii advises the Cabinet and Government departments on important legal matters and may take part in many judicial and quasi-judicial proceedings affecting the public interests, e.g. the administration of charities and patent law

iii certain criminal offences must be reported to the Attorney General and his or her consent is necessary before criminal proceedings may be taken in certain cases, e.g. bribery, incest, corrupt practices and offences against the **Official Secrets Act 1911** to **1989**, the **Misuse of Drugs Act 1971**, the **Public Order Act 1936** and various other Acts; he or she is head of the English Bar

b *The Solicitor General* is deputy to the Attorney General and his or her duties are similar. He or she is a barrister and is a member of the House of Commons. By the **Law Officers Act 1997**, any functions authorized or required to be discharged by the Attorney General may be discharged by the Solicitor General if the Office of Attorney General is vacant, if the Attorney General is absent or ill or if the Attorney General authorizes his or her deputy to act in any case.

5.4 Masters

Masters of the Senior Courts are salaried officials, lawyers of at least ten years' standing, attached either to the King's Bench Division or to the Chancery Division of the High Court.

Masters of the King's Bench Division adjudicate on all matters preliminary to a trial. These preliminaries are known as 'interlocutory matters. Thus, one party may wish to inspect documents in the possession of their opponent, or one party may wish to put questions to their opponent to clarify certain points in issue. In these circumstances, an application may be made to a master for an order for discovery or an order for interrogatories commanding the opponent to produce the required documents or to answer on oath written questions. Disputes may arise as to the most convenient time or place of trial, or whether the trial should be with or without a jury. Such disputes may be decided by a master, from whose decision appeal lies to a judge in chambers. They are appointed from barristers.

Chancery Division Masters perform similar work in their Division of the High Court. They are appointed from among solicitors.

Taxing Masters are officers of the Senior Courts whose function is the checking, determining and levying of costs to be paid by parties to the trial when the court so directs.

5.5 Director of Public Prosecutions

The office of the Director of Public Prosecutions is governed by the **Prosecution of Offences Act 1985**. The Director must be a barrister or solicitor of at least ten years' standing. This is an official appointment by the Attorney General with responsibility for the Crown Prosecution Service. This service, set up under the 1985 Act, is staffed by barristers and solicitors, certain of whom are designated Crown Prosecutors and Chief Crown Prosecutors (who are responsible for the service in each area in England and Wales).

The Director, in his or her capacity as head of the Service, is responsible for all criminal proceedings on behalf of the police (other than minor criminal offences). He or she must also conduct all binding-over proceedings instigated on behalf of the police force and any other proceedings where, because of the importance, difficulty or otherwise of the case, it may be considered necessary.

The **Crown Prosecution Service Inspectorate Act 2000** provided for the Attorney General to appoint a Chief Inspector of the Crown Prosecution Service with the power to establish an inspectorate with the primary function of inspecting the operation of the service. (This commenced 1 October 2001.)

5.5.1 The legal profession

There are two branches of the legal profession in Britain: (i) barristers and (ii) solicitors of the Supreme Court. In most other countries, including some parts of the Commonwealth, there is no such division.

5.6 Solicitors

The modern solicitor is the successor of three former ancient professions known as attorney (or representative), solicitor and proctor. These assisted judges in the King's Bench in the early stages of litigation or carried out the less skilled work in the ecclesiastical and Admiralty courts. By a succession of **Solicitors Acts, 1939** to **1974**, the profession has been unified and regulated (the 1974 Act consolidates the law).

The regulations of the Law Society provide for:

- i the scales of remuneration and fees of solicitors
- ii the terms and conditions of articles of clerkship for new entrants
- iii courses for the education and training of students
- iv the conduct of examinations
- v the discipline of all solicitors

A person who has either completed a law degree or, if a non-law graduate, has completed the Common Professional Examination and undertaken a one-year Legal Practice Course, followed by two terms as a trainee solicitor may be admitted as a solicitor by having his or her name enrolled. In addition, the legal sector now also offers solicitor apprenticeship opportunities whereby school-leavers may enter a legal workplace and secure professional-level legal employment while attending university. However, from 2020, to become a solicitor, a candidate needed to pass a series of assessments known as the Solicitors Qualifying Exam (SQE). The Solicitors Regulation Authority (SRA) to introduced the SQE in 2020 to ensure that all aspiring solicitors were assessed against the same standards regardless of their route to qualification. This applies to those with or without a law degree, legal apprentices, legal executives, paralegals and foreign lawyers. The Enrolled solicitors thereby become officers of the Supreme Court, and each receives a Certificate to Practise that is renewable annually. From 1 October 1984 solicitors are permitted to advertise on certain terms and also advertise properties for sale. In accordance with the Courts and **Legal Services Act 1990**, they are also permitted to form partnerships with foreign firms.

Discipline over solicitors is operated by the SRA with appeal from its decisions to the Solicitors Disciplinary Tribunal (SDT). Following the **Legal Services Act 2007**, the Legal Services Board was established, which oversees all approved legal regulators, including the Bar Council, which has also divested its regulatory functions in the Bar Standards Board.

Duties of a solicitor. Most solicitors are employed in private practice, either alone or in a partnership firm, with the right to incorporate with limited or unlimited liability. Others are employed in the public service, industry and commerce.

Practising solicitors are consulted by, and receive instructions from, lay clients on a wide variety of matters both civil and criminal, e.g. the making of wills, administration of estates, family matters, the formation of companies, drawing up of documents, conveyancing and criminal offences of all kinds. In cases of unusual difficulty or where a trial is to take place in the superior courts, the solicitor takes instructions from the client, prepares a brief and approaches a barrister (counsel) to give an 'opinion' or represent the client at the trial.

Solicitors' rights of audience in the magistrates' courts and county courts and limited rights of audience in the Crown Court and the Supreme Court have now been extended by the **Courts and Legal Services Act 1990**.

The relationship between solicitor and client is based on professional confidence, and a solicitor cannot be compelled to disclose in court communications made in a professional relationship. Nor is a solicitor liable for defamation in respect of statements made in court during the course of a trial. Solicitors are, however, liable to be sued for damages for negligence in the conduct of their profession; e.g. where they have carelessly lost documents entrusted to them. In certain situations, it has also been held that a solicitor might owe a duty of care in tort to a third party (*Ross v Caunters*, 1980 and *Al-Kandari v J.R. Brown & Co.*, 1987).

5.7 Barristers

Anyone wishing to become a barrister must join one of the four Inns of Court: Gray's Inn, Lincoln's Inn, Inner Temple or Middle Temple. These four Inns of Court are unincorporated bodies of medieval origin, owned and controlled by their senior members, called the Masters of the Bench.

The Senate of the Inns of Court and the Bar, formed in 1974, can be regarded as the governing body of the Bar today, since the Inns follow the general policy laid down by the Senate and the judges have agreed that disciplinary powers shall be exercised in accordance with the Senate's regulations.

Intending barristers must make a certain number of attendances (known as 'keeping term') at their Inn, and to qualify for Call to the Bar, they must either be a law graduate or, if a non-law graduate, have completed the Common Professional Examination. This is followed by a year's Professional Training course before undertaking one year's pupillage in chambers. Similar to the changes in the training for solicitors, in 2020 the Bar Standards Board (BSB) also made changes to its Future Bar Training requirements. The BSB states that these new qualifications are designed to ensure that training to become a barrister is more accessible, affordable and flexible whilst maintaining the high standards expected at the Bar. The Threshold Standard and Competence implementation schedule incorporated in these new rules will involve centralized assessments for both Civil Litigation and Professional Ethics. After six months barristers have the right of audience in any court of law in England and Wales. As noted previously, they may take instructions only from a solicitor, not from a lay client directly, but unlike the solicitor, they may not sue for their fees.

Duties of a barrister. A barrister intending to practise must choose which part of the law he or she intends to specialize in. A barrister is essentially an advocate whose task is to present his or her client's case effectively in court. Counsel's duty to put their client's case does not extend to advancing the client's unsubstantiated belief that the judge is biased and corrupt. In this case, the barrister must either refuse to comply with the client's instructions or withdraw from the case—*Thatcher v Douglas* (1996). Their work includes the drafting of opinions on difficult points of law, the settling of pleadings and advice on evidence and procedural matters.

The difference between the two branches of the profession may be summarized as follows:

a Barristers are advocates; solicitors are not necessarily so.
b Barristers have the right of audience in all courts; solicitors have only a limited right.
c Barristers specialize in certain branches of the law; solicitors tend to be general practitioners.
d Barristers deal with legal matters; solicitors may be consulted about many non-legal matters, e.g. family, business or financial matters.
e Barristers are instructed by solicitors, who are instructed by the lay client.

f Barristers cannot sue for their fees; solicitors can.
g Barristers may not be liable for negligence in the conduct of a case; solicitors may.
h Solicitors are controlled under the **Solicitors Acts 1839–1974**; barristers are controlled by their Inns of Court and the recently established Senate, non-statutory bodies.

5.8 King's Counsel

When a barrister has acquired a substantial practice, application may be made to the Lord Chancellor to 'take silk', i.e. become a King's Counsel. If the applicant's request is granted, letters patent are issued and he or she will then be called 'within the bar', thus relinquishing their former status of 'outer' or 'utter' barrister. Henceforth they wear a silk gown.

By this new status the successful applicant will expect to attract more important cases and to command higher fees. He or she will no longer draft pleadings, conveyances or similar documents. Thenceforward they will have the assistance of junior counsel who will be briefed with them. A King's Counsel is distinguished by the letters KC after their name, and is referred to as a 'Leader'.

5.9 Legal executives

The Institute of Legal Executives (ILEX) is recognized as the third arm of the legal profession. Established in 1963 it replaced the Solicitor's managing Clerks Association, which itself had been founded in 1892. In accordance with the **Legal Services Act 2007**, ILEX is the body responsible for both representing and also overseeing the education and regulation of the legal executives. It is only Fellows of ILEX who are entitled to call themselves legal executives and, in accordance with the **Legal Services Act 2007**, they are permitted to take up a position as a partner within a Legal Disciplinary Practice.

5.10 Licensed conveyancers

A licensed conveyancer is authorized to carry out the legal formalities relating to the transfer of land (**Administration of Justice Act 1985**).

The governing body of licensed conveyancers is the Council for Licensed Conveyancers, responsible for making and enforcing rules on conduct and discipline, including accounts rules. The Council is also responsible for the licensing of conveyancers, the first licence being granted on 1 May 1987.

Licensed conveyancers are permitted to practise in partnership with each other, or in partnership or association with non-licensed conveyancers (but not with solicitors). In addition to this, licensed conveyancers may practise through the medium of a 'recognized body', which means a body corporate recognized by the Council for Licensed Conveyancers.

5.11 De-regulation of legal services

The Courts and Legal Services Act 1990 has removed many restrictions on the rights of audience in certain county court proceedings. This has opened up the right of audience to authorized practitioners and lay representatives.

Besides solicitors and licensed conveyancers, conveyancing services are also permitted to be offered by authorized practitioners, who are governed by the Authorized Conveyancing Practitioners Board.

5.11.1 Tesco Law

Further reforms were introduced by the **Legal Services Act 2007** that provided in 2009 for the provision of legal disciplinary practices (LDPs) whereby a legal disciplinary practice could be established with a maximum of 25 per cent of the partners being non-lawyers and so sharing the ownership of the practice. The balance of the practice could consist of solicitors, barristers and legal executives, although an LDP would still need to have at least one solicitor partner.

This was extended in 2011 by a further provision of the Act that allowed for a wide range of legal services to be provided to the public through alternative business structures that permitted external ownership of multidisciplinary partnerships (hence the expression 'Tesco Law' on the assumption that a potential owner could be a supermarket chain). The outcome was that in March 2012, the Solicitors Regulation Authority (SRA) issued its first three Alternative Business Structure (ABS) licences, including one to Co-operative Legal Services, which has a 500-person legal business operating a face-to-face legal advice service through the Co-op's bank network.

5.12 Legal Services Ombudsman

The **Courts and Legal Services Act 1990** also provides for the Lord Chancellor to appoint a Legal Services Ombudsman to investigate allegations into the manner in which any professional legal body has dealt with any complaint made against any of its members.

5.13 Useful webpages

The Bar Council (www.barcouncil.org.uk)

The Law Society (www.lawsociety.org.uk)

Chartered Institute of Legal Executives (www.cilex.org.uk/about_cilex_lawyers.aspx)

5.14 Exercises

1. Describe (a) the appointment of and (b) the duties performed by each of the following:
   - i The Lord Chancellor
   - ii The Lord Chief Justice
   - iii The Master of the Rolls
   - iv Circuit Judges
2. Discuss the appointment and functions of the Law Officers of the Crown.
3. What are the functions of (i) Masters of the Supreme Court and (ii) the Director of Public Prosecutions?
4. Describe the duties of (i) solicitors and (ii) barristers. Is the division of the legal profession justifiable and necessary today?

Chapter 6

Human rights and the law of persons

Key points

- human rights
- nationality and domicile
- marriage and divorce
- legitimation and adoption
- corporations and unincorporated associations
- Crown proceedings

6.1 Human rights

The concept of human rights is that, without any need for an enacted law by any government, a person by virtue of being a human being has inherent, universal rights and freedoms. This was formally expressed in the Preamble to the *Universal Declaration of Human Rights* adopted in Paris by the United Nations General Assembly in 1948 as: 'The recognition of the inherent dignity and of the equal and inalienable rights of all members of the human family is the foundation of freedom, justice and peace in the world.'

As already previously explained on page 33, under 'Legal sources', the **Human Rights Act 1998** formally incorporated into English law the individual rights guaranteed by the European Convention on Human Rights.

The focus on human rights reflects the importance of the concept of human rights that emerged from an earlier feature of the English Legal System known as the 'Rule of Law'. This had as its basis the writings of A.V. Dicey, an eminent constitutional lawyer who, in his text *The Study of the Law of the Constitution*, focused on three key elements that, in his view, characterized the existence of the rule of law as he understood it:

a *An absence of arbitrary power on the part of the State*—meaning that the law controls the power of the State when it attempts to acquire and use wide discretionary powers.

b *Equality before the law*—meaning that no person is above the law, irrespective of their status in society.

c *Supremacy of ordinary law*—meaning that the English Constitution is the outcome of the only law of the land as interpreted by courts in comparison to a continental system of law, which relies on a declaration of rights in the form of a written constitution.

DOI: 10.4324/9781003422808-6

The 'Rule of Law' came into prominence again after the Second World War in 1945, when immediate post-war governments introduced legislation that had an authoritarian element considered by some lawyers to be intrusive on the rights of the individual. This also influenced the judiciary which endeavoured to exercise control over the various administrative decisions arising from such legislation, the process being described as judicial review of administrative action.

A modern view of this approach by the judiciary was better stated in 2006 by Lord Bingham, the Senior Law Lord, who explained the importance of judicial review in the following terms:

> The historic role of the courts has of course been to check the excesses of executive power, a role greatly expanded in recent years due to the increased complexity of government and the greater willingness of the public to challenge governmental (in the broadest sense) decisions. Even under our Constitution the separation of powers is crucial in guaranteeing the integrity of the courts' performance of this role.

These matters that come under the description of administrative law are dealt with in greater detail in Chapter 3, 'The courts today', section 3.5 'Administrative tribunals' and section 3.6 'Judicial control of administrative tribunals'.

6.2 Separation of powers

It follows that the concept of judicial review as an aspect of the rule of law is a process by which the courts endeavour to protect an individual from the excesses of the law. In this respect, in the United Kingdom, the process of challenging excesses against the individual was reinforced when the United Kingdom became, in 1950, an initial signatory to the European Convention on Human Rights and Fundamental Freedoms (ECHR) instituted in Europe as a means of establishing and enforcing human rights. This was reinforced in 1966 when the United Kingdom recognized the power of the European Commission on Human Rights to hear complaints from individual United Kingdom citizens, while at the same time it recognized the authority of the ECHR to adjudicate in such matters. It did not, however, at that time incorporate the ECHR into the law of the United Kingdom.

The incorporation of the ECHR into United Kingdom law took place with the enactment of the **Human Rights Act (HRA) 1998**.

The outcome of the HRA incorporating the ECHR into domestic law gave rise to the United Kingdom Courts having to decide cases in accordance with the Articles of the ECHR. These include:

a Art 2—The right to life
b Art 3—Prohibition of torture
c Art 4—Prohibition of slavery and forced labour
d Art 5—The right to liberty and security
e Art 6—The right to a fair trial (no punishment without law)
f Art 7—The guaranteed prohibition of the enactment of retrospective criminal offence
g Art 8—The right to respect for private and family life
h Art 9—Freedom of thought, conscience and religion
i Art 10—Freedom of expression
j Art 11—Freedom of assembly and association
k Art 12—The right to marry
l Art 14—Prohibition of discrimination

All human beings are 'persons' under English law. One of the most important concepts of English law is that all persons within the realm, including aliens, have rights and are subject to certain duties.

One aspect of the incorporation of the ECHR into the **Human Rights Act 1998** (HRA) is that it places a duty on states to properly investigate occurrences which could give rise to alleged offences against the various Articles of the Act. This can be illustrated by the series of cases arising out of what became known as the 'Troubles' in Northern Ireland, covering a period in Northern Ireland from approximately the late 1960s until the Good Friday Agreement in 1998. In *Brecknell v United Kingdom* (2007), this involved later evidence which gave rise to a questioning of the circumstances of the original case. In *Finucane* (2019), The Supreme Court held that there was a duty for the state to not only investigate under Article 2 of the **HRA 1998,** but it also had a separate obligation to investigate the prevention of the taking of life.

6.3 Legal persons

This situation is not universal. Slaves in early Roman and Anglo-Saxon times, for example, had no rights. They were regarded as chattels: a thing to be owned and used or even killed at the will of their master or owner. A slave had, in law, no 'legal personality'. Similarly, in early Norman times, a criminal could be declared an outlaw: someone outside the law's protection whom any man could kill with impunity. In early times also, animals that had 'misbehaved' by attacking humans or cattle were sometimes hanged; in the East, gods and idols were offered gifts or appeased in some way as if they were persons. Whether a human being or some other creation is a 'legal person' depends, therefore, on the law of the State where that being or creature is.

In English law, a legal personality generally attaches to a human being at birth and ends at death. Although certain parts of the criminal law recognize and protect the existence of a child not yet 'in being', e.g. it is an offence to commit abortion or child destruction (which means unlawfully causing the death of a child before it has an existence independent of the mother), this does not necessarily attribute legal personality to the unborn infant.

❖ CASE EXAMPLE

***Kelly v Kelly* (1997)**

A father cannot bring an action on behalf of the foetus to restrain abortion because the foetus has no legal personality and no rights which can be enforced before birth.

Death puts an end to both the physical and legal personality. For example, the defamation of a deceased person is not actionable in English law by his personal representatives or near relations.

So far, we have been dealing with human beings. We shall later discuss a different kind of legal person, the corporation, which is an artificial or juristic person, created by law, with a legal personality distinct from the individual persons who control the corporation.

6.4 Nationality and domicile

By a person's nationality, we mean their status as a citizen or member of a particular State to which they owe allegiance. Apart from stateless persons, everyone is the subject of some State to which they owe political allegiance and loyalty, for which they may be called upon to fight, pay taxes and support, and from which they may expect protection. These are broad general statements only.

For instance, although we say that all persons must be national subjects of some State or other, we know that due to upheavals of war, there are some unfortunate 'stateless' persons who have been disowned by, or expelled from, their country of birth and origin.

Nationality is of great importance in the field of public law. Thus, British subjects enjoy universal franchise, i.e. the right to vote at local and Parliamentary elections. Aliens in Great Britain have no such right. They are subject to certain restrictions concerning entry into the United Kingdom and employment after entry; furthermore, they must register certain particulars with the police. Citizens of the European Union, however, had a right to freedom of movement within the State and were not subject to the same restrictions as other aliens. The same applied to United Kingdom citizens in the European Union. However, after the EU–UK Withdrawal Agreement (Brexit), EU citizens are not covered by the agreement unless they are a family member of someone who is.

Apart from these requirements, English law treats aliens in much the same way as ordinary British subjects: for example, they are subject to the same rules of criminal law and the same laws of tort and contract. Special disabilities or restrictions will be mentioned later. Here we may note that an alien may not own, or become part-owner of, a British ship registered at a British port and sailing under the British flag.

In the following pages, we shall deal with the acquisition of British nationality and the allied question of domicile, which is becoming increasingly important as travel makes it easier for people to move from one country to another.

6.4.1 British nationality

The **British Nationality Act 1981**, which replaces the 1948 Act, divides citizenship into three classes:

i British citizenship. A person seeking to enter the United Kingdom discharges the burden of proving British citizenship by producing a British passport—*R v Secretary of State for the Home Department, ex parte* Obi (1997).

ii British Dependent Territories citizenship, conferred upon citizens of a number of specified countries, e.g. Bermuda. Note that from 1 July 1997, Hong Kong was removed from the list of dependent territories in Schedule 6 of the **British Nationality Act 1981**.
The **British Overseas Territories Act 2002** replaced references to Dependent Territory with British Overseas Territory. It also renamed British Dependent Territories citizenship as British Overseas Territories citizenship, thereby granting British citizenship to everyone who came within this new classification. As was stated in the white paper *Partnership for Progress and Prosperity: Britain and the Overseas Territories* which led to the passage of the Bill, I can announce today that we will be offering British citizenship to all residents of the overseas territories who wish to take it up. That improved status will be welcomed throughout the overseas territories. It will give their residents the right to travel freely throughout the European Union and enable their young people to support themselves through work experience while they study in Britain. (Source: https://researchbriefings.files.parliament.uk/documents/RP01-90/RP01-90.pdf)

iii British Overseas citizenship—a residual category.

British citizenship may be acquired in the following ways:

i *By birth* in the United Kingdom to a parent who is a British citizen or who is settled in the United Kingdom or who becomes a British citizen or becomes settled in the United Kingdom. The **British Nationality (Regularisation of Past Practice) Act 2023** inserted a new section 50B in the **British Nationality Act 1981** to clarify the status of those born in the United

Kingdom to EU and European Economic Area (EEA) nationals. Its aim was to disregard immigration restrictions for historical cases in which such restrictions were in practice disregarded. It retroactively changed citizenship laws to ensure that affected individuals were and always would be British citizens.

The **British Nationality (Irish Citizens) Act 2024** provides an alternative and less stringent route to British citizenship for Irish citizens who have been resident in the United Kingdom for five years. The amendments it makes to the **British Nationality Act 1981** allow Irish citizens to be entitled to British citizenship. The Act has received royal assent but has not yet come into force.

ii *By adoption* under an order made by any court in the United Kingdom authorizing the adoption of a minor who is not a British citizen.

iii *By descent*, i.e. birth outside the United Kingdom to a parent who is a British citizen by birth, adoption, registration or naturalization (not by descent). The **Nationality, Immigration and Asylum Act 2002** abolished the difference between marital and non-marital law, so that a child can now inherit British nationality from either parent, whether or not they are married.

iv *By registration*—any minor may apply for British citizenship, which is granted at the Home Secretary's discretion. Persons who are British Dependent Territories citizens, British Overseas citizens, British subjects or British protected persons may apply after satisfying periods of residence in the United Kingdom. There is a special entitlement for British Dependent citizens who are nationals of the United Kingdom for the purposes of the EEC (in practice, Gibraltarians).

v *By naturalization*—any person may apply to the Secretary of State for a certificate of naturalization. The conditions of grant (which is at the discretion of the Home Secretary) are that the applicant must be of full age and capacity, of good character, have sufficient knowledge of the English, Welsh or Scottish Gaelic language and, in accordance with the **Nationality, Immigration and Asylum Act 2002**, the applicant must now also have sufficient knowledge about life in the United Kingdom and be willing to take part in a citizen ceremony. These requirements will also apply to those seeking nationalization on the grounds of marriage to a British citizen. They must also have satisfied residence requirements and intend that the United Kingdom will be their home or their principal home. The **Citizenship (Armed Forces) Act 2014** provides for the Secretary of State to waive these requirements of residency in respect of foreign and commonwealth citizens in Her Majesty's forces who have served or are serving overseas. The Secretary of State must give notice as to the nature of any objections so as to allow representations when refusing an application—*R v Secretary of State for the Home Department, ex parte* Al-Fayed (1996); *R v Secretary of State for the Home Department, ex parte* Al-Fayed (1997).

vi *By marriage*—an alien woman who immediately before commencement of the Act was the wife of a citizen of the United Kingdom and Colonies may acquire British citizenship if she chooses to do so by registration as in (iii) above within five years, provided the marriage subsists.

vii *By statute*—the **British Nationality (Hong Kong) Act 1997** came into force on 19 March 1997 and conferred British citizenship on persons who are ordinarily resident in, or have a qualifying connection with, Hong Kong.

6.4.2 Loss of nationality

British citizenship may be lost by:

i *Renunciation*. This is affected by a person of full age and capacity making a declaration of renunciation, which must be registered with the Home Secretary. Any person who has married is deemed to be of full age. A person who has renounced British citizenship in order to retain or acquire some other citizenship or nationality may resume it but this right can only be exercised once.

ii *Deprivation*. This previously applied *only* to citizens who acquired citizenship by naturalization or by registration and may be ordered by the Home Secretary for serious misconduct, e.g. criminal acts. The **Nationality, Immigration and Asylum Act 2002** has now extended deprivation of citizenship to persons who were British by birth. The Act has introduced a process for appeal against the decision.

6.4.3 British protected persons

So far, we have been dealing with British citizens and aliens. A third group of persons, known as British Protected Persons, must be mentioned. These are members of those territories described as Protectorates, Protected States or Mandated or Trust Territories and declared as such by an Order in Council. These territories no longer exist, but some persons continue to hold protected person status. This status does not, of itself, allow residence in Britain but enables civil employment under the Crown. Citizenship may be attained by naturalization.

6.4.4 Aliens

All persons other than Commonwealth citizens, British protected persons and citizens of the Republic of Ireland are aliens. The following general restrictions apply to aliens:

i they may not vote at local or Parliamentary elections
ii they may not become Members of Parliament
iii they may not work in the United Kingdom unless specially permitted
iv they must register with the police and notify changes of address to them
v they are liable to deportation if they engage in crime

6.4.5 Removal of persons unlawfully in the United Kingdom

S.1 of the **Immigration Act 2014** provides for the substitution of s. 10 of the Immigration and Asylum Act 1999 to provide for a person to be removed from the United Kingdom under the authority of the Secretary of State or an immigration officer if the person requires leave to enter or remain in the United Kingdom but does not have such leave.

- The purpose of the Immigration Act 2016 is to tackle illegal immigration by making it harder to live and work illegally in the United Kingdom. The intention behind the Act is that, without work, it is assumed that illegal migrants will depart voluntarily, but where they do not, the Act contains other measures to support enforced removals. The Nationality and Borders Act 2022 has strengthened this legislation by adding three main objectives:

  To increase the fairness of the system to better protect and support those in need of asylum;
  To deter illegal entry into the United Kingdom;
  To remove more easily those with no right to be in the United Kingdom.
  The objectives of this legislation were extended by the **Illegal Migration Act 2023,** the purpose of which was to create a scheme whereby anyone arriving illegally in the United Kingdom would be promptly removed to their home country or to a safe third country to have any asylum or human rights claim processed. This Act built on the **Nationality and Borders Act 2022** and the measures which had been set in that legislation as a New Plan for immigration.

6.4.6 Domicile

Domicile is a concept distinct from nationality. Thus, a person may be a British subject and yet be domiciled, for example, in France.

'Domicile' defines the legal relationship between an individual and the legal system of a territory. The concept of domicile, under English law, involves two elements: (i) actual residence and (ii) *animus manendi*, i.e. the intention to remain in that place or country. Where these two elements coexist, a person is said to have a domicile in that country.

Whereas nationality implies a political relation existing between a person and the State to which they owe allegiance, domicile determines important civil rights and obligations that will be discussed later.

First, we must note that under English law, it is an inflexible rule that (i) every person must possess a domicile and (ii) no person can have more than one domicile. A person is domiciled in the country in which he or she has a permanent home—*Winons v AG* (1904).

There are three classes of domicile:

a *Domicile of origin*. This domicile attaches at birth. A legitimate child takes the domicile of the father; an illegitimate child that of its mother. A foundling (deserted infant without known parents) acquires the domicile of the place where found.

A domicile of origin cannot be entirely lost or extinguished. If a person with a 'domicile of choice' (see later) abandons his or her present domicile, the domicile of origin revives and attaches to them until they acquire a new domicile.

b *Domicile of choice*. Where a person of full age and capacity establishes their home in a country with the intention of remaining there permanently (such country being different from their last domicile), they are regarded as acquiring a domicile of choice.

c *Domicile of dependent persons*. (i) Minors take the domicile of their parent, as at (a). Children may take their mother's domicile instead of their father's, where the spouses are separated and the children make their home with their mother. (ii) A woman who marries normally acquires her husband's domicile immediately on marriage. However, under the **Domicile and Matrimonial Proceedings Act 1973**, a married woman is now capable of acquiring a domicile independent of her husband. This statute also states that a person is capable of acquiring an independent domicile when they attain the age of 16.

The preceding represent the main rules regarding the concept of domicile in English law. The law of domicile is important in regard to the following matters:

a *Jurisdiction in divorce*. For example, Atkins, a British subject domiciled in Nevada, USA, was granted a divorce by the Divorce Court in Nevada on the grounds of 'incompatibility of temperament'. The divorce is recognized in English law even though the grounds are much less than those required to sustain a divorce in England.

b *Validity of Wills of Movable Property and the distribution of such property on an intestacy*. For example, Brown, a British subject domiciled in Ruritania, makes a will attested by one witness. English law requires two witnesses to a will, whereas the law of Ruritania requires one witness only. Brown's will is regarded as valid in English law because it complies with the law of the domicile.

c *Legitimation*. This is discussed on p. 103.

d *The essential validity of marriage*. The 'essential validity' includes the form of celebration, the age of parties, etc. It is possible for an English court to decide that a marriage contracted without the form required in England is valid because it complies with the law of the domicile.

Proof of domicile. The English court decides the question of domicile by applying English law, taking account of the *intention* of the party. Evidence of intention may include correspondence, oral or written declarations, the purchase of a house or even a grave. Inquiry by the English court may range over the whole of a person's life to enable the court to establish where a domicile has been acquired.

6.5 Marriage

The legal view of marriage is that it is a contract between two persons. Because it fundamentally affects the status of each of the contracting parties and imposes rights and obligations of a special kind, marriage is accorded a particular importance legally as well as socially.

Lord Penzance defined marriage as *the voluntary union for life of one man and one woman to the exclusion of all others* (*Hyde v Hyde*, 1866).

It follows from the preceding definition that forcible marriage and marriage by deceit or by mistake must be void. Deceit means misrepresentation of the essential nature of the transaction; mistake means an essential mistake, e.g. the identity of the other party or the ceremony itself. The free and voluntary consent of the parties is essential.

The **Forced Marriage (Civil Protection) Act 2007** makes provision for protecting individuals against being forced to enter into a marriage contract without their free and full consent and also for protecting individuals who have been forced into marriage without their consent. The legislation provides the courts with new powers to make orders (FXPOs) to protect such a victim or potential victim in such circumstances.

The **Anti-Social Behaviour, Crime and Policing Act 2014** made the breach of a forced marriage protection order a criminal offence. The **Policing and Crime Act 2017**, s. 173 provides for the anonymity of a victim of a forced marriage, like those in the **Female Genital Mutilation Act 2001**.

The **Marriage and Civil Partnership (Minimum Age) Act 2022** raised the minimum age of marriage and civil partnership to 18 in England and Wales. These ended provisions allowing for 16- and 17-year-olds to marry or enter a civil partnership with parental or judicial consent.

Capacity to marry. A person domiciled in England or Wales must comply with English law as to capacity to marry. The requirements are that at the time of the marriage, neither party must be (i) under 18 years of age, (ii) already married, (iii) certified of unsound mind or (iv) within the 'prohibited degrees'.

The 'prohibited degrees' mean close members of the family, e.g. brother and sister, set out in the first schedule to the **Marriage Act 1949** as amended. Under the **Marriage (Enabling) Act 1960**, it is now lawful to contract a marriage with a sister, aunt or niece of a former wife (living or dead) or brother, uncle or nephew of a former husband (living or dead).

A marriage under English law may be contracted either (a) according to the rites of the Church of England or (b) under a certificate of a Superintendent Registrar.

a Marriage by the Church of England

Marriage by the Church of England may be solemnized provided that the following requirements have been complied with:

i *banns* have been published;
ii a *Special Licence* has been issued by the Archbishop of Canterbury under special circumstances;
iii a *Common Licence* has been issued by a bishop (or his surrogate, i.e. deputy) for the marriage of persons residing within his diocese within three months of the issue of such licence or
iv a *Certificate* has been issued by a Superintendent Registrar.

The publication of banns means an announcement made by a priest on three Sundays preceding the solemnization of the marriage. Where the parties to the marriage reside in different parishes, the banns must be published in the parish churches of both. Otherwise, they may be published in the parish church within the parish where both reside.

The marriage must be solemnized by a clergyman of the Church of England in the presence of two witnesses.

b Marriage under a Certificate of a Superintendent Registrar

The following marriages may be solemnized on the authority of a Superintendent Registrar's certificate:

- i a marriage in a registered building (e.g. a non-conformist church registered for the solemnization of marriages therein)
- ii a marriage in a register office (i.e. the office of a Superintendent Registrar)
- iii a marriage according to the usages of the Society of Friends (commonly called Quakers)
- iv a marriage between two persons professing the Jewish religion according to the usages of the Jews
- v a marriage according to the rites of the Church of England

In all these cases, the marriage must take place in the register office or in 'a building which is registered for the purpose' (except that the **Marriage Act 1983** provides for marriages of house-bound and detained persons to be solemnized at the place where they reside). Such buildings include a Roman Catholic church, a church of one of the non-established denominations (e.g. the Congregational Church), a meeting house of the Society of Friends and a synagogue of the Jewish community. A further requirement is that only 'an authorized person' may solemnize the marriage. Such a person is usually the minister or other official of the building wherein the marriage is solemnized or the Superintendent Registrar.

The **Marriage Ceremony (Prescribed Words) Act 1996** now provides for an alternative declaration and form of words.

Two witnesses must be present at the ceremony and the building must remain open throughout the proceedings to allow public access. The permitted times of marriage in a 'registered building' or in a register office are between 8 a.m. and 6 p.m.

As well as valid marriages, we need to consider marriages that are either void or voidable.

Void marriages are those destitute of legal effect. By the **Matrimonial Causes Act 1973**, a marriage after 31 July 1971 is void if:

- i the parties are within the prohibited degrees (see p. 99)
- ii either party is under 16
- iii certain formal requirements are not complied with (e.g. marriage took place elsewhere than in a registered building)
- iv either party is already legally married
- v in the case of polygamous marriages entered into outside England and Wales, either party was at the time of the marriage domiciled in England and Wales

A declaration of nullity by the High Court will have effect *ab initio*, i.e. from the date of 'celebration'.

Voidable marriages are valid until they are declared void by a competent court. The **Nullity of Marriage Act 1971** provided that in respect of a voidable marriage, the marriage is annulled only for the time after the decree and the marriage is treated as having existed up to that time.

The **Matrimonial Causes Act 1973** provides that a marriage taking place after 31 July 1971 is voidable if:

i it has not been consummated owing to incapacity of either party
ii there is wilful refusal to consummate the marriage by the respondent
iii either party did not validly consent, whether by duress, mistake, unsoundness of mind or otherwise
iv either party was suffering from a mental disorder within the meaning of the **Mental Health Acts 1959, 1983** and **2007**, of such a kind or to such extent as to be unfit for marriage
v the respondent was at the time of the marriage suffering from venereal disease in a communicable form
vi the respondent was, at the time of the marriage, pregnant by another man

Proceedings in respect of (iii), (iv), (v) and (vi) must be taken within three years of the date of the marriage. The court has a discretion to refuse a petition brought under (i) to (vi) if it would be unjust to the respondent spouse.

Any child born of a voidable marriage is legitimate irrespective of the fact that the marriage is subsequently annulled.

c Civil partnerships under the Civil Partnership Act 2004

The **Civil Partnership Act 2004** makes provision for the formation of a civil partnership as a legal relationship between two people of the same sex and provides that a civil partnership will only end on death, dissolution or annulment.

S. 2 of the Act sets out who is to be present at the registration of a civil partnership and provides that there be no religious service used while a civil partnership registrar is officiating at the signing of a civil partnership document.

In accordance with s. 3 of the Act, any two people will not be eligible to register as civil partners if either of them is already a civil partner or lawfully married, either of them is under the age of 16 or if they are within the usual prohibited degrees of relationship.

d Marriage (Same Sex Couples) Act 2013

The **Marriage (Same Sex Couples) Act 2013** makes provision for the marriage of same-sex couples to be lawful in England and Wales. The legislation provides that there is no duty on any member of the clergy of the Church of England or the Church in Wales to solemnize a marriage of same-sex couples.

e Sham marriages and sham civil partnerships under the Immigration Act 2014

This legislation changes the procedures for giving notice of marriage and civil partnerships in England and Wales, in order to provide for a new referral and investigation scheme for proposed marriage and civil partnerships involving a non-EEA national, subject to migration control.

6.6 Divorce

Under the **Matrimonial Causes Act 1973** (as amended), a consolidating Act, it is provided that the sole ground on which a petition for divorce may be presented to the court shall be that the marriage has *broken down irretrievably*. To establish this, the petitioner must satisfy the court on one or more of the following grounds:

- i the respondent has committed adultery, and the petitioner finds it intolerable to live with the respondent
- ii the respondent has behaved in such a way that the petitioner cannot reasonably be expected to live with the respondent
- iii the respondent has deserted the petitioner for a continuous period of at least two years immediately preceding the presentation of the petition
- iv the parties to the marriage have lived apart for a continuous period of at least two years immediately preceding the presentation of the petition and the respondent consents to a decree being granted
- v the parties to the marriage have lived apart for a continuous period of at least five years immediately preceding the presentation of the petition

A divorce petition cannot normally be presented within three years of the marriage. (There is an absolute bar during the first year of marriage.)

The Act contains provisions designed to encourage reconciliation of the parties, but where this is impossible and divorce is granted, the court has wide powers to order financial relief for either party.

The **Family Law Act 1996** sets out the general principles in section 1 as follows:

- i the institution of marriage is to be supported
- ii the parties to a marriage that may have broken down are encouraged to take steps to save the marriage
- iii a marriage which has irretrievably broken down should be ended with minimum distress to the parties and any children, in a manner to promote a good continuing relationship and to stop unreasonable costs from the process and any risk of domestic violence to one of the parties should be removed or diminished.

  However, in *Owens v Owens* (2018), the Supreme Court was unable to grant a divorce petition on the basis that the husband's behaviour towards his wife amounted to behaviour so unreasonable that a reasonable person could not be expected to live with him. In upholding the decision of the High Court and Court of Appeal, the Supreme Court expressed 'uneasy feelings' as to the outcome of their decision. The outcome of this decision was the enactment of the **Divorce, Dissolution and Separation Act 2020**, which, on the basis of reducing 'conflict and acrimony' between the parties, ended the need for the parties to blame each other for the marriage breakdown and introduced a 20-week minimum wait for divorce.

Under the 1996 Act, the court may make a divorce order or a separation order, as it sees fit. There is a nine-month period of reflection by the parties before an application for divorce may be made.

Presumption of death. A person who can show good grounds for believing his or her spouse or civil partner to be dead may apply to the Family Division of the High Court for an order to presume death and to dissolve the marriage. Continuous absence for a period of seven years, provided that the petitioner has no reason to believe the absent spouse to have been alive within that time, is accepted as prima facie evidence that the absent spouse or civil partner is dead.

Judicial separation. This is an order of the courts that absolves the parties from their duty of cohabitation, i.e. living together as man and wife. Whereas divorce dissolves the marriage tie, judicial separation does not. The court may still order financial relief.

Child support. In accordance with regulations made under the **Child Support Act 1991**, the Child Support Agency is responsible for assessing, collecting and enforcing maintenance payments in respect of natural children of the marriage. This applies to natural children who are under 16 years of age or under 19 and still in full-time non-advanced education (i.e. still at school).

The Act was amended by the **Child Support (Domestic Abuse) Act 2003**, which is a law that provides additional legislative protection for victims of domestic abuse who use the Child Maintenance Service (CMS). The Act allows the CMS to intervene in cases where there is abuse and use their powers to collect and make payments.

Contact orders. Part 1 of the **Children and Adoption Act 2006** is mainly concerned with providing the courts with new powers to promote contact and enforce orders made under s. 8 of the **Children Act 1989**. A 'contact order' under the **Children Act 1989** means an order requiring the person with whom the child lives, or is to live, to allow the child to visit or stay with the person named in the order or for that person and the child otherwise to have contact with each other.

Amendments have been made to this procedure regarding liability orders by s.25 of the **Child Maintenance and Other Payments Act 2008,** whilst the **Child Support (Enforcement) Act 2023** further altered the basis upon which such administrative liability orders could be made.

6.7 Domestic proceedings in magistrates' courts

Magistrates' courts exercise certain jurisdiction in regard to married persons and may make orders for (i) the protection of the spouses, (ii) the maintenance of spouses and children of the family and (iii) the custody of such children. Formerly, orders to provide maintenance could only be made against the husband, since he was traditionally regarded as the breadwinner. Since 1960, an order may be made against the wife to provide maintenance in certain circumstances for the husband and children of the family. The **Domestic Proceedings and Magistrates' Courts Act 1978** has replaced the 1960 Act.

Domestic proceedings are, as far as possible, separated from the other business of the court. The proceedings are not open to the public and press reports are limited to minimum details (**Magistrates' Courts Act 1980**). The court must contain no more than three justices, including one man and one woman.

6.8 Legitimation

A child born illegitimate becomes legitimate if his or her parents subsequently marry. By the **Legitimacy Act 1926**, an illegitimate person is legitimated by the marriage of their parents, provided that at the date of the marriage (i) the illegitimate person is alive and (ii) the father is domiciled in England and Wales.

The **Legitimacy Act 1959** further provides that it shall be no bar to legitimation that either of the parents was married to a third party at the time of the birth of the child. For example, *A* and B are married. B conceives a child (*L*) by Z. *A* then divorces B, who thereupon marries Z. The child L will be legitimated from the date of the subsequent marriage of B and Z. But in *Re Spence, deceased, Spence v Dennis and Another* (1990), it was held that a child of a void marriage born before that marriage was not legitimated in accordance with the **Legitimacy Act 1976**.

The legal effect is that the legitimated child is treated in nearly all respects as though he or she were a legitimate or a lawful child. Should the parents die intestate, the legitimated child will succeed to their property. Moreover, he or she will have the same rights of maintenance by parents as a lawful child.

6.9 Registration of births of children whose parents are not married

The **Welfare Reform Act 2009** provides that there should be joint registration of a child whose parents are neither married to each other nor civil partners of each other. This will have the effect of unmarried fathers having their names entered on the birth register and so gaining parental responsibility in accordance with the **Children Act 1989**.

6.10 Adoption

The present law is contained in the **Adoption and Children Act 2002** and the **Children Act 1989**.

The effect of adoption. An adoption order made by a court extinguishes the rights, duties and obligations of the natural parents or guardian and vests them in adopters. On adoption, the child is deemed to be the legitimate child of its adoptive parents to the exclusion, with minor exceptions, of all its former ties. The natural parent may not know who has adopted the child. The Court of Appeal has held that strong emotional curiosity on the part of a natural parent is not sufficient justification for the disclosure of information contained in the Adopted Children Register in respect of an adopted child—Re L. (Adoption; Disclosure of Information) (1997). The adopted child has the same rights of inheritance under wills, deeds and intestacies (unless the adopted child is expressly excluded) as natural children born in wedlock to the adopters. Titles of honour are, however, excepted.

A person is eligible for adoption at any age under 18, although they can include a person who is 18 before the proceedings are concluded, provided he or she is unmarried. In practice, about 90 per cent of all adoptions are of children under ten.

Who may adopt? A couple, whether married or unmarried, domiciled in the UK, may adopt jointly. Otherwise adoption by more than one person is not allowed. However, it appears from the following case that one de facto partner may adopt and that the sexual orientation of the de facto couple is irrelevant.

❖ CASE EXAMPLE

Re W. (a minor) (Adoption: Homosexual Adopter) (1997) Times, 21 May (Family Division: Singer J)

The natural mother opposed an adoption order of a single woman living in a lesbian relationship. The child had been living with the lesbian couple for two years and was 'well settled and flourishing'. *Held*: that nothing in the **Adoption Act 1976** precludes a person from seeking or obtaining an adoption order even if that person is cohabiting in a homosexual relationship at that time.

The **Adoption and Children Act 2002** states the procedure and requirements for adoption agencies to follow in determining the suitability of adoptive parents.

The applicant or both of the joint applicants for an adoption must (a) have attained the age of 21 or (b) have attained the age of 18 and be the mother or father of the infant, e.g. with an illegitimate child, the other member of the couple must have attained the age of 21. There are additional requirements imposed by the **Adoption (Inter-country Aspects) Act 1999** where the adoption involves a child from an overseas country.

Procedure. The following are the competent courts, each having jurisdiction: the High Court, the county court and the magistrates' court. The court must be satisfied that:

a the adoptive parents are suitable
b the consent of the natural parent(s) has been obtained
c the consent of the other of the two spouses, one of whom makes the application to adopt, has been obtained

❖ CASE EXAMPLE

***In Re Q S (a minor) (Adoption: Non-Patrial)* (1997)**

A British citizen of Pakistani origin who was unable to have children applied to adopt her brother's son. The boy entered the United Kingdom as a visitor and the reasons for his entry were not made clear at this time. The application was refused. The child's welfare was clearly outweighed by considerations of public policy.

The court may dispense with the natural parent's consent if, for example, the parent has abandoned the child, has persistently ill-treated the child, has seriously ill-treated the child and it is unlikely that the child will be able to live with such parent or is unreasonably withholding consent. Such consent of the natural parents may also be dispensed with where they have already indicated that they would consent to a custodianship order being made.

The court's first consideration is to safeguard and promote the welfare of the child, whose wishes and feelings (having regard to his or her age and understanding) must also be considered. So far as practicable, the court must consider the natural parent's religious preferences before placing a child for adoption.

The **Children and Families Act 2014** provided for the speeding up of the adoption process of children who are in the care of local authorities by placing them in a 'Fostering for Adoption Placement' if one is available. It also removed the explicit legal wording around a child's ethnicity so that black and minority ethnic children were not left waiting in care longer than necessary because local authorities were seeking a perfect or partial ethnic match.

In accordance with s. 9 of the **Children and Adoption Act 2006**, the Secretary of State has the statutory power to suspend inter-country adoptees from specific countries where 'because of practices taking place' in another country he has reason to believe 'it would be contrary to public policy' to permit children in certain cases to be brought into the United Kingdom for the adoption or where it concerns the entry of a child who has within the previous 12 months already been adopted through an overseas adoption process.

Further encouragement was given to the enhancement of functions to encourage adoptions by the provisions of the **Education and Adoption Act 2016**. This promoted the creation of regional adoption agencies.

6.11 Guardianship

Guardianship is the relationship existing between an infant (known as a ward) and some person who has the right of control over them and of ensuring their maintenance, education and welfare.

Such powers are, of course, normally exercised by parents who have a duty to provide care, protection and control.

Where, however, either or both parents are deceased or unable or unwilling to exercise these powers and duties, the question of appointing a successor in the form of a guardian will arise. Every infant must have an adult to safeguard their interests.

By the **Children Act 1989**, the father and mother are equally entitled to care and custody of their infant children; if either parent dies, the duties devolve on the survivor. Where a dispute arises or divorce proceedings occur, any application may be made to the court. The court will examine the circumstances and determine the matter of guardianship, bearing in mind that the *paramount consideration is the welfare of the infant.*

Appointment of guardians. Guardians may be appointed by:

a a deed or will of a parent (**Children Act 1989**);

b the High Court, county courts and magistrates' courts, where no guardian has been appointed by deed or will and the infant has no parent, guardian or other person exercising control over them;

Where an infant or minor has been made a *ward of court* (which may result where both parents are dead or divorced), all important decisions affecting the child, such as upbringing, property, investments, etc., may only be made by authority of the court, usually the Family Division. But in *Re J.S. (A Minor) (Wardship: Boy Soldier)* (1990) it was stated that the control of the High Court over the person of a ward is not absolute. Other incidents of wardship are:

i The court may appoint any person to be guardian. Thus, a parent can be appointed 'guardian' but would act under the control of the court.

ii Interference with a ward or a guardian amounts to contempt of court, punishable by imprisonment.

iii A ward may not marry or leave the country without the consent of the court.

iv A ward who refuses to carry out a direction of the court may be punished for contempt of court.

c court order under s. 4(4) of the **Family Law Reform Act 1987** regarding legal custody of the child and access to the child by the parent.

6.11.1 The guardianship of the property and financial affairs of a missing person

The **Guardianship (Missing Persons) Act 2017** created a new legal status. The Act enables the appointment by the court of a person ('the guardian') to act for a missing person, who by reason of being missing is not able to act in relation to his or her property and financial affairs. The appointment may be general or limited, but will only be made if the court considers it to be in the best interests of the missing person. The guardian, depending on the terms of the court order, may access bank accounts, authorize mortgage and insurance payments, sell or rent property or manage investments. The guardian may also make payments to dependants of the missing person to meet ongoing expenses and other needs. The appointment will be for up to four years but may be renewed.

6.12 Illegitimacy

A child born during wedlock is prima facie legitimate. Similarly, a child born within the normal time after the termination of a marriage by the death of the husband or by divorce is presumed legitimate.

A child will only be illegitimate when the mother does not marry the father. If the mother does, however, marry the father following the birth of the child, the child may be *legitimated* (see p. 103).

If the mother marries some other person, the mother and the husband may, in such a case, jointly adopt the mother's illegitimate child, although her husband will be bound to maintain the child and can claim custody as a 'child of the family'.

Custody and maintenance. An illegitimate child is in the custody of its mother, and the mother is bound to maintain it until the age of 16. The putative father, as he is generally called, is under no legal obligation to provide for the child except when an *affiliation order* has been made against him by a magistrates' court. If so ordered, the putative father is liable to maintain the child until the age of 16, although it may be extended beyond 16 if the child needs further education or training.

Property rights. Where either parent of an illegitimate child dies intestate in respect of either real or personal property, the illegitimate child enjoys the same rights of succession as if he or she had been born legitimate. Moreover, where an illegitimate child dies intestate, each of the parents can 'take any interest in the child's property to which that parent would have been entitled if the child had been born legitimate' (**Family Law Reform Act 1969**, as consolidated by the 1987 Act).

Section 15 of the Family Law Reform Act 1969 provides that in any dispositions of property (e.g. sales, gifts and trusts) after 31 December 1969, references to children and other relatives include references to, and to persons related through, illegitimate children, unless the contrary intention appears.

Similarly, section 16 provides that, from January 1970, where a testator makes a gift to his or her children or other 'issue', the reference will include any illegitimate child of the testator.

The modern law has gone a long way in assimilating the position of the legitimate and illegitimate child. The following points should be noted:

i *Domicile and nationality.* A legitimate child usually takes the father's domicile and nationality. An illegitimate child takes the mother's domicile and nationality.

ii *Surname.* A legitimate child takes the father's surname while an illegitimate child takes the mother's.

iii *Rights of succession.* Certain of these rights are different by reason of illegitimacy. The general principle is that illegitimacy is not to be taken into consideration in determining the rights of succession of an illegitimate person, the rights of succession to the estate of an illegitimate person and the rights of succession traced through an illegitimate relationship.

iv No reference on a child's birth certificate need be made as to their illegitimacy.

6.13 Infants or minors

Section 1(1) of the **Family Law Reform Act 1969** provides that, as from 1 January 1970, a person 'shall attain full age on attaining the age of 18 instead of on attaining the age of 21; and a person shall attain full age on that date if he has then already attained the age of 18 but not the age of 21'.

Section 9(1) provides that 'the time at which a person attains a particular age expressed in years shall be the commencement of the relevant anniversary of the date of his birth'. For example, a child born on 31 December 1970 will reach his or her majority at the first moment of 31 December 1988.

The following is a summary of the rights and liabilities of minors under the law:

a Under the criminal law

A child under the age of 10 is not criminally liable for any offence (*doli incapax*) and cannot, therefore, be convicted. Between the ages of 10 and 14, a child is liable for any crime they may commit if the court finds that such a child knew his or her conduct to be wrongful. This presumption was reaffirmed by the House of Lords in *C. (a minor) v DPP* (1995). Young persons over the age of 14 years are liable for criminal acts.

Children (i.e. persons under 14) and young persons (i.e. persons over the age of 14 and under 17 years) are, as a rule, tried in a Juvenile Court by magistrates. If the case is a serious indictable offence, e.g. homicide, the child or young person will usually be committed for trial at the Crown Court. No person under 17 may be sent to prison, however. Other institutions, e.g. community homes and detention centres, are used for custodial treatment or punishment. A child or young person may be fined for any offence committed.

b Under the civil law

A minor is liable for all *torts* he or she commits. (Torts are civil wrongs, which are not breaches of contracts or trust.) Usually, the minor is without means and, unless a parent or guardian is directly and personally involved in the commission of the tort, an injured party is left without remedy since a parent or guardian as such is not liable. Where the tort complained of is also a breach of contract, a plaintiff will not be able to sue in contract in respect of damage so caused. The position and liability of minors in respect of torts will be considered on p. 224.

The law as to *contracts* with minors is discussed on p. 151.

Voting rights. Under the **Representation of the People Act 1969** (now consolidated within the **Representation of the People Act 1993**), the voting age for Parliamentary and local elections is 18 years and over.

Property rights. A minor may own all kinds of personal or movable property, but cannot, however, legally own land (**Law of Property Act 1925**, s. 19).

Litigation rights. Where a minor wishes to enforce or protect rights in a civil court, a responsible person (e.g. father) must be appointed to act as 'next friend'. Where a minor is sued, a responsible person is similarly appointed to act as his or her 'guardian *ad litem*', i.e. a guardian with respect to a suit at law. In criminal proceedings a minor may act in his or her own name by taking out a summons against another person: for example, *A*, aged 16, may prosecute B, aged 25, for common assault if the police do not prosecute on behalf of the public.

Wills. Minors have no legal capacity to make a valid will. Where, however, they are serving as a member of HM Forces on military service, or as a mariner or seaman at sea, they may make an informal will.

Child trust funds. In accordance with the **Child Trust Funds Act 2004**, all children born in the United Kingdom after 31 August 2002 will have a 'child trust fund account' opened on their behalf. Currently, the treasury will provide all initial endowment of £250 for each child, increased to £500 for children in low-income families or looked after by a local authority. There will be a further Treasury payment when the child attains the age of 7 years. The account can be topped up with further contributions by parents, relatives and family friends.

No withdrawals can be made until the child attains the age of 18.

National Citizen Service. The National Citizen Service has been available since 2011 and consists of courses for young people in England and Northern Ireland, mostly aged 16 and 17, to engage in a mixture of activities, adventures, life skills and social action which encourage young people to engage with their community and develop for the future. The **National Citizen Service Act 2017** created a Trust Charter to administer the scheme. It also gave the HMRC the right to circulate to all young people eligible for the scheme.

Support for looked after children. The **Children and Social Work Act 2017** made provision for the support of looked after and previously looked after children and improving joint work at the local level to safeguard children. The term basically refers to children who have been in the care of local authorities. It also provides for better supervision of social workers under a specialist social work regulation.

Miscellaneous. Persons under 16 may not hold a driving licence to ride a motorcycle on a public road. Persons under 17 may not hold a driving licence to drive a motorcar on a public road. Persons under 16 may not contract a valid marriage. Restrictions are placed on the possession and use of firearms. Generally, persons under 18 may not consume liquor on licensed premises.

6.14 Mental capacity

The **Mental Capacity Act 2005** makes provision for a person to act on behalf of a person who is unable to decide for themselves because of a lack of capacity.

The Act applies the following principles:

a a rebuttable presumption of capacity

b a right for a person not to be treated as unable to decide unless all practicable steps to help him or her have been taken without success

c a person is not to be treated as unable to decide merely because they have made an unwise choice

d any act or decision made on behalf of a person who lacks capacity must be made in their best interests

For the Act to apply, a person is regarded as lacking capacity if 'at the material time they are unable to make a decision on their behalf because of an impairment of, or a disturbance in the functions of, the mind or the brain'.

S. 9 of the Act makes provision for a person to appoint a lasting power of attorney, which is a power of attorney under which a donee may act on a donor's behalf if the donor loses capacity, and which includes the power to make health or welfare decisions.

Changes were made by the **Powers of Attorney Act 2023** to digitise the process and make it faster, easier, more accessible and secure.

Note: This Act has been amended by the **Mental Capacity Amendment Act 2019** in relation to procedures in accordance with which a person may be deprived of liberty where the person lacks the capacity to consent.

6.15 Gender recognition

The **Gender Recognition Act 2004** aims to provide transsexual people with legal recognition in their acquired gender. This recognition in law follows from the issue of a full gender recognition certificate. This certificate is issued by the Gender Recognition Panel, which, before it is issued, must be satisfied that the applicant:

a has, or has had, gender dysphoria

b has lived in the required gender throughout the preceding two years

c intends to continue to live in the acquired gender until death

The issue of this certificate entitles the recipient to a new birth certificate and the right to marry someone of the opposite gender to his or her acquired gender.

6.16 Equality and human rights

The **Equality Act 2006** makes provision for the establishment of a Commission for Equality and Human Rights and the dissolution of the Equal Opportunities Commission, the Commission for Racial Equality and the Disability Rights Commission.

The Commission has power(s) to bring legal proceedings in respect of unlawful discriminatory advertisements (s. 25); discrimination on grounds of religion or belief (ss. 44 to 80); discrimination on grounds of sexual orientation (ss. 81 to 82), while s. 83 makes it unlawful for a public authority to discriminate or commit acts of harassment on grounds of sex when carrying out its functions. The **Equality Act 2010** harmonizes the law on sex, race and disability discrimination together with the newer post-2000 strands of discrimination such as the protected characteristics of age, gender reassignment, marriage and civil partnership, pregnancy and maternity, religion or belief and sexual orientation.

For Women Scotland Ltd (Appellant) v The Scottish Ministers (Respondent) (2025) *Held:* (Supreme Court) That the legal definition of a woman is based on biological sex. Meaning that a person who was not born as a biological female cannot obtain the legal protections the Act affords to women by changing their gender with a Gender Recognition Certificate. However, the Act still provides transgender people with protections against discrimination.

The Equality Act 2010 was further amended by s. 97 of the **Enterprise and Regulatory Reform Act 2013**, which provided for caste to be also an aspect of race. It covers public and private employment, the supply of goods, facilities, services and a great deal more (now called work and non-work). The Act also includes a strengthened public-sector duty to promote equality (of opportunity) and private and public voluntary positive action, permitting, e.g. the recruitment of a woman over an equally (or more) qualified man.

The **Worker Protection (Amendment of Equality Act 2010) Act 2023** introduced a new proactive statutory duty on all employers to take reasonable steps to prevent sexual harassment in the workplace. The Act consists of 5 sections, with s.1 introducing a duty on employers to take reasonable steps to prevent sexual harassment of their employees, and S.3 providing for compensation where there has been a breach of the employer's duty.

The law (domestic and EU) has hitherto, in accord with a constitutional concept of equality (related to fairness), prevented victims of discrimination and their advocates from discriminating. The Act intentionally crosses the line into conscious social engineering, with a sociological concept of equality (with women in the lead) which will undoubtedly be tested in the courts (both in the UK and abroad—particularly in the European Court of Justice.

There were widespread changes to the Equality Act 2010 in 2024, predominantly but not exclusively as a result of Brexit and the effect of the Retained EU Law (Revocation and Reform) Act 2023. The breadth of the changes spans aspects of the definitions of direct discrimination, indirect discrimination, pregnancy and maternity discrimination and the protected characteristic of disability; the unlawful acts of discrimination (regarding discriminatory public statements) and harassment (introducing positive duty on employers to prevent sexual harassment of employees); and changes to the equal pay provisions.

6.16.1 Safeguarding adults from abuse or neglect

The **Care Act 2014** sets out the legal framework for the provision of adult care in England. It reforms the law relating to care and support for adults and the law relating to support for carers, and it makes provision about safeguarding adults from abuse or neglect, together with the provision of care standards.

The Carer's Leave Act 2023 creates a statutory entitlement for an employee to take a week's unpaid leave to care for a dependant. The dependant does not have to be a family member. It can be anyone who relies on them for care.

6.16.2 Modern slavery protection

The **Modern Slavery Act 2015** makes provision for offences relating to modern slavery, in particular human trafficking, including social exploitation, forced labour and domestic servitude. It incorporates provisions for the protection of victims. There is also provision for an Independent Anti-Slavery Commission.

6.17 Freedom of race and religion

- The **Racial and Religious Hatred Act 2006** extended the **Public Order Act 1986** to create a new offence covering inciting religious hatred as the equivalent of the existing offences of inciting racial hatred but only to cover threatening words and behaviour, rather than extending to abusive or insulting words or behaviour and require there to be an intention to stir up racial hatred. The offences cover written material (ss. 29 B–C), plays (s. 29D), recordings (s. 29E) and broadcasts (s. 29F), as well as possession of inflammatory material (s. 29G) that makes various corporate officers or members personally liable for the acts of a company if they have consented or connived at the commission of the offence.

The **Protection from Sex-based Harassment in Public Act 2023** added a further offence whereby, if a person commits an offence under section 4A of the **Public Order Act 1986** and carried out the conduct in question because of the sex of person to whom they intended to cause harassment, alarm or distress, then that the person would be guilty of an offence.

6.17. 1 Freedom of speech

The **Higher Education (Freedom of Speech) Act 2023** aims to enhance freedom of speech and academic freedom in higher education institutions and students' unions. The Act imposes new duties on universities to protect free speech. It also introduces provisions related to the recruitment, dismissal and discipline of academic staff. Enforceable through a statutory tort and a complaints scheme. The Act is regulated by the Office for Students (OfS).

6.18 Corporations

We have mentioned that, as well as natural persons recognized as such by law, there are artificial or juristic persons called corporations. *A corporation is a legal entity, or artificial person, with a distinctive name, perpetual succession and a common seal.*

The essential feature of a corporation is that it has a legal personality distinct from that of its members or those who control it. It is clear, of course, that a corporation once created by law will only be able to act if there are human servants or agents who, for example, order goods and make contracts for it or perform other functions that the corporation itself may lawfully be empowered to do.

The next point to note is that the corporation continues in existence irrespective of the death or expulsion of any or all of its members. Its independent existence and survival are known as 'perpetual succession'. This technical expression means that once the corporation is created by law, it will continue until it is destroyed, annulled or dissolved by law. For example, a monarch may, in the past, have granted a charter to create a corporation. The corporation will continue until such time as Her Majesty or Parliament (by statute) revokes the charter. Unless the dissolution or revocation is effected by law, the corporation continues in existence forever. A corporation does not die; it must be 'killed'.

The current legislation relating to corporations is governed by the **Companies Act 2006**, which reforms company law and keeps the greater part of the former enactments relating to companies; it makes other provisions relating to companies and other forms of business organizations. It also makes provision about business names, directors and auditors and amends Part 9 of the **Enterprise Act 2002**.

6.18.1 Classes of corporations

Sir Edward Coke, L.C.J. (1552–1634) wrote: 'Persons are natural, created by God, and incorporate, created by the policy of man, and these latter are either sole or aggregate of many.' In accordance with Coke's definition, corporations may be classified as:

a corporations sole;
b corporations aggregate.

Alternatively, they may be classified according to their mode of creation:

a corporations created by charter (common law);
b corporations created by statute or
c corporations created by registration under the **Companies Acts**.

a Corporations sole

This class of corporation consists of one person only at any time. Examples include the Queen, a bishop and the Public Trustee. In all the preceding examples, there is a natural person and a 'corporation', each separate and distinct from the other. When the bishop dies, a new incumbent assumes office and there is no break in the powers vested in the corporation sole, whether of ownership of land or any other rights attaching to his office in his corporate capacity.

b Corporations aggregate

Whereas a corporation sole consists of one member only, corporations aggregate comprises many members or groups of people. Common examples include the mayor, aldermen and burgesses of a borough; the British Broadcasting Corporation; and all companies registered under the **Companies Acts** (see paragraph (f) later on).

Corporations may be classified according to their manner or mode of creation.

c By charter

Under the common law, the Crown still has the power to create corporations at the royal pleasure. The Monarch may grant a charter to groups of subjects who petition for the purpose. A local authority may wish to become a corporation to give itself added dignity and status: its council will then petition Her Majesty for the grant of a charter. The method is used today, usually to give corporate status to educational, charitable or scientific bodies, e.g. the new universities, the BBC.

d By statute

These corporations are created by Acts of Parliament. Thus, the National Coal Board (now the British Coal Corporation) was created by the **Coal Industry Nationalization Act 1946**. The County Councils were created by the **Local Government Act 1888** (and re-created by the **Local Government Act 1972**), the **Strategic Rail Authority by the Transport Act 2000**, which replaced the British Railways Board and the Independent Broadcasting Authority by the **Television Act 1954** (renewed until 1996 in 1980). Parliament has generally adopted this form of incorporation in creating all the nationalized boards.

e Community interest company

The **Companies (Audit, Investigations and Community Enterprise) Act 2004** (ss. 24 to 63) established a new type of company called a community interest company (CIC), which is a share or guarantee company with special features.

The aim of a CIC is to facilitate company work in the not-for-profit sector, so that its list of beneficiaries would not be unduly restricted. The test for creation of a CIC is whether a reasonable person would consider the activities to be for the benefit of the community.

The types of beneficiaries that it is envisaged would be covered by the CICs would be within such areas as child care, social housing, leisure and transport.

CICs have a lock on their assets, which cannot be distributed to their members. There is also a limitation imposed on the distribution of dividends and bonus shares to members. Because such companies cannot adopt charitable status, bequests to a CIC are not eligible for tax relief.

While CICs are governed by a general company law, there is a separate regulator of community interest companies to regulate and guide CICs.

f Corporations registered under the Companies Acts

From the mid-nineteenth century, **Companies Acts** were passed that conferred the benefits of incorporation and limited liability of members on previously unincorporated associations of people if they wished to achieve this by registering under the Acts. The present law is to be found in the **Companies Act 2006**, which replaced earlier Acts. The organization of companies is as follows.

Registration of a company is effected by the formation of the company in accordance with Sections 7 to 16 of the Act. In this respect, it is now possible for a single person to form a public company. In contrast to provisions under previous legislation, a company's articles of association have now become the main part of the Company's constitution, with the company's memorandum forming part of its articles in accordance with Sections 17 to 38 of the Act. In this respect, the *Memorandum of association* is a more limited document than it was under the **Companies Act 1985**. The Memorandum now states that the subscribers wish to form a company, agree to become members and, where the company is to have a share capital, to take at least one share each.

6.18.2 Share structure of a company

The capital of a company may be divided into the following classes:

a Preference shares

Holders of these shares are entitled to a dividend at a fixed rate out of profits in priority to holders of any of the company's other shares.

b Ordinary shares

The dividend paid is not fixed but fluctuates with the profits of the company.

c Deferred shares

These are shares that may receive a higher dividend after the payment of preference and ordinary share dividends.

If the capital is insufficient to run the company, additional money may be raised by means of *debentures*. These are loans to the company, such loans being usually secured by means of a charge on the company's assets.

6.18.3 The *ultra vires* rule

Previously, the doctrine of *ultra vires* ('beyond the powers') applied particularly to corporations. This meant that where a statutory or registered company exceeded the powers granted to it by statute of incorporation or the Memorandum of Association, any contract made beyond the powers laid down was void. However, in accordance with section 31, there is no requirement for a company to have to register its objects under the Companies Act 2006, and even if it does, Section 39 has now abolished the *ultra vires* doctrine liability against third parties. In fact under Section 31 a company's capacity is unlimited unless its articles specifically provide otherwise. Although Section 171 of the Act still affects its application in respect of company directors, Sections 232 to 239 now provide company directors with protection from liability in respect of conduct by the company.

6.18.4 Termination of a company

The existence of a company may be ended either (i) by the Registrar of Companies striking the name of the company off the register (after satisfying himself that it is defunct) or (ii) by winding up.

- The winding up of a company is either voluntary or compulsory. A *voluntary* winding up is begun when the members of a company resolve so to do. A *compulsory* winding up is undertaken following an order of a court on a petition presented by a member of the company, a creditor or the Department of Trade. The petition may allege one or a number of grounds: for example, inability to pay its debts, failure to commence business within a year, failure to maintain the minimum numbers or that it is just and equitable to wind up.

  As an outcome of the coronavirus outbreak in 2020, the **Corporate Insolvency and Governance Act 2020** was enacted. It was divided into two parts. The first consisted of permanent measures to update the United Kingdom insolvency regime, and the other incorporated temporary measures into insolvency law and corporate governance to assist businesses during the pandemic. An overview of the Act stated that its overarching objective was to provide businesses with the flexibility and breathing space that they need to continue trading during the difficult time of the pandemic. The intention of these measures was to help companies and other similar entities by easing the burden on businesses and helping them to avoid insolvency during a period of economic uncertainty. The Act intended to achieve this purpose by three sets of measures:
- To introduce great flexibility into the insolvency regime, allowing companies breathing space to explore options for rescue whilst supplies are protected so they can have the maximum chance of survival.

  To temporarily suspend parts of insolvency law to support directors to continue trading through the emergency without the threat of personal liability and to protect companies from aggressive creditor actions.

  To provide companies and other bodies with temporary easements on company filing and requirements relating to meetings, including Annual General Meetings (AGMS).

6.18.5 Company voluntary arrangements

Both the **Insolvency Act 1986** and the **Insolvency Act 2000**, as amended by the **Enterprise Act 2002**, have introduced procedures whereby company voluntary arrangements can be conducted and approved under the benefit of a moratorium.

6.18.6 Limited liability partnership

The **Limited Liability Partnership Act 2000** makes provision for a new form of legal entity to be known as a limited liability partnership. This is a new form of body corporate subject to many of the controls imposed upon companies, but without shareholders or directors, share capital or any of the provisions relating to meetings or resolutions. In accordance with s. 8 of the Act, the obligations imposed by such controls will be imposed on designated members in the same way as officers of a company. Its members are permitted to design their own internal mechanism with certain parts of the **Partnership Act 1890** operating by way of default.

6.19 Unincorporated associations

As the name implies, these associations of people differ from corporations in that they (the associations) do not have a distinct legal personality separate from the members themselves. Common examples include societies and clubs such as a local tennis club, a college literary society or an arts group. Trade unions and partnerships are also unincorporated associations.

6.19.1 Legal liability of unincorporated associations

The law regards these groups as a collection of persons bearing individual responsibility for the association's actions. So, where an official of an association (e.g. a secretary) makes a contract for the purchase of goods for the common use of the group, the official is personally liable on such contract either alone or jointly with the committee that authorized it.

Where a tort is committed by an individual member, that person will be responsible in law. Where a committee is appointed to act on behalf of a number of people, the committee may, however, be held liable for any action that it authorized.

❖ CASE EXAMPLE

***Brown v Lewis* (1896)**

The committee of a football club authorized the repair of a football stand for use by the public. The repair was faultily performed and a member of the public was injured when the stand collapsed. *Held*: that the committee authorizing the repair was liable.

There are certain important points of law that affect unincorporated associations with regard to:

a Ownership of land

The **Law of Property Act 1925** places certain restrictions on the number of people who may own land together. Consequently, the association may nominate four of its members to hold land as trustees. These trustees may sue and be sued in respect of the property vested in them.

b Representative action

In a representative action (class action), one representative or more may bring or defend actions on the part of the other members of the group. As stated in Part 19 of the CPR Rules and Practice Directions at https://www.justice.gov.uk/courts/procedure-rules/civil/rules/part19, '(1) Where more than one person has the same interest in a claim – (a) the claim may be begun; or (b) the court may order that the claim be continued, by or against one or more of the persons who have the same interest as representatives of any other persons who have that interest.'

c Committee

An unincorporated association may confer powers on a committee to control membership and, where necessary, to expel members. It may therefore act as a disciplinary tribunal, but while so acting, it is subject to the rules of natural justice that may be enforced by the courts. An example of such a group is the Jockey Club, the stewards of which are empowered to control members.

d Trade unions and friendly societies

Some statutory recognition has been given to both these forms of unincorporated associations, and they may, in certain circumstances, sue and be sued.

e Partnerships

These may sue and be sued in the partnership's name.

f Credit unions

These thrift and loan societies have received statutory recognition in the **Credit Unions Act 1979**.

6.20 Partnerships

A partnership is defined by the **Partnership Act 1890** as *the relation that subsists between persons carrying on business in common with a view of profit.*

The relationship between the partners may be created orally, in writing or by conduct. Frequently, of course, a deed of partnership is drawn up legally to define the rights and duties of the partners.

The carrying on of business does not necessarily imply the buying and selling of goods; the partnership may well consist in the provision of services. Where persons engage in business and they share profits, the law will presume that a partnership has been formed even though the persons have never mentioned their intention orally or in writing.

Section 128 of the **Companies Act 1989** introduced a new s. 8A into the 1985 Act, where a 'partnership company' is defined as one whose shares are intended to be held to a substantial extent by, or on behalf of, its employees.

The **Limited Liability Partnership Act 2000** introduced the concept of Limited Liability Partnership. This is a partnership in which some or all of the parties have limited liabilities. This means that each partner is not responsible or liable for another partner's misconduct or negligence, indicating an important difference from the traditional form of partnership.

The following is a summary of the main distinctions between a partnership and a registered corporation:

a Personality

A partnership has no legal personality apart from the personalities of its members. A registered company is a legal person distinct from its members.

b Management

In the absence of contrary agreement, all partners are entitled to share in managing the firm. The members of a company have no such right: they have vested the management of the company in its directors.

c Contractual authority

A partner is presumed in law to have authority to enter into contracts on behalf of the firm in the ordinary course of its business. Members of a company, as such, have no such right.

d Liability

A partner, other than a *limited partner*, is liable for the debts of the partnership to the full extent of their private estate. A shareholder member of an ordinary limited company bears liability limited to the amount, if any, unpaid on their shares. If the company is limited by guarantee, he or she is limited to the amount of its guarantee.

e Numbers

A partnership has no limit as to its number of members (previously it was limited to a maximum of 20).

f Dissolution

A partnership firm is dissolved by (i) the expiration of the agreed period of its duration; (ii) the completion of the particular undertaking for which the firm was formed; (iii) death or bankruptcy of any partner; (iv) mutual agreement or (v) by order of a competent court. Companies are wound up compulsorily or voluntarily. The death of a member of a company does not affect the existence of the corporation itself.

Where a partner commits a tort while 'in actual or apparent furtherance of the business', the partnership firm will be liable for that tort.

The law requires that partners observe the utmost good faith in their mutual dealings. This means that a partner must disclose all profits made in relation to the business so that such profits may be shared in common.

There are two types of partner, general and limited. A *general partner* is a partner in the fullest sense, while a *limited partner* is one who takes no part in the management of the firm and whose liability is limited to the amount of their capital investment. Limited partnerships must be registered under the **Limited Partnerships Act 1907**. In any such firm, however, one general partner at least must be fully liable for the partnership debts.

6.21 Trade unions and employers' associations

A trade union may be defined as a combination of workmen whose principal object is collective bargaining for wages or conditions of work.

As everyone knows, the legal control of trade unions is the subject of political debate. The **Trade Union and Labour Relations (Consolidation) Act 1974**, as amended in **1976, 1980, 1982, 1984** and **1992**, is the main statute operating today. However, the **Employment Relations Act 1999** implements a new procedure for the recognition of trade unions for collective bargaining purposes by inserting a new n. 70A and Schedule Al into the **Trade and Labour Relations (Consolidation) Act 1992**. The new Schedule set out in Schedule 1 to the 1999 Act contains the detailed mechanism relating to applications for, adjudication upon and enforcement of trade union recognition and de-recognition.

So far as the status and regulation of trade unions and employers' associations are concerned, no union can be a corporate body (s. 10). The 1992 Act provides that all unions are to have certain of the attributes of corporate bodies, e.g. the power to sue and be sued in their own names.

The Acts require the Certification Officer to maintain lists of trade unions and employers' associations and lay down administrative and accounting requirements with which trade unions and employers' organizations must comply.

The **Transparency of Lobbying, Non-Party Campaigning and Trade Union Administration Act 2014** now provides for the appointment of a qualified independent person to be an assurer to certify that the trade union has complied with the requirements of the legislation as to the registration of its members. The assurer is required to inform the Certification Officer if the union's system of compiling and maintaining the register is not satisfactory.

Employers' associations are permitted to be either (a) bodies corporate or (b) unincorporated associations (s. 127(1)).

Legal immunities currently include (in accordance with s. 219):

a protection against action for civil conspiracy
b protection for peaceful picketing
c provision prohibiting any court from ordering someone to work
d protection for persons inducing breaches of contracts of employment in contemplation or furtherance of a trade dispute

However, these immunities are subject to certain restrictions set out in s. 219 of the 1992 Act.

The **Employment Relations Act 2004** made further amendments to the legislation relating to the recognition of the taking of industrial action. The legislation also made provisions concerning the rights of members and non-members of trade unions.

The **Trade Union Act 2016** has also made further major amendments to the Trade Union and Labour Relations (Consolidation) Act 1992 as follows:

a ss. 2 and 3 set out requirements for minimum thresholds of 50 per cent turn-out in all industrial ballots and a higher level of support and specified important public services
b ss. 4 to 6 set out information relating to industrial action to be included in the ballot paper and information to be given to union members and the Certification Officer following a ballot
c ss. 7 to 9 specify the arrangements for the timing and duration of industrial action
d s.10 sets out requirements for the supervision of picketing
e ss. 11 and 12 replace the current arrangements for a union member to contribute to a union's political fund, so that positive consent is required and also place requirements on unions to include more detailed information in expenditure from political funds in the annual returns to the Certification Officer

The **Strikes (Minimum Service Levels) Act 2023** amends the legal framework governing industrial action to enable minimum service levels (MSLs) to be set in key sectors during periods of strike action. It aims to strike a balance between the right of unions and their members to strike and the need for the wider public to be able to access key services during strikes.

6.22 Employment rights—protection against victimization

The **Public Interest Disclosure Act 1998** provides protection for public interest whistleblowers against victimization where individuals have raised genuine concerns regarding malpractice, in accordance with the provisions in the Act. The legislation incorporates a new Part IVA into the **Employment Rights Act 1996** whereby an employee can claim compensation if dismissed where the reason (or the principal reason) for that dismissal was the making of that protected disclosure, and such an award will be uncapped and based on actual losses. The type of malpractices is defined within the Act and includes a good faith test, proof that there is a factual basis for their belief and, in the event of a wider public disclosure, will have either raised it internally or with a prescribed regulatory body first, unless the employee was prevented by some good reason from doing so. The protection does not apply to employment in the Security Service, the Secret Intelligence Service or the Government Communications Headquarters, nor to police officers or persons on a contract of employment with the police service.

6.22.1 Employment rights—request for more predicable working

The **Workers (Predicable Terms and Conditions Act 2023** created a new statutory right for workers on atypical contracts—such as agency workers, short fixed-term workers and those on zero-hours contracts—to request a more predictable working pattern.

Those workers who have the right to make a request where:

- there is a lack of predictability as regards any part of the work pattern (the work pattern being the number of working hours, days of the week and times on those days when the worker works and the contract length);
- the change relates to their work pattern; and
- their purpose in applying for the change is to get a more predictable work pattern.

6.22.2 Employment rights—flexible working arrangements

The **Employment Relations (Flexible Working) Act 2023** aims to enhance employees' rights to request flexible working arrangements. It allows employees to make flexible working requests, more easily fostering discussions between employers and employees regarding flexible work options.

6.23 Maternity and paternity leave/parental bereavement leave

The **Work and Families Act 2006** extended the duration of time both for maternity and paternity leave and also provides equivalent arrangements in respect of those parents adopting a child. It also permits an employee to request flexible working hours where they have caring responsibilities for an adult or for a child who is less than 18 years of age.

These rights have been further extended by the **Children and Families Act 2014** in respect of shared parental pay; unpaid time off work to attend two ante-natal appointments with a pregnant woman; and the expansion of the right to request flexible working for employees who care for parents or carers to employees. The **Neonatal Care (Leave and Pay) Act 2023** provides parents with a right to 12 weeks leave and pay when their baby requires neonatal care in addition to existing parental leave entitlements.

The Protection from Redundancy (Pregnancy and Family Leave) Act 2023 provides priority status for redeployment opportunities during redundancies for affected employees, such as those who are pregnant or have recently returned from maternity, adoption or shared parental leave.

In addition, the **Parental Bereavement (Leave and Pay) Act 2018** grants a right for employed persons to be absent from work for a prescribed period (to be set at a minimum of two weeks) following the death of a child and also to be paid during that leave.

The **Paternity Leave (Bereavement) Act 2024** provides that bereaved fathers/partners automatically receive the right to immediate paternity leave if the mother (or adoptive parent of the child) dies.

6.24 Crown proceedings

The expression 'the Crown' may be used to describe (i) the Sovereign in her personal capacity and (ii) the Sovereign as Head of State, in her corporate capacity. The Crown, in its corporate capacity, includes Her Majesty's Ministers, the Government departments and the Civil Service.

Two ancient maxims of the common law determined the relationship of the Crown to a subject: 'No action can be brought against the King (or Queen) personally, for he cannot be sued in his Courts'; and 'The King can do no wrong'. The Sovereign could not and still cannot be sued personally for any alleged wrongs he or she may have committed in person. As a corporate body, the Crown was similarly immune from legal liability. The doctrine of vicarious liability (whereby, at common law, a master is liable for the wrongs of a servant committed in the course of his employment) did not apply to the Crown.

6.24.1 The Crown as employer

The Crown is now one of the largest employers of labour in the State. Until 1971 a civil servant held office 'at the pleasure of the Crown'. Thus, he was dismissible at the Royal pleasure.

The **Trade Union and Labour Relations (Consolidation) Act 1992** applies to Crown employment in the same way that it does to other employment. The effect now is that a civil servant can no longer be dismissed at the Crown's pleasure; their dismissal will have to be a fair dismissal and the onus of proving fairness lies on the Crown. The Act does not affect members of the Armed Forces who can be discharged 'at the pleasure of the Crown'.

6.24.2 The Crown Proceedings Act 1947

This Act was passed because of the unsatisfactory state of the law regarding legal proceedings against the Crown. The main object was to place the Crown in the same position, as far as possible, as a private person or employer, i.e. able to sue and be sued for breaches of contracts or for torts committed by servants. The Act does not affect the Queen's personal immunity from legal proceedings.

Liability in contract. The Act provides that actions for breach of contract may now be brought as of right against the Crown, without the need to obtain the *fiat* of the Attorney-General.

Liability in tort. Section 2(1) of the Act provides that 'the Crown shall be subject to all those liabilities in tort to which, if it were a person of full age and capacity, it would be subject:

a in respect of torts committed by its servants or agents;

b in respect of any breach of those duties which a person owes to his servants or agents at common law by reason of being their employer; and c in respect of any breach of the duties attaching at common law to the ownership, occupation, possession or control of property.'

As an example of (b): A master is under a common-law duty to provide a reasonably safe plant and machinery for his or her employees. If, therefore, the Crown provides a faulty vehicle for use by its servant B, as a result of which C is injured, an action will lie against the Crown under s. 2(1).

As an example of (c): A private person visits the local office of the Inspector of Taxes to discuss their income tax assessment. A defective electric light fitting falls from the ceiling and cuts the caller's head. An action will lie for the tort at the instance of the injured person.

Procedure. Action is brought against the appropriate Government department. The Treasury publishes a list of the departments and names the solicitor to accept service of process on behalf of each department. Where the department is not named, or uncertainty exists as to the department's identity, the Attorney General may be made defendant.

The legal action then follows the usual procedure of a High Court or county court action. The Act provides, however, that:

a judgment against the department cannot be enforced by the ordinary methods of levying execution or attachment. The department is required to pay the amount certified due as damages;
b an injunction and a decree of specific performance are inappropriate to the Crown. Instead, the court makes an order declaratory of the rights of the parties;
c no order for restitution of property will be made against the Crown. Instead, the court may declare the plaintiff entitled as against the Crown.

Special provision is made in the Act regarding (i) the Post Office and (ii) the Armed Forces of the Crown.

The Post Office. This was formerly a government department. The **Post Office Act 1969** constituted the Post Office as a public corporation and the staff ceased to be Crown servants. The corporation is headed by a chairman and a board of control who are responsible for the day-to-day administration. The telecommunications business of the Post Office was separated off under another public corporation, British Telecom plc.

The **Postal Service Act 2000** continued the process of modernization of the Post Office to a public limited company within the meaning of the **Companies Act 2006**, but with ownership remaining with the Crown. It also established the Postal Services Commission as a new independent regulator to promote and protect the interests of the consumer while restructuring the Post Office Users National Council to strengthen consumer representation.

The corporation may sue and be sued in its corporate name. Special regulations as to compensation obtainable against the Post Office for damage or loss or mis-delivery of letters or parcels apply, and reference should be made to the Post Office Guide.

Postmen and other officials may be prosecuted for theft of postal packets, etc. in the same way as other individuals, but punishment is usually more severe by reason of their special position.

The **Postal Services Act 2011** took the modernization of the Post Office one stage further. The Act made provision to allow for an unrestricted sale of shares in Royal Mail. This included a provision for an employee share scheme and for the Post Office to remain in full public ownership, except for a possible move to a mutual ownership structure in the future.

The Armed Forces. Nothing done or omitted by a member of the Armed Forces of the Crown while on duty shall subject him or the Crown to liability for inflicting death or personal injury on another member of the Armed Forces if (i) the latter is on duty or is on any land, premises, ship, aircraft or vehicle used for the purposes of the Armed Forces and if (ii) the Minister of Social Security certifies that the victim will receive an award.

Section 10 of the **Crown Proceedings Act 1947** has now been repealed by the **Crown Proceedings (Armed Forces) Act 1987**. This allows members of the Armed Forces to sue the Crown in personal injury cases.

❖ CASE EXAMPLE

***Adams v War Office* (1955)**

A was killed on duty by a shell fired by other members of the Armed Forces on duty. The Minister certified that *A*'s death was attributable to service for the purpose of entitlement to an award, but it was also held that *A*'s father did not satisfy the conditions of the Royal Warrant under which parents might claim a pension in respect of the loss of a son.

However, the Government has reserved the right to reactivate the provisions of section 10 in the event of impending, or actual, hostilities or grave national emergency.

The **Armed Forces Act 2006** introduced a single system of law that applied to all service personnel wherever in the world they are operating. This is subject to review every three years. The **Armed Forces (Service Complaints and Financial Assistance) Act 2015** inserted in the **Armed Forces Act 2006** a new Part 14A, which set out a framework of a reformed system for the redress of service complaints. The **Armed Forces Act 2016** made minor amendments to the previous legislation relating to the testing for alcohol and drugs, investigation and charging of service offences and suspended sentences of service detention.

In addition, the **Armed Forces (Flexible Working) Act 2018** made provision for members of the regular forces to serve part-time or subject to geographic restrictions and recognized a need to make changes necessary to enable the Armed Forces to work flexibly, reflecting the realities of modern life.

The **Armed Forces Act 2021** made further amendments to service courts, summary hearings and jurisdiction. It also reinforces the Armed Forces Covenant as set out in the **Armed Forces Act 2006**. In this respect, the **Overseas Operations (Service Personnel and Veterans) Act 2021** introduced special measures that would apply when decisions were made by prosecutors in relation to the prosecution of current or former Service personnel for historical offences allegedly committed overseas.

Crown servant. Section 2(6) of the Act defines the term 'officer' (in respect of whose actions the Crown now assumes liability in tort) as follows: the 'officer' shall (i) be appointed directly or indirectly by the Crown and (ii) be paid in respect of their duties as an officer of the Crown at the material time *wholly* out of the Consolidated Fund, moneys provided by Parliament, the Road Fund or any fund certified by the Treasury.

The police are not *wholly* paid out of such funds; hence the Crown is not subject to liability for torts committed by them.

Police powers. In the United Kingdom it was always traditional for the police to be organized locally rather than as a national police force. However, this approach was modified with the **Police and Magistrates' Courts Act 1994**, making provision for the Home Secretary to 'determine objectives for the policing of the areas of all police authorities' and the subsequent **Police Reform Act 2002**, extending the powers of the Home Secretary even further. This has included granting the Minister greater supervisory powers over police forces in England and Wales. The Act also incorporated the appointment of civilians with the right to exercise police powers, in particular, community support officers who have the right to exercise limited police powers such as the right to issue fixed penalty notices and the right to carry out searches and road checks.

However, the retention of a local influence regarding policing was recognized by the provision in the **Police Reform and Social Responsibility Act 2011** for direct election of police and crime commissioners (PCC) with direct control over local police budgets, to develop policing priorities and be responsible for the appointment and determination of the positions of local Chief Constables. This legislation was further reinforced by the **Policing and Crime Act 2017**.

Concern with the development of organized crime has led respective governments to establish a Serious Organised Crime Agency (SOCA) in accordance with the provisions of the **Serious Organised Crime and Police Act 2005**. SOCA was replaced in 2013 by the National Crime Agency with even wider powers.

6.24.3 Riot compensation

The **Riot Compensation Act 2016** repealed the **Riot (Damages) Act 1886** and recognized that, because of the civil disturbances of August 2011, the Act of 1886 needed updating. The 2016 Act creates a new scheme which allows compensation to be claimed for property that is damaged, destroyed or stolen in the course of a riot. Claims for compensation may be made in respect of property that was not insured, or was not adequately insured, against such loss or damage. The Act also allows an insurance company which has settled a claim in respect of loss or damage to property during a riot to reclaim the compensation they have paid out.

6.25 Data protection

The **Data Protection Act 1998** replaces and extends the effect of the **Data Protection Act 1984** regarding the protection of individuals in respect to the processing and free movement of personal data.

In accordance with the legislation, the Data Protection Registrar was replaced by a Data Protection Commission with wider powers of investigation and enforcement. While the onus is on the individual to seek enforcement and they can apply directly to the court if they are of the view that their rights have been infringed, the Commission is now permitted to assist where cases have substantial public interest.

As of 17 October 2001, the **Data Protection Act** has been extended from its application to computerized records of personal information, to also apply to a collection of facts about individuals on paper.

The **Digital Economy Act 2010** has made provision for the online infringement of copyright, incorporating penalties for infringement of copyright and performers' rights.

Further protection was introduced by the **Data Retention and Investigatory Powers Act 2014**.

The **Investigatory Powers Act 2016** provided an updated framework for the use (by the security and intelligence agencies, law enforcement and other public authorities) of investigatory powers to obtain communications and communications data. The **Investigatory Powers (Amendment) Act 2024** made targeted changes to the **Investigatory Powers Act 2016** to enable law enforcement and intelligence agencies to continue to tackle a range of evolving threats against a backdrop of accelerating technological change that provides new opportunities for terrorists, hostile state actors, child abusers and criminal gangs.

The **Digital Economy Act 2017** introduced a new Electronic Communications code and other communications infrastructure matters, introducing better controls on online pornography and protecting persons from nuisance calls.

The **Data Protection Act 2018** updates previous data protection laws. It sets new standards for protecting personal data and gives people more control over the use of their data. It also helps the general public in the UK prepare for a future outside the EU.

Four main matters which are provided for in the Act are: general data processing, data processing for national security purposes, including processing by the intelligence services, and regulatory oversight and enforcement.

The **Online Safety Act 2023** gave further powers to the relevant Secretary of State to designate and suppress or record speech and media deemed 'harmful'. The Act introduced criminal offences related to online safety, including encouraging or assisting serious self-harm, cyber flashing and intimate image abuse. The Act also confers new powers on the Office of Communications (OFCOM), establishing it as the online safety regulator. This role includes overseeing and enforcing the new regulatory regime.

The **Digital Markets, Competition and Consumers Act 2024** has the aim of overhauling competition and consumer protection laws in the United Kingdom, with the intention of creating a new regime to enhance competition in digital markets and conferring powers on the Competition and Markets Authority (AMA). It is intended that the Act will come into effect in phases, with provisions related to consumer law enforcement expected to take effect in April 2025.

6.26 Regulation of Public Service Broadcasting

The **Media Act 2024** aims to modernize media regulations. It brings new streaming platforms under the Office of Communications (OFCOM) rules and makes changes to the public service media framework. This includes changes to on-demand programme service (ODPS) regulation in the United Kingdom.

6.27 Surveillance camera systems

S. 29 of the **Protection of Freedoms Act 2012** incorporates a code of practice relating to surveillance camera systems. This provides for the designation of a Chief Surveillance Commissioner.

6.28 Smart meters

The Smart Meters Act 2018 enables the Secretary of State to have:

a extended powers to develop, amend and oversee regulations to smart metering

b introduces a special administrative regime for the national smart meter communication and data service provided to ensure the service continues to be provided in the unlikely event of its insolvency

c provides new powers allowing Ofgem to directly modify industry codes and documents for the purposes of delivering market-wide half-yearly settlement, which uses smart metering data

6.29 Intellectual property

This is covered by the **Copyright, Designs and Patents Act 1977**, the **Registered Designs Act 1949** and the **Freedom of Information Act 2000**. The provisions of these Acts have now been extended by the **Intellectual Property Act 2014**, which intended to strengthen and simplify intellectual property law. The **Intellectual Property (Unjustified Threats) Act 2017** provides a remedy for those who are affected by threats to sue for infringement of a patent, trademark or design where they are made in respect of an invalid right or where there has been no infringement.

The **Enterprise and Regulatory Reform Act 2013**, ss. 74 to 78, makes amendments to the **Copyright, Designs and Patents Act 1988** in respect of the reduction of the duration of copyright in unpublished works other than photographs and films. S. 77 makes provision for the licensing of orphan works (where the owner of a copyright cannot be traced after a diligent search).

6.30 Useful webpages

United Nations Human Rights (www.ohchr.org/EN/Issues/Pages)

Universal Declaration of Human Rights (www.ohchr.org/EN/UDHR/Pages/UDHRIndex.aspx)

European Convention on Human Rights (www.echr.coe.int/Documents/Convention_ENG.pdf)

Lord Bingham, 'The Rule of Law' [2008] 1 *Judicial Studies Institute Journal* 121 at 136 (https://www.ijsj.ie/assets/uploads/documents/pdfs/2008-Edition-01/article/the-rule-of-law.pdf)

Coke, Edward. [1628] 1823. The First Part of the Institutes of the Laws of England, vol. 1. Edited by Butler, C. London: J. & W. T. Clarke.

6.31 Exercises

1 By what means may British nationality be acquired?

2 What are the three classes of domicile? Why is it important to establish the domicile of a person for the purposes of English law?

3 Distinguish between (i) void marriage and (ii) voidable marriage.

4 What 'domestic proceedings' may be taken in a magistrates' court?

5 What special rules apply to mentally disordered persons?

6 Define a 'corporation' in law. What are the distinguishing features of a corporation?

7 Distinguish between (i) a company limited by shares, (ii) a company limited by guarantee and (iii) an unlimited company.

8 Describe the operation of the *ultra vires* rule in regard to companies.

9 'The King can do no wrong.' How far is this maxim true today?

10 Outline the main provisions of the **Crown Proceedings Act 1947**.

11 What provisions are available for those who have suffered damage to property as a result of a riot?

12 What aspects of materials are protected under the provisions of the intellectual property legislation?

Chapter 7

The law of contract

Key points

- what constitutes a contract
- the essentials of a valid contract
- void, voidable and illegal contract
- the ways in which a contract may be discharged
- remedies for breach of contract

In his book *Principles of the Law of Contracts*, Sir William Anson defined a contract as *a legally binding agreement made between two or more parties, by which rights are acquired by one or more to acts or forbearances on the part of the other or others.* Shortly it may be defined as an agreement between two or more parties that is intended to have legally enforceable consequences.

The agreement referred to in the definition means a meeting of minds, called in law *consensus ad idem*, signifying that the parties are agreed together about the same thing. The definition also emphasizes that the parties to the contract must intend that their agreement shall be legally enforceable. Unless the law recognizes this and enforces the agreements of parties, it would be impossible to carry on commercial or business life. For this reason the law of contract plays a leading role in courses on business studies.

These contractual agreements give rise to rights and obligations that the law recognizes and enforces. But certain agreements, such as domestic and social arrangements, are not intended by the parties to be legally binding. The law allows for this. Suppose if Cumming and Gowing agree to meet for dinner and Gowing fails to turn up, the law will do nothing in the matter. The agreement was not intended to create legal rights and duties; as such, it is not a contract in law. Every contract is an agreement, but not every agreement is a contract.

The object of the law of contract is to identify those agreements that it will enforce and those that it will not. This is of prime importance and will be referred to later in more detail.

7.1 Essentials of a valid contract

An agreement will be enforced when the following essential elements exist:

a *Offer and acceptance*. There must be an offer by one party and an acceptance of it by the other.
b *Intention* to create legal relations.

DOI: 10.4324/9781003422808-7

c *Capacity* of the parties. Each party must have the legal capacity to make the contract.
d *Consent* must be genuine. The consent must not be obtained by fraud or duress (such as death threats if the contract is not entered into).
e *Consideration* must be present (except in contracts under seal, i.e. by deed; see p. 140 for a definition of consideration).
f *Legality* of object. The object of the contract must not be one of which the law disapproves.
g *Possibility* of performance.

All these elements must be present. If one or more is absent, the contract will be either (i) void, (ii) voidable or (iii) unenforceable.

Void contracts are destitute of legal effect; that is, they are not contracts, and agreements of this kind do not confer legal rights on the parties thereto. For example, a contract by an infant to buy goods other than 'necessaries'. Similarly, if *A* agrees with B to break into C's house and steal if B pays *A* £10, the contract is void for it is illegal. Neither party can recover from the other on a void contract, but goods delivered may be recovered by an action in tort because no property (ownership) passes. Money paid under the agreement may be recovered in quasi-contract (see p. 211).

Voidable contracts are those that may be made void at the instance of one of the parties. For example, a contract that is induced by fraud can be avoided by the party deceived.

Unenforceable contracts are those that are valid but are unenforceable at law because of the absence of (i) evidence of the contract or (ii) the form required by law. For example, some contracts that are not 'evidence in writing' are unenforceable at law. So, too, are contracts barred by the **Limitation Act 1980**.

7.2 Classification of contracts

Contracts may be classified under the following headings: (a) contracts of record, (b) specialty contracts and (c) simple contracts.

a Contracts of record

These include (i) judgments of a court and (ii) recognizances.

i *Judgments of a court*. The previous rights under a contract are merged in the judgment. Thus, *A* owes B £10 on a contract. B sues *A* and obtains judgment. The previous rights become merged in the judgment of the court, and execution may be levied upon *A* to enforce payment, if need be.
ii *Recognizances*. In the criminal courts an offender may on conviction be 'bound over to be of good behaviour and to keep the peace'. The person so bound acknowledges that there is a debt to the Crown of a certain sum of money (say, £10 or £20) if he or she fails to observe the terms of the recognizance.

b Specialty contracts (or contracts by deed)

This type of contract is the only formal contract in the law. Specialty contracts are used for various transactions such as conveyances of land, a lease of property for more than three years and articles of partnership.

The characteristics of a contract by deed are that it is (i) signed, (ii) sealed and (iii) delivered. Signing needs no explanation. An X will suffice if the signatory is unable to write. Sealing is today the affixing of a paper wafer, which is touched by the person making the deed.

Delivery is made by handing over the deed physically to the other party (or the agent, e.g. solicitor) or, constructively, by touching the seal and uttering the words 'I deliver this as my act and deed'.

When delivery is made subject to a condition, it is termed an *escrow*; this means that although the deed has been 'delivered' it will not become effective until the specified condition has been fulfilled. An illustration as to how this operates in practice may be illustrated by the situation in *Silver Queen Maritime Ltd v Persia Petroleum Services plc* (2010) where Persia Petroleum delivered a deed as an escrow which Silver Queen executed and returned. Once this condition had been fulfilled the deed became effective despite Persia Petroleum attempting to recall and reject the deed.

Where there are two or more parties, the deed is sometimes called an *indenture*.

The Law Commission recommended that the requirement for sealing in certain circumstances should be abolished. Acting on this recommendation, the **Law of Property (Miscellaneous Provisions) Act 1989** abolished the requirements for sealing where a deed is executed by an individual and replaced it with a rule that it must be clear on the face of the instrument that it is intended to be a deed. In order to satisfy the requirements of HM Land Registry, deeds for the transfer of land should contain the phrase 'signed as deed'.

c Simple contracts

These are contracts not under seal. They may be made (i) orally, (ii) in writing or (iii) implied by conduct.

We have considered the essential elements in a valid simple contract, and we have noted that it must be supported by valuable consideration (see p. 140). In the absence of such consideration, the contract will be void.

In addition to the preceding, we may note the following types of contract:

An *express contract* is one where the terms are stated in words (orally or in writing) by the parties.

An *implied contract* is one in which the terms are not expressed but are implied from the conduct or position of the parties. For example, if someone goes into a restaurant, takes a seat and is supplied with a meal, the law will imply a contract from the very nature of the circumstances and the customer will be obliged to pay for it. Similarly, where money that is not due is paid by mistake, the law implies a contract by the person paid to refund the money (see quasi-contract, p. 211).

An *executed contract* is one wholly performed on one or both sides. For example, on 1 June Arnold agrees to dig Basset's Garden in August if Basset will pay Arnold £10 on 1 July. When Basset pays the £10 and Arnold digs the garden the contract will be executed so far as Arnold and Basset are concerned.

An *executory contract* is one that is wholly unperformed or in which there remains something further to be done on both sides. For instance, the contract in the previously stated example is executory between 1 June and 1 July, for the contract is wholly unperformed until Basset pays Arnold £10. Many examples occur in relation to goods, as when a customer agrees to buy a car for £18,000 in the following year, payment to be made on delivery.

7.2.1 Distinction between a bilateral contract and a unilateral contract

Whereas a bilateral contract places obligations upon and grants rights to both parties, in a unilateral contract only one party makes an undertaking which they are not under an obligation to fulfil. An example of a unilateral contract is an estate agency contract—because the estate agent is not bound to find a purchaser, but if he or she does, they will be entitled to the commission.

Thus, in *Wells v Devani* (2016) the Supreme Court upheld a claim by an estate agent, Mehul Devani, that a commission became payable to him by Edward Wells, the vendor of a number of flats, on the completion of the sale of the flats to a purchaser whom Devani had to introduced to Wells.

7.3 Offer and acceptance

As already mentioned, to constitute a contract there must be an offer and an acceptance. The party making the offer is known as the *offeror*, the party to whom the offer is made is known as the *offeree*. The contract comes into existence when an offer has been *unconditionally* accepted.

How made. An offer may be made orally, in writing or by conduct. An example of an offer made by conduct is where a customer in a supermarket chooses goods and hands them to the cashier, who then accepts the customer's offer to buy.

To whom made. An offer may be made to a definite person (or group of persons) or to the whole world, i.e. generally. Where an offer is made to one person only, or a group of persons, only that person or that group may accept. Where an offer is made to the whole world, anyone may accept by complying with the terms of the offer.

❖ CASE EXAMPLE

Boulton v Jones (1857)

B bought a hose-pipe business from one Brocklehurst. J, the defendant, to whom Brocklehurst owed a debt, addressed an order to Brocklehurst for some piping. B supplied the order even though it was not addressed to him. J refused to pay B for the piping and contended that he meant to deal with Brocklehurst only because he had a set-off (contra) account against Brocklehurst. *Held*: that the offer was made to Brocklehurst and that J was not liable to B for the goods as there was no contract. 'Now the rule of law is clear, that if you propose to make a contract with *A*, then B cannot substitute himself for *A* without your consent and to your disadvantage, securing to himself all the benefits of the contract' (Pollock, C.B.).

Where a reward is offered to any person who does a certain thing, e.g. finding lost property, it follows that any person may accept. Providing the finder knows of the offer a claim may be made for any reward for returning the property.

❖ CASE EXAMPLE

Carlill v Carbolic Smoke Ball Co. (1893)

A patent-medicine company advertised that it would give £100 to anyone who contracted influenza after using their smoke ball for a certain period. Plaintiff (Mrs Carlill) bought the article, used it as directed and contracted influenza, nevertheless. She claimed the reward of £100. *Held*: that plaintiff accepted by complying with the conditions of the offer. There was an offer capable of acceptance by all who used the smoke ball, and it mattered not that the plaintiff did not communicate her acceptance to the offeror.

The offer must be communicated to the offeree. An offer must be communicated to the offeree before it can be accepted. A person cannot be said to accept an offer of which they are unaware. If A, by public notice, advertises a £100 reward to the finder of a lost brooch, and B, who is unaware of the notice and the offer, finds the brooch and returns it to the loser, B is not entitled to claim the reward.

❖ CASE EXAMPLE

***Taylor v Laird* (1856)**

A ship's captain, T, threw up his command of a vessel during a voyage, but nevertheless helped to work the ship home. He then claimed compensation for his services. *Held*: that as T had not communicated his offer to work the ship home, the defendant owners had no opportunity of accepting or rejecting the services, so T could not recover compensation.

An offer must be distinguished from an invitation to treat. An 'invitation to treat' means an invitation to make offers. Thus, when an auctioneer requests bids, potential bidders are invited to make offers. An offer is accepted by the auctioneer by the fall of the hammer.

Where goods are displayed in a shop window or on shelves in a self-service store, the display is construed as an invitation to treat, not an offer to sell. Where a customer picks up an article in a self-service store and takes it to the cashier's desk to pay, the taker's action is an offer to buy. It is for the cashier (or shopkeeper) to accept the offer and take the purchase money in payment (*Pharmaceutical Society of Gt Britain v Boots Cash Chemists (Southern) Ltd*, 1953).

❖ CASE EXAMPLE

***Fisher v Bell* (1960)**

A shopkeeper displayed in his shop window a flick-knife behind which was a ticket reading 'Ejector knife—4s.'. He was charged with offering for sale a flick-knife, contrary to the **Restriction of Offensive Weapons Act 1959**. *Held*: that the display of goods in a shop window is not in itself an offer for sale. 'According to the law of contract, the display of an article with a price on it in a shop window is merely an invitation to treat. It is in no sense an offer for sale the acceptance of which constitutes a contract' (Lord Chief Justice Parker).

As a consequence of this decision a further Act was passed in 1961 to include the words 'exposes or has in his possession for the purpose of sale', thus giving effect to the intention of Parliament.

❖ CASE EXAMPLE

Harris v Nickerson (1873)

An auctioneer, N, advertised that a sale of office furniture would take place at Bury St Edmunds. H travelled down from London to attend the sale, but found the furniture was withdrawn from the sale. H thereupon sued the auctioneer for his loss of time and expenses. *Held*: that the advertisement was a mere declaration of intention and did not create a binding contract with H when he acted on it.

However, with regard to auction sales that are advertised as 'without reserve' the courts have held in *Warlow v Harrison* (1859) (Auctioneer refused to sell to the highest bidder in an auction advertised as 'without reserve') and *Barry v Davies* (2000) (Customs and Excise refused to accept a low bid and instead sold for a higher price through a magazine—auction again advertised as 'without reserve') that the auctioneer is contractually bound to sell to the highest bidder.

A statement of price is not necessarily an offer.

❖ CASE EXAMPLE

Harvey v Facey (1893)

The following telegraph messages were exchanged between the parties. H: 'Will you sell us Bumper Hall Pen? Telegraph lowest price.' F: 'Lowest price for Bumper Hall Pen £900.' H: 'We agree to buy Bumper Hall Pen for £900 asked by you.' To this last telegram F made no reply. H claimed that there was a contract between himself and F. *Held* (by the Judicial Committee of the Privy Council): that there was no contract. The second telegram was not an offer but in the nature of an invitation to treat (i.e. the lowest price if it were decided to sell). The final message could not be looked upon as an acceptance.

Termination of an offer. An offer terminates:

a on the death of either offeror or offeree *before* acceptance;
b by non-acceptance within the time stipulated for acceptance or within a reasonable time;
c when revoked before acceptance;
d when rejected by the offeree.

Termination by methods (a) and (b) is sometimes referred to as *lapse of offer*. Students should note that although death of offeror or offeree before acceptance terminates the offer, death after acceptance has no effect on the majority of contracts. Where an offeree dies after acceptance the contract will be valid. Thus, Potts offers to sell building land to Kettle. Kettle accepts the offer but dies before conveyance. Kettle's personal representatives may compel Potts to convey the land to themselves.

As to (b), what constitutes 'a reasonable time' is a matter for the court and varies with the type of contract. Some offers must be accepted almost immediately. Where an offer is made by telegram, the mode of offer indicates prima facie that the acceptance should be quick also and, in this case, a reply by letter may be too late. Other offers may be accepted within a month or even longer.

❖ CASE EXAMPLES

Ramsgate Victoria Hotel Co. Ltd v Montefiore (1866)

M by letter on 8 June offered to purchase shares in a company. The shares were allotted on 23 November; M refused the shares. *Held*: that the offer to take shares lapsed through unreasonable delay in accepting.

Heathcote Ball & Co (Commercial Auctions) Ltd v Barry (2000)

The defendant auctioneer advertised to sell by auction without reserve two new engine analysis machines. Although the manufacturers' list price was £14,521, the claimant only bid £200 for each of the machines after which the auctioneer purported to withdraw the machines from auction. *Held*: The promise to hold an auction without reserve was an offer of a collateral contract that was accepted by the claimant by making his bid.

Revocation of offer. The offeror may decide to withdraw or revoke the offer he or she made. To be effective, the offer must be communicated to the offeree before acceptance. The revocation may be made directly by the offeror or indirectly. The important point to note is that revocation is of no effect until it is actually brought to the notice of the offeree.

❖ CASE EXAMPLE

Byrne v Van Tienhoven (1880)

On 1 October, defendant *V* offered by letter goods for sale to B. On 11 October B received the letter and accepted by telegraph immediately. On 8 October, *V* wrote to B revoking the offer. On 20 October B received the letter of revocation. *Held*: that B had accepted the offer on 11 October. Revocation to be effective must be communicated to the offeree before he has accepted. The fact that a letter of revocation had been posted or was on its way was immaterial.

Where notice of revocation of an offer does not come directly from the offeror or his or her agent, but from a *reliable source*, this is deemed indirect revocation.

❖ CASE EXAMPLE

Dickinson v Dodds (1876)

X offered to sell a house to Y, the letter stating: 'This offer to be left over until Friday, 9 a.m.' On Thursday, Y heard from *A* that X had sold the house to Z On Friday at 7 a.m. Y handed to X his acceptance of the offer. *Held*: that there was no contract between X and Y, since X had revoked his offer and the revocation had been communicated to Y by *A* before the purported 'acceptance' by Y.

Rejection of offer may take two forms: (i) where the offeree communicates his rejection to the offeror and (ii) where the offeree makes a counter-offer.

An example of (ii) occurred in the following case:

❖ CASE EXAMPLE

Hyde v Wrench (1840)

W offered to sell a farm to H for £1,000. H said he would give £950. *W* refused, and H then said he would give £1,000. When *W* refused, H sought to obtain an order of specific performance. *Held*: that there was no contract. H's offer of £950 was a counter-offer, which evidently rejected the original offer.

Where the offeree accepts subject to a condition, this also amounts to a rejection.

❖ CASE EXAMPLE

Jordan v Norton (1838)

N offered to buy J's horse if warranted quiet in harness. J agreed to the price and said he would warrant the horse quiet in *double* harness. *Held*: that N's offer was rejected.

But note that a mere request for further information of the offer does not amount to a counter-offer so as to bring about a rejection.

The methods of communicating acceptance are varied, and it is advisable to note the following decisions.

Mental acceptance. This means assenting to an offer in one's mind, but not actually communicating acceptance.

❖ CASE EXAMPLE

Felthouse v Bindley (1862)

F offered by letter to buy his nephew's horse for £30. F wrote: 'If I hear no more about him, shall consider the horse is mine at £30.' The nephew did not reply, but he asked the auctioneer who was engaged to sell the horse to keep the horse out of the sale because he had sold it to his uncle. By error, the auctioneer, Bindley, included the horse in the sale, and F sued B for conversion. *Held*: that F had no claim since his offer to buy had only been mentally accepted by the nephew. It had not been communicated to the offeror.

Particular method of acceptance. Where the offeror prescribes a particular method of acceptance, it follows that the method prescribed should normally be followed. Thus, where acceptance of an offer is to be by telegram, acceptance by air mail would be insufficient because it does not comply with the terms of the offer.

Where acceptance consists in the performance of an act, as in *Carlill v Carbolic Smoke Ball Co. Ltd* (1893) summarised on p. 129, this may be sufficient acceptance since the offer does not contemplate that the offeree should notify the offeror orally or by letter. The finder of a lost dog or other article, provided that it is returned, will be able to claim any reward offered, assuming in this case the finder knew of the reward beforehand.

Options. An option is an offer to keep a contract 'open' for a specified time. An option is not binding unless made by deed or supported by valuable consideration. Thus Potts, the owner of a building site, may give Kettle an option to buy the land, in consideration of Kettle paying £500, such offer to remain open for one month. This is not an offer to sell the land but is a contract to allow Kettle to buy it within the time (one month) on the terms of the contract. Potts is lawfully bound to sell to Kettle and, if Potts revokes the option, Kettle can on the terms of the option compel Potts to sell the land to him.

7.3.1 Rules regarding acceptance

How made. Acceptance of an offer may be made orally, in writing or by conduct. The first two models of acceptance are self-evident. Acceptance by conduct is exemplified in the case of *Carlill v Carbolic Smoke Ball Co. Ltd* (1893) summarised on p. 129.

Acceptance must be unqualified. This means that the acceptance must be absolute and must conform exactly with the terms of the offer. Thus, if the offeree is required to perform an act or to pay a sum of money, the act must be performed or the sum mentioned paid exactly.

❖ CASE EXAMPLE

Neale v Merret (1930)

M offered to sell land to N for £280. N replied purporting to accept and enclosed £80, promising to pay the balance of £200 by monthly instalments of £50 each. *Held*: that N could not enforce acceptance because his acceptance was not an unqualified one.

Acceptance subject to contract. Acceptance 'subject to contract' means that the parties do not intend to be bound and are not bound until a formal contract is prepared and signed by them. The object of the phrase, which often appears in sales of land and property, is to give the parties an opportunity to reflect on the matter, to obtain legal advice and to change their minds if need be.

❖ CASE EXAMPLES

Eccles v Bryant (1948)

The plaintiff bought a house subject to contract. The terms of the formal contract were agreed, and each party signed his part. The plaintiff posted his part, but the vendor changed his mind before posting his part. *Held*: that there was no binding contract.

Branca v Cobarro (1947)

The parties negotiated for the sale of a farm and signed a document containing the statement: 'This is a provisional agreement until a fully legalized agreement drawn up by a solicitor and embodying all the conditions herewith stated is signed.' *Held* (by the Court of Appeal): that the use of the word 'provisional' indicated that the parties intended the document to be binding, although to be replaced subsequently by a more formal contract.

Jordan Grand Prix Ltd v Vodafone Group plc (2003)

Claimant company, participants in Formula One motor racing, alleged that the defendant's director had agreed in a telephone conversation to sponsor the claimant's team for three seasons in the sum of $US150m for three years. *Held*: that nothing in the telephone conversation could sensibly be said to be 'subject to contract'. Furthermore, the director did not have actual nor ostensible authority to bind the defendants to an alleged agreement. Claimant's case plainly demonstrated to be without foundation and false and, accordingly was dismissed.

In *Walford and Others v Miles and Anor* (1992) the House of Lords held that while (i) a lockout agreement, where one party for good consideration agrees for a specific period of time to negotiate only with the other party to the exclusion of anyone else will be enforceable, an agreement to (ii) negotiate for an unspecified period of time will be unenforceable as lacking in certainty.

Acceptance by post. Where the post is the proper means of communication between the parties to a contract the following rules apply:

a An offer has no effect until it reaches the offeree. Where an offer is made by post, it takes effect (i.e. it is communicated) when it reaches the offeree, not when the letter is posted.

❖ **CASE EXAMPLE**

Adams v Lindsell (1818)

On 2 September, *L* wrote offering to sell wool at a price and requesting an answer in course of post. The letter was misdirected and reached *A* on 5 September. The reply of acceptance was sent at once and reached *L* on 9 September, but the wool had been sold on 8 September. *Held*: that there was a good contract between *A* and *L*, because the offer was accepted at once on being received.

b Where an offer is made and accepted by letters sent through the post, the contract is made the moment the letter accepting the offer is posted, even if it never reaches its destination.

❖ **CASE EXAMPLE**

Household Fire Insurance Co. v Grant (1879)

G applied for shares in a company. A letter of allotment of shares was posted to G but never reached him. *Held*: that the contract was complete on posting, and G became a shareholder of the company.

For the preceding rules to apply, the letter of acceptance must be prepaid, properly addressed and properly posted. The handing of a letter to a postman is not a proper posting.

c Revocation of an offer is communicated when the letter of revocation is received and read by the offeree. (See *Byrne v Van Tienhoven* (1800), summarised on p. 132.)

As to instantaneous communications, e.g. by telephone, the contract is complete only when the acceptance is received by the offeror at his or her end of the line. If the line 'goes dead' during the communication of the acceptance, there is no contract.

If A telephones acceptance of an offer made by B, and B does not hear *A*'s voice at the moment of acceptance, B should request *A* to repeat the message. Otherwise, B may be stopped from denying that there has been a communication of acceptance.

❖ **CASE EXAMPLE**

Entores Ltd v Miles Far East Corporation (1955)

Plaintiffs in London made an offer by Telex (teleprinter) to defendants in Amsterdam. The defendants accepted by Telex message transmitted to London. Later, defendants were in breach of contract and the plaintiffs wished to establish that the contract by Telex was made in London where the acceptance took place, in which case the legal action could be decided in English courts. *Held*: that the contract had been made in London, since the defendant's acceptance of plaintiff's offer was not complete until actually received by plaintiff. This Court of Appeal decision was upheld by the House of Lords in *Brinkibon Ltd v Stahag Stahl* (1982).

Regarding email, it has been argued that emails should also be treated as a form of instantaneous communication. This would mean that acceptance is only valid when it is received by the offeror rather than the application of the postal rule. The question arises as to when an email is deemed to have been received. It has been argued on the basis of the 'default rule', on the grounds of certainty, that this should be when the email arrives on the offeror's server and not when it is read by the offeror or ought reasonably to have come to his or her attention. As this is a default rule it can be disputed if the offeree is aware that the email has not been received or where non-receipt is the offeree's fault or within its sphere of influence.

So that in *Greenenergy SA v Memphis Biofuels* (2008), it was *held* that there was a good arguable case in the course of the negotiations such that the acceptance had taken effect in Lourdes (where the offeror received the emailed acceptance). The postal rule did not apply.

Although it did not give rise to legal proceedings a situation arose in in 1999 when Argos erroneously made an offer of a television set for £3 which was eagerly taken up by numerous customers. Argos refused to confirm any sale at this price arguing that what it had done was to make an 'invitation to treat' to its customers which Argos was entitled to withdraw.

The situation gave rise to a statement by the Advertising Standards Authority: 'This [case] is interesting because it will help determine where an advertisement ends and where a virtual shop front begins. It will define our area of jurisdiction more clearly.'

In *Neocleous v Rees* (2019) it was *held* that an automatically generated email footer could amount to a signature for the purposes of the **Law of Property (Miscellaneous Provisions) Act 1989**. This was approved by the Court of Appeal in *Hudson v Hathway* (2022).

In a Report issued by the Law Commission on 4 September 2019, it confirmed that electronic signatures could be used to execute documents, including where there is a statutory requirement for a signature. The Commission stated that

> An electronic signature is capable in law of being used to execute a document (including a deed), provided that the signatory intends to authenticate the document and that any relevant formalities, such as the signature being witnessed, are satisfied. The Commission's view is based upon the legislation and court decisions which relate to both non-electronic and electronic signatures.

Tenders. A tender is an offer. Tenders commonly arise where, for example, a corporation invites offers to supply goods or services. Two kinds of tender must, however, be distinguished: (a) where the tender is an offer to supply a *specified* or definite quantity of goods or services; and (b) where the tender is a *standing* offer, i.e. an offer to supply goods or services periodically or as required.

The rules may be summarized as follows:

a Where tenders are invited for the supply of goods or services, each tender submitted is a separate offer any one of which may be accepted. On acceptance of a tender a contract is formed. For example, *A* invites tenders for the supply of 100 tons of coal: *B* submits a tender that is accepted; the contract is formed immediately the tender is accepted.

b Where the tender is a standing offer to supply goods or services as required by the buyer (or offeree), a separate acceptance is made each time an order is placed.

❖ CASE EXAMPLE

Great Northern Railway Co. v Witham (1873)

A railway company advertised for tenders for the supply of stores. *W* made a tender and undertook 'to supply the company for 12 months with such quantities of specified articles as the company may order from time to time'. The tender was accepted. Orders were placed and goods supplied for some time, but later *W* refused to execute an order given. *Held*:*W* was bound to supply goods that had been specifically ordered but was free to refuse to supply any further goods that might be ordered in the future.

If the buyer gives no order or fails to order the full quantity of goods set out in a tender, there is no breach of contract; but where a buyer binds himself 'to buy all the goods he needs' from the person submitting a tender, the contract is broken if the buyer does need some of the goods and does not obtain them from the tenderer (*Kier v Whitehead Iron Co.*, 1918).

❖ **CASE EXAMPLE**

***Blackpool and Fylde Aero Club Ltd v Blackpool Borough Council* (1990)**

The council refused to consider a tender placed in their letter box which was cleared by the council after the specified time for submission of tenders. *Held*: (Court of Appeal) The Council was bound by the Club's action for breach of contract as the invitation to tender did contain an offer to consider tenders received by the submission of the 12-noon deadline.

7.4 Intention to create legal relations

A contract is an agreement that is intended to have legal consequences. Whether or not an agreement is intended to have such consequences is not always easily determined. We have mentioned that agreements of a purely social or domestic nature are not contracts. However, there are some 'domestic' agreements that do create legal obligations.

❖ **CASE EXAMPLES**

***Simpkins v Pays* (1955)**

S agreed with P and P's granddaughter to 'go shares' in a weekly coupon submitted in a fashion competition. A forecast by the granddaughter proved correct and the defendant received a prize of £750. Plaintiff sued for his share of £250. *Held*: that there was an intention to create legal relations. Evidence showed there was a joint enterprise, and the parties expected to share any prize won in the competition. It was not a mere domestic arrangement.

***Parker v Clark* (1960)**

An aged couple arranged by correspondence with their niece and her husband whereby the latter couple sold up their home in Sussex in order to live with the aged couple and to share the household and other expenses. The two couples subsequently quarrelled, and the Parkers were ordered to leave the house. *Held*: that there was an intention to create legal relations, and damages were awarded to plaintiff.

Wilson v Burnett (2007)

Claim of two women that they had made a binding agreement with a friend to share a bingo prize of £100,000 three ways. *Held*: The claimant had come nowhere near to rebutting the presumption with that of a 'bare-bones' account of a casual conversation.

Commercial and business agreements. In all cases coming before the courts, evidence (oral or written) will be required to substantiate the existence of a legal agreement. In commercial and business relations the law will presume that the parties entering into agreement intend those agreements to have legal consequences. Examples abound in this book.

However, this presumption may be negatived by express terms.

❖ CASE EXAMPLES

Rose & Frank Co. v J.R. Crompton & Bros Ltd (1925)

Plaintiffs were appointed selling agents in North America for the defendants, and the parties entered into an agreement that included the following: 'This arrangement is not, nor is this memorandum written as, a formal or legal agreement and shall not be subject to legal jurisdiction in the law courts.' *Held*: that this agreement was not a legally binding contract. The court stated it would respect the intention of the parties as shown in the agreement.

Blue v Ashley (2017)

A claimed £14m from B, the owner of Sports Direct, stating that he had orally agreed to pay him this sum as an incentive to do work at increasing Sports Direct share price. *Held*: (Leggatt J) that the claimant had clearly not rebutted the presumption that there was no intention to create legal relations, emphasizing factors such as the setting (in a public house), drunken social nature of occasion, jocular nature of conversation (banter), commercial implausibility of the alleged deal.

Appleson v Littlewood Ltd (1939)

A sent in a football-pools coupon, bearing a written condition that 'it shall not be attended by or give rise to any legal relationship, rights, duties, consequences.' *Held*: that in view of this condition the agreement was not actionable.

Similarly, where a coupon contains the words that the entry 'shall not give rise to any legal relationships, or be legally enforceable, but binding in honour only', the clause manifests that the agreement is not a contract creating legal relations (*Jones v Vernon's Pools Ltd*, 1938). Although the terms used in the agreements noted previously considerably limit the effect of the rights of the parties, we must observe that it is not possible to make an agreement that ousts the jurisdiction of the courts of law. Such a term is void. Access to the courts of law is open to all persons to test their rights, and it is for the courts to decide whether rights do or do not exist or whether a remedy will or will not be granted. Moreover, parties may agree to arbitration (see p. 62), which is a common method of settling disputes in commercial contracts.

7.5 Consideration

One of the fundamental rules of this branch of the law is that 'consideration' is a necessary element in the formation of a valid simple contract. In *Rann v Hughes* (1778), the principle was stated clearly that 'if contracts be merely written and not specialties (i.e. by deed), they are parol (i.e. oral) and a consideration must be proved'.

A bare promise (*nudum pactum*) is not legally binding, so that if *A* promises £10 to B, it follows that B cannot enforce the payment of the sum at law if *A* subsequently changes his or her mind. 'A promise without consideration is a gift; one made for consideration is a bargain.'

In *Currie v Misa* (1875) the term valuable consideration was defined as some right, interest, profit or benefit accruing to one party or some forbearance, detriment, loss or responsibility given, suffered or undertaken by the other. Valuable consideration means, therefore, any benefit to the promisor or detriment to the promisee, which is sufficient in law to support the promise. In other words, it is the price for which the promise of the other is bought. Executed consideration means that consideration is wholly performed on one side immediately the contract is entered into. For example, Aston sells his bicycle to Bray for £20, which Bray agrees to pay next week. If Aston delivers the machine straight away, the consideration is 'executed' by Aston.

Executory consideration is a promise to confer a benefit or to suffer some detriment at some future time. For example, so far as Bray is concerned (in the previously mentioned example) consideration is 'executory' since the £20 is payable in the future. Similarly, if M and N agree to form a partnership on 1 January of next year, both parties give mutual promises and the consideration will be executory.

7.5.1 Rules of consideration

The general rules relating to consideration are that (a) it must be real or genuine, (b) it need not be adequate, (c) it must be legal, (d) it must move from the promisee, (e) it must be possible and (f) it must not be past.

a Consideration must be real or genuine

The courts will not enforce vague or sham promises or promises in which there is no benefit at all or where no detriment is imposed on the parties. The 'reality' of the consideration will be understood by reference to the following cases.

❖ CASE EXAMPLE

***White v Bluett* (1853)**

An undertaking by a son 'to cease complaining that he was not as well treated as his brother' was held insufficient consideration and was nothing more than a promise 'not to bore' his father.

Similarly, a promise 'to do the right thing' is too indefinite and vague to support a contract.

❖ CASE EXAMPLES

Glasbrook Bros v Glamorgan CC (1925)

The managers of a colliery requested police protection during a strike and asked that police be billeted on the premises. The police arranged for this to be done, and thus gave more secure police protection than applied generally throughout the area. When sued for the cost by the police authority, the colliery owners refused to pay on the ground that the police were under a public duty to give police protection. *Held*: that police had done more than they were bound to do and that the special protection was sufficient consideration in support of the contract.

Collins v Godefroy (1831)

G obtained from the Court a subpoena requiring C's attendance as a witness for G. G promised to pay C six guineas as compensation for loss of time by C. G refused to pay and C sued G. *Held*: the issue of a subpoena imposed on C a duty to attend Court by law, and the performance by C could not be consideration for G's promise to pay the sum stated.

Ward v Byham (1956)

The father of an illegitimate child promised £1 a week to the mother provided that 'the child will be well looked after and happy'. *Held*: that the promise was binding since the mother's undertaking amounted to something more than her mere legal obligation to the child.

Shadwell v Shadwell (1860)

An uncle promised his nephew an annuity of £150 if he should marry Ellen Nicholl, to whom the nephew had already become engaged. The nephew married the lady. Certain payments were made by the uncle, and on his death, the nephew sued the uncle's executors for the balance outstanding. *Held*: that by marrying, the nephew had incurred responsibilities and changed his position and status, and the uncle had derived some benefit in seeing his nephew settled. The consideration was real, and the nephew was able to recover.

A promise to perform pre-existing contractual obligations may constitute real consideration where it secures a benefit or avoidance of detriment for the other party.

❖ CASE EXAMPLE

William v Roffey Bros & Nicholls (Contractors) Ltd (1991)

R had contracted with *W* for *W* to carry out carpentry work for £20,000 on 27 flats being built by R. *W* were in difficulty and time was of the essence for R. R agreed orally to pay an extra £10,300 to *W* being £575 per flat to ensure timely completion but failed to make the extra payments. When sued, R argued that *W* had provided no consideration for the additional amount. *Held*: There was consideration by *W* for the oral agreement because timely completion resulted in a commercial advantage to R.

b Consideration need not be adequate

The general rule of the law of contract is that the parties are free to make what contracts they desire, e.g. by naming the price for which they are prepared to sell their goods. A person cannot seek the assistance of a court of law merely because a bad bargain has been made. *Caveat emptor* ('let the buyer beware') is a basic rule. If I buy for £1 a picture that turns out to be a Rembrandt, I am lucky; the seller is not. The contract is good.

❖ **CASE EXAMPLES**

Bainbridge v Firmstone (1838)

B allowed F to weigh two boilers owned by B, on condition that they were returned as they were lent. F took them to pieces to weigh them and returned them in this condition. B sued for damages. *Held*: that there was a contract for the returning of the boilers in a complete state. The consideration given by the plaintiff, B, was the parting with the possession of the boilers for however short a period. Damages for plaintiff, B.

Haigh v Brooks (1839)

B promised to pay certain bills if H would hand over a guarantee to him. H handed over the guarantee, which turned out to be unenforceable. *Held*: that the consideration was valid as the plaintiff was induced to part with something that he might have kept, and the defendant obtained what he desired.

Where an intending litigant genuinely forbears from taking legal action, such forbearance is valuable consideration provided that the action itself is not vexatious, frivolous or one that the person forbearing knows must fail (*Callisher v Bischoffsheim*, 1870; and *Wade v Simeon*, 1846).

The adequacy of the consideration is not irrelevant where fraud is alleged. Thus, if *A* states fraudulently that a picture is a genuine Van Gogh, and B pays £50,000 for the picture, which is in fact valueless, the adequacy of the consideration is highly relevant to the intention of the seller to deceive the purchaser.

Sufficiency of Consideration. Can a promise to pay less than the amount due be consideration? The general rule laid down in *Pinnel's case* (1602) is that payment of a lesser sum than the amount due cannot be treated as satisfaction for an existing debt.

❖ **CASE EXAMPLE**

Pinnel's case (1602)

P sued C for £8 10s. due on 11 November 1600. C alleged that, at P's request, he had paid to P £5 2s. 6d. on 1 October, and that P had agreed to accept this payment in full satisfaction of the original debt of £8 10s.

Although the court gave judgment for Pinnel on a technical point, it was also laid down that *payment of a lesser sum on the day cannot be any satisfaction for the whole.* But to this general rule there are the following exceptions:

i Where the debtor, at the creditor's request, makes an *earlier* payment. The earlier payment gives the creditor something to which there is not strict entitlement, and this is consideration. A later payment of a lesser sum than the amount due, however, will not be sufficient.

ii Where the *mode of payment* is altered. The payment of a debt must be by legal tender. In *Goddard v O'Brien* (1882) it was held that the giving of a cheque for a smaller sum in satisfaction of a debt of a greater amount was the giving of 'something collateral' and the debt was thereby extinguished. The modern view is that the giving of a cheque in payment of an existing debt is not an alternation of the mode of payment: per Lord Denning in *D & C Builders Ltd v Rees* (1966), summarised on p. 146. Similarly, where *A* is bound to pay for example £20 to B at London and B requests *A* to pay £15 on the day at York, there will be a good discharge if *A* accedes to the request and pays £15 at York.

iii Where something is *added*. For example, if *A* owes £20 to B on a certain date and B agrees to accept £10 plus an article, such as a book or disposable pen (as was suggested has been supplied in Pinnel's case) or a transistor radio, however small in value, there will be a good discharge.

In these cases, the change of time or mode of payment or the addition of something of value must be with the agreement of and to the benefit of the creditor to amount to a good discharge.

iv '*Composition*' agreements. To avoid bankruptcy a debtor may reach an agreement with creditors to pay them, say, 50p in the £ in full settlement of their debts; the payment of the lesser sum discharges the greater amount. The consideration is the agreement by the creditors with each other and with the debtor not to insist on their full claims. If any creditor were to do so it would be a fraud on the others.

v Payment of a lesser sum by a third party.

c Consideration must be legal

This is obvious. A promise to break into a house for £100 must inevitably be regarded as unlawful and therefore void. No criminal would have the nerve to sue on such a contract and would receive prompt attention from the police if they did, for their agreement would amount to criminal conspiracy at least.

❖ CASE EXAMPLES

Pearce v Brooks (1866)

The owner of a cab let it out on hire to a known prostitute for use by her. *Held*: that the owner, P, could not sue for the cost of the hire since he knew of the nature of the use to which the cab would be put.

Foster v Driscoll (1929)

A contract was entered into for the shipment of whisky from England to the United States during the time when prohibition was in force. *Held*: that the consideration (whisky), the import of which was illegal (according to the law of the United States, a friendly country), rendered the contract void.

d Consideration must move from the promisee

Consideration must move from the promisee (i.e. the person to whom the promise was made). The relationship that exists between promisor and promisee is known as *privity of contract*. Since the parties to the contract must provide consideration, it follows that as a general rule a person who receives a benefit under a contract may not, unless consideration has been supplied, enforce rights under the contract. In other words, no stranger to the consideration may sue on a contract.

❖ CASE EXAMPLE

***Tweddle v Atkinson* (1861)**

T was married to the daughter of X. To assist the married couple, X promised to pay T £200 in consideration of T's father paying T £100. X, however, died before he had paid the £200 and, in consequence, T sued Atkinson, X's executor. *Held*: that T could not sue as no consideration had been given by T. Only Ts father was entitled to sue.

e Consideration must be possible

The law will not enforce a contract to do that which is quite outside human capability. Thus, a promise to go to the centre of the Earth in consideration of the payment of £100 would be absurd and impossible and brings into question whether the parties could genuinely have contemplated legal relations on that basis. However, a promise to do the impossible must be distinguished from a promise that, although possible of performance when the contract was entered into, becomes impossible subsequently. This is discussed under the doctrine of frustration (see p. 191).

f Consideration must not be past

This means that a benefit conferred in the past is not consideration for a present promise. In everyday life this may seem harsh, since most of us have received great benefits from others, e.g. parents, teachers, friends who have given a helping hand in moments of crisis. Apart from these moral obligations of indebtedness, the rule of law concerning past consideration is practical and sound.

❖ CASE EXAMPLES

***Roscorla v Thomas* (1842)**

T sold a horse to R for £30. After the actual sale, T stated that the horse was sound and free from vice. The horse proved, in fact, to be vicious, and R sued T. *Held*: that R could not recover on the warranty that the horse was not vicious. The sale had already taken place when the warranty as to the soundness and quiet temperament was given. The warranty did not, therefore, form part of the consideration.

***Re McArdle* (1951)**

The occupants carried out certain improvements and decorations to a house at a cost of £488. After the work was done, those beneficially interested in the house executed a document by which they promised, in consideration of the execution of the work, to pay £488. *Held*: that the consideration for the promise was past, as the work had been completed when the promise was made; the claim to recover £488 therefore failed.

There are two exceptions to this rule, as follows:

i **Bills of Exchange Act 1882**. Section 27 of this Act lays down that, in addition to any consideration sufficient to support a simple contract, the consideration for a bill of exchange may be any *antecedent debt or liability*, provided that such debt or liability is not that of a stranger to the instrument.

ii *Services rendered*. Where it is proved that services have been rendered at the express or implied request of the promisor, it has been held that this is sufficient consideration to support a *subsequent* promise to pay.

Today's view of such services would probably be that the defendant's request to the claimant would imply a promise to pay a reasonable sum for those services. (NB: The further exception, that a statute-barred debt could be revived by a subsequent acknowledgment or payment, was abolished by the **Limitation Act 1980**.)

Of the two foregoing exceptions, (i) is the only true exception; (ii) is looked upon merely as an *apparent* exception to the rule that consideration must not be past.

❖ CASE EXAMPLE

Lampleigh v Braithwait (1615)

B had unlawfully killed a man, and he requested L to obtain the King's pardon for him. L did as requested and went to considerable trouble to do so. B then promised L £100 for his services. *Held*: that as L's services were rendered at the defendant's request, there was consideration for defendant's promise.

Note: Lord Scarman applied the exception to the doctrine of past consideration as held in *Lampleigh v Braithwait* to his decision in *Pao v Lau Yiu Long* (1980)—see p. 178.

Promissory or equitable estoppel. Although the basic rule of common law is that consideration is essential to support a valid simple contract, there are exceptions to the rule. These exceptions demonstrate how equitable principles operate to do justice in the particular case and to soften the rigid rules of common law.

❖ CASE EXAMPLES

Hughes v Metropolitan Railway Co. (1877)

H, landlord, gave MR (lessee) six months' notice to repair some houses in accordance with the lease. A month later H negotiated with MR to purchase the freehold. Relying on this MR did not repair the houses. Negotiations failed after two months. After six months H sued for ejectment of MR for failure to repair. *Held* (House of Lords): equity should override the common law. MR relied on the negotiations as being, in effect, a promise that H would not enforce his demands while negotiations continued. So no repairs were done. H failed in his action. 'It is the first principle upon which all courts of equity proceed that if parties who have entered into definite and distinct terms involving certain legal results . . . afterwards by their own act . . . enter upon a course of negotiations which has die effect of leading one of the parties to suppose that the strict rights arising under the contract will not be enforced, or will be kept in suspense . . . the person who otherwise might have enforced those rights will not be allowed to enforce them where it would be inequitable having regard to the dealings that have thus taken place between the parties' (per Lord Cairns, LC).

Central London Property Trust Ltd v High Trees House Ltd (1947)

In 1937 the plaintiffs let to the defendants a block of flats on a 99-year lease (by deed) at a rental of £2,500 a year. Only a few flats were let owing to the outbreak of war, and the consequent departure of people from London. Plaintiffs then entered into an agreement with the defendants to reduce the rent to £1,250 a year. The defendants, who were contemplating terminating the lease, continued it in these circumstances. The agreement was in writing, not under seal and operated from 1941 to 1945. Then, when the flats were fully let, plaintiffs claimed for the full rent of £2,500 from 1941. The basis of the claim was that there was no consideration for the reduction agreed in 1941. *Held* (Denning, J.): that plaintiffs were entitled to the full rent from 1945, since implied in the 1940 agreement there was a term that the rent should revert to the original rent when the wartime situation ended. It would be inequitable to allow the plaintiffs to go back on their promise as to 1941/45 because, on the strength of it the defendants had reduced the rents to their tenants, relying on the fact that the agreement prevented the strict legal effects of the first contract from being enforced. It was a case of *equitable estoppel*.

The principle in this case is that a promise intended to create legal relations, which, to the knowledge of the promisor, will be acted upon by the promisee and which is in fact acted upon (e.g. by retaining the lease as mentioned previously), must be honoured. The law does not, however, give cause for action in damages if such a promise is broken; and it will not allow the promisor to act inconsistently with the promise, even though the promise is not supported by consideration in the strict sense.

❖ CASE EXAMPLE

D & C Builders Ltd v Rees (1966)

D & C Builders claimed £482 for work done for R, debtor. Mrs R, knowing D & C Builders were in financial difficulties, offered £300 by cheque in full settlement and stated that if the builders would not accept that sum they would get nothing. D & C Builders reluctantly accepted, but later sued for the balance of £182. *Held*: that D & C Builders could recover. There was no consideration for the builders' agreement to take less, nor were they estopped from claiming the balance, because Mr and Mrs Rees had acted inequitably by making threats to the builders. Therefore, the remedy of promissory estoppel was not available to them. The payment by cheque was not sufficient alteration of mode to amount to consideration, for it was not done at the request of the builders.

The principle operates as a shield to the party sued and is not a weapon of attack, enabling the other party to sue on a gratuitous promise.

However, it was held in *Collier v P & MJWright (Holdings) Ltd* (2007) that a *decreasing pact* is prima facie valid in equity—*promissory estoppel*. So that a creditor's agreement to redeem his (the) debtor from the remainder of the debt, or to forgo part of a debt, becomes binding on the creditor if the debtor acts on this assurance and makes a partial payment to the creditor.

Note: The debtor will not receive the benefit of this *decreasing pact* if he has been guilty of coercing the creditor into agreeing to this financial adjustment.

❖ CASE EXAMPLE

Combe v Combe (1951)

A husband and wife were divorced in 1943. The husband agreed to make an annual allowance to the wife. Accordingly, and because of this agreement, the wife failed to apply for a court order for maintenance against the husband. He, however, did not make any payments. In 1950 the wife sued the husband on his promise to pay the annual allowance. *Held* (by Lord Justice Birkett): that as the husband had not requested the wife to refrain from making an application to the court, there was no consideration for his promise moving from the wife. Therefore the action by the wife failed. 'The principle in the High Trees House case must be used as a shield and not a sword.'

It must be recognized that each type of estoppel has its own requirements although they can often be seen to be related. In *Jones v Lydon (No.1)* (2021) the parties were former members of a band known as the Sex Pistols. A dispute arose as to whether they had a continued duty to accept a decision of the majority of its members they had accepted in an agreement which the Band had made. The claimant asserted that, over a period of years, this obligation has been overridden, which had led to the establishment of certain estoppels in his favour. *Held*: that after consideration of the facts, the claimant's assertion that over the years the obligation had been overridden so as to give rise to an estoppel had failed, so that the action failed

Note:

> It is unacceptable that a man who has indicated that he is not going to insist on his strict legal rights, as a result of which the other party has altered his position, should be able at a minute's notice to insist upon his rights however inconvenient it may be to the other party's.
>
> (*Lord Cohen in Tool Metal Manufacturing Co. Ltd v Tungsten Electric Co. Ltd, 1955*)

7.6 Form

We have already seen (p. 127) that unless contracts are valid, they may be classified as either void, voidable or unenforceable. A void contract is entirely without legal effect, does not give rise to any legal rights and duties and is, in fact, no contract at all. A voidable contract is one that may be repudiated at the will of one of the parties, but until it is so repudiated, it remains valid and binding. It is affected by a flaw (e.g. fraud, innocent misrepresentation, undue influence or duress), and the presence of any one of these defects enables the person adversely affected to take steps to set the contract aside, subject to the interests of an innocent third party.

Unenforceable contracts are neither void nor voidable, but they cannot be enforced in the courts because they lack some item of evidence essential to a valid contract. Some contracts must be made by deed, some must be in writing and some must be evidenced by writing. Unless the writing (in the form laid down by law) is available, the courts will not lend their aid to the enforcement of the agreements. So, they are stated to be unenforceable, but it does not mean that they are invalid. The purpose of these formal requirements is to achieve certainty and thus avoid disputes arising in the transfer of ownership, possession or rights in various kinds of property.

Contracts that must be by deed. The following *must* be by deed; otherwise, the transaction is invalid:

- a contracts not supported by valuable consideration, e.g. promises of gifts
- b leases of land for more than three years (**Law of Property Act 1925**)
- c transfers of British ships or shares in British ships
- d transfers of title to land (**Law of Property Act 1925**) (but see p. 127)

Contracts that must be in writing. The following *must* be in writing, a requirement laid down by statute in each case:

- a bills of exchange, cheques and promissory notes (**Bills of Exchange Act 1882**)
- b a contract under the **Consumer Credit Act 1974**
- c a hire purchase contract (**Hire Purchase Act 1964 and Consumer Credit Act 1974**)
- d an assignment of copyright (**Copyright, Designs and Patents Act 1988**)
- e transfer of shares in a registered company (**Companies Act 1985**)

Contracts that must be evidenced in writing. The following will not be enforced in the courts unless a sufficient *note or memorandum* (the nature of which will be examined later) signed by the defendant or an agent is available as proof of the agreement entered into:

- a contracts of guarantee
- b contracts for the sale or other disposition of land with limited exceptions, such as public auctions (**Law of Property (Miscellaneous Provisions) Act 1989**, s. 2)
- c contracts of employment (**Employment Protection (Consolidation) Act 1978** as amended by the **Employment Act 1982**)

Contracts of guarantee. Under section 4 of the **Statute of Frauds 1677**, as amended by the **Law Reform (Enforcement of Contracts) Act 1954**, 'any special promise to answer for the debt, default or miscarriage of another person' is required to be evidenced by writing. Section 4 applies to contracts of guarantee, by which we mean the undertaking by one person to be responsible to another (e.g. a creditor) for the debt or wrongful action (tort) of a third party. For example, let us suppose that you and I enter a shop in which you want to make a purchase. The shopkeeper may not wish to sell the goods to you unless you have a guarantor, i.e. a person who will undertake to pay for the goods if you default in payment. I inform the shopkeeper that I will pay for the goods if you do not (or are unable to) pay. This is a *guarantee*. You are *primarily* liable on the contract, while I am *secondarily* liable in the event of your default. The shopkeeper should ensure that some document (the 'note or memorandum') is completed and signed by me as guarantor, signifying the agreement.

This was emphasized in *Actionstrength Limited (t/a Vital Resources) v International Glass Engineering IN. GL.EN SpA* (2003), where the claimant's action failed because the contract involved was a contract of guarantee and had not been evidenced in writing.

In *J. Pereira SA v Mecha* (2006), it was prima facie held that while an email was capable of being a sufficient note or memorandum for the purpose of satisfying section 4 of the **Statute of Frauds, 1677**, the insertion of a person's email address did not constitute a signature for the purposes of section 4.

A contract of guarantee must be distinguished from an indemnity. Thus, if you and I go into a shop and I say to the shopkeeper: 'Let him have the goods, I will ensure you are paid' (or 'I will pay for them'), I am indemnifying the shopkeeper against loss on the contract. I am primarily liable on the contract and may be sued by the creditor. Such is not a guarantee; it is an *indemnity*, and no writing is required to evidence the agreement.

Contracts subject to section 40 of the Law of Property Act 1925. Section 40 provides that:

> No action may be brought upon any contract for the sale or other disposition of land or any other interest in land, unless the agreement upon which such action is brought, or some memorandum or note thereof, is in writing, and signed by the party to be charged or by some other person thereunto by him lawfully authorized.

Contracts for the sale of land* are obviously highly important, first because land itself has always been of great value and second because the law insists that particularly strong evidence should be necessary to prove the dispositions of land by way of sale or transfer. The phrase 'or other disposition' of land refers to leases, mortgages, etc., and these too require being evidenced in writing. Further emphasis is given to this rule by section 2 of the **Law of Property (Miscellaneous Provisions) Act 1989**, which also requires the contract to be in writing and to contain all the terms agreed by the parties.

Note or Memorandum. Ideally, contracts of this kind (guarantees, sales or transfers of land) should be wholly in writing in one clearly written or printed form. Unfortunately, life is not always tidy and efficient, and the written evidence may consist of a number of documents, e.g. letters. Provided that there is some indication, oral or written, connecting them, the various documents taken together may evidence the contract and thus constitute the 'memorandum' to satisfy the evidential requirements of the law. The memorandum must contain the following:

a the names of the parties (or a sufficient description to identify them)
b the subject matter of the contract (i.e. the goods, land, etc.)
c the consideration agreed upon—this is not necessary in contracts of guarantee
d the signature of the person to be charged (i.e. the guarantor, or the person against whom the document will be used in evidence and who has accepted responsibility)

Changes made by the **Electronic Trade Documents Act 2023**. This legislation serves as a preview of the recommendations of the Law Commission to allow for the legal recognition of certain types of documents used in trade and trade law in the United Kingdom in electronic form. It does so by providing that a trade document in electronic form that satisfies the criteria set out in the act (i.e. 'electronic trade document') is capable of possession. This means that such documents (such as a bill of exchange, a promissory note or a bill of lading) will have the same legal recognition and functionality as their paper counterparts.

---

* This refers to the preliminary agreement and not to the conveyance or transfer which must be by deed.

❖ CASE EXAMPLE

***Pearce v Gardner* (1887)**

G agreed to sell P gravel situated on G's land. P sued for breach of contract and sought to put in evidence a letter signed by G and starting 'Dear Sir'. The letter did not contain P's name, but P produced the envelope, which was addressed to him and in which the letter was contained. *Held*: that the letter and the envelope together constituted a sufficient memorandum.

7.7 The doctrine of part performance

We have noted in the contracts just described that, in the absence of the required evidence in writing, the courts would do nothing. Such was the attitude of the common law: in effect a refusal to act because the parties failed to comply with the requirements laid down as to evidence. Equity, however, took a different view, and the doctrine of part performance shows how it dispensed its fairness and justice in cases where there was no note or memorandum. If, in the circumstances, the enforcement of the rigid rule of law would assist fraud rather than prevent it, equity would intervene as a matter of conscience.

In consequence of a number of judicial decisions, it is now established that the equitable remedy will be granted where:

a the contract is of such a nature that the court can effectively compel performance. The doctrine does not, therefore, apply to contracts of personal service
b the plaintiff has committed some act of part performance that is unequivocally referable to the contract
c the circumstances are such that it would be fraudulent on the defendant's part to take advantage of the lack of written evidence
d there is adequate and admissible oral evidence of the terms of the contract

❖ CASE EXAMPLES

***Wakeham v Mackenzie* (1968)**

A widow, aged 67, gave up her council house to look after a widower of 72 in poor health. He promised orally that he would leave her his house when he died. The widow contributed to household expenses but had no remuneration from her friend. *Held*: the widow's acts were consistent with the oral contract, clearly referred to it and she was entitled to specific performance to convey the house to her, despite the absence of a written memorandum.

***Rawlinson v Ames* (1925)**

Mrs *A* agreed orally to take a lease of Mrs *R*'s flat. Mrs *A* requested Mrs R to carry out certain alterations which Mrs *A* supervised. Mrs *A* refused to complete, and when sued upon the contract, pleaded the Statute of Frauds and the absence of a memorandum. *Held*: that the alterations made by Mrs R at Mrs *A*'s request clearly constituted acts of part performance and were 'unequivocally referable to the contract'. Accordingly, Mrs *A* must complete the contract by signing a proper lease.

Maddison v Alderson (1883)

Mrs M was employed as housekeeper to Mr *A*, a farmer, for a number of years. *A* made an oral promise that if M would carry on working for the rest of *A*'s life without wages, he would, by his will, leave her a life interest in the farm. *A* made a will in those terms, but it was declared void. M sued, alleging part performance. *Held*: that there were many reasons why M might have worked without wages. The work was equivocal; for example, she might have wanted a home. It did not follow that she was entitled to a life interest.

7.8 Contractual capacity

The general rule is that any person, of whatever nationality or sex, may enter into a binding contract. To this rule, there are certain exceptions. First, we remember that the word 'person' includes both natural and artificial (or juristic) persons, such as corporations. By the very nature of things, certain special rules apply to these. Second, there are special rules of common law and statute law formed for the protection of certain classes of persons who, by reason of youth or deficiency in mental ability and understanding, might be taken advantage of by experienced and mature adults.

The special rules affecting each class of person are detailed in what follows.

7.8.1 Infants or minors

As we have noted (see p. 107), a person attains his or her majority 'at the commencement of the relevant anniversary of the date of his or her birth' (**Family Law Reform Act 1969**). From the moment of reaching 18, a person assumes the full responsibilities of an adult.

Certain contracts made by a minor are classified as (a) void, (b) valid or (c) voidable.

a Void contracts

As a result of the recommendations of the Law Commission published in their Report on Minors Contracts (Law Com. No. 134), the **Minors' Contracts Act 1987** was passed with the aim of removing certain restrictions on the enforceability of contracts entered into by minors.

Previously, parts of the law of contract relating to minors, particularly those classified as 'Void' contracts, were governed by the **Infants Relief Act 1874**; section 1 of which rendered 'absolutely void' all contracts with minors for the payment of money lent or for goods supplied or to be supplied (other than contracts for 'necessaries'—the legal meaning of which is explained later on) and all accounts stated with minors.

The effect of the **Minors' Contracts Act 1987** is to disapply (i.e. repeal) the **Infants Relief Act 1874**. As a consequence, section 1 of the 1874 Act no longer governs these contracts, which are now subject to the rules of common law.

Section 1 of the **Minors' Contracts Act 1987** also repeals section 5 of the **Betting and Loans (Infants) Act 1892**, which rendered void any new agreement by a minor, after attaining full age, to repay a loan obtained during their minority; it also invalidated any negotiable instrument given in connection with such an agreement. By disapplying this provision the 1987 Act makes any future such agreement and any negotiable agreement effective.

Section 2 of the **Minors' Contracts Act 1987** provides that where:

a a guarantee is given in respect of an obligation of a party; and
b the obligation is unenforceable against him (or he repudiates the contract) because he was a minor when the contract was made, the guarantee shall not, for that reason alone, be unenforceable against the guarantor.

The effect of this section is to make a guarantee of a minor's contractual obligation enforceable against the guarantor even though the main contractual obligation is not enforceable against the minor. It ensures that the guarantee of an unenforceable minor's contract is as effective as if the minor had been an adult. Prior to this section coming into force, section 1 of the **Infants Relief Act 1874** had the effect of invalidating guarantees on the basis that the main contract itself was 'absolutely void'. This means that the rule in *Coutts & Co. v Browne-Lecky* (1947) is now repealed.

It is no longer necessary for a creditor to ensure that a separate indemnity is taken instead of a guarantee, although the distinction between them for all other purposes is apparently unaffected.

It is important to note that these changes in no way alter the circumstances in which a guarantor who has honoured the guarantee is entitled to recover against the minor. They are in the same position as any of the minor's creditors.

Section 3 of the 1987 Act alters the common law as to the recovery of property from defaulting minors under unenforceable contracts. The disappointed creditor is now allowed even in the absence of fraud and where it is 'just and equitable' to obtain a court order for the return of property acquired by a minor 'or any property representing it'. It will be necessary to wait and see how this part of the new Act will affect the decision in *Leslie v Shiell* (1914).

However, in case it should be thought that minors are free to do as they wish in regard to loans it must not be forgotten that if a minor misrepresents his age fraudulently and obtains money or goods, he renders himself liable to prosecution for 'dishonestly obtaining the property of another by deception'—an arrestable offence under the **Theft Act 1968** and punishable with imprisonment.

The decision in *Ballett v Mingay* (1943) relating to wrongful interference to goods by a minor would appear to be unaffected by the new Act.

b Valid contracts

These are of two types: (i) contracts for 'necessaries' and (ii) contracts for the minor's benefit.

i *Contracts for 'necessaries'* are contracts for 'goods suitable to the condition in life of the minor *and* to his actual requirements at the time of sale *and* delivery' (**Sale of Goods Act 1979**, s. 3). In any legal action, therefore, the courts will have to decide whether the goods in dispute are, as a matter of fact, necessaries for that particular minor having regard to his 'condition in life' (or status or standard of living).

The next question to be considered is whether, even though the goods may be 'necessaries' in themselves, the minor is in fact already plentifully supplied with the goods; for one must connect the word 'necessaries' with the minor's 'actual requirements' at the time of sale *and* at the time of delivery, where these times are different.

Examples of necessaries include such obvious things as food, clothing, medical attention and educational books. Even services such as legal advice or the hire of a car have been held to fall into this class. But in all cases, it is for the court to decide as a matter of fact whether the goods supplied or services given are necessaries to that minor. Where a minor is married, the term will include necessaries for his wife and any children he may have.

Note: Keep in mind for these cases that full age was 21 years before 1 January 1970 and 18 years thereafter.

❖ CASE EXAMPLE

Nash v Inman (1908)

Plaintiff was a Savile Row tailor and the defendant an undergraduate of Trinity College, Cambridge, who was under 21. Defendant ordered clothes (including 11 fancy waistcoats), which together amounted to £145. The plaintiff sued the defendant for the sum. Defendant's father, an architect, proved that his son was already supplied with adequate clothes suitable to his condition in life when the clothes made by plaintiff were delivered. *Held*: that in view of these facts, the plaintiff's clothes were not 'necessaries' and accordingly the action failed.

ii *Contracts for the minor's benefit*. The question of what is 'for the minor's benefit' is one for the court to decide from the particular facts of each case. Decided cases show that contracts of apprenticeship, training or education fall within this class. The court will look at the contract as a whole; isolated terms that are not for the minor's benefit will not necessarily invalidate the contract, and it may be enforced against the minor.

❖ CASE EXAMPLES

Doyle v White City Stadium Ltd (1935)

D, an infant professional boxer, made a contract with the British Boxing Board of Control. A term in the contract provided that if D were disqualified for certain reasons the prize money would be withheld. D fought a contest and was disqualified. He sued the Board to recover the money, contending that due to his infancy he was not bound. *Held*: that D's action must fail. The agreement was closely analogous to a contract of employment and the contract was, on the whole, for his benefit.

Roberts v Gray (1913)

G, a young professional billiards player, agreed with R (a leading professional player) to go on a world tour, competing against each other in matches. R accordingly made arrangements, but a dispute arose and G declined to go and repudiated the contract. R sued the infant and claimed damages for breach of their contract. *Held*: that the contract was for the infant's benefit in that he would, in effect, be receiving instruction. Damages were awarded to R.

If a minor is a trader and agrees to sell goods and receives payment for them, he or she cannot, if they have committed no fraud, be compelled to refund the money or deliver the goods.

❖ CASE EXAMPLES

***Cowern v Nield* (1912)**

N, an infant hay and straw dealer, failed to deliver a consignment of hay to C, to whom he had contracted to sell the goods. C paid for the goods. *Held*: that the contract was a trading contract that was not binding on the infant. Moreover, the infant, N, was not compelled to repay the price paid by C.

***Mercantile Union Guarantee Corporation v Ball* (1937)**

B, an infant haulage contractor aged 20, contracted to buy a lorry on hire-purchase terms for use in his business. *Held*: that the infant was not liable for the instalments due under the agreement.

c Voidable contracts

In this class we include (i) contracts of a continuing nature and (ii) contracts under which a minor acquires an interest in property of a permanent kind, e.g. leases of property, partnership agreements or the taking of shares in a company.

These contracts are described as voidable because they will be binding upon a minor unless he repudiates them before he reaches his majority or within a reasonable time thereafter.

Similarly, when a minor becomes a partner in a firm, he or she is not liable for the firm's debts contracted during his or her minority. He or she may, however, on or before reaching majority, repudiate the contract of partnership. If he or she omits so to do and continues as a partner, he or she will be responsible for all the firm's debts contracted after he or she reached 18.

❖ CASE EXAMPLES

***Steinberg v Scala (Leeds) Ltd* (1923)**

The plaintiff, an infant, applied for and was allotted shares in the defendant company. She paid sums on allotment and on the first call on the shares. She was unable to pay further calls and repudiated the contract. She requested, while still an infant, that her name be removed from the register of shareholders and also requested the return of all money she had paid. *Held*: that the infant was entitled to the removal of her name from the register, so avoiding future calls on her shares, but she could not recover the money paid because there had not been a *total* failure of consideration; although no dividends had been paid on the shares, nevertheless the shares had some value.

***Valentini v Canali* (1889)**

An infant took a lease of a house and agreed to buy the furniture in it for £102. The infant paid £68 on account. After some months, however, he repudiated the contract and then claimed to recover the sum of £68 paid. *Held*: that the infant was entitled to have the contract set aside, but having used the furniture, he could not recover the £68 already paid under the contract, for there was no *total* failure of consideration.

We have mentioned that a minor may repudiate this class of contract before or within a 'reasonable time after' he or she reached 18. What is a 'reasonable time' is a matter for decision by the court and varies with each type of contract.

Once majority is attained by a debtor, a creditor may seek ratification of a first agreement from the debtor. The **Minors' Contracts Act 1987** repealed section 2 of the **Infants Relief Act 1874**, which prevented the enforcement of promises made after attaining majority to pay debts contracted while a minor.

7.8.2 Corporations

We have already discussed the position and status of corporations in English law (see p. 111). The contractual capacity of a corporation depends on whether it is (a) a chartered corporation, (b) a statutory corporation or (c) a corporation by registration under the **Companies Act 2006**.

By the nature of things, corporations are incapable of making certain contracts of a personal nature, e.g. a contract to marry.

a Chartered corporations

These are formed by royal charter and the powers of the corporation are found in the charter, granting it corporate status. There are no legal limits to the contractual capacity of these corporations. If, therefore, contracts are made outside the powers defined in the particular charter, such contracts are not void. However, the activities of the corporation may be controlled by law to some extent. Thus, an application may be made to the court for an injunction to prevent or restrain a corporation from making contracts outside the terms of its charter. Further, the Crown that grants the charter may revoke it if the corporation wilfully persists in operating outside the limits of its powers (*Baroness Wenlock v River Dee Co.*, 1888).

b Statutory corporations

These corporations derive their powers from the statutes that create them. Sometimes the powers are increased by subsequent statutes or statutory instruments, but in all cases, any acts or contracts formed beyond the powers contained in the statutes or statutory instruments are *ultra vires* and void.

c Registered companies

In accordance with the **Companies Act 2006**, corporations entering into contracts now have, in accordance with Section 31 of the Act, an unlimited power unless their articles provide otherwise, greatly reducing the applicability of the *ultra vires* doctrine which previously applied to the law relating to corporations. The legislation also means that it is much easier for the execution of deeds by a Company so that a single director can now execute a document on behalf of a company, as a deed, by a simple signature in the presence of a witness Similarly, under the **Corporate Bodies' Contracts Act 1960**, other corporations (including local authorities) are permitted to contract in the same way as, or in the manner required of, a private person.

7.8.3 Insane and drunken persons

Contracts entered into by an *insane person* are voidable, but liability exists to pay a reasonable price for 'necessaries' (**Sale of Goods Act 1979**, s. 2).

S. 7 of the **Mental Capacity Act 2005** restates this concept as a person who lacks the capacity to contract, describing the incapacity as 'an impairment of or a disturbance in the functioning of the mind or brain' and *necessary* to mean suitable to a person's condition in life and to their actual requirements at the time when the goods or services are supplied.

Two points must be proved by the person who pleads insanity:

i that they were insane at the time of making the contract and that they were incapable of understanding the importance of the transaction
ii that the other party knew of their condition

The contracts being voidable, they may be repudiated at the will of the insane party. Unless so repudiated within a reasonable time after the disability has ceased, they will be liable. Any such contract, however, binds the other party to the contract.

Drunken or intoxicated persons are treated in the same way as those suffering from insanity.

7.8.4 Married women

By virtue of the **Law Reform (Married Women and Tortfeasors) Act 1935**, a married woman now has full legal capacity. Accordingly, a married woman has the same contractual capacity as a man or an unmarried woman.

A husband will incur liability for his wife's contracts if he expressly authorizes his wife to act as his agent or impliedly authorizes her to pledge his credit. Thus, where a wife purports to contract on his behalf and the husband pays the bills without question or demur, the law will infer that the wife has implied authority to pledge the husband's credit.

Where a wife is, for example, deserted by a husband, she may be an 'agent of necessity'. This means that for any 'necessaries' (e.g. food, shelter and clothing for herself and her family) purchased, the law infers that the husband will be liable. Where, however, the wife has means of her own or is earning her own living, the presumption of law may be rebutted.

7.8.5 Aliens

Except for being unable to acquire property in a British ship (**Merchant Shipping Act 1894**, s. 1), an alien has the same contractual capacity in peacetime as a British subject.

In wartime an enemy alien cannot enter into a contract with a British subject, and where an alien in an English court. Where, on the other hand, the alien is sued in England on such a pre-war contract, they may defend the action.

The contracts of an enemy alien present in England by licence of the Crown are valid and enforceable even during wartime.

The test of whether a person is an 'enemy alien' is not nationality but the place where they reside or carry on business. So, a British subject resident in hostile or enemy-occupied territory may be classed as an enemy alien.

Foreign sovereigns or governments cannot be sued in the English courts unless they voluntarily submit to the jurisdiction (*Mighell v Sultan of Johore*, 1894). Immunity from the jurisdiction of the English courts is extended to foreign ambassadors, High Commissioners of Commonwealth countries and certain representatives of international organizations, including the United Nations. Members of the suites of such persons enjoy similar immunity under the **Diplomatic Privileges Act 1964**.

Any such person who is sued (or even prosecuted) may claim immunity from the jurisdiction of the court by arranging for the production in court of a certificate from the Secretary of State for Foreign Affairs. Furthermore, persons enjoying this immunity may not be subpoenaed as witnesses.

7.9 Terms of a contract

We have noted that the contents of a contract may be expressed orally, in writing or by conduct. The terms of a contract define the rights and duties arising under the contract. These terms are of two kinds: (a) express and (b) implied.

a Express terms

Where a contract has been put into writing, the parties are precluded from adducing evidence to add to, vary or contradict its terms. Therefore, oral evidence will not be admitted to prove that some other term (even though agreed to orally) has been omitted from the written instrument. However, this does not prevent the rectification of a mistake in the written contract, provided that the conditions for rectification are present (see p. 170). Further, if the written contract is not complete and does not, in fact, represent the whole transaction, oral evidence will be admitted by the court to prove a collateral agreement, i.e. one that is subsidiary to the main purpose of the contract.

❖ CASE EXAMPLE

***Couchman v Hill* (1947)**

Plaintiff bought a heifer at an auction, and the catalogue described the animal as 'unserved'. The printed conditions of sale provided that the auctioneer 'gave no warranty whatever' in respect of the condition or description of any animal. Before he bid for the heifer, plaintiff asked the auctioneer and the owner of the heifer to confirm that it was 'unserved'. Both replied in the affirmative. The heifer died within eight weeks of the sale as a result of carrying a calf at too young an age for breeding. *Held* (by the Court of Appeal): that the verbal statements that the heifer was 'unserved' overrode the conditions of sale; plaintiff was able to recover damages for breach of warranty.

Certainty of terms. Unless the parties make their contract in terms that are certain, their contract will fail.

❖ CASE EXAMPLE

***Scammell and Nephew Ltd v Ouston* (1941)**

The respondents (O) agreed to purchase a motor-van from the appellants. O sent an order to appellants thus: 'This order is given on the understanding that the balance of the purchase price can be had on hire-purchase terms over a period of two years.' A dispute arose, and the appellants' defence was that there was no contract until 'hire-purchase terms' had been ascertained. *Held*: that no precise meaning could be given to the clause as to 'hire-purchase terms'. They were too vague, and as there was no previous trade practice between the parties to guide the court on what was meant, the contract failed.

Barton and Others v Morris and Another 2023

Barton, a property developer, entered into an oral contract with Foxplace, the owners of Nash House, that he would find a buyer for the property. The only express term agreed was that Barton would be paid £1.2 million if he found a buyer and the property was sold for £6.5 million. The sale was for £6m and Foxplace claimed they owed nothing to Barton. The Supreme

Court held that Barton was not entitled to any reimbursement as the £1.2 was contingent on the property being sold for £6.5 million and so there was no agreed obligation to pay in any other circumstances. There could be no implied terms, as it would be contrary to the partners' agreement.

Moreover, there cannot be a contract to make a contract. The parties cannot, in other words, make an agreement to agree in the future. The parties must agree on terms that are definite or 'capable of being made definite without further agreement of the parties'.

This case may be distinguished from the following, where, although the parties themselves had not agreed to the terms, they nevertheless agreed on a form of proceeding whereby the terms could be determined, as by conferring on a court of law or an arbitrator the power to fill in a term or gap in their agreement.

Meaningless terms are disregarded in law. If the whole contract is meaningless, the contract is void. Where the meaningless term is subsidiary, the contract may be held valid although the meaningless term is ignored.

❖ CASE EXAMPLES

Mercer v Denne (1905)

Defendant owned part of a beach and proposed to erect houses thereon. Local fisherman sought to stop him by claiming that they had a local customary right to dry their nets on the land. Witnesses proved that the custom dated back some 70 years and reputedly earlier. This raised the presumption of antiquity. *Held*: that the defendant must not build the houses on the land; the local customary right was upheld.

Foley v Classique Coaches Ltd (1934)

F sold part of his land to a motor company on condition that the company would buy all its petrol from him. The agreement between F and the company laid down that petrol would be bought from F 'at a price to be agreed by the parties in writing and from time to time'. The agreement also provided that in any dispute, the agreement should be submitted to arbitration. The price was never agreed and the company refused to purchase the petrol. *Held*: that there was a binding contract, and a method was provided by which the price could be ascertained, namely by arbitration. An injunction was granted against the company restraining them from breaching.

b Implied terms

We have noted that one of the basic rules of contract is that the parties are free to make their own terms. It is not the function of the courts to make the parties' contract for them. However, in the following exceptional cases, the law may imply terms into the contract.

- i *To give the contract business efficacy*. What is meant by 'business efficacy' can be seen from the remarks of Lord Justice Bowen in the following case.

❖ CASE EXAMPLE

The Moorcock (1889)

Appellants agreed with the respondent to use the appellants' jetty and wharf to load and store cargo from the *Moorcock*. The river bed was owned by a third party. It was beyond the appellants' control, and they had taken no steps to ascertain whether it was safe for the ship to lie, as was inevitable at low water on each tide. The ship grounded and suffered damage because of the uneven riverbed. *Held*: that appellants were liable as the jetty could not have been used without the *Moorcock* grounding. In these circumstances the appellants were deemed to have impliedly represented that they had taken reasonable care to ascertain that the river bed adjoining the jetty was in such a condition as not to cause damage to the vessel. 'What the law desires to effect by the implication is to give such business efficacy to the transaction as must have been intended at all events by both parties who are businessmen.'

- i *Officious bystander test*. This test, which often overlaps with the business efficacy test, is applied by the court if it was so obviously a stipulation that the prospective contractual parties would have assented to it forming part of their contract.

❖ CASE EXAMPLE

R Griggs Group v Evans (No. 1) (2005)

Evans was commissioned to produce a logo for the owners of *Doc Martens* footwear. He contended that it was assumed that he would retain a worldwide copyright in the logo. *Held*: (per Jacob LJ) that for such a contention to be an implied term would be regarded as 'fantastic'.

In *Attorney-General for Belize v Belize Telecom Ltd* (2009), Lord Hoffman questioned the independent application of business efficacy and the officious bystander tests. He believed that they should be viewed as overlapping ways as to how the Courts expressed the central idea of what comprised an implied term. He stated that: 'There are dangers in treating these alternative formulations of the question as if they had a life of their own.'

However, legal commentators have cautioned against adopting this view expressed by Lord Hoffman.

- i *Custom*. Terms may be implied by the custom of a locality or a particular trade. The custom, or usage as it is sometimes called to distinguish it from the general custom of the realm, must be certain, reasonable and well known (notorious) to all affected by it and must not be contrary to any statute.

ii **Sale of Goods Act 1979**. Sections 12–15 of this Act imply certain terms into contracts for the sale of goods, which are for the protection of the buyer. For example, section 13 makes it an implied condition that goods shall correspond with the description of them; section 14 provides that goods shall be of a satisfactory quality, and section 15 lays down that in a sale by sample, the bulk shall correspond with the sample. These sections were considered in *Harlingdon and Leinster Enterprises Ltd v Christopher Hull Fine Art Ltd* (1990), where the Court of Appeal held that the sale of a forged painting did not prevent it from being of merchantable quality. The **Sale of Goods (Amendment) Act 1995** implies further contractual terms, which assist the buyer when sales are made from bulk. Amending section 16, a new rule in section 18 expedites the passing of property to the buyer when sales are made from bulk. New sections 20A and 20B also provide for a buyer, in certain circumstances, to become a part-owner of bulk goods.

7.9.1 Exemption clauses

The basic rule regarding conditions contained in an offer is that the offeror can attach any conditions he or she pleases and any terms of acceptance he or she chooses. Conditions may be made orally or in writing. In the latter event the writing is generally stated on the face of the document itself (e.g. hire-purchase agreements). But, in some instances (e.g. railway tickets) an authority may impose conditions too numerous to be included on these small documents. Usually, railway tickets bear on the face the words 'For conditions, see over'. On the reverse side of the ticket may be printed: 'Issued subject to the conditions and regulations contained in the Board's publications and notices.' It follows that offerees should read such publications and notices, but only very few ever do. Such conditions are binding.

In recent years commercial companies and public authorities have imposed similar conditions in their contracts exempting or excluding themselves from liability for breaches of contract or from liability for torts, particularly negligence, arising during the contract. The rules applicable in this situation may be summarized thus:

a The offeror must do all that is reasonably necessary to bring the conditions to the notice of the offeree. This is a question of fact in each case (*Thornton v Shoe Lane Parking Ltd*, 1971).
b The conditions must be brought to the notice of the offeree either before or contemporaneously with the making of the contract (*Olley v Marlborough Court, Ltd*, 1949).
c An exemption clause printed on a receipt after the contract is not valid (*Chapelton v Barry UDC*, 1940).
d Where the party seeking to rely on an exemption clause misrepresents the extent of the clause, it will not be binding (*Curtis v Chemical Cleaning & Dyeing Co.*, 1951).
e Where the terms are signed, the parties are bound as a general rule (*L'Estrange v Graucob*, 1934).
f Where there has been a fundamental breach of contract, it is a question of construction whether the terms of the contract give an exemption from the consequences of the breach.

❖ CASE EXAMPLE

Olley v Marlborough Court, Ltd (1949)

O booked into a hotel, having paid in advance. O went to the room allotted, and on one of the walls was a notice: 'The proprietors will not hold themselves responsible for articles lost or stolen unless handed to the manageress for safe custody.' O closed the self-locking door of the bedroom and handed the key to the reception clerk downstairs.

A third person took the key and stole certain of O's furs from her room. O sued for the loss. *Held*: that the contract was completed at the reception desk and no *subsequent* notice (e.g. in a bedroom) could affect O's rights.

Note: had O previously visited the hotel and seen the notice, she would have been bound by its conditions (*Spurling v Bradshaw*, 1956).

But by the 1977 Act (see later on in the chapter), the terms must also be reasonable for O to be bound.

❖ CASE EXAMPLE

L'Estrange v Graucob (1934)

L, a shopkeeper, bought from G a slot machine. L signed a sales agreement containing the following clause: 'Any express or implied condition, statement or warranty, statutory or otherwise, is hereby excluded.' L did not read the relevant clause, which was in small print. The machine did not work, and L sued for damages. *Held*: that the clause was binding on L because she had signed the document and there had been no misrepresentation.

Chapelton v Barry UDC (1940)

C wished to hire deckchairs on a beach. He went to a stack near which was a notice: 'Hire of chairs 2*d*. per session of three hours.' He took two chairs and later he paid 4*d*. to the attendant and received two tickets which he put into his pocket without reading what was on them. Printed on the back of the tickets were the words: 'The Council will not be liable for any accident or damage arising from hire of chair.' When C sat on the chair, it collapsed and he was injured. C sued the local council which had provided the chair. *Held*: that the ticket was a mere voucher or receipt, so that the condition printed on it could not form part of the contract. The only conditions of the contract were those contained in the notice displayed near the pile of chairs. C was entitled to succeed in damages.

Curtis v Chemical Cleaning and Dyeing Co. (1951)

C took a dress with beads and sequins to defendants (cleaners and dyers) for cleaning. C was asked to sign a paper headed 'Receipt'. When C asked about the terms of the document, the defendant's assistant informed her that it exempted the company from liability for certain types of damage, such as damage to beads and sequins. C signed. In fact the paper contained a clause excluding *all* liability for damage to the garment. The dress was returned stained, and C sued. *Held*: that defendants could not rely upon the signed document because the assistant had misrepresented its terms so that C ran the risk of damage merely to beads and sequins.

Karsales (Harrow) Ltd v Wallis (1956)

W inspected a second-hand Buick car, found it in running order and arranged to purchase it for £600 through a finance company. The contract contained the clause: 'No condition or warranty that the vehicle is roadworthy or as to its age, condition or fitness for any purpose is given by the owner or implied herein.' On delivery it was found that the new tyres had been replaced by old ones, many parts were missing and other parts originally on the car when inspected had been replaced by old parts. The car would not go at all. *Held*: that the exclusion clause did not apply. The sale was for a car. What was delivered was incapable of propulsion and, therefore, not really a car at all. There had been a fundamental breach, and the plaintiffs were unable to rely on the clause.

Photo Library Group Ltd v Burda Senator Verlag GMBH (2008)

Claimants had supplied defendants with photographic transparencies accompanied by delivery notes containing terms. Defendants lost a large number of transparencies to the value of £1.2 million, so that the claimants sued for this amount in accordance with a clause in the delivery note. *Held*: That the delivery note was part of the contract between the claimants and the defendants, having been incorporated through the previous course of dealing between the parties.

7.9.2 The Unfair Contract Terms Act 1977

Judges had tried over the years to prevent the operation of exemption clauses, which often deprived a consumer of virtually all his rights, by strict interpretation of terms and by propounding the doctrine of 'fundamental breach'. The Law Commission produced a Report on the dilemma, and, as a result, the **Unfair Contract Terms Act 1977** came into force on 1 February 1978 and applies to all contracts entered into after that date. Basically, the Act limits the extent to which civil liability for breach, *or for negligence or other breach of duty*, can be avoided by means of contract terms or by warning notices.

The Act covers the supply of goods and services, contracts of employment and the liability of occupiers of premises and of land to persons entering upon or using those premises or the land. The Act primarily covers the following six areas:

Negligence liability (both in contract and tort).

i Liability for negligence resulting in death or personal injury can no longer be excluded or restricted by contract or by notice in the course of a business (s. 2(1)).

ii Liability for other loss or damage resulting from negligence can no longer be excluded or restricted in a 'guarantee' given with consumer goods (s. 2(2)) as in *Phillips Products Ltd v Hyland and Another*, 1987.

iii Except as provided for in (ii), liability for negligence not resulting in death or personal injury can be excluded or restricted, but only in so far as the contract term or notice satisfies the test of reasonableness (see later on). 'Attempts to exclude liability for negligence must be clearly and unambiguously expressed' (*Ailsa Craig Fishing Co. Ltd v Malvern Fishing Co. Ltd*, 1983).

Drax Energy Solutions Limited v Wipro Ltd (2023)

The contract involved the purchase of 30 large coaches, four of which caught fire due to a defective cooling system. The purchase agreement, which was in standard form, excluded the implied term as to satisfactory quality. It was held that the exclusion clause was potentially unreasonable and so was unenforceable. The grounds for the decision were that there was no equal bargaining strength between the parties, as one party had to rely on the standard terms of the other party. Also, when an exclusion clause denies a party any reasonable remedy (and the risk is not insured), the clause is likely to be unreasonable.

Contractual obligations. When (1) dealing with consumers or (2) on its own written standard terms, a business cannot by means of a contract term, unless the term satisfies the test of reasonableness, (a) exclude or restrict its liability for breach of contract or (b) claim to be entitled to render no performance or a performance substantially different from that which was reasonably expected of it (s. 3).

Contracts where both parties are businesses, and which are not on standard terms, are not subject to this control.

Supply of goods. The rules in the **Supply of Goods Act 1979** (which replaced the **Supply of Goods (Implied Terms) Act 1973**), in general, deal with the exclusion or restriction of liability for breach of the obligations implied by law into contracts for the sale of goods and hire purchase agreements. Work, materials, and services contracts are governed by the provisions of the **Supply of Goods and Services Act 1982**. These rules extend to all other contracts for the supply of goods (not just sales). In short, the right of the consumer to goods that (a) correspond with description or sample, (b) are of a satisfactory quality and (c) are fit for the purpose cannot be excluded or restricted by contract whether he or she (the consumer) buys the goods or obtains them by way of hire, hire purchase, exchange or under a contract for work and materials. Attempts to deny any of the corresponding rights to a business customer are subject to the reasonableness test. Terms excluding or restricting liability for breach of the implied obligations as to title (i.e. ownership) or quiet possession are also subject to control, both in consumer contracts and in contracts where both parties are businesses.

These rules have been restated in s. 31 of the **Consumer Rights Act 2015**. This means that s. 61(1) provides that Part 2 of the Act applies to all contracts between a trader and a consumer being known as a 'consumer contract'. S. 62(1) provides that an unfair term is not binding on the consumer whilst s. 62(2) provides that an unfair term of a contract is also not binding on a consumer. S.62(4) provides that the term of a consumer contract is unfair contrary to the requirement of good faith if it causes a significant imbalance in the parties' rights and obligations under the contract to the detriment of the consumer.

Auctions are exempted under s. 12(2), but there is no longer an exemption for market (market overt) sales pursuant to the **Sale of Goods (Amendment) Act 1994**.

Indemnity clauses. The reasonableness test is applied to contract terms requiring a consumer to indemnify another person (whether a party to the contract or not) in respect of the other's liability for negligence or breach of contract.

Reasonableness test. For a contract term, the test is whether 'the term is a fair and reasonable one to be included having regard to the circumstances that were, or ought reasonably to have been, known to or in the contemplation of the parties when the contract was made' (s. 11(1)). The party alleging 'reasonableness' must prove it.

For *notices* not having contractual effect, the requirement of reasonableness under the Act is 'that it should be fair and reasonable to allow reliance on it, having regard to all the circumstances obtaining when the liability arose or (but for the notice) would have arisen' (s. 11(3)).

Moreover, where a contract term or notice purports to exclude or restrict liability for negligence, a person's agreement to or awareness of it is not of itself to be taken as indicating his voluntary acceptance of any risk (s. 2(3)) as in *G. Mitchell (Chesterhall) Ltd v Finney Lock Seeds Ltd* (1983).

Fundamental breach. Section 9 of the **Unfair Contract Terms Act 1977** provides that an exemption clause may apply even where there has been a fundamental breach of contract, provided that it satisfies the requirement of reasonableness.

❖ CASE EXAMPLE

Photo Production Ltd v Securicor Transport Ltd (1980)

The plaintiff hired S, a security company, to patrol their factory premises. The security guard negligently lit a fire that caused the factory to burn down. The House of Lords held that the exclusion clause in the contract was clear and unambiguous, and it operated to relieve the security company from liability.

The **Unfair Terms in Consumer Contracts Regulations 1994** further protect consumers from unfair terms in contracts in accordance with European Union directives.

7.9.3 Conditions and warranties

At this point it is advisable to distinguish between the terms 'condition' and 'warranty' which appear in the law of contract.

A *condition* is a term (oral or written) that goes directly 'to the root of the contract', or is so essential to its very nature that if it is broken, the innocent party can treat the contract as discharged. That party will not therefore be bound to do anything further under that contract.

A *warranty* is a term of the contract that is collateral or subsidiary to the main purpose of the contract. It is therefore not so vital as to affect a discharge of the contract. A breach of warranty only entitles the innocent party to an action for damages; he cannot treat the contract as discharged.

Both conditions and warranties are terms in a contract, and it is for the court to decide in each contract whether, having regard to the intentions of the parties, a term is a condition or a warranty. The importance lies in the remedy in the event of a breach.

7.9.4 Consumer Credit Acts 1974 and 2006

The **Consumer Credit Act 1974** originally established a comprehensive code of regulations for the supply of individuals, including sole traders and partnerships, of credit not exceeding £5,000 throughout the United Kingdom. It also provided for the licensing of those who carried out a business of granting consumer credit and of ancillary credit business. The Act extended the duties and functions of the Director of Fair Trading.

The **Consumer Credit Act 2006** removed the financial limits in respect of regulated consumer credit and consumer agreements and expanded the role of the Office of Fair Trading ('OFT').

7.10 Void, voidable and illegal contracts

We have already mentioned (p. 126) that one of the essential elements in a valid contract is that there must be genuineness of consent of the parties. That consent may be vitiated (i.e. harmed) by the following factors: (i) mistake, (ii) misrepresentation, (iii) duress, (iv) undue influence and (v) illegality. Where one of these factors exists in relation to a contract, there is no true consent and the contract may be rendered void or voidable. For example, an illegal contract is void and a contract affected by misrepresentation, duress or undue influence is voidable, i.e. able to be repudiated at the instance of the party prejudiced.

However, in *Patel v Mirza* (2016), the Supreme Court held that, despite the illegal nature of an agreement considered by the court, money claimed under the terms of the contract should be repaid. Toulson LJ warned against a mechanistic approach to the issue. He stated that 'experience has shown that it is better to recognize that there may be conflicting considerations that the rules need to be developed and applied in a way which enables the court to balance them fairly'.

7.10.1 Mistake

The general rule of common law is that a mistake does not affect the validity of a contract. If I sell you a painting for £10 and, after the sale, you discover that the painting is a Rembrandt worth £100,000, you are fortunate: I am not. I merely sold a painting, not knowing that it was a very valuable old master. I mistook its real value, and the law will do nothing to assist me.

There are, however, some kinds of mistakes that operate on the agreement and really undermine it so that there is no true consent. Such a mistake is known as an 'operative' mistake, the effect of which is to render the contract void.

First, we must observe that the mistake has to be one of fact and not of law. If I make a mistake about some general rule of law, I cannot plead in court that I did not know the legal rule existed. The maxim *ignorantia juris haud excusat* ('ignorance of the law is no excuse') applies. A mistake of private rights or of foreign law is, however, treated as a mistake of fact and not of law. Thus, where *A* agrees to lease to B some land that in fact already belongs to B, such a mistake (relating to private property) is treated as a mistake of fact. The lease would, under the circumstances, be void (*Cooper v Phibbs*, 1867).

a Mistake as to the identity of the subject matter

Where two parties intend to contract and the first party intends to contract with regard to one thing while the second intends another thing, there is no true agreement and hence no contract.

❖ CASE EXAMPLES

Raffles v Wichelhaus (1864)

W agreed to buy cotton 'to arrive on the *Peerless* sailing from Bombay'. *W* intended the ship *Peerless* sailing from Bombay in October. *R* offered the cotton from another ship *Peerless* sailing in December. *Held*: that there was no binding contract between the parties as the defendant meant one ship and the plaintiff another.

Scriven v Hindley (1913)

An auctioneer put up for sale some lots of hemp and tow. Owing to ambiguity in the auction particulars, the defendant bid an excessive price for an item of tow, thinking it was hemp. From the price bid, the auctioneer must have realized there was a mistake. *Held*: that there was no contract.

Where each party makes a different kind of mistake, it is known as 'mutual' mistake; where both parties make the same mistake, it is known as 'common' mistake. Unilateral mistake means a mistake by one party, e.g. *Cundy v Lindsay* (1878)—see p. 167.

b Mistake as to the existence of the subject matter

Where both parties contract in the mistaken belief that a particular thing is in existence when, in fact, it has ceased to exist, there is a fundamental mistake that renders the contract void. For example, if I agree to sell to you my motor car, which both of us believe to be at my home, but unfortunately was destroyed by fire a day before the contract, we have both made a mistake (a 'common' mistake) and the contract is void. The law presumes in this type of situation a condition that the thing about which we agreed was in existence.

❖ CASE EXAMPLE

***Couturier v Hastie* (1852)**

A contract was made between two parties for the sale of Indian corn, which, at the time, was believed to be on the high seas. Unknown to both parties the corn had become overheated during the voyage and had been landed at the nearest port and sold. *Held*: that there was no contract. The agreement contemplated that there was in existence something to be sold and bought, but as at the time of the contract the goods had already been sold, defendants were not liable.

c Mistake as to the quality of the subject-matter

The general rule in this type of agreement is that a mistake as to the quality of the thing contracted for does not invalidate the contract. If, for example, I sell you a painting that we both think is an old master, but turns out to be a cheap imitation, the contract is good. No representation is made as to the painting. All that is bought and sold is a painting. There is no mistake as to its identity, but both parties are mistaken as to its quality. You get what you bargained for: a particular painting. In such a case the law is not concerned with the quality or the value paid, for the general rule is *caveat emptor* ('let the buyer beware').

Equity, however, may grant relief in certain circumstances, and the contract may be set aside on terms that are fair and just.

❖ CASE EXAMPLES

***Bell v Lever Bros* (1932)**

B was under a contract of service with Lever Bros Amalgamations of the company took place and B became redundant. Lever Bros contracted to pay B £30,000 as compensation for his loss of office. After the contract had been made, it was discovered that B, in breach of his employment contract, had engaged in secret trading during his service, for which he could have been summarily dismissed from office without payment of compensation. Lever Bros sought to recover the sum of £30,000 that it had paid (it was alleged) on the ground of mistake. *Held*: that the contract was not void. Lever Bros had got what it had bargained for, i.e. the termination of the agreement of service that was in existence at the time of payment. The mistake was one of quality, and this did not void the contract. (But see the decision in *Malik v Bank of Credit and Commerce International SA (in liq.)* (1977).)

***Associated Japanese Bank (International) Ltd v Crédit Du Nord SA and Another* (1988)**

Parties entered into a contract involving four machines that had never in fact existed. *Held*: (following the principles laid down previously in *Bell v Lever Bros*), that the guarantee for the purchase of the machines was void at common law due to a 'common mistake' by the parties.

Grist v Bailey (1966)

G bought a house from B for £850. Both parties believed that the house was occupied by a statutory tenant who, therefore, could not be compelled to quit. In fact, the occupier was not a statutory tenant. The value of the house with vacant possession was £2,250. *Held*: that G and B made a 'common' mistake of a fundamental kind. The contract was not void at common law, but in exercise of its equitable jurisdiction, the court set the contract aside on terms that the vendor should offer the house to the purchaser at its 'open-market' price.

d Mistake as to the identity of the other party

This type of mistake arises where, for example, *A* intends to contract with B, but by mistake contracts with C. Is the contract with C valid? The answer here depends on whether the identity of the party (in the previously mentioned case, B) is material to the contract in the sense that *A* intended to contract with B and no other person. *Boulton v Jones*, 1857, summarised on p. 129, indicates that in these circumstances, there is no contract.

Mistake of identity, therefore, will nullify the contract if it is proved

i that the identity of the party contracted with is *material* to the contract; and
ii that the party contracted with knows that he is not the person that the other party intended to enter into contractual relations with.

In ordinary contracts for the sale of goods in a shop, for example, the identity of the customer is immaterial. The person is a mere customer, and as long as he or she is willing to pay the price for the goods, the shopkeeper is usually unconcerned with personal identity. Whoever the customer, it matters not as long as a bargain is made. But in some contracts, personal identity is material, and in such cases the contracts with the mistaken person are void.

A study of the following cases shows the application of the rules. In each case the test of mistake of identity is: Did the party intend to contract with one particular person only, and none other than him or her?

❖ CASE EXAMPLES

Cundy v Lindsay & Co. (1878)

A fraudulent person named Blenkarn ordered goods from Lindsay & Co. and imitated the signature of an old customer of Lindsay's named Blenkiron. Lindsay sent the goods. Blenkarn then sold the goods to Cundy, who paid for them. Lindsay claimed the goods from Cundy who refused to part with them. Cundy claimed that the contract between the fraud (Blenkarn) and Lindsay was voidable. Lindsay claimed that their contract with Blenkarn was void by reason of the mistake of identity of the person they were contracting with. *Held*: that Cundy must return the goods. The contract was void by reason of the mistake or identity. Lindsay had only one person in mind, and that was their genuine customer, Blenkiron. There was no contract; no title passed to Blenkarn and he could not give a good title to Cundy.

Phillips v Brooks (1919)

A rogue, X, entered a jeweller's shop to purchase jewellery. The rogue offered to pay by cheque. The cheque was accepted by the jeweller, who said delivery would be delayed until the cheque was cleared by the bank. The rogue said 'I am Sir George Bullough', and gave an address at St James's Square. He asked to take some of the jewels with him. The jeweller agreed, and the rogue then went to Brooks, Ltd and pawned them for a sum of money. The cheque later proved worthless. The jeweller then sued the pawnbroker for the jewels. *Held*: that Brooks obtained a good title. The contract was not void for mistake, but voidable for fraud. At the time of the contract, the jeweller intended to deal with the person physically in his shop, and his identity was immaterial.

Note: The fraud by the rogue was that by drawing a cheque, he impliedly represented that he had an account at a bank with sufficient funds. He had no such account.

Lewis v Averay (1971)

L advertised his car for sale, X, a fraud, replied to the advertisement, met L and said he was 'Richard Green', a well-known film star. *L* and X agreed a price (£450), X drew a cheque for £450 and signed it 'R.A. Green', producing a pass to Pinewood Studios as proof of his identity. X obtained the car and sold it to *A* (a bona fide purchaser) for a sum of money. X's cheque was worthless. *L* thereupon sued *A* in conversion. *Held* (Court of Appeal): *L* intended to contract with the person (X) actually before him, despite the fraudulent impersonation as Richard Green. Judgment given for *A*, who could retain the car.

e Mistake as to the nature of the document

The general rule of law is that a person is bound by the terms of any instrument signed. This is so even though the signer did not read the document or did not understand its contents (*L'Estrange v Graucob*, 1934—see p. 161).

Where, however, a person signs a contract in the mistaken belief that it is a totally different document, liability can be avoided. In such a case, *non est factum*, i.e. 'not my deed', may be pleaded.

❖ CASE EXAMPLE

Foster v Mackinnon (1869)

M, an old man of feeble sight, was induced to endorse a bill of exchange for £3,000 on the assurance that it was a guarantee. The bill was endorsed for value to Foster, who sued M on the bill. *Held*: that M's plea of *non est factum* was good, and he was not liable on the bill.

If the document is a negotiable instrument, the plea of *non est factum* can only be used if the signer has not been negligent. Mackinnon, in the previously mentioned case, being senile and poor-sighted, was held not to have been negligent.

❖ CASE EXAMPLE

Saunders v Anglia Building Society (1970) (also known as *Gallie v Lee*)

Mrs G, an aged woman, handed over to P, her nephew, the deeds of her house. P needed money and consulted his business associate, *Lee*. The latter caused a deed to be prepared and presented it to Mrs G to sign, saying it was a deed of gift to P. Mrs G had broken her spectacles and had difficulty in reading without them. She knew the document was to raise money and that *Lee* was involved. The deed in fact transferred the property to *Lee* (a fraud), who mortgaged it to a building society for £3,000 and absconded. Mrs G sued for a declaration that the deed was void and that the building society should deliver up the mortgage. Judgment was given for Mrs G. *Held* (on appeal to the House of Lords): The plea of *non est factum* failed. 'The essence of the plea of *non est factum* is that the person signing believed the document he signed had one character and one effect whereas in fact its character or effect was quite different' (per Lord Reid). Mrs G signed a document of the same character as she intended to sign and was bound by it.

Where a person knows the nature of the document signed but is mistaken as to the contents, the contract is not avoided.

❖ CASE EXAMPLE

Howstson v Webb (1908)

A solicitor, *W*, was asked to execute a deed and did so on being told (fraudulently) it was a conveyance of property of which he was a trustee. The deed was, in fact, a mortgage of the property. *W* was subsequently sued on the mortgage. *Held*: that *W* was bound by the terms of the mortgage: the misrepresentation related to the contents, not the character of the deed.

Mistake in equity. The general rule of common law was that a mistake, by one or both parties, showed that there was no true agreement (*consensus ad idem*) and that accordingly the contract was void, as in *Raffles v Wichelhaus* (p. 165), for instance. If the mistake was, however, not fundamental, as in *Bell v Lever Bros* (p. 166), the contract was held valid or good.

Where the simple division of contracts as either void or valid is inappropriate and unfairness results, equitable principles may be applied to effect a compromise and to do justice in the particular case where a strict application of common law rules leads to hardship.

The forms of equitable relief are these:

a The court may set aside an agreement on terms that are fair and just (*Solle v Butcher*, 1950).
b It may rectify a written instrument that does not truly express the agreed intention of the parties.

In the Court of Appeal in *Great Peace Shipping Limited v Tsavliris Salvage (International) Ltd*, The Great Peace (2002) rejected the view that had been propounded by Lord Denning in *Solle v*

Butcher (1950) that there was a different treatment of common mistake at common law as compared to equity.

c It may grant an order of specific performance of a contract where appropriate. Specific performance will be refused if the contract is not found to be void, if the party seeking it acted knowing of the other parties' mistake, or if the granting of specific performance would cause hardship to the other party.

❖ CASE EXAMPLE

***Craddock Bros v Hunt* (1923)**

A orally agreed to sell a house, exclusive of an adjoining yard, to B. Owing to a mistake, the later formal and written conveyance included the house and the yard. The mistake was common to *A* and B. *Held*: that the court could rectify the conveyance to accord with the intention of the parties.

❖ CASE EXAMPLE

***Webster v Cecil* (1861)**

C wrote to *W* to offer to sell some property to *W* for £1,250. C had already refused to sell the same land to *W* for £2,000. *W*, knowing a mistake must have occurred, wrote to C accepting the offer contained in C's letter. C had intended the price to be £2,250 and immediately gave notice of the error to *W*. *Held*: that the decree of specific performance would not be granted.

Remember that all forms of equitable relief or remedy are discretionary. The plaintiff cannot claim equitable remedies as of right, as in common law, where once the claim has been proved, the plaintiff has a right to damages.

Rectification. The case of *Craddock Bros v Hunt* is a good example of the decree of rectification in action. Where the parties make an agreement, but the written instrument to which they have reduced their agreement does not accurately express the agreement, the court may rectify the instrument so as to make it express the agreement of the parties and enforce it as rectified. To obtain the equitable remedy of rectification, the following conditions must be satisfied:

a The mistake must be one of expression only.

b There must be an actually concluded contract before the written instrument is drawn up. (The court will not make a new agreement for the parties.)

c There must be clear evidence of intention.

d The mistake must be common to both parties or made by one party and suspected by the other (*Commission for the New Towns v Cooper (Great Britain) Ltd*, 1995).

e The mistake must have existed at the time of the execution of the instrument.

f The mistake must be exactly proved. The claimant must show the precise form in which the instrument should be drawn up.

All these possibilities were considered in *FSH Group Holdings Ltd v GLAS Trust Corp Ltd* (2019) and *Porter v Stokes* (2023). In the latter case the Privy Council addressed issues arising in claims based on a prior binding contract and identified the defences to such claims. This case, an appeal from Trinidad and Tobago, concerned a claim for rectification of a deed of conveyance so as to conform with a prior written agreement for sale. In its judgment the Privy Council rejected the appeal against the rectification of the original document as being inconsistent with the documentary evidence. The Privy Council endorsed the leading decision on rectification for common mistake (FHS Group Holdings Ltd), confirming that there are two distinct bases for a claim for rectification: first, to accord with a prior binding contract, whose meaning is to be construed objectively; second, to accord with the parties' common intention where it did not amount to a prior contract, which entails determining as a fact their actual, subjective intention. The judgment of the Privy Council confirmed the first of these bases. In their decision they stated that 'The result of this necessarily long analysis is that, albeit for slightly different reasons that those of the Court of Appeal, the appeal must be dismissed.'

❖ CASE EXAMPLE

***Fairstate Ltd v General Enterprise and Management Ltd* (2010)**

Defects in a guarantee form were Group sufficiently ineffective and so fundamental and extensive that they could not sufficiently be cured by rectification. *Held*: that the guarantee form was therefore ineffective as a matter of contract and in any event was unenforceable as it failed to satisfy the requirements of s. 4 of the Statute of Frauds. Accordingly, the claim was dismissed.

7.10.2 Misrepresentation

'A representation is a statement made by one party to the other, before or at the time of the contract, with regard to some existing fact or to some past event, which is material to the contract' (Cheshire and Fifoot: *Law of Contract*).

Misrepresentations are of three kinds: innocent, negligent and fraudulent.

- *Innocent misrepresentations* are those statements of fact that the maker believes to be true but are, in fact, false.
- *Negligent misrepresentations* are incorrect statements of fact that are careless (or negligent), though not dishonest.
- *Fraudulent misrepresentations* are those statements of fact that the maker knows to be false, so fraud means *dishonest belief*. Fraudulent misrepresentation is a distinct tort, known as *deceit*. Its relevance and importance to the law of contract are obvious, and for these reasons, it is treated fully in this portion of the book. The next important point to consider is the distinction between (i) representations, (ii) conditions and (iii) warranties.

Representations are those statements that are made for the purpose of *inducing* persons to make contracts. They may be made before or at the time of the contract, but are not necessarily part of the contract themselves, as is the case with conditions and warranties. *Conditions* are terms of the contract that are vital, i.e. 'go to the root of the contract'. A *warranty*, on the other hand, is a term in an agreement that is subsidiary or collateral to the main purpose of the contract. In other words, a warranty is not so vital to the performance of the contract as to enable the contract to be set aside for breach. It is not always easy, in some contracts, to distinguish the three categories or descriptions mentioned previously, and careful study of cases is usually necessary to achieve a fair understanding. But, in every case, it is for the court to determine whether a particular statement is a representation, a condition or a warranty. This can only be done by examining closely the circumstances of each case and the intention of the parties as disclosed by the evidence.

Misrepresentation is defined as *an untrue statement of fact made by one party to the other party to a contract, either before or at the time of making the contract, with the intention that the person to whom the statement is made shall act upon such misrepresentation, and he does so act*.

The features common to innocent and fraudulent misrepresentation are:

a The misrepresentation must be one of fact, not law.
b The misrepresentation must be made by a party to the contract (or his agent).
c The party seeking legal redress must have relied upon and acted upon the misrepresentation when entering into the contract.
d The plaintiff must have suffered damage as a result of the misrepresentation.

a A misrepresentation must be a statement of fact

'I am a bank manager', 'The watch is solid gold': these are obviously statements of fact. Statements of general law are immaterial and are not grounds for relief or remedy to the party suffering loss. 'Ignorance of the law is no excuse', and since this implies that everyone is presumed to know the law, a party cannot aver that he has been led into a contract by a misstatement of general law.

Statements of opinion and 'trade puffs', as they are sometimes called, are not statements of fact. 'This powder washes whitest', 'This is some of the best land in England', 'This medicine will put you on top of the world': such statements are the stock-in-trade of advertisers and are not actionable unless they are statements of fact.

A statement of intention is not, as a rule, a representation. The statement must be of a present or past fact. However, a statement of intention *may* contain within itself a representation of an existing fact.

❖ CASE EXAMPLE

Edgington v Fitzmaurice **(1885)**

A company issued a prospectus inviting the public to subscribe for its debentures. The company stated that the money raised was to complete alterations to the company's premises, to purchase horses and vans and to develop trade. Plaintiff advanced money, but it turned out that the real object of the loan was to enable the directors to pay off pressing liabilities. *Held*: that the misstatement of the purpose for which the debentures were issued was a material misstatement of fact that rendered the directors liable in deceit.

In this case Lord Justice Bowen said: 'The state of a man's mind is as much a fact as the state of his digestion.'

b The misrepresentation must be made by a party to the contract or by their agent

A representation made by a third party or a bystander is immaterial.

c The representee must have relied on the misrepresentation

If, therefore, the representee (i) never knew of the existence of the misrepresentation, (ii) did not allow the misrepresentation to affect his own judgment or (iii) was aware of the untruth, he cannot state that he relied on the misrepresentation. Moreover, the misrepresentation must relate to a material element in the contract. Thus, a misrepresentation as to a trivial matter cannot avail to enable the plaintiff to claim relief. What is material is a question for the court to decide.

❖ CASE EXAMPLE

Smith v Chadwick (1884)

A prospectus contained a false statement that a certain man was on the board of directors of a company. Plaintiff admitted that on purchasing his shares, this statement had not influenced him. *Held*: that he could not obtain relief.

Where a party makes a statement that was true when made but that subsequently becomes untrue before the other party enters into the contract, the party making the misrepresentation owes a duty to the representee to be told the true position before any action is taken.

❖ CASE EXAMPLE

With v O'Flanagan (1936)

A doctor, X, represented in January that the takings of his medical practice were £2,000. Five months later, when the contract was signed, the takings had fallen considerably due to the doctor's own illness. X failed to disclose the reduction. *Held*: that the contract could be rescinded owing to X's failure to disclose the fall in the takings.

Fraudulent misrepresentation. A fraudulent misrepresentation is an untrue statement made (i) knowingly, (ii) without belief in its truth or (iii) recklessly, careless whether it be true or false (Lord Herschell in *Derry v Peek*, 1889).

❖ CASE EXAMPLE

Derry v Peek (1889)

The Plymouth Tramways Co. had power under a special Act of Parliament to run trams by animal power and, with the Board of Trade's consent, by mechanical or steam power. The directors of the company issued a prospectus inviting subscriptions from the public for shares. The prospectus stated that the company had the authority to run trams by steam power. They assumed the Board of Trade would grant permission as a matter of course. But the Board refused permission and, in consequence, the company was wound up. A subscriber sued the directors for fraud. *Held*: that the directors were not fraudulent; they honestly believed the statement in the prospectus to be true.

As a consequence of this case the law in relation to statements in the prospectuses of companies was altered, and now, by the **Companies Act 2006**, directors are liable to pay compensation for innocent misrepresentations appearing in prospectuses.

Remedies for fraudulent misrepresentation. A party who has been deceived by a fraudulent misrepresentation has the following remedies open to him or her. They may:

a bring an action in tort for damages for deceit
b bring an action for rescission (with or without a claim for damages)
c repudiate the contract and refuse further performance
d prosecute or notify police (obtaining property or pecuniary advantage by deception: **Theft Act 1968**, see p. 366)

The party deceived may treat the contract as voidable. The contract may or may not be affirmed. In effect it is up to this person to take any of the preceding courses or to do nothing in regard to (a) to (c) and treat the contract as binding. If sued, fraud may be pleaded as a defence and a counterclaim made for damages. *Negligent misrepresentation.* A negligent misrepresentation is a statement that is made carelessly, though not dishonestly. We look at two factors:

a The *Hedley Byrne* case (1964) (see p. 250) rules that where *A* makes a negligent misstatement to B, as a result of which B suffers damage in reliance on it, B may sue *A* in tort for negligence, providing a 'special relationship' exists between *A* and B, such as banker and customer, solicitor and client, surveyor and house purchaser, etc. Hitherto the tort of negligence had been confined to acts, not words.
b The **Misrepresentation Act 1967**, s. 2(1), distinguished between (i) negligent and (ii) entirely innocent misrepresentation. Thus:

> Where a person (*A*) has entered into a contract after a misrepresentation has been made to him by another party (*B*) and as a result thereof he (*A*) has suffered loss, then, if the person making the misrepresentation (i.e. (*B*)) would be liable to damages in respect thereof had the misrepresentation been made fraudulently, that person (*B*) shall be so liable notwithstanding that the misrepresentation was not made fraudulently, unless he (*B*) proves that he (*B*) had reasonable ground to believe and did believe up to the time the contract was made that the facts represented were true. (S. 2(1))

Note: The writer has inserted (*A*) and (B) to assist in grasping the meaning of this complicated section.

Neither 'negligence' nor 'duty of care' is mentioned in this section. What the section does is to place on the defendant the burden of proving that there was reasonable ground for believing the facts represented were true; in short, that the statement did not show carelessness or negligence. In the tort of negligence, the burden of proof of duty of care and breach of duty is placed on the plaintiff. So, there is a procedural advantage to the plaintiff in suing under s. 2(1). Damages are, however, obtainable only if they would have been obtained 'had the misrepresentation been made fraudulently'.

The remedies for negligent misrepresentation in the sense we have been discussing are:

a damages, either under the *Hedley Byrne* type of action or under the **Misrepresentation Act 1967**, s. 2(1)
b rescission, either by the party misled cancelling the contract or by the court. But, in the latter case, the judge (or arbitrator) has a discretion to declare the contract as subsisting and may award damages in lieu of rescission (s. 2(2))

Remedies for innocent misrepresentation. At common law, before 1967, when a person claimed a contract was entered into as a result of an innocent misrepresentation, the party misled could not claim damages. Action could, however, be taken in court for rescission (see p. 174) or the contract could be repudiated, e.g. by notifying the other party personally that the contract was no longer regarded as binding. The contract affected by innocent misrepresentation is voidable at the option of the party misled.

The **Misrepresentation Act 1967** now governs the remedies available for innocent misrepresentation. The contracting party may:

a claim for damages (see s. 2(1) and (2) in what follows)
b apply for rescission (see s. 2(2) in what follows)
c repudiate the contract and refuse to perform further obligations under the contract
d affirm the contract

As to (a), the judge (or arbitrator) may award damages:

> if of the opinion that it would be equitable to do so, having regard to the nature of the misrepresentation and the loss that would be caused by it if the contract were upheld, as well as to the loss that rescission would cause to the other party.
>
> (S. 2(1))

As to (b), the judge (or arbitrator) 'may, if it is equitable to do so, award damages in lieu of rescission and may declare the contract subsisting'. The court must have regard to the nature of the misrepresentation, the loss that would be caused if the contract were upheld and the loss that rescission would cause to the other party (s. 2(2)).

As to (d), the party misled may choose to ignore the misrepresentation and treat the contract as binding. The contract is voidable, and it is therefore a matter for the wronged party as to what course of action should be taken.

Rescission (i.e. cancellation or annulment) is a discretionary remedy, and in any legal action on the contract it is granted subject to certain important principles. In particular the party misled will lose the right to rescission if:

i the parties cannot be restored to their original positions. This is known as *restitution in integrum*
ii the party, knowing of the misrepresentation, takes a benefit under the contract or in some other way affirms the contract
iii third parties have acquired rights under the contract
iv there has been long delay in taking legal action to rescind the contract. Delay indicates to the court that the party misled affirms the contract

❖ CASE EXAMPLE

Leaf v International Galleries (1950)

L bought a painting of Salisbury Cathedral described innocently by the seller as a genuine Constable. After five years L discovered that the painting was not a genuine Constable, and he claimed rescission on the grounds of innocent misrepresentation. *Held*: that L's claim must fail. His action was too long delayed.

Exemption clauses. Section 3 of the Act provides that if an agreement contains an exemption clause purporting to give immunity or to protect a party from liability for misrepresenting, excluding or restricting any remedy available to the represented, the exemption clause shall be void unless the court allows reliance on it as being fair and reasonable in the circumstances.

Damages for misrepresentation. The general rule of law that damages cannot be claimed for innocent misrepresentation is subject to certain exceptions as follows:

a Under the **Misrepresentation Act 1967**, just noted.
b Under the **Companies Act 2006**, where an innocent misrepresentation is included in a prospectus inviting the public to subscribe for shares in a company. In this case *compensation* is payable by the directors to a subscriber for the shares.
c In an action for breach of warranty of authority by an agent. In this case damages may be claimed from the agent who has represented an authority to act as an agent for another when in fact there is no such authority or where an agent exceeds their authority. It is immaterial that the agent acted innocently. The agent is liable in damages.

***Trade Descriptions Act* 1968**. This Act includes provisions designed to give greater protection to consumers, particularly against their being deceived by false or misleading trade descriptions. Where, therefore, a misrepresentation is made in a contract, the misrepresentor may be liable criminally under the Act, as in *Wings Ltd v Ellis* (1984). Section 11 of the Act (Misleading Price Indications) was replaced by Part III of the **Consumer Protection Act 1987**. The **Property Misdescriptions Act 1991** protects potential house purchasers from exaggerated property descriptions and is intended to ensure the accuracy of estate agents' literature and advertisements.

These powers were extended by the **Consumers, Estate Agents and Redress Act 2007**, which established a National Consumer Council to encourage industry complaints seriously. This Act amended the **Estate Agents Act 1979** by making provision for redress schemes dealing with complaints about estate agents.

7.10.3 Contracts '*uberrimae fidei*'

In the law of contract, silence by a party does not in general amount to misrepresentation. But there is one class of contracts in which disclosure of material facts must be made. Agreements falling within this class are known as contracts *uberrimae fidei* ('of the utmost good faith'). Failure to disclose material facts, whether they are asked for or not, renders the contract voidable at the option of the party prejudiced, i.e. the party to whom disclosure ought to have been made.

Note: When considering the impact of the following examples of the effect of disclosure upon an Insurance Contract notice must be taken of the effect of the provisions of the **Consumer Insurance (Disclosure and Representations) Act 2012** in relation to a disclosure and representation made by a consumer to an insurer before a consumer insurance contract is entered into or varied.

Examples of contracts to which this rule applies are as follows:

a Contracts of insurance

In contracts of marine, fire and life insurance, the insured party must disclose all facts that might influence the judgment of the other party, i.e. the insurer, whether or not to take the risk of insuring or to increase the premium. If, therefore, the insured omits the information required, the insurer may repudiate the contract. However, in *Strive Shipping Corporation v Hellenic Mutual War Risks Association* (2002), this duty of utmost good faith did not require an assured to disclose facts that it knew were of no bearing on its honesty or integrity on the basis that a suspicious person might believe otherwise. A duty of good faith is also owed by the insurer to the insured and damages may be payable upon breach of that duty (*Banque Keyser Ullmann SA v Skandia (UK) Ins. Co. Ltd and Others*, 1987).

The **Third Parties (Rights against Insurers) Act 2010** provides for rights to be transferred to a third party where an insured party is facing financial difficulties and enters into certain alternatives to insolvency, such as voluntary procedures between the insured and the insured's creditors.

b Company prospectuses

These documents invite persons to subscribe for shares in a company. In accordance with the **Companies Act 2006**, full disclosure of material facts must be contained in all prospectuses. Failure to include these facts renders the contract voidable, and the directors or promoters liable for damages (see p. 173).

c Contracts for the sale of land

A vendor of land must disclose all defects in title to the land, e.g. restrictive covenants, easements, etc. A vendor is under no duty to disclose obvious defects in the land itself that could be discovered on reasonable inspection.

d Suretyship and partnership contracts

These contracts are not, in their inception, of the utmost good faith; once the relationship is entered into, however, a duty is imposed on the surety and principal and between partners to disclose to each other all material facts affecting their fiduciary relationship.

e Family arrangements

Under this heading are included settlements of family property or agreements relating to family property and similar matters. Each member of the family is bound to disclose to the others any sums of money and details of property received without the knowledge of the remaining members.

❖ CASE EXAMPLE

***Gordon v Gordon* (1821)**

An advantage was gained under a family settlement by one brother who withheld valid information. *Held*: that the agreement should be rescinded, notwithstanding that 19 years had elapsed after its making.

f Contracts between fiduciaries

The relationship of the parties to each other may give rise to a duty in law to disclose. Thus, for example, in contracts or agreements between trustee and beneficiary, solicitor and client and principal and agent, the utmost good faith must be observed. Failure to observe this standard renders the agreement voidable at the instance of the person prejudiced.

7.10.4 Duress and undue influence

The general rule of law is that a valid agreement may be made only where the parties exercise their own free will, unconstrained by force, the fear of force or other pressure. The law takes account of two forms of pressure: (a) duress and (b) undue influence.

a *Duress* at common law means violence or threatened violence to a party to a contract or to a member of his family or threatened unlawful imprisonment. The effect on the agreement is that it is probably voidable at the instance of the party threatened, but arguably it is void.

❖ **CASE EXAMPLES**

Cumming v Ince (1847)

An agreement to give up deeds made under threat of confinement in an asylum was held not to be binding on the plaintiff.

Welch v Cheeseman (1973)

In fear of violence from the man with whom she lived, *W* transferred her home to him. *Held*: the transfer would be set aside for duress.

Barton v Armstrong (1975)

A deed executed under threats to kill was held to be void for duress.

Economic duress. More recently the courts have widened the doctrine of duress to include 'economic duress'. Scarman LJ, in a decision by the Privy Council in *Pao On v Lau Yiu Long* (1980), listed the basic requirements to be taken into account in assessing whether such duress had taken place as being:

1. Did the person claiming to have been coerced protest?
2. Did the person have other available courses of action, such as legal action?
3. Was that person independently advised?
4. After entering into the contract, did they take steps to avoid it?

❖ **CASE EXAMPLE**

Universe Tankships of Morovia v International Transport Workers Federation (1982)

Ship flying flag of convenience 'blacked' by the trade, which insisted the shipowners paid £80,000 to permit the ship to leave port (Milford Haven). Shipowners paid under protest and part went to the Seafarers International Charity Welfare Fund. Once the ship had left port the owners sued to recover money paid to the Charity. *Held*: The money was recoverable as agreement to pay it had been obtained under economic duress.

Note: The decision was extended by the High Court in *Progress Bulk Carriers v Tube City IMS LLC (The vessel Cenk Kaptanoglu* (2012) when it held that a lawful threat to commit a lawful act amounted to illegitimate pressure so as to make a contract voidable for 'economic duress'.

Pakistan International Airline Corp v Times Travel (UK) Ltd (2021)

The claimant (Times Travel—TT) was a travel agent whose business almost entirely comprised selling tickets for flights to Pakistan on planes owned by the defendants, Pakistan Airlines—PIAC. A series of disputes between the parties regarding the non-payment of commission led PIAC to threaten to end any contractual relations with TT unless it entered into a new contract whereby TT released PIAC from all claims that TT might have against them under the previous contract. The outcome was that TT sought to rescind the new contract that had been entered into for 'duress'. This would have allowed it to seek the commission that it claimed it was owed under the previous contract. *Held*: (Supreme Court—in dismissing the claim)—for a claim of economic duress to be successful, there must be a concept of unconscionability which was not present in the current claim.

Note: The Supreme Court confirmed that two essential elements were necessary for a claim to be successful in duress. First, there must be a threat by the defendant that is 'illegitimate' and secondly, that the illegitimate threat induced the claimant to enter into the contract. An additional third element, specifically in respect of economic duress, was that the claimant must have had no reasonable alternative to giving in to the threat.

b *Undue influence*, an equitable doctrine, is a more subtle form of pressure exerted upon a party to a contract. According to Ashburner the doctrine is that:

> If *A* obtains any benefit from B, whether under a contract or as a gift, by exerting an influence over B which, in the opinion of the court, prevents B from exercising an independent judgment in the matter in question, B can set aside the contract or recover the gift.

Where no special relationship exists between the parties, the party alleging undue influence has the burden of proving it.

❖ CASE EXAMPLE

Williams v Bayley (1866)

W's son had forged *W*'s signature on some promissory notes and given them to his bank. His bank manager called upon *W* and persuaded him to make a mortgage to the bank in return for the notes, under threat of prosecuting the son. *Held*: the agreement was invalid on the grounds of undue influence in that an unfair advantage was taken of *W*.

This decision was adopted by the House of Lords in *Barclays Bank plc v Coleman* (No. 2) (2001) (see later on).

But where a confidential relationship exists between the parties, undue influence may be presumed by the court, in which case the party in whom confidence is reposed has the burden of rebutting the presumption; for example, a solicitor who buys property from a client may need to show that the client has acted upon independent advice.

The special relationships that have been held by the courts to raise the presumption are solicitor and client, doctor and patient, trustee and beneficiary, guardian and ward, parent and child, religious adviser and disciple, but not husband and wife. However, the presumption may be raised in the case of other persons; the list is not closed.

This is illustrated by the following case:

❖ CASE EXAMPLE

Barclays Bank plc v O'Brien and Another (1992)

A husband who was in debt obtained his wife's signature as surety for a loan to his company from his company's bank by misrepresenting the amount and duration of the loan. *Held*: The onus was on the bank as creditor to ensure that the debtor did not take unfair advantage of the wife as surety.

This approach was adopted by the House of Lords in *Barclays Bank v Coleman* (No. 2) (2001), where the House of Lords reviewed the situation where a wife charges the matrimonial home by way of security for a loan made to the husband's business. It was held in these circumstances that a bank was put on enquiry if a solicitor tells the bank that a wife has been properly advised, unless the bank knows to the contrary. The decision means that in future, banks will be put on enquiry every time the relationship between the person providing the surety and the debtor is not commercial.

A contract induced by undue influence is voidable and confers a right to rescission. But the party seeking to avoid will be deprived of this remedy if a third party has obtained rights under the contract or if there has been a delay in asserting his or her claim. Delay implies that the party affirms the contract, and as 'delay defeats the equities', the court may, in its discretion, refuse aid to the applicant.

❖ CASE EXAMPLES

Allcard v Skinner (1887)

A, in middle age, joined a Protestant sisterhood, taking vows of poverty and obedience. She gave property to the value of £7,000 to the sisterhood in accordance with her vows. Some nine years later, she left the Order to become a Roman Catholic. Only £1,671 of her property remained with the sisterhood, the balance having been spent. *A* claimed the return of the £1,671 from S, the Mother Superior, and alleged undue influence. *Held*: that undue influence existed in this case since the plaintiff was bound not to seek independent advice while in the Order. However, the plaintiff's claim was barred by her delay of five years after leaving the sisterhood in claiming the money.

Lancashire Loans Ltd v Black (1934)

B, a young married woman, acting under the influence of her mother, made unwise moneylending contracts that were for the benefit of the mother. The moneylenders knew of the facts, and subsequently sued mother and daughter on a promissory note. *Held*: that although of full age and a married woman, B was unduly influenced by her mother. The contract was therefore voidable by B.

While inequality of bargaining power may also be regarded as undue influence, the House of Lords in *National Westminster Bank plc v Morgan* (1985) stated that there was no general principle for the granting of such relief. The decision in this case was further explained in *Goldsworthy v Brickell and Another* (1987).

7.11 Illegality

A contract is illegal if it contravenes a statute or the common law. Illegality may exist in regard to the *making* of a contract, e.g. making a contract to break into a house to steal amounts to a criminal conspiracy; or in regard to the *performance*, as in a contract to perform an illegal operation.

Contracts containing criminal elements, such as those mentioned previously, are illegal. So, too, are contracts that involve the commission of a tort. But a contract may be illegal for reasons quite unconnected with crime or tort. Thus, a contract 'in restraint of trade' is illegal, as we shall see. These and similar contracts are declared illegal because they offend certain fundamental rules of common law laid down by the judges and collectively described as 'public policy'. The broad limits of this doctrine in its application to illegal contracts will be examined later.

The general rule is that an illegal contract is void. The maxim applied by the courts is *ex turpi causa non oritur actio* ('no action arises from a base or wrongful cause').

7.11.1 Contracts declared illegal by statute

Certain statutes declare that some kinds of contracts are illegal and void. Thus, the **Gaming Act (as amended) 1845** declares certain gaming and wagering contracts to be of this kind.

❖ CASE EXAMPLE

***Lipkin Gorman (A Firm) v Karpnale Ltd* (1991)**

A partner in the firm L stole money from the firm, which was exchanged for gambling chips and used to place bets with K. *Held*: The transaction was void as a gambling contract under s. 18 of the **Gambling Act 1845** and therefore did not constitute valuable consideration for the contract.

The **Consumer Credit Act 1974** renders certain moneylending contracts void, e.g. those of an extortionate or unconscionable kind.

Note: The **Truck Acts 1831** to **1940**, which prohibited the payment or part-payment of wages in kind, have been repealed by the **Wages Act 1986**.

In *Mohamed v Alaga* & Co. (a firm) (1999), it was held that for the purpose of the doctrine of statutory liability, it did not matter whether the contract was prohibited by primary or secondary legislation.

However, on the facts of the case, the Court of Appeal permitted M to pursue a *quantum meruit* claim for reasonable remuneration for professional services that he had rendered.

7.11.2 Contracts illegal at common law

a Contracts to commit a crime or a tort

Contracts to make counterfeit coin, commit theft or maim another are examples of this kind. It is illegal in some cases to agree for a consideration not to prosecute an offender. To contract with a police officer, for a consideration, not to prosecute an offender amounts to corruption and is of course illegal.

❖ **CASE EXAMPLE**

***Beresford v Royal Insurance Co. Ltd* (1937)**

B insured his life for £50,000. This amount was to be paid on his death (even if by suicide). Some years after taking out his policy, B shot himself in a taxi-cab, intending that the insurance money should be used to pay off his heavy debts. *Held*: that B's personal representatives could not recover from the insurance company the £50,000, for it is contrary to public policy to permit B's estate to benefit by reason of the commission of a crime (suicide was at that time a crime).

An agreement to perform in a foreign and friendly country an action that is unlawful in that country is illegal and void as contrary to public policy.

❖ **FOSTER V DRISCOLL (1929)**

A partnership agreement was entered into in England for the purpose of smuggling whisky into the United States at a time when the American prohibition laws were in force. An action on the agreement was begun in England. *Held*: that the agreement was illegal and void.

b Contracts tending to sexual immorality

A contract involving prostitution is contrary to good morals and is illegal.

❖ **CASE EXAMPLE**

***Pearce v Brooks* (1866)**

A prostitute bought a brougham (carriage) on hire-purchase terms from a firm of coachbuilders. It was known that she intended to use the carriage for the purpose of attracting men customers. The woman failed to keep up her contractual payments for the carriage, and the coachbuilders sued for arrears. *Held*: that as the plaintiff knew the purpose for which the carriage was to be used, the contract was void.

c Contracts affecting the freedom of marriage

A contract in absolute restraint of marriage, i.e. to restrain a person from marrying at all, is void. Partial restraints, e.g. not to marry a person of a particular religious faith or of a particular nationality, may, if reasonable, be upheld.

Marriage-brokage contracts, i.e. contracts for reward to introduce men and women with a view to subsequent marriage, are void. This does not include introduction agencies. It is only where the contract includes marriage as a term.

d Contracts of champerty and maintenance

Maintenance occurs where one person, having no interest in the subject matter of litigation, encourages another to take civil action against a third party as, for example, by giving financial assistance. It is a good defence to show that the person assisted has a common interest with the maintaining party or that the maintenance is actuated by motives of charity.

Champerty is similar to maintenance, except that the assistance is given on the understanding that the person giving the assistance will share in the recovered damages.

Both offences were abolished by the **Criminal Law Act 1967**, but by s. 14(2), this does not affect contracts contrary to public policy.

e Agreements tending to injure the public service

A contract involving bribery and corruption and contracts to buy honours are illegal. For a definition of bribery, see **Offences under the Bribery Act 2010** (p. 385).

❖ CASE EXAMPLE

***Parkinson v College of Ambulance* (1925)**

P was induced to give a large sum of money (£3,000) to a charitable institution, the secretary of which undertook to secure a knighthood for P in return. The knighthood was not bestowed, and P sued for the return of his money. *Held*: that the agreement was illegal and void, and P was, therefore, unable to recover the sum.

These contracts are illegal at common law and also by statute (**Trading with the Enemy Act 1939**). All such contracts made with a person voluntarily residing in enemy territory during war are illegal unless permitted by licence of the Crown.

f Contracts in restraint of trade

Every agreement in restraint of trade is prima facie illegal and void. An agreement in restraint of trade will, however, be valid if it is reasonable between the parties and if it is reasonable having regard to the interests of the public. In such agreements the doctrine of public policy applies with particular emphasis. There are three classes:

- i contracts between the buyer and seller of the goodwill of a business, restraining the seller from competing with the buyer
- ii contracts between an employer and an employee
- iii contracts between traders regulating conditions of trade, price-maintenance agreements and similar agreements. These may contravene the **Competition Act 1998**, the provisions of which are noted on p. 168

i Restrictions on the sale of a business

There is said to be greater freedom of contract between the seller and purchaser of the goodwill of a business than there is between an employer and an employee. Consequently, the rule as to the 'reasonableness' of an agreement will be less strictly applied in the case of sellers and purchasers in a position of equality and competent to make their own terms and conditions.

The reasonableness of an agreement that is in restraint of trade is a matter for the court. This applies to all types of contracts, whether between employer and employee or between seller and purchaser of a business. Frequently, contracts of this kind contain several clauses, some of which may be controversial. Accordingly, where the reasonable part of a contract can be safely severed from the unreasonable, a court may, in its discretion, enforce the reasonable part only. If the contract is indivisible, however, it is void, even if parts of it are reasonable.

❖ CASE EXAMPLE

***Nordenfeldt v Maxim-Nordenfeldt Gun Co.* (1894)**

N, an inventor and manufacturer of guns and ammunition, sold his business to a company and promised that for 25 years he would not manufacture guns and ammunition henceforward in any part of the world. *Held*: that the agreement was reasonable and binding.

In this case a worldwide restraint was imposed. The fact that Nordenfeldt was liberally compensated, however, rendered the contract reasonable in itself. Also, in this case it is important to consider the broad international nature of the market for guns and ammunition.

❖ CASE EXAMPLE

***British Reinforced Concrete Co. Ltd v Schelff* (1921)**

S, the owner of a local business, sold it to the plaintiff company that had branches all over England. S covenanted not to carry on a business similar to that sold within 10 miles of any of the branches of the plaintiff company. *Held*: that the covenant was void. The restraint was more than was necessary to protect the plaintiff company and the goodwill of the business purchased from S.

ii Restraints on employees

The question arises whether an employee's contractual undertaking not to compete with an employer on leaving is enforceable when this occurs. In determining whether an agreement is reasonable, the courts pay regard to the class of business of the employer:

- the status and class of work of the employee;
- the area covered by the restriction; and
- the duration of the restraint clause in the agreement (*John Michael Design Pic v Cooke and Another*, 1987).

As to the employer's protection from competition with a former employee, we may note that a restraint has 'never been upheld if directed only to the prevention of competition or against the use of the personal skill and knowledge acquired by the employee in his or her employer's business' (*Morris v Saxelby*, 1916).

An employer may be protected against the misuse of knowledge gained by an employee of the following kinds: lists of trade connexions; trade secrets; confidential information; and lists of names and addresses of an employer's customers. An injunction may be obtained from the court to restrain the misuse of such information in suitable cases. Further, a skilled employee having access to an employer's trade secrets may be prevented by injunction from working in their spare time for a rival business (*Hivac Ltd v Park Royal Scientific Instruments Ltd*, 1946). There is an implied term in employment contracts that an employee must render faithful service during his or her employment.

An employee who is wrongfully dismissed by their employer is thereby released from liability under a restrictive agreement of the kind we are discussing here. It is, of course, otherwise where the dismissal is lawful.

In determining the reasonableness of an agreement in restraint of trade, the court has regard to the nature of the employer's business and also the capacity in which the employee serves. A wider restriction may be permissible in relation to an employee occupying a managerial position than would be upheld in the case of a subordinate employee. Moreover, some confidential relationship must subsist between employer and employee, e.g. the confidential relationship that exists between a solicitor and his managing clerk. But not all such relationships are held to be confidential in this sense and restrictive agreements between the following classes of persons have been held unreasonable and void: a newspaper proprietor and a reporter; a clothing company and a canvasser; a firm of motor-car dealers and a motor salesman; an estate agent and a clerk.

❖ CASE EXAMPLES

Attwood v Lamont (1920)

A, a tailor and draper at Kidderminster, employed *L* under a contract containing a restriction that L would not, on leaving his employment, carry on a business as a tailor within 10 miles of Kidderminster. *Held*: that the restriction was merely to prevent L from using his skill in competition with *A*, and the agreement was void.

Fitch v Dewes (1921)

D, a solicitor at Tamworth, employed F as managing clerk. A covenant in a service agreement contained a clause restraining F, on leaving D's employment, from practising as a solicitor within 7 miles of Tamworth. *Held*: that the covenant was good. F had become acquainted with the solicitor's clients and their business, and therefore could be restrained from using that knowledge to the detriment of D. Accordingly a lifelong restriction was not too wide.

M & S Drapers v Reynolds (1956)

A collector-salesman, R, working for a firm of credit drapers, covenanted that he would not, for five years after leaving his employment, canvass orders from any person on the firm's list of customers during the three years immediately preceding the determination of his employment. R sold goods in breach of the covenant and was sued by the plaintiffs. *Held*: that the restraint for five years in R's position was too long and was an unreasonable restraint of trade.

The principle was reaffirmed in *Watson v Prager and Anor* (1991), where an agreement between a boxer and his manager/promoter containing an option to extend the original term of three years for a further three years was held to be an unreasonable restraint of trade.

iii The Competition Act 1998 has repealed the Restrictive Trade Practices Legislation and the provision on anti-competitive practices in the Competition Act 1980

Part 1 of the Act provides for a new set of competition rules modelled on the provisions in Articles 85 and 86 of the **Treaty of Rome 1957**. These are known as Chapter I and II prohibition.

The Chapter I prohibition is in respect of agreements, decisions and concerted practices between or by undertakings or associations of undertakings that are implemented in the United Kingdom, the purpose or effect of which is the prevention, restriction or distortion of competition in the United Kingdom.

A Chapter II prohibition is in respect of an abuse by an undertaking or undertakings of a dominant position in the United Kingdom.

Chapter III makes provision for the investigation and enforcement of Chapters I and II prohibitions by the Director General of Fair Trading, while Chapter IV contains provisions for a newly constituted Competition Commission to replace and assume the responsibility for the work of the Monopolies and Restrictive Practices Commission. It will also act as an appeals tribunal for the enforcement of Chapter I and II prohibitions.

7.11.3 Effects of illegality

An illegal contract is void, and consequently the court will not assist a party to such an agreement either directly or indirectly: *ex turpi causa non oritur actio* ('no action arises on a base cause'). Accordingly, no money or goods delivered under such a contract can be recovered by action.

Where money or goods have passed under an illegal contract, the defendant is in a stronger position than the claimant, who seeks the aid of the court to recover his or her property. Because the court usually refuses its aid once it discovers the illegality, the defendant to whom goods have been delivered or money has been paid may sometimes keep the goods or money. The maxim applied is *in pari delicto potior est conditio defendentis* ('where there is equal wrongdoing, the position of the defendant is stronger').

There are certain exceptions to the rule. Thus (i) where the parties are not *in pari delicto* (equal in wrongdoing), e.g. where one is subservient or has entered into the contract due to the oppression, duress or fraud of the other, the innocent party may recover money paid or property transferred; (ii) where the illegal purpose of the contract has not been carried out, one party may repent and recover back any money or property transferred. There must be true repentance, and the non-performance must result from the repentance, not that the contract was frustrated for another cause.

❖ **CASE EXAMPLES**

Bigos v Bousted (1951)

P wanted to send his wife to Italy for health reasons. P agreed with D that D should make available £150 in Italian money for the purpose, contrary to the **Exchange Control Act 1947**. P deposited a share certificate with D as security, but D failed to make available the Italian currency. P claimed the return of the share certificate. *Held*: that the contract was illegal and the fact that the contract had not been carried out was not due to the repentance of P.

Berg v Sadler & Moore (1937)

B, a tobacconist, was placed on a stop list by a tobacco association for breach of its rules. B concealed his identity, and to obtain supplies, induced another member of the association to obtain tobacco for him from S & M. B paid £72 19s. for cigarettes to S & M. The latter became suspicious and refused to supply the goods or refund the money. *Held*: that B's claim failed as he had attempted to obtain cigarettes by false pretence (an illegal act).

Severance. Sometimes a contract is illegal as to a part only. In these circumstances the court may divide the contract, enforcing the valid portion and refusing assistance regarding the illegal part.

Where the whole purpose of the contract is illegal, severance of the good from the illegal is impossible and the court will do nothing to assist and will not make a new contract for the parties.

❖ CASE EXAMPLE

Napier v National Business Agency Ltd (1951)

P was employed by a company as secretary and accountant at a salary of £13 per week, plus £6 per week expenses. Both parties knew that P's expenses were never more than £1 per week. The company dismissed P, who then claimed his salary for the period in lieu of notice. *Held*: that the contract was to evade tax and was, therefore, illegal. It was impossible to sever the salary from the expenses, and the whole agreement was therefore unenforceable as tainted with illegality.

As a general rule the court will more readily sever covenants in restraint of trade affecting vendor and purchaser than similar contracts between master and servant.

7.12 Discharge of contract

A contract may be discharged by (a) agreement, (b) performance, (c) breach, (d) a subsequent impossibility or frustration and (e) operation of law.

a Discharge by agreement

Since the parties to a contract enter into their relationship by agreement, it follows that they may also, by agreement, release each other from their obligations. The mutual release of each party from their obligations under the agreement provides the consideration for the agreement to discharge the contract. This form of release is known as a *waiver*, each party waiving their rights under the contract, and is available where the consideration is still executory.

Where one of the parties has performed their obligations under the contract, an agreement to discharge the contract must (i) be supported by fresh consideration or (ii) the release must be by deed. The form of release in (i) is known as 'accord and satisfaction' and arises where the party to whom the obligation is owed agrees to accept from the other party something different in place of the original obligation. For example, Arnold agrees to dig Basset's Garden for £10. Arnold digs the garden as promised. The parties may agree to rescind the former contract and to substitute one where Basset agrees to provide Arnold with a bicycle instead of the £10. If Arnold accepts, there will be accord and satisfaction: 'accord' indicating the agreement and 'satisfaction' indicating the new consideration (the bicycle).

Substituted agreement. Where parties to a contract enter into a new agreement, the question to be determined is whether the new agreement is a variation of an existing contract or whether a new contract is substituted for the original. This is sometimes difficult to decide.

b Discharge by performance

A contract may be discharged by performance, each party fulfilling completely his or her obligations under the contract so that nothing remains to be done. Where, however, one party has done all that is required and the other has not, the contract is not discharged, for only one party has fulfilled his or her obligations.

Time. The time for performance may be agreed by the parties. Where time is 'of the essence of the contract', failure to perform within the stated time amounts to a breach. Time is 'of the essence of the contract' when the parties have expressly agreed or where it is implied from the circumstances. A contract for the supply of buns for a garden fête must be performed on the day of the event, not one day after, for obvious reasons. The general rule in mercantile contracts is that where time for performance is stated, the contract must be performed in that time; if not so performed, there is breach.

❖ TOPALSSON GMBH V ROLLS-ROYCE MOTOR CARS LTD (2023)

An agreement for the development and supply of software for a new car configuration stated: 'Time shall be of the essence regarding any date for the Supplier of goods or service specified in this agreement and the completion date'. There was a delay by the supplier in supplying the new software, and it was *Held*: that the effect of the clause was to allow the customer to terminate if the goods were not delivered by the supplier in accordance with the delivery date.

Where time is not 'of the essence of the contract', performance must be within a reasonable time.

Though time may not be 'of the essence' at the inception of the contract, it may become so on giving reasonable notice to the other party on whom performance depends.

Tender. Tender may mean 'attempted performance' of a contract. Where, therefore, performance of a contract is prevented or frustrated by the other party, it is a good defence in any subsequent action that performance was attempted (tender) but was prevented by the opponent. Accordingly, if tender of performance is made but prevented by the other party, the party tendering is freed from liability under the contract, which is thereby discharged. So, if goods are offered, as specified in the contract, but are rejected by the purchaser, the seller is freed from liability.

The second use of the word 'tender' relates to the payment of money. Where a person is obliged to pay a sum of money and attempts to do so, but payment is refused, the party tendering may, when sued, protect himself by paying into court the sum offered. If no greater sum is awarded to the claimant, the defendant will be awarded his costs incurred in the action.

❖ **CASE EXAMPLE**

***Chas. Rickards Ltd v Oppenheim* (1950)**

O ordered from R a Rolls-Royce chassis and car body, delivery to take place within six or seven months, expiring March 1948. No delivery was made. O still pressed for delivery and, in June 1948, O wrote to R instructing that the car must be delivered within four weeks, otherwise the order would be cancelled. The car was not, in fact, delivered until October 1948, and O refused to accept. *Held* (in an action by R for the price): that defendant O had waived the original time for delivery, but he was entitled on giving reasonable notice to make time 'of the essence of the contract', and did so.

A valid legal tender of money must comply with the terms of the contract as to place, mode and time of payment. Moreover, payment must be unconditional. The following points should be noted:

i The exact amount must be tendered.
ii The tender must be made to the creditor or to a duly constituted agent (e.g. solicitor).
iii The tender must be a continuing one, i.e. the party paying must always be ready and willing to pay the sum due.
iv The money must be legal tender, i.e. Bank of England notes to any amount; 50p pieces for payments not exceeding £10; 10p and 5p pieces for payments not exceeding £5; 2p and 1p pieces for payments not exceeding 20p.

A cheque is a good tender only if the creditor agrees to this method of payment. If the cheque is dishonoured the creditor may sue either under the original contract or on the dishonoured cheque, a separate action.

A receipt is evidence of payment, though not conclusive evidence. Where a receipt is lost, the payment may be proved by oral evidence of the payer or some other witness who knows the facts or by other written evidence.

Appropriation of payments. Where a debtor owes several debts to a creditor and makes a payment that is insufficient to satisfy all the debts outstanding, the question arises as to which of the several debts the one payment will be appropriated.

Certain rules have been laid down to regulate this matter as follows:

i The debtor can appropriate any payment he or she makes to any debt. The appropriation can be made expressly or impliedly. If *A* owes a £100 debt and a £50.27 debt to B, payment by *A* of a £50.27 cheque implies payment of the lesser amount, irrespective of when the smaller debt was created.
ii If the debtor fails to appropriate expressly or impliedly, the creditor may do so. Appropriation by the creditor may be to any legal or equitable claim and to debts that are statute-barred. Such debts are not extinguished; the right of action only is lost (**Limitation Act 1939**).
iii In current accounts between creditor and debtor, e.g. ordinary bank current accounts, the rule laid down in *Clayton*'s case (1816) applies. This states that if neither party appropriates expressly or impliedly, the money first paid in discharges the earliest outstanding debt.

c Discharge by breach

A breach of contract may take one of the following three forms, where a party:

i repudiates its liability under the contract before performance is due;
ii disables itself from performing his promise or part under the contract; or
iii fails to perform his obligations under the contract.

A breach of contract entitles the injured party to an action in damages. But it may also be entitled to treat the contract as discharged, provided that the injured party is able to show that the breach is of the whole contract or of some term that is vital to or 'goes to the root of' the contract. Breach of warranty, as distinct from a condition, gives a right to damages only but does not entitle the party injured to treat the contract as discharged.

Before the time for performance of the contract arrives, a party may expressly declare that there is no longer any intention to fulfil any obligations. Liability is therefore repudiated while the contract is still executory. This form of repudiation is sometimes called *anticipatory breach*, and its effect is to entitle the other party to sue immediately for breach even though time for performance has not yet arrived.

❖ CASE EXAMPLE

Hochster v De La Tour (1853)

In April 1853, *D* agreed to engage *H* as a courier for a European tour to commence on 1 June. On 11 May, *D* informed *H* that he no longer required his services. *H* began legal action. *Held*: that *D* had broken his contract by repudiation, and *H* could bring an action at once.

Repudiation may be of the whole contract or of part only. Repudiation that is sufficient to enable the contract to be discharged must be of a vital term in the contract.

Repudiation by one party entitles the innocent party (i) to sue at once (as in *Hochster v De La Tour*) or (ii) to treat the contract as still continuing and to wait until the time for performance arrives. In the latter case, the contract continuing in existence, the party in default may take advantage of any circumstances or events that may subsequently release him from liability under the contract.

❖ CASE EXAMPLE

Avery v Bowden (1855)

B chartered *A*'s ship at Odessa, and B agreed to load her with a cargo of wheat within 45 days. Before this period elapsed, B informed *A* that he had no cargo for the ship and told *A* to leave the port. But *A* refused and stayed on at Odessa, hoping B would change his mind. Before the 45 days expired, the Crimean War broke out, and performance of the contract would have been illegal. *Held*: that *A* might have treated B's refusal to load the cargo as a breach of contract. By staying on at the port he had waived his right against B. The contract was discharged, not by repudiation, but by the outbreak of war. B was accordingly under no liability.

However, in *Mediterranean Shipping Company S.A. v Cottonex Anstalt* (2016) the Court of Appeal *Held*: that upon a repudiatory breach of contract, the innocent party will not be able to affirm the contract if further performance by the defending party is not possible.

The decision further supports the Court of Appeal's recent approach to good faith in that there is no overriding principle of good faith under English law and the court is resistant to developing such a principle. The approach also draws parallels with the Court's approach to contract interpretation—whereby the answer lies within what the parties have agreed to and that in such circumstances the court should be reluctant to interfere.

d Discharge by subsequent impossibility (or frustration)

An agreement may be held to be void at the outset owing to an operative mistake, e.g. a common mistake as to the existence of subject matter. But a perfectly valid contract may be frustrated by subsequent impossibility. The common-law rule for the latter was that if the parties failed to provide for it in their contract, the party liable to perform could be sued for damages for breach. The courts have modified this rule to the extent that, though they will not regard a contract as frustrated merely because performance has become more difficult or more costly or less likely to yield the anticipated profit, they are prepared to find that a contract is discharged by frustration in the following circumstances:

i Supervening illegality

A contract, legal when made, may subsequently become illegal by the outbreak of war or by a change in the law. (*Avery v Bowden*, 1855—see p. 190.)

❖ CASE EXAMPLE

***Baily v De Crespigny* (1869)**

D leased land to B and covenanted that he (D) would not build on adjoining land that he retained. A railway company compulsorily acquired D's land under a *subsequent* statute, and the company built upon it. *Held*: that D was excused from his covenant with B, because the company's statutory powers made performance of the covenant impossible.

This case should be contrasted with the following:

❖ CASE EXAMPLE

***Walton Harvey Ltd v Walker & Homfrays* (1931)**

A contract by X, the lessees of a hotel, permitted Y *to* exhibit advertisements on the hotel roof for a period of seven years. During this time, the hotel was acquired by a local authority under powers *existing at the time* of the formation of the contract. Y sued X for breach. *Held*: that the contract was not discharged, as X was aware of the possibility of compulsory acquisition and must be taken to have accepted the risk. X was liable in damages for breach.

ii Where there is destruction of a specific thing necessary for the performance of the contract

If the contract depends on the existence of a certain thing and that thing is destroyed, the contract cannot be performed and is discharged.

❖ **CASE EXAMPLE**

***Taylor v Caldwell* (1865)**

C let a music hall to T for a series of concerts on certain days. The hall was accidentally burnt down before the concerts opened. *Held*: that the contract was discharged.

iii Where the contract depends on the happening of a certain event

If the event does not occur, the contract is regarded as discharged.

❖ **CASE EXAMPLE**

***Krell v Henry* (1903)**

Defendant agreed to hire plaintiff's flat to watch the coronation procession of Edward VII. The King was taken ill, and the procession was cancelled. *Held*: that the contract was discharged and no rent was payable by the defendant.

This case should be contrasted with the following:

❖ **CASE EXAMPLE**

***Herne Bay Steamboat Co. v Hutton* (1903)**

D agreed to hire P's steamboat on a certain day to take passengers from Herne Bay for the purpose of viewing the Royal Naval review and for a cruise round the fleet. The review was cancelled, but the fleet remained, and the steamboat might have been used for the intended cruise. D did not use the boat, however, and P claimed the hiring fee. *Held*: that the contract was not discharged as the review was not the sole foundation of the contract. Judgment for the plaintiff, P.

❖ **CASE EXAMPLE**

***RTI Ltd v BUR Shipping BV* (2024)**

A shipowner endeavoured to invoke a '*force majeure*' event (an occurrence beyond the reasonable control of the parties)—however, the Supreme Court reviewed the circumstances of the 'reasonable endeavours' proviso, whereby a party cannot rely on a *force majeure* event if that party could have avoided it by the exercise of reasonable endeavours. In the circumstances the charterer had offered to make payment in euros instead of the contracted US dollars as required by the contract. The Court did not accept this justification for creating 'needless additional uncertainty' by departing from the standard of performance provided by the terms of the contract.

iv Where there is death or personal incapacity

In contracts for personal services, the death or illness of the party who is to render the personal services discharges the contract. Thus, a pianist who contracts to give a concert performance but falls ill on the date of the concert will be excused if too ill to perform. The contract is frustrated. The illness must be sufficiently serious to go to the root of the contract (*Robinson v Davison*, 1871).

❖ CASE EXAMPLE

Condor v The Barron Knights, Ltd (1966)

C, aged 16, was a drummer employed by the Barron Knights band under a contract for five years. His duties were to play on seven nights a week when the band had engagements. C fell ill, and his doctor ordered that he was fit to play only on four nights a week. The band thereupon terminated his contract. *Held*: that, being ill, it was impossible for C to continue the contract in a business sense and the contract was properly terminated.

v Where there is a vital change in the circumstances

That is, where events occur of such gravity that they result in a greatly different situation from that contemplated by the parties when the contract was made.

❖ CASE EXAMPLES

Metropolitan Water Board v Dick, Kerr & Co. (1918)

D contracted with M to construct a reservoir within six years. After two years, a government department, acting under statutory powers, ordered D to cease work on the reservoir. *Held*: that the contract was frustrated. The character and duration of the interruption ordered by the Ministry would make the contract a really different contract based on changed conditions.

J. Constantine Steamship Line Ltd v Imperial Smelting Corporation, Ltd (1942)

I chartered a ship to go to Port Pirie, Australia, to load a cargo. The day before the ship was due to load her cargo, an explosion in her boilers occurred, the cause of which was unknown. The ship was unable to perform the charter. I sued for damages for breach of contract. *Held*: that the explosion frustrated the contract, and J was not liable in damages. Negligence against J was not proved.

There must be a fundamental change in the circumstances that, in effect, goes to the root of the contract so that to hold the parties to their agreement would be to hold them to 'a new adventure or a new agreement'. Increased costs or delay are not by themselves enough.

❖ CASE EXAMPLES

Davis Contractors Ltd v Fareham UDC (1956)

D contracted with Fareham UDC to build 78 houses for a certain sum within eight months. Because of inadequate supplies of labour and bad weather, it took 22 months to complete. Building costs rose meanwhile, and D claimed the contract was frustrated and that he was entitled to a higher sum than agreed based on *quantum meruit* (see p. 201). *Held* (by the House of Lords): that the shortage of labour and the increased costs made the contract more burdensome, but these factors did not operate to make the contract radically different from the original contract and did not frustrate it.

Tsakiroglou & Co. Ltd v Noblee Thorl GmbH (1961)

A sold a quantity of groundnuts to B, shipment being from the Sudan to Germany, c.i.f. Hamburg, November/December 1956. The usual route was via the Suez Canal, but this was suddenly closed on 2 November 1956, after the contract was made. Shipment via the Cape of Good Hope was still possible. *A* did not ship the groundnuts and B sued. *Held*: that *A* was liable for breach. The change in circumstances did not make the contract fundamentally different from that agreed upon, and shipment through the Suez Canal was not an implied term.

A contract automatically comes to an end when frustration occurs. It is not necessary for either party to give notice to the other that the contract is discharged.

The effects of frustration. The old common-law rule was that the loss resulting from the event causing the frustration lay where it fell. Money paid under the contract could not be recovered, and any sums due and payable before that time could be claimed, even though performance became impossible. These rules were formulated in the well-known case of *Chandler v Webster* (1904), but as a result of the *Fibrosa* case (1943), the law was changed and is now embodied in the Law Reform (Frustrated Contracts) Act 1943, the rules of which are summarized in the following.

Where a contract is discharged by frustration:

- i all sums paid before frustration are recoverable
- ii money payable before frustration ceases to be payable
- iii where *expenses* have been incurred before frustration, the court may allow a party to retain a reasonable sum out of money already received from the other or to recover from the other reasonable expenses if already payable under the contract
- iv where a *benefit*, other than money payment, has been conferred before frustration by one party on another, the court may permit that party to recover a reasonable sum as compensation for such benefit

The Act does not apply (i) where a contract contains special provisions in the event of frustration; (ii) where an *absolute* agreement exists, e.g. where the parties intend the agreement to be binding irrespective of frustrating circumstances; (iii) to charter parties; (iv) to carriage of goods by sea;

(v) to contracts of insurance or (vi) to any contract for the sale of specific goods under section 7 of the **Sale of Goods Act 1979**. (This section states that where goods have perished, the loss lies with the seller if ownership in the goods has not passed or with the buyer if it has.)

e Discharge by operation of law

i Lapse of time

Where a contract is entered into for a particular period of time, the contract is discharged at the expiration of that period. Apart from provisions in the contract itself, therefore, the general rule is that lapse of time does not discharge a contract.

However, lapse of time may render the contract unenforceable in a court of law, and the important statute here is the **Limitation Act 1980**, which sets out periods of time within which action must be taken by an aggrieved party. What the Act does is to extinguish the remedy by action at law. The provisions of this Act may be summarized as follows:

- Actions on simple contracts are barred after six years from the date on which the plaintiff could have first brought an action.
- Actions on specialty contracts (i.e. by deed) are barred after 12 years.
- Special time limits are set for actions in respect of certain loans.
- Actions to recover money due on a judgment by a court are barred after 12 years.

The **Limitation Act 1980** thus ensures that where a party has a cause of action, it should not be possible to keep alive the cause for a lengthy period of time, for this would be unfair to the other party and is against the public interest. By s. 29(6), a payment of part of the interest does not extend the period for claiming the remainder of the interest then due, but the payment is treated as a repayment of principal (and so restarts the limitation period running against the principal debt). Subject to what came before, s. 29(7) provides that a current period of limitation may be repeatedly extended by further acknowledgments or payment, but once a debt has become statute-barred, it cannot be revived subsequently.

Time runs not from the date of the contract but from the date when the claimant can first bring the action. Where a contracting party is under disability (such as minority or insanity) when the cause of action accrues, the period of limitation does not run against him or her until the contractual disability ends or from the death of the claimant, whichever first occurs. Once, however, time has started to run under the **Limitation Act**, any subsequent disabilities do not affect the operation of the Act.

Where the action is based on fraud or where, for example, the fraud of the defendant has prevented the claimant knowing of their right of action or where the action by the claimant is one for relief from the consequences of mistake, the period under the **Limitation Act** will begin to run when the fraud or the mistake could, by the use of reasonable diligence, have been discovered. In *Kleinwort Benson Ltd v Lincoln City Council* (1998), it was held that mistake should now be read as including mistakes of law.

Finally, where an action for personal injuries arises out of a breach of a contractual duty, the right of action is barred after three years under the **Limitation Act 1980**.

ii Statutory right

Several Statutes give the customer the right to cancel a concluded contract. The **Consumer Credit Act 1974** allows the debtor or hirer to cancel in certain circumstances, as does the **Timeshare Act 1992**. The **Consumer Contract (Information, Cancellation, and Additional Charges) Regulations** 2013 also give consumers the right to cancel distance or off-premises contracts made with traders.

iii Merger

Merger arises where a simple contract is made and subsequently the parties make a specialty contract (by deed) embodying all the former terms. The contract is said to be merged and the rights under the simple contract are discharged by this process. Similarly, where action is brought in a court of law on a simple contract and the court makes its judgment, the contract debt on which action is brought is merged in the judgment itself. Future action is brought on the judgment, e.g. by execution of the judgment, and not on the original contract.

iv Material alteration

Where parties enter into a written contract or one by deed, the written form is, in a sense, sacrosanct. Any alteration that varies the legal significance of the contract, e.g. by incorporating false dates, names or money prices, will discharge the contract. However, the insertion of a correction in a document, as by inserting 'John S. Smith' in place of 'John Smith', is immaterial and does not operate to discharge the contract.

v Bankruptcy

Where a person becomes bankrupt, a trustee in bankruptcy may be appointed and given statutory power to sue for debts due to the bankrupt party. Certain rights of action will not pass to the trustee, however, such as being unable to sue in respect of personal services to be rendered by the bankrupt. Nor may the trustee sue in respect of rights of action that the bankrupt may have in defamation. The trustee may also disclaim onerous contracts that the bankrupt may have made, thus discharging the debtor from his or her obligations.

vi Death

The death of either party to a contract discharges the contract where personal services are concerned. Thus, if a painter agrees for £100 to paint a portrait of B, the contract will be discharged if the painter dies one week after being commissioned.

Contracts other than these are not discharged, and the contractual rights and duties survive for the benefit of or against the estate of the deceased (see p. 131).

7.13 Remedies for breach of contract

On breach of contract the following remedies are available to the injured party: (a) refusal of further performance; (b) action for damages; (c) action on a *quantum meruit*; (d) action for specific performance; (e) action for an injunction; (f) rescission (see p. 174).

a Refusal of further performance

On breach of a condition of a contract, the injured party may treat the contract as at an end (or rescinded) and refuse to perform or fulfil obligations under the contract. In effect the injured party does nothing, and the initiative passes to the contract-breaker who may sue for any sums due. The injured party may in any subsequent action set up the breach as a defence and may then counterclaim for any loss sustained. Where an injured party treats the contract as rescinded, any benefits received under the contract may have to be returned (*restitutio in integrum*). Rescission is not available where the injured party has accepted the goods pursuant to sections 11(4) and 35 of the **Sale of Goods Act 1979**.

An injured party's failure to perform a contract may signify an election to repudiate the contract—*Vitol SA v Norelf Ltd* (1996).

b An action for damages

The object of this common-law remedy is to compensate the injured party for loss caused by breach of contract, i.e. to put the injured party in the same financial position as he would have occupied had the contract been performed in its entirety. The measure of damages is the value of performance to the claimant, not the cost of it to the defendant. In sales of goods the measure of damages when there is an available market for the goods is the difference between the market price at the date of breach and the contract price. Where the market price is equal to or less than the contract price, the injured party will be entitled only to nominal damages for the breach.

Not all damage resulting from or arising out of a breach of contract is recoverable. Some damage is regarded in law as too remote. No compensation will be awarded for such loss. For example, *A* takes a train journey on a certain day for an appointment for a new job. The train arrives half an hour late. *A*, in consequence, hurries through the streets and slips on the road, injuring himself. He also arrives too late for the interview. It may be said that the injuries and the loss of the job arise from the lateness of the train. But *A* may not recover damages from the railway authority for these losses, which might be held to be too remote in law. A line has to be drawn somewhere, and the law does this by applying the following principles established in certain well-known cases, of which *Hadley v Baxendale* (1854) is the most important.

The plaintiff will be entitled to:

i such damages as may fairly and reasonably be considered as *arising naturally*, i.e. according to the usual course of things, from the breach of contract; or
ii such damages as may reasonably be supposed to have been *in the contemplation of both parties*, at the time when they made the contract, as the probable result of the breach.

❖ CASE EXAMPLE

Hadley v Baxendale (1854)

A miller sent a broken crankshaft by a carrier to deliver to an engineer for copying and to make a new one. The miller informed the carrier that the matter was urgent and that there should be no delay. The carrier accepted the consignment on those terms. The miller did not inform the carrier that the mill would be idle and unable to work. The carrier had no reason to believe that the crankshaft was an essential mechanism of the mill. The carrier delayed delivery of the crankshaft to the engineer, and, as a consequence, the mill was idle for longer than it need have been. *Held*: that the carrier was not liable for the loss of profits during the period of the delay.

The court in its judgment laid down the principles as at (i) and (ii).

Hadley v Baxendale (1854) should be compared with the following. In this second type of case, loss of profits for non-delivery or delayed delivery may be recoverable if the parties concerned could reasonably have foreseen such a loss.

❖ CASE EXAMPLE

Victoria Laundry (Windsor) Ltd v Newman Industries Ltd (1949)

V, launderers and dyers, required another boiler to expand their lucrative dyeing contracts. *N* agreed to sell to *V* a second-hand boiler and to deliver it on 5 June. The boiler was damaged on being dismantled, and was not delivered till 8 November. *V* claimed for (i) loss of profits on the laundry business, which would have been earned had the boiler been delivered on time and (ii) loss of profits on a certain remunerative dyeing contract from the Ministry of Supply. *Held*: (i) that loss of profits due to the delay in the delivery of the boiler was recoverable and (ii) that the loss of the dyeing contracts, which could not have been contemplated, was not recoverable.

Two recent cases re-examining the 'remoteness rule' have been:

❖ CASE EXAMPLE

Transfield Shipping Inc. v Mercator Shipping Inc. (The Achilleas) (2008)

A charterer was nine days late in returning a ship to the claimant owners, who had already entered into a follow-on charter for the ship to the new charterers, which they were unable to do because of the defendant's breach. As an outcome of the delayed return of the ship, the owners had to reduce the rate of hire on the follow-up charter by US$8,000 per day. The charter had previously been negotiated at an exceptionally high charter rate, but because of the delay, had to be drastically reduced due to falling market rates. The lower Appeal Courts held that the claimants should be able to recover this difference in the daily rate for the new charter. *Held*: (House of Lords) that such an award was excessive and reduced the amount of damages to the difference between the lower charter and the then prevailing rate on the basis that the defendants had not been aware of the original rates negotiated for the follow-on charter. All of the Judges, except Lord Hoffman, applied the *Hadley v Baxendale* rule. In other words, the approach in *The Achilleas* might displace the standard rule by making the loss that would be recoverable under *Hadley v Baxendale* too remote (an 'exclusionary effect') or by making the loss that would be non-recoverable under *Hadley v Baxendale* not too remote (an 'inclusionary effect').

In the second case of *Supershield Ltd v Siemens Building Technologies FE Ltd* (2010) the Court of Appeal stated that while *Hadley v Baxendale* remains the standard rule and is grounded in policy, it can be displaced if, on examining the contract and the commercial background the loss in question was within or outside the scope of the contractual duty.

Mitigation of damages. The party suffering damage as a result of the breach must do all in his power to minimize his losses. If an employee is dismissed from his job, he should try to secure other suitable work, not merely sit down and do nothing. Similarly, if rooms at a hotel are cancelled by a guest, the hotelier should re-let the rooms if possible to another guest.

❖ CASE EXAMPLE

Brace v Calder (1895)

B was employed by a partnership for two years. After six months two partners died, leaving two surviving partners. A change in the partnership having taken place, this, by law, operated to dismiss all employees. The two remaining partners offered B re-employment on his previous terms, but B declined re-employment and sued for wrongful dismissal. *Held*: that B was entitled to nominal damages only since he should as a reasonable man have accepted the offer.

Damages may be classified in various ways according to the opinion of text writers. The following types are commonly found in practice:

General damages. This is pecuniary (money) compensation a judge (or jury in cases where a jury is summoned) is entitled to award on proof that a breach of contract has been committed. It is that kind of damage that the law presumes to follow from the breach of contract, and the amount is in the court's discretion, having regard to all the circumstances.

❖ CASE EXAMPLES

Kiam v Neill (1966)

K, a businessman, was wrongly reported as being bankrupt. It was held that an award of £45,000 libel damages was not excessive.

Kpoharor v Woolwich Building Society (1995)

K suffered loss of his business reputation as a result of his cheque being wrongly dishonoured by *W*, a bank, and was held to be entitled to substantial rather than merely nominal damages.

Special damages. These are damages that do not arise naturally from the breach, but must be specially proved if they are to be claimed. Thus, loss of earnings during the period of incapacity of the plaintiff, damages for medical expenses, hire of car, etc., may be claimed under this head if such damages do not follow naturally from a breach. Special damages must be brought to the court's notice and be pleaded.

Nominal damages. Where only a technical breach has occurred and the plaintiff has suffered no real loss, the court may find for the plaintiff and award a nominal sum only, e.g. £1. These damages merely acknowledge that the plaintiff has proved his case and won.

Contemptuous damages. Here the court expresses its contempt of the plaintiff in bringing the action by awarding a minimal sum, e.g. one penny. The award registers the fact that the plaintiff has technically won, but that the action ought not to have been brought at all.

Exemplary damages. These are partly punitive and serve to make an example of the defendant. They are more than would normally be awarded and may be given in tort but not contract, e.g. where the defendant's conduct is calculated to make a profit by the tort greater than normal compensation (*Cassell & Co. Ltd v Broome*, 1972).

Liquidated damages. These are damages that are ascertained and agreed beforehand by the parties to the contract. Having laid down the amount to be paid by either party on breach, it follows that the only dispute will be as to the breach itself, not the damages.

Unliquidated damages. These are unascertained damages. When a breach of contract occurs and a legal action is undertaken, it is for the court to determine the amount of such damages to be paid by the defendant, having regard to all the circumstances of the case. It is up to the plaintiff to prove the circumstances from which the court can deduce the loss.

Scope of damages remedy. Damages for breach of contract that caused distress rather than immediate financial loss were developed by the House of Lords in *Farley v Skinner* (2001). In this case damages were awarded in respect of negligent advice regarding a house in a flight path. Damages were awarded to the plaintiff for discovering the noise. The House of Lords took account of the decision in *Ruxley Electronics and Construction Ltd v Forsyth* (1996), where damages were awarded for a badly constructed swimming pool (where the water level was too shallow), even though the pool was still used by the occupiers.

Penalties. We have seen that liquidated damages are predetermined by the parties themselves, and the court normally awards the amount of liquidated damages so agreed. Sometimes, however, the amount of damages payable on breach is not merely an agreed and reasonable compensation but is more in the nature of a **penalty**. Where a minor breach occurs and a heavy payment has to be paid by way of compensation, there is obviously injustice. Accordingly, the party in breach complains against his fate. The common-law attitude was that the parties agreed to the amount payable and no relief was available. Equity took a different view, however, and has laid down certain principles in the giving of relief where the sum specified has been inserted in the contract *in terrorem*, i.e. as a *frightener* to ensure performance of the contracts.

The court will base its decision on the following principles:

i The sum agreed must be treated as a penalty if it is extravagant and unreasonable in amount by comparison with the greatest loss that can ensue from breach of the contract.
ii Where the payment of a smaller sum is secured by a larger sum, the latter is a penalty.
iii When 'a single lump sum is made payable by way of compensation on the occurrence of one or more or all of several events, some of which may occasion serious damage, and others but trifling damage', there is a *presumption* that the sum so inserted is a penalty.

(Lord Watson in *Lord Elphinstone v. Monkland Iron and Coal Co* [1886] UKHL 870)

The relief afforded by the court where a penalty is found to exist, is to excuse payment of that amount. The court has the power to substitute its own award of damages computed on the basis of compensation for loss sustained. On the other hand, where an agreed sum is in the nature of liquidated damages, no greater sum will be awarded by the court even if it is proved that the consequences of breach have been more serious than the parties had foreseen.

In the subsequent case of **Nuray Houssein & Ors v London Credit Limited & Anor (2024)**, a decision by the High Court that a default interest rate was an unenforceable penalty was reversed by the Court of Appeal on the grounds that the High Court had not applied the Cavendish test correctly.

❖ CASE EXAMPLES

Dunlop v New Garage Co. (1915)

Dunlop sold tyres at reduced rates to wholesale traders on the terms that no private customer should be supplied with tyres at a lower rate than the retail prices laid down. New Garage Co. agreed to this clause and to pay the sum of £5 as 'liquidated damages' for each tyre sold in breach of the term. New Garage Co. sold a tyre at less than the agreed current list price and was sued by Dunlop. New Garage pleaded that the £5 per tyre was a penalty. *Held* (by the House of Lords): that it was liquidated damages. The sum of £5 was really and genuinely a pre-estimate of the interest of Dunlop in the due performance of the contract.

Cellulose Acetate Silk Co. Ltd v Widnes Foundry (1925) Ltd (1933)

Manufacturers agreed to erect certain machinery within 18 weeks from the date of the final approval of drawings. They also agreed that if they took longer, the machinery manufacturers would pay £20 per week for every week exceeding 18. There was a serious delay in making the machine, and the buyers claimed £5,850, which greatly exceeded the agreed sum. *Held*: that the sum of £20 per week was agreed damages and that no more could be recovered.

However, in two recent decisions in *Cavendish Square BV v Talal El Makedessi* (2015) and *ParkingEye Limited v Beavis* (2015), the Supreme Court was asked to abolish or restrict the application of the penalty rule. It did neither but instead acknowledged the ongoing role of the penalty rule. In labelling the concept of and distinctions between 'genuine pre-estimate of loss' as and 'deterrent' as unhelpful, the Court introduced a new test emphasizing the 'legitimate interests' of the contracting party. This new test as to whether a contractual provision is penal is 'whether the impugned provision is a secondary obligation which imposes a detriment on the contract breaker out of all proportion to any legitimate interest of the innocent party in the enforcement of the primary obligation'.

Recovery of interest. The rules are that interest is payable in the following circumstances:

- i where the parties have so agreed in the contract
- ii where there is an implied agreement, e.g. from the course of dealing between the parties themselves or from a trade usage
- iii on overdue bills of exchange and promissory notes

Under the **Law Reform (Miscellaneous Provisions) Act 1934**, the court may allow interest at such rate as it thinks fit on all claims for debt or damages from the date when the claim arose to the judgment date.

c An action on a '*quantum meruit*'

In the event of a breach of contract, the injured party may have a claim other than that for damages and, in particular, may claim payment for what they have done under the contract. The right to sue on a *quantum meruit* ('as much as he has earned') arises not out of the original contract but on an implied promise by the other party who has accepted an executed consideration to pay a reasonable sum for it.

The claim arises in cases of two kinds:

i where one party abandons or refuses to perform the contract

❖ CASE EXAMPLE

Planché v Colburn (1831)

P agreed with C to write a volume on ancient armour for a periodical called *The Juvenile Library* for a fee of £100. After P had written part of his work, the defendant C abandoned the periodical. The contract could not, therefore, be completely performed, and P sued. *Held*: that the defendant had repudiated the contract and P was entitled to treat it as discharged and recover on a *quantum meruit* for the work he had already done.

Ii where work has been performed and accepted under a void contract

❖ CASE EXAMPLE

Craven-Ellis v Canons Ltd (1936)

Plaintiff was employed as managing director of Canons Ltd under a deed that provided for a salary. The directors who made the contract were unqualified (they had never obtained the required number of shares), so the deed was invalid. Plaintiff had rendered his services and now sued on a *quantum meruit* for a reasonable sum. *Held*: that he could recover on a *quantum meruit*, there being no valid contract.

A claim under *quantum meruit* does not apply, however, where the contract requires *complete* performance as a condition of payment, e.g. a contract to do one piece of work in its entirety in consideration for a lump sum payment.

❖ CASE EXAMPLES

Sumpter v Hedges (1898)

S agreed to build a house for a certain sum on H's land. When the house was half-finished, S ran out of money and could not complete. H refused payment, and S brought an action on a *quantum meruit* for the value of materials used and the labour he had expended. *Held*: that the claim must fail. The contract was to do certain work for a lump sum, which was not payable until completion. H had no choice but to accept the work.

Cutter v Powell (1795)

P agreed to pay C 30 guineas 'provided he proceeds, continues and does his duty as second mate' on a voyage from Jamaica to Liverpool. C died shortly before the end of the voyage, and his widow (C's personal representative) claimed a proportion of the agreed payment in respect of that part of the work he had completed. *Held*: that the widow's claim must fail. C's obligation remained undischarged and the contract imposed one indivisible obligation that had not been performed.

Such cases are exceptional, but if *A* agrees, for example, to make an article for B on B's promising to pay for the article when it is completed, nothing less than complete performance will bind B. But if B has the choice of rejecting or accepting partial performance, B must pay a reasonable price if they accept the work.

However, not every breach of a contractual term to complete a piece of work will absolve an employer from its promise to pay. Only a breach that goes to the root of the contract (c.f. *Sumpter v Hedges*) will enable the employer to refuse payment. It follows, therefore, that where the work is *substantially completed*, but certain small defects are manifest or differences exist from what was contractually agreed, the full amount due may be claimed, less allowances for the defects and differences.

❖ CASE EXAMPLE

Hoenig v Isaacs (1952)

An interior decorator, *A*, agreed to furnish B's flat with a wardrobe and bookcase for £750. The work was performed, but B complained that it was faulty workmanship and paid £400 only, claiming that he (B) was not liable in law to pay anything, as some of the work was defective. *A* sued for the full £750. *Held*: that the contract was a lump-sum contract; it had been substantially performed, and *A* was entitled to the contract price of £750 less a deduction in respect of the detective work amounting to £294.

d An action for specific performance

This is an equitable remedy and was available only in the courts of equity before the **Judicature Acts, 1873–5**. It is now available in all civil courts. The remedy is supplementary to the common-law remedies and is in all cases issued at the discretion of the court, so that in *Patel v Ali* (1984) the court refused specific performance on the grounds of hardship.

The order essentially instructs that the parties to a contract carry out or perform the terms of their agreement, hence its name.

The principles on which the order is granted are as follows:

i Where damages are an adequate remedy, specific performance will not be granted (see *Beswick v Beswick* (1967), p. 207).

ii Where the court cannot supervise the performance or execution of the contract, the remedy is not available. Thus, it cannot be granted in a building contract of a continuing nature where the 'performance' is usually by stage or in contracts of personal services.

iii Where one of the parties is a minor, the remedy is not granted. Equity states that there must be 'mutuality', i.e. the contract must be specifically enforceable by both parties. A contract between a minor and an adult lacks mutuality and the remedy will therefore be refused.

iv The remedy is not granted in contracts to lend money.

v The contract itself must be certain, fair and just, and the conduct of the party seeking performance must be irreproachable.

The courts are unwilling to grant specific performance to a party that has breached an essential condition as to time, even if the delay is very slight—see *Union Eagle Ltd v Golden Achievement Ltd* (1997).

The most common types of contracts in which specific performance is granted are those connected with land and contracts to take debentures in a company.

It is not ordinarily granted in the case of sales of goods, but it is a suitable remedy where the contract is for the purchase of a rare or unique article.

e An injunction

This, too, is an equitable remedy and is commonly used in torts such as where the owner of property wishes to restrain another from continual trespass to his property or goods. An injunction is an order of the court restraining a person from doing an act.

An injunction is granted only where it is just and equitable to do so, having regard to all the circumstances of the case. It is a discretionary remedy.

It will be granted to enforce a **negative** stipulation in a contract for personal services where *A* binds himself not to work for any person other than B (the other contracting party); this negative stipulation may be enforced by injunction.

❖ CASE EXAMPLES

Lumley v Wagner (1852)

W agreed to sing at *L*'s theatre for a certain period, and during that time not to sing elsewhere. Later, *W* contracted to sing at another theatre and refused to perform her contract with *L*. *Held*: that an injunction should be granted to prevent *W* from singing elsewhere. The court would not, however, grant an order of specific performance to compel *W* to sing for *L*.

Warner Bros v Nelson (1937)

N agreed to give her services exclusively for a certain period to *W*, and also during the period of the agreement, not to give her services to any other person. During the time N contracted to act for X. *Held*: that an injunction be granted restraining her from entering into the more favourable employment with X.

The court will not intervene if the granting of an injunction would compel a defendant either to work for the claimant alone or remain workless, as this would amount to an indirect enforcement of a contract for personal services. This rule is confirmed in the **Trade Union and Labour Relations (Consolidation) Act 1992**.

❖ CASE EXAMPLE

Whitwood Chemical Co. v Hardman (1891)

H was employed by *W* as manager and agreed to devote all his time to the business of the company for a term of ten years. Later he gave some of his time to a rival company and wished to relinquish his post with *W.W* sued. *Held*: that the grant of an injunction would have been in effect to compel specific performance of a contract for personal services. Other remedies were available.

f Rescission

This remedy has been described on p. 158.

7.14 Privity of contract

By its very nature, a contractual agreement is private to the contracting parties, each of whom is given rights that are enforceable at law. The general rule, therefore, is that *only a person who is a party to a contract can sue on it* (Lord Haldane in *Dunlop v Selfridge*, 1915). To permit a person who had no part in the original agreement whatsoever to obtain benefits or to impose upon such a person an obligation to which they were not a party or had never agreed would be clearly contrary to the basic rules of justice. However, these general presumptions of the rule relating to the privity of contract are now subject to the provisions of the **Contracts (Rights of Third Parties) Act 1999**.

❖ CASE EXAMPLE

Dunlop v Selfridge (1915)

D sold tyres to Dew & Co. on condition that the latter would not resell Dunlop's tyres below a certain price and that they (Dew & Co.) would obtain a similar agreement from any of their customers. Selfridge bought tyres from Dew & Co. and agreed not to sell tyres below the list price. Selfridge sold some tyres below the list price in breach of the agreement between Selfridge and Dews. The manufacturers (D) sued Selfridge for breach of the agreement. *Held*: that Dunlop could not enforce the agreement between Selfridge and Dews, because they (Dunlop) were not party to the agreement and could not therefore obtain rights under it.

This rule is distinct from the rule that consideration must move from the promise. Here, the basis of the decision is that Dunlop was not party to the agreement made between Dew & Co. and Selfridge.

The Resale Prices Act 1976 allows individual enforcement of restrictions as to minimum resale prices, so *Dunlop v Selfridge* (1915) would be decided differently today.

Once a contract is formed, there is a general duty on third persons not to interfere with the contractual relationship. If a third person, C, knowingly and without lawful justification induces *A* to break their contract with B, so causing damage to B, B may sue C in tort.

Similarly, where X threatens to do some unlawful act to Y unless Y does something that will cause loss to Z, X commits the tort of intimidation actionable at the suit of Z. Where a trade union threatened to strike if the employers did not dismiss a non-union employee, it was held that the strike, involving breach of contract of employment, would be an unlawful act and that the threat was an actionable wrong to the non-union employee (*Rookes v Barnard*, 1964). The **Trade Union and Labour Relations (Consolidation) Act 1992** now provides that such a threat shall not be actionable in tort if made in contemplation or furtherance of a trade dispute.

The doctrine of privity of contract, as stated, has existed for more than a century and has been reaffirmed in decisions ranging from *Tweddle v Atkinson* (1861) to *Scruttons Ltd v Midland Silicones Ltd* (1962).

Exceptions to the general rule as to privity of contract are listed in what follows:

❖ CASE EXAMPLE

***Scruttons Ltd v Midland Silicones Ltd* (1962)**

A and B contracted for the carriage of a cargo owned by B. A further contract existed between *A* and C regarding the unloading of the goods from B's ship. The goods were damaged through C's negligence during the unloading, and B claimed damages from C. An exemption clause existed in the contract between *A* and B, and on that clause, C relied. *Held* (by the House of Lords): that C was a stranger to the contract between *A* and B and, as a result, could not rely on the exemption clause. His defence therefore failed.

a *Action by a beneficiary under a trust*. If the facts show that the person entitled is a beneficiary (or *cestui que trust*) they may sue under the trust itself though not on the contract.
b *Certain contracts of insurance*. Section 207 of the **Road Traffic Act 1972** compels insurance against third-party risks in respect of vehicles driven on roads. If *A*, a third party, is injured, they will have rights against the negligent driver B personally and against the insurance company. The following Acts of Parliament are also relevant: The **Marine Insurance Act 1906** (s. 14); the **Married Women's Property Act 1882** (s. 11); and the **Law of Property Act 1925** (s. 47).
c Negotiable instruments (e.g. cheques).
D Restrictive covenants (see p. 312).
e Law of agency.
f *Price-maintenance agreements* under the Competition Legislation (see previous).

The following case offers an important illustration of the general rule as to privity and the effect of the **Law of Property Act 1925**, s. 56(1), which states that

> a person may take an immediate or other interest in land *or other property* or the benefit of any condition, right of entry, covenant or agreement over or respecting land or other property although he may not be named as party to the conveyance or other instrument.

The case history of *Beswick v Beswick* is interesting in that at the first hearing the court applied the general principle of *Tweddle v Atkinson* and disallowed the widow's claim; it was the Court of Appeal's verdict given previously that the widow could succeed at common law, in equity and by statute (**Law of Property Act 1925**, s. 56). The House of Lords affirmed the decision of the Court of Appeal on the ground that the widow could succeed as personal representative of the deceased and was entitled to enforce the agreement by an order of specific performance. The House of Lords expressed the view that the **Law of Property Act 1925** was a consolidating Act, and section 56 could not be construed as changing the law so as to enable the widow to sue in her personal capacity. The House of Lords reaffirmed the general principle that a person not a party to a contract cannot sue upon it, and that although the Law Revision Committee of 1937 had long ago suggested changing the rule, this change must be left to the legislature.

❖ **CASE EXAMPLE**

Beswick v Beswick (1967)

A owned a small coal round and his nephew, B, helped him to run it. *A*, being in poor health and wishing to retire from the business, drew up an agreement under which *A*, the uncle, transferred his business to the nephew, B. *A* would be retained as adviser and consultant at £6 10s. per week and on his death, his widow, C, would receive an annuity of £5 per week. *A* retired and was paid the £6 10s. per week. *A* died later, but B made no payment to the widow, C. Accordingly, C sued the nephew: (i) as administratrix of her husband's estate and (ii) in her personal capacity for the arrears of the annuity and for specific performance of the agreement. *Held*: that as administratrix, the widow could obtain an order of specific performance that would enforce the provision in the contract for the benefit of herself; but that in her personal capacity, she could derive no action from the statute.

In 1996, the Law Commission published proposals for the reform of that part of the doctrine of privity of contract that provides that a contract does not confer rights on a person who is not a party to the contract.

The Commission's recommendations were incorporated into the **Contracts (Rights of Third Parties) Act 1999**. This Act creates a two-limb test, whereby satisfaction of either limb will permit a third-party beneficiary to enforce the contract. The first limb expressly provides that a third party may enforce a contractual provision if an express provision has been made in the contract. The second limb is concerned with situations that may arise where a third party may claim that a relevant provision in a contract purported to confer a benefit on them.

In *DEFRA v Public and Commercial Services Union* (2024) where the union, whilst suffering loss because of the withdrawal by Government departments in withdrawing check-off arrangements on behalf of the union, had no original claim in breach of contract as it was not a party to the original employee contract. The outcome was that the union had to claim for its loss as a third-party beneficiary under the **Contract (Rights of Third Parties) Act 1999.** The question with which the Supreme Court was faced was whether 'on a proper construction of the contract' the parties intended the check-off arrangements to be enforceable by the union. In taking a broad view of third-party rights, the Court was of the view that there was a 'strong presumption' that the term was enforceable.

7.15 Assignment

Assignment means transfer, and we consider here the law affecting the transference of rights and liabilities to a third person who is not a party to the original contract. The general rule is that the only persons who possess rights and liabilities under a contract are the parties to it. But in certain circumstances, the contracting parties may drop out and others may take their places, thereby succeeding to the rights and liabilities. If one of the contracting parties dies, their rights and liabilities may pass to their personal representatives: this is described as an 'assignment by operation of law' (see later on). The assignment of a debt is not illegal, and the debt does not become unenforceable merely because the assignee has to commence litigation to recover the debt—see *Camdex International Ltd v Bank of Zambia* (1996).

Liabilities under a contract cannot be assigned without the consent of the other party to the contract. The only means by which a liability can be effectively assigned is by 'novation' (see later on), which requires the consent of the other party.

Rights under a contract can usually be assigned, but where the contract is for personal services and personal performance by the promisor is of the essence of the contract, rights may only be assigned with the consent of the other party.

❖ CASE EXAMPLE

***Robson and Sharpe v Drummond* (1831)**

D hired a carriage from one Sharpe, who undertook to paint it every year and keep it in repair. After three years Sharpe retired from his business and informed D that thereafter R would be responsible for the repairs. D refused to deal with R, and R sued on the agreement. *Held*: that D was entitled at law to refuse to deal with R, and further that Sharpe could not assign his liabilities under the contract without D's consent.

The assignment of rights under a contract may be carried out by: (a) novation, (b) legal assignment, (c) equitable assignment or (d) operation of law.

a Novation

This is the making of a new contract between the parties whereby *A*, the person possessing rights under a contract (e.g. a creditor), at the request of B, the person under liability (e.g. a debtor), agrees to X assuming or taking over B's liability.

The two original contracting parties, *A* and B, and the third party, X, must all agree together to form a new contract under which X undertakes B's liability to *A* in consideration of *A* releasing B.

There must be consideration for the transaction that is constituted by the release of an existing debt or other contractual obligation. Thus, a new party is introduced and a *new* contract is formed, hence the term 'novation'.

Novation arises most frequently in a partnership when, on a change in the membership of the firm, the creditors agree, expressly or impliedly, to accept the liability of the new firm and to discharge the old firm from liability.

b Legal assignment

The old rule of common law was that contracting parties could not assign rights to a third party. Equity, however, allowed assignment subject to certain conditions. The law was altered by the **Judicature Act 1873** and was re-enacted in the **Law of Property Act 1925**, s. 136, which states that all debts and other legal choses in action (see later on) may be assigned subject to equities, provided that:

i the assignment is in writing, signed by the assignor
ii it is absolute and not by way of charge
iii express notice in writing is given to the debtor, trustee or other person from whom the assignor would have been entitled to claim such a debt or chose in action

A legal 'chose in action' means a right that may only be enforced by taking legal action and not by taking physical possession. Examples include a debt, a patent right, a right under a copyright and a right under a contract. These cannot be physically touched. A 'chose in possession', on the other hand, is a tangible object, e.g. a chair, a table, a ring, a painting, coins, etc.

As a simple example of the operation of section 136 of the **Law of Property Act** 1925, let us assume that *A* owes £100 to B and B owes £100 to C. B wishes to assign to C their right in *A*'s debt. B does so by written letter assigning the £100 to C. B (the assignor) then notifies *A* (the debtor) in writing that C (the assignee) is entitled to the debt. If *A* pays the £100 to C, the debt is discharged at law.

The assignment must be 'absolute', i.e. it must be of the whole debt (£100 in our example) and not a portion of it. This is to ensure that *A* will not be inconvenienced by having to seek out and pay numerous assignees to whom B may have attempted to transfer parts of the £100. Conditional assignments or part assignments of a debt are not, therefore, absolute.

The assignment is subject to any claims or defences open to the debtor (*A*) against the assignor (B) existing at the time of the receipt of notice of assignment. Suppose that B owes *A* the sum of £10. If the debt arises out of the same contract as that under which the £100 is due, *A* will be entitled to deduct the sum of £10; then a payment of only £90 to C will be a good discharge of *A*'s obligations. This is an example of what is meant by 'subject to equities'.

The effect of the assignment is to transfer to the assignee:

i the legal right to the debt or chose in action;
ii the legal and other remedies for the debt or other legal chose in action; and
iii the power to give a good discharge, e.g. a valid receipt.

Consideration is not necessary to support the assignment of a legal chose in action.

c Equitable assignment

An assignment that does not comply with the requirements of a legal assignment (under section 136 of the **Law of Property Act**) may nevertheless take effect as an equitable assignment. But to do so, the intention to assign must be clear from the circumstances. If it is clear, no particular formalities need be complied with, e.g. the assignment need not be in writing. Notice of the assignment *need* not be given to the debtor, but it should be given for two reasons:

i The debtor can set up any defences against the assignee that he or she (the debtor) had against the assignor up to the date of their receipt of notice of the assignment. If, therefore, the debtor makes a payment to the assignor before they receive notice of the assignment, this payment is good as against the assignee.
ii To gain priority over any subsequent assignee without notice of their assignment.

❖ **CASE EXAMPLE**

***Brandt v Dunlop Rubber Co. Ltd* (1905)**

K & Co. agreed with B (plaintiff), who financed K & Co. that the purchase price of all goods sold by K &. Co. should be paid directly to B. K & Co. sold goods to Dunlop and B gave notice to Dunlop to pay the price to B. Dunlop disregarded the notice and paid K & Co. *Held*: there was evidence of an equitable assignment of the price and Dunlop was liable to pay B, notwithstanding that they (Dunlop) had already paid K & Co.

Certain assignments must be carried out in the manner laid down in the statutes appropriate to those assignments and not in accordance with section 136 of the **Law of Property Act**. For example:

- i Shares in companies are transferred in accordance with the **Companies Act 1985**.
- ii Policies of life assurance are transferred in accordance with the **Policies of Assurance Act 1867**, as amended by the **Policyholders' Protection Acts 1975** and **1997**.
- iii Bills of exchange and promissory notes are transferred in accordance with the **Bills of Exchange Act 1882**.

d Assignments by operation of law

The foregoing assignments take effect by an act of the party (or parties). The following assignments take effect by operation of law, i.e. without any voluntary act by the parties.

- i *On death*. The personal representative (i.e. executor or administrator) of a deceased person acquires the rights and liabilities of the deceased and pays the debts of the deceased to the extent of the latter's estate. Rights and obligations arising out of contracts for personal services are extinguished by the death of either party to such a contract.
- ii *On bankruptcy*. A trustee in bankruptcy has vested in him all the rights of the bankrupt. Rights of action for slander and assault, and other rights of a purely personal nature, do not pass to the trustee.

The rules relating to bankruptcy are too detailed to be examined here, but we should mention that contracts for personal services to be performed by the bankrupt are not usually affected by the bankruptcy proceedings. The trustee is primarily liable to pay the debts of the bankrupt to the extent of the estate, though the trustee can disclaim onerous contracts of the bankrupt. Any party prejudiced by such disclaimer may petition in the bankruptcy proceedings for any loss suffered thereby.

7.16 Interpretation of a contract

The general rule is that a written contract cannot be varied by parol (i.e. oral) evidence, either by the parties thereto or by others. But there are exceptions to this main rule.

The duty of the court is to interpret the contract itself and to give effect to the intentions of the parties. It does so by giving the words used in the writing their ordinary and literal sense.

Parol evidence will, however, be admitted in the following cases:

i to show that a commercial custom or a trade usage may be read into the contract (unless such custom or usage is expressly excluded)
ii to explain a latent, as opposed to a patent, ambiguity. A latent ambiguity is one that is not apparent from the face of the document. For example, *A* leaves his car by will to his nephew, John: but *A* has two nephews named John, and evidence may be admitted to explain which nephew *A* intended to benefit
iii to prove collateral terms or warranties not expressly provided for in the contract
iv to prove rescission of a written contract. Thus, where *A* and B make a contract in writing but later rescind it orally, evidence may be given of the oral rescission
v the court may receive oral evidence to imply a term to give 'business efficacy' to the contract, in accordance with the intention of the parties thereto (see *The Moorcock* (1889) at p. 159)

Note: However, in *Amald v Britton and others* (2015), which involved a leisure park with 90 chalets that were subject to an ever-increasing service charge on an annual basis, the Supreme Court *Held*: that an interpretation of the appropriate clause, where the increase every year was correct. In their reasons for making the judgment the court stated that, in interpreting a written contract, the court must identify the intention of the parties by reference to 'what a reasonable person having all the background knowledge which would have been available to the parties would have understood them by using the language in the contract to mean', focussing on the meaning of the relevant words in their documentary, factual and commercial context. However, subjective evidence of any party's intentions should be disregarded.

However, the Court of Appeal distinguished this decision in *Monsolar IQ Ltd v Woden Park Ltd* (2021) where the Court had to consider a rent review in a lease of a solar park, where a literal reading of a clause in the lease where in year 25 of the lease the rent would have increased from £15,000 to £75million. The Court followed a decision by Lord Hoffman in *Chartbrook Ltd v Persimmon Homes Ltd* (2009), where he stated that 'literal meaning of a provision can be corrected if it is clear that a mistake has been made and what the provision was actually intended to say'. The Court of Appeal distinguished the decision by drawing a distinction between an imprudent mistake, which had been made in *Arnold v Britton* and an irrational one in the current case.

7.17 Quasi-contract

We have noted that the essence of a legal contract is that it is based on the agreement of the parties. Sometimes, however, the law imposes an obligation on a party and allows an action to be brought on that obligation despite the fact that no agreement was present. These types of obligation are known as 'quasi-contracts' (quasi means 'as if it were' or 'seemingly').

The following are examples:

a a contract of record, e.g. a recognizance (see p. 127)
b an account stated
c actions for money had and received, e.g. where Smith pays money by mistake to Black instead of White; or where under a valid contract John pays money to William who fails entirely to keep his side of the bargain. Here John has a quasi-contractual remedy to recover his money as an alternative to a legal remedy in damages
d actions for money paid to the use of another, e.g. where a surety (Harry) pays the debt owed by the principal debtor (Thomas), an action will lie against Thomas

e claims on a *quantum meruit*. This type of action arises where a contract that has been partly performed by one party has become discharged by breach by the other party. Here the law implies an agreement by the person who has benefited to pay for what has been done for him or her. The right is founded not on the original contract (which is discharged or void), but on an implied agreement to pay for what has been done. See *Planché v Colburn* (1831), p. 202

7.18 Useful webpages

10 Key facts about English contract law (www.seqlegal.com/blog/10-key-facts-about-english-contract-law)

e-lawresources.co.uk, contract law (www.elawresources.co.uk/contract.php)

TransLegal, contract law (www.translegal.com/legal-english-dictionary/contract-law)

Advocates for International Development, Basic Principles of English Contract Law (http://www.a4id.org/wp-content/uploads/2016/10/A4ID-english-contract-law-at-a-glance.pdf)

Oxbridge Notes, contract law (https://www.oxbridgenotes.co.uk/revision_notes/law-contract-law)

7.19 Exercises

1 Define a contract, and state the essential elements of a valid contract.

2 Distinguish between (i) an offer and (ii) an invitation to treat.

3 What is the effect of an acceptance 'subject to contract'?

4 Describe the main rules regarding consideration.

5 Distinguish between (i) a guarantee and (ii) an indemnity.

6 What is the 'doctrine of part performance'? What are the four points that must be proved before the equitable remedy will be applied?

7 What does section 1 of the **Infants' Relief Act 1874** provide?

8 What special rules apply to contracts by corporations?

9 When will an 'implied term' be imported into a contract?

10 Distinguish between (i) a condition and (ii) a warranty in a contract.

11 What are the rules as to the mistake of the identity of the person with whom a contract is made? Discuss with reference to decided cases.

12 Define a 'representation' and distinguish between fraudulent and innocent misrepresentation.

13 Distinguish, with examples, between contracts made as a result of duress and those effected by undue influence.

14 Enumerate contracts that are illegal (i) by statute and (ii) at common law.

15 In what ways may a contract be said to be discharged? What is meant by the statement that 'a contract may be discharged by frustration'?

16 What remedies are available at law to a person who claims there has been a breach of contract?

17 Distinguish between general and special damages.

18 What is meant by 'an equitable assignment' of a debt or other chose in action? Give an example.

Chapter 8

The law of torts

Key points

- the nature of a tort
- general defences in tort
- capacity of parties
- specific torts: trespass
- specific torts: nuisance
- specific torts: negligence
- specific torts: defamation

The word 'tort' derives from the Latin *tortus*, meaning crooked or twisted, and the Norman-French *tort*, meaning wrong. In English law we use the word tort to denote certain civil wrongs as distinct from criminal wrongs.

The early Anglo-Saxons did not distinguish between civil wrongs and criminal wrongs. In the Middle Ages, however, the idea sprang up that certain wrongs of an antisocial kind, e.g. treason, murder, theft, arson and the like, were offences against the King or the State. The King's peace, as it was called, extended to every corner of the land, and all crimes were at the same time breaches of the peace. Certain other wrongs, done by one person to another, were disregarded by the King and the State. These were left to be enforced by the person claiming to be injured or wronged. The injured claimant decided whether to take action or not. The claim, if any, was for damages, i.e. monetary compensation or reparation for the injury inflicted by the defendant.

Whether or not a claimant had a right of action against another for an alleged wrong depended on the existence of a writ wherewith to begin the action. The rights available depended in practice on the writs available. The forms of action, as these were called, enshrined the rights. If there was no writ there was no remedy available in the courts of law.

The most important all-purpose writ that covered the common civil wrongs in medieval society was *trespass*. This was available for all *direct* injuries to the person, goods or lands. Thus a personal injury to another, e.g. assault and battery, damage to personal goods, to gates, hedges, lands or mere entry on lands or cattle trespass, fell within the ambit of trespass.

The writ of trespass was aptly called 'the fertile mother of actions'. After the Statute of Westminster II, 1285, there grew up offshoots of trespass, named *trespass on the case*. Whereas the writ of trespass was available for all direct and forcible injuries, the writs of trespass on the case were used for all injuries that were *indirect*.

DOI: 10.4324/9781003422808-8

For example, where *A* walks across B's land, lifts B's gate off its hinges or punches B on the nose, there is a direct and forcible injury to the property or person of another: the writ of trespass lies.

But where *A* lights a fire on his or her own property that spreads to a neighbour's house and burns it, digs a hole into which B falls or leaves a log in the road and B trips over it and is injured, *A*'s action is not direct and forcible: the writ of trespass did not lie. The claimant proceeded by trespass on the case.

8.1 The nature of a tort

First, we must examine the distinctions between (a) a tort and a crime, (b) a tort and a breach of contract and (c) a tort and a breach of trust.

a A crime

The object of criminal proceedings is primarily punishment. The police are the principal agents to enforce the criminal law, though a private person may also prosecute a criminal offence. If the defendant is found guilty the court may award the proper punishment. The object of proceedings in tort is not punishment, but compensation or reparation to the claimant, previously designated as the plaintiff for the loss or injury caused by the defendant, i.e. damages.

The same facts may disclose a crime and a tort. Thus, if *A* steals B's coat, there is (i) a crime of theft and (ii) trespass to goods (a tort) and conversion (also a tort). If X assaults Y, there is both a crime and a tort.

b A breach of contract

In contract the duties are fixed by the parties themselves. They impose terms and conditions themselves by their agreement. In tort, on the other hand, the duties are fixed by law (common law or statute) and arise by the operation of the law itself.

Here, too, the same circumstances may give rise to a breach of contract and a tort. Thus, if *A* hires a taxi-cab driven by B, and B, by dangerous driving, injures the passenger (*A*), the latter will have a cause of action for (i) breach of the contractual duty of care and (ii) the tort of negligence.

So, too, where *A* employs privately a surgeon, B, to operate on *A*'s son, B owes *A* a contractual duty of care. If B fails in that duty there will also be liability in tort to the child.

c Breach of trust

As we have seen (p. 17) a breach of trust fell within the jurisdiction of the Chancery Courts, and although compensation may be awarded for damage suffered by reason of the breach of trust, the real distinction is due to the history of equity and common law rather than to logical reasons and development.

8.1.1 Definition of a tort

'The province of tort is to allocate responsibility for injurious conduct' (Lord Denning). Such is the area of the law with which we are concerned.

A tort has been defined as 'a civil wrong for which the remedy is a common law action for unliquidated damages, and which is not exclusively the breach of a contract or the breach of trust or other merely equitable obligation' (Salmond, *Law of Torts*).

Prof. P.H. Winfield, another important authority in this field, asserts that 'tortious liability arises from the breach of a duty primarily fixed by law; such duty is towards persons generally, and its breach is redressible by an action for unliquidated damages' (*Law of Tort*).

What is the essential difference between these two writers? One school maintains there is a general principle of liability in tort, and that all harm is actionable in the absence of just cause or excuse: i.e. there is a law of tort (not torts). The other school maintains that there are a number of specific torts, and that unless the damage or injury suffered can be brought within the scope of one or more of these torts, there is no remedy.

8.1.2 Damage and liability

As a general rule, where one person suffers unlawful harm or damage at the hands of another, an action in tort for that damage or injury arises. An action in tort lies, for example, in the situation where *A* negligently collides with B's stationary car on a road and causes damage to it.

Sometimes we find instances where harm is done by one person to another, yet the law does not provide a remedy: this is described as *damnum sine injuria* ('damage without legal wrong'). Ordinary trade competition is the most common example. Let us suppose that a giant supermarket sets up adjacent to, and in competition with, a small family grocer, selling all goods cheaper. The result could well be that the family grocer, unable to compete, is forced out of business. Harm is done to the grocer and his or her family in that they lose their livelihood, yet the law offers no remedy to them.

❖ CASE EXAMPLE

***Mogul Steamship Co. v McGregor, Gow & Co.* (1892)**

The X company and the Y company were rival traders in China tea. The Y company persuaded merchants in China not to act as the X company's agents; otherwise, the Y company would withdraw its agency. *Held*: that the Y company acted with the lawful object of protecting and extending their trade and the means used were not unlawful.

In contrast to the previous, we can imagine a situation where there is a legal wrong but no loss or damage. This is described as *injuria sine damno*, and is an exception to the general rule that there must be damage or injury before action may be brought. Certain torts are actionable per se (i.e. actionable in themselves). Examples are trespass and libel: in either of these cases, no loss need be alleged or proved.

If *A* trespasses on B's land or if *A* removes B's goods without lawful authority, *A* may be sued in trespass; the mere entry on the land or the mere removal of the article constitutes in each case a trespass. Similarly in libel, as we shall see, the mere publication of the libel constitutes the wrong even though the party defamed may have suffered no loss whatsoever.

In torts not actionable per se, the claimant will succeed only if it can be proved that the defendant has infringed a legal right and that thereby the claimant has suffered damage.

In *XX v Whittington Hospital NHS Trust* (2020) the legal issue centred on the recoverability of damages for surrogacy costs following medical negligence. Not only did the case test the boundaries of public policy in the context of surrogacy, but it also considered the principles governing the award of damages in tort law, particularly concerning the extent to which damages could restore the claimant to her position before the tortious act. The claimant had become infertile due to the defendant NHS Trust's negligent failure to diagnose her cervical cancer in a reasonable manner. She therefore sought damages for her surrogacy arrangements, which involved both being undertaken in the United Kingdom and California. One of the questions which arose was the use of commercial surrogacy, which, whilst legal in California, was illegal in the United Kingdom and therefore contrary to public policy. However the Supreme Court held that damages could be awarded for the cost of surrogacy arrangements in the United Kingdom and also that it was no longer contrary to public policy to award damages for the cost of commercial surrogacy arrangements in California as this did not involve a criminal offence under United Kingdom law, even though commercial surrogacy agencies are not permitted to operate within the United Kingdom.

The judgment established that such damages were recoverable, provided the proposed surrogacy treatments were reasonable and had a reasonable prospect of success. This judgment also recognizes the expanded scope of recoverable damages in tort law to include the cost of both domestic and foreign surrogacy arrangements, considering the reasonable prospect of success and the reasonableness of the treatment. It also recognizes a progressive approach by the Supreme Court in recognising legal principles aligning with societal values.

8.1.3 Malice

Malice in its popular and narrow sense means spite and ill-will. In law the term has two distinct meanings that should be understood. Malice in its legal sense means:

i The doing of a wrongful act intentionally, without just cause or excuse. In other words, 'wilful and conscious wrongdoing'.
ii The doing of an act from some *improper motive*, i.e. a motive of which the law disapproves for the act in question.

To act maliciously means, therefore, to do the act from some wrong and improper motive, or merely to do the act intentionally.

In tort, the intention or motive for an action *is generally irrelevant*.

❖ CASE EXAMPLE

***Bradford Corporation v Pickles* (1895)**

P, with a view to inducing Bradford Corporation to buy his land at a high price, sank a shaft on his land that interfered with the water flowing in undefined channels into the corporation reservoir. The corporation applied for an injunction to restrain P from collecting the underground water. *Held*: that an injunction would not lie. P was entitled as owner to draw from his land the underground water. His 'malice', if any, in trying to force the purchase of the land, was irrelevant. No use of property that would be legal if done with a proper motive can be illegal if done with an improper motive.

A good or innocent motive will not be a lawful excuse for the commission of a tort, and a bad (malicious) motive will not make a lawful act unlawful. In general the law of tort is more concerned with the effect of injurious conduct than with the motive or intent that inspired it. It is the act, not the motive for it, that must be regarded.

❖ CASE EXAMPLE

***Wilkinson v Downton* (1897)**

A, as a practical joke, told Mrs B that her husband had met with an accident. Mrs B suffered a nervous shock and was ill as a result. Mrs B brought an action against *A* for false and malicious representation. The fact that *A* passed the information as a joke was irrelevant, and Mrs B was entitled to damages.

Malice in the sense of improper motive is, however, relevant to the following cases:

a *Malicious prosecution*. For example, *A* prosecutes B without just cause; B is acquitted. If it can be proved that *A* brought the prosecution out of private spite, B may sue *A* for the offence of malicious prosecution.

b *Malicious falsehood*. For example, *A* makes an allegation that a ship is unseaworthy; as a result the crew refuses to sail, thereby causing loss. If the allegation is proved to be untrue, *A* may be sued for the offence of malicious falsehood.

c *Defamation*. The presence of malice will destroy the defence of 'qualified privilege' in a case of defamation, and is relevant also to the defence of 'fair comment' in libel (see p. 266).

d *Conspiracy*, i.e. a combination of persons to cause illegal harm to another. Malice is relevant here in the sense of improper motive.

e *Nuisance*. See *Christie v Davey* (1893), p. 244.

8.2 General defences in tort

A frequent form of defence in an action in tort is a *denial* of the facts alleged in a claim. Thus, in a claim in negligence arising out of a road accident, the defendant may deny driving at 60 mph or that he or she was on the wrong side of the road. Sometimes the defence is on a point of law, e.g. that no duty of care was owed by the defendant to the claimant.

Certain special defences are available for particular torts, e.g. in defamation there is a special defence of qualified privilege in libel (see p. 267).

The following general defences are available to a defendant in every action for tort *where they are appropriate*.

a *'Volenti non fit injuria'* ('no injury can be done to a willing person')

This means that a person who has voluntarily consented to the commission of a tort may not sue on it. Obvious examples occur in sport. A boxer voluntarily runs the risk of being punched on the nose by an opponent, and cannot complain if this occurs. If X, a soccer player, kicks the ball towards goal and the ball strikes Y's head, Y has no cause of action against X. Participants in sport voluntarily undertake to run the lawful risks and hazards inherent in the game. On the same principle, spectators voluntarily undertake the lawful risks in attending sports meetings, and may have no cause of action if injured during the performance.

❖ CASE EXAMPLE

Hall v Brooklands Auto-Racing Club (1933)

H paid for admission to Brooklands to watch the car races. During one race, a car shot over the railings after a collision and killed two spectators. It was the first time that a car had gone through the railings. The court found the precautions taken by the defendants were adequate. *Held*: that the type of danger to spectators was inherent in the sport, and the plaintiff, H, must be taken to have assented to the risk of such an accident.

The consent of the claimant must be a true consent to both the physical and legal risks. The consent may be *expressed* (orally or in writing) or may be *implied* from the circumstances of the case. Mere knowledge (*sciens*) of a risk is not usually sufficient: there must be consent (*volens*) to the risk, for the maxim is *volenti non fit injuria*, not *scienti non fit injuria*. The distinction is important, but it is not always easy to determine.

Difficulties arise in two types of case: (i) those involving the relationship of master and servant and (ii) those where a person acting under the compulsion of a legal or moral duty undertakes risks to save others or even the person rescued if they have failed to take reasonable care for their own safety ('rescue' cases).

❖ CASE EXAMPLE

Bowater v Rowley Regis Corporation (1944)

B, a carter, was injured by a bolting horse and sued his employers, the corporation. The horse was known by B to be vicious and to have bolted on other occasions; B had protested previously to his employers about the animal. *Held*: that the corporation was liable, and the defence of *volenti non fit injuria* did not apply:

> To rely on this doctrine the master must show that the workman undertook that the risk should be on him. It is not enough that, whether under protest or not, he obeyed an order or complied with a request which he might have declined as one which he was not bound either to obey or comply with. *It must be shown that he agreed that what risk there was should lie on him.*
>
> (Lord Chief Justice Goddard)

The defence does not apply where a dangerous situation has been created by a defendant's negligent action and a person is placed in an emergency to decide to act to save or protect the lives of others or the defendant. A person of reasonable courage who acts and is injured in these circumstances cannot be described as 'acting willingly'.

❖ CASE EXAMPLES

Haynes v Harwood (1935)

Plaintiff, a constable, was injured stopping defendant's horses, which had bolted due to the defendant's negligence. *Held*: that the defendant was liable in negligence while the plaintiff, who was doing his duty, was not contributorily negligent.

Owgo v Taylor (1987)

O, a fireman, was injured by scalding caused by hose water and flames while fighting a fire in the loft of T's house. *Held*:T was liable, as his negligence had created a foreseeable risk and there had been no break in the chain of causation.

Baker v T.E. Hopkins & Son, Ltd (1959)

Two men descended a well where a petrol pump was not working properly and were overcome by fumes, causing their collapse. A doctor went to their assistance and was himself overcome and died from the poisonous fumes. *Held*: defendants were liable since they created the dangerous situation. The doctor acted under the compulsion of a moral duty and *volenti non fit injuria* did not apply.

The tests applied in such cases are: (i) Did the rescuer intervene to rescue someone who was put in peril by the negligence of another or of themselves?; and (ii) Was the act such as could be expected of a person of ordinary courage and ability situated in similar circumstances?

The case of *Haynes v Harwood* must be distinguished from the following, where the facts were different in an important respect.

Accidents on the highway show one important application of the doctrine of *volenti*. Road-users may expect to run the risk of pure accident, but not injury due to carelessness. 'For the convenience of mankind in carrying on the affairs of life, people as they go along roads must expect, or put up with, such mischief as reasonable care on the part of others cannot avoid' (*Holmes v Mather*, 1875). In this claim the claimant was knocked down by the defendant's horse, which was being ridden with proper care; the court found that the defendant was not liable.

❖ CASE EXAMPLE

Cutler v United Dairies (London) Ltd (1933)

Defendant's milk roundsman left a horse and van, two wheels of which were chained, while he delivered milk. The horse was frightened by the noise from a river steamer and bolted down the road into a meadow. The roundsman followed it, became excited and shouted for help. Plaintiff, a spectator of the incident, went to the roundsman's help and tried to hold the horse's head. The horse lunged and the plaintiff was injured. He then sued the defendant for negligence. *Held*: that in the circumstances, plaintiff freely and voluntarily assumed the risk. It was not an attempt to stop a runaway horse; there was no sense of urgency to impel the plaintiff. He knew the risk, had time to consider it and impliedly agreed to incur it.

In *Dann v Hamilton* (1939), one of the first cases involving the acceptance of a lift in a car when the driver is under the influence of drink and an accident occurs, it was held that *volenti non fit injuria* did not apply. Although D had knowledge of a potential danger and was aware of H's state when accepting the lift, she was held not to have assented to his negligent driving. Nowadays, not only does section 148 of the **Road Traffic Act 1972** prevent the defence of *volenti non fit injuria* succeeding against a passenger suing a driver in these circumstances, but the claimant's knowledge of the driver's state is treated as contributory negligence, e.g. in *Owens v Brimmell* (1976), where 20 per cent was deducted from the damages.

However, in *Morris v Murray and Another* (1990), the Court of Appeal barred the claimant's claim for injuries suffered as a passenger in a plane crash on the grounds that he was aware that the pilot was very drunk and that, therefore, the defence of *volenti non fit injuria* should apply.

b Mistake

The general rule is that mistake, either of law or of fact, is no defence in tort.

As to mistake of law, the maxim *ignorantia legis non excusat* ('ignorance of the law is no excuse') applies. To allow a defendant to say that there was a mistake or lack of knowledge of a particular law would bring the whole of the administration of justice to a standstill. Many defendants would avail themselves of such a loophole.

As to mistake of fact, there are exceptions to the rule that it is no defence. For example, in actions such as malicious prosecution or false imprisonment, a *reasonable* mistake may afford a defence. Thus where a police constable arrests X on reasonable suspicion of crime and it subsequently turns out that X is innocent and that the real culprit is Y, the constable is not liable. The test is: Had the constable who made the mistake reasonable grounds for the belief?

A trespass is actionable even if the trespasser acted under a mistaken but honest belief that the land belonged to him or her and that there was a right of entry (*Basely v Clarkson*, 1682). An auctioneer who, in good faith and without negligence, sells goods as the agent of a customer who has, in fact, no title thereto is guilty of conversion and is liable to the true owner for the value thereof (*Consolidated Co. v Curtis*, 1892).

c Necessity

In some cases damage done intentionally may be excused if done from necessity. The defence is a rare one and is available only when the defendant was compelled by the circumstances to prevent a greater evil. This is illustrated in the following cases.

❖ CASE EXAMPLES

Cope v Sharpe (1912)

Defendant (a gamekeeper) went on to the adjoining land of the plaintiff and made a firebreak in order to prevent the spread of fire to his own land where he had sitting pheasants. Plaintiff sued for trespass. *Held*: that the defendant had acted reasonably, and the threat of fire was a real one.

Leigh v Gladstone (1909)

A suffragette in prison went on hunger strike. She was forcibly fed by warders. The suffragette later sued the prison staff for assault and battery. *Held*: that the defence of necessity was good. Had the prison staff not fed the plaintiff, she would have died.

d Statutory authority

It is a defence to an action in tort to show that a statute (or subordinate legislation) authorizes the alleged wrong. The authority given by statute may be either (i) absolute or (ii) conditional. Absolute authority allows the act even though it may cause harm to other persons; conditional authority, on the other hand, merely allows the act provided that it causes no harm to others. Where the authority is imperative, it is absolute; where the authority is permissive, it is conditional only.

❖ CASE EXAMPLES

Vaughan v Taff Vale Railway Co. (1860)

A railway company was authorized by statute to run a railway that traversed the plaintiff's land. Sparks from the engine set fire to the plaintiff's woods. *Held*: that the railway company was not liable. It had taken all known care to prevent the emission of sparks. The running of locomotives was statutorily authorized.

Metropolitan District Asylum Board v Hill (1881)

A hospital authority (appellants) was empowered by statute to erect a smallpox hospital. The hospital was erected in a residential district, where it caused danger of infection to residents nearby. *Held*: that the erection of the hospital was a nuisance. The statute gave the hospital authority general power to erect such hospitals, but did not sanction the erection in places where this would constitute danger. An injunction was granted. The statutory authority was conditional.

e Illegality

A developing modern defence which has arisen is that based on the concept that no person should benefit from an illegal act, 'ex turpi causa non oritur causa'. For this defence to be successful the defendant has to be able to prove that the claimant engaged in an illegal or immoral act which incorporated a link between this conduct by the claimant and the tort which has been committed.

In *Henderson v Dorset Healthcare University NHS Foundation Trust* (2021), the appellant suffered paranoid schizophrenia. The respondent, an NHS Foundation Trust, was responsible for her care. Due to their negligence, the appellant was not admitted to the hospital when it appeared that she was having a serious psychotic episode. During this episode she stabbed her mother to death.

The outcome was that the appellant was subsequently convicted of voluntary manslaughter by reason of diminished responsibility. This led to her being sentenced to a hospital order under the Mental Health Act 1983. The appellant sued the respondent in negligence, claiming the following losses: Damages for loss of amenity, depressive disorder and PTSD which she had suffered from as a result of killing her mother; damages for the loss of liberty as a result of her prison sentence; damages for her being unable to inherit her mother's estate due to the provisions of the Forfeiture Act 1982 and future losses including having the benefit of psychotherapy and a care worker.

Held: That the defence of illegality barred the appellant's claim.

f Self-defence

A person may use reasonable force to defend him or herself (or any other person) against unlawful force. A defendant will not be liable provided that the amount of force used is reasonable and proportionate to the harm threatened.

It appears that a person may also use reasonable force in the defence of his goods.

❖ **CASE EXAMPLE**

***Cresswell v Sirl* (1948)**

A dog owned by plaintiff, C, attacked during the night some in-lamb ewes owned by S. The dog had just stopped worrying the sheep and started towards S, who shot it when it was 40 yards away. C sued for trespass to goods (dog). *Held:* S was justified in shooting the dog if (i) it was actually attacking the sheep or (ii) if left, the dog would renew the attack on them, *and* shooting was the only practicable and reasonable means of preventing renewal. The onus on justifying the trespass lay on the defendant. (Protecting livestock against dogs is now on a statutory basis: section 9 of the **Animals Act 1971**.)

An occupier of property may protect that property by using reasonable means, e.g. barbed-wire fencing. Spring guns may not be set to injure trespassers who come onto the property, nor may shots be fired at them, for such an amount of force is not proportionate to the harm or threat (*Bird v Holbrook*, 1828).

8.3 Capacity of parties

The general rule is that anyone of full age may sue and be sued in tort. Mention has already been made in Chapter 6 of certain categories of persons. Nevertheless, the following list is appropriately dealt with here since special rules apply in torts.

a The Crown

At common law the maxim 'The King can do no wrong' applied until 1947. We have seen (p. 107) that it was not possible to sue the Crown or its servants for tort. The **Crown Proceedings Act 1947** altered the common law, and section 2(1) now provides that:

> the Crown shall be subject to all those liabilities in tort to which, if it were a person of full age and capacity, it would be subject:
>
> in respect of torts committed by its servants and agents;
>
> in respect of any breach of those duties which a person owes to their servants or agents at common law by reason of being their employer; and
>
> in respect of any breach of the duties attaching at common law to the ownership, occupation, possession, or control of property.

The only respect in which the former common-law maxim applies is that no proceedings in tort may be brought against the Monarch in his or her private capacity.

The Crown is not liable for torts committed by the police or by other public officers who are appointed and paid by *local* authorities or by members of public corporations such as statutory authorities.

b Judicial immunity

Judges have absolute immunity for acts within their judicial capacity. This immunity probably also applies to justices of the peace acting within their jurisdiction. Thus, in *Law v Llewellyn* (1906), a magistrate at Bridgend court uttered words that implied that the prosecutor (Law) was a blackmailer and had brought unfounded criminal charges, whereupon Law sued. It was held that judicial immunity extended to the magistrate, Llewellyn, and there was no liability for slander.

Counsel and witnesses have similar immunity in respect of all matters relating to the case with which they are concerned.

c Foreign sovereigns and diplomats

A foreign sovereign is not liable in tort in the English courts of law unless it submits to the jurisdiction, thereby waiving its immunity from legal process. They may, however, sue in an English court. Ambassadors, High Commissioners and certain other diplomats cannot be sued in tort during their terms of office. Once the period of office is ended, such persons become amenable to the jurisdiction of the English courts and they may be sued at any time between recall and their departure from the jurisdiction.

The privilege enjoyed by ambassadors and other diplomats extends to members of their families and to some employees. A full list of such persons is maintained by the Foreign and Commonwealth Office.

d Corporations

A corporation can sue and be sued in its corporate name. It is liable vicariously (i.e. on their behalf) for torts committed by its servants or agents acting within the scope of their authority.

e Trade unions

These unincorporated bodies enjoy special protection in tort; in certain cases, in accordance with the **Trade Union Act 1984**, to ensure immunity a ballot must be held prior to a strike. Trade unions may, however, sue in tort in their registered names.

f Infants of minors

As a general rule minority is no defence in tort. Where, however, a tort is founded on malice or where negligence is a necessary ingredient of the tort, the age of the minor is relevant; through want of age, a minor may be incapable of forming the specific intent, and what may be negligent in an adult may not be so in respect of a child. If an unborn child is injured by a tort, it may sue provided it is born alive and disabled (**Congenital Disabilities (Civil Liability) Act 1976**).

Where the act complained of is also a breach of contract, the claimant cannot avoid the defence of minority by framing his or her action in tort.

❖ CASE EXAMPLE

Jennings v Rundall (1799)

An infant hired a mare for riding (not a 'necessary'). He injured the animal by over-riding her and was sued in tort for damages. *Held*: that the infant was not liable in tort for negligence since his act was substantially a breach of contract.

This means that where a minor because of the minority is not liable on a contract (e.g. a contract for the supply of an article that is not a 'necessary'), there will be no liability for a tort that arises *directly out of the contract*. Where the tort is independent of the contract, the minor will be liable.

Where a minor was in law a bailee of property and lent the property to another person contrary to the terms of the bailment, the minor was held liable in tort for detinue (*Ballet v Mingay*, 1943). However, where age was fraudulently misrepresented by a minor thereby obtaining a loan of money from a moneylender, contrary to section 1 of the **Infants' Relief Act 1874**, it was held that the minor could not be sued in deceit. To allow the plaintiff to frame the action would be to enforce a void contract (*Leslie v Shiell*, 1914).

❖ **CASE EXAMPLE**

Burnard v Haggis (1863)

A minor hired a horse for riding, but, against the express instructions of the owner, he jumped the horse and injured it. *Held*: that the minor was liable since his wrong was independent of the contract, though the injury occurred because there had been a contract.

Parents are not liable, merely because they are parents, for the torts of their children. But a parent will be liable where there has been authorization or commissioning or ordering of a tort, in which case the parent incurs vicarious liability. Second, a parent may also be held liable for personal negligence where the child has been given the opportunity to do harm.

A parent permitted his son, aged 15, to remain in possession of a shotgun, with which the son had already caused harm and in respect of which complaints had been made. The father was then held liable for injury to another boy's eye (*Bebee v Sales*, 1916). If, however, the parent took reasonable precautions and could not reasonably foresee that the child would disobey his instructions, the parent would not be liable (*Donaldson v McNiven*, 1952).

g Persons of unsound mind

Persons of unsound mind are, in general, liable for their torts. However, a person of unsound mind who is incapable of forming the intention or malice as required in the torts of malicious prosecution or deceit will not be held liable. Similarly, a person who is so insane that their actions are involuntary will escape liability.

❖ **CASE EXAMPLE**

Morriss v Marsden (1952)

Defendant took a room at a Brighton hotel. While there, he attacked the manager of the hotel (plaintiff). It was established that defendant was suffering from a disease of the mind at the time of the attack; that he knew the nature and quality of his act, but he did not know that what he was doing was wrong. *Held*: that as defendant knew the nature and quality of his act, he was liable in tort for the assault and battery. It was immaterial that he did not know that what he was doing was wrong.

h Married women

At common law a husband could not sue his wife in tort, and a wife could not sue her husband in tort except for the protection and security of her own property. This rule has been altered by the **Law Reform (Husband and Wife) Act 1962**, so that now 'each of the parties to a marriage shall have the like right of action in tort against the other as if they were not married'. Thus, if Mrs *A* is being driven by Mr *A* in his car and he negligently collides with a wall, whereby Mrs *A* is injured, she may claim damages against her husband in negligence.

The proceedings between husband and wife may, however, be stayed by the court if it appears that (i) no substantial benefit will accrue to either party from the continuation of the proceedings or (ii) that the case can more conveniently be disposed of under section 17 of the **Married Women's Property Act 1882**, which provides for the summary determination of questions between husband and wife as to the title to, or possession of, property. This has been extended and amended by subsequent legislation.

The preceding relates to actions between the spouses. The wife may now sue and be sued in tort as a feme sole (i.e. as a single woman), and the husband is no longer liable for his wife's torts by reason only of being her husband. Where, however, the wife is agent or servant of her husband, he may render himself vicariously liable (**Law Reform (Married Women and Tortfeasors) Act 1935**).

i Aliens

These fall into two classes: enemy aliens and other aliens. Enemy aliens are members of a State with which England is at war or persons (including British subjects) who 'voluntarily reside or carry on business' in that State. Such persons cannot bring an action in tort, but they may if sued defend one, and they may appeal. Other aliens have neither disability nor immunity.

8.4 Causation and remoteness of damage

A claimant is only entitled to compensation if the damage suffered is, in the eyes of the law, not too remote from the original wrong. If the damage is too remote, it follows that the defendant will not be liable for such damage.

> The law cannot take account of everything that follows from a wrongful act; it regards some subsequent matters as outside the scope of its selection, because 'it were infinite for the law to judge the cause of causes or consequence of consequences'.
>
> (Lord Wright in *Liesbosch Dredger v Edison*, 1933)

A line must be drawn somewhere. To determine where that line is, two tests have been propounded: (a) the test of directness and (b) the test of reasonable foresight.

a The test of directness

Under this test a defendant is liable for all damage that is the *direct* consequence of an act, whether such damage is or is not foreseeable by a reasonable person. This test has been superseded by (b) later on.

b The test of reasonable foresight

The second view is that the defendant is only liable for that damage that he or she, as a reasonable person, should have foreseen. Foreseeability is the test for (i) liability and (ii) remoteness of damage, as illustrated in the following case.

❖ CASE EXAMPLE

Overseas Tankship (UK) Ltd v Morts Dock and Engineering Co. Ltd (The Wagon Mound No 1 (1961))

Owing to negligence, fuel oil spilt into Sydney harbour from the appellants' ship. The oil was carried by the tide to the respondents' wharf, where their employees were welding. A piece of cotton waste on the oil was ignited by sparks from oxy-acetylene equipment. The oil burnt and set fire to the wharf, damaging the ship which the respondents were refitting. *Held* (by the Judicial Committee of the Privy Council): that the appellants were not liable. The test was that the appellants could not reasonably have foreseen that the floating oil would catch fire; they were not liable even though the damage caused was the direct result of their servants' negligence.

Under the doctrine of precedent, the decisions of the Judicial Committee of the Privy Council are of only persuasive authority on English courts. Notwithstanding this, the rule propounded in the *Wagon Mound* case has been followed in important cases: by the House of Lords in *Hughes v Lord Advocate* (1963), and by the Court of Appeal in the following case.

❖ CASE EXAMPLE

Doughty v Turner Manufacturing Co. Ltd (1964)

D was employed by the T. M. Co. A fellow employee of *D* let slip into a cauldron of molten metal an asbestos cement cover. At that time, it was unknown that asbestos cement coming into contact with the molten metal would cause an explosion. An explosion resulted and *D* was injured. No similar accident had been known to occur previously. *Held*: that the accident (though a direct result of the action of the defendant's servant) was not reasonably foreseeable, and therefore the defendants were not liable.

There is a further important rule, namely, that damage that is intended is never too remote. Moreover, although the type of damage must (to come within the rule) be foreseen, the amount of damage done need not be foreseen. For example, let us suppose that *A* negligently knocks down B with a car or strikes C an intentional blow with a fist. The injuries inflicted are very great because, as it is later found, B has a thin skull and C has a weak heart. It is no defence for *A* to claim that if B and C had been normal persons, the injuries or damage would not have occurred: the tortfeasor 'takes the victims as found'.

❖ CASE EXAMPLE

***Smith v Leech Braine & Co. Ltd* (1962)**

Plaintiff's husband was a workman employed by the defendants. Through the defendant's negligence, a piece of molten zinc flew out of a galvanizing tank and hit the husband's lip, causing a burn. Cancer developed on the site of the burn, and three years later, the man died. *Held*: that defendants were liable, although the man's death was clearly not a foreseeable result of the accident.

In this case Lord Chief Justice Parker said: 'I am satisfied that the Judicial Committee of the Privy Council did not have what are called "thin-skull" cases in mind. It has always been the common law that a tortfeasor must take his victim as he finds him.' Lord Parker also approved of the decision in the *Wagon Mound* case, but argued that it had overruled *Re Polemis* only where the actual damage differed from the foreseeable one, not only in extent but also in type. In *Smith v Leech Braine* the fatal injury to the employee differed from the foreseeable one (a burn) in extent only, but not in type.

As a result of the decision in the *Wagon Mound* case, the law as to remoteness in contract and in tort appears to be the same.

❖ CASE EXAMPLE

***Jolley v Sutton London BC* (2000)**

The claimant, aged 14, with a friend, attempted to repair an abandoned boat on amenity land. The boat was propped up but was unstable, as it fell on the claimant, causing him serious spinal injuries. *Held*: that the accident that took place was reasonably foreseeable in that the boat was a trap or allurement to children, that the local authority was in breach of its duty to J as occupier of the land and that accordingly it was liable for his injuries.

c Causation

There have been a number of recent cases speculating on whether the defendant's wrong caused the harm suffered by the claimant. Most of these involve complex issues relating to exposure to asbestos dust (mesothelioma).

8.5 Vicarious liability in tort

The circumstances in which one person will be liable for the torts of another, even though the person liable is not a party to the tort or did not commit the tort in question, must now be considered. Thus, where *A* instructs B to commit a tort against C, it is common sense and justice that *A* should be liable, whatever the liability may be that attaches to B. *A* is said to be *vicariously* liable and, therefore, may be sued for the act that had been ordered, even though *A* did not commit the tort. This subject will be dealt with under two headings: (a) the liability of a master for the torts of a servant and (b) the liability of a principal for the torts of an independent contractor.

a Master and servant

The general rule regarding the master-and-servant relationship is that the master is vicariously liable for the torts of a servant committed during the course of their employment, whether the master authorized them or not. The liability lies in respect of:

i a wrongful act or omission expressly or impliedly authorized by the master
ii a wrongful act or omission that is an unauthorized manner of doing something authorized by the master
iii a wrongful and unauthorized act or omission that is ratified by the master

In the case of an independent contractor, the principal is in general liable only for those torts that the contractor has been expressly or impliedly authorized to commit. This liability will be dealt with specifically later.

Who is a servant? The relationship of master and servant exists when one person employs another to do work on the terms that the servant is subject to the control of the employer as to the manner in which that work is to be done.

- The test is one of control. Does the master control (i) the work to be done and (ii) the way in which the work is done?
- Common examples of servants include chauffeurs, domestic servants, clerks and labourers. These persons are employed under a 'contract of *service*'.
- An independent contractor, on the other hand, is under the control of an employer as to what should be done, but the employer cannot control the actual manner in which the work is performed. Contractors are free to select their own method.
- Independent contractors are said to work under a 'contract *for services*'.

Examples of independent contractors are a builder who contracts to build a house for a client, electricians, plumbers, carpenters and the like who may be called in by a householder to effect a repair in the house. Such persons are not the servants of the householder. Similarly, a taxi-cab driver is an independent contractor, while a chauffeur is a servant.

The term 'master' or 'employer' can be applied to a body corporate, e.g. a company or local authority.

It is for the courts to decide on the evidence in each case whether a person is a servant or independent contractor: a task that is sometimes difficult, particularly in view of the expanding categories of skilled employment in modern society.

'*Course of Employment*'. Originally an employer would not be liable for a tort committed in the course of employment if the servant was performing an act solely for his or her purpose. This was known as the 'Salmond Test', which asked whether the employee's act was a 'wrongful and unauthorised mode of doing some act authorised by the master', based on the principle laid down by J. W. Salmond in his 'Law of Torts' (Stevens and Haynes, 1907). So that, for example, let us suppose that a servant (Smith) is instructed to drive the master's car from Oxbridge to Camford; but instead of proceeding directly to the destination, Smith goes off to London on a 'frolic' of his own. The master will not be liable for any tort that Smith may commit whilst deviating from the route (*Story v Ashton*, 1869).

However, this test was rejected by the House of Lords in *Lister v Hesley Hale* (2002) who replaced it with the 'So closely connected' test. In this case a Mr Grain was employed by H H Ltd as a warden of a residential facility attached to a school which specialized in teaching children with emotional and behavioural difficulties. Over the course of four years he systematically sexually abused a number of boys, including the claimants. Were the defendants, the warden's employers, vicariously liable for the warden's act of abuse? *Held* (House of Lords): that the warden's actions were 'so closely connected' with his employment that it would be fair and just to hold the employer vicariously liable. The sexual abuse was inextricably interwoven with the carrying out by the warden of his duties (Lord Seynal).

This case was further supported by the Supreme Court in *Mohamud v W M Morrison Supermarkets plc* (2016), where a petrol station attendant assaulted the claimant in a brutal and unprovoked attack at his work at the petrol station. Lord Touslon applied the Lister approach nature of the employee's job and the sufficient connection between his employment and wrongful conduct. He did not sever his employment role when he moved out from behind the counter at the service station and attacked the claimant. It was in connection with his employer's business to serve customers.

An act is done in the course of a servant's employment if it is of a class of acts that has been expressly or impliedly authorized. The master does not escape liability merely by forbidding the act that constitutes the tort: otherwise, employers would evade liability by simply prohibiting all kinds of things connected with the work (cf. *Limpus v London General Omnibus Co.* (1862), later). It is immaterial, too, that the particular act was done for the servant's own fraudulent purpose. Moreover, the master will be liable if the act complained of was merely a mode of doing what the servant was employed to do.

'Akin to employment'. This is a further test recently developed by the Supreme Court, examples of which may be seen in *Various Claimants v Catholic Child Welfare Society* (2013), involving students in a school being abused by a monastic order of Christian Brothers, the school being managed by several diocesan authorities and by a lay Roman Catholic Order ('the institute'). *Held*: Both the school and the institute were vicariously liable for the abuse which the Christian Brothers had committed. The relationship between the brothers and the institute was sufficiently 'akin to employment'.

This 'akin to employment' approach was confirmed by the Supreme Court in *Cox v Ministry of Justice* (2016), where Cox, a catering manager at HM Prison Swansea, negligently injured by a prisoner, who was carrying out paid work, under supervision at the prison when he dropped a large bag of rice on her upper back. *Held*: The prisoner's activity was 'akin to employment' even though his relationship to the prison was not voluntary.

❖ CASE EXAMPLES

Century Insurance Co. v Northern Ireland Road Transport Board (1942)

The driver of a petrol lorry was engaged in transferring petrol into an underground storage tank. The driver struck a match to light a cigarette and this caused an explosion, resulting in great damage. *Held*: that the driver was negligent in carrying out his authorized work, and his employers were therefore liable.

Limpus v London General Omnibus Co. (1862)

A bus driver racing to a stop to collect passengers deliberately obstructed the driver of a bus of a rival company, overturning the latter's vehicle. The bus driver had been given strict instructions against obstructing other buses. *Held*: that the defendants were liable. The driver was acting within the course of his employment at the time. It was immaterial whether his act was forbidden.

Beard v London General Omnibus Co. (1900)

A bus conductor drove a bus in London and negligently collided with the plaintiff. The conductor was not authorized to drive the bus. *Held*: that the servant was not acting within the scope of his employment. Accordingly the claim against the employer failed.

Lloyd v Grace, Smith & Co. (1912)

A firm of solicitors employed a managing clerk to deal with conveyancing matters. Plaintiff, a widow, wished to sell some cottages and went to the solicitors. The managing clerk induced the plaintiff to transfer the cottages to him and misappropriated certain mortgage moneys. Plaintiff sued the employers. *Held*: that the solicitors were liable to the client for the fraud of the managing clerk, though it was committed solely for his benefit.

Harrison v Michelin Tyre Co. Ltd (1985)

The plaintiff was injured by a 'practical joke' of a fellow employee. His employers argued that the employee's action constituted a 'frolic of his own'. *Held*: that two mutually exclusive questions should be asked. (1) Although unauthorized or prohibited, was the employee's action incidental to his employment? If 'Yes', *D* was liable. (2) Was it so divergent from the employment as to be plainly alien to and wholly distinguishable from the employment? If 'Yes', *D* was not liable. On the basis of the facts the answer to question (1) was 'Yes', so that the employers were vicariously liable.

It should be observed that the master *and* the servant are liable and may be sued jointly and severally. Usually the master only is sued, being the more likely to be able to pay the damages. If the master is sued, a contribution may be recovered from the employee for the loss, and, in some cases, an indemnity.

❖ CASE EXAMPLE

Lister v Romford Ice and Cold Storage Co. Ltd (1957)

L, a lorry driver employed by the company, reversed his lorry negligently and knocked down his father, who was also employed by the company. The father recovered damages from the company which was held vicariously liable for the tort of its servant, *L*. The insurers of the company paid the amount and thereupon sued *L*, in the name of the company, for an indemnity. *Held*, inter alia: that *L* had broken his obligation to the company to take reasonable care in the performance of his duties and the company could recover on an indemnity.

Where a servant is lent by one master to another, the identity of the employer is sometimes difficult to establish. Thus, Smith, the servant of *A*, is sent by *A* to work for *B*. If Smith commits a tort during 'the course of employment', is *A* or *B* liable? This question is resolved by adopting the 'control' test already mentioned, and the onus of proving that control has passed to the new employer (*B*) rests on the first employer (*A*).

b Liability for independent contractors

The general rule is that an employer is *not* liable for the torts of an independent contractor or of the servant employed by the latter. There are, however, the following exceptions to the rule:

i Where the contract is to do something that is itself a tort, e.g. a nuisance.

❖ **CASE EXAMPLE**

Ellis v Sheffield Gas Consumers Co. **(1853)**

A company that had no authority to dig up streets in Sheffield employed a contractor to open trenches in a street. The contractor's servants left a heap of stones in the road over which the plaintiff fell and injured himself. *Held*: that the defendant company was liable for the consequences of its unlawful act.

ii In operations on or adjoining a highway, other than normal use for the purpose of passage.

❖ **CASE EXAMPLE**

Tarry v Ashton **(1876)**

A was the occupier of a house from the front of which a heavy lamp protruded over the highway. The lamp fell into disrepair, and *A* instructed a contractor to inspect and renew it. The contractor negligently repaired the lamp which later collapsed and injured *T*. *Held*: *A* was liable in public nuisance. It was his duty to repair the lamp, and the duty was not discharged. It was no excuse that the injury was caused by the negligence of the contractor.

iii Under the rule in *Rylands v Fletcher* (see p. 258). In this case the employer was liable notwithstanding the fact that no negligence was imputed to the independent contractor who built the reservoir.

iv Where an independent contractor is employed to do 'extra hazardous' acts.

❖ **CASE EXAMPLE**

Honeywill & Stein v Larkin Bros **(1934)**

Plaintiffs instructed defendants (independent contractors) to take flashlight photographs of the interior of a cinema. A flash with magnesium powder caused a fire that damaged the cinema. *Held*: that the cinema owners were entitled to claim damages from the plaintiffs, who, in turn, were granted an indemnity from defendants (the photographers).

8.5.1 Joint tortfeasors

A tort may be committed by two persons acting together, i.e. jointly. Thus if *A* holds one end of a log while B holds the other, and together they heave it through a window, the law holds that *both* are liable.

The liability of joint tortfeasors is said to be 'joint and several', which means that a claimant may sue both (or all, if more than two) defendants, or may recover the full amount of the claim from one only of the tortfeasors.

Until 1935 there was no right of contribution between joint tortfeasors, but under the **Civil Liability (Contribution) Act 1978** (replacing a statutory provision in 1935), it is enacted that where one tortfeasor is sued and pays the damages, they may claim a contribution from their fellow tortfeasors. The amount recoverable is such 'as may be found by the court to be just and equitable having regard to the extent of that person's responsibility for the damage'. Thus if *A* is sued in damages for £1,000, it may be recovered from B (a joint tortfeasor) by legal action against B, such sum as the court determines, e.g. £250 if B is one-quarter responsible only.

If, in the last example, *A* were a servant of B and damages were awarded against *A* (say for £1,000), and if *A* were merely carrying out the instructions of the employer, *A* would be entitled to be indemnified by action against B for the amount of £1,000 that *A* has been compelled to pay. An indemnity may arise out of a contractual agreement as well as in the relationship of master and servant, as noted previously.

8.6 Trespass

There are three types of trespass: (a) trespass to the person, (b) trespass to goods and (c) trespass to land.

a Trespass to the person

This action takes three forms: (i) assault, (ii) battery and (iii) false imprisonment.

i Assault

Assault is an act that causes another person to apprehend immediate and unlawful personal violence. Thus, striking at another with a stick or fist (even though the party misses the aim), drawing a sword and throwing a bottle are common examples. Where *A* points a firearm at B, which *A* knows to be unloaded though B does not, and is so near that it might produce injury if it were loaded and went off, this constitutes an assault (*R v St George*, 1840).

Mere words do not constitute an assault, however. The intent must be shown in acts, not just in speech (*Wilson v Pringle*, 1986). Words are nevertheless relevant in certain circumstances and may prevent what, in other circumstances, would amount to an assault. Thus, in *Tuberville v Savage* (1669), a person laid a hand on their sword (a menace) and said: 'If it were not assize time I would not take such language from you.' This was held not to be an assault.

ii Battery

Battery consists of applying force, however slight, to the person of another hostilely or against their will. The charge of battery is usually combined with assault, namely 'assault and battery'. Common examples include giving a person a black eye, throwing water at them, holding them by the arm, spitting in their face, removing a chair from under them or throwing a squib at them (*Scott v Shepherd*, 1773).

Volenti non fit injuria (consent) is a notable defence in this type of action, e.g. where a doctor makes a medical examination of a patient with their consent. Merely touching a person (without undue force) to engage their attention is not a battery. In an action for trespass to the person it is essential to prove that the defendant acted intentionally or negligently. In *Fowler v Lanning* (1959) it was held that where the defendant shot the plaintiff accidentally, no cause of action arose in the absence of intent or negligence.

iii False imprisonment

False imprisonment consists of the infliction of bodily restraint of another without lawful justification. As with assault and battery, false imprisonment is actionable per se (i.e. in itself) without proof of damage. There need be no imprisonment such as incarceration in police cells. The mere holding of the arm of another, as when a constable makes an arrest, is sufficient.

It is not, however, necessary that actual force be used: the threat of force is sufficient. 'Stay there or I'll shoot you' may be evidence of imprisonment. Neither is it necessary for the person to know of their detention, for they may be imprisoned while asleep (applied in *Murray v Ministry of Defence*, 1988). In *R v Governor of Brookhill Prison, ex parte* Evans (No. 2) (2000) it was held that wrongful calculation of a prisoner's release date could not constitute false imprisonment.

❖ CASE EXAMPLE

***R v Bournewood Community and Mental Health NHS Trust ex parte L (Secretary of State for Health Intervening)* (1998)**

L, a severely affected mentally incapable man, became agitated at a day centre. Sedated, he was admitted informally to hospital but not detained under the **Mental Health Act 1983**. Nurses were instructed to keep him under continuous observations and to prevent him from leaving if he attempted to do so. *Held*: that this was not false imprisonment. In the circumstances the mere fact that the doctors looking after L might have had in mind to detain him compulsorily if necessary at some future point in time did not give rise to his detention in fact at an earlier date.

The restraint of another must be total or complete. Thus, to restrain a person from going in three ways but leaving them free to go in a fourth is not false imprisonment (*Bird v Jones*, 1845).

❖ CASE EXAMPLES

***Bird v Jones* (1845)**

A bridge company lawfully stopped a public footpath on Hammersmith Bridge. A spectator insisted on using the footpath, but was stopped by two policemen who barred his entry. Plaintiff was told he might proceed to another point around the obstruction, but that he could not go forward. He declined and remained for about half an hour, and then sued for false imprisonment. *Held*: that there was no false imprisonment since the plaintiff was free to go another way.

***Middleweek v Chief Constable of Merseyside and Another* (1990)**

The plaintiff, a solicitor, was arrested and detained in a police cell for one hour on suspicion of theft of a confidential police document relating to one of his clients. *Held*:

that there was no evidence to suggest that the conditions of the plaintiff's detention rendered it unlawful.

Meering v Grahame While Aviation Co. Ltd (1919)

Plaintiff was suspected of stealing paint from his employers (defendants) and was asked to accompany two works' policemen to the defendants' office to be interrogated. Plaintiff did not know he was suspected and agreed to the request. He remained in the office while the two policemen remained outside the room without plaintiff's knowledge. *Held*: that the plaintiff was imprisoned and his knowledge was irrelevant.

Jalloh, R (on the application of) v Secretary of State for the Home Department (2020)

Jalloh (Respondent) was made subject to a curfew restriction between the hours of 23.00 and 07.00 for a period between 5 February 2014 and 14 July 2016, pending potential deportation. The curfew was imposed by those acting on behalf of the Secretary of State purportedly in accordance with the Immigration Act 1971. However it was subsequently discovered that the Act did not confer a power to impose a curfew. Consequently the curfew imposed was unlawfully imposed and the Respondent issued judicial review proceedings. The High Court *Held*: That the curfew did amount to a detention for the purposes of the tort of false imprisonment. This decision was subsequently upheld by both the Court of Appeal and the Supreme Court. The Supreme Court decided that it was possible for there to he imprisonment at common law without a deprivation of liberty under article 5 of the European Convention for Human Rights (ECHR). In addition the Court declined to align or restrict the classic understanding of imprisonment at common law to the very difference and much more nuanced concept of deprivation of liberty under the ECHR.

The following *defences* may be offered to an action for trespass to the person.

i Self-defence

It is lawful for a person to defend him or herself against an assault or battery. The defence must be proportionate to the attack, no more force being used in defence of oneself than is reasonably necessary. What is reasonable or commensurate with the necessity is a matter for decision by the court on the particular facts of each case. If, for example, *A* throws a jug of water at B, which splashes B (an assault and battery), it follows that B cannot lawfully resist or claim a defence by shooting *A*.

ii Defence of property

Similar rules apply to the defence of one's property, including a house. An occupier may use reasonable force to eject a trespasser. Where the trespass is not forcible, the occupier should first request the trespasser to leave; second allow them sufficient time to do so peaceably; and finally, if they still refuse to leave, the occupier may use reasonable force to eject them.

iii Consent of claimant

The normal rules of *volenti non fit injuria* apply (see p. 218).

iv Parental or other authority

A parent may administer reasonable punishment to a child or young person. This punishment includes locking them in a room, if need be, though one must stress that in all cases, the test is reasonableness. Long imprisonment might amount to the criminal offence of cruelty to a child.

This parental authority may be delegated to another, e.g. a schoolmaster who may (providing the regulations of the Education Authority permit) also administer reasonable punishment. Thus, the detention of a child after school hours is not false imprisonment, and currently it would appear that parents are still able to administer reasonable chastisement, although this has been questioned by the European Court. However, s. 131 of the Schools Standards and Framework Act 1998 makes it an offence for any school to administer corporal punishment.

v Judicial authority

A judge who acts within judicial authority may grant a warrant of arrest, in which case the person executing the arrest may use reasonable force to detain the person named. Prisoners under terms of imprisonment in HM Prisons, for example, are there pursuant to the judicial authority of a magistrate or a judge who sentences them and signs the requisite committal warrants.

vi Preservation of the peace

All persons owe a duty not to disturb the public peace, either by committing a crime or causing public disorders and the like. The police have wide common law and statutory powers to make arrests to enforce the law and to preserve the peace. If the individual constable acts lawfully, no action lies against him or her in trespass, provided that they use no more force than is reasonably necessary to effect the arrest.

vii Protection from harassment

In accordance with the **Protection from Harassment Act 1997**, a civil tort is created in England and Wales (delict in Scotland) where a person has been involved in a course of conduct amounting to harassment of a person or where such a person fears that violence will be used against them. In these circumstances an order can be sought restraining such harassment. If that order is breached, that will constitute an offence.

b Trespass to land

Trespass to land may take three forms:

i entry on the land of another;
ii remaining on the land of another; and
iii placing or throwing any material object upon the land of another.

Again, it may be noted that it is not necessary to prove actual damage to the land, the tort being actionable per se.

'Land' includes not only the soil itself but things under the soil, and buildings or houses affixed to the surface. The general rule is that the owner of the land owns all the land below the surface and all the space above the land (*cujus est solum ejus est usque ad caelum et ad inferos*). Trespass may, therefore, occur by delving into the subsoil, e.g. to lay a cable or to take coal from another's mine.

Common examples of trespass to land include putting a hand on a fence or through an open window of a house, entering another's forecourt, removing a dustbin and throwing bricks onto another's land. (Merely to allow bricks from a chimney which is ruinous and in disrepair to fall on a neighbour's land constitutes a nuisance, but is not trespass.)

As to the flight of aircraft over land, it is provided by the **Civil Aviation Act 1982**, that:

> no action shall lie in respect of trespass or nuisance by reason only of the flight of aircraft over any property at a height above the ground which, having regard to wind, weather and all the circumstances of the case is reasonable or the ordinary incidents of such flight.

But the Act makes the owner of the civil aircraft (not RN, Army or RAF aircraft) strictly liable for any damage caused.

The sign 'Trespassers will be prosecuted' is not true. Mere trespass on land is not a *crime* and no *prosecution* for it may be brought, though a civil action may be. If, however, the trespass is accompanied by damage, e.g. by breaking fences or treading down growing corn, an offence of wilful damage is committed contrary to the **Criminal Damage Act 1971**. In civil trespass no damage need be proved. Moreover, a person may be sued even though he or she did not know they were trespassing, for mistake is no defence.

Personal entry on land of another may be lawful, as for example, where the occupier grants permission on payment (by licence) or gratuitously. Where permission to enter and remain on land is revoked or where the time limit for entry has expired, a person may become, from that moment, a trespasser. Subject to the foregoing rules the trespasser may be requested to leave, given time to do so, and if they still refuse to go, ejected.

Trespass 'ab initio'. Where a person enters on the land of another by authority of law (as distinct from authority conferred by the claimant occupier), they may become a trespasser if, by their subsequent conduct, they abuse their right of entry. This doctrine is known as trespass *ab initio* and is exemplified by the ancient case given later on. The subsequent conduct that abuses the right of entry may be stealing an article from the occupier. The abuse relates back to the *original* entry and he or she becomes a trespasser. The abuse must consist of a *misfeasance* (i.e. some positive act of wrongdoing, such as stealing), not a *non-feasance* (i.e. an omission to do something, such as failing to pay for food or drink).

Who may sue and be sued. Trespass is essentially a wrong against possession, not against ownership. Thus an owner out of possession cannot sue, but if they later recover possession, the right relates back to the time when their right of entry accrued, and they may sue for any trespass committed in the meantime. A landlord may sue in trespass only if some permanent injury has been done to the property or its value has been seriously impaired. This means that a landlord cannot sue in respect of a trespass to land in the occupation and possession of a tenant. A mere licensee, e.g. a person attending a theatre as a member of an audience, a lodger or a guest at a hotel, is not deemed to be 'in possession' of land (theatre, hotel, etc.) so as to enable them to sue in trespass to that land.

❖ **CASE EXAMPLE**

The Six Carpenters Case (1610)

Carpenters entered an inn (entry being the exercise of a public and lawful right). They ordered bread and wine, for which they paid. They then ordered more wine, but refused to pay. *Held*: that they were not trespassers *ab initio* because they had authority by law to enter the inn and their offence was one of *non-feasance*, not *misfeasance*.

Justification for entry. We have noted that to constitute actionable trespass, an entry on land must be unlawful. Nevertheless there are several instances where the supposed trespasser may claim that entry is justified either by common law or by statute. The justification may, therefore, be a defence, as follows:

- i entry by lawful authority: e.g. by police to make an arrest or to search premises (**Criminal Law Act 1967**); or by bailiffs to distrain for rent or to eject a tenant
- ii entry to abate a nuisance in emergency (see p. 244)
- iii entry made to retake a chattel owned by defendant provided the chattel is placed there by the claimant (occupier of the land) or, possibly, by a third person, and the claimant acts reasonably
- iv entry by licence or permission of the occupier, express or implied. A licence is 'that consent which, without passing any interest in the property to which it relates, merely prevents the acts for which consent is given from being wrongful' (Pollock)
- v peaceable entry on the land by a person entitled to possession of it

Remedies for trespass to land. The following remedies are available to a claimant.

- i *Damages*. This is in general the amount by which the value of the property is diminished as a result of the trespass, not the cost of reinstatement.
- ii *Injunction*. This may be used to prevent the continuance or repetition of the act of trespass. The claimant may apply to the court for both damages and an injunction.
- iii *Ejection*. The occupier of the land may eject a trespasser after they have been requested to leave and allowed peaceably so to do. No more force may be used than is reasonable in the circumstances; otherwise, the occupiers themselves may be sued for assault.
- iv *An action of ejectment* may be brought for recovery of land.

Where trespass consists in entry by cattle or sheep on the land of another, the occupier's rights are now governed by the **Animals Act 1971**, which replaces the common-law rules.

S. 4(1) provides that where the defendant's livestock strays on the claimant's land, the defendant is, generally, liable for the damage done to the land or to the property on it and for any expenses reasonably incurred by the claimant in keeping the livestock, while it cannot be restored to the defendant, or while it is being detained for certain other purposes.

S. 7 gives the occupier of land onto which livestock strays limited rights of detention and sale in certain cases.

Dispossession means wrongfully depriving another of possession of land. This may occur where, for example, *A* enters a field or a house and assumes possession of it, or where *A* retains possession of land after the expiration of any lease granted. If now B claims possession of the land or house in the preceding example, B's proper course, should *A* prevent possession, is to take action in the courts for recovery of possession of the property. The court will then examine the respective claims of *A* and B and make an order as to the right of possession to the one who has the stronger claim. Where B is successful in regaining possession, damages may be claimed, which include the right of mesne (i.e. intermediate) profits. These are profits of the land during the period when it was wrongfully possessed by *A*.

The general rule is that a claimant to possession must prove the claim by the strength of their own title; they may not support their claim by alleging that a third party has a better title than that claimed by the party in possession. This right outstanding in a third party is known as the *jus tertii*.

Re-entry on land. Where a person is lawfully entitled to take possession of land, those rights should be exercised peaceably; otherwise, they themselves will be rendered liable. Where a person is *wrongfully* in possession, it is no tort for a person claiming under a legal title to eject the wrongful possessor forcibly, provided that no more force is used on the wrongful possessor or their goods than is reasonably necessary (*Hemming v Stoke Poges Golf Club*, 1920). The Statute of Forcible Entry,

1381, which made forcible entry, even by the person entitled to possession, a criminal offence, was repealed by the **Criminal Law Act 1977**.

When B (the person lawfully entitled to possession) has re-entered, the possession re-vests in them and the former occupant *A* (i.e. the person against whom the incoming tenant re-entered) becomes a trespasser. Action may, therefore, be taken against *A* for trespass.

c Trespass to goods

The wrong of trespass to goods is the intentional or negligent interference with the possession of goods of another. The interference must be direct and forcible (though a mere touching may be trespass). Trespass is actionable per se.

An omission does not give rise to an action in trespass unless it was done intentionally or negligently (*NCB v Evans*, 1951; and *Fowler v Lanning*, 1959). Accidental touching of goods is not actionable.

As examples it may be noted that it is a trespass to throw another's book out of the window, to remove a bicycle from a shed or to remove the wheels of another's motor-car.

Trespass is essentially a wrong to possession, as distinct from ownership. To maintain trespass, the claimant must show possession of the goods at the time of the trespass. Thus, a borrower, hirer or a bailee of goods (e.g. a shoemaker to whom shoes are sent for repair) possesses the goods lent, hired or bailed, and action may be maintained against any person who wrongfully interferes with the goods in their possession. It follows, therefore, that a bailor cannot sue in the trespass during the term of bailment.

8.7 Interference with goods

Detinue means 'the wrongful detention of the goods of another to the immediate possession of which that other is entitled', e.g. *A* lends a book to B for one week and B refuses to return it at the proper time; X hands a watch to Y, a watchmaker and Y declines to return it after demand by X. The essence of the claim was for the return of the claimant's property of which they were owner.

Conversion is defined as 'an act or complex series of acts of wilful interference, without lawful justification, with any chattel in a manner inconsistent with the right of another, whereby that other is deprived of the use and possession of it' (*Salmond on Torts*).

In practice the torts of (a) trespass to goods, (b) detinue (detention) and (c) conversion of goods overlapped and archaic procedures applied to each. The **Torts (Interference with Goods) Act 1977** abolished the tort of detinue and simplified the law and procedure. Each of the various torts is now treated in the same way.

Wrongful interference with goods is defined as:

a conversion of goods (also called trover);
b trespass to goods;
c negligence so far as it results in damage to goods or to an interest in goods; or
d any other tort so far as it results in damage to goods or to an interest in goods (s. 1).

Detention of goods now becomes conversion, including such cases as loss or destruction of goods by a bailee in breach of a duty to the bailor, e.g. where B (see previously) loses the book, or Y (previously) destroys the watch, is now conversion.

Court's powers. The court may order: (a) specific delivery of goods, (b) damages or (c) specific delivery, with the alternative to the defendant of paying damages. Specific delivery is a *discretionary* remedy, and may be ordered subject to conditions.

Damages. Payment of damages or settlement extinguishes the title to the goods of the claimant, including where damages are reduced by reason of contributory negligence of the claimant.

If the defendant improved goods, e.g. *A* has a car that B steals and sells to C, a bona fide purchaser, who fits a new engine, then the defendant (C) is entitled to an allowance to the value of the goods attributable to the improvement (s. 6).

Jus tertii. This rule is abolished and a defendant is now entitled to prove that a third party has a better right to the goods than the claimant. The plaintiff must now give particulars of their title and identify any person who, to their knowledge, has or claims to have any interest in the goods, and the defendant may apply to join any person in the action (s. 8(2)). The court determines the respective claims to the goods at one time.

Co-ownership is not a defence to an action (a) in conversion or (b) trespass to goods where the defendant, without the authority of the co-owner:

a destroys the goods, disposes of the goods in a way giving a good title to the entire property in the goods or otherwise does anything equivalent to the destruction of the other's interest in the goods; or

b purports to dispose of the goods in a way that would give a good title to the entire property in the goods if he or she was acting with the authority of all co-owners of the goods (s. 10(1)).

Conversion may be committed in the following ways:

i *By taking*. Where *A* takes chattels out of the possession of B (the true owner) without lawful justification with the intention of exercising dominion over the goods permanently or even temporarily. Every simple theft, as when X steals Y's jacket, is a conversion. Mere shifting the goods of another, as where a station porter puts suitcases at the side of a railway platform, may be trespass but not conversion.

ii *By detention*. Where *A* detains goods of B in defiance of B's right to the chattels, B may sue in conversion.

iii *By wrongful delivery*. If *A*, without lawful justification, delivers B's goods to C (a stranger), *A* is liable in conversion. Similarly, if a bailee of goods sells them before the period of the bailment has expired, the bailee is rendered liable in conversion.

iv *By destruction*. The wilful and unlawful destruction of another's goods amounts to conversion. There must be complete destruction; the mere damage of goods is insufficient.

❖ CASE EXAMPLES

Fouldes v Willoughby (1841)

W was the manager of a ferry boat. F embarked his horses on the ferry. *W* and F had a dispute, and in order to induce F to leave the boat, *W* turned the horses off onto the highway. F remained on the boat and crossed to the other side of the river. F then sued *W*. *Held*: that there was trespass to the horses, but no conversion.

Hollins v Fowler (1875)

A cotton broker, acting on behalf of a customer for whom he had often made purchases, bought cotton from a person who had obtained it by fraud. The broker sold it to the customer and received only his commission. *Held*: that the broker was liable in conversion for the entire value of the goods.

Armory v Delamirie (1722)

A chimney sweep's boy found a jewel and handed it to a jeweller for valuation. The latter took the jewel from the setting and refused to return it to the boy, who thereupon sued the jeweller in trover (the original form of conversion). *Held*: that the jeweller was liable; the finder had a good title except as against the true owner. (This case was applied by the Court of Appeal in *Parker v British Airways Board* (1982), where the plaintiff passenger at London Airport found a gold bracelet in the executive lounge, and it was held that his claim prevailed.)

8.8 Nuisance

Nuisances are of two kinds: (i) public and (ii) private.

A public nuisance is some unlawful act or omission that endangers or interferes with the lives, safety or comfort of the public generally or of some section of the public, or by which the public, or some section of it, is obstructed in the exercise of a common right.

It is a public nuisance to keep a brothel; to obstruct the public highway; and to erect a factory that emits excessive smoke, fumes or dirt so as to cause discomfort to persons in the locality.

A public nuisance is a *crime*, punishable at common law on indictment before a jury. Usually the criminal proceedings are undertaken by the police. Action may also be taken by the Attorney-General on behalf of the public, who may *sue* also for an injunction to restrain further offences. In addition, a private person may also *sue* (not prosecute) the person committing the public nuisance if it can be shown that he or she has suffered peculiar damage over and above that suffered by the public generally. Thus, to dig a trench in a public highway without lawful authority is a public nuisance and a crime. If *A* falls into the trench, or if the trench interferes with *A*'s right of way into his or her own premises, *A* may show peculiar damage to himself or herself and sue the person who excavated the trench.

Statutory nuisances. Statutes may also forbid nuisances. Some of these are the **Public Health Act 1936**, the **Clean Air Act 1956**, the **Noise Abatement Act 1960**, the **Control of Pollution Act 1974**, the **Deposit of Poisonous Wastes Act 1972** and the **Noise Act 1996**.

❖ CASE EXAMPLES

Lyons, Sons & Co. v Gulliver (1914)

G were the occupants of a theatre. Popular performances at 2.30 p.m. and 6.30 p.m. caused queues to form that obstructed customers to an adjacent shop. *Held*: that L suffered particular damage, and the nuisance was actionable at the suit of the adjacent shop owner.

Attorney-General v PYA Quarries, Ltd (1957)

PYA owned and used a quarry at which blasting of rocks took place. Some stones and splinters were hurled out of the quarry, and dust and vibration caused discomfort to nearby dwellers. *Held*: that this was a public nuisance.

Miller v Jackson (1977)

Balls were often struck out of a cricket ground (long used for the game) onto M's house, recently built nearby. The Court of Appeal awarded damages for negligence and nuisance, but discharged an injunction against playing cricket. The court was of the opinion that, on balance, the interest of the public in playing cricket should prevail over the private interests of individuals who must have realized when buying their property that balls would sometimes strike it.

A private nuisance is an unlawful interference with a person's use of his or her property or with his or her health, comfort or convenience. It is, in fact, a wrongful act or omission causing (i) material injury to property or (ii) sensible personal discomfort.

There are two main classes of private nuisance: (i) interference with the enjoyment of land generally and (ii) injuries to servitudes. Of these two classes the first is the more important; the second deals with servitudes or easements (e.g. rights of way, rights of light and rights of support to land) and is more appropriate to a specialized study of English land law rather than the present book.

There are, of course, many varied acts that may constitute nuisance. Noise, vibrations, fumes, smell, smoke, dirt and damp are fairly obvious ones and are part of a person's existence in some degree or other.

Nuisance is not (in contrast to trespass) actionable per se. Some damage must have occurred to the plaintiff to enable them to sue.

The basic rule is that you should use your property so that you cause no harm to another (expressed by the Latin maxim: *sic utere tuo ut alienum non laedas*). More simply, one should 'live and let live' and be reasonable as to one's acts or omissions in regard to neighbours.

> A balance has to be maintained between the right of the occupier to do what he likes with his own, and the right of a neighbour not to be interfered with. It is impossible to give any precise formula, but it may broadly be said that a useful test is perhaps what is reasonable according to the ordinary uses of mankind living in society.
>
> (Lord Wright in Sedleigh-Denfield v O'Callaghan, 1940)

The following points are relevant to private nuisance and are helpful in understanding the field of law affecting this tort:

i *Health and comfort.* There need be no direct injury to health. It is sufficient that a person has, to an appreciable extent, been prevented from enjoying the ordinary comforts of life.

ii *Standard of comfort.* The standard of the 'ordinary comfort of life' varies with the locality affected. Thus, for example, in London there is a difference between Mayfair and Stepney. One area may be relatively quiet and peaceful, another bustling and noisy. The only exception, under this head, seems to be that an interference with light to a building will be dealt with equally whether it occurs in one area or another, for 'one requires as much light to sew in Belgravia as in Whitechapel'.

iii *Variety.* The modes of annoyance are infinitely diverse: stenches, filth, the use of radio, church bell ringing and circus performing may all be nuisances. Interference with television reception, however, does not constitute an action in nuisance (*Hunter v Canary Wharf Ltd*, 1997).

iv *Several wrongdoers.* A nuisance may be caused by the combined operation of several wrongdoers. Their joint action or cumulative action (if operating separately) may result in a nuisance. If for instance *A*, *B*, *C* and *D* are the persons involved, a plaintiff may sue all jointly or one only, *A* for example, for the total damage. If this is done, *A* will have a right of contribution from *B*, *C* and *D*, the joint tortfeasors, for their portion of the damage caused.

v *Extra sensitivity*. Reasonableness is, as we have observed, the test. A person cannot take advantage of their personal sensitivity or that of their property. Moreover, one cannot expect the same standards to be obtained in a crowded industrial city as those that hold in a country market town. There must be 'give and take'. 'By living in such flats, the claimants made themselves unusually vulnerable to this invasion of their privacy' (*Fearn v Trustees of the Tate Gallery*, 2019).

vi *Utility of the nuisance*. Pig sties, tanneries, lime kilns, quarries and fried-fish shops are perhaps useful for the general well-being, but if their operation causes serious or appreciable discomfort, they are a nuisance. The allegation that the trade or industry is 'for the public benefit' is no defence in law.

vii *Natural nuisances*. *Leakey v National Trust for Places of Historic Interest or Natural Beauty* (1980) established that an occupier could be liable for damage to neighbouring property caused by a state of affairs arising on his or her own property. However, in *Holbeck Hall Hotel Ltd v Scarborough Borough Council* (2000) it was held that for this to happen the danger must have been patent (the occupier saw or should have seen the danger on their land) and not latent (not where the threat to neighbouring property could only be discovered by further investigation).

viii *Malice or evil motive*. This may in some cases be the essence of the tort, inasmuch as the wrongdoer's improper motive may show that they are not acting reasonably and lawfully. The wantonness of an act to annoy a neighbour may therefore be a nuisance (*Hollywood Silver Fox Farm v Emmett* (1936), see p. 241).

ix *Prescription*. A person may acquire a right to commit a nuisance by long usage, e.g. 20 years' continuous operation since the act complained of first became a nuisance. Prescription is a defence in private nuisance, but *not* in public nuisance (which is a crime).

Who may sue and be sued. The occupier of the property (e.g. a tenant) affected by the nuisance is the person who brings the action (*Malone v Laskey*, 1907). A landlord may, however, sue in some cases, e.g. where a permanent injury is caused, or will be caused, to the property.

The person to be sued is the one who creates the nuisance. Where premises are leased, a landlord may, however, be liable if (i) the landlord creates the nuisance and then leases the property; or if (ii) the landlord authorized, expressly or impliedly, a tenant to commit or continue the nuisance (*Harris v James*, 1876).

Defences. The following defences may be raised in nuisance.

i *Statutory authority*. It is a defence to show that a statute authorizes the act or omission in question (see p. 201 for further discussion on this defence).

ii *Triviality*. A defendant may prove that the act or omission is small and trivial, e.g. smoke from an ordinary garden fire on one morning only. The maxim is *de minimus non curat lex* ('the law does not concern itself with trifles'). Minimum discomfort must be expected on the basis of 'give and take'.

iii *Lawful use of land*. The defendant may prove that the use of the land does not give rise to a nuisance (*Mayor of Bradford v Pickles*, 1895).

iv *Reasonableness*. The act or omission is reasonable, having regard to the locality concerned.

The following defences are *ineffectual*:

i that the claimant came to the nuisance. If a person goes to the place where a nuisance exists, he or she is not barred from his or her claim. The question is whether the act is reasonable in that locality (*Sturges v Bridgman*, 1879; and *Bliss v Hall*, 1838)

ii that the particular act is for the public benefit
iii that all care and skill have been used to prevent a nuisance

Remedies. The following legal remedies exist:

i *Abatement.* This means 'self-help'. The injured party may stop the nuisance by removing the cause. But the abater must not, in the process, infringe another's rights, e.g. by trespassing on a neighbour's property or land or injuring an innocent person's rights, such as a tenant's. Abatement is not favoured as a remedy by the law, and where entry on another's land is contemplated, notice to the alleged tortfeasor should first be given to remedy the alleged nuisance before entry is effected, unless there is an emergency (*Lemmon v Webb*, 1895). A common example of abatement is the cutting of roots and branches projecting from a neighbour's trees: such roots and branches may be sawn off, but they remain the property of the person owning the tree (*Mills v Brooker*, 1919).
ii *Damages.* This is the ordinary common-law remedy.
iii *Injunction.* Application may be made to the court for an order to restrain further acts constituting the nuisance if it can be proved that the nuisance will recur and do irreparable damage to the plaintiff.

Distinction between trespass and nuisance. The torts of nuisance and trespass to land are similar in that both affect land. Nevertheless, there are important distinctions as indicated in the following.

	Trespass	Nuisance
1	Actionable per se.	Must prove *damage*.
2	*Direct* physical interference to land (e.g. placing rubbish on a neighbour's land).	Need not be direct (e.g. allowing bricks from a ruinous chimney to fall on a neighbour's land).
3	Wrongful *entry* of an object or person on another's land.	No entry necessary. Can be created on defendant's own land.
4	May consist of *one act* only.	Usually more than one act is necessary.
5	Trespass to land is not a crime.	Public nuisance is a crime.

❖ CASE EXAMPLES

Robinson v Kilvert (1889)

Defendant manufactured paper boxes in a cellar of a house, and leased the floor above to the plaintiff. Defendant heated the cellar with hot, dry air. This raised the temperature of the plaintiff's premises above which was used for storing brown paper, which (because of its special quality) lost its value. Plaintiff sued in nuisance. *Held*: that defendant was not liable. His heating of the premises would not have damaged ordinary brown paper, though it did damage the plaintiff's particularly sensitive paper.

Christie v Davey (1893)

C, a music teacher, used her house for frequent practice and musical evenings. *D*'s premises were separated by a party wall. *D* became exasperated with the playing and retaliated by knocking on the wall, beating trays, whistling and shrieking. *Held*: that the defendant acted maliciously and unreasonably and was liable. He purposely annoyed the plaintiff.

Baxter v Camden London Borough Council (1999)

The case was concerned with the issue as to whether the ordinary use of residential property can be actionable in nuisance (also landlord and tenant). Claimant rented a first-floor flat in a converted house owned by defendant council. The defendant's use and enjoyment of the flat was substantially affected by noise from flats above and below due to poor soundproofing, not the unreasonable behaviour by other tenants. *Held*: that no action lay in these circumstances, since 'the ordinary use of residential premises was not in itself capable of amounting to an actionable nuisance'.

St Helen's Smelting Co. v Tipping (1865)

Fumes from a factory injured the plaintiff's trees and shrubs. *Held*: that this was an actionable nuisance.

Hollywood Silver Fox Farm v Emmett (1936)

Plaintiff bred silver foxes on land where they erected a sign. Defendant owned an adjacent field. A dispute arose over the sign, and defendant sent his son to discharge a 12-bore shotgun near the plaintiff's land, which frightened the vixen, affected their breeding habits and caused them to miscarry their young. Plaintiff sued in nuisance. *Held*: that this was an actionable nuisance. Defendant's malicious motive rendered his actions a nuisance, and an injunction was granted to restrain him in future.

Adams v Ursell (1913)

A fried-fish shop was alleged to be a nuisance that caused the plaintiff's house to be permeated with the odour and vapour from the stoves. *Held*: that an injunction be granted. It was immaterial that the shop served a working-class area and supplied a public need.

Castle v St Augustine's Links (1922)

A taxi-cab driver, plaintiff, lost an eye when he was hit by a sliced golf ball. The golf links adjoined a road, and the golf hole was near it. *Held*: that there was a public nuisance.

Bolton v Stone (1951)

A cricket field was near a highway, and it was proven that only six or ten cricket balls during 35 years had been known to be hit into the road. No one had been previously injured until the plaintiff was struck by a ball. *Held*: that there was no nuisance.

Sturges v Bridgman (1879)

Defendant, a confectioner and baker in Wigmore Street, London, used a pestle and mortar for some 20 years on his premises. Plaintiff, a doctor, built consulting rooms in his garden next to the confectioner's premises. Noises and vibration interfered with plaintiff's practice, and, accordingly, he sued defendant in nuisance. *Held*: that although defendant could acquire a prescriptive right to create a nuisance, the nuisance in this case arose only when the doctor's consulting room was built.

8.9 Negligence

Negligence is one of the most important and common torts in the law. Although its origins are to be found in trespass and trespass on the case, the action was developed and formulated only in the nineteenth century; it now exists in its own right as a separate and independent tort.

In the law of tort, negligence may mean:

i a state of mind in which a particular tort may be committed, e.g. where *A* commits a trespass through inadvertence or carelessness; and
ii an independent tort. It is this aspect alone that will be dealt with in the following pages.

The claimant suing in negligence must prove three points to maintain a successful claim:

i that the defendant was under a *duty of care* to the plaintiff
ii that there had been a *breach* of that duty
iii that as a result the plaintiff has suffered damage

The duty of care. It has been said that a person may be as negligent as they please towards the whole world, if they owe no duty to it (*Le Lievre v Gould*, 1893). This is of course true, and it is good law. If, having given no one permission to be in my field and having no knowledge of any other person's presence, I enter my property, I can do what I like there. I can drive my tractor, shoot a rabbit and hit a golf ball anywhere I please. I owe no duty to anyone and I can be as negligent as I please.

Negligence is not a ground of liability unless the person whose conduct is impeached is under a duty of taking care (*Butler v Fife Coal Co. Ltd*, 1912). The important question we may ask is, when does such a duty of care arise in real life? There are, of course, many situations where one person owes a duty of care to another; the most common arise on the highways. All persons, whether driving motor cars, riding pedal cycles or merely walking as ordinary pedestrians, owe a duty of care to all other road users. Doctors owe a duty of care to patients; employers to work people; and teachers to students. The list is endless, and the forms of negligence and the situations in which the duty of care arises are varied. In *Harris v Perry* (2009) it was held, on appeal, that where a child was seriously injured on a bouncy castle, it was not reasonably foreseeable that physical injury would be likely to be serious, let alone as severe as the injury sustained by the claimant. However in *Sherrat v The Chief Constable of Great Manchester sub nom Beevers (Deceased), Re* (2018) it was held that the police owed a duty of care to the deceased from failing to follow up on a 999 call by a mother that her daughter might self-harm. 'The categories of negligence are never closed' (Lord Macmillan in *Donoghue v Stevenson*, 1932).

❖ CASE EXAMPLE

Donoghue v Stevenson (1932)

A friend of the plaintiff bought from a retailer a bottle of ginger beer manufactured by the defendant. The bottle was given to the plaintiff, who became ill from drinking the contents. The bottle contained the decomposed remains of a snail. The bottle was opaque so that the noxious substance could not have been seen and was not discovered until the plaintiff was refilling her glass. The consumer sued the manufacturer in negligence. *Held* (by the House of Lords): that the manufacturer was liable to the consumer in negligence.

The consumer had no cause of action in contract against either the retailer or the manufacturer, because it was not she but her friend who bought the bottle. In this most important case, Lord Atkin laid down a broad definition of the duty of care:

i 'You must take reasonable care to avoid acts or omissions which you can reasonably foresee would be likely to injure your neighbour.'

ii 'Who then is my neighbour? The answer seems to be persons who are so closely and directly affected by my act that I ought reasonably to have them in contemplation as being so affected when I am directing my mind to the acts or omissions which are called in question.'

(Lord Atkin in *Donoghue v Stevenson* (1932) AC 562, 580)

The rule enunciated has been applied to manufacturers of foodstuffs, clothing, hair-dyes and similar matters. *Recognized duties in law*. The list is not exhaustive.

i *Highway*. This duty of care for other users has already been mentioned. The duty of care applies to railways, shipping at sea and canal navigation. However, a common law duty of care does not apply to a highway authority to promote the safety of road users—*Stovin v Wise (Norfolk County Council Third Party)* (1996).

ii *Employers' liability*. An employer owes a duty of care to employees (*Pape v Cumbria CC*, 1992). He or she is expected to provide a reasonably safe system of work, reasonably safe machinery and competent fellow employees.

❖ CASE EXAMPLE

Pape v Cumbria CC (1992)

It was held that employers had not discharged their duty of care towards their employee cleaner, who contracted dermatitis, by the mere provision of rubber gloves. They should have instructed and encouraged her to wear the gloves at all times.

Under the **Employers' Liability (Compulsory Insurance) Act 1969**, an employer must insure against liability for bodily injury or disease sustained by his or her employees in the course of their employment. This applies even where the injury is caused by defective equipment supplied by a third party (**Employers' Liability (Defective Equipment) Act 1969**).

iii *Professional persons*. Doctors, surgeons, dentists, solicitors and similar professional persons owe a duty of care in the discharge of their duties to their patients, clients or other persons with whom they are in a professional relationship. In *Anns v LB of Merton* (1977), where a building inspector had passed defective foundations of a house, the House of Lords held that a local authority owes a duty of care in the application of its bye-laws to owners and occupiers who might suffer injury as a result of its negligence. However, it overruled this decision in *Murphy v Brentwood District Council* (1990), where it was held that a local authority was not liable in negligence to an owner or occupier of a building where the cost of remedying a dangerous defect resulted from the negligent failure of the local authority to carry out its statutory functions of control over building operations.

In *Carr-Glyn v Frearsons* (a firm) (1998), the court held that a solicitor owed a duty of care to a disappointed beneficiary who had suffered because of negligence.

iv *Carriers*. These owe a duty of care for the passengers and goods, whether fee-paying or not, independently of the contractual terms of their agreement to transport.

v *Schools*. A duty of care is owed to the children, and this duty is also owed to third parties injured by the children: *Carmarthenshire CC v Lewis* (1955).

vi *Police*. A duty of care owed to the general public, but not to an individual in respect of losses caused by their failure to apprehend a criminal: *Hill v Chief Constable of West Yorkshire* (1988).

As stated earlier, the categories are not closed. New categories are held to exist as the case law develops. The following cases are examples of this development.

❖ CASE EXAMPLES

Smoldon v Whitworth (1996)

S, a rugby player, was injured by an opposing player during a scrum in a match and W, the referee, had not taken a tight grip on the general lines to be expected of a reasonably competent referee. The referee was held to owe a duty of care to the players to protect them from the unnecessary and dangerous aspects of the game.

Margereson v J. W. Roberts Ltd; Hancock v J. W. Roberts Ltd (1996)

M's late husband and H played together as children in the loading bays of a factory where the level of asbestos contamination was very high, and, as adults, they developed mesothelioma. The company was held to have breached a duty of care as they ought to have reasonably foreseen a risk of pulmonary injury to the children.

However, the categories are not without limits, as seen in the case of *John Munroe (Acrylics) Ltd v London Fire and Civil Defence Authority* (1996), where it was held on the grounds of public policy that the fire brigade is not under a common law duty of care in carrying out its firefighting functions.

In *Khan v Meadows* (2021) the Supreme Court, in unanimously dismissing an appeal, confirmed that losses outside the scope of the duty of a doctor's care are not recoverable.

The standard of care. Granted a person in a given situation must use care to another; the question is what standard of care is he or she required in law to use? The answer here is that the standard of care is that of an ordinary prudent person. In other words, that care which a reasonable person would use or show in the circumstances of the particular case under consideration. The degree or amount of care (to be distinguished from the standard) is variable. For example, one is expected to take more care in handling a loaded gun than in handling a walking stick. Where serious consequences may follow from carelessness in a particular situation, the greater the degree of care that must be exercised. One expects a manufacturer of, or dealer in, explosives, poisons or drugs to manifest a high degree of care.

Where a person sets themselves up as possessing a particular skill, e.g. a surgeon, industrial chemist or accountant, they must exhibit in following their calling that skill which is usually found in such a person. A plumber, carpenter or labourer may not display the same amount of skill as a highly qualified heart specialist, but the same legal standard applies to both. The test to be applied is: What is reasonable in the circumstances of the case, having regard to the particular profession or occupation?

❖ CASE EXAMPLES

Dorset Yacht Co. Ltd v Home Office (1969)

Some boys escaped from a borstal institution, set adrift and damaged a motor yacht in Poole harbour. The Yacht Co. (owners) sued the Home Office as the Government department responsible for prisons and borstals. *Held*: that the Home Office was liable for damage done by persons who escaped from custody or while on parole if the escape was due to the negligence of prison or borstal officers.

Smith & Others v Littlewoods Organisation Ltd (1987)

Vandals started a fire in the defendant's empty building which damaged adjoining property. *Held*: occupier's duty did not extend to preventing deliberate acts of third-party vandals in these circumstances.

Yachuk v Oliver Blais Co. (1949)

A boy of 9 persuaded a garage attendant to let him have a tin of petrol by a false tale that his mother's car had run out of petrol some distance from the garage. The boy poured the petrol over some timber and then set it alight. The fire caused an explosion, and the boy was seriously injured. *Held* (by the Judicial Committee of the Privy Council): that it was negligence on the part of the garage attendant to entrust the child with such a dangerous commodity as petrol.

Dunnage v Randall and another (2016)

Randall was suffering from schizophrenia and, while visiting his nephew (the claimant), poured petrol over himself, causing him to die and leaving the claimant with serious burns. The claimant sought damages from his estate and household insurers. *Held*: Randall owed Dunnage a duty of care not to carelessly injure him despite his supposed lack of capacity and mental illness.

McLoughlin v O'Brian (1983)

One of the plaintiff's children was killed and her husband and two other children were badly injured in a road accident caused by the defendant's negligence. The plaintiff was at home two miles away when she was informed of the accident and taken to the hospital, where she saw the injured members of her family and heard her daughter had been killed. She suffered severe nervous shock. The House of Lords extended the doctrine of nervous shock, holding that her injury was foreseeable by the defendant, who owed her a duty of care, and was liable.

Note: Decision extended to shock of seeing damage caused to own property (*Attia v British Gas plc*, 1987) but not to seeing simultaneous television pictures of persons suffering death or injury at a football match (*Alcock v Chief Constable of South Yorkshire Police*, 1991). Neither did it apply to the police officers who suffered psychiatric injury while they were on duty and carried out rescue work arising from the same football match (*White v Chief Constable of South Yorkshire Police*, 1999).

Brice v Brown (1984)

Mother was alarmed by injuries to her daughter when both were passengers in a taxi involved in a collision caused by the negligence of the defendant. *Held*: defendant liable in negligence for the mother's resulting mental illness.

Paul and Anor v Royal Wolverhampton NHS Trust (2024)

The claimants were two children aged 9 and 12, the daughters of a Mr Paul, who were present when he suffered a cardiac arrest and died in distressing circumstances. They claimed that as a result of witnessing the shocking circumstances of their father's death, they had suffered psychiatric illness and claimed damages for this outcome. *Held*: (Supreme Court) that a duty of care was not owed by physicians to their patients' family members in order to prevent them from suffering harm as a result of witnessing the death, caused by medical negligence of their relative (father). Note: The court also found that psychiatric harm should not be treated any differently from physical harm in tort law. This decision has obviously raised questions regarding decisions in previous cases of a similar kind, meaning that it will be difficult for claims by secondary victim onlookers in future cases, in that they cannot generally recover damages in cases of clinical negligence unless very specific criteria apply.

Negligent misstatement. Formerly the general rule was that a person was liable for negligent acts but not for negligent words. Where, therefore, a negligent statement was made even though it was intended to be acted on by the claimant, previously designated as the plaintiff, and was, in fact, acted on by them to their loss, no liability fell on the defendant.

We must distinguish *fraudulent misrepresentations* that give rise to an action of deceit (cf. *Derry v Peek*, 1889) from *negligent misstatements*.

In *Candler v Crane, Christmas & Co.* (1951), it was held that an accountant who negligently prepared certain accounts for a particular transaction was under no liability in tort in respect of those accounts, even though a claimant in reliance on the accounts invested money in a company and suffered financial injury as a consequence.

This case was overruled by the following:

❖ CASE EXAMPLE

Hedley Byrne & Co. Ltd v Heller & Partners Ltd (1964)

H. B. contacted *A*'s bankers, H. & P. (defendants), for references. H. & P. gave a favourable report of *A*'s creditworthiness. H. & P. headed the document 'Without Responsibility'. H. B. acted on the misleading report, gave substantial credit and suffered a heavy loss when *A* went into liquidation shortly after. H. B. sued H. & P. in negligence. *Held* (House of Lords): the defendant bankers (H. & P.) would have been liable in negligence had they not expressly disclaimed liability.

> Where in a sphere in which a person is so placed that others could reasonably rely on his judgment or his skill or on his ability to make careful inquiry, a person takes it on himself to give information or advice to, or allows his information or advice to be passed on to, another, who, as he knows or should know, will place reliance on it, then a duty of care will arise.
>
> (per Lord Morris)

In *Caparo Industries plc v Dickman and Others* (1990), the House of Lords held that the auditors of a company's accounts did not owe a duty of care in negligence to either a shareholder or potential shareholder.

Since the **Unfair Contract Terms Act 1977** (which, despite its name, also affects the law of torts), the 'without responsibility' clause will only be effective if it is 'reasonable' having regard to all the circumstances.

In *Clay v A.J. Crump & Sons* (1963), an architect inspected a site in the course of demolition and negligently stated that a particular wall was safe and could be left. However, the wall collapsed, injuring a labourer. It was held that the architect was liable for his negligent statement.

In *Arthur J.S. Hall & Co. (a firm) v Simons* (2000), the House of Lords abolished the long-standing immunity from negligence claims that had been enjoyed by advocates in respect of the conduct of both civil and criminal proceedings.

Res ipsa loquitur. Where the duty is so plain as to admit of no denial, the presumption that failure in performance indicates fault is expressed by the maxim *res ipsa loquitur* ('the thing speaks for itself').

As a general rule, the claimant, previously designated as the plaintiff, must prove that the defendant has by their act or omission been negligent in the discharge of a legal duty owed to the plaintiff.

There must be reasonable evidence of negligence, but where the thing is shown to be under the management of the defendant or their servants, and the accident is one that in the ordinary course of things does not happen if those who have the management use proper care, it affords reasonable evidence, in the absence of explanation by the defendant, that the accident arose from want of care (*Scott v London and St. Katherine's Docks Co.*, 1865). If the defendant produces a reasonable explanation, equally consistent with negligence or no negligence, the burden of proof of negligence remains with the plaintiff. The presumption is one of fact, not law.

Similar examples of *res ipsa loquitur* are found in the following cases. A pedestrian was knocked down by a car that mounted the pavement and struck him from behind (*McGowan v Scott*, 1923); two trains collided on the same railway line (*Skinner v L.B. & S.C. Rly*, 1850); excess sulphites were present in underwear, causing claimant dermatitis (*Grant v Australian Knitting Mills*, 1936); collapse of scaffolding (*Kealey v Heard*, 1983). Although in *Mahon v Osborne* (1939) it was said the doctrine could not apply to surgical cases, the modern trend is to allow it (*Cassidy v Ministry of Health*, 1951).

❖ **CASE EXAMPLE**

***Byrne v Boadle* (1863)**

A barrel of flour fell from an open door on an upper floor of the defendant's warehouse, injuring a passerby in the street. *Held*: that this was evidence to go to the jury without further explanation. Barrels that are properly handled do not generally so fall, and a jury might reasonably infer negligence on the part of the defendant.

8.9.1 Contributory negligence

Before 1945 a defendant could escape liability by showing that the accident would not have happened had not the claimant contributed to it by their own negligence. This common-law rule was altered, and the present law is contained in the **Law Reform (Contributory Negligence) Act 1945**, which adopts the principle applied in regard to collisions of ships at sea. Section 1(1) of the Act provides that:

> Where any person suffers damage as a result partly of his or her own fault and partly of the fault of any other person or persons, a claim in respect of that damage shall not be defeated by reason of the fault of the person suffering the damage, but the damages recoverable in respect thereof shall be reduced to such extent as the court thinks just and equitable having regard to the claimant's share in the responsibility for the damage.

So that in *Platform Home Loans Ltd v Oyston Shipways Ltd and Others* (1999) the court held that where defendant valuers had been negligent in their valuation, the damages should be reduced by 20 per cent due to the claimant's imprudent lending policy.

To take a simple illustration, let us suppose that X is a pedestrian who negligently walks into the path of a car driven carelessly along the road by Y. X claims damages for injuries sustained to the extent of £6,000 from Y. The court may find that X was one-third to blame for the accident. Accordingly, damages may be awarded of £4,000 (i.e. £6,000 less one-third).

Doctrine of novus actus interveniens. A *novus actus interveniens* (a new act intervening) occurs when some act of a third person intervenes between the wrongful act or omission of the defendant and the subsequent damage to the claimant.

In this type of case it is for the court to decide whether the new act ought reasonably to have been foreseen by the defendant. If it ought to have been foreseen the defendant remains liable. Thus in *Scott v Shepherd* (1773), *A* lit a squib at a market fair and threw it onto *B*'s stall. *B* threw it away to *C*'s stall, and *C* threw the squib to *D*'s stall, where the squib exploded, injuring *D*. *Held*: *A* was liable to *D*. The chain of causation was not broken by the actions of B and C.

If the defendant could not foresee the intervening actions, the originator(s) of the *novus actus may* be liable, and the defendant's act or omission will not be treated as the cause of the damage.

Where a person is placed in imminent personal danger by the negligence of another, any unwise act they do in 'the agony of the moment' (as it is put) is not treated as contributory negligence. There is a qualification that the person so acting imprudently should show as much judgment and control as can reasonably be expected in the unusual and dangerous circumstances. This is sometimes referred to as the doctrine of alternative danger.

For example, a motor-coach being driven negligently gets out of control going down a hill. A passenger, realizing the situation, decides to jump from the coach as it moves on and is injured in the fall. The coach subsequently comes to rest safely. The passenger is not debarred from his or her claim against the driver of the coach merely because, had he or she (the passenger) remained seated, no harm would have come to them. In such circumstances the passenger is not contributorily negligent for acting on the spur of the moment in a difficult situation.

❖ CASE EXAMPLES

Sayers v Harlow UDC (1958)

The plaintiff, a woman, entered a public lavatory owned and operated by the defendants. Owing to a defective lock without a handle, she could not get out of the cubicle. Her bus was due to leave, and she tried to climb over the door. She placed her foot on a revolving toilet roll, fell to the ground and injured herself. She sued the local authority. *Held*: (i) that the defendants were negligent and (ii) that plaintiff herself was guilty of contributory negligence in trying to balance on a revolving object. Her claim would be reduced by one-quarter.

Froom and others v Butcher (1976)

B drove a car negligently on a road and collided with F's car, injuring the driver, F, who was not wearing a seat belt. The accident was *solely* caused by B. *Held*: (CA): F's claim for damages was reduced by 25 per cent, because F was contributorily negligent in not wearing the seat belt.

Jones v Boyce (1816)

A horse-drawn coach got out of control going down a hill due to the defendant's negligence. A passenger (plaintiff) feared the coach would overturn, jumped and was injured. *Held*: that plaintiff was not guilty of contributory negligence.

O'Connell v Jackson (1971)

A rode a moped and had no crash helmet. B negligently collided with *A*, who received severe head injuries. *Held*: although the accident was caused by B, the absence of a crash helmet was a contributory causative factor in the damages. *A*'s claim was reduced.

Vernon v Bosley (1996)

B was the nanny of *V*'s two children. She had a car accident and crashed into a river. *V* arrived at the scene and watched the unsuccessful attempts to rescue his children, who both died, and he suffered severe trauma as a result. B argued his suffering was from grief and would have occurred whether or not he saw the accident, but the court held that the plaintiff could recover damages for nervous shock, notwithstanding that the nervous shock and post-traumatic stress disorder were also a pathological consequence of the bereavement suffered by him.

8.10 Breach of statutory duty

A claimant, previously designated as the plaintiff, may have a right of action in tort as the result of a breach of duty imposed by a statute: originally most breach of statutory duty claims arose out of industrial injuries (e.g. under the **Mines and Quarries Act 1954** and the **Factories Act 1961**). Provisions under the **Health and Safety at Work Act 1974** and health and safety regulations of general application are gradually repealing statutory provisions applicable to particular industries. The focus is upon the type of process involved, rather than the trade in which that process is carried out. For example, the **Provision and Use of Work Equipment Regulations 1992** repealed the **Factories Act 1961** ss. 12–17 and the **Mines and Quarries Act 1954**, ss. 81(1), 82.

8.11 Death: survival of actions

At common law the general rule known as *actio personalis moritur cum persona* ('a personal action dies with the person') applied. Thus, if an injury were done either to the person or property of another for which damages were the only remedy, the action died with the person to whom (the would-be claimant) or by whom (the would-be defendant) the wrong was done. If *A* negligently drove a car and knocked down a pedestrian (B) walking along a footpath, and either *A* or B died before action was brought, the claim died too.

The common-law rule was mitigated to some extent by the **Fatal Accidents Act 1846**, under which certain dependants of the deceased may recover damages from a tortfeasor responsible for the death, if the dependants can show that they have suffered financial loss. The **Fatal Accidents Act 1976** (as amended by the **Administration of Justice Act 1982**), consolidates the law. The following points should be noted:

a The specified class of relatives who may sue are: (i) wife, husband, former spouse or any person who at the deceased's death and for at least two years before had lived with the deceased as his or her husband or wife, (ii) children including posthumous, illegitimate, stepchildren or those treated by the deceased as a child of his or her family, (iii) grandchildren, (iv) parents, step-parents or treated by the deceased as his or her parent, (v) grandparents, (vi) brothers and sisters and their issue and (vii) uncles and aunts and their issue.
b The claimant must show that the death was caused by the wrongful act, neglect or default of the defendant. Non-tortious acts will not qualify.
c The claimant must have suffered some 'actual pecuniary loss' (this term includes reasonable probability of financial benefit) and the loss must arise out of the death of 'the breadwinner'.
d Action must be brought by the deceased's personal representatives on behalf of the claimant relative(s).
e Action must be commenced within three years of the death.

The old common-law rule referred to in the preceding list was fundamentally altered by the **Law Reform (Miscellaneous Provisions) Act 1934**, as amended by section 4 of the **Law Reform (Limitation of Actions) Act 1954**. The 1934 Act provided that on the death of any person, 'all causes of action subsisting against or vested in him or her shall survive against, or, as the case may be, for the benefit of, his or her estate'. The following points are relevant here:

a Actions in defamation do not survive.
b The cause of action must exist at the time of death.
c Damages may be recovered for (i) pain and suffering, (ii) loss of earnings (during the period between the injury and the death) and (iii) medical and hospital expenses. The **Administration of Justice Act 1982** abolished loss of 'expectation of life' as a separate head of general damages but the knowledge of such reduction is to be taken into account in assessing damages in respect of pain and suffering.
d Exemplary damages cannot be awarded in favour of the deceased plaintiff's estate.
e Funeral expenses may be recovered if not already recovered under the **Fatal Accidents Act**.
f The following special periods of limitation apply:

    i If the tortfeasor dies, no action may be brought against the estate unless either the proceedings were pending at the date of death, or proceedings are begun not later than six months after personal representatives have taken out representation. (Unless this rule were made, the personal representatives would never be able to wind up the estate.)
    ii If the injured (i.e. aggrieved) person dies, there is no special period of limitation; the ordinary rules apply in such a case.

However, in *Knaver v Ministry of Justice* (2016) the Supreme Court *Held*: that the correct date to assess the multiplier when assessing damages for future loss in claims under the Act should be the date of trial and not the date of death.

❖ CASE EXAMPLES

Reeves v Commissioner of Police of the Metropolis (1999)

A Mr Lynch hanged himself while in custody due to the negligence of police who knew he was a suicide risk. *Held*: police were liable to partner in accordance with the **Fatal Accidents Act 1976**, but damages were reduced by one half on the grounds of contributory negligence by the deceased.

Daley v National Trust (2001)

Claimant's husband drowned while swimming in a pool at Hardwick Hall owned by the National Trust. An inconspicuous notice warned of the danger of catching 'Well's disease' from swimming in the pool. Claimant argued failure of National Trust to place notices was a breach of common-law duty under s. 2 of the Act. *Held*: No breach by the National Trust. No special or hidden dangers under the Act.

8.12 Occupiers' liability

Before 1957 at common law the liability of an occupier to a person coming on to his or her premises depended on the category in which the entrant fell, i.e. whether as an *invitee* or a *licensee*, and the **Occupiers' Liability Act 1957** was passed to simplify the position.

The Act abolished the distinctions between the categories and the varied duties of care applicable to each. The Act now establishes one category of persons, namely that of *visitor*. A visitor is anyone who has express or implied permission to be on the property, e.g. a guest at dinner, a postman, a shopper and so on. Section 1 of the **Occupiers' Liability Act 1984** has introduced statutory rules for the safety of persons outside the scope of the 1957 Act.

❖ CASE EXAMPLES

Staples v West Dorset District Council (1995)

Defendants occupied a sea wall known as 'the Cobb' at Lyme Regis, which was covered in seaweed and algae and obviously very slippery. Plaintiff slipped on algae and suffered serious injuries as a result of the accident. Plaintiff stated that he noticed that the algae was slimy and wet and could foresee that this could be slippery. *Held*: Defendants not liable. The duty owed to the plaintiff by the defendants under the **Occupiers' Liability Act 1957** was a duty to warn the visitor as to the extent of a risk that he was unaware. However, the plaintiff had acknowledged he was aware of the risk.

English Heritage v Taylor (2016)

Claimant sustained a serious head injury after falling over a sheer drop while on a day out with his grandchildren at Carrisbrooke Castle. *Held*: Claimant's injury was caused by the defendant's breach of s. 2 of the Act in failing to warn visitors by means of a sign of the danger which gave rise to the accident. However, the claimant was 50 per cent to blame on the basis of contributory negligence.

8.12.1 Dangerous premises

Section 2 of the **Occupiers' Liability Act 1957** provides as follows:

a An occupier of premises owes the same duty, the 'common duty of care', to all his or her visitors, except in so far as he or she is free to and does extend, restrict, modify or exclude his or her duty to any visitor by agreement or otherwise. (This section allows, therefore, an occupier to contract with a visitor to absolve themselves from liability.)

b The 'common duty of care' is a duty to take such care as, in all the circumstances of the case, is reasonable to see that the visitor will be reasonably safe in using the premises for the purpose for which they are invited or permitted by the occupier to be there.

c The circumstances relevant for the present purpose include the degree of care and want of care, which would ordinarily be looked for in such a visitor. For example:

  i an occupier must be prepared for children to be less careful than adults; and

  ii an occupier may expect that a person, in the exercise of their calling, will appreciate and guard against any special risks ordinarily incident to it, so far as the occupier leaves them free to do so.

d In determining whether the occupier of premises has discharged the common duty of care to a visitor, regard is to be had to all the circumstances. For example:

  i where damage is caused to a visitor by a danger of which they had been warned by the occupier, the warning is not to be treated as absolving the occupier from liability, unless in all circumstances it was enough to enable the visitor to be reasonably safe; and

  ii where damage is caused to a visitor by a danger due to the faulty execution of any work of construction, maintenance or repair by an independent contractor employed by the occupier, the occupier is not to be treated as answerable for the danger if in all the circumstances they have acted reasonably in entrusting the work to an independent contractor and has taken such steps (if any) as they reasonably ought in order to satisfy themselves that the contractor was competent and that the work had been properly done.

e The 'common duty of care' does not impose on an occupier any obligation to a visitor in respect of risks willingly accepted by the visitor.

f Persons who enter premises for any purpose in the exercise of a right conferred by law are to be treated by the occupier to be there for that purpose, whether they in fact have his or her permission or not.

For example, a police officer may enter premises under the authority of a search warrant; the 'common duty of care' is owed to him or her while he or she is so exercising the right conferred by law.

Defences. The following defences deserve note:

i that the occupier warned the visitor (see previous paragraph (d) (i))

ii that the claimant, previously designated as the plaintiff consented, *volenti non fit injuria* (see preceding paragraph (e))

iii that the occupier employed a competent independent contractor (see preceding paragraph (d) (ii))

❖ **CASE EXAMPLE**

***O'Connor v Swan & Edgar and Carmichael Contractors* (1963)**

Plaintiff was working as a demonstrator in a store when part of the ceiling fell and injured her. Plaintiff sued the store owners (as first defendants) and the plasterers (independent contractors employed by first defendants). *Held*: that first defendants (store owners) were not liable; second defendants (plasterers) were liable since they had been guilty of faulty workmanship in plastering the ceiling.

Under the **Defective Premises Act 1972**, the builder, the specialist subcontractor, the developer and the professional people involved come under a non-excludable statutory duty of care in respect of new houses towards the purchaser and their successors in title, unless the National House Builders Registration Council scheme, or a similar scheme of protection, applies.

8.12.2 Trespassers

A trespasser has been defined as 'one who goes on to the land without any invitation of any sort and whose presence is either unknown to the proprietor, or, if known, is practically objected to' (*Addie and Sons v Dumbreck*, 1929).

A burglar or a poacher is clearly a trespasser, but difficulties can arise in borderline cases, e.g. hawkers or canvassers, unless there is a notice specifically excluding them.

The general rule is that an occupier of premises owes no active duty to trespassers. A trespasser enters the property of another at their own risk. Where, however, a trespasser is known to be present, an occupier may not inflict damage on them recklessly or intentionally. An occupier may not create dangers intentionally to injure a trespasser. Thus, they may not set spring guns (*Bird v Holbrook*, 1828), though it is possible to take defensive measures, such as covering the tops of high walls with broken glass.

8.12.3 Children

The general rules as to trespass apply to children. There are, however, some special points that should be noted.

a An occupier must be prepared for the fact that children are less careful than adults.
b What may be a warning to an adult may not be so to a child.
c If with the knowledge of child trespassers on their land, the occupier makes no attempt to prevent recurrence of the trespass, e.g. by repairing fences, such inactivity might be evidence of implied permission, in which case the child may qualify as a 'visitor'.
d Where a child is lawfully on land and there is something on the land that acts as an 'allurement' to a child, e.g. machinery or attractive poisonous berries, the occupier may be liable even though the child is a trespasser so far as the allurement itself is concerned.

As to (d), an occupier of land is entitled to assume that young children will be in the charge of competent adults. In *Phipps v Rochester Corporation* (1955), where a boy aged 5, who was accompanied by his sister aged 7, fell into a hole and broke his leg, it was held that the responsibility for the safety of young children rests primarily with their parents.

❖ CASE EXAMPLES

British Railways Board v Herrington (1972)

H, aged 6, trespassed through a defective fence adjoining an electrified railway line and was badly injured. H sued the Board in negligence for permitting the fence to be in a dilapidated condition. The Board knew previous trespasses had occurred. *Held* (House of Lords): the Board was liable. An occupier's liability to a child trespasser depends on what a conscientious, humane man (with his knowledge, skill and resources) could reasonably have been expected to have done or refrained from doing that would have avoided the accident. A poor person would often be excused where a large organization would not (per Lord Reid).

Cooke v Midland Great Western Railway of Ireland (1909)

Defendants kept a turntable on their land near a public road. To the knowledge of the defendants, children habitually came onto the land and played with the turntable. Defendants took no effective steps to prevent them from doing so. A child aged 4 injured himself on the turntable. *Held*: that there was sufficient evidence to find the defendants liable. As they had acquiesced in the trespasses by the children, the particular child was in the position of a visitor, and to him the turntable was an allurement.

Glasgow Corporation v Taylor (1922)

A child, 7 years of age, picked some attractive, but poisonous, berries growing on a shrub in a public park controlled by Glasgow Corporation. The child died after eating the berries. Defendants (the corporation) knew the berries were poisonous and that children went to the park, but they had done nothing to give an effective warning, intelligible to children, of their danger. *Held*: that the corporation was liable in an action by the child's parent; the berries constituted an allurement.

8.13 The rule in *Rylands v Fletcher* (1868)

> A person who for his own purposes brings on his lands and collects and keeps there anything likely to do mischief if it escapes, must keep it in at his peril, and, if he does not do so, is prima facie answerable for all the damage which is the natural consequence of its escape.
>
> (Per Blackburn J in the Court of Exchequer Chamber)

The circumstances of the case were that the defendant employed independent contractors to construct a reservoir on his land and to use the water power for his mill. In the course of construction the contractors came across some disused mine-shafts and passages filled with earth and marl that, unknown to defendant and the independent contractors, communicated with the claimant's mines. When the reservoir was filled, the water escaped through the shafts and flooded the claimant's mine. It was found as a fact that the defendant had not been negligent. Nevertheless the defendant was held liable, first by the Court of Exchequer Chamber and second on appeal to

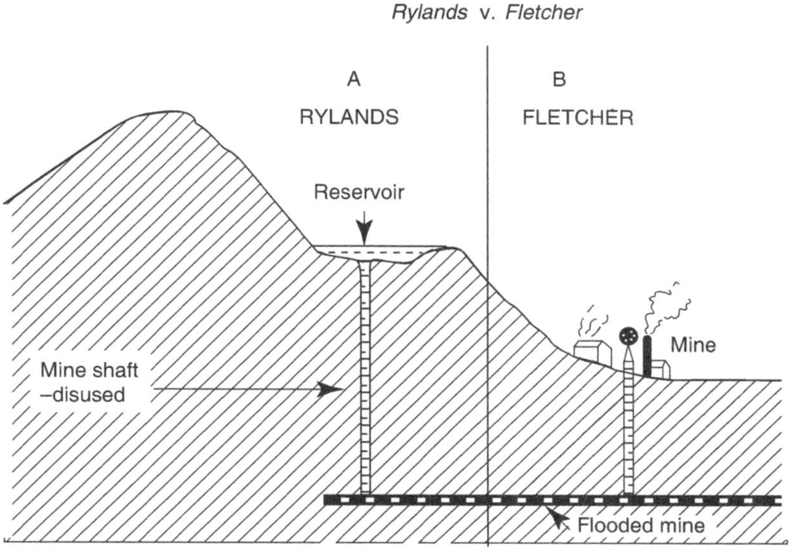

FIGURE 8.1 *Rylands v Fletcher*

the House of Lords, where the judgment was confirmed but the rule was restricted to damage due to a non-natural user of the land.

Note: The original action was brought by *Fletcher* (the mine owner) against *Rylands* (the mill owner), the names being reversed on appeal.

The rule is one of strict liability, i.e. the defendant is liable independently of wrongful intent or negligence. The rule in *Rylands v Fletcher* was reconsidered by the House of Lords in the following case:

> The rule has been applied to various kinds of 'escape', for example: electricity (*National Telephone Co. v Baker* (1893)), yew trees (*Crowhurst v Amersham Burial Board*, 1878), wire fencing (*Firth v Bowling Iron Co.*, 1878), sewage (*Jones v Llanrwst UDC*, 1911), and explosives (*Rainham Chemical Works v Belvedere Fish Guano Co.*, 1921).

The tort is not actionable per se; some damage must be proved to sustain a successful claim.

There are several important points to observe in the rule. One is that the defendant is liable notwithstanding their employment of a competent independent contractor, and whether or not there is any default by the contractor.

❖ CASE EXAMPLES

Cambridge Water Co. Ltd v Eastern Counties Leather plc (1994)

In this case the court held that a prerequisite of liability was foreseeability by the defendant of the relevant type of damage in the event of an escape. It stated that the rule in *Rylands v Fletcher* was a rule of strict liability in the sense that the defendant could be liable notwithstanding the lack of negligence in 'allowing' the escape.

Northumbrian Water Ltd v McAlpine Ltd (2014)

The defendants, McAlpine, a construction company, were redeveloping a site in Newcastle's town centre, which required large foundations to be sunk. During these excavations, a private sewer not shown on any public plan (only on a 1908 plan in the Newcastle Discovery Museum) was breached and concrete ran through that gap into Northumbrian Water Company's public sewers, causing extensive damage. *Held*: no actionable nuisance. Redevelopment of an urban city centre was a reasonable and normal use of the land. In this case the defendant was not engaged in any unusual methods of piledriving when constructing a new building in the city. There was no claim in negligence either. Further the claim had been based on *Rylands v Fletcher*. Neither was the escape of concrete foreseeable in the sense used in *The Wagon Mound (No. 2)* (1967).

Where the subcontractor of a contractor employed by a property owner is negligent in the performance of works involving inherently dangerous operations, only the ultimate employer and the subcontractor have (coexistent) liability for the negligent performance of those works.

Further, there must be an actual 'escape' or leakage from the defendant's land of the dangerous or harmful thing, and the dangerous thing must move from the defendant's land to the plaintiff's.

Things 'naturally on land' include thistles, insects, rats (unless their numbers increased as a result of defendant's acts or omissions) or rocks (when these crumble and fall naturally there is no liability on the defendant, though it would be otherwise if the fall were due to negligent quarrying or if increased falls resulted from quarrying). Liability for such things may, however, be actionable in nuisance or trespass. Many things are brought onto land by landowners, and the question arises as to whether their introduction and use amounts to 'non-natural usage'. Natural usage includes the working of mines and the planting of trees, though if these are poisonous and they escape, the defendant will be liable. The storage of water in quantities and the storage of electricity have been held as non-natural.

Defences. The defences to this tort are:

i *Act of God*. The defendant may evade liability if they can prove that there was an escape due to what is described as an Act of God, e.g. extraordinary rainfall that could not reasonably have been anticipated (*Nichols v Marsland*, 1876).

ii *Act of a stranger*. The defendant can evade liability if they can prove that the escape was due to the unlawful act of a third party ('stranger') over whom the defendant had no control (*Rickards v Lothian*, 1913).

iii *Default of claimant*. If the escape from the dangerous thing was caused by the default of the claimant.

iv *Consent of claimant*. Where the claimant voluntarily consented to the presence or existence on the defendant's land of the dangerous thing or source of the mischief. For example, fire extinguishers, water pipes or water cisterns in a block of flats. Common benefit is evidence of consent.

v *Statutory Authority*. A local authority or public-utility corporation may escape liability if the terms of the statute are clear (*Green v Chelsea Waterworks Co.*, 1894). This does not apply to the escape of water from reservoirs (**Reservoirs Act 1975**).

❖ CASE EXAMPLES

Rickards v Lothian (1913)

R, the lessee of a building, sublet the second floor to L. A third person unknown blocked the waste pipes of a washbasin on the fourth floor (which was in R's control) and turned the tap on. L's stock on the second floor was damaged by the overflow of water. *Held*: that R was not liable since the damage was due to the act of a stranger which R could not reasonably have prevented.

Home Brewery Co. Ltd v William Davis & Co. (Leicester) Ltd (1987)

Defendants filled in a clay pit, which caused water to percolate onto the plaintiff's land and also temporary flooding. *Held*: *Rylands v Fletcher* did not apply as there was no escape and the defendants were liable either in trespass or nuisance for temporary flooding.

Peters v Prince of Wales Theatres Ltd (1943)

Defendants leased to P a shop in a building used as a theatre. The theatre, with knowledge of P, contained a water-sprinkler system against fire risk, the system extending to P's shop. During a frost, water poured from the system, damaging P's stock. P claimed damages under *Rylands v Fletcher*. *Held*: that the water-sprinkler system had been installed for the common benefit of plaintiff and defendant; the rule in *Rylands v Fletcher* did not apply; and, as there was no negligence on the part of defendant, there was no liability under that head.

Green v Chelsea Waterworks Co. (1894)

Defendants were authorized by statute to lay a water main. The main burst and flooded the plaintiff's premises. *Held*: that statutory authority precluded liability under *Rylands v Fletcher*; and as there was no negligence on the part of the defendants, they were not liable.

Crowhurst v Amersham Burial Board (1878)

Yew trees were planted by the defendants on the boundaries of their land. The yew-tree branches protruded over the land occupied by the plaintiff. The plaintiff's horse ate some leaves and was poisoned and died. *Held*: that defendants were liable, for it was a non-natural use of land to plant such poisonous trees, and the branches had 'escaped' into plaintiff's field.

Read v Lyons (1947)

Plaintiff was an inspector of the Ministry of Supply and was injured by an explosion in defendant's munition factory while she was carrying out her duties. The plaintiff was unable to prove negligence by the defendants, but she alleged that they were liable under the rule of *Rylands v Fletcher*. *Held* (by the House of Lords): that there had been no escape sufficient to render the defendant liable under the rule. The House gave the opinion (not part of the decision) that the making of munitions in wartime was a natural usage of land.

Giles v Walker (1890)

The occupier of land ploughed it up, and shortly afterwards a large crop of thistles grew up. As a consequence, thistle seeds were blown onto the land of neighbours.

Held: that the rule of *Rylands v Fletcher* did not apply. The defendant had not brought the thistles onto his land, for they had accumulated there naturally. (The case has been overruled in *Leakey v National Trust* (1980) on the ground that there would now be liability in nuisance.)

8.14 Defamation

Defamation is the publication of a statement that exposes a person to hatred, ridicule or contempt or causes them to be shunned or avoided by right-thinking members of society generally. In other words it is a 'false statement about a person to their discredit'.

There are two classes of defamation: (i) *libel*, which is a statement made in *permanent* form and (ii) *slander*, which is a statement in *transitory* form.

The permanent form, as far as libel is concerned, may be in a written or printed statement, an effigy, a statue, a caricature or a film. Section 1 of the **Defamation Act 1952** made defamation by broadcasting (radio and television) libel, not slander. A talking film was held to be libel in *Youssoupoff v Metro Goldwyn Mayer Ltd* (1934).

The transitory form, as far as slander is concerned, is usually by speech or gesture.

Two further distinctions may be drawn. Libel, if it tends to a breach of the peace, is a crime. Slander, as such, is not a crime.

Third, libel is actionable per se, i.e. on mere publication, and the claimant need not show that any pecuniary loss has been suffered following the libel. In slander the claimant must prove actual damage (i.e. financial loss) except in the following cases:

i imputation of any crime that is punishable by imprisonment
ii imputation that the claimant is suffering from a contagious disease rendering the person so infected liable to be excluded from society, e.g. venereal disease
iii imputation of unchastity in a woman (**Slander of Women Act 1891**). This includes lesbianism (*Kerr v Kennedy*, 1942)
iv imputation of unfitness for any office, profession, calling, trade or business held or carried on by the claimant at the time of the publication (*Defamation Act* 1952). Thus, it is defamatory to say of a solicitor that they know no law or of a carpenter that they cannot make a simple joint

In a trial the question whether the statement is defamatory or is one of fact is to be decided by the jury. As a matter of practice and law, however, the judge first decides whether the statement is *capable* of being defamatory, i.e. whether a reasonable person could take such a view; it is for the jury to say whether the statement is *in fact* defamatory.

Proof of defamation. In a successful claim in defamation the claimant must prove four points:

i that the statement was defamatory
ii that the statement referred to him or her
iii that the statement was published
iv that damage was suffered (in slander, outside the four exceptions)

Defamatory statement. The variety of the forms of defamation can be gleaned from the definition appearing at the head of this section. Moreover, a study of the examples that follow will assist in grasping how the law is applied in the particular circumstances of each individual case.

One special form of defamation that needs particular mention is *innuendo*. Although words may not on the face of them appear defamatory, they may nevertheless be such by reason of peculiar surrounding circumstances or facts, or because a special meaning is attributable to them. There is, we may say, a hidden meaning or implication, possibly more telling and harmful in its effect than a bold and obvious statement. In such cases, the plaintiff who alleges defamation by innuendo must show that the facts were known to the person to whom the defamatory statement was made, and that reasonable persons would interpret the words used as defamatory. To say '*A* drinks a lot' is ambiguous: it may be a harmless statement, or it may insinuate that *A* is a heavy drinker of intoxicants and may, in certain circumstances, be defamatory.

❖ CASE EXAMPLES

Cassidy v Daily Mirror Newspapers Ltd (1929)

A newspaper published a photograph of a man and a woman. Underneath appeared the words 'Mr C and Miss B whose engagement has been announced'. Mr C was already married to Mrs C, and the latter sued the newspaper proprietors, alleging that the words imputed 'by innuendo' that she was immorally cohabiting with Mr C and that several friends thought this to be the case. *Held*: that the plaintiff should be awarded £500 damages, although the defendants acted quite innocently.

Tolley v Fry (1931)

Defendants, chocolate manufacturers, published without the plaintiff's consent an advertisement that showed the plaintiff, a golfer, with a packet of their chocolate in his pocket. Plaintiff alleged an innuendo that he had prostituted his amateur golf status. *Held*: that defamation was proved; damages were awarded to the plaintiff.

Reference to claimant. The claimant must prove that he or she was the person marked out by the words, i.e. identified. Nevertheless, they need not be the person to whom the defendant intended to refer. The question to be asked is: Would a reasonably minded person who knew the claimant connect the defamatory statement with them?

It follows from what has been stated that a *class* of persons cannot as such be defamed. To say 'All lawyers are rogues who fleece the public' or 'All priests are immoral and dishonest' is not defamatory.

❖ CASE EXAMPLES

Hulton v Jones (1910)

A newspaper article contained words that defamed one Artemus Jones, who was intended to be a fictional character in a fanciful sketch of life in Dieppe. Artemus Jones was described as a churchwarden at Peckham. Unfortunately, the name Artemus Jones was also that of an English barrister and journalist. Evidence was adduced that those who knew him thought the article referred to the barrister and journalist. *Held*: that the newspaper was responsible for the libel. Damages were awarded to the respondent, Jones.

Newstead v London Express Newspaper, Ltd (1940)

Defendants published in their newspaper a report of the trial and conviction of bigamy of one 'Harold Newstead, a thirty-year-old Camberwell man'. The account was true of a barman of that name. But it so happened that there was also another man, Harold Newstead, 30 years old, and living in Camberwell. The latter sued the defendants. *Held*: that plaintiff was entitled to damages.

Publication consists of making known in writing, orally or in another form, to some person other than the claimant. If *A* orally tells B that B is a thief or a rogue, this is not actionable. If C is present and overhears the remark, there is publication to C. Where *A* authorizes another, say B, to make a defamatory statement, *A* is liable. Moreover *A* will be liable if the likelihood of a publication, which had been initiated by *A* could have reasonably been foreseen.

Where a postcard is sent through the post, there is a 'publication'. The presumption is that a postcard is likely to be read by post office staff. However, it was accepted that this rule does not apply to a letter, either sealed or unsealed, for it cannot reasonably be foreseen that someone other than the addressee will open it and read the contents. However, in *Theakery v Richardson* (1962), the defendant wrote to the plaintiff accusing her of being a 'very dirty whore and low down brothel keeping whore and thief'. He put it in an envelope on which he typed the plaintiff's name and put it through her letter box. Her husband, thinking that it was an election address, opened it. *Held*: a jury, allowing her claim and awarding her £500 damages, found that it was reasonably foreseeable that someone other than the plaintiff might open the envelope.

Where the author of a letter reveals its contents to a secretary or to the writer's clerks or officials, there is a publication. In such cases, however, the occasion may be privileged.

Special rules apply to communications between husbands and wives. The communication of a statement that defames a third person made by a husband to his wife is not publication. The same rule applies where the communication is made by a wife to a husband. So if H (husband) writes a letter defaming X (a third party) and shows the letter to *W* (H's wife), there is no publication of the letter sufficient to sustain an action in libel by X. Where X, a third party, writes a letter defaming H (husband), and X shows the letter to *W* (H's wife), there is a publication. Where a servant wrongfully opened his master's letter, it was held that there was no publication to the servant (*Huth v Huth*, 1915).

Publication has now been extended to include websites (*Godfrey v Demon Internet*, 2001), tweets (*Monroe v Hopkins*, 2017), blogs (*Cruddos v Adams*, 2013) and internet hyperlinks (*Islam Expo Ltd v the Spectator*, 2010).

Repetition and dissemination. The repetition of a defamatory statement orally or in writing is a fresh 'publication'. It is no defence in such cases to plead that the person who repeats the statement did not originate it.

Repetition is highly relevant to the press. Where a book or newspaper article is defamatory, the printer and the publisher are each liable as well as the author. Subsidiary distributors such as booksellers and newsvendors are not liable, however, if they can prove the following points. The distributor must show that:

i it was not known that the statement was libellous;
ii there were no circumstances that ought to have given rise to the suspicion that the book or paper was libellous; and
iii the lack of knowledge was not due to negligence.

The **Defamation Act 1996** created a new statutory defence that modifies these common law rules relating to innocent dissemination. The Act extends the common-law defence of innocent dissemination to secondary publishers such as printers, broadcasters of live television programmes, communication network service operators and computer systems providers. The burden of proof would be on them to prove that they had no reason to know or believe that the publication was defamatory and had taken reasonable care in relation to publication. The previous record of the publishers in publishing defamatory material would also be taken into account.

❖ CASE EXAMPLE

***McManus v Beckham* (2002)**

Consideration was given as to whether a defendant in a claim for defamation can be made liable for damages alleged to have been suffered by the claimant as the consequence of the re-publication of the original defamatory statement by a third party, specifically by the media. *Held*: in the circumstances, there was a possibility that the claimant could establish that the defendant knew or ought reasonably to have known that there was a significant risk that what she said would be repeated in whole or in part in the press.

A circulating library is in the same position as a bookseller or a newsvendor.

❖ CASE EXAMPLE

***Vizetelly v Mudie's Select Library Ltd* (1900)**

A book contained a libel. Defendants, librarians, had copies in stock, but were unaware of the libellous consents. They employed a reader of their books and took other precautions, but they did not observe in a trade publication that the publishers of the libellous book requested the return of all copies for correction. The library continued to lend the book. *Held*: that the library was negligent and thus liable in damages as 'publishers' of the particular libel in the book.

Defences. The following defences may be raised in defamation:

a justification
b fair comment
c privilege
d apology
e offers of amends

a Justification

It is a good defence to plead that the alleged defamatory statement is *substantially true*, even though some details may be untrue. If an alleged defamatory statement is true, the claimant cannot, by the nature of things, have suffered damage to his or her reputation.

In an action for libel or slander in respect of words containing two or more charges against the claimant, the defence of justification will not fail merely because the truth of every charge is not proved, if the unproved charges do not materially injure the claimant's reputation having regard to the truth of the remaining charges (**Defamation Act 1952**, s. 5).

In practice justification is only rarely pleaded. If the defence fails, the defendant will usually be required to pay substantial damages by reason of having persisted in the assertion of the truth of the defamatory statement.

b Fair comment

This defence is restricted to fair comment on *a matter of public* interest. What constitutes 'a matter of public interest' is for the judge to decide in each individual case. The following subjects fall within this category: central and local government; the conduct and speeches of persons in public offices and affairs generally; trade unions; the police; works of art; books; plays; television and other broadcasts. The private lives of authors, actors and playwrights are not matters of public interest in this context.

As to the meaning of 'fair comment', the defendant must be able to prove that the remark is honest, relevant and free from malice or improper motive. The defendant's statement must consist of opinion or comment and not a statement of fact. Proof of actual spite or of malice towards an author (and similar persons) negatives the defence. Moreover, the statement must not be a comment on a person's moral character.

Banks v Cadwalladr (2022) involved journalistic comments by Cadwalladr that Banks, the Claimant had inappropriate Russian connections. *Held*: That in all the circumstances the defendant had established that her belief that publishing her talk was in the public interest was reasonable.

In each case the judge decides whether a reasonable person might consider the comment as fair. The jury decides in each case whether it is unfair.

c Privilege

This defence protects certain defamatory statements from action at law on the grounds of public policy. The free expression of opinion and facts in Parliament is so important to our democratic way of life that this freedom (protected by absolute privilege) overrides any private right or interest of the person who might be defamed. No action may be taken against the person, e.g. a Member of Parliament, giving utterance to their words. There are two classes of privilege: absolute and qualified.

Absolute privilege exists in the following cases:

i *Statements made in Parliament*. Whatever is said in Parliament cannot be the subject of legal proceedings (Bill of Rights, 1689).

ii *Reports ordered to be published by either House of Parliament*. For example, 'Hansard' and Government White Papers (**Parliamentary Papers Act 1840**).

iii *Judicial proceedings*. Statements made in the course of judicial proceedings by a judge, jury, parties, witnesses and advocates. The proceedings must be judicial. Statements made in the course of licensing applications dealt with by magistrates enjoy qualified privilege only, the proceedings being administrative, not judicial.

iv *Matters of state*. Communications between one Officer of State and another in the course of their duty. Secretaries of State and Ministers fall within the category of 'Officer of State', but it is uncertain how far this privilege extends to those in subordinate rank. Such persons would, however, be protected by qualified privilege (*Chatterton v Secretary of State for India*, 1895).

v *Communications between solicitor and client*, i.e. statements made in the course of their professional relationship. (There is some doubt as to whether this privilege is absolute or qualified, but its importance in the administration of the law justifies inclusion here as absolute.)

Qualified privilege means that the defence is qualified to the extent that the statement in question was made without malice and with an honest belief in its truth. If a statement is made maliciously, the law withdraws the protection of privilege and the defendant will be liable for defamation.

Qualified privilege exists in respect of the following matters:

i *Legal or moral duty*. Statements where the maker has a duty to inform, or an interest in informing, some person who has a duty or interest to receive the information. For example, where employer *A* writes to employer B concerning X, an applicant for a post with B.

ii *Private interests*. Statements in protection of one's private interests.

iii *Statements to authorities*. Letters of complaint or report to a proper authority, e.g. petitions to Parliament, complaints to local government officials and police.

iv *Reports of Parliamentary proceedings*. Fair and accurate reports of Parliamentary proceedings.

v *Reports of judicial proceedings*. Fair and accurate reports of public judicial proceedings.

vi *Reports of public proceedings*. Fair and accurate reports of various matters of public interest and importance, such as proceedings of the UN International Court of Justice, British courts martial outside the UK, and proceedings of public meetings of local authorities, public authorities, public companies or any tribunal or body exercising functions under an Act of Parliament.

In *Reynolds v Times Newspaper Ltd* (1998) Lord Bingham CJ gave guidance as to the circumstances in which qualified privilege will attach to publications made to the general public. In his view the 'necessary ingredients' incorporated the following three tests that needed to be answered in relation to any individual publication:

a the duty test

b the interest test

c the circumstantial test

❖ CASE EXAMPLES

Addis v Crocker (1961)

The plaintiff (not a solicitor) alleged he was libelled by the findings of the Disciplinary Committee of the Law Society. *Held*: that the Disciplinary Committee, a statutory committee, was exercising judicial functions, and the publication of its findings was absolutely privileged.

Chatterton v Secretary of State for India (1895)

Plaintiff alleged that a letter from the Secretary of State for India to his Parliamentary Under-Secretary, giving material with which to answer a Parliamentary question, was libellous. *Held*: that the statement was absolutely privileged, since it concerned a matter of State.

Osborn v Thomas Boulter & Son (1930)

Plaintiff was a licensee of an inn. He wrote to the defendants (his brewers) complaining of the quality of the beer. Defendants sent one of their men to investigate and report. After receiving the report, defendant (Boulter) dictated a letter to his secretary suggesting that plaintiff had been adding water to the beer, and pointed out the penalties attaching to this practice. Plaintiff sued, alleging publication to the secretary and other clerks. *Held*: that the occasion was privileged; as the plaintiff could not prove malice, his claim failed.

Jackson v Hopperton (1864)

A prospective employer, *A*, wrote to a former employer, B, concerning the character of C, an employee, of B. B replied. *Held*: that information about the character of the employee, C, was privileged.

d Apology

By the **Libel Act 1843** (as amended by the **Libel Act 1845**), a defendant in an action for libel contained in a newspaper and other periodical may plead:

i that the publication was made without malice or gross negligence;
ii that a full apology was published at the earliest opportunity; and
iii that compensation has been paid into court.

This is a special plea, but it is seldom used since no other defence can be set up if the statutory apology under this Act is relied on.

e Offer of amends

Previously the defence of offer of amends under section 4 of the **Defamation Act 1952** was available when the words had been published innocently, i.e. if the publisher used reasonable care and had either not intended to publish them; or did not know of the circumstances by which words innocent on the face of it might be understood to be defamatory of the plaintiff. Within the 1952 Act an offer of amends did not mean the payment of money.

Section 2 of the **Defamation Act 1996** has replaced the provisions of section 4 of the 1952 Act by extending the opportunity to offer to make amends to anyone who has published a statement alleged to be defamatory of another while the previous requirements of the 1952 Act with regard to the publication of a correction and apology are retained, the **Defamation Act 1996** does provide for an offer of amends to incorporate the payment to the aggrieved party of 'such compensation (if any) and such costs, as may be agreed or determined to be payable'.

A procedure is provided for in section 3 of the **Defamation Act 1996** with regard to accepting an offer to make amends and section 4 where there is a failure to accept such offer to make amends by the aggrieved party.

Remedies. The main legal remedies for defamation are (i) damages and (ii) injunction. We have noted that in slander, as a general rule, some damage must be proved as grounds for the action. A loss of the voluntary hospitality of friends has been held in one case as sufficient. Damages may be compensatory (i.e. recompense for the actual loss sustained) or exemplary.

The following matters may, however, be taken into account in mitigation of damages:

i if the defendant made a full apology at the earliest practicable moment
ii if the claimant had a bad reputation

iii if there was provocation by certain counter-libels
iv if the claimant had already recovered damages for the publication of words to the same effect as those in which the action is brought
v if the damage was too remote

Injunctions may also be granted, but the court is reluctant to grant an interim injunction since this involves a decision that prima facie the case is one of libel before the jury has itself decided this important fact. The claimant must act quickly in the petition for an injunction, and prove that the offending publication will be made or continued and that any such intended or continued publication will entail immediate and irreparable injury.

❖ CASE EXAMPLE

PJS v News Group Newspapers Ltd (2016)

Celebrity claimant applied for an injunction preventing publication of his name and his partner's alleged involvement in an extramarital threesome. *Held*: injunction granted despite widespread knowledge of the celebrity outside the jurisdiction and widespread overseas media coverage.

This area of the law is subject to much criticism, as injury to reputation often pays more in damages than personal injury. It was held in *John v MGN Ltd* (1995) that public opinion is offended by damages for defamation often being greater than damages for personal injuries that leave a claimant helplessly crippled. Therefore, juries in defamation actions are given guidance by references to appropriate awards, although they are not bound by them. Exemplary damages cannot exceed the minimum sum necessary to meet the purpose of punishment and deterrence.

Note: That whilst the courts have continued to refuse to recognize a tort of privacy, cases such as *PJSV News Group Newspapers Ltd* (2016) quoted previously continue to arise. In *Linklaters LLP & Another v Mellish* (2019), the question arose as to whether an injunction should be granted to restrain an ex-employee from disclosing confidential information obtained from and relating to his employment by the claimants. In granting the injunction the court noted that the applicants for an interim injunction of this kind must meet some threshold conditions and subsequently that it is likely to establish that publication should not be allowed. The court was satisfied that the likelihood that the claimant would succeed at a trial and sufficient that relief should be granted

In *ZXC* v *Bloomberg LP* (2020) the Supreme Court *Held:*. Dismissal of an appeal holding the appellant liable for violation of the respondent's right to privacy in relation to information relating to a criminal investigation into his activities. The respondent, ZXC, and his employer were the subject of a criminal investigation by a United Kingdom Legal Enforcement Body. In the context of that investigation, the Legal Enforcement Body sent a confidential Letter of Request to a foreign state seeking, among other things, information and documents relating to the respondent. The appellant, a media company, obtained a copy of the Letter of Request and published an article referring to the fact that information had been requested in respect of the respondent and detailing the matters in respect of which he was being investigated. The respondent brought a successful claim in the High Court against the appellant for misuse of private information. The appellant's appeal against that judgment was dismissed by the Court Appeal, and their subsequent appeal to the Supreme Court was also dismissed when the

Court held that a person under criminal investigation has, prior to being charged, a reasonable expectation of privacy in respect of information relating to the investigation. It reasoned that a balancing exercise must be done in such cases to determine whether respondents' right to privacy or the publishers' right to freedom of expression should prevail, with neither of the rights having the right or precedence over the other.

These cases should be compared with *Sutherland v Her Majesty's Advocate* (2020), where the Supreme Court considered an appeal where the appellant had entered into sexualized communications with a decoy from a 'Paedophile Hunter' (PH) Group, believing he was a child. After being reported to the police, he was convicted of three charges related to sexually motivated communications with a child using the evidence which had been obtained through the PH Group. The appeal concerned the admissibility of this evidence. *Held:* That on two grounds there had been no interference with the appellant's rights to respect for private life and correspondence under articule 8 (1) of the ECHR. Firstly, the 'reprehensible nature 'of the communication in question did not attract the protection of article 8, because they did not reflect values which the ECHR 'exists to protect and promote'. Secondly, the court held that the appellant had no reasonable expectation of privacy in respect of the communications—an important indicator of whether the right to respect for private life and correspondence is engaged.

8.14.1 The Defamation Act 2013

In September 2009, the Ministry of Justice published a consultation paper: *Defamation and the internet: the multiple publication rule*. This was followed by other consultation papers relating to defamation law, which subsequently led to the enactment of the **Defamation Act 2013**. The Ministry of Justice press release stated that: 'The Defamation Act 2013 reverses the chilling effect on freedom of expression current libel law has allowed, and the prevention of legitimate debate we have seen in the past.'

The Act makes a number of substantive and procedural changes to the law of defamation including:

a. A new 'serious harm' threshold to prevent people from bringing trivial claims, and a requirement that bodies trading for profit show serious financial harm.
b. Codifying and updating the common law and statutory defences of justification, fair comment and privilege.
c. A new defence of qualified privilege for the publication of articles in peer-reviewed academic and scientific journals.
d. A new defence of publication on a matter of public interest.
e. A new defence for operators of websites hosting third-party content, provided a specific process is followed to facilitate contact between the claimant and the author.
f. A single publication rule to prevent repeated claims in relation to the same material.
g. Tightening of jurisdictional rules in order to restrict libel tourism.
h. A new defence for secondary publishers where it is reasonably practicable to pursue an action against the primary publisher.
i. Reversing the presumption in favour of jury trials.

The Press Release also stated that: 'These changes were accompanied by changes to the civil procedure rules and cost rules designed to reduce the length of cases and consequent chilling effect brought about by the threat of disproportionate costs.'

Lachaux v Independent Print Ltd (2020) was one of the first cases where the Supreme Court considered the impact of the 'serious harm' test, incorporated in the 2013 Defamation Act, on the common law test for defamatory publication.

8.15 Deceit

Fraudulent misrepresentation (or deceit) has already been discussed in the law of contract (see p. 153). Deceit is a separate tort, and its essential features are considered later.

The tort of deceit consists in making a wilfully false statement with the intent that the claimant shall act in reliance on it, and with the result that harm is suffered as a consequence of acting upon it (*Bradford Building Society v Borders*, 1941). In *Alliance and Leicester Building Society v Edgestop Ltd* (1993), it was held that as far as the tort of deceit is concerned, a person cannot plead by way of defence that the victim was guilty of contributory negligence either at common law or by virtue of the **Law Reform (Contributory Negligence) Act 1945**.

The essentials of the tort are:

a a statement of fact
b that the maker knew it to be false or had no genuine belief in its truth
c that it was made with *intent* that it should be acted upon
d that it was acted upon
e damage was suffered

a Statement of fact

Mere expressions of opinion are insufficient. The statements are usually made orally or in writing, but a 'statement' or representation may be made by conduct, without words, even. Thus, where a person at Oxford, who was not a member of the university, went into a shop, wearing a cap and gown, and obtained goods, as a result of the fraud, this was held to be a sufficient 'false pretence' (*R v Barnard*, 1837).

b The representation was false

The classic definition of fraud is in *Derry v Peek* (1889). It is 'a false representation of fact, made with knowledge of its falsity or without belief in its truth, or recklessly careless whether it be true or false'. The test is whether the defendant had an honest and genuine belief in the truth of the statement. Recklessness indicates the absence of such a belief; and if the defendant honestly believed the representation to be true in the sense in which he or she understood it, however erroneously, this will be a good defence.

c The intent

The statement must be made with the intent that the claimant should act upon it, and that the claimant did so act.

If the claimant was not deceived by the statement, he will not be able to recover.

d The statement must be acted upon

The claimant must have relied on the fraudulent misrepresentation, and in consequence of the deceit must have acted upon it, e.g. by transferring goods or money to the defendant.

e Damage

Damage or loss must have been suffered by the claimant.

❖ **CASE EXAMPLES**

Peek v Gurney (1873)

Plaintiff, in reliance on a fraudulent prospectus issued by company promoters, bought shares that were already in the market and so suffered a loss. *Held*: that plaintiff could not recover. The purpose of a prospectus is to induce persons to apply for shares from the company, not to induce them to purchase shares in the market and already issued. The plaintiff was not, therefore, one of the persons intended to act on the false representation in the prospectus.

Burrows v Rhodes (1899)

Defendant induced the plaintiff to take part in the Jameson Raid in South Africa by the false statement that British women and children needed protection. Plaintiff lost certain property (his kit) and suffered personal injuries in the loss of a leg. *Held*: that he could recover.

Langridge v Levy (1837)

A gun maker sold a gun to *A* for the use of *A* and his (*A's*) sons, and fraudulently represented the gun to be sound. While B, one of *A's* sons, was using it, the gun burst and B was injured. *Held*: that B could bring an action in deceit by the gun maker because the statement as to the soundness of the gun, though made to *A*, was intended to be communicated to and acted upon by B.

8.16 Malicious falsehood

This tort is committed when a person causes damage to another by making false and injurious imputations. The damage here contemplated is damage to business interests, not to reputation.

The essentials of malicious falsehood are:

i that the statement is false
ii that there is *malice*, i.e. a desire to injure, or some other improper motive
iii that it tends to make *others* act on the statement to the plaintiff's detriment

The distinction from deceit is that in deceit, the claimant is induced by the false representation to act to his or her own detriment; and the distinction from defamation is that in defamation, the person's reputation is primarily attacked.

There are three types of injurious or malicious falsehood:

a *Slander of title*, where a defendant falsely and maliciously disparages or denies another person's title to property in a manner calculated to cause him damage. An example occurs where *A* falsely and maliciously alleges that B is offering certain goods for sale, in infringement of a patent vested in C (*Wren v Weild*, 1869).
b *Slander of goods*, e.g. where a person falsely and maliciously disparages goods manufactured or sold by another, though the motive may be to boost the first person's sales. But a false statement that one's own goods are the best is not actionable. The court will not allow

litigation to be used as a method of advertising by using the forum of the court to give publicity to a litigant's products.

c *Other false words that damage a person's business.* Thus, where a defendant falsely and maliciously published in a newspaper that the claimant had ceased to carry on business, it was held that the claimant was entitled to recover damages for loss of trade attributable to the false statement (*Ratcliffe v Evans*, 1892).

8.17 Limitation of actions

The law governing this matter is found in the **Limitation Act 1980**, which has replaced earlier Acts.

Actions in tort must be brought within six years of the cause of action accruing. This is the general rule, and the calculation of the period presents little difficulty where the tort consists of one independent and simple tort. Time begins to run from the date of that event. Where, however, the damage arising from a tort does not become immediately apparent, e.g. where a person by continual digging on their own land disturbs the supports of a neighbour's property (a nuisance), time begins to run from the date of the damage accruing.

❖ CASE EXAMPLES

Pirelli General Cable Works Ltd v Oscar Faber & Partners (1983)

Defendants designed a chimney that was constructed from unsuitable materials in June and July 1969. As a result cracks developed in the chimney in April 1970, although the plaintiffs did not discover the damage until November 1977. In October 1978 the plaintiffs brought an action for negligence. *Held*: although it was agreed that the damage could not with reasonable diligence have been discovered before October 1972, the claim was statute-barred as the action accrued when the damage came into existence and not when the damage was discovered or could have been discovered with reasonable diligence.

Dove v Banhams Patent Locks Ltd (1983)

Defendants fitted an insecure security gate to the plaintiff's premises. The house was burgled in 1979 when thieves forced the top of the security gate. The defendants pleaded that the cause of action arose in 1967 when the gate was installed. *Held*: that the plaintiff's cause of action was not statute-barred. The damage and, therefore, the cause of action arose in 1979 from the forcing of the gate and the resulting burglary.

Where the tort consists of a continuing wrong, e.g. noise, vibration or stench (nuisances), a new cause of action arises daily. Where any such nuisance has been continuously committed for, say, nine years, the claimant will be able to recover only for the six years immediately preceding the date action commences. The first three years in this example are outside the limit, and damage occurring within that time is not actionable.

If the injured party was under disability (e.g. a minor or of unsound mind) when the cause of action accrued, the period runs from the time when the disability ceases or the injured party dies, whichever first occurs.

Special periods of limitation operate in the following cases.

i **Fatal Accidents Act 1976**. Action must be commenced within three years after the death of the deceased person. If the deceased person is the tortfeasor, the limitation period is six months from the date of death (see p. 254).

ii *Personal injuries*. Action for damages for negligence or nuisance where *personal injuries* are involved must be begun within three years from the date on which the cause of action accrued, or the date (if later) of the claimant's knowledge.
The date of the claimant's knowledge where the claimant has undergone major surgery (as a result of the alleged act or omission) arises as soon as the claimant has had a reasonable time to overcome the shock of the injury, take stock of his disability and seek expert advice—see *Forbes v Wandsworth Health Authority* (1996).
The court has a discretionary power to override the time limit if it thinks it is equitable to do so (*Conry v Simpson*, 1983), although any resulting prejudice to the defendant must also be taken into account (*Donovan v Gwentoys Ltd* (1990)). In accordance with s. 6 of the **Administration of Justice Act 1982**, provisional damages can be awarded where there is a possibility of further serious disease or deterioration.

iii *Defamation*. The **Administration of Justice Act 1985**, s. 57, has reduced the limitation period for libel and slander actions from six to three years.

iv **Latent Damage Act 1986**. Provides that in actions relating to property, where the damage is latent, the time limit is either six years from the date on which the action accrued, or three years from when both the knowledge and the right to bring the action were acquired.
No claim, however, may be brought more than 15 years after the negligent act or omission occurred.

v *Joint tortfeasors*. A tortfeasor wishing to recover contribution from a joint tortfeasor must bring his action within two years from the date when judgment was entered against him.

8.18 Useful webpages

Tort law summary (http://lawskool.co.uk/content/uk_tort_law_sample_2011.pdf)

The law of tort—e-law resources.co.uk (www.e-lawresources.co.uk/Tort-law.php)

English tort law Wikipedia (http://en.wikipedia.org/wki/English_tort_law)

8.19 Exercises

1 Define a tort, and distinguish a tort from (i) a crime and (ii) a breach of contract.

2 How far is malice and intention relevant to an action for a tort?

3 How far is mistake a defence in tort?

4 Discuss the defence in tort of (i) necessity and (ii) inevitable accident.

5 The liability of two or more persons who together commit a tort is said to be 'joint and several'. What is meant by this statement?

6 'A person may be imprisoned without being conscious of the fact.' Explain.

7 Distinguish between (i) detinue and (ii) conversion.

8 Explain, with examples, what is meant by 'a public nuisance'.

9 What do you understand by 'the duty of care' in relation to the tort of negligence?

10 How far is it true to say that negligent misstatement is now a tort?

11 Distinguish between (i) the liability of joint tortfeasors and (ii) contributory negligence?

12 Summarize the provisions of the **Occupiers' Liability Act 1957** in relation to visitors on premises.

13 Define 'defamation'. List the points to be proved in a successful claim for libel.

14 What special rules govern 'publication' in the law of libel?

15 Distinguish, with examples, between (i) absolute privilege and (ii) qualified privilege in regard to the law of libel.

Chapter 9

Trusts

Key points

- definition of a trust
- differences between private and public (or charitable) trusts
- trustees
- liability for breaches of trusts

The modern trust derived from the feudal 'use', which was invented by medieval lawyers in order to overcome the hardship of the common-law rules preventing land from being devised (i.e. left by will), and the harshness of the feudal burdens imposed on freehold tenants.

Suppose that *A* was a feudal tenant who wanted to escape the heavy burdens and services attached to the holding. *A* would 'enfeoff' three friends, X,Y and Z, of the land to the 'use' of a son, B. (Enfeoff means to transfer the interests in land to another.) So far as the lord of the manor was concerned, X,Y and Z were the legal owners. On *A*'s death no feudal dues were payable, because the legal ownership in the land was vested in X,Y and Z. If one friend died there was no interruption of ownership since the property passed to the remaining two, and if one of these died the property passed to the survivor under the doctrine of survivorship, which applied at common law to joint tenants (see p. 305).

If X,Y and Z attempted to deal with the land in a way incompatible with their obligations towards B (e.g. by using the land themselves or selling it), the Court of Chancery would intervene on B's behalf. B could not, however, obtain any redress in the courts of common law, for these were concerned only with the legal rights and the legal owner or owners.

B's right, at least originally, was a personal one against the legal owners X,Y and Z. But it was soon realized that to permit the remedy to prevail against only the feoffees to 'uses' was to open the door to fraud. Consequently, a remedy for B was afterwards made available against a purchaser from the legal owners (i.e. the feoffees), provided that the purchaser took the land *with notice* of the 'use' attached to it. If, however, the purchaser bought the legal estate in the land without notice of the rights of the beneficiary, the latter had no right against them either at law or in equity. Herein lies the origin of the doctrine of 'the purchaser for value of the legal estate without notice' (see p. 287).

The adoption of the 'use' led to the loss of income and valuable rights that were exacted from the tenants by the feudal lords and landowners, particularly the Crown, the greatest landowner of all. The Statute of Uses, 1535, was passed to stop evasion of death duties and feudal dues or

DOI: 10.4324/9781003422808-9

payments. The statute enacted that where land was granted 'To *A* to hold it for the use of B', B should be regarded as the legal owner and *A* should be excluded from the grant. B was intended to bear responsibility for the discharge of the feudal burdens. However, the statute was unpopular, and lawyers invented technical ways of evading its operation. Uses persisted and came in due course of time to be called 'trusts'. Gradually they achieved popularity and came to be one of the most distinctive features of English law.

9.1 Definition of a trust

> A trust is the relationship which arises wherever a person called the trustee is compelled in Equity to hold property, whether real or personal,. . . for the benefit of some persons (including themselves) or for some object permitted by law, in such a way that the real benefit of the property accrues, not to the trustee, but to the beneficiaries or other objects of the trust.
>
> (Professor Keeton, *The Law of Trusts*)

The trust device is used for many different purposes, notably:

i to enable property to be held for persons who cannot hold the legal title themselves, e.g. a minor cannot be the legal owner of land, but land can be held in trust for a minor
ii to enable property to be used to benefit persons in succession, e.g. settlements
iii to enable two or more persons to own land
iv to further a charitable purpose
v to avoid or minimize liability to various forms of taxation

The distinctive feature of the trust is the duality of ownership. The **trustee** is the legal owner; the *beneficiary* is the equitable owner. This split in ownership is possible because, while admitting that the trustee has the legal title, equity acts on the trustee's conscience and will compel them to hold the property for the beneficiaries.

Trusts may be classified as (a) private trusts and (b) charitable trusts. These must be considered separately as there are important differences between them.

9.2 Private trusts

Private trusts can be categorized as (a) express, (b) implied or (c) constructive.

a Express trusts

An express trust is one expressly created by the settlor *inter vivos* (i.e. during life), or by will, for the benefit of one or more specified persons or a group of persons. It may be created in writing, by deed, by will or merely orally in certain cases.

The essential elements of an express private trust were laid down in *Knight v Knight* (1840) by Lord Langdale, who declared that three 'certainties' are necessary for the creation of a trust: (i) certainty of intention, (ii) certainty of subject matter and (iii) certainty of objects.

i *Certainty of intention*. The settlor must show by his or her words a clear intention to create a trust. The words must be imperative, not precatory (i.e. words merely beseeching or hoping): there must be a positive command that a thing shall be done and that a trust shall be created. If there is a lack of certainty of intention, the grantee can take the property absolutely. Thus in *Re Adams and the Kensington Vestry* (1884), the testator left property in his will to his widow 'in full confidence that she will do what is right as to the disposal thereof between my children'. This was held not to create a trust so the widow took the property for herself.

ii *Certainty of subject-matter*. This refers both to the property to which the trust is to apply and to the interests in the property that the beneficiaries are to take. Thus, if a testator attempts in a will to create a trust of 'the bulk' of his or her property or a trust of 'a nice round sum', the trust will fail. Again, if a settlor conveys houses to trustees to hold some in trust for Mary and the rest for Ann, the trust will fail and the trustees will hold the houses on a resulting trust (see later on) for the settlor.

iii *Certainty of objects*. This means that the persons whom the trust is intended to benefit must be ascertainable or at least capable of ascertainment. Note: In *Wang v Derby* (2002) it was *Held*: That cryptocurrencies can in theory constitute trust property. If a settlor has conveyed property to trustees and the objects of the trust are uncertain, the trustees will hold on a resulting trust for the settlor.

Completely and incompletely constituted trusts. A settlor can create a trust either:

i by declaring him or herself to be a trustee; or
ii by conveying the property to trustees.

If the settlor chooses (ii), the trust will not be fully constituted (i.e. complete and enforceable) until the legal title is vested in the trustees. What the settlor must do depends on the type of property involved, e.g. if it is unregistered land there must be a conveyance; if it is a chattel (such as a painting) it must be physically handed over; if it is shares the share transfer must be registered in the company's books; if the trust is created by will then the will must comply with the formalities of the **Wills Act 1837** (see p. 324).

Once a trust is fully constituted, equity will assist any beneficiary under the trust to enforce their rights. Before the trust is fully constituted, however, it does not exist—an incompletely constituted trust is no trust at all—and no person can have any rights as beneficiary under a trust that does not exist.

Equity will assist would-be beneficiaries under an incompletely constituted trust if they have provided consideration. Consideration in equity's eyes means either valuable consideration in the common-law sense (money or money's worth) or marriage consideration, i.e. where the would-be beneficiaries are the spouse and children of the settlor and the settlement was made before and in consideration of marriage. Equity will assist them by compelling the settlor to convey the property to the trustees, thus completely constituting the trust.

If, however, the would-be beneficiaries have provided no such consideration, then they are known as 'volunteers' and equity will not help them to completely constitute the trust. This is summed up in the maxim 'Equity will not assist a volunteer'.

However, this principle has been questioned in recent cases where the question of the outcome might give rise to unconscionability, which might constitute an exception to the rule. In *Khan v Mahmood* (2021). This arose because of an ineffective transfer of the land involved. The outcome was that the land constituting the trust was not registered, neither was the registration fee paid. *Held*: The transfer was valid on the principle that a failed gift will always be upheld where unconscionability is present.

b Implied trusts

An implied trust is based upon the presumed intention of the settlor. The most common type of implied trust is the **resulting trust**. For example, suppose a settlor conveys property to trustees to hold on trust for B for life. If the settlor does not state where the property is to go on B's death, then when B dies, the trustees will hold on a resulting trust for the settlor; thus the equitable interest returns to the settlor. Similarly, if a settlor conveys property to trustees but the trusts are void, e.g. because they offend one of the rules against perpetuities, then the trustees hold on a resulting trust for the settlor.

Another example of a resulting trust can be seen in the following situation: suppose *A*, a purchaser of property, has it conveyed into the name of B. In the absence of any evidence to show that *A* intended to make a gift of the property to B, equity will treat B as holding the property on a resulting trust for *A*, i.e. there is a presumption of a resulting trust. Sometimes there is a presumption the other way; this is known as the presumption of advancement. Thus if the person providing the purchase money has the property conveyed into the name of his wife or child, it is presumed that a gift was intended. In this case there is no resulting trust and the recipient can enjoy the property for himself. These presumptions can be rebutted by evidence of what was actually intended.

One outcome of the resulting trust has been the concept of the Quistclose Trust. This originally arose from the decision in *Barclays Bank v Quistclose* (1970) where money was loaned for the express purpose of the payment of a dividend. When the dividend was not paid due to the liquidation of the payee, the Court (House of Lords) declared that a resulting trust had arisen in favour of the provider of the money. This arose where money was provided for a particular purpose only and that purpose had failed. In *Twinsectra v Yardley* (2002) *Held*: That a Quistclose trust involves a species of resulting trust designed to protect lenders of funds transferred to borrowers solely to promote designated purposes. However, in *Prickly Bay Waterside Ltd v British American Insurance Co Ltd* (2022) was distinguished by the Privy Council, where the monies involved had not been set aside for a particular purpose (e.g. by being paid into a segregated account) so that no *Quistclose* trust arose.

c Constructive trusts

These are trusts imposed by equity regardless of the intention of the parties. An important example of this type is where a trustee, X, in breach of trust conveys the trust property to another person, Y, who knows of the breach of trust but nevertheless accepts the trust property. In these circumstances, Y will be treated as a 'constructive trustee' and will be compelled by equity to hold the property on trust for the beneficiaries. Y will be a constructive trustee whether there is consent or not.

A person will also be treated as a constructive trustee where he or she acquires a benefit under the trust to which they are not entitled. The constructive trustee will be compelled by equity to hold the benefit for the beneficiaries, as in the following cases:

❖ CASE EXAMPLES

Keech v Sandford (1726)

A trustee held a lease of Romford Marker on trust for an infant beneficiary. The trustee attempted to renew the lease for the benefit of the infant, but the lessor refused to grant a renewal to the infant. The lessor agreed, however, to renew the lease in favour of the trustee personally. The lease was accordingly made out to the trustee. *Held*: that the trustee held the new lease on a constructive trust for the infant.

AGIP (Africa Ltd) v Jackson (1991)

The plaintiffs requested the defendants not to arrange for the transfer of money in their possession to a third party as it had been obtained by fraud by one of the P's employees. D ignored the request. *Held:* D were liable as constructive trustees.

Amin v Amin and Others (2020)

The claimant Mrs Amin failed in a claim for beneficial interest of a property. The case is important in that it highlights the importance of evidence, common intention and detrimental reliance in constructive trust claims.

9.3 Public (or charitable) trusts

For a trust to be charitable it must satisfy three requirements:

a It must be charitable in the legal sense

'Charity' in a legal context does not accord with the popular meaning of the word. For example, fee-paying public schools such as Eton or Harrow are charitable in the legal sense and enjoy the same privileges, including tax exemptions, as, say, Barnardo's or the Spastics Society.

There is no statutory definition of a charity. The preamble to the Statute of Charitable Uses, 1601, listed a number of charitable objects, but the classification most frequently quoted is that of Lord Macnaghten in *Income Tax Special Commissioners v Pemsel* (1891), who classified charitable trusts under four heads:

i for the relief of poverty
ii for the advancement of education
iii for the advancement of religion
iv for other purposes beneficial to the community

The last category includes such purposes as the welfare of animals, the provision of public works such as bridges and museums, the setting up of fire brigades and distress funds and the promotion of efficiency in the armed forces. Trusts for political purposes are not charitable and will therefore fail (re *Koeppler's Will Trusts v Slack*, 1985).

The **Charities Act 2011** was intended to consolidate the **Charities Act 1993** and the other enactments that relate to charities. With regard to charitable purposes, the classification (iv) in Pemsel's Case expanded to include such purposes as: *The advancement of health and the saving of lives, the advancement of citizenship community development* and *the advancement of amateur sport*. It also clarified the meaning of: *public benefit requirements*.

❖ CASE EXAMPLES

In re South Place Ethical Society (1980)

This was an agnostic society; it held public meetings and gave high-quality concerts. Its objects were held to be charitable under heads (ii) and (iv), but not wider head (iii).

Inland Revenue Commissioners v McMullen (1980)

The Football Association Youth Trust was set up to promote football and other sports in schools and universities. The House of Lords held that this was a charitable trust within the preceding head (ii), as the physical development of the young is part of their education.

Nuffield Health v London Borough of Merton (2021)

Held: That the provision of gyms could be regarded as charitable under the 'advancement of health'. However, the application failed on the requirement of public benefit, due to members having to pay a membership fee which had not been reduced for poorer members, and also, there were very few services available for non-members.

The enactment of the **Charities Act 2022** was intended to effect to the Law Commission's recommendations to reform various technical issues in the law governing charities. It does so primarily by amending the **Charities Act 2011** with the intention to significantly improve the efficiency of the sector, release more funds for use on charitable purposes rather than administration and reduce unnecessary and excessive bureaucratic regulation that not only increases the sector's costs but also is a factor in discouraging people from volunteering to become trustees.

The **Recreational Charities Act 1958** was introduced following the decision in the *Commissioner of Inland Revenue v Baddeley* (1955). Under the **Recreational Charities Act 1958**, it is charitable to provide facilities for recreation or leisure-time occupations if the facilities improve the conditions of life of the persons for whom they are primarily intended. The persons must have need of the facilities by reason of age, youth, infirmity, disablement, poverty or social or economic circumstances; or the facilities must be available to members or female members of the public at large. Trusts in favour of Women's Institutes would thus be held valid.

b It must benefit the public as a whole or at least a section of it

If the main intention of the trust is to benefit certain specified individuals, no charitable trust arises. Thus a trust to provide for the education of the lawful descendants of three named persons is not charitable (*Re Compton*, 1945). Employees of a company do not form a section of the public for this purpose. Thus a trust to educate children of employees of a company has been held not charitable (*Oppenheim v Tobacco Securities Trust Co. Ltd*, 1951).

Trusts for the relief of poverty are, however, exempt from this public benefit requirement. Such trusts are charitable even if restricted to the relatives of the donor or to the employees or ex-employees of his firm.

c It must be wholly and exclusively charitable

This requirement is not satisfied if, under the terms of the trust, the property can be applied to non-charitable as well as to charitable purposes. Thus trusts for 'charitable or benevolent purposes' have been held void.

d Charities Act 1992

Among the major reforms of this Act was a provision whereby the Secretary of State could order that charitable trustees would not be bound by the 'half/half' rule in s. 2(1) of the **Trustee**

Investments Act 1961 (see p. 285). It also amended the requirements relating to fundraising and street collections, introducing a cooling-off period for charitable donations in excess of £50.

9.4 Differences between private and charitable trusts

a The persons to benefit

Private trusts are created for the benefit of specified persons or classes of persons; charitable trusts are created to further a purpose that will benefit society at large or an appreciable part of it.

b The application of the perpetuity rules

See 9.5 below.

c Taxation

Charities are wholly or partially exempt from many taxes that affect private trusts, and they also enjoy reduced rates. The income of a charity, if used for charitable purposes, is largely exempt from income tax.

d Uncertainty of objects

If the persons who are to be beneficiaries under a private trust are not defined with sufficient certainty, the trust will fail. However, a trust whose objects are clearly charitable will not fail merely because those purposes are vague; the court can order a scheme for the application of the property.

e The cy-près doctrine

This applies only to charitable trusts. Where the literal execution of a charitable trust is or becomes inexpedient or impractical, the court will apply the property cy-près, i.e. to some charitable purpose as near as possible to the original purpose named by the donor. This is done by means of a scheme established by the Charity Commissioners or the court.

The **Charities Act 1960** (as amended by the **Charities Acts 1992** and **1993**) extended the doctrine of cy-près to include cases where:

i the original purposes have as far as possible been fulfilled or cannot be carried out;
ii the original purposes provide a use for part only of the property
iii the property given can be more effectively employed if used in conjunction with other property applied for similar purposes
iv the original purposes were laid down by reference to an area that has ceased to be a unit, or by reference to a class of persons that has ceased to be suitable
v the original purposes since being laid down have been provided for by other means, or have ceased to be an effective method of using the property

If the charitable gift fails from the start, then the property cannot be applied cy-près unless the court can find a *general charitable intention*, i.e. an intention on the part of the donor to benefit charity in any event. Thus, if there is a gift by will to a charity that ceases to exist before the testator's death, the gift cannot be applied cy-près in the absence of a general charitable intention.

f Enforcement

Private trusts are enforced by the beneficiaries; charitable trusts are enforced by the Attorney-General on behalf of the Crown.

g Registration

Most charities must be registered with the Charity Commissioners, who have general supervision over charities. They may sanction new charitable schemes and authorize legal proceedings.

9.5 The rules against perpetuities

a The rule against remoteness of vesting

As a matter of policy, the law has always discouraged the tying up of land or other property for excessive periods of time. Two rules have been developed to deal with this, both of which apply to private trusts.

This was laid down in *Cadell v Palmer* (1833):

> Every attempted disposition of land or goods is void unless, at the time when the instrument creating it takes effect, one can say that it *must* take effect (if it takes effect at all) within a life or lives *then* in being and 21 years after the termination of such life or lives, with the possible addition of the period of gestation.

This has now been amended by the **Perpetuities and Accumulations Act 1964**. The effect now is that where property is held on trust, the beneficiaries must become absolutely entitled to the property either within a period no longer than that of a life in being at the time when the trust came into existence, plus 21 years after the end of that life, *or* within a period not exceeding 80 years specified in the trust instrument. Under the pre-1964 rule, *possible* events, and not actual or likely events, had to be considered. Where a gift might have failed under the pre-1964 rule because there was a *possibility* that it would vest outside the perpetuity period, the Act introduces a 'wait-and-see' rule. The effect is that such a disposition is to be treated as if it were not affected by the rule against remote vesting until such time as it is established that the disposition will *in fact* vest outside the perpetuity period.

For a recent case example dealing with the **Perpetuities and Accumulations Act 1964**, please refer to *Adam v Shrewsbury & Anor* (2005).

Charitable trusts *are* basically subject to this rule.

b The rule against perpetual trusts

This renders void any disposition that attempts to tie up property for a period longer than a life in being plus 21 years. This rule does *not* apply to charitable trusts, which can therefore continue indefinitely.

9.6 Trustees

Most of the law relating to trusts has evolved from the decisions of the Court of Chancery, but there are also important statutory provisions, notably the **Trustee Act 1925**.

Any person of full age, sound mind and legal capacity may be a trustee under an express trust. An infant cannot be an express trustee, though he or she may become a *constructive* trustee or hold property on a *resulting* trust in certain circumstances.

If the trust property is land, a maximum of four trustees is permitted. Where land is sold, at least two trustees (or a trust corporation) are needed to give a valid receipt for the purchase money.

9.7 Trust corporations

A trust corporation is empowered to act as a trustee. Because this is not a human trustee, there is never any problem of the trustee dying or retiring. Common examples include the trustee departments of banks and large insurance companies. The Public Trustee is a trust corporation and a government office: if the Public Trustee acts improperly, the State makes good any loss.

9.8 Appointment of trustees

The initial trustees are usually appointed by the settlor in the trust instrument. It is one of the maxims of equity that a trust shall never fail for want of a trustee. Thus, if a testator creates a trust by will but does not name trustees, or if those named refuse to act, then the testator's personal representatives must act as trustees until others are appointed.

Subsequent trustees are appointed by the person given power to appoint in the trust instrument; failing that, the existing trustees or the personal representatives of the last surviving trustee can appoint. As a last resort the court can appoint under section 41 of the **Trustee Act**.

Under section 36 of the **Trustee Act** a new trustee can be appointed by writing. This can be either an additional trustee or a replacement trustee for one who is (i) dead, (ii) remains outside the UK for more than 12 months, (iii) wishes to retire, (iv) refuses to act, (v) is unfit or incapable of acting, or is an infant or (vi) is a corporation that is dissolved.

A person may decline to accept the office of trustee, but unless this is done promptly they may be presumed to have accepted.

9.9 Termination of trusteeship

Apart from death, this may be effected either:

a By removal

A trustee can be removed under an express power in the trust instrument, under section 36 of the **Trustee Act** (where a replacement trustee is appointed), or, in extreme cases, by the court; or

b By retirement

This can be effected under section 36 of the **Trustee Act** if a replacement trustee is appointed. If no replacement trustee is appointed, a trustee can retire under section 39 provided (i) at least two trustees or a trust corporation will remain, (ii) the consent of the co-trustees and any person empowered to appoint trustees is obtained and (iii) the retirement is by deed. As a last resort a trustee can apply to the court to be discharged.

9.10 Duties and powers of trustees

a Administration

A trustee must take the same care of the trust property as an ordinary business person would take of their own property. Moreover, a professional trustee must exercise the special skill that they profess to have (*Bartlett v Barclay's Bank Trust Co.*, 1980). If a trustee is careless or fails to comply strictly with the terms of the trust they may be personally liable for losses. They will not, however, be liable for mere accidental losses or errors of judgment. A trustee must actively consider exercising all powers—equity does not countenance a sleeping trustee. Control of the trust property must be obtained and all debts owing to the trust must be collected, legal action being taken if this is necessary.

Schedule 1, para. 7 of the **Trustee Act 2000** does provide for a trust instrument to include an exclusion of a duty of care.

b Investment

The **Trustee Investments Act 1961** placed restrictions on trustees with regard to certain categories of investments. The **Trustee Act 2000** introduced a new concept of 'standard investment criteria', whereby a more specific duty was placed on a trustee to take a more balanced view with regard to risk and return across the whole trust investment portfolio. These statutory powers are often extended by a clause in the trust instrument that may give unrestricted powers of investment. Trustees must select investments of a type suitable to the trust and must secure a balance between income-producing and capital-producing investments so that all beneficiaries are treated fairly. Where charitable trustees hold investments, they must aim for the highest yield consistent with commercial prudence. When investing, they should not try to accommodate the different views of potential beneficiaries or financial supporters if this would mean a significant financial detriment to the trust funds (*Harries and Others v The Church Commissioners for England and Another*, 1992).

The **Trustee Act 2000** now also permits a trustee to buy freehold or leasehold land in the United Kingdom for any purpose. (Note that the Trust instrument may fetter the trustees' rights in this respect.)

c Trustees must not profit from their trust

This rule is strictly applied. If a trustee makes an unentitled profit, it must be accounted for: *Keech v Sandford*.

d Delegation of duties

A trustee can employ and pay an agent provided the agent is employed in their professional area, e.g. a solicitor to prepare a mortgage deed, a surveyor to carry out a valuation. Normally, a trustee cannot delegate their discretion; they must always be considered, e.g. a stockbroker may be employed to give advice on investments and to make the investments, but the decision as to the choice of investments must be made by the trustee. The statutory powers are narrow but may be widened by the provisions of the trust deed.

In accordance with the amendments made by the **Trustee Delegation Act 1999**, a trustee is permitted to delegate his or her functions by power of attorney, subject to certain limitations. However, the trustee will still remain liable for the acts or omissions of the attorneys.

The **Trustee Act 2000** gave even wider power to trustees of non-charitable trusts to delegate any of their functions to agents except with regard to the distribution of trust assets; allocation of fees between capital and income; appointment of trustees; powers conferred by legislation; powers conferred by the trust instrument; and the appointment of nominees or custodians.

e Keeping accounts

Trustees must keep proper accounts and must produce them for inspection by a beneficiary.

f Variation of trusts

If all the beneficiaries are of full age and capacity and are entitled to the whole beneficial interest in the trust, they may together authorize the trustees to deal with the trust in any manner desired. Apart from this, the trustees have no power to vary the trust. However, under the **Variation of Trusts Act 1958** where the beneficiaries belong to certain specified classes (e.g. those under incapacity by age or unsoundness of mind), the court may approve an arrangement varying or revoking any of the trusts or enlarging the trustees' powers. The court must be satisfied that the variation is for the benefit of those persons on whose behalf it is giving its approval.

g Remuneration of trustees

The **Trustee Act 2000** provides that, contrary to previous legislation, whereby the character of remuneration was a benefit under the trust, it is now recognized as a payment for services. This means that, subject to the terms of the trust instrument, trust corporations and professional trustees may be paid for work done even where it could be done by a lay trustee.

9.11 Liability for breaches of trust

Where a loss occurs to the trust estate from some improper act, neglect, default or omission of the trustee, the following actions are available to the beneficiaries:

i an action against the trustees to compensate the trust for the loss sustained
ii a criminal prosecution in certain cases (**Theft Act 1968**, see p. 366)
iii 'following' the trust property (see what follows)

A trustee is liable only for their own acts or defaults, not being liable for losses occasioned by the acts or defaults of co-trustees or of other persons with whom trust money is deposited, unless this happens through wilful default (section 30, **Trustee Act 1925**). 'Wilful default' means deliberate intention to commit a breach of trust, or reckless carelessness as to whether there is a breach of trust or not.

Where more than one trustee is liable for a breach of trust, their liability is joint and several. Thus, the beneficiaries may sue any one or more of those trustees liable for the breach and may recover from them the whole amount of the loss. Where a single trustee is compelled to satisfy a claim, this may be recovered by way of contribution from the co-trustees such amount as the court thinks just (**Civil Liability (Contribution) Act 1978**).

In three cases a trustee will be bound to indemnify co-trustees:

i where the trustee is a solicitor to the trust and the breach of trust resulted
ii where the trustee has obtained the benefit of the breach of trust

Where one of the trustees is a beneficiary, and in particular where the beneficiary instigated the breach, the breach will be made good out of that interest so far as possible.

However in **Bishop of Leeds v Dixon Coles and Gill (2021)**, where a partner had stolen from her firm's clients, it was *Held*: That the two remaining partners could not have been 'party or privy' to the fraud merely by being her partners. If they had absolutely no knowledge of the fraud and did not benefit from or ratify it, as was accepted by the litigants, then they were innocent trustees within s. 21 of the Limitation Act 1980 and could plead a six-year limitation defence. The Court of Appeal stated that 'The Partnership Act 1980, makes a partner liable for the sins of fellow partners but does not make a partner "party or privy" to them.'

9.12 Following the trust property (tracing)

This remedy is best understood by example. Suppose that X, a trustee, holds a valuable painting in trust for B. If X, in breach of trust, sells the painting to Q, the question arises as to whether the beneficiary, B, can sue Q for the return of the painting. B has a right of action against X for the money realized on the sale. If Q had no notice, actual or constructive, that the painting purchased was held on trust, then the painting may be kept. Q in this case falls within the category of a person who bona fide (i.e. in good faith) purchased trust property without notice that it is such, and is thus protected. B's only remedy is against X, the trustee. If, instead of selling the painting to Q, X had *given* it, the beneficiary (B) may lawfully claim the painting from Q, for the latter is not a bona fide purchaser. Therefore, the beneficiary can follow (i.e. trace) the trust property.

Another example of tracing is where the trustee, in breach of trust, uses trust money to purchase an asset, say land. The beneficiaries can trace into the land, i.e. they can claim the land because it is identifiable as their property, albeit in a different form.

If a trustee or a recipient of trust property (e.g. money) mixes it with personal monies, special tracing rules apply that are outside the scope of this book.

A tracing claim has two important advantages over a personal action for damages. First, if a person who has received trust property becomes bankrupt, a beneficiary who can trace will, in effect, gain priority over that bankrupt's creditors. Second, a beneficiary may reap the benefit of any increase in the value of property into which it can be traced.

9.13 Relief from liability for breach

The standard of care required of a trustee is high. Some breaches occur even though there was no deliberate intent to defraud or harm the beneficiaries or diminish the trust fund. Accordingly, relief may be granted by the court to a trustee if honest and reasonable action has been taken and ought fairly to be excused (section 61, **Trustee Act 1925**).

Under the **Limitation Act 1980**, an action for breach of trust cannot usually be brought more than six years from the date of the breach. Exceptions to this rule may be made where there has been fraud by the trustee, or other circumstances obtained that prevented the time from running, e.g. where a breach was not discovered until sometime after it was committed.

9.14 Exercises

1 Define a trust and give a short history of its development.

2 What are 'the three certainties' of an express private trust?

3 When is a trust said to be completely constituted?

4 What is (i) a 'resulting trust' and (ii) a 'constructive trust'?

5 What are the four heads of charitable trusts laid down in *Income Tax Special Commissioners v Pemsel* (1891)?

6 Certain special rules apply to charitable trusts. Describe them. What are the main provisions of the **Charities Act 1960**?

7 What is a 'trust corporation'? What advantages do these have over other types of trustee?

8 'Equity never wants for a trustee'. Explain.

9 What are the main duties of a trustee? What standard of care must a trustee adopt in regard to trust property? May he or she delegate any of his or her duties? If so, to whom?

10 What types of action are available to a beneficiary who alleges breach of trust and loss of trust funds caused by a trustee?

11 Describe the advantages of a tracing claim over a personal action for damages.

Chapter 10

The law of property

Key points

- the distinction between ownership and possession
- classification of property
- the division of estates into freehold and leasehold
- comparison of the strict settlement and the trust for sale
- the role of easements and servitudes
- creation and termination of the various forms of mortgage

10.1 Ownership

Ownership has been described as 'the entirety of the powers of use and disposal allowed by law' (Pollock: *First Book of Jurisprudence*). The owner of a thing has an aggregate of rights, namely (i) the right of enjoyment, (ii) the right of destruction and (iii) the right of disposition, subject to the rights of others. Thus, if *A* owns a hat he or she can wear it, alter it, burn it or merely throw it away. There are, however, limits to these rights. If *A* throws the hat at B, this might be an assault on B (or a battery if the hat strikes B), for under the general law B has a right not to be interfered with. Similarly, regarding land, *A* may enjoy and use it, sell it or give it away; but use of this land is subject to the rights of others as allowed by law, e.g. in nuisance and tort. Today a landowner's rights are much circumscribed by legislation aimed at social control, e.g. the **Town and Country Planning Acts 1971** and **1990**, the **Countryside and Rights of Way Act 2000** and the **Neighbourhood Planning Act 2017**. Further control has been extended by the **Environment Act 2021** which first provides both for a legal framework for environmental governance and secondly makes provision for specific improvement of the environment, including measures on water and resource efficiency, air quality and environmental recall, water, nature and biodiversity and conservation covenants. To speed up the planning system the Government introduced the **Levelling-up and Regeneration Act 2023** with the aim of holding developers accountable, reducing bureaucracy and encouraging more local councils to enable the building of new homes. The **Building Safety Act 2022** has extended the government's control over building safety legislation as an outcome of the adverse effects of the Grenfell Tower fire in 2017. The Permission for any change in the use of the land owned must be obtained from the local planning authorities. Moreover, Government departments and local authorities may compulsorily acquire privately owned land and use it for

DOI: 10.4324/9781003422808-10

public purposes, e.g. as a site for a school or college. A person may own land notwithstanding that another has an easement, such as a right of way, over it.

As already mentioned, the ownership of land grew out of possession. An early landowner's rights were possessory, and in medieval law, title to the land was based on the concept of *seisin* (a possessory right). The word 'ownership' was not found in use in England before 1583, and the word 'property' was uncommon before the nineteenth century. People spoke of 'possessions' and 'estates'.

In course of time the idea of ownership grew with an advancing industrial and capitalistic economy. The *right of possession* changed into the *right of ownership* which we know today.

Ownership may be acquired in the following ways.

a Originally

Ownership may be thus obtained by (i) *creating* something, e.g. a clay jar or a picture; (ii) *occupation*, where a person claims something not owned by anyone, e.g. a wild bird or animal, by occupation of property abandoned by another; or (iii) *accession*, e.g. if *A* owns an animal that begets young, the young animals become the property of *A* by accession.

b Derivatively

Through sale, gift or compulsory acquisition by law, e.g. where goods or land are compulsorily acquired by statute, or taken by distress in execution of judgment.

c By succession

On the death of a previous owner, another person may succeed to the property and thus acquire ownership, e.g. a beneficiary under a will.

10.2 Possession

Possession in law is based on possession in fact. It involves two concepts:

a the *corpus possessionis*, meaning the control over the thing itself which may be exercised by a person, their servant or agent

b the *animus possidendi*, which is the intent to exercise exclusive possession of the thing itself and thus to prevent others from using it

Possession is, therefore, largely a question of fact, as is borne out by common experience. Thus, if *A* lends a pen to B for examinations, B is in temporary physical possession of the pen. If *A* sends shoes to the shoe repairer, B, to be mended, the repairer possesses them while the articles are under repair. In each case B is known as a *bailee* in law. The *ownership* of the pen and the shoes remains in both cases with *A*, while the *possession* resides with others who exercise temporary control.

Possession may be obtained lawfully and unlawfully.

- Lawful possession needs no explanation, as the preceding examples demonstrate.
- As to unlawful possession we may note that if X, a thief, steals Y's watch, X acquires possession but *not* ownership. Clearly X acquires no rights to the watch as against the lawful owner. Moreover, if X sells the watch to another person, Z, the rights of ownership in Y are not destroyed. Nevertheless, the thief has possession, and usually endeavours to maintain

exclusive control over the thing stolen until such time as a decision is made to sell it, discard it or throw it away.

It is possible to possess things without being aware of them. I possess the books in my library, even though they may be individual books on my shelves whose existence or particular disposition I have forgotten. I nevertheless control them and, as I have the intent to exclude others, I possess them in law. Possession is not lost even though I may have temporarily mislaid an article.

In English law even wrongful possession may, if continued for a length of time, ripen into a claim that is indistinguishable from ownership itself. Thus, where a squatter occupies derelict land or land in respect of which the true owner is unknown or untraceable, and continues in uninterrupted possession for 12 years, using it in a way inconsistent with the true owner's right, the owner's title to the land is destroyed. The squatter thereupon acquires a lawful title of ownership with rights against the whole world.

The law acknowledges that wrongful possession of land for 12 years, and goods for six years, may mature into lawful ownership, thereby destroying the previous owner's title and even the legal right to recover the land or goods by action (**Limitation Act 1980**).

Although possession is, as we have noted, largely a question of fact, it also has considerable legal significance. When we speak of 'possession being nine points of the law', we refer to the legal rights attaching to possession itself and to the protection given to it by law.

- First, actual possession is evidence (though not conclusive evidence) of ownership. Proof of ownership of a thing is sometimes difficult. Let us suppose that I purchase a dictionary from a bookshop. I may not keep the receipt, and there may be many similar dictionaries. Conclusive and incontrovertible proof that the dictionary is mine becomes difficult. I may only be able to prove that it is mine by my signature on the book and by my having had possession of it for some time, so that I can identify it.

Similarly, it is sometimes difficult to prove ownership of land. *A* may claim ownership of land by right of inheritance or purchase from some other person, C, who may be able to prove ownership or 'a good root of title', e.g. by a deed showing the devolution of the property. If one can go back far into the past, the title may be traced ultimately to someone who took possession, so originating the ownership of the particular portion of land in dispute. All ownership of land finally derives from possession. *A*'s claim may, of course, be defeated by a rival claimant, C, who can prove that their predecessors in title were in possession or that *A* wrongfully dispossessed C. The law has always protected the rights of possession.

- Second, the law protects possession by various procedural rules. Suppose X possesses something (e.g. a pen) to which Y lays claim. If the latter uses force in retaking (called in law *recaption*), the physical act of recovery may involve an assault or breach of the peace for which Y may be held responsible. As regards premises, the **Criminal Law Act 1977** provides that squatters may be charged with criminal offences in certain circumstances.

  Also, in *Wolverhampton City Council and Others v London Gypsies and Travellers and Others* (2023) it was *Held*: (Supreme Court) that where a landowner can apply for an injunction to prevent unlawful occupation of their land (in this case by gypsies and travellers camping on their land, but as they did not know the identities of the individuals who could change from day to day) they were entitled to 'newcomer injunctions'.

  These were an entirely new form of injunction which could be granted without prior notice against persons who cannot be known at the time of the injunction being granted.

  They, therefore, could potentially apply to anyone in the world. However, it was recognized that they should be used only under specified circumstances, such as in this particular situation, as a compelling need to enforce public law and should be subject to procedural safeguards to protect newcomers' rights.

A finder of goods is entitled to them as against all persons other than the true owner (*Hannah v Peel*, 1945). As a general rule the right to take action in respect of trespass to land inheres in the occupier (i.e. the person in possession), for it is the right of possession or the enjoyment of possession that is disturbed or infringed by trespass.

10.3 Property

The word 'property' has several meanings, and in law we must be careful to distinguish between two of them.

i Property may mean the thing or things *capable* of ownership. In this sense the word includes not only physical (or corporeal) things such as a pen, desk, watch and land, but also non-physical (incorporeal) things such as patent rights, copyrights, debts, etc. This is the popular sense of the term 'property'.

ii Property may mean *ownership*. Thus, we may say in law that '*A* has the property in a watch', or in other words, '*A* owns a watch'. Both statements mean the same. In a sale of goods where, for example, a student buys a pen, the shop assistant hands the pen to the buyer and, at the same time, passes 'the property in the goods' (i.e. the ownership) to the buyer by delivery on the sale.

Classification of property. English law has classified property in various ways. Land, the main source of wealth, is by the very nature of things treated differently from most other kinds of property, as we shall see later. Property may be divided into two classes:

a *real property* (i.e. freehold interests in land); and
b *personal property*, which may be subdivided into:

 i chattels real and
 ii chattels personal.

'Chattels real' means leaseholds in land. 'Chattels personal' comprises *choses in action* and *choses in possession*.

The meaning of the terms mentioned previously is explained in the following pages.

Real property. In medieval law property was said to be 'real' if the courts of law would restore to a dispossessed owner the thing (*res*) itself. For example, if *A*, the owner of freehold land (the term freehold will be explained later) were dispossessed or evicted or turned out of their land by B, *A* could bring a 'real' action against B for the recovery of the land.

If B took away, let us say, a car owned by *A*, the remedy available to *A* was a personal action at civil law against B for the recovery of the specific property (i.e. the car) or its value. The car in the present example is referred to as *personalty* and land is referred to as *realty*.

A right *in rem* (sometimes called a real right) corresponds to a right against persons in general. In other words, the owner of the right has a right against the whole world not to be interfered with in relation to the thing (the *res*), e.g. land owned by them. A right *in personam* is a personal right only against one person or a group of persons; the commonest example is an ordinary contract made between, say, *A* and B, where each has a right against the other under the agreement.

As a result of these historical and procedural rules, a distinction was made between real property and personal property, and the distinction continues to this day. On the Continent, and in most other legal systems, the division of property is into 'movables' and 'immovables'. Land is

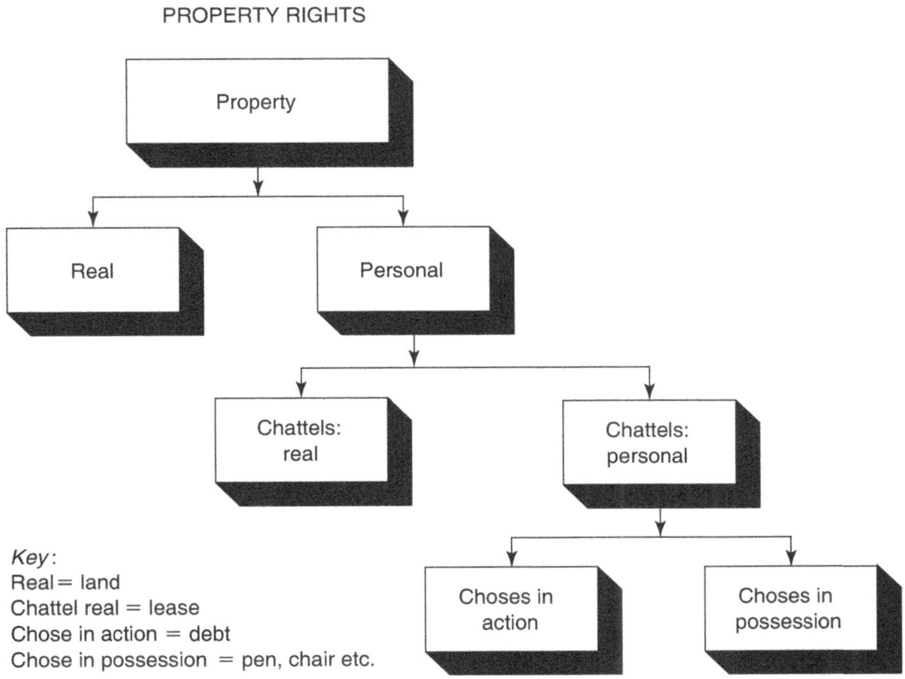

FIGURE 10.1 Property rights

immovable, while all other things that can be taken up and carried away (and are not permanently affixed to the land) are regarded as movable.

The term 'real property' in general signifies all interests in land. An important exception exists in regard to *leaseholds*, or 'terms of years' as they are sometimes called. A leasehold arises, for example, where *A*, the owner of land, grants to B a lease for (say) two years. *A* is called a lessor, and B is a lessee.

In the past a dispossessed leaseholder had no right at law to recover the land from anyone except the lessor who granted the lease. Until the thirteenth century the lessee could recover damages, but not possession. Later, in 1499, a lessee was permitted to recover the land itself by action. The law had by this time come to look upon leases as personalty and has done so ever since. A lease has, therefore, acquired a different status in the eyes of the law. Even today, if, for example, X dies leaving his or her realty to *A* and his or her personalty to B, any leaseholds held by X on death will pass to B.

The relationship of landlord to tenant is mainly contractual; the tenant pays the rent to the landlord who, for his or her part, agrees to allow the tenant to occupy the land or house, as the case may be. The lease in law is classified as personalty, but it is also specially described as a *chattel real*. The word 'chattel' derives from the Latin *cattala* (cattle) and means, in general terms, 'goods'. The word 'real' signifies, as we have noted, connexion with land. A lease partakes of both goods and land, and to distinguish it from 'real property' and from 'personal chattels', it is called a chattel real.

Chattels personal. There are, as we have noted, two types: (i) choses in possession and (ii) choses in action. The word 'chose', derived from the French, means in law 'a thing'.

Choses in possession. The characteristic of a chose in possession is that it is a physical thing and can be touched. A pen, book, chair and a horse are all choses in possession. As each has a physical existence, they are sometimes called corporeal (i.e. material) chattels to distinguish them from the so-called choses in action.

Choses in action. The main characteristic of a chose in action is that it can be owned but not touched. It has no physical existence. A common example is a debt, which is a 'thing' in law yet has no tangible existence. If *A* owes B £10, this is obviously of value to B, who may sue on the debt to recover the amount of £10 from the debtor *A*. We have discussed (see p. 208) the transfer or assignment of the right that B has. Provided that certain formalities are complied with, B may assign to C, a third party, the right to the debt and the right to sue *A*.

The phrase 'chose in action' provides a clue to another characteristic. It is not possible to take *physical* possession of a debt, but it is possible to assert the right by taking *legal action* for the debt; hence, it is called a chose *in action*.

Other examples of choses in action include patent rights, copyrights, rights in trademarks, stocks and shares, registered designs, goodwill of a business, insurance moneys and cheques.

All rights existing in the items listed previously can be protected, enforced or transferred at law by taking action, if need be, in the courts. Care must be taken to distinguish the thing itself from the rights that attach to it. A cheque, for example, is in common experience merely a piece of paper on which appear words and figures. That is its physical manifestation. However, *in law* it represents certain rights, the most important of which is the right (enforceable by action) to payment of a sum of money.

10.4 Freehold and leasehold land

The basic rule of English land law was that all land in England was owned by the Crown. When William I defeated the English, grants of land were made to his followers, to certain of the English barons and to those who submitted to his control. The grantees thereupon became holders or 'tenants' of the land. Since under feudal law there could not be two owners (the King was lord paramount and owned the land by right of conquest), it follows that the interest in the land possessed or held by a grantee was certainly less than that of the royal grantor.

Tenure. The grants of land were made in return for services to be rendered by the tenant. The terms on which the tenant held (called the tenure) were of various kinds. The chief division was between free and unfree tenure. *Free tenure* included the following:

i *Military tenure*. This consisted of the provision of armed horsemen and knights for a certain number of days in each year (Knight Service).
ii *Spiritual tenure*. This consisted of praying for the lord and saying masses for him. Spiritual tenure was sometimes called Frankalmoign.
iii *Socage tenure*. This consisted of services of a non-military kind, usually agricultural, e.g. provision of crops and beasts to a lord.
iv *Serjeanty*. This consisted of a personal service to the King or a lord.

These forms of tenure were for *fixed* services. Once the specified services were performed by the tenant, his time was his own and he was free to use the land as he desired. In course of time all four tenures became known as *freehold*, as distinct from copyhold (villeinage) tenure or *unfree tenure*.

Medieval serfs (or villeins) held their land by unfree tenure and were under the complete domination of their lord. Their services were not defined or limited as were those of free tenure. They were in a real sense bound to the soil and could not leave the holding. In the course of time

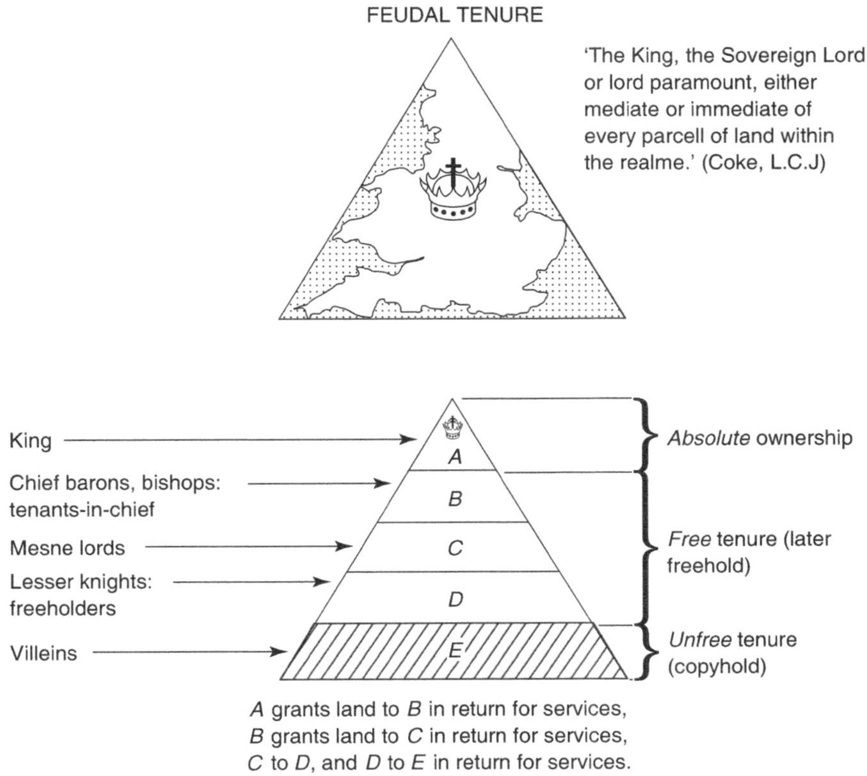

FIGURE 10.2 Feudal tenure

the tenure of land became known as *copyhold*, because a tenant's right to land depended on the possession of a copy of the rolls of the manorial court kept by the steward of the court. Copyhold tenure was finally abolished in 1922, the land becoming freehold.

In the limited space available it is impossible to give more than a very brief outline of the history of the land. The accompanying diagram shows the structure of the feudal grants of land and the sub-grants made by one person to another. A person sub-granting a freeholding estate to two or more tenants became a 'lord of the manor'. Subinfeudation, as this process was called, was stopped by the statute of *Quia Emptores*, 1289.

The feudal system broke down in the Middle Ages, and the various forms of tenure already described disappeared after 1660, with the exception of socage tenure, which was retained as the only form of free tenure.

In early land law, the possession that a freeholder of land had or enjoyed was of a special kind known as *seisin*. Seisin was, therefore, the interest of a freeholder in land. Right of seisin was protected in the courts of common law and was enforced against all persons except those with a prior right to seisin acquired by lawful means.

The meaning of estate. A person who owned the seisin in land owned a collection of rights in relation to it. The tenant's interest in land was known as an *estate*. Estates in land were of various kinds, and they differed as to the length of time for which they might exist. The word 'estate' does not, in law, mean the vast areas of land often implied in the everyday use of the word.

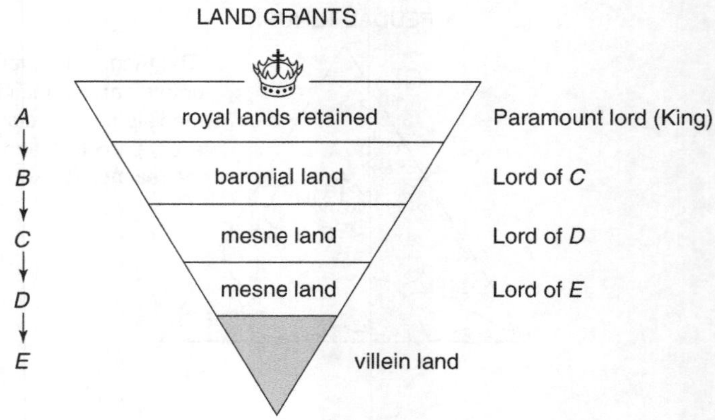

B held land of *A* (King) as tenant-in-chief.
C held of *B*, and *D* of *C*. Sub-infeudation (i.e. grant of land to another over whom the grantor became lord) was abolished by Statute of *Quia Emptores*, 1289.

FIGURE 10.3 Land grants

Classification of estates. Estates are classified according to the duration of a tenant's rights to the land as either:

a estates of freehold (of uncertain length of duration); or
b estates less than freehold (e.g. leaseholds), where the duration is either certain or may be ascertained from the terms of the grant.

Estates of freehold may be subdivided into: (i) estates in fee simple, (ii) estates in fee tail, (iii) estates for life and (iv) estates *per autre vie* ('for another's life').

i *The estate in fee simple* is the greatest estate in land that may be held. In broad terms it is equivalent to complete ownership; so if in common speech today we refer to *A* as owner of a certain portion of land, we mean that they enjoy an estate in fee simple in the land. This estate will be dealt with in more detail later.
ii *The estate in fee tail* may be best illustrated by example. Where a parent owned lands in fee simple and had sons who were dependent, they might wish to make a grant of a portion of land to son *A*, but so limited that the land be kept within the family. They could, therefore, make a grant of an estate in fee tail, which meant that on *A*'s death the land would devolve on *A*'s lineal descendants only. If there were no lineal descendants the estate reverted to the grantor, or, if already dead, to the (the grantor's) own successors, i.e. the next son.
iii *The estate for life.* Where an owner (X) in fee simple wished to grant an estate for the life of the grantee only, this could be done at common law. A formal grant was merely made to indicate the intentions: 'To *A* for life.' *A* became the owner of a limited estate in that it was unable to be disposed of at will. On *A*'s death the land reverted to the grantor, X. The interest of X was known as an interest in reversion. Sometimes the grant could be: 'To *A* for life, remainder in fee simple to B.' In this case the estate would not revert to the grantor, but it would vest in B. The interest of B was known as an *interest in remainder*, so called because the estate remained away from the grantor, X.
iv *The estate 'pur autre vie'*, endured for the life of a person other than a tenant. Assume X is the owner in fee simple of land granted to *A* in the following terms: 'To *A* for the life of B.'

A becomes the tenant of the land for the duration of the life of B. On B's death the estate terminates and will revert to the grantor or become vested in some other person to whom the 'remainder' has been granted.

10.5 Reform of the land law

In the course of some 900 years following the Norman invasion, the English land law became highly complex, highly technical and artificial. The distinction between real property, chattels real and personal property is one example. The rules of the devolution of property on death differed as to real property and personal property. A multitude of rights and interests in relation to land were created, making the transfer of land a most complicated task and sometimes impossible. Certain interests were legal interests, while others, known as equitable interests, took effect only in equity. Landowners tried to keep the land within their families, and constantly endeavoured to tie up the land so as to prevent alienation (i.e. transfer, by sale or otherwise) by a tenant for life. The public policy of the law was against tying the land up, and hence, there arose a battle of wills and wits.

Some attempts at piecemeal reform had been undertaken, but it was left to one of the most famous of English Lord Chancellors, Lord Birkenhead, to undertake a thorough reform of the land law. Lord Birkenhead's reforms resulted in the following five Acts of Parliament.

- i **Law of Property Act 1925**
- ii **Settled Land Act 1925**
- iii **Administration of Estates Act 1925**
- iv **Land Charges Act 1925**
- v **Land Registration Act 1925** (now repealed by the **Land Registration Act 2002**—The reforms introduced under the 2002 Act were aimed at ensuring that the future ownership of land took the form of 'title by registration' rather than 'registration of title'. Major changes introduced by the Act included the registration of shorter leases, encouraging voluntary land registration, changing the system of third-party rights, and reforming and modernizing the law of adverse possession—often known as 'squatters rights').

The main aims of the 1925 legislation were:

- a to abolish the distinction between real property and chattels real, and to assimilate the law relating to land as far as possible into the law relating to chattels
- b to simplify land law, and thus to make it cheaper and easier to transfer land
- c to make the rules for intestate succession the same for all forms of property
- d to abolish the antiquated form of tenure of land known as copyhold tenure
- e to reduce the number of *legal* estates in land to two
    - i a fee simple absolute in possession
    - ii a term of years absolute
- f to reduce the number of legal *interests* to five

Reduction of the number of legal estates. Under section 1 of the **Law of Property Act 1925**, the number of legal estates and interests that can exist in land has been reduced as follows:

- a The only estates in land that are capable of subsisting or of being conveyed or created at law are:
    - i an estate in fee simple absolute in possession
    - ii a term of years absolute

b The only interests or charges in or over land that are capable of subsisting or of being conveyed or created at law are:

i an easement, right or privilege for an interest equivalent to either of the previously mentioned estates (thus 'an easement for life' would not be a *legal* interest)
ii a rentcharge in possession issuing out of or charged on land being either perpetual or for a term of years absolute (a rentcharge is a right which, independently of any lease or mortgage, entitles the owner of it to a periodical sum of money with the payment of which the land is charged. For example, where the owner in fee simple of Whiteacre charges the land with the payment of £500 per annum for John Smith)
iii a charge by way of legal mortgage
iv land tax and other similar charge on land that is not created by an instrument (this means a land tax, etc., created by a statute)
v rights of entry exercisable over or in respect of a legal term of years absolute, or annexed, for any purpose, to a legal rentcharge

It should be noted that the section does not provide that all the estates and interests mentioned at (a) and (b) are necessarily *legal*, but no *other* estate or interest can be a *legal* estate or interest. All other estates in land can now only exist as *equitable* interests.

10.5.1 Reform of Land Law—Modern Reforms

The year 2022 signalled a period of change in modern land law. **The Leasehold Reform (Ground Rent) Act 2022** ensured that freeholders/landlords were no longer able to make financial demands for ground rent. The Act also prohibited the charging of administration charges in relation to peppercorn rents. The **Leasehold and Freehold Reform Act 2024** was the second part of this legislative package to reform English property law. It empowered homeowners:

a By banning the sale of new leasehold houses, so that all new houses had to be freehold.
b Made it easier and cheaper for existing leaseholders in houses and flats to extend their lease or buy their freehold.
c Increased the standard lease extension term from 90 years to 990 years for both houses and flats, with ground rent reduced to a peppercorn.
d Removed the requirements for a new leaseholder to have owned their house for two years before they could extend their lease or buy their freehold and for flats before they could extend their lease.
e Increased the 25 per cent 'non-residential' limit, preventing leaseholders in building with a mixture of homes and other uses such as shops and offices, from buying their freehold or taking over management of their buildings—to allow leaseholders in buildings with up to 50 per cent non-residential floorspace to buy their freehold or take over its management.

Note: Also, the reforms which are taking place to **10.12 Commonhold** (see p. 312).

10.6 An estate in fee simple absolute in possession

This is one of the two estates in land that, since 1925, may exist as *legal* estates. The expression is admittedly a technical one, but the meaning may be ascertained by analysis of each of the terms used.

'*Fee*' denotes that the estate is an estate of inheritance, i.e. one that may be inherited under the laws of intestacy or given by will.

'*Simple*' denotes that the estate is not a fee tail (an estate limited to certain lineal descendants only of the grantee). 'Simple' means that the estate is capable of passing to the *general heirs* of the grantee.

'*Absolute*' signifies the grant is not subject to a condition but will continue forever, and distinguishes it from a fee or an estate that may be determinable on the happening of an event.

'*In possession*' signifies that the grantee must be entitled to immediate possession of the estate. This *may* be physical possession, though not necessarily, for the phrase 'in possession' includes 'the receipt of rents and profits and the rights to receive rents and profits'. A grantee need not, therefore, take physical possession to qualify as being 'in possession'.

A tenant in fee simple absolute in possession is, for all practical purposes, in the same position as the owner. Those ownership rights extend down to the centre of the earth and up to the sky (*usque ad inferos et usque ad caelum*).

Owners are not, of course, absolutely free to do what they like with their own property, be it land or any other thing. They are subject to the general law of torts, including nuisance, negligence and particularly to modern statute law which circumscribes the rights of the individual owner in the interest of the community, e.g. **Town and Country Planning Acts** and, in accordance with the **Countryside and Rights of Way Act 2000**, the constraints of the rights of the public in relation to access to land. Moreover, certain mineral rights (e.g. coal, iron ore and petroleum) in an owner's land have been taken away and vested in the State.

❖ CASE EXAMPLE

Graham v K.D. Morris and Sons Pty Ltd (1974)

At frequent intervals the jib of the defendants' crane projected over the plaintiff's land. *Held*: The invasion of the plaintiff's airspace by the projection of the crane jib was a trespass and not just a nuisance.

Creation of an estate in fee simple absolute in possession. It is clear that a legal owner of land wishing to transfer the ownership may do so in various ways, e.g. gift, sale or by will. Land is transferred by means of a *conveyance*, which is a legal document conveying the ownership of the property from one person to another. Words in the conveyance must be used with exactness to define or delimit the right to be transferred. The words marking out the interest in the land to be taken by another are known as 'words of limitation'.

The common-law rules on words of limitation were exceedingly strict, but section 60 of the **Law of Property Act 1925** states that the 'grantee will take the whole interest which the grantor had power to convey in such land, unless a contrary intention appears in the conveyance'. Today, therefore, where X who let us say, owns the fee simple in Blackacre, wishes to transfer the land to Y, Blackacre may be conveyed. In such a case, Y will 'take the fee simple in the land known as Blackacre'. The same rules regarding words of limitation apply to wills as to conveyances.

Words of limitation must be distinguished from 'words of purchase'. Words of limitation *define* or *delimit* an estate or interest; words of purchase *confer* one. To make this clearer, let us suppose that a grant of land is made thus:

a 'To *A* and his heirs.' The entire phrase is taken together to delimit *A*'s estate. *A* receives the fee simple estate which can be sold or given away or left by will. There is no interest conveyed to the heirs.

b 'To X for life, remainder to Y.' The effect of this grant is that X takes a life interest, and on X's death, the estate will pass to Y. The effect of the words of purchase here is to confer an interest on the two persons, X and Y.

In example (a), the words are words of limitation. In example (b), the words are words of purchase, since they define or mark out and *confer* the estate or interest to be taken by X and Y. Words of purchase do not necessarily mean that the recipient bought the estate. They mean that the estate or interest was handed over by grant, which may take the form of a sale or a gift, as distinct from entitlement arising by operation of law (as when an owner dies intestate).

To understand the meaning and legal effect of the phrase 'an estate in fee simple absolute in possession', it is useful to mention some forms of grant that may be made today and to consider what interest passes to the grantee. A grantor may today use such phrases as 'To X for life'; 'To X and the heirs of his body'; 'To X provided he adopts the name of Dickens'; 'To X in fee simple absolute from 1984'; 'To X in fee simple' and 'To X and his heirs'.

The common law had formed rigid rules of interpretation before 1925, and these have been carried over into current use. They must now, however, be interpreted in the light of the **Law of Property Act 1925** and its provisions.

i *'To X for life.'* A grant in this form does not create a legal estate. It is of limited duration and can now take effect only as an equitable interest.
ii *'To X and the heirs of his body.'* This again does not create a legal estate. This form of words formerly created an entailed estate capable of being inherited only by the lineal descendants of X. It now creates an entailed interest that is equitable.
iii *'To X provided he adopts the name of Dickens.'* This does not create a legal estate, for it is not absolute, being subject to the condition of the adoption of the name Dickens.
iv *'To X in fee simple absolute from 1984.'* This does not create a legal estate. It does not take effect in possession, being postponed until 1984. It is not of a certain duration since X may not be alive in 1984.
v *'To X in fee simple.'* This does create a legal estate in fee simple absolute in possession. The **Conveyancing Act 1881** enabled this phrase to be used to convey the whole interest of the grantor. Where the date for possession is not mentioned, the estate is deemed to take effect in possession immediately, i.e. forthwith.
vi *'To X and his heirs.'* This phrase creates a legal estate in fee simple absolute in possession. The words here used are words of limitation and not words of purchase. The mention of the words 'his heirs' does not transfer to them any interest in the property.

The interests in (i), (ii), (iii) and (iv) that are passed will take effect, if they take effect at all, as equitable interests. Only in cases (v) and (vi) do the words create a legal estate, i.e. a fee simple absolute in possession.

10.7 Future estates

Before 1925 there were three main varieties of future legal estates:

a reversions and remainders
b shifting and springing uses
c executory devises

a Reversions and remainders

Where a grant of land is made by a tenant in fee simple to another for life or in fee tail, the grantor loses the right to present possession and enjoyment of the land. The estate becomes a future estate and is called a *reversion*.

Suppose the tenant (*A*) owner in fee simple of Blackacre makes the following grant: 'To B for life.' When B's life comes to an end, the 'particular estate' carved out of *A*'s fee simple estate also ends, and the estate reverts to *A* in possession. The same rule applied to the fee tail when the lineal descendants of the grantee became extinct.

Where a grant was made by *A* (fee simple owner of Blackacre): 'To B for life, then to C in fee simple', the future interest to be taken by C was known as a *remainder*. And even if C died before B, the effect would be that C's heirs would take the fee simple in Blackacre.

The tenant for life and the tenant of the fee tail estate were known as 'limited owners', as distinct from the tenant in fee simple when in possession, who was a full owner.

b Shifting and springing uses

These kinds of future interests were created by means of a trust (which evolved from the medieval 'use'), and were always equitable as they are today.

c Executory devises

These future interests were created by means of wills. The details need not concern us.

10.8 Settlements and trusts for sale

In former times, where a person owned considerable land, ways might be considered for the provision of the family out of the estate's income. It was also a matter of family pride to keep the land within the family. These were the main reasons for the creation of family settlements.

A settlement is a legal instrument by which land or other property is limited in trust for a number of persons successively. Settlements fall into two classes: (a) strict settlements and (b) settlements by way of trust for sale.

a Strict settlements

The means adopted to keep the land within the family was the trust. The land was so limited that it descended as a whole from father to the eldest son. If the father had no son, it was so arranged that the land descended to daughters. The claims of the other members of the family, i.e. his wife (or widow), and other sons and daughters dependent upon the father, were satisfied by giving them an income or capital sum charged upon the land.

We remember that before 1 January 1926, the life estate and the estate tail existed as legal estates. These forms were used to affect the intention of the creator of the trust or settlement.

The operation of the strict settlement may best be explained by example. Let us go back in time to before 1926 and suppose that William Smith was the owner of property known as Blackacre and that he was about to marry Jane. A so-called 'marriage settlement' would be executed, transferring the estate in Blackacre to trustees on the following trusts.

i To William Smith (the owner) to hold for a life interest in Blackacre.
ii With remainder to the eldest son in tail, and successive remainders should the eldest son die without issue.

iii A provision for his wife (Jane), i.e. an annual payment (called a *jointure*) during widowhood.
iv A provision for other children of the marriage who would be granted *portions*, i.e. capital sums of money raised out of the estate in Blackacre.

The jointure to the wife and the portions to the children were secured on the property by means of a *rentcharge*. Payment of these annual sums was a first charge on the proceeds and profits arising out of the land. These grants could be enforced at law (they were legal grants) and the person liable could be used for them, if need be. The person liable was the life tenant or other person entitled to the estate.

It was the practice when the son reached maturity for the father and the son to join together to make a resettlement of the property. If William had a son, Robert, who reached 21 years, the land was then re-conveyed to the trustees in trust to hold on the following terms:

i To William Smith for the rest of his life.
ii An annual charge upon the land is secured to Robert Smith, with remainder to Robert Smith for life, with remainder to Robert Smith's son in tail.

On the death of William Smith, Robert Smith would, as life tenant, take the place of the father. In due time when he himself had a son, Robert Smith would make a similar resettlement with his eldest son to avoid the possibility of the son barring the entail. The process was continued generation by generation.

The exact details of these settlements varied from family to family, but the main principles outlined previously to keep the land with the Smith family prevailed almost universally among those persons with sufficient land at their disposal. Consequently, there was no person, not even the life tenant, having the power of sale. This led to unfortunate consequences, however laudable the family motives might be. The tenant for life, while paying for all repairs, maintenance, taxes, etc., was unable to pay for improvements or to secure capital for these from the estate. The chief limitation was the inability to sell the estate. In later times increased taxation added to the burdens facing life tenants.

The policy of the law generally was that land ought to be freely alienable, i.e. transferable from person to person, and at long last, the **Settled Land Act 1882** and the **Settled Land Act 1925** were passed.

10.8.1 The Settled Land Act 1925

The Settled Land Act 1925 applies to settled land and not to land held on trust for sale (to be described later). Since 1 January 1926, where land is settled, the *legal* estate in the land is vested in the tenant for life. The tenant is now in a dual position: he or she is (i) absolute owner for the purpose of any disposition (e.g. sale) of the land; but as regards their interests under the settlement they are (ii) a trustee of the settled land on behalf of themselves and the other beneficiaries under the settlement.

The Act further provides that settlements must now be made by two deeds: (a) the vesting deed and (b) the trust instrument.

The *vesting deed* must contain:

i a description of the settled land;
ii a statement that the land is vested in the life tenant on the trusts of the settlement;
iii the names of the settlement trustees;
iv the names of the person(s) entitled to appoint additional trustees; and
v a statement of any additional powers of the tenant for life over and above those conferred by the Act.

There is no mention in the vesting deed of the trusts upon which the tenant for life holds the land.

The *trust deed*, which is made out at the same time, contains the description of the trusts on which the land is held, i.e. giving the details of the beneficiaries and the interests that each is to have (following the pattern of the settlement already described) which will necessarily be equitable interests.

Where a settlement arises under a will, the will itself is treated as the trust instrument, and the testator's personal representatives (the executors of the will) hold the land on trust to vest the legal estate in the first person entitled as life tenant. This is done by means of a vesting assent in writing.

The advantage of creating these two instruments (vesting deed and trust instrument) is that a purchaser of the land is normally only permitted to examine the vesting deed that deals with the legal estate they are purchasing. As far as the purchaser is concerned, the owner of the land is the tenant for life—not the trustees. The details of the trust on which the land has been settled, contained in the trust deed, are not disclosed to the buyer. They lie behind the curtain of the vesting deed, and they can be overreached by the purchaser of the land, provided the purchase money is paid to the trustees of the settlement, not to the tenant for life. It is the duty of the trustees on receipt of the purchase price to ensure that the trusts of the settlement are discharged, i.e. by paying to the beneficiaries their interests that attach to the money, and not to the land once the sale has taken place. This is what is meant by 'overreaching'.

The **Settled Land Act 1925** also lays down the powers of the tenant for life concerning the settled land. These powers include the general management of the settled property, in regard to which it may be used at their own discretion. But, to protect the interests of the beneficiaries of the settlement, the tenant may exercise certain powers only after giving notice to the trustees or, in some cases, obtaining their consent. Thus consent is required where the tenant for life proposes to sell the principal mansion house, to cut and sell timber, to use capital money for improvements and to modify restrictive covenants attaching to the land.

b Trusts for sale

The strict settlement just described must be distinguished from a settlement by way of trust for sale.

- In the latter case the purpose of creating a trust was not to keep the land in the family but to sell the land and to provide a regular income for the beneficiaries out of the money realized on the sale.
- Accordingly, the trust for sale imposes on the trustees an absolute duty to sell the land, and to hold the proceeds of the sale and the rents and profits until the sale for the beneficiaries.
- The trustees were usually given power to postpone the sale at their discretion and to manage the land until the sale. As long as it produced a satisfactory income, the land could be retained. Often the consent of the beneficiaries under the trust was made necessary before a sale could take place.
- The effect of creating a trust for sale was that, even before sale, the rights of the beneficiaries were deemed to be rights in personalty, not in the land. Since there was a *binding obligation* to sell the land, the beneficiaries were treated as having immediate interests in the purchase money into which the land would ultimately be converted, but they had no interest in the land itself.
- This doctrine, known as *conversion*, was based on the principle that equity 'looks upon that as done which ought to be done'. Thus, from the moment of the conveyance of the property to the trustees, whether there has been an actual sale or not, the land was regarded in equity as

if it were *purchase money* already. The doctrine of conversion was abolished by section 3 of the **Trusts of Land and Appointment of Trustees Act 1996**.

- In a trust for sale there is no need for a 'tenant for life'. The trustees exercise the power of sale, since they are the legal owners. Moreover, under section 28(1) of the **Law of Property Act**, the trustees for sale are given all the powers of a tenant for life under a settlement, e.g. they have power to exchange the land for other land, to grant leases, to obtain mortgages, to manage the property and to make improvements to the land. The trustees may delegate their powers of leasing, accepting surrenders of leases and management, at any time before sale to 'any person of full age for the time being beneficially entitled in possession to the rents and profits' under the terms of the trust.
- Since the rights that encumber the land are (in theory) rights only in respect of a share of the purchase money, notice of them will have no effect upon a purchaser. Once the latter pays the trustees on the sale, the distribution of the money among those beneficially entitled is the responsibility and business of the trustees; the purchaser takes the land free from those interests, which again are said to be overreached. There is, therefore, no need for special machinery (e.g. the making of two deeds) to conceal these rights. Although only one deed is strictly necessary in a trust for sale, in practice and for the sake of simplicity, two are generally used.

Trusts for sale may arise (a) expressly, as where land is deliberately limited by a settlor on trust for sale or (b) by operation of law. The most common circumstances under which a trust for sale arises by operation of law are:

i where there is co-ownership of land by two or more persons (**Law of Property Act 1925**, s. 36); and
ii where a person dies intestate (**Administration of Estates Act 1925**, s. 33).

c Trusts of land

The **Trusts of Land and Appointments of Trustees Act 1996** has replaced, with a single system, the dual system of trust for sale and strict settlements. The effect of the Act is that in the future, most new trusts that include land will be known as *trusts of land*. There is an exception for existing strict settlements created under the **Settled Land Act 1925**, which will continue to be governed by that Act.

10.9 Co-ownership

Although property rights in relation to land are often held by one person only at a time, it is, of course, possible for two or more persons to own land together, e.g. a husband and wife may both own the matrimonial home. This form of ownership is known as co-ownership, and is of two kinds: (a) joint ownership and (b) ownership in common.

a Joint ownership

The owners are known as *joint tenants* and each is the owner of the whole land, though, of course, the rights of ownership of each are subject to the right of the other party or parties.

b Ownership in common

In this case each owner is regarded as owning an individual share in the property, though not a specific part; e.g. if there are three owners in common, each is entitled to a third.

There are important distinctions between these two forms of ownership.

- In the first place, a joint tenancy arises where land is conveyed to two or more persons and no words of severance, such as 'in equal shares', are used in the grant. Thus, a grant: 'To *A* and B' or 'To *A* and B jointly' creates a joint tenancy, while a conveyance 'To *A* and B equally' or 'To *A* and B in common' creates a tenancy in common.
- Wherever land is granted in such a way as to suggest that the grantor intends the tenants to have *distinct* shares, even though the land remains physically undivided, a tenancy in common arises. Words that show this intention of distinct shares are known as *words of severance*.

The difference between the two forms of ownership is best observed by looking at the position when one owner (joint or in common) dies.

- Where a joint owner dies, the share in the property passes to the survivor(s). Let us suppose that *A*, B and C are joint tenants. When C dies, the share in the property passes automatically to *A* and B equally. When B dies, the share in the property passes to *A*, who thereupon becomes the sole owner of the land. This is known as the *jus accrescendi* or right of survivorship.
- If, however, the land is held in common, the deceased owner's share will pass to the heir and does not accrue to the surviving co-tenant. Thus, where *A*, B and C are tenants in common, on the death of C his share will form part of C's estate and will be disposed of accordingly.
- The advantage of the joint tenancy was that it avoided splitting the estate into many different parts, and thus prevented the creation of too many interests in one portion of land.
- A joint tenant cannot leave any part of the jointly owned property by will.
- With a joint tenancy, there would be only a few persons whose consents and signature are necessary for a sale and conveyance of the land to a purchaser.
- With land held in common, however, the transfer of ownership raised difficulties as each co-owner had to sign the necessary deeds of transfer or conveyance.
- Moreover, each co-owner may leave their interest by will, thus creating further complications.
- A joint tenancy as described previously is of course unjust in that the right to the sole ownership depends on the length of one's days, and longevity is uncertain.

The **Law of Property Act 1925** amended the law in respect of co-ownership. After 1925 a tenancy in common cannot exist at law and all co-owners (or the first four named in the grant if there are more than four) are joint tenants of the legal estate, which is subject to a trust for sale.

- The right of survivorship applies to the joint tenancy, so that on the death of one trustee, the legal estate automatically vests equally in the remaining trustees.
- In equity, however, they and any other co-owners will be either joint tenants or tenants in common according to the terms of the grant or the presumptions of equity. For example, equity will presume a tenancy in common of the equitable estate where two or more purchasers contribute the purchase money in unequal shares, or where partners purchase land.
- The effect is that anyone buying property from co-owners (joint or in common) is concerned with, at the most, only four persons as legal owners from whom they take a conveyance of the legal estate.
- The rights of the co-owners attach to the sum resulting from the sale in proportion to the shares held by each.
- If, therefore, a co-owner who is a tenant in common in equity dies, the heirs will succeed not to the interest in the land, but to the interest in the money realized on the sale and held in trust for them.

- If a co-owner who is joint tenant in equity dies, however, the right of survivorship applies to the equitable joint tenancy and the share accrues equally to the other equitable joint tenants. This is the form of co-ownership used very frequently, where a husband and wife purchase the matrimonial home as co-owners.

10.10 Leaseholds

We have already mentioned that before 1925, a freeholder could grant leases of his land to others. Much of the property (land and houses) in the United Kingdom is occupied by tenants under leases. As a result of the 1925 legislation the only legal estate in land other than the fee simple absolute in possession is the *term of years absolute*, which is the interest created by a lease.

The essential nature of a lease is that it is a grant by a landlord to a tenant of exclusive possession of the property leased, together with an intention to create the relationship of landlord and tenant. In doubtful cases it is for the courts to decide whether the agreement (oral, in writing or by conduct) into which the parties have entered is a tenancy agreement in law. The further essential feature of a leasehold interest is that it will start and end at some definite time in the future and will not continue indefinitely, i.e. it is of a determinate nature.

The expression 'a term of years' is misleading in that it includes weekly, monthly, quarterly or yearly tenancies (called *periodic tenancies*), as well as long leases for 99 years or 999 years which are common in practice. Other types of tenancies are known as *tenancies at will* and *tenancies at sufferance*.

A leasehold interest may subsist as a legal estate even though the tenant is not to take possession at once. Thus, a *term of years* can be made to take effect in, say, five years' time. Under section 149(3) of the **Law of Property Act 1925**, a term granted at a rent must be limited to take effect within 21 years. Any grant purporting to postpone the taking effect of the term for a longer period than 21 years is invalid.

10.10.1 Tenancies

a Lease for a fixed period

The characteristics of this tenancy are (i) that it is created by express agreement and (ii) that the commencement and the termination of the lease must be certain or ascertainable before the lease comes into effect.

b Yearly tenancies

A yearly tenancy continues from year to year or until determined by proper notice. It may be created (i) expressly or (ii) by implication, e.g. where a person occupies land with the owner's consent and pays rent that is calculated on an annual basis. The period of notice necessary to determine the tenancy is agreed upon between the parties. If no such agreed notice has been arrived at, a yearly tenancy must be determined by at least half a year's notice to expire at the end of the year of the tenancy; where the tenancy began on one of the official quarter days, this means two-quarters' notice. Quarterly, monthly or weekly tenancies (which are included under this classification) are determined by notice for the full period, i.e. Quarter, month or week.

c Tenancy at will

This arises where a person takes possession of property with the owner's consent (i.e. not as servant or agent) on the understanding that the term can be brought to an end at any time by either party giving notice. The tenancy may be rent-free, but unless this has been expressly agreed between the parties, the tenant must pay rent. In addition to notice, the tenancy may come to an end if either landlord or tenant does some act inconsistent with the tenancy and automatically terminates after 12 months. Where there is no agreement as to rent, the tenancy can become a periodic tenancy if the tenant pays and the owner accepts rent paid at given periods of time.

❖ **CASE EXAMPLE**

***Burrows v Brent London Borough Council* (1996)**

If a council tenant's secure tenancy has come to an end, but the council allows him or her to remain in occupation subject to conditions, the tenant is considered a tolerated trespasser whom the council has decided not to evict.

d Tenancy at sufferance

This can only arise by implication of law. It comes into existence where, on the expiration of the tenancy, a tenant holds over without the landlord's permission. The distinction between this and the tenancy at will is that in the one case, the landlord does not consent, but does in the other. No rent is payable, but the tenant must compensate the owner by a payment (called *mesne profits*) for the use and occupation of the land. The tenancy may be brought to an end at any time, or it may be converted into a periodic tenancy if rent is paid and accepted periodically.

Statutory *protection*. Because of the shortage of houses and accommodation, the Government has more and more interfered in the landlord and tenant relationship, which was originally purely contractual. This involves detailed legislation that cannot be described here. The main purpose is to give some degree of security to tenants and to restrict rents. The most important statutes are:

a the **Agricultural Holdings Act 1986**, as amended
b the **Landlord and Tenant Acts 1985, 1987** and **1988**
c the **Leasehold Reform Acts 1967** and **1979**, under which a tenant holding a long lease may, in certain cases, acquire the freehold or the extended long lease of the house where he resides
d the **Rent Act 1977**, which imposes certain rent control and gives some security of tenure in respect of unfurnished lettings, and imposes rent control and, again, a limited security in respect of furnished lettings
e the **Leasehold Reform, Housing and Urban Development Act 1993** and the **Leasehold Reform (Amendment) Act 2014**
f the **Homelessness Reduction Act 2017**, which provides for local authorities to intervene at earlier stages to protect against homelessness and to take reasonable steps to help those who become homeless to share accommodation
g the **Social Housing (Regulation) Act 2023** which focuses on the needs of tenants and ensures that landlords are held to account for their performance

10.10.2 Creation of leases

a Leases for more than three years

This type must be created by deed in order to become a legal estate. A mere written lease (not a deed) creates only an equitable interest that is capable of being converted into a legal estate by order for specific performance. If the lease is merely oral, it may be enforced by equity as mentioned previously, provided that the equitable doctrine of part performance applies (see p. 150).

b Leases for not more than three years

These need not be by deed to be legal; a written or oral lease will suffice, so long as the lease takes effect in possession at once at the best rent obtainable and without payment of a capital sum.

10.10.3 Duties of landlord and tenant

In any lease the lessor may require the tenant to sign certain express covenants, e.g. to insure against fire. Apart from these expressed covenants there are certain implied covenants.

Landlord's duties. The following are the main duties owed by the landlord to the tenant:

a The landlord has to ensure that the tenant gets 'quiet enjoyment' of the land. This does not mean there will be no noise, but that the lessor guarantees to the tenant that no third party will be lawfully able to question the title of the tenant to the land.
b The landlord must not derogate from the grant, i.e. the tenant's enjoyment of the premises must not be interfered with. Therefore, nothing must be done that would render the land unfit for the purpose for which it was let, e.g. by using the adjoining premises in a manner inconsistent with the lease.
c Previously the landlord had no obligation to ensure that the premises should be fit for habitation. However, the Homes (Fitness for Human Habitation) Act 2018—an Act to amend the Landlord and Tenant Act 1985—requires that residential rented accommodation is provided and maintained in a state of fitness for human habitation. There is an implied covenant that a furnished house that is let must be fit for human habitation at the time of the letting. Houses let at an annual rental of less than £52 (£80 in London) must be fit for human habitation at the time of letting and maintained in that state during the tenancy (Landlord and Tenant Act 1985).
d Certain statutes and cases now impose a limited obligation on the landlord to repair.

Tenant's duties. The main duties of the tenant are:

a to pay the rent
b to pay rates and taxes, except those that are legally the landlord's personal obligation
c not to commit waste; this means that the property must not be deliberately damaged or allowed to depreciate unreasonably by neglect

10.10.4 Express covenants

The most important express covenants usually contained in a lease are: (i) to pay rent; (ii) to pay rates and taxes; (iii) to repair; (iv) to permit the lessor to enter and inspect the state of repair; (v) to obtain insurance; (vi) not to carry on any trade or business and (vii) not to assign or underlet without consent.

Two of the preceding covenants call for mention:

a Covenant not to assign or underlet

Where such a covenant exists, the tenant may neither assign nor underlet; in the absence of such a covenant a tenant may do so. In an assignment, the lessee parts with the whole interest to the purchaser, who becomes the tenant of the freeholder. Such an assignee is bound, as long as the leasehold interest is owned, to observe and perform all the covenants binding on the vendor (the assignor) that touch and concern the land. In an underletting, the original lessee grants an underlease to the purchaser for the residue of the lease, less the last few days. For example, *A* is the fee simple owner and leases Blackacre to B for 20 years. B, the lessee, may then sublet Blackacre to

C (who becomes sub-lessee) for the residue of the term held by B less the last ten days thereof. B will, therefore, retain the reversion of ten days on the expiration of C's underlease. Generally, the sub-lessee is not bound by the covenants in the lease granted by the freeholder, but will be bound by those in the underlease of the sub-lessee.

Where a landlord imposes a covenant permitting the lessee to assign or underlet but only with the landlord's consent, there is a statutory duty on the landlord not to withhold consent unreasonably (section 19(1)(a) of the Landlord and Tenant Act 1927). To justify a refusal to consent, the landlord must have a good reason, e.g. the unsuitability of the use to which the subtenant proposes to put the land.

The Court of Appeal in *International Drilling Fluids Ltd v Louisville Investments (Uxbridge) Ltd* (1986) set out seven propositions that can be deduced from the authorities on the reasonableness of withholding consent.

b Covenant to repair

In long leases the tenant usually covenants to repair. In short leases the landlord frequently assumes the liability for external repairs and structural repairs, and the tenant assumes responsibility for internal repairs only. The standard of repair is the standard that a reasonable landowner would adopt in relation to their own premises.

If the lease makes no mention of the liability to repair, neither party is liable. The tenant is liable for committing waste, and must generally keep the property in a reasonable state of repair (an implied duty).

10.11 Servitudes

In addition to the ordinary rights of property that landowners may exercise over their own land, the law recognizes certain rights that extend over the land of a neighbour. These are known as *servitudes* and may be either (a) easements or (b) profits à prendre.

a Easements

An easement may be defined as the right to use, or to restrict the use of, the land of another person in some way. The most important easements are rights of way, rights of light, rights to abstract water and rights to the support of buildings.

The main features of an easement are as follows:

i There must be a *dominant* and a *servient* tenement. The land in favour of which the easement exists is known as the dominant tenement; that in respect of which the right is exercised is called the servient tenement. Thus, if X gives Y permission to cross the land, Y will have no easement. It is a personal grant only and, at most, may be a licence so that Y does not become a trespasser. If, however, X, the owner of Blackacre, grants a similar right to Z, the owner of neighbouring Whiteacre, this is an easement. In this example, Whiteacre is the dominant tenement and Blackacre is the servient tenement. The easement must contribute in some way to the better enjoyment of the dominant tenement, e.g. by facilitating access to house or land, and not merely benefit the owner personally in a way unconnected with the enjoyment of the dominant tenement.

ii The easement must be capable of forming the subject matter of a grant by deed. Thus there must be a capable grantor and a capable grantee, and the grant must relate to something that is capable of reasonable definition and have the characteristics of an easement.

iii There must be separate ownership of the dominant and servient tenements. If the two pieces of land are under the same ownership, or at some future date come under the same ownership, the easement will cease to exist.

In *Parker and Another v Roberts* (2019) it was *Held*: (Court of Appeal) that if land ceases to be used for an ancillary purpose. it can no longer be accessed via a right-of-way benefitting adjoining land.

Note: In *Regency Villas Title Ltd v Diamond Resorts Europe Ltd* (2018) it was held that rights of timeshare owners to use recreational facilities could amount to an easement—obviously such determination was a matter of fact. Common law should accommodate itself to new types of property ownership and new ways of enjoying land. Timeshare developments were such a new type and recreational easements had become widely recognized in common law.

b Profits à prendre

A *profit à prendre* is the right to take something from the land of another, e.g. a right of fishing in another's river, grazing rights for cattle, a right to collect firewood or to cut turf. The right to draw water from another's river or stream is an exception since it is treated in law as an easement, not a profit. (This apparent anomaly is based on the proposition that running water cannot be privately owned.) The distinctions between a profit and an easement are:

i An easement must, as it is put, be appurtenant to land (i.e. there must be a dominant and servient tenement), while a profit may exist *in gross*, which means that it may be enjoyed by its owner or owners independently of any dominant tenement and unconnected with the enjoyment of land.

ii A profit may be a 'several profit', i.e. enjoyed by one person only to the exclusion of all others, or a 'profit in common', i.e. enjoyed by many people. Thus, *A* may have a right to shoot game on B's land (a several profit), and all the inhabitants of a certain village may have a right to graze cattle on B's land (a profit in common).

Easements and profits may be created by (a) statute, (b) grant (express, implied or presumed) and (c) prescription.

a By statute

Where these exist, the statute is usually a local one. An exception to this rule is the **Access to Neighbouring Land Act 1992**. This enables people who need access to their neighbour's land in order to ascertain types of repair and maintenance work on their own land to get a court order authorizing entry.

b By grant

This is the most usual method of acquisition of a servitude. *Express* grants exist where the owner of the servient tenement creates the servitude by deed. An *implied* grant is one implied by law. Let us suppose that *A* owns a field and a bungalow in the middle of it. If *A* sells the field, without reserving a right of way from the bungalow to the road, they will have no means of access. A reservation of way is, therefore, implied in favour of the bungalow retained by *A*. This is called an easement or 'way of necessity'.

c By prescription

At common law, proof of use of a servitude from 'time immemorial', i.e. since 1189, is regarded as giving a prescriptive right to the servitude. In practice, the courts regard any long usage as

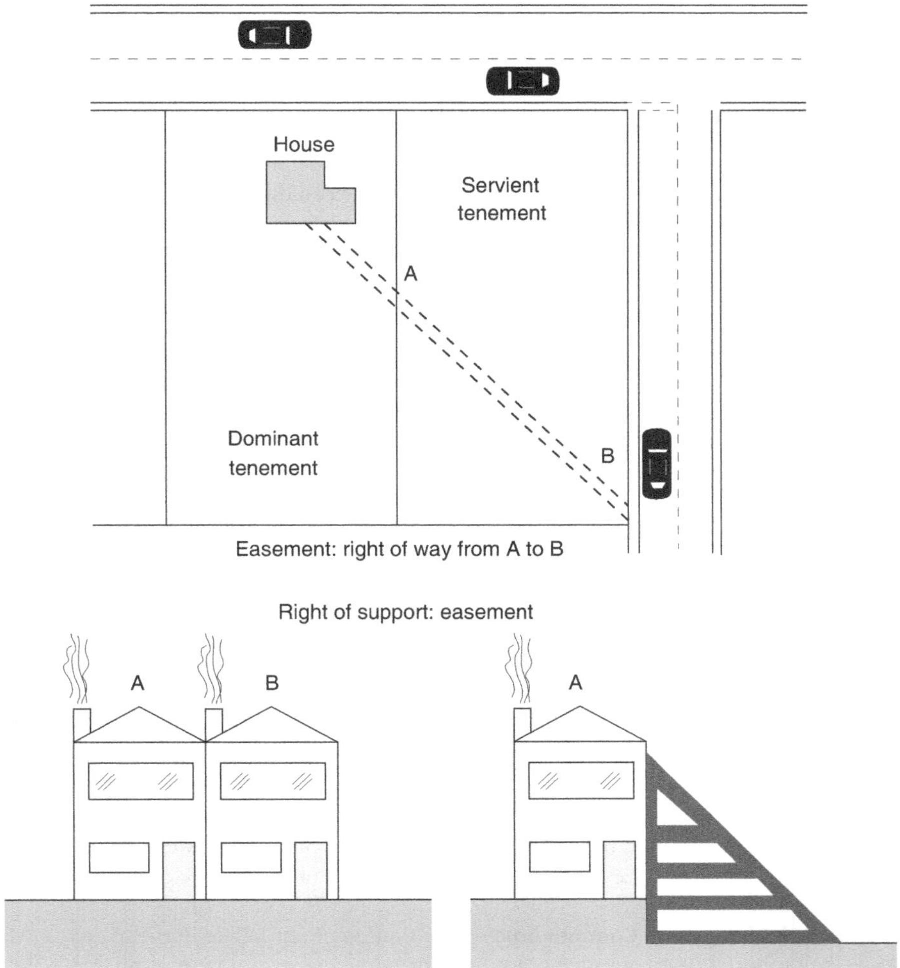

FIGURE 10.4 Right of way from A to B

sufficient to raise the presumption that the right has existed since 1189, but the presumption may be rebutted by proof that the right did not exist, or by its nature could not have existed, at some time since 1189.

Because of the obvious difficulty of proof of continuous use since 1189, the courts evolved the doctrine of the *Lost Modern Grant*. Under this doctrine a court will sometimes presume, provided that long use (usually 20 years) can be proved, that a grant was made at some time since 1189 but that it has subsequently been lost (*Bridle v Ruby and Another*, 1988). While a grantee (user) of a right of way is entitled to repair it, any improvements beyond this would amount to a trespass (*Mills and Another v Silver and Others*, 1991).

Under the **Prescription Act 1832**, which was passed to remedy some of the defects in the common law prescriptive rights, the grant of a servitude may be presumed from long usage of the right involved. In the case of an easement, the usage must be for 20 years, and in the case of a profit, 30 years. Where the servitude has been held or enjoyed by right of *oral* permission from the owner of the servient tenement, the periods of prescription are (under the **Prescription Act 1832**) 40 years for an easement and 60 years for a profit. Written permission defeats prescription.

The **Rights of Light Act 1959** provides for a permanent change in the methods of preventing the acquisition of a right of light by enjoyment of the right for a period of 20 years. Under the **Prescription Act 1832**, a servient owner could avoid the creation of a right of light by statutory prescription only if they (i) gave written permission or (ii) interrupted the enjoyment of the right for a continuous period of one year. This interruption could be affected by, for example, putting up a screen to prevent access of light to the dominant premises. The latter method may not always be practical because the permission of the planning authority is necessary for the erection of such a physical structure, and that permission is discretionary. Now, under the **Rights of Light Act 1959**, a servient owner may substitute for the actual screen a 'notional' screen. This may be done by registering in the register of local land charges a statutory notice indicating the exact site of the screen that they would have liked to erect. The effect of such registration is the same as if the access to light of the dominant tenement had been obstructed for one year.

10.12 Commonhold

Commonhold is a form of land tenure introduced by the **Commonhold and Leasehold Reform Act 2002**. The concept is that each unit owner (usually a half-owner) can purchase the freehold of their unit, but attached to the unit will be a share in the Commonhold Association, a company limited by guarantee. The unit holders' estate is known as a 'freehold estate in commonhold'. The Commonhold Association owns and is responsible for the maintenance of the common parts of the property, e.g. roadways, recreation areas and staircases and so on. While this form of tenure will usually be adopted by new developers, it is possible for current tenants to convert their leaseholds into commonholds, but in order for this to be effected, the conversion must be agreed to by all interested parties, for example, all leaseholders in an existing block of flats together with the owner of the freehold.

Proposed Changes to Commonhold—The Commonhold White Paper dated 3 March 2025—The proposed new commonhold model for home ownership in England and Wales—is intended to phase out property ownership by making commonhold the default tenure for homes, aiming to phase out the leasehold system. Matthew Pennycook, the Minister of State for Housing and Planning stated in the White Paper that: 'Commonhold was introduced in England and Wales in 2002, but for a variety of reasons it failed to establish itself and is now out of date.' The paper proposes a reinvigorated commonhold model implementing recommendations from the Law Commission on its report on commonhold, to enable commonhold to work for all types of developments, including mixed-use buildings.

10.13 Restrictive covenants

Restrictive covenants are agreements restricting the use of freehold land that are enforceable not only between the original contracting parties, but also between assignees of the respective lands. In spite of the doctrine of privity of contract, such a contract may be enforced by applying the principles of equity, namely that a person who acquires property with knowledge that some other person has rights in relation thereto will, in conscience, be bound to observe those rights provided that certain conditions are satisfied. An example will help to make this clear:

❖ **CASE EXAMPLE**

Tulk v Moxhay (1848)

Tulk sold the central part of Leicester Square to Elms, who covenanted on behalf of himself, his heirs and assigns not to build on the land. The land was later sold to Moxhay, who knew of this covenant, but nevertheless proceeded to build on the land. *Held*: that Moxhay was bound by the covenant. It would be inequitable that Elms, who gave a small price for the land because of the restrictions, should be able to sell it for a larger price free from those restrictions.

It was laid down in the preceding case that the purchaser was bound, even if they had only 'constructive' notice of the covenants, i.e. those covenants that they would have discovered if they had made a proper investigation of title. We may note here also that, under the doctrine of constructive notice, any sub-lessees are deemed to have notice of the contents of the head lease and are, therefore, bound in equity by any negative covenants contained therein.

Restrictive covenants may be enforced today subject to the following conditions:

i The covenant must be *negative* in nature, i.e. one that does not require the expenditure of money. For example, a covenant not to use dwellings as shops is negative, but a covenant to build or maintain a house or a wall is positive.

ii The covenant must 'touch and concern' the land, i.e. it must in some way be beneficial in protecting the value of the land or the amenities of some other piece of land or a house in respect of which the covenant was created.

iii The land in respect of which the covenant is claimed must be owned by the person who seeks to enforce it.

iv Where the claimant of the benefit of the covenant is not the original covenantee, they must show that the benefit of the covenant has been expressly assigned to them or that it was originally annexed to the land, or relates to land subject to a building scheme or a scheme of development.

The requirements for strict observance of these conditions were emphasized in *Churston Golf Club Ltd v Haddock* (2019), where a covenant to fence was held to be a positive covenant and the burden could not pass to the Golf Club as successors in title.

By section 78 of the **Law of Property Act 1925**, the benefit of a covenant entered into after 1925 is deemed to be annexed to the covenantee's land, and by section 79, the burden is deemed to be annexed to the covenantor's land.

Under the **Land Charges Act 1925**, all restrictive covenants entered into since 1 January 1926 are registrable as 'land charges'. Thus, the doctrine of notice no longer applies to them, although they remain equitable interests. It is, therefore, no longer necessary to prove that the buyer of land bought it with knowledge of the existence of the covenant, registration of the covenant being treated as notice to any subsequent purchaser. The doctrine of notice still applies, however, to covenants entered into before 1 January 1926.

10.14 Mortgages

A loan of money may be obtained in various ways:

- The borrower may approach a friend who may agree to the loan quite freely, making no charge.

- The borrower may obtain a loan from a stranger who may insist on some form of security against repayment.
- This security may be personal, e.g. where a third person (a guarantor) undertakes to repay the loan should the borrower default.
- Alternatively, the lender may agree to advance the required loan provided that the borrower offers some form of property against which the lender may lawfully make a claim should the borrower default in repayment of the debt.
- Personal property (e.g. a gold watch) is a simple form of security; it is easily deliverable and is the kind sometimes transferred to a pawnbroker as security for a loan that the latter is prepared to advance to the borrower (the pawner).
- When the loan is repaid with interest on the date agreed, the property is returned to the borrower.
- Real property, such as valuable lands and houses, provides a good form of security, but by the very nature of things, this form of property cannot be 'delivered' in the straightforward way applicable to personal property; the lands or houses must be *conveyed*, which means the preparation of a formal deed.
- The *mortgage* (Norman-French, meaning 'dead pledge') is the name given to the transaction by which a borrower (a mortgagor) obtains a loan from another person (a mortgagee) on the security of property.

Before the **Law of Property Act 1925**, the usual method of creating a mortgage of freehold land was for the borrower (the mortgagor) to convey the fee simple, i.e. the freehold estate, to the lender (the mortgagee) with the condition that if the mortgagor repaid the loan plus interest on a specified date (usually six months later) the mortgagee would reconvey the land.

- In the early days the common-law courts held the parties to their agreement (into which they had freely entered), strictly construed the contract and enforced its terms.
- If the loan was not repaid on the date named in the mortgage deed, the borrower would be deprived permanently of the land, the land then becoming a 'dead pledge'.
- This caused some hardship; the lender obtained the land itself (more valuable than the loan advanced), and in addition could sue the mortgagor on the agreement to repay the sum advanced, plus interest thereon.
- Mortgagors could obtain no relief from this situation from the common law courts, and eventually approached the Court of Chancery.
- As a result, equity intervened in the mortgage transaction and gave borrowers certain rights, the most notable being the right to get back their lands (taken as security) if the loans were able to be repaid at some time later than the date of redemption named in the contract.
- This right became known as the 'Equity of Redemption'. As was said by Lord Nottingham in 1675, 'The principal right of the mortgagee is to the money, and his right to the land is only as a security for the money.'
- From the earliest days equity gave valuable rights to mortgagors on the ground of conscience, such rights being termed equitable rights.

Since the **Law of Property Act 1925** it is no longer possible to create a mortgage in the way just described, i.e. by transferring the whole of the interest of the mortgagor in the land to the mortgagee, but the principle of the 'equity of redemption' remains, with other equitable principles, today. The forms of mortgages of land today are (a) legal mortgages and (b) equitable mortgages.

a Legal mortgages

These take two forms: (i) mortgage by demise (i.e. lease) and (ii) a charge by deed expressed to be by way of legal mortgage.

i *Mortgage by demise*. This is effected by the creation of a lease. Suppose *A* is owner of Blackacre in fee simple. *A* (mortgagor) wishes to borrow money from B (mortgagee). *A* may grant to B a legal term of years, usually for 3,000 years, with a proviso in the deed that if the principal loan plus interest is repaid on a date named (usually six months later), the term of years shall cease. *A* further agrees that they will repay the sum due plus interest on the date named.

ii *Charge by way of legal mortgage*. This is created by a short deed that confers on the mortgagee a legal *interest*, not a legal estate. The legal interest entitles the mortgagee to the same remedies as if the mortgage were by lease for a long term of years as in (i).

Where the mortgagor owns leasehold property (this is sometimes as valuable as freehold, e.g. where the lease is for 999 years), the mortgagor may adopt one of two methods:

i A grant of a sublease to the mortgagee for a term of years subject to the proviso that the sublease will cease or determine on repayment of the principal sum secured plus interest. The sublease will be at least one day shorter than the lease vested in the mortgagor. In practice the term of the first sublease is usually for ten days less than that held by the mortgagor.

ii A charge by way of legal mortgage. The advantage of the charge by way of legal mortgage over the mortgage by demise is that where the mortgagor owns both freeholds and leaseholds, he or she may, on one document, charge both types of property with the mortgage debt. Moreover, where a holder of a lease wishes to create a mortgage on the lease, he or she may be obliged to obtain the lessor's consent to sublet. No consent is required if the charge by way of legal mortgage is adopted.

b Equitable mortgages

An equitable mortgage is one in which the mortgagee receives merely an equitable interest in the land. There are two distinct types:

i A mortgage of an equitable interest owned by the mortgagor, e.g. a life interest or other interest under a trust. In these cases, the mortgagor may assign their equitable interest to the mortgagee with a proviso for reassignment of the equitable interest on repayment of the debt, plus interest.

ii An informal mortgage of a legal estate or legal interest. Sometimes a borrower requires a loan urgently and wishes to avoid the trouble and expense of drawing up a formal legal mortgage. In cases of this type an agreement in writing to create a mortgage or the deposit of title deeds as an act of part performance of an oral agreement operates to create an *equitable* mortgage. This will be treated in equity as a mortgage since 'equity looks upon that as done which ought to be done'.

The three usual methods of creating such equitable mortgages are:

i a written agreement (signed as required by section 40 of the **Law of Property Act 1925**) which is not accompanied by a deposit of title deeds

ii a deposit of deeds alone, without written agreement, if the deposit of the deeds amounts to part performance of an agreement to give security
iii a combination of (i) and (ii), i.e. a written agreement *plus* a deposit of deeds

The agreement is usually by deed as this gives the mortgagee certain valuable remedies under the **Law of Property Act 1925**.

Remedies of the mortgagee. The mortgagee of a legal mortgage has the following rights:

a To sue for the debt

The amount due on the mortgagor's covenant to repay is the principal sum plus interest.

Where the date fixed for redemption has passed, the mortgagee may sue for that amount.

b To take possession

This remedy is available to the mortgagee as the legal tenant of the land. Possession may be taken at once or 'before the ink is dry on the mortgage' (per Harman J. in *Four Maids Ltd v Dudley Marshall (Properties) Ltd*, 1957). The remedy of taking possession is not, in practice, desirable since the mortgagee is strictly accountable to the mortgagor for any loss occasioned by the default. The mortgagee is not only accountable for such rents and other income from the property received, but also for those rents, incomes, etc. that *might* have been received had due diligence and proper management been exercised. A mortgagee's right to obtain possession of a dwelling house is restricted by the **Administration of Justice Acts 1970** and **1973**.

Mortgagees must now take account of the effect of the **Mortgage Repossessions (Protection of Tenants Etc.) Act 2010** which gives an unauthorized tenant the right to apply to the court for the postponement of a warrant of possession for a period not exceeding two months.

c To foreclose

If the mortgagor fails to pay the sum due for an unreasonable time, the mortgagee may obtain a court order extinguishing the mortgagor's equitable right to redeem the property and vesting the full legal estate in the mortgagee. The first order is a *foreclosure order nisi*, which directs that the money due must be repaid within a given time, e.g. six months. If not so paid, the court order is made *absolute*, and the property then vests in the mortgagee free from the equity of redemption. Foreclosure is a rare remedy in practice since the court may reopen the foreclosure, thus giving the mortgagor a further opportunity to redeem the mortgage. Also, the mortgagor may apply to the court for an order for sale instead.

d To sell the land

This is the most frequently used right and is implied in all mortgages made by deed. Subject to the exceptions that follow, the mortgagee has the power to sell the property as soon as the legal date for redemption has passed. The power of sale cannot be exercised until:

i three months' notice has been served on the mortgagor requiring repayment of the debt, and the notice has expired; or
ii interest on the loan is in arrears for two months; or
iii there has been a breach of some covenant in the mortgage other than the covenant to repay.

Mortgagees cannot purchase the land for themselves. The sale of the property is usually by public auction. Out of the proceeds of sale the mortgagee may recover (i) any expenses incurred in the sale of the property and (ii) the principal sum due, plus interest. Any surplus money belongs to the mortgagor. A sale with vacant possession is preferable, but where a husband mortgaged the matrimonial home, of which his wife was in actual occupation and to which she had contributed, the mortgagee was refused an order for possession: *Williams and Glyn's Bank Ltd v Boland* (1981).

In *Cuckmere Brick Co. Ltd v Mutual Finance Ltd* (1971), the mortgagee failed to mention the existence of planning permission when advertising the land for sale and selling it at auction. The Court of Appeal held that there had been a breach of duty.

e To appoint a receiver

The power to appoint a receiver is also implied in all mortgages by deed, unless a contrary intention is expressed. The receiver's duties are to receive the rents and profits on the mortgagee's behalf in order to discharge the sum due. The receiver is deemed in law to be the agent of the mortgagor, and the latter is liable for the receiver's acts or defaults, unless the mortgage otherwise provides. For this reason, it is usually more advantageous to appoint a receiver than for the mortgagee himself or herself to take possession.

Where the mortgage is equitable and is created by deed, the mortgagee has practically the same remedies as those stated previously. Unless, however, the power to do so is expressly reserved, the equitable mortgagee has no right to take possession. If the mortgage is created by a deposit of title deeds, the mortgagee must apply to the court for an order to sell the property and for an order appointing a receiver.

Remedies of the mortgagor. The main weapon of the mortgagor is the right to redeem the mortgaged property on payment of the principal sum borrowed, plus interest. This amount falls due on the contractual date specified (usually six months later). The equity of redemption evolved by the Court of Chancery applied two equitable principles in its jurisdiction: 'Once a mortgage, always a mortgage' and 'Equity looks at the intent rather than the form'. Accordingly, even after the date for redemption had passed, the mortgagor could get back the land when in a position to repay the debt plus interest.

As long as an order of foreclosure has not been issued by a court, that right of redemption exists. But there are conditions. The mortgagor must show proper conduct themselves, and must, for example, give to the mortgagee six months' notice of desire to redeem (or give six months' interest in lieu), unless the legal charge states some shorter period. This period gives the mortgagee, who regards the mortgage transaction as an investment, time to reinvest the money in a suitable security elsewhere.

Equity treated the right of redemption with special care. Any provision in the mortgage deed that tended to make the mortgage irredeemable, that encumbered the property or land or that encumbered the mortgagor's enjoyment of it in the future, after paying off the sum due, was regarded as inequitable. The mortgagor had the right, in essence, to get the property back in exactly the same condition as it was before the mortgage deed. Any term in a mortgage deed that greatly benefits the mortgagee at the expense of the mortgagor has always been viewed with suspicion.

❖ CASE EXAMPLES

Carritt v Bradley (1903)

B held most of the shares in a tea company. He mortgaged them to C. The mortgage contained a term that B, as a shareholder, would induce the company to employ C as the company's agent to sell tea. The company paid off the mortgage and ceased to employ

C, whereupon C claimed damages for breach of the agreement to employ him. *Held*: that the proviso in the mortgage as to the employment of C ceased to exist after the mortgage was paid off.

Noakes v Rice (1902)

The tenant of a 'free' public house, under a 26-year lease, mortgaged the premises to a brewery company as security for a loan and covenanted that during the remainder of the 26 years he would not sell any beers except those provided by the brewery company (the mortgagee). The tenant paid off the mortgage three years later and sued for a declaration that he was free from the covenant. *Held*: that the covenant was inconsistent with the express proviso for redemption (which entitled the tenant to demand a reconveyance of the premises upon repayment of the loan with interest) and was a clog upon the equity. Tenant became entitled to trade as a 'free' public house.

Nevertheless, not every collateral advantage to the mortgagee is void, as will be seen from the following case.

❖ CASE EXAMPLE

Kreglinger v New Patagonia Meat and Cold Storage Co. (1914)

A firm of woolbrokers (mortgagees) lent £10,000 to a meat company on mortgage. The woolbrokers agreed not to demand repayment for five years, but the mortgagors (the meat company) could repay the debt earlier on giving notice. The parties also covenanted that the meat company would not sell sheepskins to anyone except the woolbrokers for five years from the date of the agreement, as long as the woolbrokers were willing to purchase the skins at the agreed price. The loan was paid off before the five years. *Held*: that the option of purchasing the sheepskins did not end on repayment, but continued for five years. It was a collateral contract and did not affect the right to redeem.

Where the parties to a mortgage agree to postpone redemption for a long period, it is a matter for decision by the court in each case whether it is unreasonable. In *Knightsbridge Estates Ltd v Byrne* (1939), where the mortgagee required a long-term investment, it was held that the postponement of the period of repayment for 40 years was not oppressive or unconscionable in the circumstances, although such a period would be unreasonable between *private* persons who mortgage property of small value in return for a small loan.

10.15 The sale of land

The sale of land involves two elements: (a) the contract of sale and (b) the delivery of the land and transfer of title in it.

As to the contract of sale, the general rules of the law of contract already considered apply. The parties to the sale must have contractual capacity, the contract must not be illegal, there must be an 'agreement', and the acceptance of the offer must be unconditional. Where the offer of the sale is made 'subject to contract', no agreement comes into effect until a formal contract is approved by both parties. The decision in *Alpenstow Ltd v Regalian Properties plc* (1985) illustrates an exception to this rule.

Under section 40 of the **Law of Property Act 1925**, contracts for the sale of land must be evidenced in writing. In the absence of a 'note or memorandum' the contract is unenforceable by legal action, although valid. The preceding are the general rules and are subject to the proviso that where the doctrine of 'part performance' applies, the contract may be enforced notwithstanding that the agreement does not comply with section 40 of the **Law of Property Act 1925**. The memorandum must contain: (i) an agreement for sale, (ii) a description of the parties, (iii) a description of the property, (iv) a statement of the price and (v) it must also be signed by the person to be charged or the agent (see p. 185). The normal procedure would be to use the Standard Conditions of Sale that came into effect on 21 March 1990. These form part of the protocol for domestic conveyancing intended to standardize, simplify and speed up the conveyancing process.

Under an *open* contract for sale (i.e. a contract that does not set out the terms of the sale, but merely specifies the names of the parties, the description of the property and the price), there is a most important condition implied by law that the vendor must show title for at least 15 years, starting with 'a good root of title'.

A good root of title may be defined as a disposition of the land dealing with the whole of the legal and equitable estate in the property to be sold, containing an adequate description of the property and revealing no defect in title thereto. The vendor must, at their own expense, abstract and, if under their control, produce the document that forms the root of the title and all subsequent documents that affect the legal estate. They must also prove all facts that have affected the legal estate. They must also prove all facts that have affected the legal estate in the last 15 years. This is called 'deducing title'. The purchaser on their part 'investigates the title'.

Upon the satisfactory investigation of the title the transaction proceeds to the *conveyance* of the property to the purchasers.

The stages in this process are as follows:

i the preparation of the contract
ii the exchange of contracts between the vendor's solicitor and the purchaser's solicitor, when the purchaser pays a deposit (usually 10 per cent of the purchase money). In *Morris v Duke-Cohan & Co.* (1975), it was stated that it may be negligent of a solicitor to accept less than the 10 per cent deposit without first obtaining his or her client's authority. The transaction has now become binding on both parties
iii delivery by the vendor's solicitors of an 'abstract of title'
iv examination of this title by the purchaser's solicitor and comparison of the abstract with the title deeds to check accuracy. The time allowed for this is usually 14 days
v the purchaser's solicitor may deliver requisitions (i.e. written questions) on title to the vendor to give the purchaser full details of the property concerned, and to clear up doubts
vi search by purchaser's solicitor in the Land Charges Register and in the register maintained by the local authority to ascertain what encumbrances exist in relation to the property
vii once the conveyance has been drawn up, it has to be completed. Completion is usually carried out at the office of the vendor's solicitor. The purchaser hands over the money and the vendor hands over the signed conveyance, together with the title deeds of the property. The deed must be stamped as required by the **Stamp Act 1891**, as amended

Registration of land charges. It is of great importance to a prospective purchaser of land to discover what charges exist in favour of third parties. Certain rights and charges are legal and will bind the purchaser in all cases; e.g. a purchaser would be bound by a legal lease of the property.

The 1925 legislation has greatly affected the 'doctrine of notice' to which reference has been made previously. By the very nature of land, there may be many rights of others in relation to a property. *A* may be a fee simple owner of Blackacre, but the property may be in the occupation of B, under a lease, and may be subject to an easement (e.g. a right of way) in favour of C and *D* may have an equitable mortgage on the property. Before 1926 the rule was that a purchaser from *A* was bound by the *legal* rights of B, C and *D*, irrespective of notice. However, a purchaser from *A* would be free from any *equitable* interests only if the legal estate for value had been acquired *without notice of* equitable rights.

To simplify the investigation as to these rights, the **Land Charges Act 1925** introduced the principle of registration of certain equitable interests and charges affecting land. Registration of such interests constitutes notice to a purchaser, whether he or she knows of them or not. Conversely, an interest requiring registration and that is not in fact registered is not binding on a purchaser even though they know that such an interest exists.

The most important charges that should be registered are:

a *puisne mortgages*, i.e. legal mortgages not protected by a deposit of title deeds
b *limited owners' charges*, i.e. an equitable charge on settled property arising by statute in favour of the tenant for life of such property, e.g. where they pay estate duty out of their own pocket
c *general equitable charges*, i.e. an equitable charge not secured by a deposit of documents relating to the legal estate. For example, an equitable mortgage not protected by deposit of the title deeds; or the right of an unpaid vendor who has parted with the deeds
d *estate contracts*, i.e. contracts by estate owners to convey or create a legal estate. The object of registration is to protect the purchaser's rights under the contract against other purchasers who may acquire a legal estate from the vendor before the completion of the purchase
e *restrictive covenants* (see p. 312)

In addition to the preceding, section 15 of the **Land Charges Act 1972**, which contains the modern law on the subject, requires local authorities to keep registers of local land charges. These charges are constituted under various statutes: for example, the **Private Street Works Act** enables local authorities to recover the cost of road construction, etc., from local property owners; and certain plans and orders made under the **Town and Country Planning Acts** have to be registered. If the charges are not registered, they are void against a purchaser of the legal estate, and they take the estate free from them.

10.16 Registered land

The investigation of title of land is sometimes very difficult and complicated. The parties to the conveyance are responsible for ensuring accuracy.

- In many countries a system of compulsory land registration is in force, the purpose of which is to provide an official guarantee certifying who is the owner of a particular piece of land and disclosing certain of the encumbrances to which the land is or may be subjected. A purchaser need only consult a single publicly operated register to find out whether the vendor has a good title to the property and the nature of the rights and encumbrances affecting the land they propose to buy.
- The **Land Registration Act 1925** introduced the system of land registration into Britain. In areas to which an Order in Council has made the system applicable, registration of title is compulsory upon sale of freeholds or of leaseholds having more than 40 years to run. Section 1 of the **Land Registration Act 1997** now extends the range of events to include gifts, dispositions by personal representatives and certain mortgages.

- In accordance with section 4 of the **Land Registration Act 2002**, any dealing in a legal estate that has an unregistered title will make it subject to compulsory registration.

The mechanism of registration is as follows:

- The Government lawyers of the Land Registry or a district registry investigate the title of every freehold or leasehold sold after the appropriate date once and for all.
- If they are satisfied that it is in order, they record the owner as registered proprietor of the land with absolute (freehold) title or good leasehold title, as the case may be.
- The title is, in effect, guaranteed by the State.
- Where the title does not come up to the previously mentioned standard, or where there is doubt, the person in possession of the land may be granted a possessory title only, which can be subsequently upgraded in accordance with section 1 of the **Land Registration Act 1986**.
- The Land Registry issues to the registered proprietor a *land certificate*, certifying that a registered title of the appropriate kind has been granted. This corresponds to the title deeds of property.
- In any further transactions affecting that particular land, the purchaser's solicitors need not concern themselves (except in rare cases) with the original deeds: the land certificate and the certified statements made therein can generally be relied upon.
- The name of the new registered proprietor is entered by the Land Registry officials when a transfer is made in their favour, or a grant of a lease is made to them.
- In addition to the Property Register giving details of land, and the Proprietorship Register giving details of title (absolute, good leasehold, qualified or possessory) and the name and address and description of the proprietor, there is a Charges Register that contains charges and encumbrances affecting the land, all dealings with registered charges and encumbrances and notices relating to covenants, conditions and other rights *adversely* affecting the land. It contains all the matters that would be registered under the **Land Charges Act 1972** if the title to the land were unregistered.
- *Brown (Respondent) v Ridley and another (Appellants)* (2025) is a good example of the process involved in the registration of 'disputed land—adverse possession. This involved the appellants relying on a claim of reasonably believing that a ten-year period of occupation of the disputed land was sufficient. *Held*: (Supreme Court) In allowing the appeal, that the appellants had satisfied one of the relevant conditions for adverse possession of the land in dispute under registration in accordance with the **Land Registration Act 2002.**
- It is important to note that the **Land Registration Act 2002**, s. 91 makes provisions for conveyancing by electronic means. The introduction of electronic conveyance will mean not just the simple replacement of conventional documentation, but provides for entries to be placed on the register electronically. The current three-stage process of operating an interest, application to the registry and entry on the registry will be collapsed into one stage of electronic transaction of entry on the register. This will necessitate the creation of a land registry network whereby all conveyances will have network access agreements (s. 92, Schedule 5). It is anticipated that a pilot scheme will commence in 2007.

10.17 Useful webpages

History of English land law—Wikipedia (http://en.wikipedia.org/wiki/History_of_English_land-law)

Modern land law—Martin Dixon—Google books—Routledge (books.google.com/Law/Land Use)

Property law—Wikipedia (http://en.wikipedia.org/wiki/Property-law)

Law and lawyers—English land law—No. 1 Estates in land and tenure (http://obiterj.blogspot.com.au/2011/09/english-land-law-no1-estates-in-land.html)

An introduction to land law (http://www.fds.oup.com/www.oup/pdf/13/9780199593408.pdf)

10.18 Exercises

1 'Possession' and 'ownership' are common terms in ordinary life, yet in law each has a special significance. Discuss the two concepts and explain what 'possession is nine points of the law' means.

2 Distinguish between (i) real property and (ii) personal property and between (iii) choses in possession and (iv) choses in action.

3 Describe the main aims of the 1925 legislation.

4 Explain in detail what is meant by the phrase 'an estate in fee simple absolute in possession'.

5 What are the main duties of (i) a landlord and (ii) a tenant?

6 How may an equitable mortgage be created?

7 Outline the remedies available to a mortgagee of a legal mortgage.

8 The sale of land involves two major steps: (i) the contract for sale and (ii) the delivery. Enumerate the stages leading to 'completion'.

9 What do you understand by 'registered land'? Explain 'registration of land charges'. Estimate the importance of registration to the rational development of land law.

Chapter 11

Succession

Key points

- formalities and revocation of a will
- variation of a will in favour of family members
- appointment and duties of personal representatives
- intestacy

When *A* transfers property to B it may be said that B 'succeeds' to that property, i.e. takes over the rights owned by the transferor. In law the word 'succession' has a special meaning. When we speak of 'universal succession', it may refer to two classes: (a) succession on death and (b) succession on bankruptcy. This chapter deals with succession on death.

Obviously, a person cannot own property or exercise rights over property when dead. The law bows to inevitable facts: other persons will succeed to the property owned or possessed by the deceased. All systems of law have certain rules of succession that lay down how, and to whom, the property of a deceased person is to be distributed.

Where a person makes a valid will stating how their property is to be distributed, they are said to die 'testate' (from the Latin word *testari*, to make a will). Where a person leaves no will, or an invalid will, they are said to die 'intestate'.

11.1 Wills

From an early date the law recognized the right of a person to make a will showing to whom *personal* property should descend. In medieval times a person had no right to dispose of freehold land, as the strict feudal law laid down that the land had to devolve on the heir at law. Later, the **Statute of Military Tenures 1660** permitted a male freeholder to devise (i.e. leave by will) lands, and the introduction of the 'use' provided a further means of making dispositions of freehold property on death.

Birth, marriage and death have always been of immediate concern to the Church. In Norman and medieval times, the Church courts (separate from the lay courts) adjudicated on wills of personal property, including leaseholds. The **Court of Probate Act 1857** transferred the jurisdiction relating to wills to the ordinary civil courts, where it has been exercised ever since.

DOI: 10.4324/9781003422808-11

However, many of the rules applied today are derived from the early Church courts which applied canon law (i.e. Church law), not the common law.

Nature of a will. A will is a declaration of a person's intentions concerning the descent of property after death. A will is said to be *ambulatory* (i.e. not permanent: subject to revocation or alteration) until the death of the testator. The will speaks from death. If *A* makes a disposition of 'All my property to Z', the successor (Z) will receive all the property that *A* owns at the moment of death. The gift will include property that *A* acquires between the time of making the will and death. It will not, however, include property that *A* has disposed of between these times.

Testamentary capacity. The general rule is that any person of full age and sound mind may make a valid will. The testator is presumed sane at the time when the will was made, but if the will is contested on the ground that the testator was of unsound mind, the person propounding the will has the burden of proving the sanity of the testator.

Married women were formerly incapable of making valid wills, but legislation in the past century has remedied this, so that now they have full testamentary capacity (**Married Women's Property Acts 1882** and **1892** and the **Law Reform (Married Women and Tortfeasors) Act 1935**).

An infant (i.e. a person under the age of 18) cannot make a valid will, but there is an exception regarding infant soldiers, sailors and airmen (see p. 325).

Testamentary intent. Testamentary intent means an intention to make a revocable ambulatory disposition of the testator's property taking effect on death; to possess the necessary intent, the testator must intend that the disposition comes into play immediately and is not postponed by some future event or condition—see *Corbett v Newey* (1996).

Formalities. The **Wills Act 1837** is the main Act governing this important matter. Its main provisions are:

a *Writing.* A will must be in the form of a written document. Any document, e.g. a letter, can suffice and may include other documents existing at the time the will was made and referred to in the will. Oral evidence may be given to identify these documents if they are so referred to. 'In writing' includes handwriting, print and typescript.

b *Signature.* The will must be signed by the testator or by someone in their presence and by their direction. Initials, a partial signature, a mark (e.g. a cross) or a thumbprint in ink may be used, as long as the mark is clearly ascribable to the testator. A seal stamped with the testator's initials has been held to be a signature.

The **Administration of Justice Act 1982**, s. 17 substituted a new section for section 9 of the **Wills Act 1837** and the **Wills Act Amendment Act 1852**, dealing with the signing and attestation of wills and relaxing the law governing the position of the testator's signature and the acknowledgement of signature by an attesting witness. The result of this new section 9 is that the signature by or on behalf of the testator can be anywhere on the will provided that the testator intended by their signature to give effect to the will (confirmed in *Wood v Smith*, 1992).

Attestation. The signature of the testator 'shall be made or acknowledged by the testator in the presence of two or more witnesses present at the same time' and 'each witness either attests and signs the will or acknowledges their signature in the presence of the testator (but not necessarily in the presence of any other witness)'.

The purpose of attestation is to authenticate the testator's signature. The witnesses need not be present at the time of the actual signing of the will by the testator. They must, however, both be *present together* at this time *or* at some later time when the testator acknowledges the signature. Although in practice a witness signs or acknowledges the signature in the presence of the other witness, this is not a legal requirement. Addresses and occupations are added to assist in identification and subsequent tracing. If a dispute should arise over the validity of the will, the evidence of the witness will be vital. Witnesses need not read the will or know its contents.

A blind person may not 'witness' a will or a codicil, because they cannot 'see' the signature (*Re Gibson*, 1949). A person under the age of majority is a competent witness for the purpose of attestation, provided that they satisfy the other criteria.

Section 9 of the **Wills Act 1837** expressly provides that no particular form of attestation shall be necessary. It is enough if the witnesses merely subscribe their names, their initials (*In the Goods of Christian*, 1849) or their marks (*In the Goods of Ashmore*, 1843).

All amendments made to the **Wills Act 1837** introduced by the **Administration of Justice Act 1982** came into operation on 1 January 1983, but did not affect the wills of testators who died before that date.

Additions and alterations. A will, having been made, is alterable. Any changes may be made in the body of an existing will, *provided* that they are initialled by the testator and the witnesses. Moreover, additions may be made even below the testator's signature if they are signed and attested in the same manner as the will itself. Further, a will may be supplemented or added to by properly signed and attested codicils.

Anyone to whom, or to whose husband or wife, the testator had left property and who acted as a witness was not entitled to benefit under the will (**Wills Act 1837**, s. 15). The **Wills Act 1968** restricts the operation of this section and provides that if a will is attested the person who is, or whose spouse is, a beneficiary, the gift will not be avoided if the will is duly executed without his attestation.

Provided there are two qualified witnesses, the attestation of any other witnesses can be disregarded and they become entitled to any dispositions made to them under the will.

Rectification and extrinsic evidence. The **Administration of Justice Act 1982** introduced some further measures to assist the court in carrying out the testator's intentions. Section 20 provides for rectification of a clerical error or failure to understand the testator intentions (*Wordingham v Royal Exchange Trust Co. Ltd and Anor*, 1992); section 21 for admission in certain circumstances of all available extrinsic evidence (*Re Williams* (dec.) *v Madgin*, 1985).

As a matter of public policy no one convicted of murder or manslaughter may benefit under the will of their victim (**Forfeiture Acts 1970** and **1982**).

Wills of soldiers, sailors and airmen. Roman law allowed a soldier 'in the field' to make an informal will. During hostilities, death in battle is likely; a soldier may have no legal advice nearby, and pen and paper are not readily available. The law, by the very nature of things, cannot apply stringent rules in the abnormal situations mentioned. It has, therefore, allowed oral declarations and other informal dispositions to take effect notwithstanding their noncompliance with the technical rules of regular law applicable to civilians.

These practical rules found their way into English common law, and they are now incorporated in section 7 of the **Wills Act 1837** as extended by the **Wills (Soldiers and Sailors) Act 1918**. The effect of these provisions is to grant special privileges to soldiers, sailors and airmen who are *on actual military service* and to seamen who are *at sea* (under any conditions). Such persons may make wills even though infants, and such wills may be made informally.

Where a soldier about to embark overseas declared orally, 'If anything happens to me this is for R', the disposition was held to be a valid will. When a privileged testator writes a will, there is no need for witnesses. Whether the declaration is oral or written, the court will give effect to its terms, provided that the person wanted it to be a binding will. The phrase 'actual military service' means that the serviceman or woman is called up for service, is engaged in hostilities, is about to proceed to a hostile engagement or is on embarkation leave for a foreign station in connexion with operations of war, imminent or taking place. In *Re Wingham* (1949), it was held that a trainee pilot on a RAF instructional course in Canada was on 'actual military service'. A soldier in England in *peacetime* is not. Sailors (including those serving in the Merchant Navy) may make informal wills when at sea or about to embark for a voyage, but not if they are on leave and do not have orders to join a ship (*Re Rapley's Estate, Rapley v Rapley* (1983)).

Persons serving as army nurses, typists, etc., under military or naval orders enjoy the same privilege as soldiers on 'actual military service'.

An informal will made by any of the previously mentioned persons remains valid even after the testator ceases to be a sailor or completes his or her service in the Armed Forces.

Revocation. It is of the very nature of a will, according to English law, that it shall be revocable until the testator dies. Revocation may be express or it may be implied from the conduct of the testator.

Revocation may be affected by (a) subsequent will or codicil, (b) a writing executed like a will, (c) subsequent marriage (*per subsequens matrimonium*) or (d) destruction of the will with *animus revocandi*.

a Revocation by a subsequent will or codicil

A will usually begins with a clause revoking all former wills. If such a clause is not inserted, the later will (or codicil) does not revoke the former will except in so far as it is inconsistent therewith. Thus, if a testator, T, in a first will leaves a specified named house to A, and in a later will leaves the same house to B, the house goes to B. If, however, T in the first will leaves £500 to X, and in a later will (which does not contain a revocation clause) leaves £500 to Y, both X and Y will receive legacies of £500.

b Revocation by writing executed as a will

A will may be revoked by a writing that, though not itself a will, is signed and attested. It is sufficient that it should declare the testator's intention to revoke the will without containing any dispositions in lieu of those contained in the instrument revoked. Thus, a letter signed by a testator and attested by two witnesses directing a will to be destroyed has been held sufficient to revoke the will (*In the Goods of Durance*, 1872).

c Revocation 'per subsequens matrimonium'

A will is revoked by the subsequent marriage of the testator, whether the testator be male or female (**Wills Act 1837**, s. 18). The **Administration of Justice Act 1982** has substituted a new section for section 18 and has added a new section 18A to the Act while repealing section 177 of the **Law of Property Act 1925**. It has re-enacted the general rule that a testator's will is revoked by marriage, but provides that where it appears from a will that at the time it was made the testator was expecting to be married to a particular person and that it was intended that the will should not be revoked by the marriage, the will is not revoked by marriage to that person. In addition, where it appears from a will that at the time it was made the testator was expecting to be married to a particular person and that it was intended that a disposition in the will should not be revoked by marriage to that person, then that particular disposition shall take effect. Any other disposition will also take effect unless it appears from the will that the testator intended the disposition to be revoked by the marriage. Section 18A provides that, except where there is a contrary intention in the will, where a marriage of a testator has ended by divorce, annulment or by being declared void, any appointment of a former spouse as an executor or executor and trustee will be ineffective, as will any gift to such a former spouse.

d Revocation by destruction of the will with 'animus revocandi'

This is effected by the testator (or someone present and under direction) destroying the will, provided that the act of destruction, e.g. burning, tearing, is done with the intention to revoke the will (**Wills Act 1837**, ss. 20 and 21). The following points must be proved: a physical destruction; an intention (*animus revocandi*) to revoke by such destruction; and the destruction must be effected by the testator or someone in his presence and by his direction.

As to destruction, a partial destruction is sufficient if there is clear evidence that cancellation of the will was intended, e.g. tearing off the signature and attestation clause or, as in *Re Adams, Deceased* (1990), where the signatures of the testatrix and attesting witnesses had been obliterated by ballpoint pen scribbling. 'All the destroying in the world without the intention will not revoke a will, nor intention without destroying. There must be the two' (Lord Justice James in *Cheese v Lovejoy*, 1877).

The destruction cannot be delegated to a solicitor or other agent unless the will is destroyed in the presence of or by the authority of the testator. 'If it was not done by the testator's authority at the time . . . no amount of authority afterwards can be brought into play so as to ratify an act done without authority at the time' (*Gill v Gill*, 1909).

Where a will is lost or is destroyed without being revoked, its contents may be proved by other evidence, e.g. a copy, a draft or oral evidence (*Sugden v Lord St Leonards*, 1876).

Revival of revoked wills. Where a will has been revoked in any of the previously mentioned ways it may nevertheless be revived either by re-execution as a will or by a properly executed codicil that expresses a clear intention that the earlier will shall stand. We may note here that it is not possible to revive a will that has been revoked by a later will merely by destroying the later will. For example, let us suppose a testator makes will no. 1; later, will no. 2 is made revoking will no. 1. The testator now desires to revive will no. 1. It is not possible to do this merely by destroying will no. 2. The only effect of this is that the testator would have left no will at all and would die intestate.

Doctrine of dependent relative revocation. Where a testator revokes a will with the intention of making a new one, and for some reason (e.g. dies before executing it) fails to make a new one, the original (i.e. the revoked will) remains valid and is treated as the will of the testator. This applies only where the court is satisfied that the testator did not intend to revoke the will *absolutely*, but merely revoked it as a first step towards making a new will. For example, a person destroyed a will, made out in favour of the spouse, under the mistaken belief that all property would pass automatically to the spouse if the death occurred while intestate. It was held in these circumstances that a copy of the will could be admitted to probate (*In the estate of Green street*, 1930).

11.2 Legacies and devises

A *devise* is a disposition of freehold land contained in a will. A *legacy* or a *bequest* is a disposition of any other form of property, including leaseholds. The terms used for recipients of the gift by will are 'devisees' and 'legatees', respectively.

Classes of dispositions. A legacy (or bequest) may be (a) a general legacy, (b) a specific legacy or (c) a demonstrative legacy.

a *A general legacy*. Where a gift is made that does not refer to a specific or particular object, it is described as a general legacy. For example, a gift of 'a horse', 'a motorcar' or '£1,000'.

b *A specific legacy*. This is a gift that is specifically described. For example: 'my Rover car' or 'my Chippendale chairs'.

c *A demonstrative legacy*. A gift of a sum of money to be paid out of a particular fund is referred to as demonstrative. For example: 'a sum of £500 from my Post Office deposit account'.

In the specimen will on p. 328, mention is made of a 'residuary gift'. The residue of an estate is that which remains after all the debts have been paid, and the devises and legacies have been distributed. Unless the residue is disposed of, e.g. by gift to some person, the testator will be presumed in law to be intestate as to that part.

The importance of distinguishing these different classes of legacies will be seen when we come to discuss the effect of abatement and ademption.

Lapse of gifts. Where a legatee or devisee dies before the testator, and is not issue of the testator, the intended gift lapses. The property allocated to the deceased beneficiary falls into the residue of the estate. Where, however, the deceased beneficiary is issue, the **Wills Act 1837** raises the fiction that the child (grandchild, etc.) who had died before the testator had in fact died immediately after the testator. It is, of course, open to a testator to make provision against the contingency of death of a legatee or devisee, but in the absence of such a provision the property will fall into residue for the benefit of the residuary legatee or devisee.

Abatement. The first duty of the personal representative responsible for winding up the testator's estate is to pay the testator's debts before the estate is distributed among the beneficiaries. Where there is insufficient property remaining after the debts have been paid to satisfy all the beneficiaries, it follows that some of the legacies will have to be reduced or even repudiated altogether. The legacies are said to 'abate', and they will do so in a certain order. Residuary gifts abate first, then general legacies, then specific legacies. Demonstrative gifts will not abate unless the fund out of which they are to be paid is itself exhausted. If that happens the demonstrative legacies will be treated as general legacies and will abate with them.

Ademption. If a specific thing to be given by will to a legatee is not in existence or no longer belongs to the testator at the time of the testator's death, the gift is 'adeemed', and the legatee gets nothing. Thus, if X bequeaths a specific painting to Y, and the painting is destroyed by a fire before X dies, Y will get nothing. The rule as to ademption does not apply to general legacies or to demonstrative gifts.

11.3 Specimen will[1]

I, EDWARD COKE, of 14 Acacia Avenue, Oxbridge, in the County of Somerset, company director, HEREBY REVOKE all Wills and testamentary documents heretofore made by me AND DECLARE this to be my LAST WILL

1 I APPOINT my wife *Gladys Coke*, and my solicitor, *Thomas B. Macaulay*, to be jointly the executors of this my will.

2 I DEVISE my freehold cottage known as THE LILACS, at Tone Dale, Oxbridge, unto my son, *Hugh Coke*, in fee simple.

3 I BEQUEATH the following specific legacies:

   i To my son, *John Coke*, any motor-car I may own at the date of my death.

   ii To my daughter, *Carolyn Coke*, all my ordinary shares in the company known as Imperial Chemical Industries plc.

   iii To my said wife all my personal chattels not hereby bequeathed for her absolute use and benefit.

4 I BEQUEATH the following pecuniary legacies:

   i to my daughter *Rosalyn Coke* the sum of Three Thousand Pounds.

   ii to my daughter *Elizabeth Coke* the sum of Three Thousand Pounds.

5 I DEVISE AND BEQUEATH all the residue of my real and personal estate whatsoever and wheresoever not hereby or by any codicil hereto otherwise expressly disposed of as to my freeholds in fee simple and as to my personal estate absolutely unto my said wife *Gladys Coke* for her own absolute use and benefit.

1 This is meant to be only an example of a will—it is not to be adopted as the basis for the drafting of any actual will. Please seek the advice of a practising lawyer. No liability is accepted by the author.

6 I DIRECT that any executor of this my Will being a solicitor or a person engaged in any profession or business may be so employed and act and shall be entitled to make all proper professional charges for any work done by him or his firm in connexion with my Estate including work which an executor not being a solicitor or a person engaged as aforesaid could have done personally.

7 IN WITNESS whereof I the said *Edward Coke* the Testator have to this my LAST WILL set my hand this thirty-first day of March One Thousand Nine Hundred and Ninety-Three.

SIGNED AND ACKNOWLEDGED by the above-named Edward Coke the Testator as and for his LAST WILL in the presence of us both present at the same time who at his request in his presence and in the presence of each other have hereunto subscribed our names as witnesses:	Edward Coke (signed)

Thomas More, (signed)
6 High St.,
Oxbridge,
Somerset.
Clerk.

Jeremy Bentham, (signed)
3 North St.,
Oxbridge,
Somerset.
Chartered Accountant.

11.4 Family provision

Until 1938 a testator had complete freedom to dispose of property, in any manner thought fit. There was no obligation to make any will. Moreover, if a husband made a will, he was not obliged by law to include any provision for his wife and children, and he could leave to any other person the whole of his property if he so decided. Such was testamentary freedom.

By the **Inheritance (Family Provision) Act 1938**, as amended by the **Intestates' Estates Act 1952**, the court was given power to vary a will on the application of certain persons. Where the court considered that either the dispositions of the will or the law relating to intestacy did not make reasonable provision for certain **dependants** of a deceased person, payment of reasonable provision out of the net estate might be ordered for his or her maintenance.

The **Inheritance (Provision for Family and Dependants) Act 1975** replaced the 1938 Act (as amended) and applies to the death, on or after 1 April 1976, of a person domiciled in England and Wales.

The 1975 Act expands the list of claimants surviving the deceased to include:

a the wife or husband
b a former spouse who has not remarried
c a child
d any person who was treated by the deceased as a child of the family (in relation to any marriage of his)
e any person who immediately before the death of the deceased was being maintained by the deceased without reciprocal consideration

A partner or other person with whom the deceased was cohabiting may claim under (e), stated previously.

Any such person (a) to (e) may apply to the court for an order on the ground that the disposition of the deceased's estate effected by the will or the law relating to intestacy is not such as to make *reasonable financial provision* for such person.

- 'Reasonable financial provision' means in the case of a surviving spouse, other than one under a continuing separation following a decree of judicial separation, 'such financial provision as it would be reasonable in all the circumstances of the case for a husband or wife to receive, whether or not the provision is required for his or her maintenance'. In other cases, the financial provision should be such as 'would be reasonable in all the circumstances of the case for the applicant to receive for his or her maintenance'.
- Application under the Act must be made within six months from the date on which representation in respect of the estate is first taken out.
- The court may make an order for periodical or lump sum payments from the estate. In making the order, the court must have regard to a number of matters, including, e.g. the applicant's resources, the size of the estate and the applicant's conduct towards the testator (or the person dying intestate). There are wide powers under the Act to upset dispositions intended to defeat or frustrate applications under the Act.
- An objective test of 'reasonable financial provision' is made. As to the nature of the conduct of an applicant spouse living with the deceased at the time of his or her death, this is of marginal effect only in the majority of cases. In *Wachtel v Wachtel* (1973), Lord Denning, MR, stated (in regard to financial provision in divorce proceedings) that the conduct of a party was relevant only where it was '"both obvious and gross", so much so that to order one party to support another whose conduct falls into this category is repugnant to anyone's sense of justice.' In *Miller v Miller; McFarlane v McFarlane* (2006), Lord Nicolls of Birkenhead noted that fairness does not require consideration of the parties' conduct. Rather, conduct should only be considered in exceptional cases where the statute permits. Baroness Hale of Richmond found that the 'both obvious and gross' test is not only the just test but also the practical test. An unmarried daughter who devoted considerable time to looking after the deceased at considerable sacrifice will have a strong moral claim for provision—*Re Cook* (1956). A child who lost contact with the deceased for a long time and was not dependent on him or her in any way has little, if any, claim on the deceased for provision—*Re Andrews* (1955). In *Re Callaghan (dec.)* (1984), it was held that 'child' was not limited to a minor or dependent child but could include a stepson if treated as one of the family or as in *Re Leach* (dec.) (1985), an adult stepdaughter.

In *Miles v Shearer* (2021), which involved two adult daughters, the defendant argued that the claimants had not demonstrated a financial need for maintenance. The Court *Held*: that it would not make an award for financial provision for an adult child where it considers they are not in financial need, even where there is a large estate.

11.5 Personal representatives

It is a feature of the English legal system that a deceased's estate does not vest in the persons to whom it has been left by will or among whom it has by law to be distributed on an intestacy. The estate vests, in the first instance, in the deceased's personal representatives. These are interposed, as it were, between the estate and the beneficiaries.

The personal representatives are recognized by law as representing the deceased person for all purposes under the law of property and for most purposes under the law of contract and tort.

In general terms the deceased's rights and liabilities are transferred or transmitted to the lawfully appointed personal representatives, and can be enforced by or against them as soon as they are officially able so to act.

There are two *classes* of personal representative:

a *Executors*, who are appointed usually by a testator in the will. Sometimes an appointment may be implied, as when a testator nominates a certain person to pay off his or her debts. In this event, the executor is technically called 'an executor according to the tenor'.
b *Administrators*, i.e. personal representatives of someone who has died intestate.

There is a danger of oversimplifying the division between these two classes, because although a testator may appoint an executor in a will there is no certainty that the appointee will act when the time comes. Where no executor is appointed or where an executor dies, becomes incapacitated through illness or refuses to act, the court itself will appoint a person to administer the estate 'with the will annexed'. This means that the appointee will administer the estate in accordance with the terms of the will as though an executor. This special type of administrator is called an *administrator cum testamento annexo*.

If an infant is appointed an administrator, an adult will be required to act during the minority. Such an appointee is called an *administrator durante minore aetate* ('during infancy').

An executor appointed under a will of which the validity is in dispute cannot take office, for the authority would be void if the will should be declared invalid. In this type of case an *administrator pendente lite* ('during the litigation') has to be appointed; they may proceed with the administration but must not distribute the property among the beneficiaries.

11.5.1 Probate and letters of administration

An executor can begin duties immediately following the death of the testator. The *right to dispose of the estate* is not complete, however, until a *grant of probate* of the will has been obtained.

Probate (from the Latin *probatum*, 'proved') is nothing more than an official acceptance that the will is a genuine one, and that the executor's right to administer the estate is officially sanctioned. Probate may be obtained in two ways: (a) Probate in Common Form (the usual one); and (b) Probate in Solemn Form.

Application for probate may be made by the executors in person at the Principal Probate Registry (First Avenue House, High Holborn, London) or at a district registry. Applicants should present the following documents: (i) the will, if any; (ii) a certificate of death; (iii) particulars of property liable to capital transfer tax and (iv) a list of debts and funeral expenses.

Where the deceased has many complicated business interests, the collection of information as at (iv) stated previously may take some time. If the documents are in order, and payment of estate duty is made, probate can then be granted and a *copy* of the will handed to the executor. The original will is retained at the Probate Registry.

Probate in common form is usually a matter of course. Where a dispute arises as to the validity of the will, *probate in solemn form* will have to be obtained. This involves an action taken usually before a judge of the Chancery Division of the High Court in London.

Letters of administration are granted at the registries mentioned previously, and in broadly the same way as probate of a will. Whereas an executor is selected because, at least in the opinion of the deceased, he or she is an honest and prudent person, an administrator enjoys no such confidence. Therefore, the court will not usually appoint an administrator unless they produce what is called an 'administration bond'. This is a solemn undertaking by the administrator to pay to the Principal Registrar double the value of the estate if they do not administer it in accordance with the law. Two sureties who guarantee to be liable if the administrator defaults in this obligation are also obtained.

Who may be appointed. The naming of an executor is within the discretion of the testator. Usually more than one executor is nominated, because it is always open to a sole executor to refuse to act, but only the first four named can act. Probate will not be granted to more than four executors. Nor will it be granted to (a) a person of unsound mind or (b) an infant during their minority.

As to administrators, the appointment is within the discretion of the court. The order of priority of appointment follows that of the persons entitled to take on intestacy: surviving spouse, children, father and mother of deceased, etc. Sometimes a creditor may be appointed, e.g. where the estate is insolvent.

Not more than four administrators may be appointed. Where an infant is beneficiary there must normally be at least two, although a trust corporation may act as sole trustee. Trust corporations include the Public Trustee and any corporation, such as a bank, which is either appointed by the court to act as custodian trustee, or is qualified as such under the Public Trustee (Custodian Trustee) Rules, 1926.

Powers and liabilities of personal representatives. The personal representatives have absolute power to dispose of the property for the purpose of administering the estate. On a total intestacy a trust for sale automatically arises, and the powers of trustees for sale are conferred upon the executors (**Administration of Estates Act 1925,** s. 39).

Personal representatives have one year in which to wind up the estate, such time being extended if need be. Where a beneficiary or creditor is prejudiced by delay, a complaint may be made to the court, but it will have to be proved that neglect on the part of the personal representatives was the cause of the delay.

❖ CASE EXAMPLES

James v Scudamore and others (2023)

The deceased died in 2010 with a will and codicil leaving his share of the family home to his wife and executor. In 2013 one of the deceased's sons wrote to the wife alleging that the codicil was invalid and that as a result she should only have a life interest in the home. The wife responded to the son's letter refuting his claim and then heard nothing more from him. The wife subsequently died in 2018.

The claimant in 2020 issued a claim against the dead wife's executor seeking revocation of the probate of the former codicil, basing his claim on evidence of a sole surviving attesting witness, who stated that the codicil had not been properly executed. *Held*: The Court, in dismissing the claim due to unjustified delay on the basis that where the claimant had a right to intervene in existing probate proceedings, but deliberately abstained from joining in them, he or she is bound by the result. That whilst delay is not generally enough to bar a claimant from taking probate proceedings, if there is unjustified delay when possibly evidenced by acts amounting to a waiver of the claimant's right, this will bar their right, particularly where this delay has led to others having a detrimental reliance on this inaction, leading to the distribution of the estate and to the death of witnesses prior to the claim being lodged.

Personal representatives hold a fiduciary position in respect to the administration and are therefore in the position of trustees. If they distribute the estate imprudently, e.g. by paying the beneficiaries before the creditors, they render themselves personally liable. However, the court has the power to relieve a personal representative who has acted honestly and reasonably and ought fairly to be excused.

Revocation. A grant of probate or letters of administration may be revoked if good reason can be shown. For example, if the grant was obtained by fraud, if a later will has been discovered, if it can be shown that the testator is alive or, if probate was granted to the wrong persons or was irregular, there would be good reason for revocation.

Duties of personal representatives. The four main duties of personal representatives are:

a to collect all debts due to the estate
b to pay all the debts and satisfy all the liabilities of the estate
c to convert unauthorized investments into authorized ones (if need be). There is usually power to postpone this duty for as long as the personal representatives think fit
d to distribute the remainder of the estate according to (i) the will or (ii) the rules of intestacy

In accordance with s. 12 of the **Insolvency Act 2000** where the deceased person immediately before their death was beneficially entitled to an interest in any property as a joint tenant, the court can make an order requiring the survivor to pay to the trustee an amount not exceeding the value lost to the estate. (Note that it does not provide for the transfer of that property right as such.)

Where the estate is sufficient to pay off all debts and the beneficiaries in full, there is no difficulty. Where, on the other hand, the estate is insolvent, there will necessarily be conflicting claims. Accordingly, rules must be laid down as to the order or priority of payment.

Insolvent estates. The following rules apply where the estate is insufficient to meet the claims of creditors in full:

a Funeral expenses, testamentary expenses and the costs of administration have first priority. They must be paid in full, if possible.
b Debts have next priority. These are paid in the order set out in the **Insolvency Act 1986**, thus:
    i preferred debts, e.g. arrears of rates and taxes for one year, and wages of clerks and workmen (up to £200) due for a period of four months prior to the death
    ii ordinary debts. These are debts not falling into the categories of preferred or deferred
    iii deferred debts, e.g. claims by a husband or wife for money lent to the deceased for the purpose of business, and claims for money lent to the deceased on terms that it is to bear interest at a rate varying with the profits of the deceased's business

Secured creditors, e.g. persons holding a mortgage, charge or lien on property, are also entitled to special rights in regard to payment.

11.6 Intestacy

Before 1926, the freehold land owned by a person dying intestate passed to the heir at law, while personalty (including leaseholds) passed to the next of kin.

Descent upon an intestacy is now governed by the **Administration of Estates Act 1925**, the **Intestates' Estates Act 1952** and the **Inheritance and Trustees' Powers Act 2014**. After paying funeral expenses, testamentary expenses and debts, the administrators hold the estate on trust for sale (with power to postpone the sale), and distribute the proceeds of sale according to rules laid down in what follows.

Five main groups of people must be considered: (i) a surviving husband, wife or civil partner; (ii) surviving children; (iii) surviving parents; (iv) surviving brothers and sisters of the whole blood and (v) surviving relations of remoter degree.

The right of the intestate's widow, widower or civil partner depends largely on whether there are any children of the marriage or relationship.

a Where the intestate leaves a surviving spouse or civil partner

If there is no issue and no surviving parent or brothers and sisters of the whole blood, the estate passes to the surviving husband, wife or civil partner. If there is issue, the surviving husband, wife or civil partner takes:

i personal chattels, e.g. furniture, motorcars and jewellery, but not chattels used for business purposes; and
ii £250,000 free of death duty and costs, with (if possible) interest at 4 per cent; and
iii half of the residue above the first £250,000. The remaining property then goes to the issue on 'the statutory trusts' (see later on).

Note: Prior to the **Inheritance and Trustees' Powers Act 2014**, if there was no issue, surviving parents and brothers or sisters of the whole blood had certain entitlements. These have now been abolished under the **Rules of Intestacy Act 2014**.

Section 14 of the **Family Law Reform Act 1969** provides that where either parent of an illegitimate child dies intestate in respect of all or any of their real or personal property, the illegitimate child (or, if they are dead, their issue) shall be entitled to take any interest therein to which they would have been entitled if they had been born legitimate.

Where an illegitimate child dies intestate, each of the parents (if surviving) shall be entitled to take any interest therein to which that parent would have been entitled if the child had been born legitimate.

b Where the intestate leaves no surviving spouse or civil partner

The residue is held on 'the statutory trusts' for the issue, if any.

If there is no issue but one or both parents survive, the residue passes to the parents absolutely.

If there is neither issue nor parents, but other relatives survive, the property is distributed in the following order:

i brothers and sisters (or their issue) of the *whole* blood
ii brothers and sisters (or their issue) of the *half* blood
iii grandparents absolutely, if there is no one in class (i) and (ii)
iv uncles and aunts (or issue) of the *whole* blood
v uncles and aunts (or issue) of the *half* blood

In cases (i), (ii), (iv) and (v), the property is held on 'the statutory trusts'.

Where the deceased leaves no relatives whatsoever, the property goes to the Crown as *bona vacantia* ('ownerless property').

The statutory trusts. This means that the administrators are to divide the property equally among the beneficiaries within the class, each share vesting at the age of majority or on a prior marriage of the beneficiary. Where a beneficiary predeceases the intestate, the share goes to the issue (if any). If they have no issue, the property falls into the common fund.

We should note in passing that on an intestacy the surviving spouse has, in normal circumstances, the right to require the personal representatives to appropriate to him or her the matrimonial home. The market value of the home on such an appropriation has to be deducted from the other benefits accruing to the surviving spouse under the intestacy.

Where a testator fails to dispose of all their property, they are described as dying 'partially intestate'. The property not disposed of specifically is taken by the residuary legatee, if any. In the absence of such a person, the property not disposed of by will is distributed by the testator's executors in accordance with the rules of intestacy as set out previously.

Hotchpot. In a total intestacy, s. 47(1)(iii) of the **Administration of Estates Act 1925** requires money or property transferred to a child by the intestate during their lifetime to be brought into account on the division of the residuary estate under the statutory trusts, and treated as having been paid on account of the child's share under the intestacy, unless a contrary intention is shown. This is called the hotchpot rule.

Similarly, in a partial intestacy, under section 49 a surviving spouse must bring into hotchpot any beneficial interest received under the operative part of the will; and so must children bring into account any substantial benefit received from the deceased during his lifetime; and issue, any beneficial interests under the operative part of the will.

11.7 Gifts '*inter vivos*'

So far in this section we have considered the disposition of a person's estate in the event of death. A person may make dispositions of property with the intention that they be effective or become operative during their lifetime.

A gift may be defined as *a transfer of property whereby the transferor* (the donor) *receives no valuable consideration from the transferee* (the donee). Gifts may be made by deed or, more usually, by a transfer of the property by the donor to the donee with the intention that the *ownership* in the goods (as distinct from mere possession) shall be transferred. A gift is not complete therefore until *possession* of the thing has actually been transferred to the donee: the mere intention alone is insufficient; there must be an actual transfer of possession. Where the gift is by deed, the physical transfer of possession or delivery is not necessary. A donee can, of course, refuse a gift. The law presumes that a donee has accepted the gift unless it has been shown clearly that they do not wish to do so.

Once a gift is made, it is irrevocable. On the Continent, however, some legal systems permit a donor to revoke a gift on the grounds of ingratitude by the donee. A gift may be conditional. Thus a gift of an engagement ring may be conditional on the fiancée being prepared to marry the donor of the ring.

11.8 'Donatio mortis causa'

- A *donatio* (gift) *mortis causa* (in anticipation of death) is the delivery of property to another in contemplation of the donor's imminent death on condition that the gift is not to be absolute until the donor dies.
- A *donatio mortis causa* resembles a gift by will in that the donor has the right to revoke the gift; the gift lapses if the donee happens to die before the donor; the gift is subject to death duties and is also liable for the donor's debts.
- A *donatio* resembles a gift *inter vivos* ('between the living') in that it takes effect when the delivery occurs, subject to the condition (as stated previously) that the gift will only become absolute if the donor dies. The donor must be in imminent peril of death, i.e. *in extremis*, either by illness or otherwise.
- Revocation of the gift is automatic on recovery of the donor from his illness. Revocation may be express, as where the donor informs the donee that the gift is revoked; or implied, as where the donor resumes possession of the property.
- Delivery of the gift may be actual or constructive. Actual delivery occurs where, for example, *A*, who is about to die, hands a ring to B. Constructive delivery occurs where, for example, *A* hands the keys of their safe where the property is kept to B, the donee, coupled with the intention to transfer ownership.
- Anything capable of passing by mere delivery can be the subject of a *donatio*. Examples include a Post Office Savings Book, National Savings Certificates and a Bank Deposit Book. Freehold land and leasehold land cannot pass by means of a *donatio* (*Sen v Headley*, 1990). However, in *Re Basham* (1986), a claimant was awarded the whole of a deceased's estate.

❖ CASE EXAMPLES

King v Chiltern Dog Rescue (2015)

The deceased, four to six months prior to her death, handed title deeds to her nephew, who purported that she had said 'this will be yours when I go' or similar words. After her death, the nephew claimed that this statement, with the deeds, constituted a donation mortis causa (a DMC). This claim was accepted in the lower court as an effective DMC gift but rejected on appeal when the court *Held*: that it did not satisfy the first requirement of a DMC, 'impeding death', and the second requirement, 'not consistent with it being a gift conditional on death within a limited period of time'.

Keeling v Keeling (2017)

The claimant and his wife stated that the deceased, his sister, had made a DMC to his wife and himself of her unregistered property. *Held*: That this was a hopeless failure of a death-bed DMC. The gift had not been made in contemplation of death. The deeds had been passed to the claimant for safekeeping, not as a gift, and also that the deceased had been suffering from dementia and therefore lacked capacity to manage her affairs.

Masudur Rahman v Dewan Raisul Hassan & Ors (2024)

Al Mahmood died on 23 October 2022, apparently leaving his £2.8 million estate to his brother-in-law and nieces under a will made in 2015. However, on 20 October 2022, Mahmood told his distant relative and long-time carer, Masudur Rahman, that all his assets were his. To support this statement, he gave him all the security devices, logins and passwords which would be needed for accessing his financial accounts. He also gave Rahmin the land certificate for his London house and all the documents relating to the flats he owned in Sutton in the London suburbs. *Held*: That they were all valid DMC, except for the furniture and household contents, as there had been no delivery of these.

11.9 Useful webpages

Government UK—Wills, probate and inheritance (www.gov.uk/wills-probate-inheritance/if-the-person-didnt-leave-a-will)

Shedden family law—Inheritance Act Fact Sheet (www.sheddenfamilylaw.co.uk/inheritance-act-fact-sheet.php)

11.10 Exercises

1 Outline the main provisions of the **Wills Act 1837**.

2 What is the purpose of 'attestation' in regard to a will?

3 How may a will be revoked?

4 What is meant by the doctrine of dependent-relative revocation?

5 What are the three kinds of legacies? Give an example from your own experience of each.

6 Draw up a specimen will for yourself, disposing of all your property.

7 Name the powers, duties and liabilities of personal representatives.

8 Outline the legal provisions in regard to intestacy. State the Acts that apply particularly to this part of the law and show how an estate devolves (i) where an intestate leaves a surviving spouse or civil partner and (ii) where an intestate leaves no surviving spouse or civil partner.

9 In relation to the law of intestacy, what is meant by the phrase 'the statutory trusts'?

10 Explain the law in regard to *donatio mortis causa*.

11 Consider the importance of the changes made to the Law of Wills by the **Administration of Justice Act 1982**.

Chapter 12

Criminal law

Key points

- structure and classification of a criminal law
- the elements of criminal liability
- offences against the person
- offences against property

12.1 Definition of crime

Criminal law is concerned with conduct that the State considers should be punished, whereas civil law is concerned with private rights. A crime may be regarded as a public wrong, but conduct that is harmful to the public is not necessarily criminal. 'Crimes, then, are wrongs which the judges have held, or Parliament has from time to time laid down, are sufficiently injurious to the public to warrant the application of criminal procedure to deal with them' (Smith and Hogan). Nor is immoral conduct necessarily criminal; but conduct that would not be regarded as immoral may be criminal on grounds of social expediency. 'The domain of criminal jurisprudence can only be ascertained by examining what acts at any particular period are declared by the State to be crimes' (Lord Atkin).

This means that crime can only usefully be defined by reference to procedure: 'A crime (or offence) is a legal wrong that can be followed by criminal proceedings which may result in punishment' (Glanville Williams).

12.2 Sources

a Common law

Many criminal offences were originally created by the common-law courts and the definitions of some of these offences are to be found even today only in case law, e.g. murder, involuntary manslaughter, common assault.

An offence remains a common-law offence even when statute provides defences or penalties, e.g. **Homicide Act 1957**.

DOI: 10.4324/9781003422808-12

Today the courts have no power to create new offences, and this was acknowledged by the House of Lords in *Knuller v DPP* (1973). In an earlier case before the House of Lords, *Shaw v DPP* (1962), Lord Simonds LC seemed to be claiming otherwise when he stated that 'there remains in the courts of law a residual power to enforce the supreme and fundamental purpose of the law to conserve not only the safety and order but also the moral welfare of the State'.

b Textbooks

These are not sources, but certain early works—e.g. Coke, Foster, Hawkins, Hale—are accepted by the courts as authoritative of the law as it stood at the time when the book was written.

Modern books are not authoritative but may be used persuasively by counsel and thus influence the courts, e.g. Kenny, Williams, Smith and Hogan.

c Statute

This is the main source of law today. Some statutes may merely amend common-law offences, e.g. **Homicide Act 1957**. Others may abolish earlier law and start afresh, e.g. **Theft Act 1968, Criminal Damage Act 1971**. But a great number of modern statutes that have no apparent connexion with criminal law contain criminal offences, e.g. **Income Tax Acts, National Insurance Act, Health and Safety at Work Act**. Ministers appear to accept that the best way to ensure compliance with the statute is to have a criminal law sanction, and as most of the charges are heard by unpaid magistrates, this is no doubt an economic method. But it may be doubted whether the criminal law should be so vastly widened since even the minor offences involve prosecution before the criminal courts (see, for example, 'Breaking the Rules'—a report by Justice 1980).

d Subordinate legislation

Statute may empower a minister or some other body, e.g. a local authority, to make rules, orders or byelaws that may contain offences. If the minister exceeds the authority given by the statute, he is said to have acted *ultra vires*, and the rule will be invalid.

12.3 Classifications

Crimes may be classified as follows:

a According to source

See Definition and Classifications of a crime.

b According to method of trial

The **Criminal Law Act 1977** provides as follows:

i indictable offences—triable in the Crown Court by judge and jury; e.g. murder, robbery
ii summary offences—triable by lay or stipendiary magistrates; e.g. most traffic offences
iii offences triable either way; e.g. theft

c Treason, arrestable offences, other offences

Treason is an offence against the State. Arrestable offences are the more serious offences for which arrest may be made without a warrant. By s. 2 of the **Criminal Law Act 1967** they are ones that have a fixed penalty, e.g. murder, or for which a person, not previously convicted, may under any enactment be sentenced for a term of five years, or attempts to commit such offences. Also, a statute may declare an offence that has a lesser sentence than five years to be arrestable, e.g. s. 12 of the **Theft Act 1968**.

'Other offences' are the less serious ones.

12.4 Criminal liability

Almost all common-law offences and serious statutory offences require two elements, *actus reus* and *mens rea*; in the words of the Latin maxim *actus non facit reum nisi mens sit rea*. The easiest way to understand these elements is to think of *actus reus* as the physical act and *mens rea* as the intent to do that act. *Mens rea* is the Latin for 'guilty mind' and traditionally refers to the state of mind of the person committing the offence. Some offences are satisfied with negligence instead of *mens rea*. Many minor statutory offences require proof only of the *actus reus*: these are called strict liability offences. In addition, a person may sometimes be vicariously liable in criminal law for the act and even *mens rea* of another person. Lastly a corporation, a non-human, may be held personally liable for acts of its directors or servants.

This is the prohibited act that is necessary for all crimes and is to be found in the definition of the crime. Professor Glanville Williams defines *actus reus* as 'the conduct that is forbidden by the rule of the criminal law on the assumption that any necessary *mens rea* is found to exist . . . the external elements of the offence, including the negative of defences'. The *actus reus* may consist of three elements: (i) the willed movement or omission, (ii) the surrounding circumstances and (in some cases) (iii) the prohibited consequences.

The following may amount to conduct:

i a physical act, e.g. a blow
ii words, in such offences as incitement, conspiracy, blackmail and where the words induce an act by an innocent agent
iii an omission, where there is a legal duty to act either at common law, by statute or by undertaking, e.g. a parent has a duty to provide food and medical attention for his or her children

❖ CASE EXAMPLE

***Instan* (1893)**

A niece who had undertaken to look after her elderly aunt at her aunt's expense and failed to provide food and to call medical assistance when the aunt was seriously ill was convicted of manslaughter.

iv possession, e.g. drug offences
v a state of affairs, e.g. 'being found in a dwelling-house for an unlawful purpose'
vi conduct of others in vicarious liability

If the conduct is not willed by a person, it will not count as his or her act, e.g. where *A* is pushed by B into C, it is not *A*'s act. Similarly, the conduct of a sleepwalker in his or her sleep is not willed conduct (see *automatism*, p. 346).

The word 'unlawfully' in the definition of a crime indicates merely that there are defences.

12.4.1 Mens rea

This consists of intention or recklessness. It is necessary to distinguish them since some crimes require nothing less than intention, e.g. attempt and wounding with intent under section 18 of the **Offences Against the Person Act 1861** (Belfon, 1976).

a Intention

The hallmark of intention is desire or purpose. Professor Williams defines it as 'a volitional movement (or omission), knowledge of the relevant circumstances and a desire that any relevant consequences shall follow'. Foresight of certainty without desire must also be counted as intention. The Law Commission has proposed the following definition: 'A person intends an event not only (a) when his purpose is to cause that event but also (b) when he has no substantial doubt that the event will result from his conduct.' Intention is a subjective concept: a court is concerned purely with what the particular defendant was intending at the time of the offence, and not what a reasonable person would have intended in the same circumstances. The words 'has no substantial doubt' seem less clear than 'is certain'.

b Recklessness

Here there is foresight of the consequences but not desire. The Law Commission has proposed the following definition:

> A person is reckless if (a) knowing that there is a risk that an event may result from his conduct or that a circumstance may exist, he takes that risk, and (b) it is unreasonable for him to take it having regard to the degree and nature of the risk which he knows to be present.

However, in *Caldwell* (1981), where D, while drunk,* had set fire to a hotel and was indicted for arson, the House of Lords stated that recklessness had a wider meaning than that which had previously been ascribed to it. It was used as an ordinary English word and as such included not only deciding to ignore a risk that one has recognized as existing but also failing to give any thought to whether or not there is a risk in circumstances where, if any thought were given to the matter, the existence of risk would be obvious. The decision in this case and in *Lawrence* (1981) has been to bring a marked change in the approach to recklessness, very different from that recommended by the Law Commission. This test of recklessness was followed in *Miller* (1983) where D was convicted of reckless arson and *DPP v K. (A Minor)* (1990), where D was convicted of assault occasioning actual bodily harm.

The principle of objective recklessness espoused in Caldwell was abolished by the House of Lords in *R v G* (2003). In this case the defendant boys, aged 11 and 12 years old, set fire to newspapers and proceeded to place the newspapers into a large wheelie bin. The fire spread to the adjoining shop, causing damage of approximately one million pounds. The basis of the Caldwell test is therefore: Can a defendant properly be convicted under section 1 of the **Criminal Damage Act 1971** on the premise that he was reckless or had disregard for the risk as to whether the property was destroyed or damaged? However, in this situation, by reason of his age and/or personal characteristics, would the risk not have been obvious to him even if he had thought about it? The House of Lords was persuaded by the unfairness of convicting children on the strength of what someone else (a responsible adult) would have objectively apprehended.

---

* Note: In this chapter, D denotes the defendant and P the prosecutor or the person affected by D's act.

12.4.2 Negligence

Mens rea involves foresight or awareness. Negligence does not; it is conduct that fails to measure up to the conduct of a reasonable person, i.e. the test is objective. Negligence has been long established in the law of tort, e.g. the negligent motorist will have to compensate anyone injured by his or her act. In criminal law there is less scope for this since the sanction is punishment. Some writers doubt therefore whether negligence ought to feature at all in criminal law (e.g. Hart). There are, however, some statutory offences based on negligence, e.g. careless driving, neglect of children and some offences under the **Health and Safety at Work Act 1974**; and some offences may be regarded as offences of negligence where there is a defence of due diligence, e.g. **Trade Descriptions Act 1968**. There is also one serious offence, manslaughter, which can be committed by grossly negligent conduct. In *R v Evans* (2009) the elder half-sister of the victim supplied her with heroin. The victim showed signs of overdosing. The defendant failed to seek medical assistance. In the morning, the victim was dead. The Court of Appeal held that the defendant was guilty of grossly negligent manslaughter.

12.4.3 Strict liability

Common-law offences require *mens rea*, and until the middle of the nineteenth century the courts always presumed that a statutory offence also required *mens rea* even where the statute did not expressly say so. However, when the courts came to construe the social legislation that Parliament had begun to pass, they felt that the statutes would be rendered more or less ineffective if the prosecution had to prove *mens rea* before the lay magistrates, who heard these minor cases. The courts therefore began to hold in this class of offence, called 'public welfare offences' in America, that where the statute neither expressly nor by necessary implication required *mens rea*, then Parliament had intended that it was not necessary, and thus the prosecution could succeed by proving merely the *actus reus*. What follows are two examples of this:

❖ CASE EXAMPLES

***Parker v Alder* (1899)**

D was convicted under the **Food and Drugs Act** of selling impure milk. He had sent pure milk by train to London, but when it was delivered it was found to have been adulterated by water and the culprit was unknown.

***Quelch v Collett* (1948)**

Provisions as to third-party insurance in the **Road Traffic Act** were held to be strict and D was liable even though he was without fault.

Offences that the courts have construed in this way are to be found in such statutes as **Sale of Food and Drugs Act, Road Traffic Acts, Trade Descriptions Act, Consumer Protection Act, Pollution Act, Factories Acts** and similar statutes whose object is the protection of the public against such activities. In *Westminster City Council v Croyalgrange Ltd* (1986) it was stated that caution should be exercised in reaching a guilty verdict where the word 'knowingly' is incorporated into the offence. Occasionally the courts have extended the notion of strict liability to offences outside the field of social legislation. For example:

❖ CASE EXAMPLE

Prince (1875)

A conviction under s. 55 of the **Offences against the Person Act 1861** of unlawfully taking an unmarried girl under 16 out of the possession and against the will of her father was upheld even though D believed on reasonable grounds that the girl was over 16, the court holding that it was an offence of strict liability so far as the age of the girl was concerned.

In tort an employer may be liable for the tort of an employee committed in the course of employment. At common law there was no vicarious liability in criminal law (*Huggins*, 1730). But from the late nineteenth century the courts began to hold that it could arise in statutory offences in the following circumstances:

i where the statute expressly says so (see, for example, the **Medicines Act 1968**, s. 69)
ii in licensing cases, (a) where the licensee knows and fails to stop an employee contravening the statute; or (b) where the licensee has delegated control of the business

❖ CASE EXAMPLE

Allen v Whitehead (1930)

The licensee of a refreshment house employed a manager for it and instructed him not to allow prostitutes to frequent the house. The manager knew that they were resorting to it. The licensee did not, but was convicted because he had delegated control to the manager.

iii where the offence is one of strict liability and the employer can legitimately be regarded as coming within the *actus reus*. An employer can be held guilty of a 'selling' or 'using' offence even though the act is that of an employee. But an employer will not be held liable for a 'driving' offence by an employee

❖ CASE EXAMPLES

Harrow London BC v Shah & Anor (1999)

D1 and D2 were proprietors of a newsagent's whose employee sold lottery tickets to a person under the age of 16, contrary to s. 13 of the **National Lottery Act 1993** and the **National Lottery Regs 1994**. *Held*: that this was an offence of strict liability and the prosecution was not required to prove that D1 and D2 or their agent was aware of the buyer's age or was reckless as to his age.

Coppen v Moore (1898)

The owner of a shop was convicted under the **Merchandise Marks Act** of selling goods to which a false trade description was applied, when, without his knowledge, an assistant sold an American ham as a 'Scotch ham'.

Green v Burnett (1955)

A company was convicted under the Motor Vehicles (Construction and Use) Regulations of using a vehicle on the road with defective brakes, even though the defect leading to the failure could only have been discovered by dismantling the cylinder.

There are one or two other cases that cannot be brought under the previous headings, e.g. *Newton v Smith* (1962).

A corporation may be liable (i) vicariously where an ordinary employer can be liable (see what was stated previously) and (ii) under the '*alter ego*' doctrine.

Under (ii) a corporation can be held personally liable for most offences provided:

a it is a fineable offence
b it is committed by a 'controlling mind', i.e. a director
c it is committed in the course of corporate duties

❖ CASE EXAMPLES

ICR Haulage (1944)

A company, its managing director and persons outside the company were indicted for conspiracy to defraud. The Court of Criminal Appeal held that the company could be liable through its director.

Henshall v Harvey (1965)

A weighbridge operator employed by a company allowed, by oversight, an overladen lorry to be driven away. The company was held not guilty of aiding and abetting the driver's offence, since the knowledge of an inferior servant is not knowledge of the company.

12.4.4 Corporate manslaughter

Attorney General's Reference (No. 2 of 1999): On 19 September 1997, a high-speed train from Swansea crashed into a freight train from Southall, resulting in the death of seven people. The trial judge ruled that it was a condition precedent to a conviction for manslaughter by gross negligence, for a guilty mind to be proved and that where a non-human defendant was prosecuted, it could only be convicted via the guilt of a human being with whom it could be identified.

Two questions of law were asked:

1 Can a defendant be properly convicted of manslaughter by gross negligence in the absence of evidence as to that defendant's state of mind? The response by the Court of Appeal to

this question was that evidence of a defendant's state of mind was not a prerequisite to a conviction for manslaughter by gross negligence. However, this might be relevant to the jury's consideration when assessing the grossness and criminality of his or her conduct.

2 Can a non-human defendant be convicted of the crime of manslaughter by gross negligence in the absence of evidence establishing the guilt of an identified human individual for the same crime? The response by the Court of Appeal to this second question was that a non-human defendant, such as a corporation, could not be convicted in the absence of evidence establishing the guilt of an identified human individual for the same crime.

The **Corporate Manslaughter and Corporate Homicide Act 2007** creates the offence of corporate manslaughter with the main elements to be established for the offence being that the organization that owes the deceased a 'relevant duty of care' must be in breach of that duty in which its actions were managed or organized with causing the person's death, and the management's failure must amount to a gross breach of duty of care owed to the person. An organization guilty of corporate manslaughter will be liable on conviction on indictment to a fine. The organizations listed in the legislation as coming within the terms of the legislation are: companies and other incorporated bodies, government departments, police forces, partnerships and trade unions or employer associations.

12.5 Exemptions from liability

a The sovereign

b Foreign sovereigns, ambassadors

The Crown cannot be prosecuted, nor can government departments.

Visiting foreign sovereigns and diplomats are exempt from criminal liability; so are members of armed forces unless a statute provides otherwise.

c Children

There is an irrebuttable presumption that a child under 10 cannot commit a crime. If a child is between 10 and 14, there is a rebuttable presumption that he or she cannot do so; but the prosecution can rebut this by evidence of 'a mischievous discretion', i.e. that he or she knows that what he or she is doing is gravely wrong (*Gorrie*, 1919).

The criminal liability of children over 14 is the same as for adults.

12.6 Parties to a crime

By s. 1 of the **Criminal Law Act 1967**, which abolished the distinction between felonies and misdemeanours, parties may now all be charged as principals. But there are reasons for distinguishing the parts actually played: (i) for the purpose of punishment; (ii) an accessory cannot be guilty of an offence unless they have *mens rea*, whereas a principal may in strict liability offences; (iii) duress is available to an accessory as a defence in murder but not to a principal.

The courts therefore distinguish between a principal or perpetrator who does the act and the accessory who counsels, procures, aids or abets. However, the parties may be charged as joint principals. A person who commits an act through an innocent agent will be charged as a principal. So will the employer be in vicarious liability.

To constitute counselling or procuring, there must be instigation, not mere knowledge, or facilitating the commission of the offence by providing the instrument knowing that it is to be used for a crime of the type committed. In *Bainbridge* (1960) D's oxygen cutting equipment was used for burglary.

Prior to 1967 aiding and abetting was assisting at the scene of the crime: there had to be help or encouragement, not mere presence; common purpose; power to prevent the offence. Since the Act, presence would not seem to be necessary.

If the principal exceeds the agreed purpose, the accessory will not be held liable for the excess if he or she did not agree.

❖ CASE EXAMPLE

***Davies v DPP* (1954)**

The agreed purpose was common assault, but D had a knife and killed. D's confederates were held not to be parties to the homicide.

Both the principal and the accessory may be liable for unforeseen consequences:

❖ CASE EXAMPLE

***Buck* (1960)**

D carried out an illegal abortion on P at the request of her friend E. The girl died. The Court of Criminal Appeal held that D was rightly convicted as principal and E as accessory to manslaughter.

Normally a person cannot be convicted as an accessory if there is no principal—*Thornton v Mitchell* (1940). But there are a number of exceptions to this rule.

The *mens rea* may consist of knowledge of the circumstances, knowledge of the type of crime planned or in some cases 'wilful blindness' (*Carter v Mace*, 1949). Negligence is not sufficient.

12.7 General defences

It is convenient to group these together, although mistake is no more than a negating of *mens rea*.

12.7.1 Automatism

If the act is involuntary, there is no act in law. This means that it would be a defence even to an offence of strict liability.

According to Lord Denning in *Bratty* (1963), automatism is confined to acts done while D is unconscious and to spasms, reflex actions and convulsions. The usual instances are: sleepwalking or other behaviour during sleep (*Boshears*, 1961), concussion, epilepsy, hypoglycaemia (*Quick*, 1973) and dissociative states or hysterical neurosis. An act that does not arise from automatism may nevertheless be involuntary, e.g. where a driver's brakes fail without his fault (*Burns v Bidder*,

1967) or where a driver is attacked by a swarm of bees and loses control of the vehicle (*Hill v Baxter*, 1958).

A successful defence of automatism entitles the defendant to an absolute acquittal. But the courts have qualified the defence in three ways: (i) D will not be entitled to the defence if there was prior fault, e.g. failure to stop upon realizing that he or she is likely to fall asleep; (ii) self-induced intoxication will never amount to automatism; (iii) if the automatism arises from disease of the mind the M'Naghten rules will be applied (see below under 'Insanity'). Devlin J. in *Kemp* (1957) held that the issue of insanity was a question of law for the judge, and this was approved by Lord Denning in *Bratty*.

In *Quick* (1973), D, a diabetic, had taken insulin that had produced a hypoglycaemic episode during which a patient was assaulted. Following *Kemp* and *Bratty* the trial judge did not allow the jury to consider the defence of automatism. The Court of Appeal in quashing the conviction distinguished *Kemp* on the ground that the blackout resulted from inherent disease, whereas in *Quick* it resulted from an external event, i.e. the insulin injection, and therefore D was entitled to the defence of non-insane automatism.

In putting forward the defence, D must put it on a proper foundation; and, according to Lord Denning, D's own word must be supported by medical evidence.

12.7.2 Mistake

According to the maxim, ignorance of the law is no defence. But ignorance or mistake may be a defence where:

i the definition of the crime involves a concept of civil law, e.g. bigamy—being married
ii there is a claim of right—this is a defence to theft and criminal damage (*Smith*, 1974)

Mistake of fact may be a defence if it negates the *mens rea* of the offence, e.g. if A takes B's umbrella by mistake, there will be no *mens rea* for theft. The House of Lords in *Morgan* (1976) held that mistake will be a defence if it is an honest mistake; except in bigamy, where the mistake must be based on reasonable grounds, i.e. an objective test (*Tolson*, 1889). In other than bigamy cases courts have sometimes held that the mistake must be reasonable. But the ruling in *Morgan* presumably now applies to such cases, though not apparently to mistake as to a defence (*Rose*, 1884).

12.7.3 Insanity

According to the *M'Naghten rules*, which a committee of judges stated in 1843, an accused is presumed sane until proved otherwise. In order to succeed in the defence of insanity, it must be shown that at the time of committing the act, D was labouring under such a defect of reason, from diseases of the mind, as to:

i not know the nature and quality of the actions; and
ii have no realization of wrongdoing.

The judges added that if the accused 'labours under a partial delusion only, and is not in other respects insane, we think it must be considered in the same situation as to responsibility as if the facts with respect to which the delusion exists were real'.

The accused who puts forward this defence must prove on balance of probabilities that (i) medically there is insanity and (ii) that the situation comes within the M'Naghten rules. If the defence is successful, the verdict is not guilty by reason of insanity, but the accused will be detained in a hospital such as Broadmoor.

Since the abolition of the death penalty, this defence is rarely used, diminished responsibility being preferred. But if the accused raises the defence of diminished responsibility or automatism the prosecution will be allowed to rebut with evidence of insanity—see *Kemp* (1957).

The courts have also given a wide meaning to disease of the mind:

❖ CASE EXAMPLE

***Kemp* (1957)**

D injured his wife in a blackout caused by arteriosclerosis. His defence was automatism. Devlin J. ruled that physical disease of the brain could amount to disease of the mind and could therefore come within the rules.

This decision was approved by Lord Denning in the House of Lords case of *Bratty* (1963), where he said,

> It seems to me that any mental disorder that has manifested itself in violence and is prone to recur is a 'disease of the mind'. At any rate it is the sort of disease for which a person should be detained in hospital rather than be given an unqualified acquittal.

But in Attorney General's Reference (No. 3 of 1998) (1999) and *R v Antonine* (1999), *D* was fit to plead on a charge of aggravated burglary, but it was agreed that at the time of entering the property where the offence was committed he was legally insane. It was held in the Attorney General's Reference that when assuming insanity the Crown merely has to prove the ingredients that constituted the *actus reus* of the crime. There was no requirement for them to prove *mens rea* of the crime alleged.

❖ CASE EXAMPLE

***DPP v H* (1997)**

At the first instance a defendant charged with driving with excess alcohol was acquitted on the ground of insanity. On appeal it was held that the defence of insanity was only available in respect of offences requiring a *mens rea*. As this was a strict liability offence, an insanity plea was not available.

***R v Keal* (2022)**

The defendant was found guilty of attempted murder of his father, mother and grandmother. During this frenzied attack, he stated, 'I am sorry; this isn't me, it's the devil'. He appealed his conviction on the grounds of insanity. *Held:* In dismissing his appeal, the Court of Appeal (Criminal Division) stated that (i) In order to establish the defence of insanity within the M'Naghten Rules of not knowing that the act was 'wrong', the defendant must establish both that (a) he did not know that his act was unlawful (i.e. contrary to law) and (b) he did not know that his act was 'morally' wrong (also expressed as wrong 'by the standards of ordinary people'). 'Wrong' means both against the law and by the standards of ordinary reasonable people. (ii) Under the M'Naghten

Rules, the defence of insanity is not available to a defendant who, although he knew what he was doing was wrong, believed that he had no choice but to commit the act in question. (iii) The current law on insanity cannot be interpreted as involving an element of 'choice', as significant changes to our criminal law that have remained undisturbed for long, laden with policy choices as they would be, are more properly for Parliament. (iv) The Judge's direction of law in the present case was appropriate.

12.7.4 Intoxication by drink or drugs

In the House of Lords case of *DPP v Beard* (1920), Lord Birkenhead stated the law with regard to this defence as follows:

i If the intoxication causes actual insanity, e.g. delirium tremens, then the M'Naghten rules will be applied.

ii Intoxication is a defence if it rendered *D* incapable of forming the specific intent essential to constitute the crime.

iii Intoxication not negating *mens rea* will be no defence if its only consequence is merely to lead *D* more readily to such behaviour.

The charge in *Beard* was murder, and in (ii) Lord Birkenhead was no doubt drawing a distinction between murder and negligent manslaughter which needs no intent; just as Lord Denning was doing in *A.-G. for Northern Ireland* (1963) when he referred to the case of the nurse at a christening party who was so drunk that she put the baby on the fire in mistake for a log of wood; Lord Denning said there would be a defence to murder but not to manslaughter. However, later courts held that intoxication was a defence only to crimes of 'specific intent'; and over the years held that murder, wounding with intent, theft, robbery, burglary with intent to steal, handling stolen goods, criminal damage under s. 1(2) of the **Criminal Damage Act 1971** and attempt were such offences; whereas manslaughter, malicious wounding, assault occasioning actual bodily harm, common assault, indecent assault, assault on a constable, rape, criminal damage under s. 1(1) of the Act and taking a conveyance without consent have been held to be offences of basic intent not requiring a specific intent and therefore intoxication is no defence. Only the decisions will show which is which. The leading case today is *Majewski* (1976) in which the House of Lords considered the history of the defence and approved the classification adopted by the courts after *Beard*. The actual decision was that intoxication was not a defence to assault occasioning actual bodily harm.

- In *Pordage* (1978) the Court of Appeal held that the question to be asked is not whether *D* had the capacity to form the intent, but whether in fact it was formed.
- In *O'Grady* (1987) the Court dismissed an appeal that the blows causing the death of the victim had been struck by *D* under a drunken and unreasonable mistake that a deadly attack was being made.
- However, as was explained in *R v Scarlett* (1993) and *R v Owino* (1995) the courts will apply the rule in a manner that takes account of the motives of the accused and that is no longer wholly objective.
- In *R v Dietschmann* (2003), the appellant, who was on trial for murder, pleaded the defence of diminished responsibility. The trial judge directed the jury to consider whether, on the balance of probabilities, the appellant had satisfied them that if he had not taken drink (1) he would have killed as in fact he did; and (2) he would have been under diminished responsibility when he did so. If they have satisfied you that the answer to both questions is

'Yes', then this was a case of diminished responsibility. But if the answer to either question is 'No', then it is not. The direction reflected the two-stage test developed by the Courts over the years to deal with such cases.

- See, for example, *R v Egan* (1992). In this case the defence was removed from an accused if he had killed because of intoxication, irrespective of the determination that he was suffering from a mental abnormality which itself substantially impaired his mental responsibility. The House of Lords referred the case back to the Court of Appeal with the focus on mental disorder outside of alcohol abuse and the killing occurred under the remit of diminished responsibility. *Held*: The defendant was convicted of murder.
- In *R v TAJ (Simon)* (2019) the decision in *Majewski* was followed where the Court of Appeal (Criminal Division) dismissed an appeal against conviction for an attempted murder on the basis that 'attributable to intoxication' was therefore not confined to cases in which alcohol or drugs were still in the defendant's system.

The principles are the same whether the intoxication is by alcohol or drugs.

❖ CASE EXAMPLE

***Lipman* (1970)**

D took LSD and during hallucination killed his girlfriend not knowing what he was doing. D's conviction of manslaughter was upheld.

The defence will not apply where the drink or drugs were ingested with a view of committing a criminal act once intoxicated.

There is very little authority on involuntary drunkenness. It is open for the courts in a *Lipman* situation, where D's intoxication was not self-induced and where there was no fault in any way, to hold that D was in a state of automatism and so not liable for murder *or manslaughter*.

12.7.5 Prevention of crime: arrest

S. 3(1) of the **Criminal Law Act 1967** provides that a person may use such force as is reasonable in the circumstances in the prevention of crime or in effecting or assisting in the lawful arrest of offenders.

As Williams points out, this 'gives no clear guidance on what we are allowed to do', especially on what offences are so serious that extreme force is justified to prevent them.

12.7.6 Private defence

This will excuse crimes against the person or property, provided the force used is necessary to avoid the attack and is reasonable. If D is mistaken in the belief that there is a need for defence, D will be excused only if the belief is reasonable (*Rose*, 1847).

At common law there were rules as to the duty to retreat if possible before acting in defence. It is not clear whether those rules remain or have been replaced by s. 3(1) of the **Criminal Law Act 1967**; but according to Williams they have not; also queried in *Bird* (1985).

The occupier of premises may use force against a trespasser, provided it is necessary and reasonable. In *Hussey* (1924) it was assumed by the Court of Criminal Appeal that it was still good law for a person to defend their dwelling against unlawful eviction even to the extent of taking life. However, it is doubtful whether the courts would take that view today.

Under s. 6 of the **Criminal Law Act 1977** a displaced residential occupier may use necessary and reasonable force to re-enter. Similar force may be used to prevent the dispossession of chattels.

12.7.7 Necessity

Is it a defence for *D* to break the law in order to prevent greater harm? In the American case of '*The William Gray*' it was held that the captain of a ship was justified against regulations in entering port during a storm in order to save the ship, lives and cargo.

Opinions differ as to whether necessity is a general defence at common law or whether it is confined to the definitions of particular offences. Some statutes contain a defence in respect of acts done in an emergency, e.g. **Control of Pollution Act 1974**; in other offences a justification may be implied, e.g. careless driving. At common law there are a number of cases in which necessity has been held to be a defence, e.g. prisoners leaving prison, which was on fire, pulling down a house to prevent a fire spreading, jettisoning cargo in a storm at sea for the safety of passengers, force-feeding prisoners on hunger strike in gaol. But it is not clear how far the defence extends beyond such cases. Williams has argued that there must be a general defence; otherwise, the doctor who operates on an unconscious victim of a road accident would have no defence to assault.

In the English case of *Dudley & Stephens* (1884) some shipwrecked crew killed and ate the cabin boy to save their own lives. This was held to be no defence to a charge of murder. Nevertheless, there are no doubt circumstances where necessity would be a defence to murder.

12.7.8 Duress

If *D* commits any crime, other than murder, as a principal in the first degree (*Abbott*, 1977) and some forms of treason (*Oldcastle*, 1419), under the threat of immediate death (*Gill*, 1963) or serious personal violence (*A.-G. v Whelan*, 1934) there may be the defence of duress. In *Howe* (1987) the House of Lords held that duress was not available as a defence in murder to either a principal or secondary party. Duress was also held to involve an objective as well as a subjective test.

A threat to property is not sufficient (*Conway*, 1988).

D was chased in a car by plainclothes detectives who believed the passenger was a victim of an assassination attempt. The Court of Appeal (Criminal Division) held that the question of duress, as to whether *D* had reason to believe that he was doing this to avoid death or serious injury was a matter that should be left to the jury to decide.

The fact that the defendant is of low intelligence is not relevant for the jury to take into account, as it does not make him or her any less able to withstand threats or pressure. However, the fact that a defendant suffers from mental illness or a recognized psychiatric condition may be a relevant characteristic—*R v Bowen* (1996).

In *R v Hasan* (2005) the Court of Appeal (Criminal Division), in allowing the defendant's appeal, upheld a defence of duress on the basis that the jury should have been directed to consider whether the defendant knew he was likely to be subjected to threats to commit a crime of the very type with which he was charged (aggravated burglary).

12.7.9 Coercion

By s. 47 of the **Criminal Justice Act 1925**, on a charge against a wife for any offence other than treason or murder, it shall be a good defence to prove that the offence was committed in the presence of and under the coercion of the husband.

Whereas duress amounts to physical compulsion, coercion is concerned with 'moral or spiritual' influence. But it is seldom put forward as a defence; the only reported case seems to be *Pierce* (1941).

12.7.10 Superior orders

That a person was acting under the orders of a superior does not normally constitute a defence to a criminal charge. It has been held in the South African case of *Smith* (1900) that a soldier would have a defence if it was honestly believed that there was a duty to obey the commands of a superior and the orders were not so manifestly illegal that a person ought to have known them to be unlawful.

12.8 Inchoate offences

There are three such offences:

a Incitement

Previously it was an incitement to counsel, procure, advise, encourage or persuade a person to commit a crime, even though that crime was not committed. If the crime was committed, the inciter became an accessory to the crime. This common-law crime of incitement was abolished by the **Serious Crime Act 2007** and replaced with three new offences. These were:

i intentionally encouraging an offence
ii encouraging or assisting an offence, believing it will be committed
iii encouraging or assisting offences, believing one or more will be committed

b Conspiracy

By the **Criminal Law Act 1977** it is a statutory conspiracy for two or more persons to agree to commit a crime, even though the offence is not committed. The Act in abolishing common-law conspiracy nevertheless preserved three conspiracies at common law: conspiracy to defraud, to corrupt public morals and to outrage public decency.

❖ CASE EXAMPLES

Yip Chieu-Chung v The Queen (1995)

C-C was convicted of conspiracy to traffic heroin. He claimed that he did not have the necessary *mens rea* as his motive in agreeing to act as a courier was to bring the criminal gang to justice. The House of Lords rejected his claim by stating that his intention that the crime be carried out constituted the necessary *mens rea* and his motive was, therefore, irrelevant.

Scott v Metropolitan Police Commissioner (1975)

The House of Lords held that D was rightly convicted of conspiracy to defraud where he had agreed with employees of cinema owners to pay them for lending him, without the owners' consent, films that he could copy in breach of copyright and sell for profit. An agreement dishonestly to deprive a person of something that is his or to which he might be entitled or to injure some proprietary right of his suffices for the offence.

This offence is therefore wider than agreements to commit offences under the **Theft Act**.

❖ CASE EXAMPLE

Nock (1978)

The House of Lords held that an agreement to do what was in fact impossible was not a common-law conspiracy. The court therefore quashed a conviction for conspiracy to produce a controlled cocaine-based drug from powder that in fact contained no cocaine.

It seems likely that the courts will treat Nock as applying also to statutory conspiracies.

c Attempt

It is an offence at common law to attempt to commit any indictable offence or an offence triable either way.

The *mens rea* for an attempt is nothing less than intention to commit the crime aimed at; recklessness is not sufficient (*Mohan*, 1976). Attempted murder requires the intent to kill (*Whybrow*, 1951).

The act must be 'proximate' to the crime attempted. The courts have said that to be proximate, it must go beyond mere preparation.

❖ CASE EXAMPLE

Robinson (1915)

A jeweller was held not guilty of attempted obtaining by false pretences where he had staged a fake robbery of his jewellery, insured against theft and allowed himself to be found by the police, bound and gagged. He had not gone beyond preparation since he had not claimed from the insurance company.

Today *Robinson* could be charged under s. 5(2) of the **Criminal Law Act 1967**, of causing the wasteful employment of the police.

The courts have not had much success in laying down more precise rules as to what constitutes a proximate act, and prosecutions often fail on this score. Another difficulty of attempt is the question of impossibility. Until recently a long line of authorities as far back as 1870 had held that factual impossibility was not a defence to attempt, and thus *D* could be convicted of attempting to steal from a pocket that was in fact empty (*Ring*, 1892) or attempting to obtain by false pretences where the person approached was not deceived (*Hensler*, 1870). But in *Haughton v Smith* (1975) the House of Lords restated the rules with regard to this aspect in holding that *D* could not be guilty of attempting to handle goods that had in fact ceased to be stolen. The aim of the **Criminal Attempts Act 1981** was to clarify the law relating to attempts generally and, in particular, to reverse these decisions. S. 1(2) of the Act provides that a person may be guilty of attempting to commit an offence, even though the facts were such that the commission of the offence would have been impossible.

In *Shivpuri* (1986), the House of Lords held that since the Act, impossibility was no bar to a conviction for attempt. This decision overruled their previous decision in *Anderton v Ryan* (1985), which tried to exclude some situations of impossibility from the effect of s. 1 of the Act.

12.9 Burden of proof

In criminal cases the burden is throughout on the prosecution to establish the case against the accused beyond reasonable doubt. If the jury or magistrates have such a doubt, then they should acquit (*Woolmington*, 1935).

At the close of the prosecution case, counsel for the defence may submit that there is no case to answer; if the judge agrees, the jury will be directed to acquit.

Normally, if the accused puts forward a defence it does not have to be proved, but sufficient evidence must be adduced to go to the jury (the evidential burden) and if it creates a reasonable doubt in the minds of the jury, they should acquit. In some cases, however, a defence on balance of probabilities must be proved, i.e. the civil burden of proof, e.g. insanity, diminished responsibility and under the **Prevention of Corruption Act 1916** (s. 2), where a gift shall be deemed to have been given or received corruptly unless D proves the contrary.

In the Crown Court the judge directs the jury on the relevant law and the jury apply the law to the facts of the case in returning a verdict of guilty or not guilty.

In R v K (2003), the Court of Appeal, Criminal Division, made it clear that the aim of ss. 34–38 of the **Criminal Justice and Public Order Act 1994** did not include police cross-examination of a suspect on his account over and above the disclosure of that account, although the making of a pre-prepared statement gave no automatic immunity against adverse inferences being drawn under s. 34 (drawing inferences from silence).

12.10 Offences against the person

Homicide, the killing of a person, may be lawful if it is done for self-defence or prevention of violence or if it is accidental, i.e. without *mens rea* or negligence.

The forms of unlawful homicide are murder, manslaughter, infanticide and causing death by reckless driving.

12.10.1 Murder

Coke C.J. defined murder as:

> [W]hen a person of sound memory and of the age of discretion unlawfully killeth any reasonable creature *in rerum natura* under the King's peace, with malice aforethought, either expressed by the party or implied by law, so as the party wounded, etc., die of the wound or hurt, etc., within a year and a day after the same.

'A person of sound memory, etc.' means a person who is responsible according to the general principles of criminal law. 'Under the King's peace' excludes only an enemy in time of war. A killing by a citizen of the UK and Colonies may be murder or manslaughter even if committed outside the UK. Killings on a British ship or aircraft by anyone are triable in the UK. 'A reasonable creature, etc.' means any human being, but a foetus does not become a person until it has an existence independent of the mother, and a person becomes a corpse when the brain is dead.

The rule known as the 'year and a day rule', whereby if death occurred more than a year and a day after injury, it was not unlawful homicide, was abolished by the **Law Reform (Year and a Day Rule) Act 1996**. One exception provided by this Act is that if the injury that is alleged to have caused the deaths occurred more than three years before the death, then proceedings may only be instituted by or with the consent of the Attorney General.

In homicide, problems of causation can arise. D will be liable only if his or her act was a substantial cause of the death. For example, if the victim received medical treatment after the injury, the court will have to determine whether the injury or the treatment was the cause.

❖ CASE EXAMPLES

Jordan (1956)

D stabbed P, who was admitted to hospital, was given an antibiotic after intolerance had been shown and died a few days later. The Court of Criminal Appeal quashed D's conviction, holding that the cause of death was the 'palpably wrong' (negligent?) treatment, not the wound which had almost healed.

Smith (1959)

D stabbed P, another soldier, in a fight. When being carried to the medical centre P was dropped twice by his comrades. The medical officer considered the wound to be superficial, whereas in fact it had pierced a lung, and consequently gave the wrong treatment. D's conviction of murder was upheld on the ground that at the time of death, the original wound was still an operating and substantial cause.

The common-law rule that neglect of the injury by P does not exempt D (*Holland*, 1841) was applied in the recent case of *Blaue* (1975), where D stabbed P, a young girl, and pierced her lung. As a Jehovah's Witness she refused a blood transfusion, which she was told was necessary to save her life. She died from loss of blood; her refusal to have a transfusion was held not to have broken the chain of causation, and D's conviction of manslaughter was upheld.

Killing means accelerating death, even if P is in any case expected to die within a short time (*Adams*, 1957).

The malice aforethought for murder has traditionally been regarded as follows:

i intention to kill (*Salisbury*, 1553)

ii intention to cause grievous bodily harm (*Vickers*, 1957—approved by the House of Lords in *DPP v Smith* (1961) and followed by the Court of Appeal in Ellerton, 1978)

iii recklessness as to death (*Desmond*, 1868, and *Serne*, 1887) or grievous bodily harm (*Barnes v Richards*, 1940, *Buckett*, 1964)

In spite of the authorities, in (iii), recklessness has been an uncertain *mens rea* and such cases have usually been treated as manslaughter.

Today the leading case on malice aforethought is *Moloney* (1985), where D and his stepfather were very drunk, following a family party. As a result of a challenge by the stepfather to load and fire a shotgun, D fired without aiming and blew the stepfather's head off. He admitted manslaughter but maintained that he had no foresight whatsoever of the possibility of death or injury to his victim. The House of Lords held that D should be acquitted of murder if, in his drunken state, he might have failed to foresee death or injury at all and that only intent to kill or cause serious harm would suffice for malice aforethought. This decision has been followed in both *Hancock* (1986) and *Nedrick* (1986). The emphasis is on distinguishing intent from foresight.

Defences to murder. D is entitled to be acquitted of murder if the killing was carried out in the execution or advancement of justice, in self-defence or prevention of violence or if the death was accidental.

In *R (Officer W80) v Director General of the Independent Officer for Police Conduct* (2023), the case arose from a fatal shooting by a police firearms specialist in the honest but mistaken belief that the suspect was armed. The Supreme Court had to decide whether the test for self-defence in police disciplinary proceedings should be that applied in civil law or criminal law? It *Held*: That in the circumstances, the correct test was the civil law test.

12.10.2 Manslaughter

The two types of manslaughter are:

a Voluntary manslaughter

D may have the malice aforethought for murder, but if one of the following mitigating circumstances is present, the jury may convict of manslaughter instead of murder.

i Provocation

A classic definition of the common-law rule, approved by the Court of Criminal Appeal, was stated by Devlin J. in *Duffy* (1949):

> Provocation is some act, or series of acts, done by the dead person to the accused, which would cause in any reasonable person and actually causes in the accused, a sudden and temporary loss of self-control rendering the accused so subject to passion as to make them for the moment not masters of their minds.

This rule has been modified by s. 3 of the **Homicide Act 1957**, which provides:

> Where on a charge of murder there is evidence on which the jury can find that the person charged was provoked (whether by things done or by things said or by both together) to lose his self-control, the question whether the provocation was enough to make a reasonable man do as he did shall be left to be determined by the jury; and in determining that question the jury shall take into account everything both done and said according to the effect which, in their opinion, it would have on a reasonable man.

The 'reasonable man' is one of the same age and characteristics as the accused and other characteristics relevant to how the provocation would affect him—see *R v Camplin* (1978). Self-induced provocation may also be a good defence—see *R v Johnson* (1989). If a defence of provocation is raised to a murder charge, the defendant's obsessiveness and eccentricity ought to be left to the jury to decide whether a reasonable man in the defendant's position would lose his self-control—see *R v Dryden* (1995).

The Court of Appeal in *Ahluwalia* (1992) stated that while delay between the final provocation behaviour and D's reaction is not fatal to the defence, lack of self-control must still be sudden and temporary. In *Brown* (1972) it was laid down that the judge should ask the jury two questions and in this order:

1 Did D as a result of the provocation lose self-control? If so,
2 Was the provocation enough to make a reasonable person do as D did?

Even if the judge thinks the evidence is slight, it should be left to the jury to decide whether D did lose control (*Bullard*, 1957). One matter that will be important is whether there has been time for the blood to cool (*Hayward*, 1833).

S. 3 prevents the judge from withdrawing the defence from the jury on the ground that there is no evidence on which a jury can find that no reasonable person would have been provoked; or that the mode of retaliation was not reasonably related to the provocation. It also presumably prevents the judge from telling the jury to disregard physical or mental peculiarities of D. In *Camplin* (1977) the House of Lords held that the jury could consider what effect the provocation would have on a reasonable boy of 15, the age of D, and also that severe depression could have the effect of reducing D's threshold for erupting with violence (*Smith*, 1998). But in *Wardrope* (1960) Edmund Davies J. directed the jury that 'the reasonable man is not a violent-tempered man, not a drunken man'. *McCarthy* (1954) seems therefore still to be good law; in that case the jury was directed that they were not entitled to consider the fact that D was drunk and therefore more likely to lose self-control.

In *Davies* (1975) it was held that under s. 3 the provocation could come from a third party.

ii Diminished responsibility

S. 2 of the **Homicide Act 1957** provides:

> Where a person kills or is a party to the killing of another, they shall not be convicted of murder if they were suffering from such abnormality of mind (whether arising from a condition of arrested or retarded development of mind or any inherent causes or induced by disease or injury) as substantially impaired their mental responsibility for their acts and omissions in doing or being a party to the killing.

A jury can convict of manslaughter instead. S. 2(2) puts the burden of proof on D, and in *Dunbar* (1958) it was held that the standard of proof was on balance of probabilities.

By s. 6 of the **Criminal Procedure (Insanity) Act 1964**, as amended by the **Criminal Procedure (Insanity and Unfitness to Plead) Act 1991**, on a plea of diminished responsibility, the Crown may adduce evidence of insanity.

In *Byrne* (1960) the Court of Criminal Appeal indicated the scope of 'abnormality of mind': 'It appears to us to be wide enough to cover the mind's activities in all its aspects . . . also the ability to exercise willpower to control physical acts in accordance with that rational judgment.' Thus irresistible impulse, which had never been recognized under the M'Naghten rules, is admitted under the new defence.

It should be noted that the courts have power under s. 60 of the **Mental Health Act 1959** to make hospital orders committing persons who have committed imprisonable offences to a mental hospital or to guardianship of a health authority as extended by the **Criminal Procedure (Insanity) Act 1964** and the **Criminal Appeal Act 1968**.

However, the judgment in *R v Hussain (Imran)* (2019) *Held*: That the prosecution is entitled to pursue a charge of murder and to challenge the medical evidence.

iii Killing in the course of a suicide pact

S. 4 of the **Homicide Act 1957** provides that 'it shall be manslaughter . . . not murder, for a person acting in pursuance of a suicide pact between him and another to kill the other or be a party to the other being killed by a third person'. The burden of proof of the pact is on the defence.

By the **Suicide Act 1961** suicide is no longer a crime; but it is an offence to aid, abet, counsel or procure the suicide of another or an attempt by another to commit suicide (*Attorney-General v Able*, 1983). Whether D is guilty of manslaughter or of the offence under the 1961 Act will depend on who does the act that kills.

iv Excessive self-defence

There is some old authority for the rule that if *D* in self-defence kills by using more force than is allowed, *D* is entitled to a verdict of manslaughter, not murder. But in *Palmer* (1971) the Privy Council and in *McInnes* (1971) the Court of Appeal did not accept this rule. It seems therefore that in such cases *D* should rely on the defence of provocation, not self-defence.

However, the difficulties in judging the reasonability of force used in self-defence has given rise to the enactment of further legislation to clarify the existing defences relating to self-defence. The **Criminal Justice and Immigration Act 2008**, s. 76, stated that a defendant was to be judged on the facts as he or she believed them to be (s. 76 (3)); and that the defendant was to be entitled to rely on a generally held, albeit mistaken belief, as regards the existence of any circumstances, whether or not it was a reasonable mistake for the accused to have made (s. 76 (4)). Further, s. 148 of the **Legal Aid, Sentencing and Punishment of Offenders Act 2012** amended previous provisions of legislation relating to reasonable force for the purpose of self-defence to be interpreted as a possibility that the defendant could have retreated as a factor to be taken into account, rather than giving rise to a duty to retreat.

In *R (Collins) v Secretary of State for Justice* (2016) the High Court *Held*: that this law is compatible with the European Human Rights legislation. However, the **Crime and Courts Act 2013**, s. 43 extended s. 76, so that the householder has complete defence (and therefore could be acquitted) if the force used was reasonable and was exercised either in defence of him or herself or another in the prevention of crime—in fact the force used against burglars in defence of one's home does not have to be reasonable provided that it not 'grossly disproportionate'. This is known as the 'householder defence'. In *R v Cheesman (Steven)* (2019) such a defence was *Held*: Not available where the injured person had entered a building lawfully, but had thereafter become a trespasser.

b Involuntary manslaughter

There appear to be three types:

a Killing by gross negligence

The classic definition of this is by Lord Hewart in *Bateman* (1925):

> [W]hatever epithet be used and whether an epithet be used or not, in order to establish criminal liability the facts must be such that, in the opinion of the jury, the negligence of the accused went beyond a mere matter of compensation between subjects and showed such disregard for life and safety of others as to amount to a crime against the State and deserving of punishment.

This definition was approved by Lord Atkin in *Andrews v DPP* (1937) and has been followed by many judges. The test envisaged by it is clearly an objective one. But in some later cases judges have directed in terms of recklessness (*Cato*, 1976, *Lowe*, 1973) or equated recklessness with criminal negligence (*Lamb*, 1967). Even Lord Atkin in *Andrews* used 'reckless' obscurely. This is unfortunate since the legal meaning of recklessness differs from its everyday meaning.

❖ CASE EXAMPLE

***R v Wacker* (2003)**

Fifty-eight illegal Chinese immigrants died from suffocation in a lorry on a ferry crossing to Dover. *Held*: The Court of Criminal Appeal found the defendant guilty of manslaughter, the principles of the law of negligence, including the doctrine of *ex turpi causa non oritur action* applied as the defendant owed a duty of care.

b Killing by intentionally doing an unlawful and dangerous act (constructive manslaughter)

It is not sufficient that the act is unlawful; it must also be dangerous (*Franklin*, 1883).

In *Church* (1966) the Court of Criminal Appeal stated that 'the unlawful act must be such as all sober and reasonable people would inevitably recognize must subject the other person to at least the risk of some harm resulting therefrom, albeit not serious harm'. This was approved and applied by the House of Lords in *DPP. v Newbury* (1976), which also held that the test of dangerousness is objective, i.e. D need not have known of the risk. In this case two 15-year-old boys threw part of a paving stone from a railway bridge onto an oncoming train, they said, in order to hit the train. It went through a window and killed the guard. Since the unlawful act here is criminal damage, and an offence against property has hitherto been regarded as not sufficient for manslaughter, the House of Lords in upholding the conviction of manslaughter appears to be overruling *Franklin*, which however, was not referred to in the speeches.

In *Mitchell* (1983), following an argument in a shop queue, M struck *A*, who, as a result, fell accidentally onto B, an elderly lady, who, in turn, fell to the ground suffering a fatal injury. M was convicted of unlawful act manslaughter, the unlawful act being the battery committed by M on *A*.

Of this type of manslaughter Williams says:

> The present position is that (it) is committed only by a killing in the course of certain kinds of unlawful acts and then only when the defendant is negligent as to causing bodily injury . . . apart from the special case of abortion, constructive manslaughter now requires a criminal act of actual or constructive aggression, whether by force or by poisoning.

In *Williams* (1992) the Court of Appeal held that when a victim is killed, a jury can only convict of manslaughter if the threats were a cause of death.

In *R v Tas (Ali)* (2018), where the appellant went with two friends to look for a victim and one of the friends stabbed a victim, subsequently being picked up by the accused in his car, it was *Held*: That he was convicted of being involved in a joint enterprise intending to harm the victim and the victim having died as a result, then the appellant was guilty of manslaughter.

c Killing by an intentional act, being reckless whether bodily harm less than grievous bodily harm results

If recklessness as to grievous bodily harm is sufficient for murder, it is logical that recklessness as to a lesser degree of harm should suffice for manslaughter, but the authority is slight.

❖ CASE EXAMPLE

***Pike* (1961)**

D caused his consenting mistress to inhale the vapour of a cleaning chemical as an aphrodisiac. He had done this to other women over several years with no ill effects except temporary loss of consciousness. On this occasion the woman died. The jury was directed that D was guilty of manslaughter if he knew that inhaling would expose P to physical harm and yet recklessly caused her to inhale. The Court of Criminal Appeal approved this direction.

Today the charge might perhaps be gross negligence.

❖ CASE EXAMPLE

***R v Rogers (Stanley John)* (2004)**

The appellant/landlord, not being a registered installer of gas appliances and having no relevant experience, fitted used gas fires into the premises. The carbon monoxide escaped into the flat, causing the death of two tenants. *Held*: although Rogers had not intended to cause death, he had been reckless and was therefore guilty of manslaughter.

In a 1996 report (*Legislating the Criminal Code: Involuntary Manslaughter*) setting out its recommendations for reforming the law relating to involuntary manslaughter, the Law Commission recommends the abolition of the present unlawful act of manslaughter, the creation of offences of reckless killing and killing by gross carelessness and a separate offence of corporate killing.

12.10.3 Causing or allowing the death of a child or vulnerable adult

S. 5 of the **Domestic Violence, Crime and Victims Act 2004** creates an offence of causing or allowing the death of a child or vulnerable adult. The offence may only be committed by an unlawful act of a person who is the parent of the deceased or is at least 16 years of age, who is a member of the same household as the deceased and who has frequent contact with the deceased.

S. 6 of the Act introduces the concept of *familial homicide*, involving two or more householders in respect of whom it is not possible to prove who performed the fatal act. In this respect s. 6 makes evidential and procedural provisions that apply where a person is charged in the same proceedings and in respect of the same death with murder or manslaughter and the causing or allowing the death of a child or vulnerable adult. By s. 1 of the **Domestic Violence, Crime and Victims (Amendment) Act 2012**, this offence has been amended to incorporate both death and sufferers of serious physical harm.

12.10.4 Infanticide

S. 1(i) of the **Infanticide Act 1938** provides that where a woman causes the death of her child under the age of 12 months but at the time the balance of her mind was disturbed by reason of not having fully recovered from the effect of giving birth to the child she shall be guilty of infanticide, not murder, and dealt with as for manslaughter.

12.10.5 Causing death by dangerous driving

Causing death by careless or inconsiderate driving. This is a new offence introduced by s. 20 of the **Road Safety Act 2006**, as is *Causing death by driving: unlicensed, disqualified or uninsured drivers* in accordance with s. 21 of the Act.

Since juries have always been reluctant to convict fellow motorists of manslaughter, the police therefore do not prosecute for it. Parliament provided the offence of causing death by dangerous driving, with an objective test for danger.

In this respect s. 143 of the **Legal Aid, Sentencing and Punishment of Offenders Act 2012** has extended this offence to include causing serious injury by dangerous driving. Serious injury is construed by the legislation to be grievous bodily harm for the purposes of the **Offences Against the Person Act 1861**.

S. 20 of the **Road Safety Act 2006** has introduced a new offence of causing death by careless or inconsiderate driving, while s. 21 of the Act extends this to causing death by driving in respect of unlicensed, disqualified or uninsured drivers.

12.10.6 Child destruction and abortion

It is not murder to kill a child in the womb or while being born. But it may be one of the following offences:

i By the **Infant Life (Preservation) Act 1929** it is child destruction for any person who with intent to destroy the life of a child capable of being born alive by any wilful act causes a child to die before it has an existence independent of its mother, provided that the act was not done in good faith for the purpose only of protecting the life of the mother. Evidence that at the material time the woman had been pregnant for 28 weeks or more shall be prima facie proof that she was pregnant with a child capable of being born alive.

ii As regards an earlier stage of pregnancy, s. 58 of the **Offences against the Person Act 1861** makes it an offence for a pregnant woman with intent to procure her miscarriage, unlawfully to administer to herself any poison or other noxious thing or use any instrument or other means whatsoever; or for another person to do such act with intent to procure the miscarriage of a woman, whether or not she is pregnant. This is the offence of illegal abortion.

iii By the **Abortion Act 1967**, medical termination of pregnancy is protected if two medical practitioners are of the opinion that continuance of the pregnancy would involve risk to the mother's life or injury to her physical or mental health, account being taken of environmental factors; or that there was a substantial risk that if the child were born it would suffer from such physical or mental abnormalities as to be seriously handicapped. The operation must be carried out in an NHS hospital or other approved place. One medical practitioner may perform the operation in an emergency. Abortions performed otherwise than within the terms of this Act are unlawful; and thus even a doctor may be prosecuted under s. 58 of the **Offences against the Person Act** (*Smith*, 1974).

12.10.7 Assault and battery

At common law these are two distinct offences: assault is any act by which D intentionally or recklessly (*Venna*, 1975) causes P to fear immediate and unlawful personal violence; battery is the intentional or reckless infliction of unlawful personal violence on P. The courts, however, often use 'assault' to cover both.

If P does not observe D's act, it is not an assault, nor if it is obvious that D cannot carry out the threat. Words may 'unmake' an assault, as in *Tuberville v Savage* (1669), where D, laying his hand on a sword, said 'If it were not assize time I would not take such language'. But it is questionable whether words alone will constitute an assault, although there is a dictum of Lord Goddard that they may (*Wilson*, 1955). It seems neither offence can be committed by omission, e.g. in *Fagan* (1968), where D, in parking his car accidentally, ran a wheel onto a policeman's foot and took some time in removing it. This was held to be battery by a continuing act, not by an omission.

Because of the serious implications of domestic violence in common assault incidents, the **Domestic Violence, Crime and Victims Act 2004** made common assault an 'arrestable offence' without a warrant.

Consent, either express or implied, may be a defence to both offences. It is implied, for example, in taking part in sports or in everyday contact in buses, trains or streets. But it will not be a defence where the victim is too young to understand the nature of the act, where it is obtained by duress or fraud or in sexual offences against children. P cannot consent to serious bodily harm, except in surgical operations for medical purposes. Consent can be given to some degree of likely bodily harm in lawful sport, but consent does not apply to deliberate injury outside the rules of the game (*Billinghurst*, 1978). Also, on grounds of public policy, the courts may refuse the defence even when there is only a slight degree of harm, e.g. *Donovan* (1934), apparently because of the element of indecency.

Two other defences are: lawful physical chastisement (i.e. moderate and reasonable) by parents of their children, or by school teachers in respect of children at school or on the way to or from school as well as self-defence.

12.10.8 Assault occasioning actual bodily harm

This offence is provided by s. 47 of the **Offences against the Person Act 1861**. The harm need not be serious, but presumably there must be some harm, e.g. a bruise. If the harm was reasonably foreseeable, the prosecution need not prove that *D* foresaw it; the *mens rea* for the assault is sufficient (*Roberts*, 1971). Consent to sadomasochistic assaults is no defence (*Brown*, 1992). However, the Court of Appeal has held that a husband who, at the instigation of his wife, burnt marks onto his wife's body was not guilty of assault occasioning actual bodily harm—see *R v Wilson* (1996).

The question of the degree of consent in lawful sport was reconsidered by the Court of Appeal (Criminal Division) in *R v Barnes* (2005), where on appeal the defendant was found not guilty of unlawfully and maliciously inflicting grievous bodily harm contrary to s. 20 of the **Offences Against the Person Act 1861** in respect of causing serious injury in a soccer match.

The Court stated that criminal proceedings should be reserved for situations where the conduct was sufficiently grave to be properly categorized as criminal. Most sports have their own disciplinary proceedings.

In addition to criminal prosecution, there was the possibility of the injured player obtaining damages in a civil action. Whether the conduct reached the objective threshold for it to be considered criminal depends on the circumstances.

In *Haystead* (2000), *D* was found guilty of common assault by beating (battery) when he struck the victim twice in the face while she was, to his knowledge, holding her baby, which caused her to drop the child which was injured when it struck the floor.

It is interesting to observe the development of the law in this area by considering the following two cases. In *R v Ireland* (1996), silent phone calls were held to be capable of constituting assault occasioning actual bodily harm under s. 47 of the **Offences Against the Person Act 1986**. Two months later, in *R v Burstow* (1996), the defendant had made silent phone calls to his victim and sent her hate mail, as a result of which she suffered severe depression. The Court of Appeal held that s. 20 of the **Offences Against the Person Act 1986** covers psychiatric injury and therefore a 'stalker' can be convicted under this section even if he has not applied physical violence either directly or indirectly to the body of his victim. In both of the preceding cases the conduct involved silent phone calls, but in one case it was *Held*: to fall under s. 20 and the other under s. 47.

In *R v Rowe (Daryll)* (2018), the first case of its kind to be prosecuted in England and Wales, the defendant, who was HIV-positive, intentionally infected others through unprotected sex, having assured partners he was free from infection. *Held*: Guilty of grievous bodily harm.

12.10.9 Malicious wounding

By s. 20 of the **Offences Against the Person Act 1861** it is an offence unlawfully and maliciously to wound or inflict any grievous bodily harm upon any other person. 'Grievous' means 'really serious' (*DPP v Smith*, 1961). 'Maliciously' means 'intentionally or recklessly' (*Cunningham*, 1957).

In *Parmenter* (1991) it was held that it was necessary for *D* to have actually foreseen that some physical harm would result from the act.

12.10.10 Wounding with intent

By s. 18 of the same Act it is an offence unlawfully and maliciously to wound or cause any grievous bodily harm to any person with the intent to do some grievous bodily harm to any person or with intent to resist or prevent the lawful apprehension of any person. The maximum penalty is life imprisonment. 'Wounding' means to break the two layers of skin, so that an internal injury cannot constitute a wound, as there must be a break in the skin (*C (a minor) v Eisenhower*, 1983). 'Causes' is wider than 'inflicts' in s. 20. S. 18 requires intention; recklessness is not sufficient (*Belfon*, 1976). If D intentionally strikes at P but hits X, the intention can be transferred to X (transferred malice).

12.10.11 Administering poison

Sections 23 and 24 of the same Act provide two offences of administering poison or other noxious thing to another person.

12.10.12 Assault on, resistance to or obstruction of a police constable in the execution of his or her duty

These offences are in s. 89 of the **Police Act 1966**. Such an assault is considered more serious than common assault, but by the **Criminal Law Act 1977**, it becomes a summary offence only. There is much case law on 'execution of their duty' (*Collins v Wilcock*, 1984, and *R v Riley*, 1989).

12.10.13 Protection from harassment

The **Protection from Harassment Act 1997** makes it an offence to pursue a course of conduct amounting to harassment of a person or give them cause to fear that violence will be used against them. The court also has power to make an order preventing further harassment, which, if breached, will constitute an offence.

This power was further extended by s. 12 of the **Domestic Violence, Crimes and Victims Act 2004**, so that a restraining order may also be made on conviction or acquittal for any offence where the court considers it is necessary to do so to protect the victim from harassment.

12.10.14 Preventing and Combating Violence and Domestic Violence

The **Preventing and Combating Violence Against Women and Domestic Violence (Ratification of Convention) Act 2017** was enacted in order to at some time in the future ratify the Council of Europe Convention on preventing and combating violence and domestic violence (the Istanbul Convention). It prevents violence against women, protects victims and survivors of abuse and prosecutes perpetrators. The outcome was that the Secretary of State introduced the **Domestic Abuse Act 2021** with the purpose of which was to raise awareness and understanding of domestic abuse and its impact on victims, to further improve the effectiveness of the justice system in providing protection for victims of domestic abuse and bringing perpetrators to justice and to strengthen the support for victims of abuse and their children provided by other statutory agencies. The Act, which is seven Parts, incorporates at Part 2 the office of Domestic Abuse Commissioner and at Part 3 provides for a new civil preventative order regime—the Domestic Abuse Protection Notice (DAPN) and Domestic Abuse Protection Order (DAPO).

12.10.15 Firearms and offensive weapons

In an endeavour to prevent serious offences against the person, the **Firearms Act 1968** as amended by the **Firearms (Amendment) Acts** of **1988, 1992** and **1997**, regulates the manufacture, sale, use and possession of firearms (as explained in *Hall v Cotton* (1986)). The **Prevention of Crime Act 1953** prohibits the carrying of offensive weapons in public places without lawful authority or reasonable excuse. S. 142 of the **Legal Aid, Sentencing and Punishment of Offenders Act 2012** extended this offence to include an offence of threatening with a blade, point or offensive weapon in a public place or school premises. The Court of Appeal extended this to include a situation where a sawn-off shotgun had been left in a locked car (*Pawlicki*, 1992 and *Swindell*, 1992). In the latter Act, the wide definition includes three categories of articles: (i) those made for causing injury; (ii) those adapted for such use; and (iii) those carried for causing injury (*Simpson*, 1983 and *Court*, 1986).

The courts have construed 'reasonable excuse' narrowly and have held that even if *D* carries a weapon only for self-defence, to have an excuse it must be shown that there was 'an imminent particular threat' (*Evans v Hughes*, 1979). In *Bradish* (1990) it was ruled that possession of a prohibited weapon was an offence of strict liability.

Further, the **Criminal Justice and Public Order Act 1994** empowered senior police officers to stop and search in anticipation of violence. This power has been extended by the **Knives Act 1997** to include knives and other offensive weapons.

The **Firearms (Amendment) Act 1997** extends the prohibition in respect of firearms further by completely prohibiting certain small firearms. It also makes widespread changes to the licensing and regulation of gun clubs, besides increasing the control on the possession and sale of firearms and ammunition. The exemption which had been granted in firearms law (section 11 (4)of the **Firearms Act 1958**) which allowed the exemption of operators of miniature rifle ranges to operate without a firearms licence has now been amended by the **Firearms Act 2023**, so that such operators will have to apply for a firearms licence and undergo the necessary security checks. Further restrictions have been imposed by the **Policing and Crime Act 2017**, whilst the **Offensive Weapons Act 2019** is to help reduce violent crime by prohibiting the possession of corrosive substances in a public place, strengthening the arrangements for controlling the sale of bladed weapons and prohibiting the possession of certain offensive weapons and firearms.

12.10.16 Assaults on Emergency Workers (Offences) Act 2018

This Act creates a new triable offence of assault and battery committed against an emergency worker with an increased maximum penalty when tried on indictment. The Act seeks to improve the protection for emergency workers. It will also apply where other assaults, including sexual assaults and assault related offences, are committed against emergency workers.

12.10.17 Modern slavery

To combat this increasing form of organized crime of human trafficking in the United Kingdom, the Government enacted the Modern Slavery Act 2015 in order to deal with its various forms, such as sexual exploitation, forced labour and domestic servitude. The Act is in seven parts. Part 1 consolidates and clarifies the existing offences of slavery and human trafficking whilst increasing the maximum penalty for such offices. Part 2 provides for two new civil preventative orders, the Slavery and Trafficking Prevention Order and the Slavery and Trafficking Risk Order. Part 3 provides for new maritime enforcement powers in relation to ships. Part 4 establishes the office of Independent Anti-slavery Commissioner and sets out its functions. Part 5 introduces a number of measures focussed on supporting and protecting victims, including a statutory defence for slavery or trafficking victims and special measures for witnesses in criminal proceedings. Part 6 requires certain businesses to disclose what activity they are undertaking to eliminate slavery and trafficking from their supply chains and their own business. Part 7 requires the Secretary of State to publish a paper on the role of the Gangmasters Licensing Authority.

12.10.18 Sexual offences

The main Act is the **Sexual Offences Act 2003**. The offences include:

a Rape

The Act has radically reformed the law on rape by including both non-consensual oral sex and buggery within the definition of rape.

By s. 1 of the Act a man commits rape if he intentionally penetrates the vagina, anus or mouth of a woman with his penis and the woman does not consent to the penetration and the man does not reasonably believe that there has been consent.

S. 1(2) states that whether the belief by the man is reasonable has to be determined having regard to all the circumstances, including any steps the man may have taken to ascertain whether the woman had consented.

In the circumstances the jury will be required to assess all the surrounding circumstances of a case before deciding whether or not the belief was reasonable.

In *R v Adams* (2021) the Supreme Court addressed the issue of consent in sexual offences. *Held*: That it is insufficient for the defendant to rely solely on the complainant's apparent consent. It would be necessary for the defendant to demonstrate that the complainant had the freedom and capacity to choose whether to engage in sexual activity.

b Assault by penetration

S. 2 of the Act creates a new offence of assault by penetration in respect of which the *mens rea* is similar to that required for rape, in accordance with s. 1. Unlike rape it is possible for the offence to be committed by either a male or female.

c Sexual activity without consent

S. 4 makes it an offence when any person causes the penetration or other sexual activity of another without that person's consent. In theory it could include the actions of a woman who forces a man to penetrate her and will also involve exploitation of prostitution where a woman is forced to have sexual intercourse as a prostitute for the financial gain of a third party.

d Protection of children

Ss. 9 to 15 reflect the fact that the protection of children was one of the primary objectives of the Act. Any offence against a child 13 years of age or under will be treated as a 'strict liability' offence, a child not being regarded as capable of giving consent to any form of sexual activity. S. 15 introduces the new offence of 'sexual grooming' whereby arranging a meeting through the internet or by the use of text messaging a child with the intention of committing a sexual act will be regarded as an offence.

e Abuse of a position of trust

Such offences committed by a person who is involved in a position of trust, such as caring or supervising a child, is covered by ss. 16 to 29.

f Protection of person with a mental disorder

Sexual offences against a person with a mental disorder are covered by ss. 30 to 37; care workers who take advantage of their position in relation to a person with a mental disorder can be prosecuted in accordance with ss. 38 to 44. The **Mental Health Units (Use of Force) Act 2018** makes provision about the oversight and management of the appropriate use of force in relation to people in mental health units, and to make the provision of body cameras by police officers in the course of their duties in relation to people in mental health units.

g Miscellaneous provisions

Other relevant provisions of the Act provide that an offence will be committed in relation to indecent photographs of children (ss. 45 to 46); abuse of children through prostitution and pornography (ss. 47 to 51), whilst s. 176 of the **Policing and Crime Act 2017** added: 'or streamed or otherwise transmitted to include situations where such images are streamed (such as via the internet) or transmitted by some other technological means, such as CCTV'; exploitation of prostitution (ss. 52 to 54); trafficking for sexual exploitation into the UK (s. 57), within the UK (s. 57) and out of the UK (s. 59); exposure (s. 68); voyeurism (s. 67); intercourse with an animal (s. 69) and with a corpse (s. 70).

The Digital Economy Act 2017, s. 14 makes it an offence for a person to make pornographic material available on the internet to persons in the United Kingdom on a commercial basis if the material is normally available to persons under 18 years of age. This provides that there must be an age verification in place.

h Protection of children

The **Protection of Children Act 1999** as extended by the **Criminal Justice and Court Services Act 2000** creates a list (Department of Health's Consultancy Service Index—CSI) which identifies individuals who are unsuitable to work with children (i.e. a person under the age of 18). However, someone who is on the CSI will not be committing a criminal offence if they subsequently do work with children.

i Notification by sex offenders

Part I of the **Sex Offenders Act 1997** requires persons convicted or cautioned in respect of certain sex offences to notify the police of their names and addresses.

j Sexual offences and sex establishments

The **Policing and Crime Act 2009** introduces new offences in relation to sexual services of a prostitute subjected to force, human trafficking, child prostitution of women and the regulation of lap dancing and other sexual entertainment venues.

k Sexual offences committed outside the United Kingdom

In accordance with s. 72 of the **Criminal Justice and Immigration Act 2008**, if a United Kingdom national commits a sexual offence in a country outside the United Kingdom that would constitute a sexual offence if committed in the United Kingdom, then the national would be considered to have committed the offence within the United Kingdom.

12.11 Offences against property

12.11.1 Offences under the Theft Act 1968

a Theft

S. 1 defines theft as dishonestly appropriating property belonging to another with the intention of permanently depriving the other of it. So that in *Hinks* (2000) the House of Lords held that where D took advantage of a person with limited intelligence to make a gift to her, this would constitute theft contrary to s. 1(1).

S. 1(2) provides that 'it is immaterial whether the appropriation is made with a view to gain, or is made for the thief's own benefit'.

The *actus reus* is appropriating property belonging to another. S. 3(1) provides that:

> [A]ny assumption by a person of the rights of an owner amounts to an appropriation, and this includes where he has come by the property (innocently or not) without stealing it, any later assumption of a right to it by keeping or dealing with it as owner.

The term obviously covers a taking, and such cases as characterized in the case given as an example:

❖ CASE EXAMPLE

Rogers v Arnott (1960)

The bailee of a tape recorder offered to sell it to another person. It was held that his offer, even though it was not taken up, amounted to conversion as a bailee.

The Court of Appeal has interpreted the term widely in *Monaghan* (1979), where a shop assistant was held to have appropriated money when she put cash in the shop till without registering it; and in *Anderton v Wish* (1980) where a customer swapped labels on tins in a supermarket to pay a lower price. The House of Lords has widened this concept of theft so that if D assumes any right of the owner, even with the owner's full consent, over the property of another, that person has committed the *actus reus* of theft. There will, of course, still be proof of *mens rea*, i.e. dishonesty and an intention to deprive the owner of his or her property permanently.

❖ CASE EXAMPLE

Gomez (1993)

D, assistant manager of an electrical shop, induced the manager to authorize the sale of goods in return for two building society cheques, which D knew to be stolen. *Held:* D was guilty of theft instead of obtaining property by deception.

It is arguable that in each case, D did no more than a preparatory act.

If a shop assistant sells an employer's goods at less than the correct price, this is an appropriation since the person has exceeded their authority. In *Pilgram v Rice-Smith* (1977) D's conviction for theft was upheld when, in a supermarket, she had charged a customer friend less than the price of the goods. Whether there is an appropriation will depend on the intention with which an act is done. In a supermarket the contract is made at the cash desk (*Pharmaceutical Society v Boots*), so that in *Eddy v Niman* (1981), D, who had placed goods in a receptacle with the intention of stealing them, and had then changed his mind and left the store without them, was held not to have appropriated the goods. However, in *Macpherson* (1973) it was held that a customer appropriates when goods are taken from a shelf in a manner that is clearly dishonest, e.g. putting them in a pocket intending not to pay for them.

S. 3(2) excepts a bona fide purchaser for value from s. 3(1).

S. 4 defines 'property' widely to include 'money and all other property real or personal, including things in action and other intangible property', e.g. debts, patents. But land can only be stolen by:

i a trustee who appropriates the land for their own purposes
ii a person not in possession who appropriates by severing the land, e.g. cuts down a tree or takes away the top soil
iii a tenant who appropriates fixtures or structures let to be used with the land, e.g. selling a greenhouse

- Things growing wild cannot be stolen unless the whole plant is taken or the flowers, etc., are picked for a commercial purpose.
- Wild creatures cannot be stolen unless the creature is tamed or ordinarily kept in captivity or it has been reduced into possession of another person and possession has not since been lost or abandoned.
- To be stolen, property must belong to another; thus abandoned property cannot be stolen, nor can it be if *D* believes it to be abandoned. But there are some situations where the property in the goods is by s. 5 notionally put in another person for the purposes of the Act.
- By s. 5(1) 'property shall be regarded as belonging to any person having possession or control of it, or having in it any proprietary right or interest'. Therefore the owner can steal from someone with a lesser but prior interest, e.g. a bailee. In *Rose v Matt* (1951) *D* pawned his clock and then retrieved it when the broker was not looking, and was convicted of what would now be theft.
- By s. 5(2) a trustee, who has the legal ownership of the trust property, is regarded as stealing from the person having the right to enforce the trust.
- S. 5(3) provides that:

  where a person receives property from or on account of another, and is under an obligation to the other to retain or deal with it in a particular way, the property or its proceeds shall be regarded as belonging to the other.

- By s. 5(4):

  where a person gets property by another's mistake, and is under an obligation to make restoration (in whole or in part) of the property or its proceeds or the value thereof, then . . . the property . . . shall be regarded . . . as belonging to the person entitled to restoration and an intention not to make restoration shall be regarded accordingly as an intention to deprive that person of the property or proceeds.

In *Ghosh* (1982) the Court of Appeal stated that it had to be shown that *D* acted dishonestly by the standards of ordinary people and, if so, must have realized that the acts were dishonest by those standards. It has been held (in *Attorney-General's Ref. (No. 1 of 1983)* that the same situation would apply where an employer mistakenly instructs their bank to credit an employee's bank account with a sum in excess of the employee's proper entitlement.

- To be theft, the appropriation must be made dishonestly and there must be the intention to deprive the other person of the property permanently.

S. 2 does not define dishonesty, but it provides that a person is not dishonest if he or she appropriates:

i 'in the belief that he has in law the right to deprive the other of it' (claim of right);
ii 'in the belief that he would have the other's consent if the other knew of the appropriation and the circumstances of it'; or

iii 'in the belief that the person to whom the property belongs cannot be discovered by taking reasonable steps', e.g. where he or she finds lost property.

If none of these provisions applies, the accused may still be found not dishonest, the matter being left to the jury (*Feeley*, 1972), e.g. where the manager of a shop, against the rules, takes money from the till knowing that it can be repaid within a few days. S. 6 provides that a person shall be:

> regarded as having the intention of permanently depriving if his intention is to treat the thing as his own to dispose of regardless of the other's rights, even without meaning the other permanently to lose the thing itself; and a borrowing or lending of it may amount to so treating it if . . . the borrowing or lending is for a period and in such circumstances making it equivalent to an outright taking or disposal.

12.11.2 Robbery

By s. 8 robbery is:

> stealing and immediately before or at the time of doing so, and in order to do so, using force on any person or putting or seeking to put any person in fear of being then and there subjected to force.

❖ CASE EXAMPLE

***Skivington* (1968)**

D went to his sister's firm to collect wages due to her. When the cashier refused to pay him on that day, he obtained the money by threatening the cashier with a knife. *Held*: not robbery because not theft since *D* had a claim of right.

The penalty is life imprisonment. If there is no theft, there is no robbery.

Force must be used upon the person in order to obtain the property. Force against a third person is sufficient, e.g. a passerby who intervenes.

The Court of Appeal in *Hale* (1979) held that appropriation is a continuing act and it is for the jury to decide when it is over. In consequence, they upheld a conviction of robbery where the force was used some minutes after the theft.

By s. 8(2) an assault with intent to rob carries the same penalty as robbery.

12.11.3 Burglary

By s. 9 burglary is either:

a entering a building or part of a building or an inhabited vehicle or vessel as a trespasser with intent therein to steal, to inflict grievous bodily harm, to rape or to do unlawful damage; or

b having entered as a trespasser to steal or attempt to steal therein or inflict or attempt to inflict grievous bodily harm.

'Entering' is not defined; thus the common-law rules no doubt apply. According to these, insertion of any part of the body was sufficient entry. In *Davis* (1823), *D* pushed in a pane and his finger was seen to be inside. In *Machent v Quinn* (1970) *D* broke a shop window and stole from the window display; he was convicted of burglary. In *Collins* (1972) the Court of Appeal spoke of 'substantial entry' but did not elaborate. If an instrument is inserted, it will amount to an entry if inserted for the purpose of committing the ulterior offence, even though no part of the body enters, e.g., the barrel of a gun inserted to shoot a person inside. But not if it is inserted only to gain entry.

The trespass must be intentional or reckless, and it will not be trespass if the entry is negligent or involuntary. In *Jenkins and Jenkins* (1983) it was held that assault is not an essential requirement of inflicting grievous bodily harm within s. 9. Entry obtained by a false pretence is probably trespass, since fraud usually negatives consent.

By s. 10 it is aggravated burglary if a person commits burglary 'and at the time has with him any firearm or imitation firearm, any weapon of offence or any explosive'.

12.11.4 Removal of articles from places open to the public

Borrowing does not amount to theft, subject to the provisions of s. 6; but the borrowing of exhibits in museums and of vehicles had become a nuisance that needed controlling. S. 11 provides that it is an offence without lawful authority to remove from a building or its grounds articles displayed or kept for display where the public has access to the building in order to view the building or a collection housed in it. 'A collection made or exhibited for the purpose of effecting sales or other commercial dealings' is not within the section.

12.11.5 Taking a motor vehicle or other conveyance without authority

This is the other borrowing offence. By s. 12 it is an offence if a person:

> [W]ithout having the consent of the owner or other lawful authority, takes any conveyance for his own or another's use or, knowing that [it] has been taken without such authority, drives it or allows himself to be carried in or on it.

It is not an offence if the act is 'done in the belief that he has the lawful authority to do it or that he would have the owner's consent if the owner knew of his doing it and the circumstances of it'.

If *D* has authority to use a vehicle for one purpose but uses it for another, then an offence may have been committed (*McKnight v Davies*, 1974).

In *Bogacki* (1973) the Court of Appeal held that 'taking' involved some element of movement, however small, and therefore where *D* boarded a bus and tried to start the engine but the bus did not move, an offence had not been committed.

'Conveyance' means one 'constructed or adapted for the carriage of a person or persons whether by land, water or air'. A conveyance for the carriage of goods is not included unless it has a place for a driver, e.g. a lorry, but not a goods trailer.

By s. 12(5) the taking of pedal cycles is a summary offence.

12.11.6 Dealing in stolen vehicle parts

In accordance with s. 12 of the **Vehicles (Crime) Act 2001** it is an offence to give false particulars relating to the sale of a motor vehicle to a person carrying on the business of a motor salvage operator. S. 28 makes it an offence to sell or supply counterfeit vehicle registration plates, while s. 29 makes it an offence to supply motor vehicle registration plates to an unregistered person.

12.11.7 Abstracting of electricity

Electricity cannot be stolen and therefore cannot be the subject of burglary. But by s. 13 it is an offence dishonestly to use without due authority, or dishonestly cause to be wasted or diverted, any electricity. The penalty is up to five years' imprisonment. If there is no dishonesty, there is no offence. In *Boggeln v Williams* (1978) *D*'s supply had been cut off; *D* reconnected it to the meter and informed the electricity board; *D* was held not to have been dishonest.

12.11.8 Obtaining property by deception

The difference between this offence and theft is that here the owner has voluntarily handed over the property in consequence of the fraud of *D*. By s. 15(1) the offence is committed by 'a person who by any deception dishonestly obtains property belonging to another, with the intention of permanently depriving the other of it'.

❖ CASE EXAMPLE

***R v Preddy* (1996)**

The House of Lords has held that no identifiable property passes from the payer to the payee where a payment is made between two bank accounts by cheque or by telegraphic or electronic transfer, and therefore a payee cannot be guilty of dishonestly obtaining property belonging to another under s. 15(1) of the 1968 Act.

'Obtain' includes obtaining for another or enabling another to obtain or retain. *D* obtains property under s. 15 if he or she obtains ownership, possession or control of it; thus if *D* obtains possession by a trick, that is theft by a trick, it is also obtaining by deception and it would be better to charge *D* under s. 15.

As a result of this decision, the **Theft (Amendments) Act 1996** created a new s. 15A of the **Theft Act 1968**, as amended by the **Theft Act 1978**. This provides that, in effect, the action by Preddy would now be a specific offence.

Note: Further amendments have been made in accordance with the **Fraud Act 2006**. The new s. 15A is entitled 'obtaining a money transfer by deception'.

The obtaining must be induced by the deception, therefore it is not the offence if *P* is not deceived, but it is an attempt (*Hensler*, 1870, approved by the House of Lords in *Haughton v Smith*, 1975); and the obtaining must not be too remote, as in *Clucas* (1949) where *D*, by a false pretence, induced bookmakers to accept credit bets, the practice being not to pay if the horse did not win, but to collect the winnings if the horse did win; on this occasion it won and the court held that the effective cause of obtaining the money was not the deception but backing the winner.

The deception may be by 'words or conduct and as to fact or as to law, including a deception as to the present intentions of the person using the deception or any other person'. Active concealment of defects would amount to 'conduct'; as would going into an Oxford tailors wearing an undergraduate gown if the person is not a member of a college (*Barnard*, 1837).

A promise made not intending to fulfil it is sufficient; and so is an implied promise, as where a person orders a meal in a restaurant (*Jones*, 1878).

S. 15 says nothing about statements of opinion, but on principle, it should count as deception where the opinion is not honestly held.

The deception may be 'deliberate or reckless'. With regard to statements, the House of Lords in *Derry v Peek* (1889), a case on the tort of deceit, held that the defendants could not be liable if they honestly believed what they had said (see p. 156).

'Property' is wider than in theft: the s. 4 limitations do not apply.

Apart from being 'deliberate or reckless', the deception must be dishonest. If the same view as in *Feely* (1973), a theft case, is taken, then the matter of dishonesty should be left to the jury.

12.11.9 Obtaining a pecuniary advantage by deception

Since s. 16(2)(a) has been repealed, this offence is committed by a person who, by deception, dishonestly obtains for him or herself or another one of the following advantages:

> He is allowed to borrow by way of overdraft, or to take out any policy of assurance or annuity contract, or obtains an improvement of the terms on which he is allowed to do so; or he is given the opportunity to earn remuneration or greater remuneration in an office or employment, or to win money by betting.

Clucas (1949) would now come within this section. In *Callender* (1992) Davas was convicted of pretending to hold accountancy qualifications contrary to s. 16(2)(C).

'Deception' has the same meaning as in s. 15 and must be made deliberately or recklessly and dishonestly.

12.11.10 False accounting

This offence, wider than the last offence and forgery, is by s. 17:

> [W]here a person dishonestly, with a view to gain for himself or another or with intent to cause loss to another:
>
> destroys, defaces, conceals or falsifies any account or any record or document made or required for any accounting purpose; or
>
> in furnishing information for any purpose produces or makes use of any account or any such record or document as aforesaid, which to his knowledge is or may be misleading, false or deceptive in a material particular.
>
> A person who makes or concurs in making in an account or other document an entry which is or may be misleading, false or deceptive in a material particular, or who omits or concurs in omitting a material particular from an account or other document, is to be treated as falsifying the account or document.

In *Golchha* (1989) and *Choraria* (1989) it was stated that 'with a view to gain' has to be something more than an act that induces forbearance on the part of the victim—this would also apply to s. 16 (mentioned previously).

The records or documents are restricted to those made or required for any accounting purpose, e.g. ledgers, cash books, meters, cash tills. The section is useful particularly as it covers omissions as well as acts. In *Shama* (1990) it was held that *D* was guilty of falsification where there was an omission to use a required standard form.

12.11.11 Liability of company officers for offences by the company

By s. 18 if an offence by a corporation under sections 15, 16 or 17 is proved to have been committed with the consent or connivance of a director, manager, secretary, etc., he shall also be guilty of the offence. This offence is wider than aiding and abetting.

12.11.12 False statements by company directors, etc.

By s. 19 it is an offence for an officer of a corporation, with intent to deceive members or creditors of the corporation about its affairs, to publish or concur in publishing a written statement or account that to his knowledge is or may be misleading, etc.

A false statement in a prospectus is also covered by s. 993 of the **Companies Act 2006**.

12.11.13 Suppression of documents

Under s. 20 a person who dishonestly, with a view to gain for himself or another or with intent to cause loss to another, destroys, defaces or conceals any valuable security, any will, etc. (the conduct of Squeers in *Nicholas Nickleby*) or by deception procures the execution of a valuable security, shall be guilty of an offence (*Beck* (Brian), 1985).

In *King* (1991) it was held that a CHAPS (Clearing House Automated Payment Service) order/form was a valuable security.

12.11.14 Blackmail

By s. 21 it is blackmail if, with a view to gain for himself or another or with intent to cause loss to another, a person makes any unwarranted demand with menaces; and it is unwarranted unless he makes it in the belief:

i that he has reasonable grounds for making the demand
ii that the use of the menaces is a proper means of enforcing the demand

'Menaces' was used in the previous Act and no doubt Lord Wright's definition in *Thorne v Motor Trade Association* (1937) is likely to be followed:

> I think the word 'menace' is to be liberally construed and not as limited to threats of violence but as including threats of any action detrimental to or unpleasant to the person addressed. It may also include a warning that in certain events such action is intended.

The test for whether the demand is warranted is clearly subjective.

No doubt *Skivington* (1968) could have been charged under this section; and *Bernhard* (1938) would probably be acquitted on a claim of right as under the old law; she believed she had a legal right to enforce a promise of payment of a sum of money made by her ex-lover and threatened that unless he paid she would tell his wife of their association.

12.11.15 Handling stolen goods

This offence carries a penalty of 14 years, which is higher than the penalty for theft. By s. 22:

> [A] person handles stolen goods if (otherwise than in the course of the stealing) knowing or believing them to be stolen goods he dishonestly receives the goods, or dishonestly undertakes or assists in their retention, removal, disposal or realization by or for the benefit of another person, or if he arranges to do so.

Goods are 'stolen' for the purposes of this section if obtained by an offence under sections 1, 15 or 21 or, if obtained in a foreign country, the act would have been a crime in that country and would have been an offence under sections 1, 15 or 21 if done in England or Wales (s. 24(1) and (4)).

D must know or believe the goods to be stolen; and they must actually be stolen at the time of the offence. If they have ceased to be stolen by being taken into the possession of the owner or the police, *D* cannot be convicted of the offence or an attempt (*Haughton v Smith*, 1975).

The forms of the offence are:

i receiving
ii arranging to receive
iii undertaking or assisting in their retention, etc.
iv arranging to undertake or assist

Where *D* is charged with receiving, to be guilty, they must have the *mens rea* at the time. Nor will they be guilty of theft if they were bona fide purchasers for value and only later knew that the goods were stolen (s.3(2)).

To be guilty of undertaking, etc., *D* must be acting for the benefit of another person.

❖ CASE EXAMPLE

***Pitchley* (1973)**

D's son stole £150 and gave it to *D* to look after. *D* paid it into his bank account and only later learned that it was stolen; he did nothing about it. *Held*: he was guilty of assisting in retaining.

This decision is open to the objection that *D* alone retained; therefore, *D* could hardly be said to assist. A better charge would have been theft, since *D* would not come within s. 3(2).

The *mens rea* of the offence is knowledge or belief. The test is subjective and therefore negligence is not sufficient; nor is mere suspicion or wilful blindness, since knowledge and belief are something positive (*Ismail*, 1977; *Stagg*, 1978).

Dishonesty is an essential ingredient. Therefore if *D* knows the goods are stolen but intends to return them to the owner (*Matthews*, 1950), *D* will not be guilty.

Proof of *mens rea* in handling cases is assisted by s. 27(3) which enables evidence of previous handling or of previous convictions of theft or handling to be given, and by the common-law rules that enable a jury to infer guilty knowledge where *D* is in possession of recently stolen property and gives no satisfactory explanation.

12.11.16 Offences under the Theft Act 1978

This Act was passed to remedy certain defects of the 1968 Act and provides for three offences:

- **Obtaining services by deception**

By s. 1 it is an offence dishonestly to obtain services from another by deception, i.e. 'where the other is induced to confer a benefit by doing some act, or causing or permitting some act to be done, on the understanding that the benefit has been or will be paid for'.

The liability need not, it seems, be legally enforceable.

- **Evasion of liability by deception**

S. 2 covers three situations:

a Where a person by any deception

i dishonestly secures the remission of the whole or part of any *existing liability* to make a payment, whether his own liability or another's; or

ii with intent to make permanent default in whole or in part on any *existing liability* to make a payment, or with intent to let another do so, dishonestly induces the creditor or any person claiming payment on behalf of the creditor to wait for payment (whether or not the due date for payment is deferred) or to forgo payment; or

iii dishonestly obtains any exemption from or abatement of liability to make a payment.

In this section 'liability' means legally enforceable liability (s. 2(2)). S. 2(3) provides that a person who takes in payment a cheque, etc., 'by way of conditional satisfaction of a pre-existing liability is to be treated not as being paid but as being induced to wait for payment'.

- **Making off without payment**

Unlike the other two offences this does not require any deception and was designed to cover the 'bilking' cases.

By s. 3(1) it is an offence if:

> [A] person who, knowing that payment on the spot for any goods supplied or service done is required or expected of him, dishonestly makes off without having paid as required or expected and with intent to avoid payment of the amount due.

'Payment at the time of collecting goods on which work has been done or in respect of which service has been provided' is included (s. 3(2)). *D* can only be guilty of this offence if there is intent to avoid payment permanently (*Allen* (Christopher), 1985).

The section does not apply where the supply of goods or the service is contrary to law or where payment is not legally enforceable.

The section is intended to catch such cases as:

❖ CASE EXAMPLE

***Edwards v Odin* (1976)**

D asked an attendant to fill his car tank with petrol. When this had been done, he decided he could not wait and drove off without paying. *Held*: that he had not stolen the petrol because the property in it passed to him when it was put in the tank, therefore it was not property belonging to another.

The offence is expressly made an arrestable one (s. 3(4)).

The **Theft (Amendment) Act 1996** amends the 1968 and 1978 Acts and creates two new offences. The first is obtaining money by deception and the second is retaining credits from dishonest sources.

12.11.17 Criminal damage

The **Criminal Damage Act 1971** contains one basic offence, one aggravated offence and two subsidiary offences.

The basic offence by s. 1(1) is without lawful excuse destroying or damaging any property *belonging to another* intentionally or recklessly. For the interpretation of the meaning of 'recklessly' see *Caldwell* (1981) and *Miller* (1983) on p. 307. 'Destroy' means to break up, demolish, etc. 'Damage' may be slight, but there must be some perceptible physical harm.

❖ CASE EXAMPLE

***'A' (a juvenile)* (1978)**

D, a football supporter, spat on a constable's raincoat. The prosecution argued that it must have been damaged because it needed dry-cleaning. *Held*: a raincoat is not damaged in this way, though, for example, a satin wedding dress might have been.

'Property' is widely defined by s. 10(1) as of a tangible nature, whether real or personal, including money and wild creatures reduced into possession, but excluding mushrooms, flowers, fruit or foliage of a plant growing wild on any land. It belongs to another by s. 5 if another has custody or control of it, any proprietary interest in it or a charge on it.

By s. 5, *D* will have a lawful excuse where:

i *D* believes P had consented or would have consented had he known of the damage and the circumstances (as in *Denton*, 1981); or
ii *D* is protecting property or a right or interest in the property and at the time *D* believes:

  a the property was in immediate need of protection; and
  b the means adopted were reasonable in the circumstances.

Here it is a question of honest belief, not reasonable belief.

❖ CASE EXAMPLE

***Lloyd v DPP* (1992)**

D damaged a clamp placed on his car, which was unlawfully parked in a private car park. *Held*: *D* had committed criminal damage as he had no right to damage or destroy the clamp.

Also, existing defences in law are preserved by s. 5(2), e.g. infancy, necessity.

D also has a defence if he or she believes wrongly that he or she owns the property or has a claim of right.

❖ CASE EXAMPLE

Smith (1974)

D wrongly believed that the wiring that he had installed in his flat belonged to him and removed it when he left. In law it had become a landlord's fixture. *Held*: honest belief that the property was his own was a defence.

The aggravated offence by s. 1(2) is without lawful excuse to destroy or damage any property, *whether belonging to D or another*:

a intending to destroy or damage it or being reckless as to that; and
b intending by the destruction or damage to endanger the life of another or being reckless as to that (*Sangha*, 1988).

The House of Lords in *Steer* (1987) explained that in the case of aggravated criminal damage, the element of the *mens rea* relating to the endangering of life must refer to the endangering resulting from the damage, as opposed to the means used to cause the damage.

This offence does not require intent to kill and is therefore wider than attempted murder; it is also wider because a preparatory act may suffice that is not sufficient for attempt.

S. 5 does not apply to this offence; but since the definition itself includes the words 'without lawful excuse', there must be circumstances that would excuse. Smith and Hogan suggest that such a case would be where the police damage property to prevent a serious offence against a person, even though they know it might endanger D's life.

If the offence under s. 1(1) or s. 1(2) is committed by fire, it must be charged as arson (s. 1(3)) and the penalty is life imprisonment, the same as for s. 1(2).

The two subsidiary offences are based on threats and possession.

By s. 2, a person is guilty of an offence 'who without lawful excuse makes to another a threat, intending that that other would fear it would be carried out:

(a) to destroy or damage any property belonging to that other or a third person; or
(b) to destroy or damage his own property in a way which he knows is likely to endanger the life of that other or third person.

By s. 3, a person is guilty of an offence 'who has anything in his custody or under his control intending without lawful excuse to use it or cause or permit another to use it:

(a) to destroy or damage any property belonging to some other person; or
(b) to destroy or damage his own or the user's property in a way which he knows is likely to endanger the life of some other person.'

The maximum penalty under s. 1(1), s. 2 and s. 3 is ten years' imprisonment.

S. 8, which is now superseded by s. 1 of the **Criminal Justice Act 1972**, empowered all courts, on application or otherwise, on conviction of a person to order them to pay compensation for the destruction or damage to the person to whom the property belonged.

It should be noted that sections 35, 36, 47, 58 and 72 of the **Malicious Damage Act 1861**, dealing with railways and shipping, were not repealed by the 1971 Act. The charge against the protestors who in July 1980 halted a train carrying nuclear waste in Gloucestershire was under s. 35, which makes it an offence 'to place wood, etc., on railway lines with intent to obstruct . . . an engine'.

12.11.18 Forgery

S. 1 of the **Forgery and Counterfeiting Act 1981** provides that a person is guilty of forgery if they make a false instrument in order that it may be used as genuine: s. 8 defines instrument as either any formal or informal document or any form of sound recording such as a disc, tape or soundtrack. In accordance with s. 2 it is now a separate offence to make a photostat copy of a forged document.

At common law 'document' usually means a writing. A painting with a false signature has been held not to be a document (*Closs*, 1858), and so has a printed wrapper on a baking powder (*Smith*, 1858).

At common law the rule was that 'a document must not only tell a lie, it must tell a lie about itself'.

❖ CASE EXAMPLE

***Re Windsor* (1865)**

A teller in a bank fraudulently entered in his journal a greater sum than the actual asset. *Held*: not a forgery since the journal did not tell a lie about itself.

However, in the later case of *Hopkins and Collins* (1957) the Court of Criminal Appeal did not follow this rule and held, on similar facts, but where a figure had been altered, that the document was a forgery. Even under the **Forgery and Counterfeiting Act 1981**, it is not clear what the present position is. However, in *Donnelly (Ian)* (1984), the Court of Appeal held that the Act is a reforming statute and that an instrument that would not be a forgery under the old law could fall within the definition provided by the new Act.

The House of Lords has held that the log-on procedure for assessing computer databases such as Prestel does not constitute forgery.

❖ CASE EXAMPLE

***Gold and Schifreen* (1987)**

Illicit access to a database obtained by using someone else's identity number. *Held*: not forgery.

However, the misuse of a password may be an offence under the **Computer Misuse Act 1990**.

Buckley J. in *re London and Globe Finance Corporation Ltd* (1903) defined defraud and deceive as 'to deceive is by falsehood to induce a state of mind; to defraud is by deceit to induce a course of action'. The House of Lords in *Welham v DPP* (1961) held that defrauding is not confined to an economic loss, and D was held to have intended to defraud where his intention was to cover up a breach of credit regulations to avoid prosecution.

❖ CASE EXAMPLE

***Bassey* (1931)**

D was held to have an intent to defraud where he forged documents in order to gain admission as a student to the Inner Temple. S. 13 has now abolished the offence of forgery at common law.

12.11.19 Trespass

In recent years, squatting has caused problems, and in order to give some, though limited, legal protection against it, five offences were enacted in the **Criminal Law Act 1977**:

i S. 6 provides that it is an offence for any person without lawful authority to use or threaten violence for the purpose of securing entry into any premises for himself or another, provided that:

  a there is someone present on those premises at the time who is opposed to the entry; and
  b the person using or threatening the violence knows that that is the case.

  The violence may be against a person or property. The right to occupy the premises will not excuse a violent entry, but a displaced residential occupier has a defence provided the force used is reasonable.

ii By s. 7 any person on the premises as a trespasser having entered as such is guilty of an offence if they fail to leave on being required to do so by or on behalf of:

  a a displaced residential occupier of the premises requiring the premises for occupation as a residence; or
  b an individual who is a protected intending occupier of the premises, i.e. a person who has purchased a freehold interest, a leasehold interest with not less than 21 years to run or a person authorized to occupy by, for example, a local authority or a housing association.

  In both cases the person must be excluded by a trespasser and must hold a written statement or a certificate as to occupation as a residence.

iii S. 8(1) makes it an offence for a trespasser on any premises having entered as such to have with them, without lawful authority or reasonable excuse, on the premises any weapon of offence.

iv By s. 9(1) a person who enters or is on foreign diplomatic or consular premises as a trespasser is guilty of an offence.

v S. 10(1) provides that it is an offence to resist or obstruct an officer of the court engaged in executing process issued by the court for the purpose of enforcing any judgment or order for the recovery of any premises or for the delivery of possession of premises.

However, s. 144 of the **Legal Aid, Sentencing and Punishment of Offenders Act 2012** created the offence of squatting in a residential building where the offender has entered as a trespasser and intends to live there for any period.

12.11.20 Unlawful eviction and harassment of a residential occupier

This is made an offence by s. 1 of the **Protection from Eviction Act 1977**.

12.12 Other offences

12.12.1 Bigamy

S. 57 of the **Offences Against the Person Act 1861** provides that 'whosoever, being married, shall marry any other person during the life of the former husband or wife, whether the marriage shall have taken place in England or Ireland or elsewhere', commits the offence.

But it will not be bigamy if at the time of the second ceremony the first marriage had been dissolved or annulled by a court of competent jurisdiction; or if the second ceremony took place abroad and the defendant is not a citizen of the United Kingdom and Colonies; or if the spouse shall have been continually absent from the other spouse for the past seven years and not known by that spouse to be living within that time.

It has also been held that *D*'s reasonable belief that the spouse was dead shall be a defence, even though there has not been seven years' absence (*Tolson*, 1889).

In *King* (1964) the court accepted that *D* would have a defence where he believed on reasonable grounds that the alleged first marriage was void. Similarly, in *Gould* (1968) *D*'s reasonable belief that he was divorced was held to be a defence.

The elements that must be proved for the offence are: the first marriage, that it was still subsisting at the time of the second ceremony; and a second ceremony known to and recognized by law. It is immaterial that the second ceremony is invalid for other reasons, e.g. non-compliance with residential requirements.

Problems have arisen in recent years with regard to polygamous marriages. Is such a marriage a basis for bigamy? The position seems to be that the first marriage must be a monogamous marriage, but marriages potentially polygamous when contracted may become monogamous through change of domicile or by legislation, in which case *D* may commit bigamy.

❖ CASE EXAMPLE

***Sagoo* (1975)**

D married in Kenya, where he was domiciled. The Kenyan government later converted the marriage into a monogamous one. He came to England and married another woman. *Held*: bigamy.

No one domiciled in England can contract a polygamous marriage. If a person acquires a domicile in England, a marriage contracted where they were earlier domiciled will be converted into a monogamous marriage.

12.12.2 Road traffic offences

Offences under the **Road Traffic Acts** are construed strictly unless *mens rea* is expressed or implied or the offence is one of negligence. Some of the offences are:

> *Careless driving*. By s. 3 of the 1983 Act it is an offence to drive 'a motor vehicle on a road without due care and attention'. The standard is objective and is the same for learner drivers as for experienced ones (*McCrone v Riding*, 1938); i.e. it is an offence of negligence. In *Simpson v Peat* (1952) Lord Goddard stated the test as: 'Was the accused exercising that degree of care and attention that a reasonable and prudent driver would exercise in the circumstances?'

The same facts may amount to some other offences as well as careless driving; in which case D should not be convicted of both.

Inconsiderate driving. It is also an offence by s. 3 to drive 'a motor vehicle on a road without reasonable consideration for other persons using the road'. For this offence other persons must be using the road. Instances are: D drives slowly and holds back following traffic; D drives through an avoidable puddle near the kerb and splashes pedestrians.

Dangerous driving. By s. 2 of the 1983 Act, a person who drives a motor vehicle on a road recklessly shall be guilty of an offence.

Causing death by dangerous driving has already been discussed (see p. 360).

Driving under the influence of drink or drugs. By s. 4 of the 1983 Act a person who, when driving or attempting to drive or when in charge of a motor vehicle on a road or other public place, is unfit to drive through drink or drugs shall be guilty of an offence.

In view of the indulgent attitude of juries to fellow motorists, this offence has been found difficult to prove; therefore, most prosecutions for drinking and driving are brought under s. 5 in spite of its procedural difficulties, because it has an objective test; but s. 4 must be used when drugs are concerned. *Driving with a blood-alcohol concentration above the prescribed limit*. By s. 5 it is an offence if a person drives or attempts to drive or is in charge of:

> a motor vehicle on a road or other public place, having consumed alcohol in such a quantity that the proportion thereof in the blood, as ascertained from a laboratory test for which the person subsequently provides a specimen under s. 7 of the Act, exceeds the prescribed limit at the time the specimen is supplied.

There is much case law on this section, including the breathalyzer cases.

The **Criminal Law Act 1977** has reduced the offences under sections 5 and 6 to summary offences, with a penalty of six months' imprisonment and/or a fine of £1,000.

In accordance with the **Road Traffic Offence Act 1988**, s. 14, conviction under s. 4 or s. 5 of driving or attempting to drive also carries a mandatory disqualification from driving for at least 12 months, unless there are special reasons for the court to do otherwise; and for at least three years if the defendant has previously been convicted within a period of ten years.

Offence of keeping a vehicle that does not meet insurance requirements. S. 22 of the **Road Safety Act 2006** extends the requirements of s. 143 of the 1983 Act requires motor vehicle insurance of the registered keeper of a vehicle to cover risks to third parties.

12.12.3 Control of dangerous dogs

The **Dangerous Dogs Act 1991** provides for criminal penalties against the owners of any breed of dog that acts in a dangerous fashion. The purpose of the Act is specifically to control the ownership of certain types of dogs deemed to represent a particular danger to the public. In these circumstances the Act reverses the normal rules relating to the burden of proof so that it is presumed that a dog is of the type unless the owner can prove to the contrary. Where the owner of a prescribed dog does not comply with the requirements of the Act relating to such matters as having the dog registered, muzzled and on a lead in a public place, etc., then the court may order the dog to be destroyed.

The **Dangerous Dogs (Amendment) Act 1997** allowed a court to exercise a discretion in deciding whether to destroy a prohibited dog previously listed under the **Dangerous Dogs Act 1991**. The **Anti-Social Behaviour, Crime and Policing Act 2014** extended the provisions of the previous legislation so that an offence was not confined to a public place but to 'any place in England and Wales' and that after 'injures any person' should be included 'or assistance dog'.

12.12.4 Offences involving theft of animals

The **Pet Abduction Act 2024** introduces new criminal offences in relation to the taking or detaining of a dog from the lawful control of any person and the taking of a cat from the lawful control of any person. The act also introduces an enabling power to amend the Act or to apply or replicate the offences through secondary legislation to other species of animal commonly kept as pets when certain conditions are met.

12.12.5 Prevention of terrorism

The **Terrorism Act 2000** completely reformed the laws for the prevention of terrorism, incorporating elements of preventive legislation such as the **Prevention ofTerrorism (Temporary Provisions) Act 1989** and the **Criminal Justice (Terrorism and Conspiracy) Act 1998**. 'Terrorism' as now defined by the Act is 'the use or threat of action which is designed to influence the Government or to intimidate the public or a section of the public where it is made for the purpose of advancing a political, religious or ideological cause'. The type of action coming within this definition would have to constitute some:

> [S]erious violence against a person or some serious damage to property or danger to life or serious danger to life or serious risk to public health or safety, or serious interference to or disruption of an electronic system ('cyber terrorism').

The use of firearms or explosives is regarded as terrorism without the need to prove that there was a design to influence the Government or to intimidate the public. Within the context of this legislation is the concept of dealing with terrorism in the political context ('proscribed organization') and the plotting of terrorism abroad. This includes the granting of jurisdiction to United Kingdom courts over acts of conspiracy in the United Kingdom in respect of offences committed or intended to be committed abroad, and there is no requirement that anything be done in the United Kingdom.

The Prevention of Terrorism Act 2005 was introduced following the decision in *A and Others v Secretary of State for the Home Department* (2004). In that case the House of Lords held that the detention without trial of nine foreigners in accordance with Part IV of the **Anti-Terrorism, Crime and Security Act 2001** was unlawful. The **Prevention of Terrorism Act 2005** gives the Home Secretary authority to impose control orders on any person suspected of involvement in terrorism. These control orders may include restrictions that the Home Secretary or, by virtue of s. 1 (3) of the Act, a court 'considers necessary for purposes connected with preventing or restricting involvement by that individual in terrorism-related activity'.

On 30 March 2006 the **Terrorism Act 2006** came into force. The legislation was enacted because of the London bombings. Part 1 of the Act imposes criminal sanctions for the encouragement of terrorism; the dissemination of terrorist publications; the preparation of a terrorist act; training for terrorism; and so on. Part 2 of the Act arms the Home Secretary with wider powers, including the power to extend the detention of terrorist suspects. Part 2 of the Act also gives Intelligence services wider powers and warrants to intercept communications are given wider effect. By virtue of Part 3 of the Act, the Secretary of State must appoint a person to review the operation of the provisions of the **Terrorism Act 2000** and of Part 1 of the **Terrorism Act 2006**.

The jurisdiction relating to these offences has been extended by the **Anti-Terrorism, Crime and Security Act 2001** and the **Crime (International Co-operation) Act 2003** and the **Terrorism Prevention and Investigation Measures Act 2011**. Further provisions relating to temporary restrictions on travel and temporary exclusion orders were introduced by the **Counter-Terrorism and Security Act 2015**. S. 21 of the Act also incorporates a power given to the Secretary of State by amendment of the Data Retention and Investigatory Powers Act 2014 to require communications service providers to retain data that would allow relevant authorities to identify the individual or their device that was using a particular internet protocol address at any given time. The purpose of the **Counter-Terrorism and Sentencing Act 2021** was to strengthen the approach taken to the sentencing and release of terrorist offenders and to enhance the management of terrorism risk through civil powers. It was also meant to ensure that serious and dangerous terrorist offenders would spend longer in custody, reflecting the seriousness of the offence which they had committed.

The **National Security Act 2023** introduced new offences in respect of espionage, prohibited places, sabotage, foreign interference and obtaining benefits from foreign intelligence services. It also introduced a Foreign Influence Registration Scheme requiring the registration of arrangements for political influence activities in the United Kingdom which had been directed by a foreign power.

The **Covert Human Intelligence Sources (Criminal Conduct) Act 2021** was drafted in response to a court ruling in December 2019 which permitted, in a marginal decision, MI5 and other agencies to commit crimes in order to prevent more serious crimes from occurring.

12.12.6 Disruptive or drunken people on aircraft

The **Aviation (Offences) Act 2003** introduced new police powers whereby they could exercise powers of arrest, without a warrant, of disruptive or drunken passengers on an aircraft.

12.12.7 Prevention of violence or disorder at football matches

The **Football Spectators Act 1989** conferred powers on courts to make an order prohibiting a person from attending a prescribed football match. This power was extended by the **Football (Offences and Disorder) Act 1999** which empowered courts to make an international football banning order preventing a person from travelling overseas to attend a football match.

The **Football (Disorder) Act 2000** further extended this power by providing for the making of banning orders that combined the effect of domestic football banning orders and international football banning orders.

12.12.8 Assisting arrestable offenders

By s. 4(1) of the **Criminal Law Act 1967**, where a person has committed an arrestable offence, any other person who, knowing or believing him to be guilty of such an offence, does without lawful authority or reasonable excuse any act with intent to impede his apprehension or prosecution, is guilty of an offence.

It was necessary to enact this offence to replace that of being an accessory after the fact to a felony.

12.12.9 Concealing an arrestable offence

By s. 5(1) of the same Act, where a person has committed an arrestable offence, any other person who, knowing or believing that such an offence has been committed, and that they have information that might be of material assistance in securing the prosecution of an offender for it, shall be guilty of an offence if they accept or agree to accept for not disclosing that information any consideration other than the making good of loss or injury caused by the offence or the making of reasonable compensation for the loss or injury.

12.12.10 Causing wasteful employment of the police

By s. 5(2) of the same Act it is an offence to cause:

> [A]ny wasteful employment of the police by knowingly making to any person a false report tending to show that an offence has been committed, or to give rise to apprehension for the safety of any persons or property, or tending to show that he has information material to any police inquiry.

12.12.11 Illegally dealing in cultural objects

The **Dealing in Cultural Objects (Offences) Act 2003** makes it an offence to trade in cultural property that has been stolen, illegally excavated or exported to specified countries. This legislation has been strengthened by the **Cultural Property (Armed Conflicts) Act 2017**.

12.12.12 Computer misuse

It is an offence under s. 2 of the **Computer Misuse Act 1990** to cause a computer to perform a function with intent to secure unauthorized access to any program or data in any computer and with intent to commit a further offence.

However, police officers who accessed the police national computer for an unauthorized purpose at an authorized level did not commit an offence contrary to the **Computer Misuse Act 1990**, s. 1—see *DPP v Bignell* (1997). Further, the House of Lords has held in relation to the **Data Protection Act 1984** that information retrieved for an improper purpose that is displayed on a computer screen and is read, but no further action is taken, does not constitute a 'use' for the purposes of the Act—see *R v Brown* (1996).

- The **Serious Crime Act 2015** has extended the provisions of the **Computer Misuse Act 1990** to include unauthorized acts causing or creating risk of serious damage (s. 41) and obtaining articles for purposes relating to computer misuse (s. 42).
- The **Online Safety Act 2023** established a new regulatory regime to address illegal and harmful content online. It imposed legal requirements on:
  - Providers of internet services which allow users to encounter content generated, uploaded or shared by other users (user-to-user services);
  - Providers of search engines which enable users to search multiple websites and databases ('search services'), and

- Providers of internet services on which provide pornographic content (pornographic content that is published by a provider and is not user-generated) is published or displayed.

12.12.13 Misuse of telecommunications system

The **Communications Act 2003** incorporates provisions for offences for fraudulent and improper use of licensed and public telecommunication systems. This includes offences relating to scanners and mobile phones. The Act was amended by the **Telecommunications (Security) Act 2021** which introduced a new security framework for the United Kingdom telecoms sector. This was in order to ensure that public telecommunication providers would operate secure and resilient networks and services and manage their supply chains appropriately. Further regulation was introduced by the **Product Security and Telecommunications Infrastructure Act 2022** to make consumer connectable products ('smart' products) more secure against cyber-attacks whilst incorporating changes to the Electronic Communications Code.

12.12.14 Pornography

The **Criminal Justice and Immigration Act 2008** makes it an offence to be in possession of extreme pornographic images (s. 63) or indecent photographs of children (s. 69). This has also been extended by the **Criminal Justice and Courts Act 2015** to include offences involving sexual grooming (s. 36) or extreme pornographic images or rape or other grossly offensive, disgusting or images of an obscene character (s. 37).

12.12.15 Bribery

By s. 1 of the **Bribery Act 2010**, the offence of bribery is committed where a person offers, promises or gives a financial or other advantage to another person. S. 6 of the Act includes an offence of the bribery of a foreign public official. S. 7 of the Act creates a new strict liability offence for corporations and partnerships for failing to prevent bribery occurring within their organization.

12.12.16 Provision of Contract Cheating Services—Further Education Students

The **Skills And Post-16 Education Act 2022** made it an offence for individuals and organizations to provide or arrange for another person to provide in commercial circumstances, contract cheating services for students at post-16 institutions, sixth forms and higher education providers in England and any other person over compulsory school age who has been entered to take an examination relating to a regulated qualification at a place in England and the advertising by them of those services.

12.12.17 Representation of the People Act 1983—Election Offences

There are existing offences under the **Representation of the People Act 1983** to safeguard the secrecy of voting and prevent voters from being subject to inappropriate or undue influence from other persons when casting their vote. It is an offence for a person to carry out a particular activity for the purpose of inducing or compelling a voter to vote in a particular way (or refrain from voting), to interfere with or attempt to interfere with a voter while they are voting or to find out or attempt to find out in a polling station for whom they are about to vote or have voted.

The **Ballot Secrecy Act 2023** introduces new offences to provide that a voter should enter a polling booth alone when completing a ballot paper and not be accompanied by another person (unless they are a companion of a disabled voter who has made the required written declaration acting in that capacity: the presiding officer assisting the voter acting in that capacity; or a child under the voter's supervision).

12.13 Provisions for combating crime and disorder

The **Criminal Justice and Police Act 2001** was enacted to combat crime and disorder. Many of its provisions are related to disorderly behaviour and/or concern young persons on the streets, in public places or licensed premises. It introduced the power for the police to make on-the-spot fines for disorderly behaviour such as throwing fireworks in a thoroughfare, making a false alarm to a fire brigade or throwing stones at trains. It also introduced the power to place restrictions on drug trafficking offenders, further measures to deal with the intimidation of witnesses and child curfew schemes for children under the age of 16.

The **Public Order Act 2023**—the purpose of this Act is to strengthen police powers to tackle dangerous and highly disruptive tactics employed by a minority of protesters.

12.14 Anti-social behaviour

The **Anti-social Behaviour Crime and Policing Act 2014** was principally concerned with making provision for an order on conviction to prevent behaviour which causes harassment, alarm or distress, including powers for the police to disperse people causing such an offence, apart from being able to close premises involved in such behaviour. It also creates provisions to respond to complaints of anti-social behaviour.

12.15 Organized, serious and gang-related crime

Part 3 of the **Serious Crime Act 2015** introduced a new participation offence in England and Wales to tackle serious organized crime which is gang-related. The new participation offence (s.b45) encompasses not just those who carry out an act of serious crime, but those who provide materials, services or related infrastructures. The scope of this Act has been greatly extended by the provisions of the **Serious Crime Act 2015** for wider use of confiscation orders, civil recovery, seizure and forfeiture of cash and criminal taxation. In addition, the **Criminal Finances Act 2017** provides law-enforcement agencies and partners with capabilities and powers to recover the proceeds of crime, tackle money laundering and corruption and counter-terrorism funding. It also introduced the concept of Unexplained Wealth Orders (UWOs) that require a person who is suspected of involvement in, or association with, serious criminality to explain the origin of assets that appear to be dis-appropriate to their known income (s. 1). The **Economic Crime (Transparency And Enforcement) Act 2022** reformed the UWO regime to enable law enforcement to investigate the origin or property and recover the proceeds of crime. The measures of the Act aim to strengthen the United Kingdom's fight against serious economic crime, to clarify the scope of UWO powers and to increase and reinforce operational confidence in relation to UWO powers. The second part of this legislative package was the **Economic Crime and Corporate Transparency Act 2023**, whose aim was to prevent the abuse of United Kingdom corporate structures and tackle economic crime. The main objectives of the Act were to prevent organized criminals and others from using corporate entities to abuse the United Kingdom's economy, to strengthen the United Kingdom's broader response to economic crime and to support enterprise by enabling Companies House to provide a better service for all United Kingdom companies.

12.16 Effective action against crime and deliver a fair justice system

The **Police, Crime, Sentencing and Courts Act 2022** was enacted to include specific commitments to protect and empower the police and introduce 'a new court order to target known knife carriers, making it easier for officers to stop and search those convicted of knife crime.' It also included commitments to empower courts to tackle crime particularly by introducing 'tougher sentencing for the worst offenders and [ending] automatic release from prison for serious crimes.'

The purpose of the Act was stated to be:

- protect the police and other emergency workers
- protect the public by giving the police the tools needed to tackle crime and disorder
- ensure that the most serious violent and sexual offenders spent time in prison that matched the severity of their crimes
- to tackle repeat and prolific offenders through robust community sentences
- modernize the delivery of criminal justice by overhauling existing court processes to provide better services for all court uses

12.17 Criminal injuries compensation board

This Board, established in 1964 and created as a Statutory Body by s. 108 of the **Criminal Justice Act 1988**, consists of a chairman of wide legal experience and seven other legally qualified members appointed by the Home Secretary and Secretary of State for Scotland after consultation with the Lord Chancellor. Its function is to entertain applications for *ex gratia* payments of compensation, in certain circumstances, to victims of crimes of violence in Great Britain or on a British vessel or aircraft, including since 1979 victims within the family.

It must be shown that the injury is one for which compensation of at least £150 would be awarded by the courts. The circumstances of the injury must have been reported to the police without delay or have been the subject of criminal proceedings in the courts. An applicant must have given the Board all reasonable assistance to substantiate his claim. Compensation, which is assessed on the basis of common-law damages, amounts to several million pounds per annum. About 12,500 applications are made yearly to the Board. Monthly reports are issued by the Board giving details of the amount of compensation paid and some of the more important cases.

The scheme does not apply to Northern Ireland, where there is statutory provision in certain circumstances for compensation from public funds for criminal injuries and also for malicious damage to property.

12.18 Assets recovery agency

The Agency was established by the **Proceeds of Crime Act 2002**. It provides for the appointment of a Director of the Agency whose functions will include the provision of certification orders in respect of persons who could benefit from criminal conduct, making of restraint orders in respect of property gained as a result of criminal conduct and the taking of action in respect of money laundering.

12.19 Circumstances to be considered by Parole Board when considering parole of an offender

The **Prisoners (Disclosure of Information About Victims) Act 2020** places a statutory duty on the Parole Board to consider the non-disclosure of information about victims in its decision-making. The duty applies to cases involving the non-disclosure of information about the whereabouts of a victim's remains (sometimes referred to as *Helen's Law*) and the non-disclosure of information about the identity of child victims in indecent images.

12.20 Independent advocate to support victims of major incidents

The **Victims and Prisoners Act 2024** established the appointment of an Independent Advocate to support victims of major incidents. It also made changes to the parole system to allow government ministers to veto the release of some prisoners. It also granted power to government ministers to restrict marriage in prisons for those serving whole-life orders.

12.21 The Proposed Criminal Justice Act 2025 (Criminal Justice Bill 2023–24)

The Progress of this Bill, first introduced to the House of Commons on 14 November 2023, has been continually delayed and a second reading is now proposed for May 2025. However, because of some of the contentious issues incorporated into the legislation there can be no guarantee as to when it becomes law, but it will probably be after this book has been published. Nevertheless, it is important that readers should be aware of its contents, although there will obviously be some further changes to the text before it is finally enacted.

The Government states that the Criminal Justice Bill contains various measures which will protect the public, give the police the powers they need to cut crime and anti-social behaviour, improve public confidence in the police, introduce tougher sentencing for sexual and violent criminals and strengthen the supervision of offenders on release from prison.

These measures currently include:

New criminal offences relating to items used in serious crime, theft or fraud, including 3D printer firearms templates and table presses, electronic devices for use in theft, SIM forms, knives and offensive weapons.

The introduction of a broader offence of encouraging or assisting serious self-harm and new offences relating to the taking of intimate images without consent.

- Changes to the law on corporate criminal liability to extend criminal liability from individual senior managers, to include their organization.
- The expansion of existing police powers to test suspects in police detention for drugs, to seize bladed articles and search and seize stolen goods.
- Provisions for IP address and domain name suspension orders, allowing law enforcement agencies to apply for a court order to prevent access to IP addresses and domain names that are being used for criminal purposes.
- Extending and clarifying the existing law, allowing police and law enforcement officers to access driver licence records.
- Powers for courts order the attendance of offenders at sentencing hearings and punish them if they do not attend.
- New aggravating factors increasing the seriousness of child sex offences where there was grooming and of murder where it took place in connection with the end of a relationship with the victim.
- Provisions to make certain offenders convicted of coercion or controlling behaviour automatically subject to multi-agency public protection arrangements.
- Changes to the confiscation regime in England and Wales giving effect to the Government's acceptance of a number of Law Commission recommendations and provisions to allow the creation of a Suspended Accounts Scheme.
- Changes to the law on serious crime prevention orders to expand the circumstances in which orders can be applied for and made and by enabling the use of electronic monitoring and standardized notification requirements to improve compliance and enforcement.
- A new framework of nuisance begging directions, prevention notices and prevention orders, together with broadly identical nuisance rough sleeping directions, notices and orders and an offence of trespassing with intent to commit a criminal offence.
- Amended powers to tackle anti-social behaviour (ASB), including expanding the timeframe for which a dispersal order can be put in place, lowering the minimum age at which a Community Protection Notice (CPN) can be imposed to 10 years old, extending powers to apply for a Public Space Protection Order (PSPO), extending Community Safety Accreditation Scheme powers to breaches of PSPOs and CPNs, increasing the upper limit of fixed penalty notices for breaches of CPNs and PSPOs to £500 and creating a duty for local policing bodies to raise awareness of ASB case reviews in their police areas.
- The Bill has also committed the College of Policing to issue a Code of Practice about ethical policing and a power for the Secretary of State to make certain regulations about appeals by chief officers of police and local policing bodies to the Police Appeal Tribunals.

12.22 Useful webpages

English Criminal Law—Wikipedia (http://en.wikipedia.org/wik/English_criminal_law)

Oxford Law—Faculty of Law—University of Oxford—Criminal Law (www.law.ox.ac.uk/theme/criminlaw)

A bonfire of criminal laws?—Office of Parliamentary Counsel (www.opc.gov.au/calc/docs/Loophole_papers/Reid_May2011.pdf)

English Criminal law—Wikibooks (http://en.wikibooks.org/wiki/English_Criminal_Law)

12.23 Exercises

1 What are 'arrestable offences' and 'other offences' under the **Criminal Law Act 1967**?

2 *Actus non facit reum nisi mens sit rea*. Explain. Are there any exceptions to this principle?

3 Describe what is meant by an 'attempt to commit crime'.

4 Describe the defence of 'diminished responsibility'.

5 'Mistake is no defence to a prosecution for crime'. Do you agree? How far is duress a defence?

6 How far may drunkenness be a defence to a criminal charge?

7 Can a corporation be indicted for crime? Give examples, if any.

8 Define 'murder'. What is meant by 'malice aforethought' and 'under the Queen's peace'?

9 Define 'bigamy'. What are the facts of *R v Tolson* (1889)?

10 Define 'theft'. What is meant by 'appropriation' and 'property' under the **Theft Act 1968**?

11 Explain three offences under the **Criminal Damage Act 1971**.

12 Discuss the offences under s. 3 of the **Road Traffic Act 1983**.

13 What is the Criminal Injuries Compensation Board and what are its functions?

Chapter 13

European Union law

Key points

- the effect if European Union law on the development of English law
- primary and secondary sources of European Law
- the six key institutions of the European Union
- the different forms of European legislation
- repeal of the European Communities Act 1972

13.1 Introduction

European Union law has had an enormous impact on the development of English law today, and represents a source of law (see p. 17). The following pages outline the development, the institutions and the substantive law of the European Union.

Note: The Treaties were renumbered by the Treaty of Amsterdam. Where it is relevant, the post-Amsterdam number has been placed in brackets after the original number.

13.2 Background

Cooperation between countries in Western Europe in the fields of politics, economics and defence, following the Second World War, led to the development of the Council of Europe in 1949 and the North Atlantic Treaty Organization (NATO) that same year. The Council of Europe continues to operate as a separate institution and currently consists of 44 Member States.

Germany and France, despite their historical differences, came to realize that the industrial resources of Germany complemented the agricultural resources of France. The Treaty of Paris (1951) expanded this cooperative arrangement to Belgium, Luxembourg, the Netherlands and Italy, and laid the foundations of unity in Europe.

The Treaty of Rome in 1957 (now the European Treaty) provided further organizational and legal structures and created the European Economic Community (EEC). The overall aim was to integrate economically, politically and legally the Member States to create a common market. Subsequent treaties renamed the EEC the Economic Community (EC) and then, finally, the European Union (EU).

DOI: 10.4324/9781003422808-13

13.3 Sources of European law

There are two main sources of European law. The first are the treaties (primary source law) and the second are laws created under the authority of the treaties by the Community institutions (secondary source law).

13.3.1 Primary source law

There are three founding treaties:

i European Coal and Steel Community (ECSC) Treaty, signed in 1951, to regulate a common market for coal and steel

ii European Atomic Energy Community (Euratom) Treaty, signed in 1957, to create a common market for atomic energy

iii European Economic Community (EEC) Treaty, signed in 1957, to promote (a) a harmonious development of economic activities, (b) a continuous and balanced expansion, (c) an increase in stability and (d) an accelerated raising of the standard of living and a strengthening of political relations between Member States

The Treaty on European Union, signed on 7 February 1992 (the 'Maastricht Treaty' or the TEU), amended all three treaties and created new areas of union such as education and culture. The TEU created the European Union, which replaced the former European Community and established common policies in the Member States in relation to foreign and security policy, and justice and home affairs.

The EEC Treaty of Rome (now the European Treaty) is the most legally relevant of the three founding treaties and will be the focus of the following discussion.

Further amending legislation is the **European Communities (Amendment) Act 1998** which incorporated the Treaty of Amsterdam 1997 into United Kingdom law, which came into effect in May 1999.

The basic aims of the legislation were to improve processes, increase effectiveness and bring the EU closer to the ordinary citizen. Among the changes incorporated in the legislation were a new numbering of the EC Treaty, authority to create legislation aimed at prohibiting discrimination and, in preparation for enlargement of the EU, the European Parliament to be capped at 700 Members of the European Parliament (MEPs) and the Commission at 20.

The **European Union (Amendment) Act 2008** was designated to make provision with the Treaty of Lisbon or the Lisbon Treaty, which was signed by the EU Member States on 13 December 2007, and entered into force on 1 December 2009. It amended the Maastricht Treaty and the Treaty of Rome. The most prominent changes made by the Lisbon Treaty were a change in the voting arrangements of the Council of Ministers, a more powerful European Parliament, a consolidated legal personality for the EU, together with the creation of a long-term President of the European Council. It also made the EU's bill of rights, the Charter of Fundamental Rights, legally binding.

13.3.2 Secondary source law

Secondary legislation comprises the bulk of European Union law and includes regulations, directives, decisions, recommendations and opinions of the Council of the European Union and the European Commission. The secondary legislation of the Union is published officially in the *Official Journal*.

13.4 The European Union today

There were 15 Member States in the European Union, namely France, Germany, Italy, Belgium, the Netherlands, Luxembourg, the United Kingdom, Denmark, the Republic of Ireland, Greece, Spain, Portugal, Austria, Sweden and Finland. On 1 May 2004, they were joined by a further ten States: Czech Republic, Cyprus, Estonia, Hungary, Latvia, Lithuania, Malta, Poland, Slovakia and Slovenia.

In accordance with the **European Union (Accession) Act 2006**, Bulgaria and Romania joined on 1 January 2007, while Croatia joined on 1 July 2013 in accordance with the **European Union (Croatian Accession and Irish Protocol) Act 2013**, making the total Member States now 28.

13.4.1 Institutions of the European Union

The six key institutions of the European Union are those bodies created by treaties. They have the power to take binding decisions and consist of elected representatives.

The institutions of the European Union are:

i the European Parliament (called the 'Assembly' in the founding treaties)
ii the European Council
iii the Council of the European Union (Council of Ministers)
iv the Commission of the European Communities (European Commission)
v the Court of Justice of the European Union
vi the General Court

13.4.2 The European Parliament

The European Parliament consists of elected representatives from the Member States, with a final maximum of 72 MEPs from the United Kingdom as authorized by the **European Parliament (Representation) Act 2003**. The way in which United Kingdom MEPs were elected was fundamentally changed by the **European Parliamentary Elections Act 1999** and further consolidated by the **European Parliamentary Elections Act 2002**. Subsequent to this Act, Gibraltar is included in the south-west region of the UK for the purposes of European elections. The 'first past the post' method was replaced by a 'regional list' method. These representatives participate in political supervision, law-making and budgetary processes. The Parliament meets to draw up proposals and to give its assent or advisory opinion on the adoption of Union acts. The Secretariat of the Parliament is based in Luxembourg, while plenary sessions take place in Strasbourg, with most committee meetings taking place in Brussels. The powers of the Parliament have increased over successive treaties. It can appoint an Ombudsman and set up a temporary Committee of Inquiry to investigate alleged contraventions of Community law, except where the matter to be investigated is already before the European Court of Justice. Any citizen of the EU has the right to petition the Parliament directly on matters affecting that citizen directly.

13.4.3 The European Council

The Council is made up of heads of State or of the government of the Member States, together with foreign ministers, and meets at least twice a year to discuss matters of foreign policy and strategy. It was established first by convention and then officially under Article 2 of the **Single European Act 1986**. The Council makes decisions on whether or not to adopt measures developing or extending the primary rules in the treaties. The Council coordinates general economic policy, which plays a very important role considering the movement towards Economic and Monetary Union (EMU).

13.4.4 The Council of the European Union (Council of Ministers)

The Council of Ministers consists of a representative from each Member State at ministerial level, who represents the different national interests. In practice, the foreign ministers attend general sessions and specific ministers attend meetings applicable to their area. For example, if the meeting focused on environmental law, the environmental minister from each Member State would attend. The Council has the power to take decisions and may confer on the European Commission the power to implement its rules.

13.4.5 The European Commission

The European Commission is composed of three tiers:

i The College of Commissions consists of 27 commissioners coming from each Member State. Each commissioner is assigned a portfolio that makes each commissioner responsible for a particular policy area. It is headed by the President, the only commissioner without a portfolio, who is appointed by the national governments of the EU, with the appointments being subject to the approval of the European Parliament. It is the President who nominates the other commissioners in consultation with the Heads of Government.

ii It was agreed, at the Treaty of Nice, that when the EU reached a size of 27 States, the number of commissioners would become less than the total of Member States. An intergovernmental conference approved (Art I-26 (5) CT) that the composition of the College would gradually be reduced to between 16 and 18 commissioners appointed on a strictly rotational basis, but taking into account the demographic and geographical range of all the Member States.

iii The Directorates-General (DG) are the equivalent of ministries within a national government. The majority of the Commission's employees work for the DG, of which there are currently 27.

iv The Cabinets, formally appointed by the President, are the office of each commissioner. Each Cabinet is composed of six officials, with the President's Cabinet larger with ten officials. The Cabinets act as the interface between each commissioner and the DGs.

13.4.6 The Court of Justice of the European Union

The Court of Justice of the European Union, now known as the CJEU (formerly the ECJ), consists of 27 judges and ensures that the interpretation and application of the law of the European Union is correctly observed. The Court is assisted by eight Advocates-General, who act independently to make reasoned submissions on cases before the Court.

All members are appointed by common accord of the governments of the Member States and must possess the qualifications required for appointment to the highest judicial offices in their respective countries or of recognized competence (in the case of academic lawyers).

Less important cases are handled in a chamber; more important cases by plenary session. The Court receives cases on appeal from Member States.

13.4.7 The General Court, originally known as the European Court of First Instance

The European Court of Justice requested the Council to establish a court to deal with specific cases so that the ECJ (now the CJEU) could focus upon its task of ensuring uniformity in the interpretation of Union law. The Court of First Instance (CFI) was established in October 1988 and now consists of 27 justices. It has the jurisdiction to hear actions brought by citizens of the Union and cases relating to such areas as agriculture, fisheries and transport. It was renamed by the Lisbon Treaty in 2009 as the General Court.

13.4.8 The Court of Auditors

This body consists of 27 members, one from each Member State. The members are appointed by the Council, in consultation with the Parliament. Each member is assigned a specific sector of activity in relation to the accounts of the Union.

The Court of Auditors conducts annual audits and submits observations and opinions on matters requested by other Community institutions. It may also carry out investigations in the Member States concerning the application of Union law by that State, e.g. the collection of customs duties.

13.4.9 Bodies of the European Union

The 'bodies' of the European Union are other organs whose decisions are not generally binding and that act mainly in an advisory capacity or in a specific area. Bodies of the European Union include:

i the Committee of Regions
ii the Economic and Social Committee
iii the European Central Bank

13.4.10 The Committee of the Regions and the Economic and Social Committee

Both institutions were established to assist the Council and the Commission. They act only in an advisory capacity and have no real decision-making power. The Committee of Regions consists of representatives of regional and local bodies and the Economic and Social Committee consists of representatives from producers, farmers, carriers, workers, craftsmen, professional occupations and the general public. These representatives are appointed by the Council. Both bodies have 317 members.

13.4.11 The European Central Bank

The European Central Bank (ECB) was established in 1998 and gained official status as an Institution of the European Union under the Lisbon Treaty in 2009. The ECB has the exclusive right to authorize the issue of euros. It sets the short-term interest rates for those States that have the euro as their currency. It has certain enforcement powers so that it can bring national banks, who fail to comply with their obligations under EC law, before the Court of Justice. The decision-making bodies of the ECB are the Executive Board and the Governing Council.

13.5 European Union law in the United Kingdom

The **European Communities Act 1972 (UK)** achieved the result of incorporating the laws of the European Communities into the domestic law of the United Kingdom. The Act has since been amended to reflect the current legal status of the European Union. The courts and law enforcement agencies are to apply Union law as part of domestic law, unless there is an intentional and express repudiation of Union law in the United Kingdom legislation. In practice, only provisions of Union law with direct effect have force equal to a statute. There is some debate as to the status of Union law in relation to later statutes enacted by the Parliament of the United Kingdom.

13.6 Principle of direct effect

The principle of direct effect is that individuals can rely on European Union law in actions before national courts. It was first raised in the case of *Van Gend v Nederlandse Administratie der Belastingen* (case 26/62). This was known as a 'vertical' direct effect between an individual and a State. The notion of 'horizontal' effect occurs where a treaty obligation is raised between individual and individual.

13.7 Freedom of movement

The **European Treaty 1957** (formerly known as the Treaty of Rome) provides for the free movement of goods and services, persons and capital, with a view to achieving a common market. The policy basis is economic and social.

13.7.1 Free movement of goods

Articles 9–29 (23–27) of the European Treaty provide for the establishment and maintenance of a customs union, which prohibits customs duties on goods moving between Member States. A distinction is drawn between internal controls (between Member States) and external controls (between a Member State and a non-EU country). No customs duties should apply in the former case and, in the latter, a common customs tariff (CCT) is set so that the tariff paid by the non-EU country is the same regardless of their point of entry into the EU.

Articles 30–37 (28–31) eliminate quantitative restrictions and equivalent measures that can be a barrier to the free movement of goods. This includes, for example, licences and restricted hours of opening for accepting goods. Article 95 (90) prohibits discriminatory taxation.

13.7.2 Free movement of persons

The aim of an integrated labour market is to avoid areas of high unemployment, so workers in these areas would move to areas of high demand for labour.

Article 3c (6) of the European Treaty removes obstacles to the free movement of persons and services. Article 6 prohibits discrimination on the grounds of nationality (see p. 87).

The European Treaty applies only to three categories of people, all of whom were economically active:

a free movement of workers—Article 48
b right of establishment of self-employed persons—Article 52
c free movement of service providers—Article 5

Under Article 48, a worker is free to enter a State and do work. Upon entry the worker is entitled to the same employment conditions and treatment as the national workers of that State. The worker can stay on once the work is finished and can retire there if he or she so chooses.

Secondary legislation includes Directive 68/360 and Regulation 1612/68.

'Worker' is a community concept, which means it is defined by the Community and not the individual Member States, so that there is a more uniform and less discriminatory treatment of individuals. An individual can be classified as a worker provided the work is a genuine economic activity, regardless of the amount of payment, or whether the work is full-time or part-time. There are also rights of movement, which attach to the worker, for persons dependent upon them.

Recently, the principle has been expanded, subject to satisfying certain conditions, to include students, retired persons and persons of independent means (without employment but able to support themselves).

Limitations to free movement of workers include those in public service appointments that require loyalty to their State and refusal of movement on the grounds of public policy, public security or public health.

The rights in (b) and (c) mirror the rights of workers in relation to access, residence and general equality of treatment. The main issues regarding establishment are the nationality restrictions in some occupations and whether the academic qualifications are recognized in the host State.

13.8 Competition law

The aim of competition law in the European Union is to prevent undertakings from distorting competition in the internal market (Article 3G), so that the market will be efficient and so that small and medium-sized firms are able to compete alongside the large multinationals.

Articles 85 and 86 provide detailed rules to achieve these objectives. Article 85 covers collusion between undertakings, such as cartels setting artificial prices in the market. Article 86 is concerned with dominance, in particular with the abuse or exploitation of a dominant position. This would be the case if an undertaking had a monopoly and set ridiculously high prices.

The law in this area refers to 'undertakings' rather than 'companies', although an undertaking is not defined in the Treaty. It is a union concept that is very broad and is not limited to companies. For example, it could include a non-profit organization, a pension fund, an inventor or even a performer.

Competition law is enforced by the Commission, which conducts an investigation into any alleged breaches. The Commission has extensive powers. It can require information to be supplied and can gain access and search the premises of an undertaking at any time. The Commission can issue a decision that is legally binding, subject to appeal to the European Court of Justice.

13.9 Social policy

Article 119 provides for equal pay for work of equal value. It is a brief article that has been used to develop extensive rights in the sex discrimination area and was initially inserted into the treaty for economic reasons, so that those States that could pay women less would not have a competitive advantage. There is also a social aim, to improve social progress and promote the living and working conditions in the Member States.

In order to apply the provision, we need to know what constitutes 'pay' and what constitutes 'work of equal value'. 'Pay' has been held to include salary, pensions, concessions and any other benefit derived from the employment relationship. 'Work of equal value' is broadly similar work according to qualitative criteria, focussing on the nature of the work.

There are two types of discrimination: direct and indirect. Direct discrimination is openly discriminatory and cannot be justified. Indirect discrimination, which is neutral on the face but discriminatory in effect, cannot be justified by the employer as a reasonably proportionate means of achieving another purpose.

13.10 Current outcomes

The European Union has resulted in a common market that affords businesses in Europe many advantages. Firms can source the place of lowest cost for purchasing supplies and sell finished goods in the market with the highest demand. Companies must be highly efficient, organized and productive to withstand the force of increased competition. Consumers also gain enormously from more competitive pricing of goods and a vast choice of goods.

The Union is now moving towards greater political and economic unity through the adoption of a single currency and the coordination of Member States in relation to areas of State policy, such as defence and security, and justice and home affairs. In order to achieve such union, there must be further sacrifice of national sovereignty and an acceptance by the governments and people of the Member States of the further constraints placed upon them in the interests of the Union.

13.11 Brexit—the future

Currently, dealing with European Union law has to be carried out with some caution. This is due to the outcome of the **European Union Referendum Act 2015** which made provision for the holding of a referendum in the United Kingdom and Gibraltar on whether the United Kingdom should remain a member of the European Union. The outcome of this referendum was that a majority of the electorate voted for the United Kingdom to leave the European Union.

13.11.1 European Union (Notification of Withdrawal) Act 2017

Further to this legislation, the **European Union (Notification of Withdrawal) Act 2017** was enacted. The Act was introduced as a result of the decision of the Supreme Court in *R (on the application of Miller and Don Santos) v Secretary of State for Exiting the European Union* (2017) when the Supreme court held that a prior Act of Parliament was required giving authority to the Prime Minister to give notice to the European Union under Article 50 (2) of the Treaty of European Union to withdraw from the European Treaties. The Supreme Court also considered whether the consent of the devolved legislatures in Scotland, Wales and Northern Ireland was required before notice to withdraw was served. By a unanimous decision of the court, it was held that the European Union and other foreign affairs matters are reserved to the United Kingdom and Parliament and that the devolved legislatures do not hold a veto on the United Kingdom's decision to withdraw from the European Union.

13.11.2 European Union (Withdrawal) Act 2018

This Act repeals the **European Communities Act 1972** (ECA) on the day the United Kingdom leaves the European Union. The Act ends the supremacy of European Union law in United Kingdom law and converts European Union law as it stands at the moment of exit into domestic law. It also creates temporary powers to make secondary legislation to enable correction to be made to the law that would otherwise no longer operate appropriately once the United Kingdom has left, so that the domestic legal system continues to function correctly outside the European Union. The Act also enables domestic law to reflect the content of the withdrawal agreement under Article 50 of the Treaty on European Union once the United Kingdom leaves the European Union, prior to the enactment of a statute of Parliament approved by the final terms of withdrawal.

The Act performs four main functions:

- i it repeals the **European Communities Act 1972**
- ii it converts European Union law as it stands at the moment of exit into domestic law before the United Kingdom leaves the European Union

iii it creates powers to make secondary legislation, linking temporary powers to enable corrections to be made to the law that would otherwise no longer operate appropriately once the United Kingdom has left the European Union and to implement a withdrawal agreement (subject to the prior enactment of a statute by Parliament approving the final terms of the withdrawal

iv it maintains the current scope of devolved decision-making powers in areas currently governed by European Union Law

13.11.3 European Union (Withdrawal) Act 2019

This is expressed to be the Act to make provision in connection with the period of negotiations for withdrawing from the European Union. The Bill for this Act was passed by an unprecedented procedure, as part of the political difficulties around Brexit in respect of which the Government lacked an effective majority in either Houses of Parliament. As a result of a controversial process, a group of backbench members of Parliament effectively took over the Government's business procedure and presented and passed the Bill for this Act on the back of business motions in the House of Lords. The Bill passed all stages in both Houses of Parliament and received the Royal Assent on 8 April 2019. The Bill incorporated a motion: 'that this House agrees for the purposes of s. 1 of the **European Union (Withdrawal) Act 2019** that the Prime Minister seek an extension of the period specified in Article 50 (3) of the Treaty of European Union to a period ending on [30 June 2019]. The effect of this motion is to recall Parliament to debate a motion to require the Prime Minister to seek an extension to the period in which the United Kingdom is to negotiate the terms of its withdrawal from the European Union ('Brexit') under Article 50 (3) of the Treaty on European Union. The motion must be moved on the day the Act received Royal assent or the next day, 8 or 9 April 2019. If Parliament passes the motions, then the Prime Minister is legally obliged to comply with and seek an extension to a date chosen by Parliament.

13.11.4 European Union (Withdrawal) (No. 2) Act 2019

This Act which received the Royal Assent on 9 September 2019 requires the Prime Minister to seek an extension to the Brexit withdrawal date (originally 31 October 2019) should he not be able to agree a withdrawal agreement with the European Union and obtain approval from the House of Commons for it by 19 October 2019.

13.11.5 European Union (Withdrawal Agreement) Act 2020

An Act to implement and make other provision in connection with the agreement between the United Kingdom and the European Union under Article 50 (2) of the Treaty on European Union, which sets out the arrangements for the United Kingdom's withdrawal from the European Union. This Acts was required to implement the Withdrawal Agreement for it to have domestic legal effect and to enable the United Kingdom government to ratify the Withdrawal Agreement.

13.12 Ending of rights to the free movement of persons under retained EU law

The purpose of the **Immigration and Social Security Co-Ordination (EU Withdrawal) Act 2020** is to end the free movement of persons in United Kingdom law and make European (EU), other European Economic Area (EEA) and Swiss citizens and their family members, subject to United Kingdom immigration controls. The Act ends the EU's rules on free movement that are retained in United Kingdom law by the **European Union (Withdrawal) Act 2018**, whilst repealing other retained EU laws relating to immigration, as amended by subsequent legislation.

13.12.1 United Kingdom regains full control of its fishing rights

The **Fisheries Act 2020** gives the United Kingdom full control over its fishing waters for the first time since 1873. It allows the United Kingdom to set annual Total Allowable Catches (TACs) based on scientific information, while considering the needs of fishermen. It establishes a framework for fisheries management, following the end of the Brexit transition period moving away from the Common Fisheries Policy.

13.12.2 Interim arrangements for disclosure of information prior to Free Trade Agreement

The **Trade (Disclosure of Information) Act 2020** allowed Her Majesty's Revenue and Customs and other public authorities to share data relating to the flow of traffic, goods and services into and out of the United Kingdom prior to the enactment of the Trade Act 2020. It was stressed that these powers granted in the Act were critical to support the use and sharing of trade-related data between Government.

13.12.3 Provision for the prevention of internal trade barriers within the United Kingdom

The purpose of the **United Kingdom Internal Market Act 2020** was to prevent internal trade barriers within the United Kingdom and to restrict the legislative powers of the devolved administrations in economic policy. It is one of several pieces of legislation concerning trade that were passed following the establishment of the European Union.

13.12.4 United Kingdom—European Union Trade and Cooperation Agreement

The **European Union (Future Relationship) Act 2020** implemented the EU–UK Trade and Cooperation Agreement agreed between the United Kingdom and the European Union and Euratom in December 2020.

13.12.5 Promotion of procurement obligations

The Trade Act 2021 was enacted to ensure that the United Kingdom could implement procurement obligations that would arise from the United Kingdom acceding to the Agreement on Government Procurement (GPA) in its own right and not as a member state of the European Union.

13.11.6 Recognition of professional qualifications gained overseas

The **Professional Qualifications Act 2022** revoked the current European Union-based system for the recognition of professional qualifications which had been gained overseas and established a new approach based on regulator autonomy and the delivery of international agreements. Its aim is to enable the United Kingdom to access international talent by assessing individuals with overseas professional qualifications or experience.

13.11.7 Revocation of European Laws

The **Retained (EU Law and Reform) Act 2023** revoked approximately 800 laws which originally implemented European Law (known as retained EU law) following the United Kingdom's exit from the European Union. The Act which took effect on 1 January 2024, ended EU law supremacy within the United Kingdom. The outcome was that retained laws no longer need to be interpreted in accordance with European Union law principles.

13.11.8 Revocation of European Union Law relating to financial services

The **Financial Services and Markets Act 2023** implemented the outcomes of the Future Regulatory Framework (FRF). It therefore revoked retained EU law relating to financial services and also enabled HM Treasury and the financial services regulators to replace it with legislation designed specifically for United Kingdom markets.

13.13 Useful webpages

European Union Law (http://www.en.wikipedia.org/wiki/European_Union_Law)

Europa—Summaries of EU legislation—Primary Law (http://europa.eu/legislation_summaries/institutional_affairs/decisionmaking_process/I14530_en.htm)

The ABC of European Union Law by Professor Klaus-Dieter Borchardt (http://www.europea.eu/documentation/legislation/pdf/oa8107147_en.pdf)

EUR-LEX Access to European Union Law (http://eur-lex.europa.eu/en/index.htm)

EUROPA-EU law (http://europa.eu/eulaw)

13.14 Exercises

1 Outline the major sources of European law.

2 Describe the six key institutions of the European Union and explain their influence on the future development of the European Union.

3 Describe and explain the differences between Court of Justice of the European Union and General Court.

4 Explain, with examples, the influence that European law has on the domestic law of the United Kingdom.

Appendix 1

Glossary of terms

ab initio	from the beginning
actio personalis moritur cum persona	a personal action dies with the person
ad litem	with respect to a suit at law
administrator cum testamento annexo	administrator with the will annexed (which the court appoints him to administer)
administrator durante minore aetate	administrator during infancy (of the true appointee)
administrator pendent lite	administrator during the litigation (of a disputed will)
animus manendi	the intention to remain in that place or country
animus revocandi	the intention to revoke
audi alteram partem	hear the other side
bona fide	in good faith
bona vacantia	ownerless property
caveat emptor	let the buyer beware
certiorari	to be informed (an order of certiorari is explained on page 60)
cestui que trust	the person for whose benefit a trust is created; a beneficiary
chattels personal	personal goods
chattels real	a lease, forming part of personalty
chose in action	a thing in action; a personal right of property which can only be claimed or enforced by an action at law and not by taking physical possession
chose in possession	a thing that is the subject of physical possession (contrast with chose in action)
consensus ad idem	mutual agreement on the same point
cujus est solum ejus est usque ad caelum	the owner of land owns all the land below the surface and all the space above the land
cum testamento annexo	with the will attached
Curia Regis	the King's Court
cy-près	so near; as nearly as possible
damnum sine injuria	damage without legal injury (or wrong)
de facto	existing in fact
del credere	in the belief that (the buyer is solvent)
delegatus non potest delegare	one to whom power has been delegated cannot delegate that power to another
de minimis non curat lex	'the law takes no notice of trifles'
de novo	anew
distress damage feasant	the right of an occupier of land to seize animals doing damage thereon
donatio mortis causa	a gift in anticipation of death
durante minore aetate	during infancy

ejusdem generis	of the same kind, or nature
equitas sequitur legem	equity follows the law
escrow	a sealed writing delivered conditionally, which condition being performed it operates immediately as a deed
estoppel	a rule of evidence whereby a party is precluded by some previous act to which he was party or privy from asserting or denying a fact. For example, a party cannot aver that a state of things is different from what he has led the other party to believe if the other party has acted upon such belief and changed his position to his detriment
ex gratia	as a matter of favour
ex nudo pacto non oritur actio	a bare promise (without consideration) does not give rise to any action
ex officio	arising from an official position, by virtue of his office
ex parte	on the application of (an *ex parte* hearing is one at which only one side is represented)
ex post facto	after the event
expressio unius est exclusio alterius	the express mention of one thing implies the exclusion of another
ex turpi causa non oritur actio	no action arises out of a base cause
ibid. ibidem; in the same place	
ignorantia juris haud excusat	
ignorantia juris neminem excusat	ignorance of the law excuses no one
ignorantia juris non excusat	
in consimili casu	in similar case to
in extremis	in imminent peril of death
in pari delicto potior est conditio defendentis	of two wrongdoers it is better to be the defendant
in pari delicto potior est conditio possidentis	where two parties are equally in the wrong, the condition of the possessor is the stronger
in personam	an act, proceeding or a right in land which is good against a specified person who is aware of it—but not valid against any other person—such as a buyer of the property who is not aware of the right
in re	in the matter of
in rem	against a thing; a right *in rem* is a right in property such as land which is good against the whole world
in terrorem	as a threat, to cause fear
indenture	a deed to which there are two or more parties
injuria sine damno	legal wrong without damage
inter alia	among other matters
inter se	among themselves
inter vivos	during life
jus accrescendi	right of survivorship
jus tertii	the right of a third party
laches	delay, e.g. in pursuing a remedy at law
lex loci contractus	the law of the place where the agreement was made
locus sigilli	the place of the seal
Magnum Concilium	the Great Council
mandamus	we command (an order of mandamus is explained on page 60)

mens rea	guilty mind
mesne	intermediate
nec per vim, nec clam, nec precario	peaceably, openly and as of right
nemo dat quod non habet	no one can give what he does not have *nemo judex in causa sua*
	no one shall be a judge in his own case
non est factum	'not my act'
noscitur a sociis	the meaning of a word can be gathered from its context
novus actus interveniens	a new development intervening (to change the legal situation)
obiter dicta	sayings by the way
overt	open
pendente lite	during the litigation
per capita	by the number of individuals
per incuriam	by oversight (of a judge)
per se	by itself, by or through himself
per subsequens matrimonium	by subsequent marriage
prima facie	at a first view
puisne	lesser in importance
pur autre vie	for another's life
quantum meruit	as much as he has deserved
quasi	as if, as it were
quid pro quo	a mutual consideration; tit for tat
qui facit per alium facit per se	he who does a thing through another does it himself
ratio decidendi	the reason for the decision
res	thing
res extincta	the thing having ceased to exist
res ipsa loquitur	'the thing speaks for itself'
res sua	the thing being his own property
restitutio in integrum	restoration to the original position
sans recours	without recourse
sciens	knowing
scienti non fit injuria	one who knows cannot be harmed
seisin	effective possession of land by a freeholder
sic utere tuo ut alienum non laedas	so use your own property as not to injure your neighbour's
sine die	without fixing a day
stare decisis	to stand by past decisions
status quo	the state in which a thing exists
sue	to take proceedings in a civil action
sui juris	of full legal capacity
surrogate	deputy
tortfeasor	a person liable on a civil wrong other than a contractual or trust matter
trover	an early form of conversion in which a finding (trover) of the goods was alleged
uberrimae fidei	of the utmost good faith
ubi jus ibi remedium	where there is a right there is a remedy
ubi remedium ibi jus	where there is a remedy there is a right
ultra vires	beyond the powers of
viva voce	by word of mouth
volens	willing
volenti non fit injuria	no wrong can be done to one who consents to what is done

Appendix 2

Examination technique

At the end of each chapter you will find questions to enable you to test your knowledge. Use these questions constantly throughout your course, for revision is a vital requirement in all studies and particularly in law. However able your tutor may be, in the final result the examination will test *your* knowledge and *your* learning. Constant revision is vital for those of us with average powers. The secret of success is adequate preparation.

Law questions

These are usually of two types: (a) a textbook type of question and (b) a problem question. The approach to each is slightly different.

a Textbook questions

These seek to test your knowledge of a particular portion of the law. A question may call for a description of a development in legal history or a court: for example, 'How was the common law of England formed?' 'What is the composition and jurisdiction of a county court?' A thorough knowledge of the textbook will enable you to answer all such questions normally asked. Deal with historical questions in chronological order as a general rule; and if you are tackling a question on the courts, deal with it in the order asked, i.e. (i) composition and (ii) jurisdiction.

b Problem questions

These usually set down facts, based on one or more decided cases. The question may ask you to discuss the problem or to consider the liability of persons named in the case. These questions test your knowledge of the law and, second, your application of the law to the facts. The general approach here is first to set down quite clearly the general rule of law, which may be statutory or a decided case. Then lead on to the exception to the general rule, which may be the result of another case decided in the courts and, therefore, law. In all your statements on the law, quote authorities, i.e. statute law or case law. At this stage apply the law to the facts in question, noting any distinctions you may observe and come to a conclusion.

The following simple rules will guide you in answering all law examination questions:

i read the question *carefully*
ii read it again, underlining the *key word or words*
iii make *rough* notes of your answer
iv arrange your points in *order*
v write your answer from your *plan*

English style. Examiners want clear and concise answers. Remember the 'ABCD Rule':

A = Accurate
B = Brief

C = Clear
D = Direct (i.e. be relevant)

Legal text-writers, judges and examiners prefer simple, clear and direct statements. Avoid showy, extravagant and facetious language or comments. This wastes time, earns no marks and may be penalized. Aptness and suitability should be the aim.

Spelling, grammar and handwriting. Whatever views we may personally hold on these matters, the fact remains that a grammatically correct, well-paragraphed and well-written paper will commend itself to any examiner. Untidy, blotched and scribbled efforts ask for the red pencil and will not justify good marks.

Citing authorities. Examiners seek to test your knowledge of English law. Include your authorities for your statements, e.g. 's. 136 of the Law of Property Act 1925', or (if your authority is a decided case) '*Nash v Inman* (1908)', '*Roscorla v Thomas* (1842)' and so on. It is customary practice in law examinations to underline the titles of cases. This helps to draw the attention of the examiner to the important references you make. If you do not know the name of the case, or if it escapes your memory, give the facts and the principles of law that it demonstrates.

Example 1

QUESTION: What do you understand by equity? What reasons led to the creation and growth of the Court of Chancery?

ROUGH NOTES: Definition of equity: supplementary to common law. Creation of Court of Chancery: petitions of King; reference to Council, then Chancellor; Court set up by the end of the fifteenth century.

GROWTH: Earl of Oxford's case 1616; principles established, case law developed; finally, delays and abuses till Judicature Act 1873–5; now Chancery Division.

MODEL ANSWER: Equity in a general sense corresponds to natural justice or fairness in the adjustment of conflicting interests or controversies. As administered in the courts, however, equity means that portion of natural justice that eventually formed itself into technical rules operating according to certain clear-cut principles. Before the Judicature Acts, 1873–5, equity comprised those rules administered and enforced by the Court of Chancery in cases where the courts of common law gave no remedy or gave an inadequate remedy to a plaintiff, notwithstanding that there was a right, based on conscience, to relief. In this sense, therefore, equity may be looked upon as a gloss (or appendix) to the common law, filling in the gaps and making the English legal system more complete.

The germ of the idea of equity lies in the notion of the King as 'fountain of justice' to whom a subject could present a petition for relief in any cause and for any reason. Where no relief was obtainable in the common law courts or under the common law, a subject sent his petition to the King. The petitions became numerous and were sometimes examined by the King and his Council, relief being granted, as a matter of grace, or refused. Owing to the pressure of business in the Council the petitions were sent to the Chancellor, who, as Chief Secretary of State and Keeper of the King's Conscience, eventually dealt with them alone.

By the end of the fifteenth century the Chancellor had established his own court, the Court of Chancery, and assumed a jurisdiction in disputes, applying his own procedures (e.g. subpoena and interrogatories) and granting relief by decree (e.g. specific performance of contracts and injunction). In due course of time the Chancellor's jurisdiction grew because of its popularity.

Eventually his jurisdiction competed with and conflicted with the common law itself and resulted in open dispute in the celebrated Earl of Oxford's case (1616) in which the King personally interposed his will. Thereafter, where the rules of common law and equity conflicted, equity prevailed.

Despite its initial popularity, equity as administered in the Chancery Court came under criticism. Jurisdiction grew, particularly in the administration of trusts and mortgages, but abuses occurred and there were frequent delays in dealing with cases, so that in course of time the Court became the exact opposite of its original intention and purpose.

Finally the **Judicature Acts, 1873–5**, were passed which brought into being a new system of courts and a fusion of the administration of law and equity. The Court of Chancery was abolished, but was re-created as one of the divisions of the High Court and named the Chancery Division. It retained most of its original jurisdiction, but may now grant in any case coming before it not only its traditional equitable remedies (referred to previously) but also common law remedies.

Example 2

Question: (a) Discuss the meaning of trespass to the person and distinguish between the different forms that it may take. (b) State with reasons whether F and G are guilty of the tort of assault in the following cases:

i F, a farmer, after a quarrel with his neighbour, H, points his gun at him. In fact, unknown to H, the gun is not loaded.

ii G, who with his wife has been playing cards with Mr and Mrs K, has an argument with Mr K, who has accused him of cheating. G says to Mr K: 'If there were no ladies present, I should give you the biggest hiding you ever got' (A.E.B.).

ROUGH NOTES

a Three forms of trespass: assault, battery and false imprisonment. Cases: *R v St George*, *Bird v Jones*.

b (i) Assault even if gun unloaded, *R v St George*. (ii) No assault here, *Tuberville v Savage*.

MODEL ANSWER

a Trespass to the person comprises three kinds: (i) assault, (ii) battery and (iii) false imprisonment.

i An assault is an act that causes another to apprehend immediate and unlawful personal violence. An assault may be committed by striking at another person with a stick or a fist or by throwing water or a stone at another; it is immaterial that the person who aims the blow misses his aim. It has been held that words alone do not constitute an assault; there must be some force used by the defendant.

ii Battery consists of *applying* force to the person of another hostilely or against their will. It is a battery even if the amount of force applied is slight. Common examples include giving a man a 'black eye', throwing water over another, which splashes him and holding a man by the arm (as where a police officer arrests a prisoner).

iii Merely touching a person to draw his attention to some matter does not constitute an assault; similarly, it is no assault where a pedestrian collides with another on the footpath accidentally. It appears that it is essential in this type of case to prove that the defendant acted intentionally or negligently: *Fowler v Lanning* (1959).

iv False imprisonment consists in the infliction of bodily restraint on another without lawful justification. There need be no imprisonment, such as detention in police cells. The mere holding of the arm of another is sufficient, provided that the detention is complete. Thus, to restrain a person from going in three ways while leaving a fourth way open to him is not false imprisonment: *Bird v Jones* (1845). Similarly, it was held that there was no imprisonment where employers refused to allow miners employed at the coal face to come to the surface to discuss a dispute, where the miners were working on a shift that had not been completed: *Herd v Weardale Steel etc. Co.* (1915).

b

i Applying the rules stated at (a)(i), the test is: Did the neighbour, H, fear violence from F? Pointing a gun is a threat to apply unlawful force to the person of another. Therefore an assault has been committed if H is put in fear, as would be the case with any reasonable person in his position. It is material whether H knew the gun was loaded or unloaded: *R v St George* (1840). In the circumstances, H may sue F for assault.

ii Words alone do not constitute an assault, it is said, but may 'unmake' it. In the present case G qualifies his statement by the words. 'If there were no ladies present . . .'. There is no decided case where these particular words have been uttered in the circumstances shown, but it was held in *Tuberville v Savage* (1669) that where a defendant uttered 'If it were not assize time, I would not take such language from you' and at the same time put his hand on his sword (a threat), there was no assault. Arguing by analogy from this early case, we may state that G has committed no assault.

Appendix 3

List of abbreviations: law reports

[1891] A.C	The Law Reports, Appeals to the House of Lords and the Judicial Committee of the Privy Council and Peerage cases, from 1891 onwards.
Ad. & El	Adolphus and Ellis's Reports, Queen's Bench. 12 volumes. 1834–40.
[1936] All E.R	All England Law Reports from 1936 onwards.
[1923] All E.R. Rep	All England Reports Reprint.
App. Cas	The Law Reports, Appeals to the House of Lords and the Judicial Committee of the Privy Council. 15 volumes. 1875–90.
B. & Ad	Barnewall and Adolphus's Reports, King's Bench. 5 volumes. 1830–4.
B. & Ald	Barnewall and Alderson's Reports, King's Bench. 5 volumes. 1817–22.
B. & S	Best and Smith's Reports, Queen's Bench. 10 volumes. 1861–70.
Beav	Beavan's Reports, Rolls Court. 36 volumes. 1838–66.
Bing	Bingham's Reports, Common Pleas. 10 volumes. 1822–34.
Bing. N.C	Bingham's New Cases, Common Pleas. 6 volumes. 1834–40.
Bro. Parl. Cas	Brown's Parliamentary Cases. 8 volumes. 1702–1800.
C.B	Common Bench Reports. 18 volumes. 1845–56.
C.B. (N.S.)	Common Bench Reports, New Series. 20 volumes. 1856–65.
C. & P	Carrington and Payne's Reports, Nisi Prius. 9 volumes. 1823–41.
C.P.D	The Law Reports, Common Pleas Division. 5 volumes. 1875–80.
[1891] Ch	The Law Reports, Chancery Division, from 1891 onwards.
1 Ch.D	The Law Reports, Chancery Division. 45 volumes. 1875–90.
Cha. Ca	Choyce Cases in Chancery. 1557–1606.
Cl. & F	Clark and Finelly's Reports, House of Lords. 12 volumes. 1831–46.
Co. Rep	Coke's Reports. 13 parts. 1572–1616.
Cox C.C	Cox's Criminal Law Cases. 1843–1945.
Cro. Car	Croke's King's Bench Reports during the time of King Charles I. 1 volume. 1625–41.
Curt	Curteis's Ecclesiastical Reports. 3 volumes. 1834–44.
De G. M. & G	De Gex, Magnachten and Gordon's Reports, Chancery. 8 volumes. 1851–7.
Dowl	Dowling's Practice Reports. 9 volumes. 1830–41.
E. & B	Ellis and Blackburn's Queen's Bench Reports. 8 volumes. 1852–8.
Eq. Case. Abr	Abridgement of Cases in Equity. 2 volumes. 1667–1744.
Exch	Exchequer Reports (Welsby, Hurlstone and Gordon). 11 volumes. 1847–56.
Ex.D	The Law Reports, Exchequer Division. 5 volumes. 1875–80.
Foster	Foster's Crown Cases. 1 volume. 1708–60.
Gal. & Dav	Gale and Davision's Queen's Bench Reports. 3 volumes. 1841–3.
H. & C	Hurlstone and Coltman's Exchequer Reports. 4 volumes. 1862–6.
H. & N	Hurlstone and Norman's Exchequer Reports. 7 volumes.1856–62.

H. & T	Halls and Twells's Chancery Reports. 2 volumes. 1846–50.
H.L.C	Clark's House of Lords Cases. 11 volumes. 1847–1866.
Jur	Jurist Reports. 18 volumes. 1837–54.
[1901] K.B	The Law Reports, King's Bench, from 1901 onwards.
Keb	Keble's King's Bench Reports. 3 volumes. 1661–79.
Kel	Sir John Kelying's Reports, Crown Cases. 1 volume. 1662–1707.
L.J.Ch	Law Journal Reports, Chancery. 118 volumes. 1831–1949.
Lev	Levinz's King's Bench Reports. 3 volumes. 1660–97.
[1951] Lloyd's Rep	Lloyd's List Law Reports, cited by date from 1951 onwards.
L.J.C.P	Law Journal Reports, Common Pleas. 1831–75.
L.J.Ex	Law Journal Reports, Exchequer. 1831–75.
L.J.(o.s.)	Law Journal, Old Series. 1822–31.
L.J.P	Law Journal Reports, Probate, Divorce and Admiralty. 1875–1946.
L.J.P.C	Law Journal Reports, Privy Council. 1865–1946.
[1947] L.J.R	Law Journal Reports. 1947–9.
L.R.App.Cas	The Law Reports, Appeals to the House of Lords and the Judicial Committee of the Privy Council. 15 volumes. 1875–90.
L.R.C.C.R	The Law Reports of Crown Cases Reserved. 2 volumes. 1865–75.
L.R.C.P	The Law Reports, Common Pleas. 10 volumes. 1865–75.
L.R.Ex	The Law Reports, Exchequer. 10 volumes. 1865–75.
(1875) 7 H.L.1	The Law Reports, English and Irish Appeals to the House of Lords. 7 volumes, 1865–75.
L.R.P. & D	The Law Reports, Probate and Divorce. 3 volumes. 1865–75.
L.R.Q.B	The Law Reports, Queen's Bench. 10 volumes. 1865–75.
L.T	Law Times Reports. 1859–1947.
L.T.(o.s.)	Law Times, Old Series. 34 volumes. 1843–60.
Leach	Leach's Crown Cases. 2 volumes. 1730–1815.
M. & W	Meeson and Welsby's Exchequer Reports. 16 volumes. 1836–47.
Mer	Merivale's Chancery Reports. 3 volumes. 1815–17.
Mod. Rep	Modern Reports. 12 volumes. 1669–1755.
Moo. & S	Moore and Scott's Reports, Common Pleas. 4 volumes. 1831–4.
Moore K.B	Sir F. Moore's Reports, King's Bench, Folio. 1 volume. 1485–1620.
New Rep	New Reports. 6 volumes. 1862–5.
[1891] P	The Law Reports, Probate, Divorce and Admiralty Division, from 1891 onwards.
P.D	The Law Reports, Probate Division. 15 volumes. 1876–90.
Ph	Phillips's Reports, Chancery. 2 volumes. 1841–9.
Q.B	Queen's Bench Reports (Adolphus and Ellis, New Series). 18 volumes. 1841–52.
[1891] Q.B	The Law Reports, Queen's Bench Division, from 1891 onwards.
Q.B.D	The Law Reports, Queen's Bench Division. 25 volumes. 1875–90.
Rep. Ch	Reports in Chancery. 3 volumes. 1615–1710.
Rob. Eccl	Robertson's Ecclesiastical Reports. 2 volumes. 1844–53.
Smith L.C	Smith's Leading Cases. 2 volumes.
Sol. Jo	Solicitor's Journal, from 1856 onwards.
S.T	State Trials. 34 volumes. 1163–1820.
State Tr. (N.S.)	State Trials, New Series. 8 volumes. 1820–58.
Str	Strange's King's Bench Reports. 2 volumes. 1716–47.
Starkie	Starkie's Reports, Nisi Prius. 3 volumes. 1814–23.

T.L.R	The Times Law Reports. 1885–1952.
Term. Rep	Term Reports (Durnford and East). 8 volumes. 1785–1800.
Toth	Tothill's Transactions in Chancery. 1 volume. 1559–1646.
Ves	Vesey Junior's Chancery Reports. 19 volumes. 1789–1817.
W. & T.L.C	White and Tudor's Leading Cases in Equity. 2 volumes.
W. Bl	Sir William Blackstone's King's Bench Reports. 1746–80.
[1953] W.L.R	Weekly Law Reports, from 1953 onwards.
W.R	Weekly Reporter. 54 volumes. 1852–1906.
W.N	Weekly Notes. 1866–1952.

Index

Note: Page numbers in *italics* refers figures.

D

E

M

N

Q

R

T

For Product Safety Concerns and Information please contact our EU representative GPSR@taylorandfrancis.com Taylor & Francis Verlag GmbH, Kaufingerstraße 24, 80331 München, Germany